HARDPRESS.NET
HOME OF HARD-TO-FIND BOOKS

The Lost Solar System of the Ancients Discovered

by John Wilson (Writer in Astronomy.)

Address:
HardPress
8345 NW 66TH ST #2561
MIAMI FL 33166-2626
USA
Email: info@hardpress.net

THE ANCIENTS

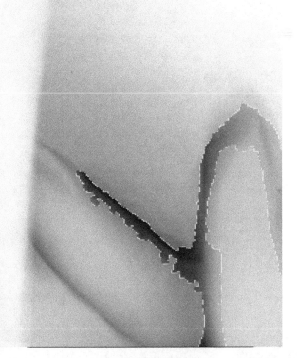

THE LOST

SOLAR SYSTEM OF THE ANCIENTS

DISCOVERED.

VOL. II.

LONDON :
Printed by SPOTTISWOODE & Co.,
New-street-Square.

THE LOST

SOLAR SYSTEM OF THE ANCIENTS

DISCOVERED.

BY JOHN WILSON.

IN TWO VOLUMES.

VOL. II.

LONDON:

LONGMAN, BROWN, GREEN, LONGMANS, & ROBERTS.

1856.

CONTENTS

OF

THE SECOND VOLUME.

PART VII.

PART VIII.

PART XI.

LOST SOLAR SYSTEM OF THE ANCIENTS DISCOVERED.

PART VII.

DRUIDICAL REMAINS IN ANGLESEA AND SCOTLAND. — STONE CIRCLE AT STENNIS.—CALERNISH.—RICHBOROUGH, IN KENT.—THE RECULVER. — CIRCLE OF SWINSHEAD, IN LINCOLNSHIRE. — JEWRY WALL IN LEICESTER. — DRUIDICAL REMAINS IN THE ISLE OF MAN. — GLEN DARRAGH. — PEEL CASTLE. — THE TINWALD. — FAIRY HILL. — CIRCLE IN PORTUGAL. — ECBATANA, IN CENTRAL ASIA. — ATHENS. — ITS CIRCUIT. — PARTHENON. — TEMPLE OF JUPITER OLYMPUS. — AREOPAGUS. — CECROPS, THE FIRST KING OF ATHENS, CAME FROM SAIS; HE CIVILISED THE PEOPLE, AND INTRODUCED THE EGYPTIAN RELIGION AND ARTS. — BRAHMANICAL TEMPLE AT DWARKA. — RAMISSERAM. — HILL FORT AT DOULUTABAD. — TRIPETTY, IN THE CARNATIC. — CONJEVERAM. — BALBEC. — KARNAC. — LABYRINTH OF MŒRIS.— PALMYRA.—PERSEPOLIS.—ASSYRIAN MOUND OF KHORSABAD. — ANCIENT ENCLOSURE. —KALAH SHERGAT. — MUJALLIBAH. — BIRS NIMROUD, AT BABYLON. — KOYUNJIK, AT NINEVEH. — ROCK-CUT TEMPLES IN INDIA. — ELEPHANTA. — ELLORA. — PYRAMIDAL TEMPLE OF CHALEMBARAM.— PAGODA OF TANGORE. — TEMPLES AT BRANDANAN, IN JAVA. — ROME. — CAPITOLINE HILL. — COLISEUM. — PANTHEON. — AMPHITHEATRE AT VERONA. — TEMPLE OF DIANA AT EPHESUS. — SEGESTA.

PENNANT found in Anglesea the Brya Gwya or Brein Gwyn (royal tribunal), belonging to the Arch-Druid. It is a circular hollow of 180 feet diameter, surrounded by an

immense agger of earth and stones.   Not far from it was
one of the Gorseddau, now much dispersed, but once consisting of a great copped heap of stones, upon which the
Druid sat aloft while he instructed the people.   A stone
circle and cromlech were adjacent.

Diameter of circle = 180 feet = 155 units,

Circumference   = 486   ,, ,

$\quad$ = twice the side of the Tower of Belus,

486^3 = circumference of earth,

or cube of circumference of circle = circumference of the
earth.

In the Isle of Man is a great stone chair, placed at the
entrance of Ruthin Castle, for the governor, and two smaller
for the dempsters, where they sat and tried civil causes.

In Britain there were two Arch-Druids; one resided in
Anglesea, and the other in the Isle of Man.

There has just been discovered at Tynrich, a small Druidical circle, which had hitherto been concealed by masses of
broom and bramble.   This olden temple, if temple it were, is
about 18 feet in diameter, and quite entire, each of its huge
stones standing erect and in its proper place; but there is an
additional interest attached to it from the fact that, while
digging and levelling the interior, four huge urns, about
2 feet in height, and 1 foot in diameter at the mouth, were
exhumed, quite full of calcined bones, besides three or four
stone coffins, formed of thin, unshaped slabs, evidently from
the adjacent ground, and likewise containing the mortal
remains of the ancient Caledonians of a pre-historic period.
Unfortunately, either from the extreme brittleness of the
urns, or want of care on the part of the labourers, the whole
were broken to pieces.   They were of the very coarsest
manufacture, in shape remote from classical, and with no
pretension to decoration, but a profusion of scratchings without method on the outside of the upper portion of each.   The
coffins were equally unceremoniously dealt with, but it is
worthy of remark that they lay in no particular order in
reference to the compass, but, if anything, rather inclined to

south and north; indeed, one of them lay directly in that direction. The general notion is, that Druidical circles were temples, and nothing else; but the trenching of this one shows that they were also used as burying-places, like churches in the present times, for great men, probably the higher orders of the priesthood.—*Perthshire Advertiser.*

10 times diameter $= 10 \times 18 = 180$ feet $= 155$ units,
$$\text{circumference} = 486 \text{ ,, .}$$

Cube of circumference of circle 10 times diameter,

$= 486^3 =$ circumference of the earth,

or cube of Tynrich circle $= \frac{1}{1000}$ circumference of the earth.

The stone Circle of Stennis.

" The road to Kirkwall," says Barry, "crosses a dreary moor of great extent, passing by a bridge, a narrow stream communicating between the bay and a large salt water loch. A natural embankment separates this Loch from Loch Stennis, a broad sheet of water. It is the site of the well-known stone circles. Their situation, so similar to that of the circles of Calernish in Lewis, was probably chosen with reference to the vicinity of water, necessary, perhaps, to the ceremonies or the safety of the people by whom they were erected. Their number is also the same. Of one of them there are four stones remaining, of which three are standing. They are about 18 to 20 feet in length. The principal circle is very large; its diameter, extending to the outside of the fosse, is 360 feet, and it is surrounded by a fosse 20 feet broad and 12 feet deep; the stones of which it is composed are from 12 to 14 feet high. There are several tumuli in the neighbourhood of the circles, and detached stones of the same description are found in all the Orkney Islands.

Diameter of principal circle $= 360$ feet $= 310$ units,

Circumference $= 2 \times 486$ units $= 4$ stades,
$$= \text{perimeter of Tower of Belus.}$$

Cube of circumference $= 8$ circumference of the earth.
Width of fosse $= 20$ feet $= 17$ units.

Diameter of circle to the middle of fosse

$$= 310 + 17 = 327 \text{ units.}$$

Circumference $\quad = 1028.$

Cube of circumference $= 1028^3 =$ distance of the moon.

The ancient inhabitants of the Isles of Orkney were Picts, to whom are ascribed the conical towers found in various parts of the coast of Scotland, one of which exists near Kirkwall.

The cathedral of Kirkwall is an object of much interest; and there is something peculiarly striking and imposing in the massy pile and lofty towers, and the more so when this cathedral, standing on the northern shore of Orkney, is viewed as almost the only unimpaired specimen of these stately monuments of ecclesiastical grandeur which adorned Scotland previous to the Reformation. Its architecture is a respectable specimen of the style of the twelfth century. The small size of the windows, and the heavy character of the building, are characteristic of that age.

The length of the cathedral from east to west is 236 feet, its breadth 56 : the arms of the cross or transept are 30 feet in breadth; the height of the roof is 71 feet, that of the steeple 140. The roof of the nave is vaulted by Gothic arches, supported on each side by a triple row of columns; the lowest tier consists of 14, each measuring 15 feet in circumference. The tower is supported by 4, measuring each 24 feet in circumference. The effect of the massy and regularly formed columns is imposing.

Here, near Druidical circles erected at an unknown period, we find a cathedral, built in the style of the twelfth century, having the height of the roof $\frac{1}{4}$ of a stade, and the height of the steeple $\frac{1}{2}$ a stade. That these dimensions were adopted on account of a traditional association of the stade with sacred architecture may be possible; though the relation between the stade and the earth's circumference had been forgotten ages before that period.

The length of the cathedral from east to west $= 236$ feet, and breadth 56.

If $5\frac{1}{2}$ feet be deducted from each of the two sides for the thickness of the walls, then the length of the interior will be $230\frac{1}{2}$ feet, and breadth $50\frac{1}{2}$ feet,

$$230\frac{1}{2} + 50\frac{1}{2} = 281 \text{ feet} = 1 \text{ stade.}$$

The four sides will equal 2 stades; but $2\frac{3}{4}$ feet is too small an estimate for the thickness of the walls of such an ancient structure. If $5\frac{1}{2}$ be allowed for the thickness, then the perimeter, measured from the middle of the walls, will equal 2 stades.

Height of steeple $= \frac{1}{2}$ height of tower of Belus.

Perimeter of cathedral $= \frac{1}{2}$ perimeter of the tower of Belus.

Cube of $\frac{1}{2}$ perimeter of cathedral $= 1$ cubic stade $= \frac{1}{8}$ circumference,

$\frac{1}{3}$ cube $=$ content of tower of Belus $= \frac{1}{24}$ circumference.

Cube of perimeter $= 8$ cubic stades,

$\qquad\qquad = $ cube of side square that enclosed the tower of Belus,

$\qquad\qquad = $ circumference of the earth.

Sides of cathedral are

$$230 \cdot 5 \text{ by } 50 \cdot 5 \text{ feet,}$$
$$232^3 : 50^3 :: 100 : 1.$$

The diameter of the circle at Calernish, according to Macculloch, is 63 feet from north to south, and 62 from east to west. It contains 14 stones in the circumference, with one in the centre. The central one is 12 feet high; one near the end of the long line measures 13; a few are found reaching to 7 or 8, but the height of the greater number does not exceed 4.

The recent removal of the peat-moss, in which the stones were half buried, from the sides of one of them, exhibits not only the surprising growth of this vegetable production, on a height where it could not receive any alluvial contributions, or deposit of extraneous decayed vegetable matter, but also the method employed by the rude architects who erected them, to fix them on those bases on which they have remained unmoved for centuries. The stone is inserted in a hole, filled up with small loose fragments of the same material. The elevation of the stones of the central circle must have amounted to 30 feet above the ground. Where exposed to view, the substance is as white as a bleached bone, contrasting singularly with the grey hue produced by the atmosphere.

The extensive appendage to the circle at Calernish, which distinguishes it from other circles, consists of four avenues of stones directed towards it, from the four principal points of the compass. The other two circles in the neighbourhood are composed of much smaller stones; one is incomplete, the other has a double row still standing, and arranged in an oval form. The people have no tradition respecting them.

Diameter = 63 feet = 54·6 units,
$$100 \times 54 \cdot 6 = 5460,$$
and $= 5460^3 =$ distance of Mercury.

Or cube of 100 times diameter = distance of Mercury,
$$= 150 \quad \text{,,} \quad \text{moon,}$$
150 cubes   ,,   = ,, Belus.

Diameter of circle   =   54·6 units,
,,   circumference =   171·6
$$10 \times 171 \cdot 6 = 1716$$
$$\tfrac{1}{2} = \quad 858$$
$$858^3 = \tfrac{50}{9} \text{ circumference,}$$
$$(2 \times 852)^3 = \tfrac{400}{9}.$$

Cube of 10 times circumference $= \tfrac{400}{9}$ circumference of earth,
$$(3 \times 2 \times 858)^3 = \tfrac{400}{9} \times 3^3 = 1200.$$

30 cubes of 30 times circumference of circle,
$$= 36000 \text{ circumference of earth,}$$
$$= \text{distance of Saturn.}$$

Cylinder having height = diameter of base = 54, &c. units
$$= 24 \text{ minutes,}$$
Sphere -   -   = 16   ,,
Cone   -   -   = 8   ,,

Circumference = 171·6,

$\quad$ 6 × 171·3, &c. = 1028,

Distance of moon = 1028³.

Cube of 6 times circumference = distance of the moon.

Cube of 60 $\quad$,, $\qquad$ = 1000.

Cube of 96 $\quad$,, $\qquad$ = 4096.

Diameter of Jupiter $\quad$ - $\quad$ = 4090³.

Thus cube of 100 times diameter = distance of Mercury.

Cube of 96 times circumference = diameter of orbit of Jupiter nearly.

Cube of 40 times circumference = diameter of orbit of Mercury.

Or diameters $\qquad$ 63 by 62 feet,

$\qquad$ = 54·45 by 53·6 units,

Circumferences = 171, &c. by 168, &c.

$\quad$ 171³, &c. = $\frac{4}{90}$ circumference,

$(3 × 171, \&c.)^3 = \frac{4}{90} × 3^3 = \frac{12}{10}$,

$(10 × 3 × 171, \&c.)^3 = \frac{12000}{10} = 1200$.

30 cubes of 30 times greater circumference,

$\qquad$ = 1200 × 30 = 36000 circumference,

$\qquad\qquad$ = distance of Saturn,

$\qquad$ 168³, &c. = $\frac{4}{900}$ distance of the moon,

$(30 × 168, \&c.)^3 = \frac{4}{900} × 30^3 = 120$.

30 cubes of 30 times less circumference = 3600,

$\qquad$ = 3750 − 150,

$\qquad$ = distance of Saturn − distance of Mercury,

$\qquad$ = distance between Mercury and Saturn.

Sum of 2 diameters = 54·45 + 53·6 = 108 units,

$\qquad$ 3 × 108 = 324,

$\qquad$ 324³, &c. = $\frac{5}{10}$ circumference.

Cube of 30 times sum of 2 diameters = 300 circumference.

Extracts from "Old England" descriptive of Richborough, in Kent: — "At the distance of two or three miles we distinctly see that this is some remarkable object. It is not a lofty castle of the middle ages, such as we sometimes look upon with tower and bastion crumbling into picturesque ruins; but here, on the north side, is a long line of wall, without a single aperture, devoid of loophole or battlement, and seemingly standing there only to support the broad masses of ivy which spread over its surface in singular luxuriance. This is indeed a mighty monument of ages that are gone. Let us examine it with somewhat more than common attention.

Ascending the narrow road which passes the cottage built at the foot of the bank, we reach some masses of wall that lie below the regular line. Have these fallen from their original position, or do they form an outwork connected with fragments which also appear on the lower level of the slope? This is a question not easily to decide from the appearance of the walls themselves. Another question arises, upon which antiquarian writers have greatly differed. Was there a fourth wall on the south-eastern side facing the river? It is believed by some that there was such a wall, and that the castle or camp once formed a regular parallelogram. It is difficult to reconcile this belief with the fact that the sea has constantly been retiring from Richborough, and that the little river was once a noble estuary. Bede, who wrote his "Ecclesiastical History" in the beginning of the eighth century, thus describes the branch of the river which forms the Isle of Thanet, and which now runs a petty brook from Richborough to Reculver:—"On the east side of Kent is the Isle of Thanet, considerably large, that is, containing, according to the English way of reckoning, 600 families, divided from the land by the river Wantsum (Stour), which is about 3 furlongs over, and fordable only in two places, for both ends of it run into the sea."

Passing by the fragments of which we have spoken, we are under the north (strictly north-east) wall,—a wondrous work, calculated to impress us with a conviction that the people who built it were not the petty labourers of an hour, who were contented with temporary defences and frail resting-places. The outer works upon the southern cliff of Dover, which were run up during the war with Napoleon at a prodigious expense, are crumbling and perishing, through the weakness of the job and contract. And here stand the walls of Richborough, as they have stood for 1800 years, from 20 to 30 feet high; in some places with foundations 5 feet below the earth, 11 or 12 feet thick at the base, with their outer masonry in many parts as perfect as at the hour when their courses of tiles and stones were first laid in beautiful regularity. The northern wall is 560 feet in length. From the eastern end, more than two-fifths of its whole length, it presents a surface almost wholly unbroken. It exhibits seven courses of stone, each about 4 feet thick, and the courses separated from each other by a double line of red or yellow tiles, each tile being about $1\frac{1}{2}$ inches in thickness. The entrance to the camp through this north wall is very perfect. This was called by the Romans the Porta Principalis, but in after times the Postern-gate. We pass through this entrance, and we are at once in the interior of the Roman castle. The area within the walls is a field of five acres, covered, when we saw it, with luxuriant beans. Towards the centre of the field, a little to the east of the Postern-gate, was a large space where the beans grew not. The area within the walls is much higher, in most places, than the ground without; and therefore the walls present a far more imposing appearance on their outer side. As we pass along the north wall to its western extremity, it becomes much more broken and dilapidated, large fragments having fallen from the top, which now presents a very irregular line. It is considered that at the north-west and south-west angles there were circular towers. The west wall is very much broken down, and it is held that one of the openings was the Decuman gate (the gate through which ten men could pass abreast). The south wall is considerably dilapidated, and from the nature of the ground is at present of much less length than the north wall. Immense cavities present themselves in this wall, in which the farmer deposits his ploughs and harrows, and the wandering gipsy seeks shelter from the driving north-east wind and rain. One of these cavities in the south wall is 42 feet long, as we roughly measured it, and about 5 feet high. The wall is in some places completely cut through. So that here is a long low arch, with 15 or 18 feet of solid work, 10 feet thick, above it, held up almost entirely by the lateral cohesion. Nothing can be a greater proof of the extraordinary solidity of the original work. From some very careful engravings of the external sides of the walls, given in King's " Munimenta Antiqua," we find that the same cavity was seen in 1775.

Leland, in describing Ratesburgh, says, " there is a great likelihood that the goodly hill about the castle, and especially to Sandwich-ward, hath been well inhabited. Corn groweth on the hill in marvellous plenty; and in going to plough there hath, out of mind, been found, and now is, more antiquities of Roman money than in any place else of England. Surely reason speaketh that this must be Rutu- pinum. There is a good flight shot off from Ratesburgh, towards Sandwich, a great dike, cast in a round compass, as it had been for fence of men-of-war. The compass of the ground within is not much above an acre, and it is very hollow by casting up the earth. They call the place there Lytleborough. Within the castle is a little parish church of St. Augustine, and an hermitage. I had antiquities of the hermit, the which is an industrious man."

In the bean-field within the walls of Richborough there was a space where no beans grew, which we could not ap- proach without trampling down the thick crop. We knew what was the cause of that patch of unfertility. We had earned from the work of Mr. King, who had derived his information from Mr. Boys, the local historian of Sandwich, that there was, " at the depth of a few feet, between the soil and rubbish, a solid regular platform, one hundred and forty-four feet in length and one hundred and four feet in breadth, being a most compact mass of masonry composed of flint stones and strong coarse mortar." This great plat- form, " as hard and entire in every part as a solid rock," is pronounced by King to have been " the great parade, or augurale, belonging to the Prætorium, where the Sacellum for eagles and ensigns, and where the sacrifices were offered."

But upon this platform is placed a second compact mass of masonry, rising nearly five feet above the lower mass, in the form of a cross, very narrow in the longer part, which extends from the south to the north (or, to speak more correctly, from the south-west to the north-east), but in the shorter transverse of the cross, which is forty-six feet in length, having a breadth of twenty-two feet. This cross, according to King, was the site of the Sacellum. Half a century ago was this platform dug about and under, and brass and lead and broken vessels were found, and a curious little bronze figure of a Roman soldier playing upon the bagpipes. Again has antiquarian curiosity been set to work, and labourers are now digging and delving on the edge of the platform, and breaking their tools against the iron concrete. The workmen have found a passage along the south and north sides of the platform, and have penetrated under the platform to walls upon which it is supposed to rest, whose foundations are laid twenty-eight feet lower. Some fragments of pottery have been found in this last excavation, and the explorers expect to break through the walls upon which the platform rests and find a chamber. It may be so. Looking at the greater height of the ground within the walls, compared with the height without, we are inclined to believe that the platform, which is five feet in depth, was the open basement of some public building in the Roman time. To what purpose it was appropriated in the Christian period, whether of Rome or Britain, we think there can be no doubt. The traveller who looked upon it three centuries ago tells us distinctly, "within the castle is a little parish church of St. Augustine, and an hermitage." To us it appears more than probable that the little parish church of St. Augustine which Leland saw had this cross for its foundation, and that when the church was swept away—when the hermit that dwelt there, and there pursued his solitary worship, fell upon evil times—the cross, with its crumbling walls, proclaimed where the little parish church had stood, and that this was then called St. Augustine's cross. The cross is decidedly of a later age than the platform; the masonry is far less regular and compact.

The sides of the solid rectangular platform are

$$144 \quad \text{by} \quad 104 \text{ feet.}$$
$$= 124{\cdot}5 \quad \text{,,} \quad 89{\cdot}92 \text{ units.}$$
$$(10 \times 123{\cdot}8)^3 = 1238^3 = \tfrac{50}{3} \quad \text{circumference}$$
$$(2 \times 10 \times 123{\cdot}8)^3 = \tfrac{50}{3} \times 2^3 = \tfrac{400}{3} \quad \text{,,}$$
$$(3 \times 2 \times 10 \times 123{\cdot}8)^3 = \tfrac{400}{3} \times 3^3 = 3600 \quad \text{,,}$$
$$= \tfrac{1}{60} \, 216000$$

Cube of 60 times greater side $= \tfrac{1}{60} \, 216000$ circumference

$$= \tfrac{1}{60} \text{ distance of Belus}$$

less side $\qquad = 89{\cdot}92$ units

$$(10 \times 89{\cdot}8)^3 = 898^3 = \tfrac{4}{3} \text{ distance of moon.}$$

3 cubes of 10 times less side

$$= 2 \text{ distance of moon}$$
$$= \text{diameter of orbit of moon.}$$

Sum of 2 sides $= 123{\cdot}8 + 89{\cdot}8 = 213{\cdot}6$ units.

$$214^3 = \tfrac{9}{1000} \text{ distance of moon}$$
$$(10 \times 214)^3 = \tfrac{9000}{1000} = 9$$
$$(5 \times 10 \times 214)^3 = 9 \times 5^3 = 1125.$$

20 cubes of 50 times sum of 2 sides
or of 25 times perimeter

$$= 20 \times 1125 = 22500 \text{ distance of moon}$$
$$= \text{distance of Belus.}$$

Sides are 124·5 by 89·92 units
if 126·4 ,,   91

then $\qquad 60 \times 126{\cdot}4 = 7584$

distance of earth $= 7584^3$

and $\qquad 60 \times 91 = 5460$

distance of Mercury $= 5460^3$.

Cube of 60 times greater side
$$= \text{distance of earth.}$$

Cube of 60 times less side
$$= \text{distance of Mercury.}$$

Sum of 2 sides $= 126{\cdot}4 + 91 = 217{\cdot}4$

$$40 \times 217\cdot4 = 8696$$
distance of Mars = about 8690^3.

Cube of 40 times sum of 2 sides
  or of 20 times perimeter of platform
    = distance of Mars.

Cube of 60 times sum of 2 sides
    $= (60 \times 217\cdot4)^3 = 13040^3 =$ distance of Jupiter.

Sides of the cross are   46 by 22 feet
        = 39·76 ,, 19 units

$$(10 \times 39\cdot8)^3 = 398^3 \qquad = \tfrac{1}{18}\ \text{circumference.}$$
$$(10 \times 10 \times 39\cdot8)^3 = \tfrac{1000}{18}$$
$$(3 \times 10 \times 10 \times 39\ 8)^3 = \tfrac{1000}{18} \times 3^3 = \tfrac{1000}{2} = 1500$$
$$(2 \times 3 \times 10 \times 10 \times 39\cdot8)^3 = 1500 \times 2^3 = 12000.$$

3 cubes of 600 times greater side

    36000 circumference = distance of Saturn

6 cubes   ,,   ,,   ,,   =   ,,   Uranus
18 cubes   ,,   ,,   ,,   =   ,,   Belus.

  Less side =   19 units
100 × 19   = 1900 ,,
  1900³ =   60 circumference.

Cube of 100 times less side = 60 circumference.
Sum of 2 sides $= 39\cdot8 + 18\cdot96 = 58\cdot56$ units

    $10 \times 58\cdot56 = 585\cdot6$
    585^3 &c. $= \tfrac{5}{27}$ distance of moon
$(3 \times 585$ &c.$)^3 = \tfrac{5}{27} \times 3^3 = 5.$

Cube of 30 times sum of 2 sides
        = 5 times distance of moon.

Cube of 60 times sum of 2 sides
        = 40 times distance of moon.

10 cubes of 60 times sum of 2 sides
    = 400 distance of moon = distance of earth.

30 cubes of 30 times sum of 2 sides
    30 × 5 = 150 distance of moon
        = distance of Mercury.

The northern wall is 560 feet in length.

Two stades equal 562 feet = 486 units = the side of the square that enclosed the tower of Belus.

The three sides in the plan appear of equal length, so that, if the four sides of the Richborough area were equal, the enclosed area at Richborough would equal the enclosed area at Babylon.

Cube of side of enclosure = circumference.
  „ 2 sides   „   = 8
  „ perimeter „   = 64
60 cubes of perimeter   = 3840 circumference
                        = distance of earth.
Cube of 60 times side   = 60^3 circumference
                        = distance of Belus
or cube of 15 times perimeter = distance of Belus.

From these few data it would appear that Richborough most probably ranks under the Babylonian standard; if so, its origin will date from a period anterior to the Roman conquest of Britain, and the building (like many other sacred structures which we have noticed) had been converted into a fortress.

The Roman remains still existing at Reculver are less interesting than those at Richborough, chiefly because they are of less magnitude, and are more dilapidated. Very close to the ruins of the ancient church, whose spires were once held in such reverence that ships entering the Thames were wont to lower their top-sails as they passed, is an area, now partly under the plough, and partly a kitchen garden. It is somewhat elevated above the surrounding fields; and, descending a little distance to the west of the ruined church, we are under the Roman wall, which still stands on the western and southern sides with its layers of flat stones of concrete, defying the dripping rain and the insidious ivy. The castle stood upon a natural rising ground, beneath which still flows the thread-like stream of the river Stour or Wantsum. Although it was once the key of the northern mouth of the great estuary, it did not overhang the sea on the northern cliff, as the old church ruin now hangs. When the legions were here encamped, it stood far away from the dashing of the northern tide, which for many generations has been here invading the land with an irresistible power. Century after century has the wave been gnawing at this cliff; and, as successive portions have fallen, the bare sides have presented human bones, and coins, and fragments of pottery, and tessellated pavements, which told that man had been here, with his comforts and luxuries around him, long before Ethelbert was laid beneath the floor of the Saxon church, upon whose ruins the sister spires of the Norman rose, themselves to be a ruin, now preserved only as a sea-mark. Reculver is a memorable example of the changes produced in the short period of three centuries. Leland's description of the place is scarcely credible to those who have stood beneath these spires, on the very margin of the sea, and have looked over the low ruined wall of the once splendid choir, upon the fishing-boats rocking in the tide beneath, — " Reculver is now scarce half a mile from the shore." In another place, " Reculver standeth within a quarter of a mile or a little more from the sea-side."

Through the once broad channel of the Wantsum the Roman vessels from the coast of Gaul sailed direct into the Thames, without going round the North Foreland; and the entrance to the estuary was defended by the great castle of Richborough at the one end, and by the lesser castle of Reculver at the other.

In a short account of Swinshead, in Lincolnshire, the following paragraph appears: — Near the town is a circular Danish encampment, 60 yards in diameter, surrounded by a double fosse, all remarkably perfect to the present day. This was, doubtless, a port of importance, when the Danes, or Northmen, carried their ravages through England, in the time of Ethrelred I.; and the whole country passed permanently into the Danish hands about A. D. 877. The inner fosse is almost encircled with willows, and the whole work, except to the eye of the antiquarian, is scarcely associated with the strategies of war and siege.

Circumference of circle having a diameter of $59\frac{3}{4}$ yards, or 179 feet $= 562$ feet $= 2$ stades $= 486$ units.

Cube of circumference of circle $= 486^3 =$ circumference of earth in units.

($684^2 =$ circumference of earth in stades.)

Diameter $59\frac{3}{4}$ yards $= 179$ feet $= 154$ units.

Cylinder having height $=$ diameter of base

$= 153$ &c. units	$= \frac{1}{10}$	circumference	$= 36$ degrees,
sphere	$= \frac{1}{15}$	,,	$= 24$	,,
cone	$= \frac{1}{30}$	,,	$= 12$	,,

If the circumference of the fosse $= 514$ units,
cube of circumference $= 514^3 = \frac{1}{8}$ distance of the moon,
cube of 2 circumference $\qquad =$ distance of the moon.

The side of the square enclosure of the tower of Belus

$$= 2 \text{ stades} = 486 \text{ units.}$$
$$514 - 486 = 28$$
$$\tfrac{1}{2} = 14.$$

Hence if the thickness of the wall $= 14$ units,

cube of inner side would $\qquad =$ circumference of the earth,

cube of outer side $\qquad = \frac{1}{6}$ distance of moon,

cube of twice outer side $\qquad =$ distance of moon,

cube of circumference of circle $\qquad =$ circumference of the earth,

cube of 60 circumference of circle $= 60^3 = 216000$ circumference of earth,

$\qquad =$ distance of Belus,

$\qquad =$ cube of Babylon,

sphere $\qquad =$ distance of Neptune,

pyramid $= \frac{1}{3}$ cube $\qquad =$ distance of Uranus,

$\qquad =$ diameter orbit Saturn,

cube of $\frac{1}{4}^\circ$ diameter $\qquad = \frac{1}{3}$ circumference of the earth.

The great power of the Druids brought upon them the vengeance of the Romans, who in other instances were seldom intolerant. The pretext for this was the cruelty committed by the Druids in their sacred rites; but the true reason was, their influence over the people. The authority of the Druids in Gaul was by various means so much reduced in the time of Claudius, that this emperor is said to have destroyed them altogether about A. D. 45; and in Britain, Suetonius Paulinus, the governor of that country under Nero, having taken the island of Anglesey, not only cut down the sacred groves of the Druids in that place, and overturned their altars, but also burnt many of the Druids themselves in those fires which they had kindled for sacrificing the Roman captives, if the Britons had gained the victory. So many of the Druids were destroyed on this occasion, and in the subsequent revolt under Queen Boadicea, that they never afterwards made any figure. Their religion, however, continued, and prevailed even long after the introduction of Christianity.

The remains of the " Jewry Wall " at Leicester, supposed to have been a Roman station, may also, from its dimensions, have probably been originally a Druidical enclosure. It is stated in the Archæological papers, that in the western quarter of the town of Leicester stood a massive pile of ancient masonry, known as the Jewry Wall. Leicester was the Rata of the Romans. It has been thought that the probability is strongly in favour of a temple dedicated to Janus, as the principal of the gods, and the representative of the early Sol might have been erected in such a station. A reference to a modern map of Leicester would show that three sides of a parallelogram might yet be discerned in the outline of the present streets, and if a dotted line were drawn from a point in the north wall, near the river Soar to a corresponding point near the south gates, parallel with the eastern wall, that line would pass through the Jewry Wall, and complete a quadrangular area, giving the whole enclosure a circuit of about 2800 yards, the extent of some of the ancient Roman stations.

Circuit = 2800 yards = 8400 feet = 7263 units,
4 times circuit   = 29052 units,

distance of Belus $= 29160^3$ units
$= 120^3$ stades $=$ cube of Babylon.

If 4 times circuit of the Jewry Wall $= \frac{1}{4}$ circuit of the walls of Babylon, then cube of 4 times circuit of Jewry Wall

$=$ distance of Belus,

Sphere	$=$	,,	Neptune,
Pyramid	$=$	,,	Uranus,

$=$ diameter of orbit of Saturn.

The most perfect remains of a Druidical temple in the Isle of Man are to be found at Glen Darragh. It is formed of stones of moderate size, placed erect and at moderate distances, enclosing a circle 14 yards in diameter.

Diameter 14 yards $= 42$ feet $= 36 \cdot 3$ units,
Circumference $= 114$,,

$10 \times 114 \cdot 8 = 1148$
1148^3 &c. $= \frac{40}{3}$ circumference.
$(3 \times 10 \times 114 \cdot 8 \ \&c.)^3 = \frac{40}{3} \times 3^3 = \ 360.$
$(2 \times 3 \times 10 \times 114 \cdot 8 \ \&c.)^3 = 360 \times 2^3 = 2880.$

Cube of 60 times circumf. of circle $= 2880$ circumf. of earth,
$=$ diameter of the orbit of Mercury.

Cube of 30 times circumf. of circle $= 360$ circumf. of earth,
$= \frac{1}{8}$ diameter of the orbit of Mercury.

So that the diameter of the orbit of Mercury will $=$ about 6890^3.

If the diameter $= 36 \cdot 64$,
then $36640^3 =$ diameter of the orbit of Belus;

Or, cube of 1000 times diameter $=$ diameter of the orbit of Belus.

Glen Darragh, in the Manks' language, signifies "the Vale of Oaks." Whence it would appear that it was originally planted with those trees, which the Druids held in great veneration. The spot of ground on which their remains are situated is barren, bleak, and uncultivated.

Peel Castle stands on a small rocky island. Here are the remains of two churches: one dedicated to St. Patrick,—the era of its erection unknown; the other, called St. German's, or the cathedral, constructed about the year 1245. About the middle of the area, a little to the northward of the churches, is a square pyramidical mound of earth, terminating obtusely. Each of its sides faces one of the cardinal points of the compass, and measures about 70 yards. Time and weather have rounded off its angles; but, on a careful observation, it will be found to have been originally of the figure here described. Tumuli of this kind are not uncommon in the island.

$$70 \text{ yards} = 210 \text{ feet} = \tfrac{3}{4} \text{ stade.}$$

Thus the circuit of the mount will equal 3 stades.

Side $= 210$ feet $= 181$ &c. units.

Cube of side $= 181^3$ &c. $= \tfrac{1}{19}$ circumference $= 19$ degrees.

Thus the cube will be the reciprocal of itself.

$182^3 = \tfrac{1}{180}$ distance of the moon.

So 180 times the cube of the side equals the distance of the moon from the earth.

$$(10 \times 182)^3 = \tfrac{1000}{180} = \tfrac{50}{9} = \text{distance of the moon.}$$
$$(3 \times 10 \times 182)^3 = \tfrac{50}{9} \times 3^3 = 150.$$

Cube of 30 times side $= 150$ distance of the moon,
$= $ distance of Mercury.

150 cubes $=$ distance of Belus.

Circuit of mount $= 3$ stades,
$= 729$ units.

$$(723)^3 = \tfrac{1}{3} \text{ circumference.}$$
$$(3 \times 723)^3 = \tfrac{1}{3} \times 3^3 = 90.$$

30 cubes of 3 times circuit $= 2700$ circumference,
$= $ distance of Venus.

Cube of 6 times circuit $= 90 \times 8 = 720$.

300 cubes $= 216000$ circumference $=$ distance of Belus;

or, cube of 1 stade $= 243^3 = \tfrac{1}{8}$ circumference.

cube of 3 stades $= 729^3 = \tfrac{27}{8}$.

Cube of twice circuit $=$ cube of 6 stades $= 27$ circumfer.

100 cubes $= 2700$ circumference $=$ distance of Venus.

Cube of 40 times circuit = cube of 120 stades

$\qquad$ = cube of Babylon = distance of Belus.

Sphere $\qquad$ = distance of Neptune;

or, $\qquad 182^3 = \frac{1}{180}$ distance of the moon.

$(4 \times 182)^3 = \frac{1}{180} \times 4^3 = \frac{64}{180}$.

Cube of perimeter $= \frac{64}{180}$.

$(5 \times 4 \times 182)^3 = \frac{64}{180} \times 5^3 = \frac{400}{9}$.

9 cubes of 5 times perimeter = 400 distance of the moon,

$\qquad$ = distance of the earth.

$(3 \times 5 \times 4 \times 182)^3 = \frac{400}{9} \times 3^3 = 1200$.

Cube of 15 times perimeter $= 1200$.

Pyramid $= \frac{1}{3}$ cube = 400 distance of the moon

$\qquad$ = distance of the earth.

Again, $(3 \times 182)^3 = \frac{1}{180} \times 3^3 = \frac{27}{180} = \frac{3}{20}$ dist. of moon.

$(10 \times 3 \times 182)^3 = \frac{3000}{20} = 150$.

Cube of 30 times side = 150 distance of the moon

$\qquad$ = distance of Mercury.

20 cubes of 3 times side = 3 times distance of the moon.

Tynwald, in the Isle of Man, is described as a round hill of earth cut into terraces, and ascended by steps of earth like a staircase, on one side. Here the Lord or King of Man was crowned. He sat in a chair of state, with his face to the east, towards a chapel, where prayers and a sermon were made on the occasion. His barons, viz., the bishop and abbot, with the rest in their degrees, sat beside him. His beneficed men, counsellors, and deemsters, were before him : his gentry and yeomen were in the third degree. The commons stood without the circle, with three clerks in surplices. The entrance into the area had stone jambs, covered with transverse imposts, like those of Stonehenge. Grose calls these terraced barrows Danish mounts.

In Train's " History of the Isle of Man," the Tynwald, or Judicial Hill, is described as an ancient mound, of a circular form. It was formerly surrounded by a wall of about 100 yards in circumference. The approach to the top is by a flight of steps. There are three circular seats, or benches, below the summit, which are regularly advanced 3 feet above each other. The circumference of the lowest is about 80 yards. There is a proportionable diminution of the circumference of width of the two higher. The diameter of the top is 6 feet. It has been the site of great battles in the thirteenth century; but it derives its principal celebrity from being the place where the laws of the island have been promulgated from an unknown period of antiquity.

Tumuli are numerous,—some of them of very large size; Cronk-ny-maroo being 40 feet long by 20 broad: while Cranck-na-moar, or as it is called by the inhabitants, "the fairy hill," is a truncated cone, nearly 40 feet high and upwards of 400 in diameter. Its summit forms an area of 25 feet square, surrounded by elevated edges in the form of a parapet 5 feet high. As this round mound was surrounded by the remains of a fosse, it was most probably an artificial hill-fort, and the work doubtless of the earliest inhabitants. Cromlechs and cairns are also of frequent occurrence. In the kist-vaens, however, sometimes found beneath the cairns, a skeleton has been discovered, with the thigh-bones folded on the breast.

Druidism appears to have flourished in the Isle of Man. Its central situation in respect to England, Wales, Ireland, and Scotland, probably pointed it out as a convenient gathering-place for the ministers of that religion.

There were two Arch-Druids: one resided in the Isle of Man, the other in Anglesea.

"To the westward of the ancient city of Pantinamit, in Guatemala, is a little mount," observes Fuentes, "on which stands a small round building, about 6 feet in height. Seated round this building, the judges heard and decided causes; and ιere also their sentences were executed, after the oracular, black, transparent stone in the ravine below had been consulted."

Several of the pyramids of Saccara have lost their casing, and present naked sides of sand and rubbish. The principal one here is, in descriptive truth, not a pyramid; but vast, square, altar-like steps, six in number, rise in graduated lessening proportions to a flat summit.   Arab tradition calls it the Seat of Pharaoh, and states it to have been the spot whence the ancient kings of Egypt promulgated their laws to their assembled subjects.   (Scenes and Impressions in Egypt.)

Circumference of Tynwald $=100$ yards $=300$ feet $=259$ units.

$$258^3, \&c. = \tfrac{8}{800} \text{ distance of the moon.}$$
$$(10 \times 258)^3 = \tfrac{8000}{800} = 16.$$
$$(5 \times 10 \times 258)^3 = 16 \times 5^3 = 2000.$$

Cube of 50 times circumference $=2000$ distance of moon.
$$=5 \text{ times distance of the earth.}$$

$(5 \times 258, \&c.)^3 = \tfrac{8}{800} \times 5^3 = \tfrac{1000}{800} = 2$ distance of the moon.

Cube of 5 times circumference $=$ diameter orbit of moon.
$$(8 \times 5 \times 258, \&c.)^3 = 2 \times 8^3 = 1024.$$

2 cubes of 40 times circumference $= 2048$ distance of the moon.

Distance of Jupiter $=2045$.

Circumference of lowest seat $=80$ yards $=240$ feet $=207$ units.

$$208^3, \&c. = \tfrac{8}{1000} \text{ distance of the moon.}$$
$$(5 \times 208)^3 = \tfrac{8}{1000} \times 5^3 = 1.$$

Cube of 5 times circumference $=$ distance of moon.
Cube of 10 times circumference $=8$,,
50 cubes of 10 times circumference $=400$,,
$$=\text{distance of earth.}$$

$$(16 \times 5 \times 208)^3 = 1 \times 16^3 = 4096 \text{ distance of moon.}$$
Cube of 80 times circumference $=4096$,,
Diameter of orbit of Jupiter $=4090$,,

The cube of the circumference of the wall is double the cube of the circumference of the lowest seat.

If circumference $=257$ units,
$$4 \times 257 = 1028.$$
Distance of the moon $= 1028^3$.

Cube of 4 times circumference = distance of the moon.

If circumference = 261 units,

Cube of 50 times circumference = 13050^3 = distance of Jupiter.

If circumference = 252·8 units,

$$30 \times 252\cdot8 = 7584.$$

Distance of the earth = 7584^3.

Cube of 30 times circumference = distance of the earth.

Diameter of highest seat = 6 feet = 5·2 units.

Circumference = 16·3 ,,

$$10 \times 16\cdot3 = 163.$$

163^3, &c. $= \frac{4}{1000}$ distance of the moon.

Hence cube of circumference of lowest seat : cube of 10 times circumference of highest seat :: $\frac{8}{1000}$: $\frac{4}{1000}$ distance of the moon :: 2 : 1.

Or cube of circumference of lowest seat : cube of circumference of highest seat :: 2 : $\frac{1}{1000}$ :: 2000 : 1.

If the circumference of the base = 16·6 units, then twice circumference of base to the power of 3 times 3 = 33·2⁹.

= twice distance of Belus.

= twice cube of Babylon.

= cube of Nineveh.

= distance of Ninus.

Thus it appears that the Druidical circle is symbolical of infinity or eternity.

$$(10 \times 16\cdot3)^3 = \tfrac{4}{1000} \text{ distance of the moon.}$$
$$(10 \times 10 \times 16\cdot3)^3 = \tfrac{4000}{1000} = 4.$$
$$(5 \times 10 \times 10 \times 16\cdot3)^3 = 4 \times 5^3 = 500.$$

Thus cube of 500 times circumference at the top,

= 500 times distance of the moon.

Cube of circumference : cube of 500 circumference.

$$:: \frac{4}{1000^2} : 500.$$

:: 4 : 500,000,000.

:: 1 : 125,000,000.

2 circumference at base = 33·2 units.

$33\cdot2 : 33\cdot2^9 :: 2$ circumference : 2 distance of Belus.

   $:: 2$ circumference of circle : 2×60^3 circumference of earth.

   $::$ circumference of circle : 60^3 circumference of earth.

    Hence 2 circumference of circle : $(2$ circumference$)^9$.

      $:: 2$ circumference   ,,   : distance of Ninus.

      $::$ circumference   ,,   : distance of Belus.

      $::$ $16\cdot6$ units   : 216000 circumference

of the earth.

    $:: 16\cdot6 : 243 \times 684^2 \times 216000$ units.

    $:: 16\cdot6 : 243 \times 684^2 \times 60^3.$

    $::$ circumference of circle : $\frac{1}{4}$ $(2$ circumference of circle$)^9$,
or 2 circumference : $(2$ circumference$)^9$.

    $:: 33\cdot2 : 486 \times 684^2 \times 60^3.$

If diameter of base of highest seat $= 6$ units, then $6^{12} =$ diameter orbit of the moon.

If circumference of base $= 33\cdot7$ units, cube of 200 times circumference $= 6740^3.$

         $=$ distance of Venus.

Tumulus 40 by 20 feet $= 34\cdot58$ by $17\cdot29$ units.

      $(10 \times 34\cdot4)^3 = \frac{3}{80}$ distance of the moon.

      $(2 \times 10 \times 34\cdot4)^3 = \frac{3}{10}.$

      $(10 \times 2 \times 10 \times 34\cdot4)^3 = \frac{1000}{10} = 300.$

Cube of 200 times greater side $= 300$ distance of the moon $=$ diameter orbit of Mercury.

Cube of 1000 times greater side $= 300 \times 5^3 = 37500$ distance of moon $= 10$ times distance of Saturn.

Cube of less side $= \frac{1}{8}$ cube of greater.

Perimeter $= 3$ times greater side.

Cube of 10 times perimeter $(3 \times 10 \times 34\cdot6)^3 = \frac{3}{80} \times 3^3 = \frac{81}{80}$ distance of the moon.

Hence if cube of 10 times perimeter $=$ distance of the moon,
              perimeter will $= 102\cdot8$ units.

    Greater side $= \frac{1}{3} 102\cdot8 = 34\cdot26$, &c.

    $(30 \times 34\cdot26, \&c)^3 = 1028^3 =$ distance of the moon.

Cube of 30 times greater side = distance of the moon.

150 cubes = distance of Mercury.

150^2 cubes = distance of Belus.

Cube of 10 times perimeter = distance of the moon.

Tumulus 40 by 20 feet = 34·58 by 17·29 units.

$200 \times 34·4 = 6880.$

Diameter orbit of Mercury = 6880^3.

$200 \times 17·2 = 3440.$

$\frac{1}{8}$ diameter orbit of Mercury = 3440^3.

= 360 circumference of the earth.

Cube of 200 times greater side
= diameter orbit of Mercury.

Cube of 200 times less side
= $\frac{1}{8}$ diameter orbit of Mercury.

Sum of 2 sides = $34·4 + 17·2 = 51·6$,

$20 \times 51·4 = 1028$,

distance of the moon = 1028^3.

Cube of 20 times sum of 2 sides
= distance of the moon.

Cube of 200 times sum or of 100 times perimeter
= 1000 distance of the moon.

or $200 \times 34·45 = 6890$,

diameter orbit of Mercury = 6890^3.

Conical Hill.

Diameter of base is upwards of 400 feet, or 346 units.

Say diameter = 350, &c.

Cylinder having height = diameter of base = 350, &c. units
will = 350^3, &c. × ·7854.

$= \frac{3}{10}$ circumference = 108 degrees

Sphere $= \frac{2}{3} = \frac{2}{10}$,, = 72 ,,

Cone $= \frac{1}{3} = \frac{1}{10}$,, = 36 ,,

Cylinder having height = diameter of base = 10 × 350, &c.
will = $\frac{1000}{10} = 300$ circumference.

Sphere ,, = 200 ,,

Cone ,, = 100 ,,

Or 351^3, &c. $=\frac{1}{2\cdot5}$ distance of the moon.

$(10 \times 351)^3 = \frac{1000}{2\cdot5} = 40.$

10 cubes of 10 times diameter $= 400$ distance of the moon $=$ distance of the earth.

If diameter $= 347\cdot6$ units,
circumference $= 1092$

$\frac{1}{2}$,, $= 546,$

$546^3 = \frac{3}{2\cdot0}$ distance of moon,

$(10 \times 546)^3 = \frac{1000}{2\cdot0} = 150,$

$=$ distance of Mercury,

$(10 \times 2 \times 546)^3 = 150 \times 2^3 = 1200$ distance of the moon,

pyramid $= \frac{1}{3}$ cube $= 400,$

$=$ distance of the earth.

This cube of 10 times $\frac{1}{2}$ circumference of circle or of 5 times circumference $=$ distance of Mercury.

Cube of 10 times circumference $= 1200$ distance of the moon.

Pyramid $= 400 =$ distance of the earth.

12 times circumference $= 12 \times 1092 = 13104.$

Distance of Jupiter $= 13040^3.$

If diameter $= 350,$ &c. units,
circumference $= 1100,$,,

$(2 \times 110,$ &c.$)^3 = \frac{1}{100}$ distance of the moon,

$(10 \times 2 \times 110,$ &c.$)^3 = \frac{1000}{100} = 10.$

Cube of twice circumference $= 10$ distance of the moon.

Cube of $2 \times \frac{10}{4}$ or of 5 diameter $= 5$,,

If circumference $= 1136,$ &c. units, circumference will $= \frac{1}{100000}$ circumference of earth.

If circumference $= 1085,$ &c. units, circumference will $= \frac{1}{1000000}$ distance of the moon.

$=$ one millionth part distance of the moon.

The Druid's Stone.

" While toiling along these wastes (in Portugal), I observed a little way to my left a pile of stones of rather a singular appearance, and rode up to it. It was a Druidical altar, and the most perfect and beautiful one of the kind which I had

ever seen. It was circular, and consisted of stones immensely
large and heavy at the bottom, which, towards the top, became thinner and thinner, having been fashioned by the hand
of art to something of the shape of scollop shells. These
were surmounted by a very flat stone, which slanted down
towards the south, where was a door. Three or four individuals might have taken shelter within the interior, in which
was growing a small thorn tree. I gazed with reverence and
awe upon the pile where the first colonies of Europe offered
their worship to the unknown God. The temples of the
mighty and skilful Roman, comparatively of modern date,
have crumbled to dust in its neighbourhood. The churches
of the Arian Goth, his successor in power, have sunk beneath
the conqueror of the Goth : where and what are they ? Upon
the rock, masses of hoary and vanishing ruin. Not so
the Druid's stone ; there it stands on the hill of winds as
strong and as freshly new as the day, perhaps thirty centuries back, when it was first raised by means which are a
mystery. Earthquakes have heaved it, but its copestone has
not fallen ; rain floods have deluged it, but failed to sweep it
from its station ; the burning sun has flashed upon it, but
neither split nor crumbled it ; and time, stern old time, has
rubbed it with his iron tooth, and with what effect, let those
who view it declare. There it stands, and he who wishes to
study the literature, the learning, and the history of the
ancient Celt and Cymbrian, may gaze on its broad covering,
and glean from that blank stone the whole known amount.
The Roman has left behind him his deathless writings, his
history, and his songs ; the Goth, his liturgy, his traditions,
and the germs of noble institutions ; the Moor, his chivalry,
his discoveries in medicine, and the foundations of modern
commerce ; and where is the memorial of the Druidic races ?
Yonder ; that pile of eternal stone ! "—*Borrow's Bible in
Spain.*

The Brahmins of Asia and the Druids of Europe were
constantly to be found in the recesses of the sacred grotto,
and in the bosom of the embowering forest, observes Maurice. Here, undisturbed, they chanted forth their devout

orisons to their creator; there they practised the severities of bodily mortification; here they taught mankind the vanity of wealth, the folly of power, and the madness of ambition.

It will be seen that the Brahmins, like the Druids, made use of the Babylonian standard in the construction of their temples.

Herodotus states that the strong and magnificent walls, which now go under the name of Ecbatana, were built by Deioces, the first king of the Medes. These walls are of a circular form, one within the other, and of equal heights. The situation of the place, rising like a hill, was favourable to the design. But the industry of man has strengthened it more than nature; for it is enclosed by seven walls, and the palace of the king, where the treasures are kept, is built within the last. The first and most spacious of these walls is equal in circumference to the city of Athens, and white from the foot of the battlements. The second is black, the third of a purple colour, the fourth blue, and the fifth of a deep orange. All these are coloured with different compositions; but of the two innermost walls, one is painted on the battlements with a silver colour, and the other gilded with gold.

We find the fortress of Ecbatana, like the pagoda of Seringham, encompassed by seven walls. In the centre of the fortress were placed the palace and treasures of the king. In the centre of the pagodal enclosures were placed the temple and treasures of the priests.

Next let us compare the fortress of Herodotus, at Ecbatana, in Central Asia, with the fortress of Humboldt, Xochicalco, in Central America. Each appears to have been formed from a natural hill, by the hands of man, into a succession of walled terraces. One has seven and the other five terraces. Both have platforms at the top, or both are terraced, truncated, conical hills, or teocallis.

When Deioces became sovereign, and had intrenched himself in the centre of this great teocalli, he ordered that no one should be admitted to the king's presence, but should transact all affairs with him by messengers, thus rendering access to his presence as difficult as it was to approach the idol in the temple of Seringham.

Deioces, like Montezuma, appears to have been sovereign pontiff. Deioces was named, and, with great applause and general consent, elected king. Montezuma ascended to the throne by unanimous election, in 1502. He was esteemed a person of great bravery, and was likewise a priest. The Medes observing the equity of the conduct of Deioces, chose him for their judge ; and he, aspiring to sovereign power, performed that office with all possible regard to justice. When Deioces became sovereign he ordered messengers to communicate with him on affairs of state, and that none should be permitted to see him ; and that either to laugh or spit in his sight should be accounted indecent. Montezuma, having ascended the throne, decreed that no one should enter the palace, either to serve the king, or to confer with him on any business, without pulling off his shoes and stockings at the gate. No one was allowed to appear before the king in any pompous dress, as it was deemed a want of respect to majesty. When he gave audience he listened attentively to all that was communicated to him, and answered everyone by his ministers or secretaries.

It may be observed that the sides of the seven terraces at Ecbatana were all differently coloured, and the central terrace was of gold (symbolical of the sun). The dome of the cavern of Mithra, as described by Porphyry, represented orbs of different metals, symbolical of the sun and planets performing their ceaseless and undeviating revolutions.

The city of Athens at first consisted of nothing but the citadel, built on the top of a high rock, 60 stadia round, called Cecropia, from Cecrops, the first king of Athens. When, from the increase of inhabitants, the lower ground was built upon, the citadel was called Acropolis.

The citadel was, in after times, surrounded with a strong wall, of which one part was built by Cimon, and another by some Pelasgi, who lived at the bottom of the citadel.—(*Pausanias.*)

There was but one entrance to the citadel, by stairs. The

vestibules to it, called Propylæa, were built of white marble.

In the citadel were several magnificent edifices, the chief of which was the temple of Minerva, called Parthenon. It was burnt by the Persians, and rebuilt with the finest marble by Pericles. It is still standing, and esteemed one of the noblest remains of antiquity; about 229 feet long, 101 feet broad, and 69 feet high.

From whatever quarter a person came to Athens this splendid edifice was to be seen. The two architects employed by Pericles in building it were Ictinus and Callicrates.

Sides of the Parthenon

$$229 \text{ by } 101 \text{ feet,}$$
$$= 198 \text{ ,, } \quad 87 \cdot 3 \text{ units.}$$
$$198^3, \&c. = \tfrac{5}{700} \text{ distance of the moon.}$$
$$(10 \times 198, \&c.)^3 = \tfrac{5000}{700} = \tfrac{50}{7} = 7 \text{ nearly,}$$
$$40 \text{ cubes} \qquad = 7 \times 40 = 280,$$
$$\text{Distance of Venus} \qquad = 281,$$

40 cubes of 10 times greater side
$$= \text{distance of Venus,}$$
$$(10 \times 88)^3 \qquad = 880^3 = 6 \text{ circumference,}$$
$$(4 \times 10 \times 88)^3 = 6 \times 4^3 = 384,$$
$$10 \text{ cubes} = 3840$$
$$\text{Distance of the earth} = 3840.$$

10 cubes of 40 times less side
$$= 3840 \text{ circumference} = \text{distance of the earth.}$$

Sum of 2 sides $= 198, \&c. + 88 = 286, \&c.$
$$287^3 = \tfrac{2}{90} \text{ distance of the moon.}$$
$$(10 \times 287)^3 = \tfrac{2000}{90} = \tfrac{200}{9},$$
$$(3 \times 10 \times 287)^3 = \tfrac{200}{9} \times 3^3 = 600.$$

Cube of 30 times sum of 2 sides or of 15 times perimeter,
$$= 600 \text{ distance of the moon.}$$

604 distance of the moon,
$$= \text{distance of Mars.}$$

Cube of 15 times sum of 2 sides

$$= 75 \text{ distance of the moon.}$$

2 cubes of 15 times sum of 2 sides

$$= 150 \text{ distance of the moon,}$$
$$= \text{distance of Mercury,}$$

Height = 69 feet,

¼ stade = 70¼,

which is the estimated height of the walls of Babylon above the canal.

The Pelasgi were employed in building the strong wall that surrounded the citadel. The Pelasgi appear to have belonged to the wandering masons, whose laborious and scientific works have been traced over the world. It would seem the Pelasgi were the first who erected the temple on the Acropolis, which was burned by the Persians, and afterwards rebuilt by Pericles on the foundation of a temple originally constructed by the architects of a philosophical mission of religion, science, and civilization, to whom Greece was indebted for the early excellence she attained in architecture and the fine arts over the other European nations.

The Pelasgi seem not only to have civilized Greece, but also to have instructed that nation in the early mythology of Egypt and other ancient kingdoms; for the most ancient king of Thessaly was Deucalion, and Pyrrah was both his wife and sister. As Osiris and Isis were brother and sister, husband and wife, so were Manco Capac and Mama Ocallo, both brother and sister, husband and wife; they were called the children of the sun, and pretended to deliver their instruction in his name and by his authority to the Peruvians.

Of the temples in the lower city of Athens, the most remarkable, and indeed one of the most magnificent in the world, was that of Jupiter Olympus. It was supported on marble columns, the first that were built in Athens, and which Sylla afterwards carried to Rome. The temple was four stadia in circuit. It was founded by Pisistratus; some say by Deucalion (Pausanias), but not finished till the time of Adrian.

The stade of Herodotus equals the stade of Babylon, equals that of the Sabæans and wandering masons.

The circuit of the temple of Jupiter equals the circuit of the temple of Belus, equals 4 stades.

The circuit of Athens was originally 60 stades, which equals $\frac{1}{2}$ the side of the square of Babylon, $=\frac{1}{2}$ 120 stades.

60^3 stades $=\frac{1}{8}$ distance of Belus,

$\qquad = \frac{1}{8}$ cube of Babylon.

Cube of twice the circuit of Athens equals cube of side of square of Babylon, equals distance of Belus, equals cube of Babylon.

Athens had also its judicial mount, like the seat of the Pharaohs in Egypt, the Tinwald in the Isle of Man, the mount of the ancient city of Pantinamit, in Guatemala, America.

On an eminence, at a small distance from the citadel, was the place of meeting of the Areopagus (Herodotus), the most ancient tribunal of judges in Athens.

Opposite to the Areopagus was another eminence called Pnyx, where the assemblies of the people used sometimes to meet.

In the temple of the Parthenon was the celebrated colossal statue of Minerva, made by Phidias under the direction of Pericles, 26 cubits high, of gold and ivory.

The cubit of Babylon $=8\cdot43$ inches; 26 cubits $=18\cdot26$ feet English.

Cecrops, the first king of Athens, is said to have come from Sais, in Egypt (Diodorus), about 400 years before the Trojan war, or 1582 B. C. He first induced the inhabitants of Attica, formerly scattered over the country, to live in small towns.

The period of Cecrops' arrival at Athens from Sais corresponds with that of the 18th Egyptian dynasty, when the most magnificent architectural works were executed in Egypt. Ramses II., who reigned 1500 B. C., erected the two obelisks in front of the Luxor, and built the Propylæa. This was about the time of Sesostris, who was called Ramses II. or III.

There was a colossal statue at Sais, 75 feet high (*Herod.*).

75 Babylonian feet = 50 cubits,

       ,,   ,,   = 34·75 feet English.

This statue was placed by Amasis before the temple of Phtha.

Athens, like Sais, had a temple of Minerva, and a colossal statue.

Cecrops was the first who called Jupiter supreme, or the highest, and offered to him only the fruits of the earth. (Pausanias.) He taught his subjects to cultivate the olive, and instructed them to look upon Minerva as the watchful patroness of their city. He gave them laws and regulations, and introduced among them the worship of those deities which were held in adoration in Egypt.

Cicero speaks of five Minervas; one, a daughter of the Nile, who was worshipped at Sais in Egypt.

Dodona, in Epirus, built by the Pelasgi, was famous for the temple and oracle of Jupiter, the most ancient in Greece.

The Greeks borrowed the names of their deities from the Egyptians, according to Herodotus, who also states that two black doves took their flight from the city of Thebes, in Egypt, one of which flew to the temple of Jupiter Ammon, and the other to Dodona, where they acquainted the inhabitants of the country that Jupiter had consecrated the ground, which in future should give oracles. The extensive grove which surrounded Jupiter's temple was endowed with the gifts of prophecy.

Here we find the sacred grove, like that of the Druids, and two missions sent by the religious college at Thebes to Epirus, and the oasis of Ammon.

The fountain at Dodona was totally dry at noon-day, and was restored to its full course at midnight, from which time till the following noon it began to decrease, and at the usual hour it was again deprived of its water.

Ten days' journey from Thebes, says Herodotus, the territories of the Ammonians begin, who have a temple resembling that of the Theban Jupiter. The image of Jupiter, which is placed in the temple of Thebes, has the head of a ram. They have likewise a fountain, which in the morning is tepid ; and growing cold during the hours of walking abroad, becomes very cool about noon, and is then used in watering their gardens. As the day declines, this cold gradually diminishes, till about the setting of the sun the water becomes tepid again, and continues to increase in heat, boils at midnight like a tide, and from that time till the morning cools by degrees. This fountain is called the Fountain of the Sun.

Gliddon thus describes the present state of ancient Sais. Here Apries was strangled by his rebellious subjects 588 B. C., but his body was allowed honourable burial in the tomb of his ancestors, within the precincts of the temple of Neith (a goddess whom the Greeks call Minerva) at Sais, in Lower Egypt. Sais is now Sa-el-Hagar, — Sais the Stony — lying in the delta of Lower Egypt, about two miles from the river. A lake overgrown with sedge, and teeming with wild fowl, indicates the site of the one whereon the priests of Neith performed their annual aquatic processions ; mounds of crude and red brick, with fragments of pottery, marble columns, granite friezes, and other broken relics — proofs of departed greatness — mark the position of the once stupendous temple ; a granite sarcophagus, protruding from the soil, establishes the location of the once vast necropolis. Having been there every season for some years, I have netted ducks on Minerva's lake ; shot jackalls amid the ruins of the sanctuary of Neith ; chased wolves in the commercial part of the city ; speared the wild hog where Apries was strangled ; and scared the owl and bittern from the sepulchre of Amasis.

" In 1816," observes Wallace, " I belonged to the field-force sent against the pirates of Okamundel. After rooting out several nests, we invested Dwarka, and the chief of that place was forced to surrender it. On approaching Dwarka, I was struck with the magnificent external appearance of the temples : within the wall which surrounds the town there are two very large ones, and four much smaller. They stand on very elevated ground. One is an immense pyramid, at least 140 feet high, crowned with glittering balls, having a flag near the top, with a sun and moon. It is curiously carved from bottom to top, like the pagodas in the south of India, and composed of prodigiously large stones. There are seven stories in the pyramid, and two in the base on which it rests. The other great pagoda is not so high, but it is broader; the roof is carried up curiously, by one retirement after another, till it ends in a circular form, surmounted by a ball and flag, Round the outside of that temple, both above and below, there are curious galleries or virandas, which are crowded with Brahmans, who live in the upper part of the temples. The four small pagodas are pyramids, with flags and glittering tops, but they are not very striking objects compared with the two large temples; all these are built in the ancient Egyptian style of architecture. A handsome dome is put over the entrance to one of the pagodas, but I conceive this to have been a modern addition.

" It should be mentioned that the Dwarka pagodas are enclosed in a square, whose side is about 200 yards, by a wall 14 feet high, and of considerable thickness. Besides the great gate from the sea face, there are other small ones, which communicate with the town. The town of Dwarka was taken by escalade by our troops in 1820, upon which occasion the pirates and Arabs, in the service of Moolao Maniek, took post in the pagodas, where they might have defended themselves for a long time. Their priests, apprehensive for the safety of the temples, persuaded the garrison to evacuate the sacred precincts, when our men were getting over the wall, after sustaining some losses. The Arabs and pirates then took post in a swamp, where they were surrounded, and forced to surrender by discharges of grapeshot.

" The pirates are of Wagur origin, having come, it is said, originally from Cutch. Their appearance is wild and barbarous. It may be said they live by plunder. In courage and enterprise they are not surpassed by any people of India. The reliance they place on their deities at Dwarka and Bate inspires them with confidence to undertake anything. Runchor, the god of Dwarka, is supposed to protect them while at sea. His priests are the chief instigators of piracy.

Many vessels are fitted out in his name, as sole owner, and actually belong to the temple, which receives the plunder they bring back; as well as a part from all private adventurers.

"Runchor, the supreme, is on a throne in the great temple, and I could see that he was gorgeously dressed, and covered with gold brocade. His face was frightfully painted, and he looked horrible amidst the glare of lamps that surrounded him in his abode, from which the light of day is excluded. I was nearly crushed to death by the pressure of the crowd. The great drums were beating; the trumpets were sounding; large conch shells were roaring; shrill instruments of music were heard in all directions; the Brahmans were praying aloud, and extorting offerings from the unwilling devotees, some of whom were most anxious to purchase their certificates at as cheap a rate as possible; the devotees were prostrating themselves, and muttering various dialects; and, in short, the whole was a scene of noise and confusion, which to be conceived must be experienced."

At Dwarka we find a pyramidal temple having the height of 140 feet $= \frac{1}{2}$ stade $= \frac{1}{2}$ the height of the pyramidal temple of Belus.

The side of the square enclosure at Dwarka is stated to be about 200 yards.

The pyramid at Dwarka has 7 stories, and the base 2.

The pyramid of Belus had 8 stories.

The sun and moon, the standards of the Sabæans, who first erected pyramidal temples, still waved over the temples at Dwarka, which are built in the Egyptian style.

The height of the surrounding wall at Dwarka $= 14$ feet $= \frac{1}{10}$ the height of the pyramid $= \frac{1}{20}$ stade.

As the wall is of considerable thickness, the difference between the external and internal measurements of the sides would be considerable.

At Dwarka we find the priesthood performing their religious duties at the pyramidal temples; as Cortez found the priesthood officiating at the pyramidal temples in Mexico; and as we still find the hyperbolic temples of the Burmese consecrated to religion, and the priests residing within the sacred enclosure of the temple.

Ramisseram is an island situated in the straits between the island of Ceylon and the continent. It is eleven miles in length by six in the average breadth. There is a pagoda here of great antiquity. The entrance is through a lofty gateway one hundred feet high, covered with carved work. Its door is forty feet high, composed of single stones, placed perpendicularly, with others crossing over. The square of the whole is about six hundred feet, and is certainly one of the finest pieces of architecture in India.

The side of the square enclosure, both at Dwarka and Ramisseram, is about 200 yards = 600 feet = 518 units.

$$514^3 = \tfrac{1}{8} \text{ distance of moon}$$
$$(10 \times 514)^3 = \tfrac{1000}{8} = 125$$
30 cubes of 10 times side = 3750 distance of moon
$$= \text{distance of Saturn}$$
$$(4 \times 514)^3 = \tfrac{1}{8} \times 4^3 = 8 \text{ distance of moon.}$$
50 cubes of 4 times side = 400
$$= \text{distance of earth}$$
$$(8 \times 514)^3 = \tfrac{1}{8} \times 8^3 = 64 \text{ distance of moon.}$$
Cylinder height = diameter of base = 8×514
$$= 50 \text{ distance of moon}$$
3 cylinders $\quad = 150$ distance of moon
$$= \text{distance of Mercury.}$$
8 ,, $\quad = 400$ distance of moon
$$= \text{distance of earth.}$$
or cylinder height = diameter of base
$$= 16 \times 514 = 400 \text{ distance of moon}$$
$$= \text{distance of earth.}$$
Cube of twice side = $(2 \times 514)^3$ = distance of moon
Cube of perimeter $\quad = \quad 8$,,
Cube of 5 times perimeter $\quad = 1000$,,
If side of square $\quad = 521$ &c. units
$$521^3 \text{ \&c.} = \tfrac{1}{4} \text{ circumference.}$$
$$(2 \times 521 \text{ \&c.})^3 = \tfrac{1}{4} \times 8 = 10$$
Cube of twice side = 10
Cube of perimeter = 80 circumference.

When Dowlutabad was taken by Allah-ud-Deen, it was called Deoghir, or Tagara, which means the city of God. It belonged to a powerful Hindoo rajah; and from the immense treasure found in it, the Moguls changed its name to Dowlutabad, which means the rich city.

One of the greatest curiosities of the Deccan is the hill fort of Dowlutabad, in which the Nizam had a garrison. Wallace describes it as being cut out of the solid rock, and apparently impregnable; for the perpendicular height of each face is about 90 feet; and it has a wet ditch, 30 feet broad and 20 feet deep. From the capital of the scarp, the hill shelves up to a point, so gradually, that even if the besiegers could mount the first perpendicular, their labour would be but little more than commenced. The hill itself may be about 350 feet high from the base, and it is cut nearly into a square. It is quite a shell, the fort being excavated out of it, with tanks for the retention of water, and winding passages, which astonish those who have visited its interior. These excavations were made before the invention of gunpowder, and the immense body of solid stone cut away was transported from its original situation to various parts of the fort and city, by the tedious means of human labour.

Height   = 350 feet,
$\frac{5}{4}$ stade = 351$\frac{1}{4}$ feet.

Height of each terrace = 90 feet,
$\frac{1}{4}$ of $\frac{5}{4}$ stade   = 88 feet.

Thus the number of square terraces will be four, like the teocalli of Cholula; but the height of the hill-fort will equal twice the height of the teocalli, equal to $2 \times \frac{5}{8}$, equal to $\frac{5}{4}$ stade.

One of the pyramids at Dashour has the height to apex = 350 feet, and side of the square base = 700 feet.

The content equals $\frac{1}{3}$ circumference, = 120 degrees.

Height 350 feet = 303 units,

$300 \cdot 5 = \frac{1}{2}601 = \frac{1}{2}$ side of Cephrenes' pyramid, the cube of side = $601^3 = \frac{1}{4}$ distance of the moon.

So cube of the height $= 300 \cdot 5^3 = \frac{1}{40}$ distance of the moon.

Or 40 cubes $=$ distance of the moon.

$305^3 = \frac{1}{4}$ circumference.

Tripetty, in the Carnatic, is so sacred, that it is said no European or Mohammedan ever saw its interior. An incarnation of Vishnu is worshipped here. The natives say that the pagodas are built of great carved stones, like those which excite our wonder at Chillambaram, Dwarka, &c., and covered with plates of gilt copper, so curiously ornamented with figures, that they are pronounced the works of superior beings. At the famous pagoda of Malla-cargee and Brahma Rumbo, situated on the south bank of the Krishna, in a desert, 118 miles from Hyderabad, the idols are shown only by flashes of a brass speculum, that fall upon them so as to leave imagination to form a sublime picture, from a faint outline of something which cannot be described.

These temples are enclosed in a great wall, forming a square, 600 feet long by 510, and covered with curious sculptures. But to enter into the description of such fabrics in India, says Wallace, would fill volumes. They are nearly all in the Egyptian style of architecture, and so massy, that they have endured, amidst the wreck of matter around them, for times of which there is now no trace. By what powers of mechanism they were constructed is a curious question for the antiquarian.

Sides of the enclosure are

$$600 \text{ by } 510 \text{ feet,}$$
$$= 518 \quad ,, \quad 440 \text{ units.}$$
$$514^3 = \tfrac{1}{8} \text{ distance of the moon,}$$
$$(2 \times 514)^3 = 1 \qquad ,,$$

Cylinder height $=$ diameter of base,
$$= 8 \times 514,$$
$$= 50 \text{ distance of the moon.}$$

3 cylinders $= 150 \qquad ,,$
$$= \text{distance of Mercury.}$$

Cylinder height   = diameter of base,

                 = 16 × 514,

                 = 400 distance of the moon,

                 = distance of the earth.

440^3 = $\frac{1}{4}$ circumference,

$(2 \times 440)^3$ = $\frac{1}{4} \times 2^3 = 6$,

$(10 \times 2 \times 440)^3$ = 6000.

Cube of 20 times side

                 = 6000 circumference,

                 = $\frac{1}{6}$ distance of Saturn,

                 = $\frac{1}{12}$,,   Uranus,

                 = $\frac{1}{37}$,,   Belus.

Hence cube of twice less side

                 = 6 circumference.

Cube of twice greater side

                 = distance of the moon.

Sum of 2 sides   = 514 + 440 = 477 × 2,

477^3 = $\frac{1}{10}$ distance of the moon,

$(2 \times 477)^3 =$ = $\frac{8}{10}$,,   ,,

$(10 \times 2 \times 477)^3$ = $\frac{8000}{10} = 800$.

Cube of 10 times sum of two sides, or of 5 times perimeter

                 = 800 distance of the moon,

                 = diameter orbit of the earth.

Supposing 514 by 440 units to be the interior dimensions, and allowing 4 units for the thickness of the walls, the external dimensions of the sides will be 514 + 8 and 522 + 8, or 522 by 448 units,

522^3 = $\frac{10}{8}$ circumference,

$(2 \times 522)^3$ = 10   ,,

Mean of the 2 sides = $\frac{1}{2}$ (522 + 448) = 485,

                 and $485^3 = \frac{1}{10}$ circumference.

Thus the cube of twice greater side = 10 circumference.

The cube of the mean of 2 adjoining sides = circumference.

So the cubes will be as 10 : 1;
or 522 by 448 units may be supposed to be the rectangle of the middle of walls, or mean between the external and internal dimensions,

$$522 + 448 = 970 \text{ units,}$$

and 969^3 = 8 circumference,

9690^3 = 8000,

9 cubes = 72000 circumference = distance of Uranus,

27 ,, = 216000 circumference = distance of Belus,

449^3 = $\frac{8}{10}$ circumference,

$(5 \times 449)^3$ = $\frac{8}{10} \times 5^3 = 100,$

$(3 \times 5 \times 449)^3$ = $100 \times 3^3 = 2700.$

Cube of 15 times less side

= 2700 circumference,

= distance of Venus.

Cube of 30 times less side

= $2700 \times 2^3 = 21600$

10 cubes = 216000 circumference,

= distance of Belus.

" Conjeveram is a town of considerable size in the Carnatic, 46 miles south of Madras. The pagoda here is dedicated to Mahadeva, or the mother of the gods. It is a magnificent structure. There is an edifice near it for the accommodation of pilgrims, supported by 1000 stone pillars, carved with figures of Hindoo deities in a very masterly manner."

"The platform at Balbek is 1000 paces long, and 700 feet broad, built entirely by the hands of men, of hewn stones, some of which are 50 or 60 feet long, and 15 or 16 high, but the greater part from 15 to 30 in elevation. This hill of granite was seen by us at its eastern extremity, with its immeasurable foundations and walls, in which three pieces of stone gave a horizontal line of 180 feet, and near 4000 feet superficies.

" We proceeded to the south side of the platform, where the six gigantic columns reared their heads above the horizon of ruins.   To arrive there we were obliged to clear the outer walls, and the steps, pedestals, and foundations of altars, which everywhere obstructed the space between those columns and us.   We reached their bases at last.   Silence is the only language of man when, what he feels surpasses the ordinary measure of his impressions.   We thus remained mute when contemplating these columns, and surveying with the eye their diameter and height, and the admirable sculpture of their architraves and cornices.   They are 7 feet in diameter, and more than 70 feet high; they are composed of only two or three blocks, so perfectly joined together that it is scarcely possible to distinguish the lines of junction; their material is a stone of a slightly gilded yellow, and of a colour between marble and sandstone.

"On the northern side of Balbek, an immense tunnel in the sides of the platform yawned before us," says Lamartine. "We descended into it.   The light which penetrated it by the two extremities enabled us to see sufficiently.   We followed it in all its length of 500 feet, reaching under the whole extent of the temples.   It is 30 feet high, and the walls and arch are formed of blocks, which astonished us by their size, even after those which we had just contemplated.   They are of unequal proportions, but the greatest number are from 10 to 20 feet long.   The stones of the arch are joined without cement; we were unable to divine its purpose.   At the western extremity this tunnel has a branch higher and wider, which is prolonged under the platform of the small temples, which we had first visited.   We threw a superficial glance, as we passed, upon four temples, which would have been considered wonders at Rome, but which are here like the works of dwarfs.

"*The Quarries near Balbek.*—These vast hollows of stone, the walls of which still show the deep traces of the chisel, exhibit various gigantic blocks half detached from their bases, and others completely hewn, on the four sides, which seem to be waiting for the waggons and arms of a giant race to move them.   One of these masses was 62 feet long, with a breadth of 24, and a thickness of 16 feet; such a mass would crush the man of our times, — man would shrink before his own works, — 60,000 men would need their united powers to simply raise this stone, and the platforms of Balbek contain some still more colossal reared 25 and 30 feet above the ground, to support colonnades proportioned to their bases.

" The imagination of the Arabs even, daily witnesses of these wonders, does not attribute them to human power, but to that of genii or supernatural beings. When we consider that these blocks of hewn granite are in some instances 56 feet long, 15 or 16 broad, and of an unknown thickness, and that these prodigious masses are raised one upon the other, 20 to 30 feet above the ground; that they have been cut out of far-distant quarries, conveyed here, and hoisted to such a height to form the pavement for temples, we recoil before such a proof of human capacity. The science of our days has nothing which explains it, and we need not be surprised that people take refuge in the supernatural.

" These masses are evidently of a different date from the temples. They were mysteries to the ancients as well as to us. They belong to an unknown era, possibly antediluvian, and have, in all likelihood, borne a variety of temples, sacred to a successive variety of creeds. To the simple eye, five or six generations of monuments are apparent upon the hill of ruins at Balbek, all of different epochs. Some travellers and some Arab writers attribute these primitive substructions to Solomon, 3000 years before the present time. They say he built Tadmor and Balbek in the desert. The history of Solomon fills the imagination of the orientals; but this supposition, at least, concerning the gigantic substructions of Balbek is utterly improbable. How could a king of Israel, who possessed no port on the sea, lying 10 leagues from his mountains, who was reduced to borrow the ships of Hiram, king of Tyre, to bring him cedars from Lebanon, have extended his dominion beyond Damascus, and as far as Balbek? How could a prince, who, intending to build the temple of temples, the house of the only God, in his capital city, employed in its erection fragile materials, incapable of resisting time, or leaving any durable record, have raised, 100 leagues from his kingdom, in the midst of deserts, monuments built of such imperishable materials? Would he not have rather employed his wealth and power at Jerusalem? And what remains at Jerusalem indicative of such monuments as those at Balbek? Nothing. Solomon can therefore have had nothing to do with them. Whatever may be the fact, some of these Balbek stones, which are 62 feet long, 20 broad, and 15 thick, are the most prodigious masses that humanity has ever lifted. The largest stones in the pyramids of Egypt do not exceed 18 feet, and these are peculiar blocks, placed in certain positions, to give a finishing of special solidity."

Sides of platform

$$1000 \text{ paces by } 700 \text{ feet}$$
$$= 6000 \text{ feet} \quad ,, \quad 700 \quad ,,$$
$$= 5188 \text{ units} \quad ,, \quad 605 \text{ units.}$$

If the greater side $= 5140$ units,

$$514^3 = \tfrac{1}{8} \text{ distance of the moon,}$$
$$(10 \times 514)^3 = \tfrac{1000}{8} = 125.$$

Cube of side $= 125$ distance of the moon,

$$30 \text{ cubes} = \text{distance of Saturn,}$$
$$60 \quad ,, \quad = \quad ,, \quad \text{Uranus,}$$
$$180 \quad ,, \quad = \quad ,, \quad \text{Belus.}$$

Should greater side $= 5460$ units,

Cube of greater side $= 5460^3$,
$$= \text{distance of Mercury.}$$

If less side $= 601$ units,

Cube of less side $= 601^3 = \tfrac{1}{8}$ distance of the moon,
Height $= 40$ feet $= 34 \cdot 6$ units.

Then content of terrace will

$$= 5460 \times 601 \times 34 \cdot 6 = \text{circumference of the earth.}$$

Sphere having diameter 601 units $=$ circumference.
Or if the sides be as 5490 by 610 units.

Then, as at Cholula, $5490^3 =$ distance of Mercury,

$$610^3 = 2 \text{ circumference.}$$

Sum of 2 sides $= 5490 + 610 = 6100$,

$$6100^3 = 610^3 \times 1000 = 2000 \text{ circumference.}$$

Cube of sum of 2 sides $= 1000$ times the cube of the less side $= 2000$ circumference,

Cube of perimeter $= 16000$ „

Cube of perimeter + cube of 2 sides,

$$= 16000 + 2000 = 18000 \text{ circumference,}$$
$$= \tfrac{1}{2} \text{ distance of Saturn,}$$
$$= \tfrac{1}{4} \quad . \text{„} \qquad \text{Uranus,}$$
$$= \tfrac{1}{12} \quad \text{„} \qquad \text{Belus.}$$

Cube of twice perimeter + cube of twice sum of 2 sides

$$= 128000 + 16000 = 144000 \text{ circumference,}$$
$$= \text{diameter of orbit of Uranus,}$$
$$= 100 \text{ times distance of Mercury.}$$

Or 9 cubes of perimeter

$$= 144000 \text{ circumference,}$$
$$= 100 \text{ times distance of Mercury,}$$
$$= 100 \text{ times cube of greater side.}$$

The sides of a court at Balbek are

$$350 \text{ by } 336 \text{ feet } (Volney),$$
$$= 302{\cdot}5 \quad \text{„} \quad 290{\cdot}4 \text{ units,}$$
$$30{\cdot}7^9 = \text{distance of Belus,}$$
$$29160^3 = \text{distance of Belus,}$$

$\tfrac{1}{10}$ greater side to the power of 3 times 3,

$$= \text{cube of } 100 \text{ times less side}$$
$$= \text{distance of Belus.}$$

The avenue leading from Karnac to Luxor is nearly half a league long, and contains a number of sphynxes, some of them in very good preservation. They are now partly shaded by a row of palm-trees, and the two parallel lines are 63 feet asunder. The sphynxes are only 12 feet apart in the line, are made of sandstone, and each has between its fore-legs a mummy-shaped figure with its hands crossed on the breast, and in each hand what is commonly called the sacred tau.

The length of the avenue is nearly ½ a league, or 1½ mile.

Another account makes the length to exceed 1 mile.

1 mile = 18·79 stades = 4549 units.

The cube of 5492 or 5460 units, or of 22·6 or 22·46 stades = distance of Mercury from the sun.

"As we leave the great front of the Luxor, which is on the north side, we pass along an avenue of sphynxes with female heads for the distance of 1500 feet. Here the avenue divides into two branches, nearly at right angles to one another. One avenue leads up to a temple, which is called in the French plan the great Temple of the South. It is lined on each side by a row of colossal rams, the sacred rams of Ammon. This temple, which we may call small, when compared with the enormous structure at a short distance from it, bears all the marks of ancient simplicity ; and yet it is partly built with the materials of a still more ancient temple."

$$1500 \text{ feet} = 1296 \text{ units,}$$
$$1296^3 \quad = 2 \text{ distance of the moon,}$$
$$= \text{diameter of orbit of moon.}$$

Another description makes the avenue about 6560 feet,
$$= 5670 \text{ units;}$$
$$566^3 = \tfrac{1}{6} \text{ distance of moon,}$$
$$= \tfrac{60}{6} = 10 \text{ radii of the earth,}$$
$$5660^3 = \tfrac{1}{4} \ 1000 \text{ distance of the moon,}$$
$$= 10000 \text{ radii of the earth.}$$

The side of the square at Palmyra = 566 units = $\tfrac{1}{10}$ the length of the avenue of sphynxes.

The cube of Cheops = $648^3 = \tfrac{1}{4}$ distance of moon.

Thus the cube of the length of the avenue = the cube of twice the side of the base of Cheops' pyramid = twice the distance of the moon.

$$75 \text{ cubes of } 1296 = \text{distance of Mercury}$$
$$200 \qquad ,, \qquad = \qquad ,, \qquad \text{the earth.}$$

" The second branch, the direction of which makes somewhat more than a right angle with the main avenue, is also lined with sphinxes, having female heads, and runs 600 feet in a straight line."

600 feet $= 518$ units,

and 514^2 units $= \frac{1}{2}$ distance of the moon.

The cube of twice the side, or the cube of the sum of the two sides $= (2 \times 514)^3 =$ distance of the moon.

" The colossal entrance of the magnificent propyla of the building is about 360 feet long, and 148 high, but without sculptures ; the great door in the middle is 64 feet high."

360 feet $= 311$ units,

148 ,, $= 128$,,

The cubes are as 2 : 30 or 1 : 15.

" The whole length of the palace of Carnac, from the western extremity to the western wall, is about 1215 feet. This is the length of the real building itself, not taking into account any propyla that may have existed on the eastern side, or any part beyond the walls of the edifice. The breadth of the narrowest part is 321 feet ; the longest line of width being that of the front propylon, which we have already stated to be about 360 feet."

1215 feet $= 1050$ units,

$1044^3 = 10$ times circumference of the earth.

12^2 times the cube of $1044 = 144 \times 10$ circumference,

$= 1440$ circumference,

$=$ distance of Mercury.

Length $311^3 = \frac{1}{36}$ distance of the moon,

$(6 \times 311)^3 = \frac{1}{36} \times 6^3 = 6$,

$(5 \times 6 \times 311)^3 = 6 \times 5^3 = 750$.

10 cubes of 30 times side $= 7500$ distance of the moon,

$=$ distance of Uranus.

30 cubes of 30 times side $=$,, Belus,

30 spheres $=$,, Neptune.

Height of the doorway $= 55$ units.

$\frac{1}{2} 55 = 27\cdot5$,

and $26\cdot9^2 =$ distance of Uranus.

Height of propyla $= 128$ units,

$$128^3 = \tfrac{4}{270} \text{ circumference,}$$
$$(3 \times 128)^3 = \tfrac{5}{270} \times 27 = \tfrac{5}{10} = \tfrac{1}{2}.$$

Cube of 3 times height $= \tfrac{1}{2}$ circumference ;

or 129^3, &c. $= \tfrac{2}{1000}$ distance of the moon,
$$(10 \times 129, \text{ \&c.})^3 = \tfrac{2000}{1000} = 2.$$

Cube of 10 times height $=$ diameter of the orbit of the moon.

According to Lepsius the stone roof of the great hall at Carnac is supported by 134 pillars, covering a space of 164 feet in length, and 320 in breadth. Each of the 12 middle columns is 36 feet in circumference, and is, up to the architrave, 66 feet high; the other columns, 40 feet high, are 27 feet in circumference.

Hall 164 by 320 feet
$= 141 \cdot 74$ by $276 \cdot 6$ units

141^3, &c. $= \tfrac{1}{40}$ circumference $= 9$ degrees,
$279^3 \qquad = \tfrac{1}{50}$ distance of the moon.

Sum of 2 sides $= 141 \cdot 7 + 279 = 420 \cdot 7$ units, and 423^3, &c. $= \tfrac{2}{3}$ circumference $= 240$ degrees.

Cube of perimeter $= (2 \times 423)^3 = \tfrac{16}{3}$ circumference.
Cube of less side $= 141^3$, &c. $= \tfrac{1}{40}$,,
$$(10 \times 141, \text{ \&c.})^3 = \tfrac{1000}{40} = 25,$$
$$(10 \times 10 \times 141, \text{ \&c.})^3 = 25000.$$

Inscribed cylinder $= 19635 =$ distance of Jupiter, or cylinder, height $=$ diameter $= 100$ times the side 141, &c., $=$ distance of Jupiter.

Before this hall is an open court about 270 by 320 feet
$= 233 \cdot 37$ by $276 \cdot 5$ units,

235^3, &c. $= \tfrac{8}{70}$ circumference,
$279^3 \qquad = \tfrac{1}{50}$ distance of the moon.

Sum of 2 sides $= 235 + 279 = 514$, and $514^3 = \tfrac{1}{8}$ distance of the moon.

Cube of perimeter $= (2 \times 514)^3 =$ distance of the moon.
Cube of perimeter of hall $= \tfrac{16}{3}$ circumference,
$$(3 \times \text{perimeter})^3 = \tfrac{16}{3} \times 3^3 = 144.$$

10 cubes of 3 times perimeter $= 1440 =$ distance of Mercury,
150×10 cubes of 3 times perimeter $= 216000 =$ Belus.

Cube of greater side $= 279^3 = \frac{1}{10}$ distance of the moon,

$$(10 \times 279)^3 = \frac{1980}{88} = 20.$$

20 cubes of 10 times greater side $= 400$ distance of the moon $=$ distance of the earth.

141^3, &c. $= \frac{1}{10}$ circumference,
$$(40 \times 141, \&c.)^3 = \frac{1}{10} \times 40^3 = 1600,$$

$(3 \times 40 \times 141, \&c.)^3 = 1600 \times 3^3 = 43200 = \frac{1}{5}$ distance of Belus, or cube 120 times less side $= \frac{1}{5}$ distance of Belus, and $\frac{1}{5}$ cube of 120 stades $= \frac{1}{5}$ cube of Babylon $= \frac{1}{5}$ distance of Belus.

Thus cube of 120 times less side $= \frac{1}{5}$ cube of 120 stades $= \frac{1}{5}$ distance of Belus.

The great plan of the temple terminates a length of 1170 feet, without reckoning the row of sphinxes before its exterior pylon, and without the private sanctuary which was erected by Ramses Miaum directly against the furthest wall of the temple, and in the same area, but in such a manner that the entrance to it was on the opposite side. This enlargement reckoned with it would make the whole length nearly 2000 feet, to the southernmost gate of the outer wall, which makes the whole place about the same breadth. The later dynasties, who found this principal temple completed on all sides, and yet could not renounce the idea of doing honour to this centre of Theban worship, began by erecting small temples on the great plain surrounded by the outer wall, and afterwards gradually enlarging these again.

1170 feet $= 1011$ units,
$1005^3 = 9$ circumference,
and $1028^3 =$ distance of the moon.

Whole length $= 2000$ feet nearly,
$= 1729$ units.

1756^3, &c. $= \quad 5$ distance of the moon $= 300$ radii of earth.
30 cubes $\quad = 150 \quad\quad ,, \quad\quad ,, \quad\quad = $ distance of Mercury.
$1758^3 \quad\quad = \quad 48$ circumference.
30 cubes $\quad = 1440 \quad\quad ,, \quad\quad = $ distance of Mercury.

The cube of twice side = 40 distance of the moon.
$$10 \text{ cubes} = 400 \qquad \text{,,} \qquad \text{,,}$$
$$= \text{distance of the earth.}$$

The side of the outer wall is not given.

$$1170 \text{ feet} = 1011 \text{ units,}$$
$$20 \times 1011 = 20220,$$
distance of Uranus = about 20300^3,
$$2000 \text{ feet} = 1729 \text{ units,}$$
$$4 \times 1729 = 6916,$$
diameter of orbit of Mercury = about 6890^3.
$$1011 + 1729 = 2740,$$
$$2 \times 2740 = 5480,$$
distance of Mercury = 5480^3.

This remarkable place, which in the lapse of 3500 years had grown from the little sanctuary in the midst of the great temple into an entire temple-city, covering a surface of a quarter of a geographical mile in length, and about 2000 feet in breadth, is also an almost unbroken thread, and an interesting standard for the history of the whole new Egyptian empire, from its commencement in the old empire down to its fall under the Roman rule.

1 geographical mile = 5263 units,
$$\text{length} = \tfrac{1}{4} \quad \text{,,} \quad = 1316$$
If length = 1365,
then cube of $4 \times 1365 = 5460^3 =$ distance of Mercury.

If breadth = 1720 units,
cube of 4 times breadth = 6880^3,
$$= \text{diameter of the orbit of Mercury.}$$

The cubes of the sides are as 1 : 2.

Lepsius thus describes the labyrinth of Mœris and the Dodecarchs. " There is a mighty knot of churches still existing, and in the midst is the great square, where the Aulæ stood, covered with the remains of great monolithic pillars of granite, and others of white, hard limestone, gleaming almost like marble.

" We found, on a cursory view of the districts, a number of

confused spaces, as well super as subterranean, and the principal mass of the building, which occupied more than a stadium (*Strabo*), was distinctly to be seen. Where the French expedition had fruitlessly sought for chambers, we literally found hundreds, by and over each other, little, often very small, by larger and great, supported by diminutive pillars, with thresholds and niches, with remains of pillars and single wall slabs, connected together by corridors, so that the description of Herodotus and Strabo are quite confirmed in this respect.

" The disposition of the whole is, that three mighty clumps of buildings, of the breadth of 300 feet, surround a square 600 feet in length and 500 in width; the fourth side is bounded by the pyramid lying behind, which is 300 feet square, and, therefore, does not quite come up to the side of the wings of the buildings.

" When viewed from the heights of the pyramid, the regular plan of the whole lies before one like a map. The labyrinth of chambers runs along here to the south. The Aulæ lay between this and the northerly pyramid opposite, but almost all traces of them have disappeared. The dimensions of the place alone allow us to suspect that it was divided into two parts by a wall, to which the twelve Aulæ, no longer to be distinguished with certainty, adjoined on both sides, so that their entrances were turned in opposite directions, and had close before them the innumerable chambers of the labyrinth. Who was, however, the Maros, Mendes, Imandes, who, according to the reports of the Greeks, erected the labyrinth, or rather the pyramid belonging to it, as his monument ?

" In the royal lists of Manetho, we find the builder of the labyrinth towards the end of the twelfth dynasty, the last of the old empire shortly before the irruption of the Hyksos. The fragments of the mighty pillars and architraves, that we have dug out in the great square of the Aulæ, give us the cartouches of the sixth king of this twelfth dynasty, Amenemha III.; thus is this important question answered in its historical portion. We have obtained an entry into a chamber covered with piles of rubbish that lay before the pyramid, and here we also found the name of Amenemha several times. The builder and possessor of the pyramid is therefore determined. But the account of Herodotus, that the construction of the labyrinth was commenced two hundred years before the time of the Dodecarchs, is not yet confuted. In the ruins of the great masses of chambers surrounding the great square, we have discovered no inscriptions."

The sides of the great square are 600 by 500 feet,

$$= 518\cdot5 \text{ by } 432\cdot1 \text{ units,}$$
$$521^3, \&c. = \tfrac{4}{4} \text{ circumference,}$$
$$433^3 \quad = \tfrac{4}{7} \quad \text{,,}$$

Cubes of the sides are as $\tfrac{4}{4} : \tfrac{4}{7}$
$$:: 7 : 4.$$

Sum of the two sides $= 521 + 433 = 954$ units, and 954^3 $= \tfrac{4}{4}$ distance of the moon.

Cube of the side 521 : cube of the sum of the two sides 954.

$$:: \tfrac{4}{4} \text{ circumference} : \tfrac{4}{4} \text{ distance of the moon,}$$
$$:: \tfrac{5}{4} \qquad \text{,,} \qquad : 48 \text{ radii of the earth.}$$

Sides of square $518\cdot5$ by $432\cdot1$ units,
if   521 by $434\cdot5$,,
then $6 \times 521 = 3126$
$\tfrac{1}{10}$ distance of Venus $= 3126^3$
$$20 \times 434\cdot5 = 8690$$
Distance of Mars $= 8690^3$.

Thus cube of 6 times greater side $= \tfrac{1}{10}$ distance of Venus, cube of 20 times less side $=$ distance of Mars.

Sum of 2 sides $=$ $521 + 434 = 955$
$$10 \times 955 = 9550$$
Diameter of the orbit of the earth $= 9550^3$.

Cube of 10 times sum of 2 sides, or of 5 times perimeter, $=$ diameter of the orbit of the earth.

If sides $= 514$ by 433 &c. units,
$514^3 = \tfrac{1}{8}$ distance of the moon,
$(2 \times 514)^3 =$ distance of the moon,

433^3 &c. $= \frac{2}{40}$ distance of the moon,

$(2 \times 433$ &c.$)^3 = \frac{2}{5}$,, ,, ,,

Cube of sides are as $1 : \frac{1}{5} :: 5 : 3$.

Sum of 2 sides $= 514 + 433$ &c. $= 947$ &c.

$948^3 = \frac{30}{4}$ circumference,

$(2 \times 948)^3 = \frac{30}{4} \times 2^3 = 60$.

Cube of perimeter $= 60$ circumference.

$(4 \times 2 \times 948)^3 = 60 \times 4^3 = 3840$.

Cube of 4 times perimeter $= 3840$ circumference,

$= $ distance of the earth.

$(2 \times 521)^3 = 10$ circumference.

$(3 \times 2 \times 521)^3 = 10 \times 27 = 270$.

10 cubes $= 2700 = $ distance of Venus;

or 10 cubes of 6 times 521 $= $ distance of Venus.

$(12 \times 2 \times 512)^3 = 10 \times 12^3$.

$\frac{1}{12}$ cube of 24 times greater side

$= 10 \times 12^2 = 1440$ circumference $= $ distance of Mercury.

$\frac{150}{12}$, or $12\frac{1}{2}$ cubes $= 216000$ circumf. $= $ distance of Belus.

$954^3 = \frac{1}{2}$ distance of the moon.

$(10 \times 954)^3 = \frac{1000}{} = 800$.

Cube of 10 times sum of 2 sides, or of 5 times perimeter,

$= 800$ distance of the moon $= $ diameter of orbit of the earth.

Less side $= 433$ &c. units.

30×433 &c. $= 13000$.

Distance of Jupiter $= $ about 13040^3,

or, cube of 30 times less side $= $ distance of Jupiter.

Side of base of pyramid $= 300$ feet $= 259 \cdot 2$ units.

262^3 &c. $= \frac{1}{60}$ distance of the moon

$= $ radius of the earth.

$(60 \times 262)^3 = \frac{1}{60} \times 60^3$ $= 3600$ distance of moon

$= 3750 - 150$

$= $ distance between Saturn and Mercury.

If side $= 257$ units, then cube of perimeter of base $= (4 \times 257)^3 = 1028^3 = $ distance of the moon, and cube of side of base $= \frac{1}{64}$.

■ 3

262^3 &c. $= \frac{1}{60}$ distance of the moon.

$(20 \times 262$ &c.$)^3 = \frac{1}{60} \times 20^3 = 113 \cdot 3$ &c.

3 cubes of 20 times side, or of 5 times perimeter

$\qquad = 3 \times 133 \cdot 3 = 400$ distance of the moon
$\qquad =$ distance of the earth.

$(432 \times 3)^3 =$ diameter of orbit of the moon,

$(432 \times 2^4)^3 =$ diameter of orbit of Mercury.

Palmyra.

Extracts, from the "Philosophical Society," of a journey from Aleppo to Palmyra, made by an English party in 1691:—

"The whole enclosed space where the temple at Palmyra stood is a square of 220 yards on each side, surrounded with high and stately walls, built of large square stone, and adorned with pilasters within and without, to the number of 62 on each side, as near as can be computed from those that are left; and upon the cornices which are remaining are to be seen some of the most curious and exquisite carvings in stone that can be met with. The two stones which supported the sides of the great gate are each of them 35 feet in length, artificially carved with vines and clusters of grapes, exceeding bold, and to the life. They are both standing in their places, and the distance between them, which gives the wideness of the gate, is 15 feet; but the space is now walled up, excepting a narrow doorway, which is left.

"On the entrance into the court are seen the remainders of two noble rows of marble pillars, 37 feet high, with their capitals of most exquisitely carved work; but of these only 58 are remaining entire: but there must have been many more, because they appear to have gone round the whole court, and to have supported a spacious double piazza, or cloister. The space within this once beautiful inclosure our travellers conceived to have been an open court, in the midst whereof stood the temple, encompassed with another row of pillars, of a different order and much higher than the former, being 50 feet high, of which there are but sixteen remaining at present; and the whole space contained between these last pillars was 59 yards in length, and 28 in breadth; in the midst of which space is the temple, extending in length 33 yards and upwards, and in breadth 13 or 14. It pointed north and south, having a most magnificent entrance on the west, exactly in the middle of the building; and just over the door may be still discerned part of the wings of a large spread eagle, extending the whole wideness thereof. There is nothing standing of this temple, at present, but the outward walls, in which the windows were not large, but adorned with excellent carving, and narrower at the top than at the bottom.

" Another curiosity at Palmyra are the sepulchres, which are square towers, built of stone or marble, four or five stories high. They stand on the north part of the city, on both sides of a hollow way, for a mile together. They are all of the same form, but of different dimensions and splendour. Two of them were larger than ordinary steeples; the outside of these was of common stone, but the partitions and floors within of good marble, beautified with lively carvings and paintings, and figures of men and women as far as the breast and shoulders, but miserably defaced and broken.

In another description of Palmyra we find, in addition to what has been stated, that north of the temple is an obelisk, consisting of seven large stones, besides its capital and the wreathed work about. At the distance of a quarter of a mile from this obelisk, to the east and west, are two others, besides the fragment of a third, so as to lead to the supposition that there was originally a continued row.

" About 100 paces from the middle obelisk, straight forward, is a magnificent entry to a piazza, 40 feet in breadth, and more than half a mile in length, enclosed with two rows of marble pillars, 26 feet high, and 8 to 9 feet in compass. Of these there still remain 129; and, by a moderate computation, there could not have been originally less than 560. The upper end of this piazza was shut in by a row of pillars, standing somewhat closer than those on each side. A little to the left are the ruins of a stately building, which appears to have been a banqueting-house; it is built of better marble, and finished with still greater elegance than the piazza. The pillars by which it was supported were each of one entire stone, so strong that one of them which had fallen down had not received the slightest injury. It measures 23 feet in length, and in compass 8 feet 9 inches.

" Among these ruins are many sepulchres, ranged on each side of a hollow way, towards the north part of the city, and extending more than a mile. They are square towers, four or five stories high, alike in form, but differing in magnitude and splendour. The outside is of common stone, but the floors and partitions of each story are of marble. A walk crosses the centre of this range of buildings, and the space on each side is subdivided by thick walls into six partitions, the space between which is wide enough to receive the largest corpse. In these niches six or seven are piled on one another."

Sides of the square inclosing the temple

$$= 220 \text{ yards} = 660 \text{ feet} = 570 \text{ units},$$
$$566^3 = \tfrac{1}{6} \text{ distance of the moon}.$$

Thus cube of side $= \tfrac{1}{6}$ distance of the moon,

$$= \tfrac{60}{6} = 10 \text{ radii of the earth}.$$

Sides of temple inclosed by the square

$$= 33 \text{ yards by } 13 \text{ or } 14 \text{ yards},$$

$$33 \text{ yards} = 99 \text{ feet} = 85 \cdot 6 \text{ units},$$
$$13 \quad ,, \quad = 39 \quad ,, \quad = 33 \cdot 4 \quad ,,$$
$$(10 \times 86 \cdot 7)^3 = \quad 867^3 = \tfrac{1}{6} \text{ distance of the moon},$$
$$(10 \times 10 \times 86 \cdot 7)^3 = \quad 8670^3 = \tfrac{3600}{6} = 600,$$
$$8690^3 = 604 \text{ distance of the moon},$$
$$= \text{distance of Mars}.$$

Cube of 100 times greater side $=$ distance of Mars.
Less side $= 33 \cdot 4$ units

$$(10 \times 33 \cdot 1)^3 = 331^3 = \tfrac{1}{36} \text{ distance of the moon}.$$

Cubes of the sides are as $\tfrac{1}{36} : \tfrac{3}{8} :: \tfrac{1}{36} : \tfrac{18}{8} :: 1 : 18$,

$$\text{or } (100 \times 33 \cdot 7)^3 = 3370^3 = \tfrac{1}{8} \text{ distance of Venus},$$
$$(2 \times 3370)^3 = 6740^3 = \text{distance of Venus}.$$

Cube of 200 times less side = distance of Venus.
Sum of 2 sides = 85·6 + 33·4 = 119 units,

$$(119·4, \&c.)^3 = \tfrac{3}{200} \text{ circumference,}$$
$$(10 \times 119·4)^3 = \tfrac{3000}{200} = 15,$$
$$(8 \times 10 \times 119·4)^3 = 15 \times 8^3 = 7680.$$

Cube of 80 times sum of 2 sides,
    or of 40 times perimeter,
= 9552³ = 7680 circumference = diameter of orbit of earth.
30 cubes = diameter of orbit of Neptune.
The whole space within the pillars is 59 yards by 28,

    59 yards = 177 feet = 153 units,
    and 153³ = $\tfrac{1}{300}$ distance of the moon.
28 yards = 84 feet = 72 units,
    and 71·3³ = $\tfrac{1}{3000}$ distance of the moon.

Cubes of the sides are as 1 : 10.
Sum of 2 sides = 153 + 71·3 = 224·3 units,

    and 224³, &c. = $\tfrac{1}{10}$ circumference,
    $(10 \times 224)^3 = \tfrac{1000}{10} = 100,$
    $(3 \times 10 \times 224)^3 = 100 \times 3^3 = 2700,$
                = distance of Venus,

    $(6 \times 10 \times 224)^3 = 100 \times 6^3 = 21600.$
10 cubes = 216000 = distance of Belus.
Thus cube of 30 times sum of 2 sides,
    or of 15 times perimeter,
        = distance of Venus.

 10 cubes of 60 times sum of 2 sides,
    or of 30 times perimeter,
        = distance of Belus.

Side of the inclosing square = 566 units,
        566 = $\tfrac{1}{4}$ distance of the moon,
    $(12 \times 566)^3 = \tfrac{1}{4} \times 12^3 = \tfrac{1728}{6} = 288,$
    distance of Venus = 281 distance of the moon.
Again $(3 \times 566)^3 = \tfrac{27}{6},$
        $(10 \times 3 \times 566)^3 = \tfrac{21000}{6} = 4500.$

5 cubes of 30 times side $= 22500 =$ distance of Belus.
5 spheres $=$ distance of Neptune.
5 pyramids $=$ „   Uranus.

Length of the piazza is more than $\frac{1}{2}$ a mile.

$$1 \text{ mile} = 18\cdot79 \text{ stades,}$$
$$\tfrac{1}{2} = 9\cdot39 = 2281 \text{ units.}$$

If length equal about 13·8 stades,
   or 3365 units,
   then $3365^3 = \frac{1}{8}$ distance of Venus.

Breadth $= 40$ feet $= 34\cdot6$ units,
   say $= 33\cdot65$ „

The cube of 100 times breadth

   $=$ cube of length,
   $= 3365^3 = \frac{1}{8}$ distance of Venus.

Cube of twice length $=$ distance of Venus.

Another account makes the length of the piazza nearly 4000 feet.

$$4000 \text{ feet} = 3457 \text{ units.}$$

Length of piazza is more than $\frac{1}{2}$ a mile, or 9·39 stades.

10 stades $= 2430$ units,
If length $= 2730$ „
then $2730^3 = \frac{1}{8}$ distance of Mercury,
$(2 \times 2730^3) = 1$ „

Cube of twice length $= 5460^3$
   $=$ distance of Mercury.

Breadth $= 40$ feet $= 34\cdot6$ units,
   $(10 \times 34\cdot4)^3 = \frac{1}{16}$ distance of the moon,
   $(2 \times 10 \times 34\cdot4)^3 = \frac{8}{16} = \frac{1}{2}.$

Cube of 20 times breadth $= \frac{1}{2}$ distance of the moon.
Cube of 40   „ $= 4$ „

If breadth $= 33\cdot65$ units,
   $100 \times 33\cdot65 = 3365$
$\frac{1}{8}$ distance of Venus $= 3365^3$

Cube of 100 times breadth $=\frac{1}{8}$ distance of Venus.
Cube of 200   ,, $=1$,,

Side of square $=$ 570 units,
        if $=$ 573 ,,
     $12 \times 573 = 6880$,,

Diameter of orbit of Mercury $= 6880^3$.
Cube of 12 times side,

   or of 3 times perimeter,
       $=$ diameter of orbit of Mercury.

Sides of inclosed temple 85·6 by 33·4 units.
Sum of 2 sides $= 119$,

$$80 \times 119, \&\text{c.} = 9550.$$

Diameter of orbit of the earth $= 9550^3$.
Cube of 80 times sum of 2 sides,

   or of 40 times perimeter,
       $=$ diameter of the orbit of the earth.

Or if sides $= 86·9$ by 33·7,

$$100 \times 86·9 = 8690,$$
$$\text{distance of Mars} = 8690^3,$$
$$200 \times 33·7 = 6740,$$
$$\text{distance of Venus} = 6740^3.$$

Cube of 100 times greater side,
       $=$ distance of Mars.

Cube of 200 times less side,
       $=$ distance of Venus.

Fraser, describing Persepolis, says, — " One of the most striking considerations which arises from examining these splendid monuments is the great mechanical skill and exquisite taste evinced in their construction, and which indicates an era of high cultivation and considerable scientific knowledge. We see here, as in Egypt, blocks of stone, 40 or 50 feet long, and of enormous weight, placed one above another with a precision which renders the points of union almost invisible ; — columns 60 feet high, consisting of huge pieces, admirably

formed, and jointed with invariable accuracy; and a detail of
sculpture which, if it cannot boast the exact anatomical proportions and flowing outline of the Greek models, displays at
least chiselling as delicate as any work of art on the banks of
the Nile."

We have met with no measurements of the monuments of
Persepolis.

"Not only," says Heeren, "is Persia Proper memorable on
account of its historical associations, but also from the architectural remains which it continues to present. The ruins of
Persepolis are the noblest monuments of the most flourishing
era of this empire which have survived the lapse of ages. As
solitary in their situation as peculiar in their character, they
rise above the deluge of years, which for centuries have overwhelmed all the records of human grandeur around them or
near them, and buried all traces of Susa and of Babylon.
Their venerable antiquity and majestic proportions do not
more command our reverence, than the mystery which involves their construction awakens the curiosity of the most
unobservant spectator. Pillars which belong to *no known
order* of architecture; inscriptions in an alphabet which continues an enigma; fabulous animals which stand as guards at
the entrance; the multitudes of allegorical figures which
decorate the walls, — all conspire to carry us back to ages of
the most remote antiquity, over which the tradition of the
East has shed a doubtful and wandering light. Even the
question what Persepolis really was, is not so perfectly
ascertained as to satisfy the critical historian."

"The most striking feature on the approach to Persepolis,"
remarks Morier, "is the staircase and its surrounding walls.
Two grand flights, which face each other, lead to the principal platform. To the right is an immense wall, of the finest
masonry and of the most massive stones. To the left are
other walls, equally well built, but not so imposing. (No
dimensions of the platform are given.) This staircase leads
to the principal compartment of the whole ruins, which may
be called a small plain, thickly studded with columns, sixteen
of which are now erect.

" In the rear of the whole of these remains are the beds of aqueducts, which are cut in the solid rock. They occur in every part of the building, and are probably, therefore, as extensive in their course as they are magnificent in their construction. The great aqueduct is to be discovered among a confused heap of stones, not far behind the buildings described above, on that quarter of the palace, and almost adjoining to a ruined staircase. Its bed, in same places, is cut 10 feet into the rock. This bed leads east and west : to the eastward its descent is rapid for about 25 paces; it there narrows, but again enlarges, so that a man of common height may stand upright in it. It terminates by an abrupt rock."

No mound, it is said, has hitherto been so fully explored as that of Khorsabad; and no other gives us such an insight into the plan of the cities, as well as the temples, of the Assyrians.

The following are the dimensions of this double mound, taken as correctly as the unequal inclinations and the irregularities would allow : —

Length from north-west to south-east -   - 983 feet,
Breadth of the large rectangle   - - - 983 ,,
Breadth of the little rectangle   - - - 590 ,,

The common summit is nearly flat, although not everywhere of the same level.

Besides the mound of Khorsabad, Botta distinctly traced the walls of a city forming nearly a perfect square, two sides of which are 5750 feet, the other 5400, or rather more than an English mile each way; all the four angles being right angles. The wall surrounding the enclosure, which at the present day looks like a long tumulus of a rounded shape, is surmounted, but at regular intervals, by elevations which jut out beyond it, inside as well as outside, and indicate the existence of small towers. The direction of the rectangle is such that its diagonals are directed towards cardinal points. The wall which forms the south-eastern side is very distinct. This is also the case with the ditch which bounds it for its whole length. The outward wall exhibits traces of eight towers.

Botta supposes this vast enclosure was destined to contain the gardens of the palace constructed upon the mound. Fergusson gives it as his opinion, that at first sight it might be supposed that the enclosure, formed by what he presumes to have been the city walls, was only a *paradisus*, or park, attached to the palace. The immense thickness and solidity of the wall, however, he thinks, entirely destroys such a theory; and he goes on to state that it does not require walls 45 feet thick, and more than 30 feet in height, to enclose game; whereas, too, if they were meant for defence, there must have been inhabitants to defend them; for a mere guard could not man a wall more than four miles in length. He considers, therefore, that there are good grounds for considering this enclosure as the site of the city of Khorsabad, and as such it would, allowing 50 square yards for each individual, contain a population of between 60,000 and 70,000 souls,—a large number for a city in those days. The perfect facility with which the city walls can be traced, as well as those opposite Mosul, Ferguson considers, is in itself quite sufficient to refute the idea of those who would make the old city extend from Nimroud to Khorsabad; for neither between nor beyond these ruins, nor connecting them in any way, can any trace of walls or mounds be found. He also observes, that if they can be traced so distinctly in these two localities, traces of them would be found elsewhere, had they ever existed; and considers that, till they are found, we are justified, even from this circumstance alone, in assuming what every other consideration renders so probable, that they never existed, but that these two were independent cities, and quite as large, too, as the country would well support.

The mean of the two sides of the square enclosure

$$= \tfrac{1}{2} (5750 + 5400) = 5575 \text{ feeet};$$

and 5620 feet = 20 stades.

Thus the four sides, or perimeter of the square, will = about 80 stades = $\tfrac{1}{8}$ the circuit of the walls of Babylon. The height of the walls at Khorsabad is more than 30 feet. The south-eastern wall at Khorsabad is very distinct, as well as the ditch.

The walls of Babylon were surrounded by a ditch. Towers were erected along the walls of both cities.

The side of Babylon = 120 stades.

If the mean of the two sides of Khorsabad = 20 stades, then the sides of the two cities will be as 20 : 120 :: 1 : 6; their cubes as 1^3 : 6^3 :: 1 : 216.

The cube of Babylon = 216000 circumference,
∴ the cube of Khorsabad = 1000 ,,

Greater side of mound = 983 feet = 850 units,
Less side ,, = 590 ,, = 510 ,,

$$853^3 = \tfrac{4}{7} \text{ distance of the moon}$$
$$(7 \times 853)^3 = \tfrac{4}{7} \times 7^3 = 196.$$

7 cubes of 853 = 4 distance of the moon.
Cube of 7 times 853 = 196 ,,

$$514^3 = \tfrac{1}{8} \text{ distance of the moon,}$$
$$(2 \times 514)^3 = 1 \qquad \text{,,}$$

150 cubes of twice side = 150 distance of the moon,
= distance of Mercury,
150^2 cubes ,, = ,, Belus.

Sum of 2 sides = 853 + 514 = 1368 units,
$$4 \times 1368 = 5472.$$

Distance of Mercury lies between
$$5460^3 \text{ and } 5490^3.$$

Side of pyramid of Cholula = 1373.
Cube of perimeter = $(4 \times 1373)^3$ = distance of Mercury.

We do not understand this description of the mound called double. It may mean that there are two terraces. No height is mentioned. We have not seen Botta's work.

Sides are 850 and 510 units.
$$30 \times 850 = 25500,$$
$$50 \times 510 = 25500.$$

Diameter of orbit of Uranus = 25440^3,
if sides were 860 and 514,
$$8 \times 860 = 6880.$$

Diameter of orbit of Mercury $= 6880^3$,

$$2 \times 514 = 1028,$$

distance of the moon $= 1028^3$.

The sides of the city of Khorsabad are

5750 by 5400 feet,

$$= 4972 \text{ ,, } 4670 \text{ units,}$$

$497^3 = \frac{9}{80}$ distance of the moon,

$$4970^3 = \frac{9000}{80} = \frac{900}{8},$$

$$(2 \times 4970)^3 = 900.$$

Cube of twice greater side $= 900$ distance of the moon,

$$= 6 \text{ times distance of Mercury,}$$

$$= 1\tfrac{1}{2} \text{ ,, } \text{Mars.}$$

25 cubes $= 22500 =$ distance of Belus,

25 spheres $=$,, Neptune,

25 pyramids $=$,, Uranus,

$468^3 = \frac{81}{90}$ circumference,

$$4680^3 = \frac{81000}{90} = 900,$$

$$(2 \times 4680)^3 = 7200.$$

Cube of twice less side $= 7200$ circumference,

$$= \tfrac{1}{10} \text{ distance of Uranus,}$$

$$= \tfrac{1}{30} \text{ ,, } \text{Belus,}$$

$$\text{Sphere} = \tfrac{1}{30} \text{ ,, } \text{Neptune.}$$

Cube $= 5$ times distance of Mercury.

Cube of twice greater side : cube of twice less side :: 6 : 5 times distance of Mercury.

Cube of twice greater side : cube of less side :: 900 distance of moon : 900 circumference.

Sum of 2 sides $= 4970 + 4680 = 9650$ units,

mean $= 4825,$

484^3, &c. $=$ circumference,

$$(10 \times 484, \text{ &c.})^3 = 1000,$$

$$(6 \times 10 \times 484, \text{ &c.})^3 = 6^3 \times 1000 = 216000.$$

Thus cube of 3 times sum of 2 sides of the walls of Khorsabad $= 216000$ circumference,

$$= \text{cube of side of Babylon,}$$

$$= \text{distance of Belus,}$$

Sphere $=$ distance of Neptune,

Pyramid $=$,, Uranus.

Cube of sum of 2 sides

$$= (2 \times 10 \times 484, \&c.)^3 = 8000 \text{ circumference,}$$

9 cubes $= 72000 =$ distance of Uranus,
27 „ $= 216000 =$ „ Belus,
27 spheres $=$ „ Neptune.

Thickness of the walls $= 45$ feet,
$= 39$ units.

If 4970 by $4680 = 9650$ units be the external dimensions, then the internal dimensions of the two sides will

$$= 9650 - (4 \times 39) = 9650 - 156 = 9494,$$
Diameter of orbit of the earth $= 9560^2$.

If the two sides were measured on the middle of the top of the walls, the sum of two sides would

$$= 9650 - (2 \times 39) = 9572 \text{ units,}$$
and diameter of orbit of the earth $= 9560^2$ „

The Kalah Shergat, a triangular mound situate in the midst of a most beautiful meadow, well wooded, watered by a small tributary of the Tigris, washed by the noble river itself, and backed by the rocky range of the Jebel Khánúkah, is thus described by Ainsworth. Although familiar with the great Babylonian and Chaldean mounds of the Birs Nimroud, Mujallibah, and Orchoe, the appearance of the mass of construction now before us filled me with wonder. On the plain of Babylonia to build a hill has a meaning; but there was a strange adherence to an antique custom, in thus piling brick upon brick, without regard to the cost and value of labour, where hills innumerable and equally good and elevated sites were easily to be found. Although in places reposing on solid rock (red and brown sandstones), still almost the entire depth of the mound, which was in parts upwards of 60 feet high, and at this side 909 yards in extent, was built of sun-burnt bricks, like the Aker Kuf and the Mujallibah, only without intervening layers of reeds. On the side of these lofty artificial cliffs numerous hawks and crows nestled in security, while at their base was a deep sloping declivity of crumbled materials. On this northern face, which is the most perfect as well as the highest, there occurs at one point the remains of a wall built with large square-cut stones, levelled and fitted to one another with the utmost nicety, and levelled upon the faces, as in many Saracenic structures; the top stones were also cut away as in steps. Ross, who formerly visited this structure, deemed this to be part of the still remaining perfect front, which was also the opinion of some of the travellers now present; but so great is the difference between the style of an Assyrian mound of burnt bricks and this partial facing of hewn stone that it is difficult to conceive that it belonged to the same period, and, if carried along the front of the whole mound, some remains of it would be found in the detritus at the base of the cliff, which was not the case; at the same time its position gave to it more the appearance of a facing (whether contemporary with mound or subsequent to it I shall not attempt to decide) than of a castle, if any castle or other edifice was ever erected here by the Mahommedans, whose style it so greatly resembles.

Our researches were first directed towards the mound itself. We found its form to be that of an irregular triangle, measuring in total circumference 4685 yards; whereas the Mujallibah, the supposed tower of Babel, is only 738 yards in circumference; the great mound of Borsippa, known as the Birs Nimroud, 762 yards; the Kasr, or terraced palace of Nebuchadnezzar, 2100 yards; and the mound called Kóyunjik, at Nineveh, 2563 yards.

But it is to be remarked of this Assyrian ruin on the Tigris, that it is not entirely a raised mound of sun-burnt bricks; on the contrary, several sections of its central portions displayed the ordinary pebbly deposit of the river, a common alluvium, and were swept by the Tigris; the mound appeared chiefly to be a mass of rubble and ruins, in which bricks, pottery, and fragments of sepulchral urns lay embedded in humus, or alternated with blocks of gypsum; finally, at the southern extremity, the mound sinks down nearly to the level of the plain. The side facing the river displayed to us some curious structures, which, not being noticed by Ross, have probably been laid bare by floods subsequent to his visit. They consisted of four round towers, built of burnt bricks, which were 9 inches deep, and 13 inches in width outwards, but only 10 inches inwards, so as to adapt them for being built in a circle. These towers were 4 feet 10 inches in diameter, well built, and as fresh looking as if of yesterday. Their use is altogether a matter of conjecture; they were not strong enough to have formed buttresses against the river; nor were they connected by a wall. The general opinion appeared to be in favour of hydraulic purposes, either as wells or pumps, communicating with the Tigris.

The south-western rampart displays occasionally the remains of a wall constructed of hewn blocks of gypsum, and it is everywhere bounded by a ditch, which, like the rampart, encircles the whole ruins.

All over this great surface we found traces of foundations of stone edifices, with abundance of brick and pottery, as observed before, and to which we may add, bricks vitrified with bitumen, as are found at Rahabah, Babylon, and other ruins of the same epoch; bricks with impressions of straw, &c., sun-dried, burnt, and vitrified; and painted pottery with colours still very perfect; lastly, we picked up a brick close to our station, on which were well-defined and indubitable arrow-headed characters.

The perimeter of the triangular mound = 4685 yards = 14055 feet = 50 stades. The perimeter of Cheops' pyramid = $10\frac{3}{4}$ stades.

Here we find burnt bricks adapted so as to form a circle or semi-circular arch. It follows that the builders of these towers were familiar with the construction of the arch.

Mound of Kóyunjik = 2563 yards = 7689 feet = 6638 units.

$$662^3 = \tfrac{A}{50} \text{ distance of the moon,}$$
$$(10 \times 662)^3 = \tfrac{A000}{30} = \tfrac{A00}{3}.$$

3 cubes of circuit = 800 distance of the moon,
= diameter of orbit of the earth,
6730^3 = distance of Venus.

Circuit of Birs Nimroud = 762 yards.

Circuit of the walls inclosing the tower of Belus (the supposed Birs Nimroud) was 8 stades $= 762\frac{2}{3}$ yards.

Circuit of the Ksar, or terraced palace, is 2100 yards $= 6300$ feet $= 5447$ units,

and $5460^3 = 1440$ circumference $=$ distance of Mercury.

The northern side of the triangular mound is 909 yards $= 2727$ feet $= 2357$ units,

$$235^3, \&c. = \tfrac{6}{800} \text{ distance of the moon,}$$
$$(10 \times 235, \&c.)^3 = \tfrac{6000}{800} = 12.$$

Cube of side $= 12$ distance of the moon,

$$(5 \times 10 \times 235, \&c.)^3 = 12 \times 5^3 = 1500.$$

5 cubes of 5 times side $= 7500$ distance of the moon,
$$= \text{diameter of orbit of Saturn,}$$
$$= \text{distance of Uranus,}$$
$$= \tfrac{1}{3} \quad ,, \qquad \text{Belus,}$$
$$6 \times 2357 = 13142.$$

Distance of Jupiter $= 13040^3$.

Cube of 6 times side $=$ distance of Jupiter.
Cube of 5   ,, $= 1500$ distance of the moon,
$= 10$ times distance of Mercury.

Or $\tfrac{1}{4}$ cube of 5 times side $=$ diameter of orbit of Mercury.
15 cubes   - $=$ distance of Belus.

Perimeter of triangular base of mound $= 4685$ yards $= 14055$ feet $= 12153$ units $= 50$ stades,
$$= \tfrac{4}{12} \text{ side of Babylon.}$$

Should perimeter $= 12200$ units,
$$\tfrac{1}{2} = \quad 6100 \quad ,,$$
$$610^2 = 2 \text{ circumference,}$$
$$6100^3 = 2000,$$
$$(2 \times 6100)^3 = 12200^3 = 16000,$$
$$(3 \times 12200)^3 = 16000 \times 3^3 = 432000.$$

Cube of 3 times perimeter $= 423000$ circumference,
$$= \text{diameter of orbit of Belus,}$$
$$\text{Sphere} = \qquad ,, \qquad \text{Neptune,}$$
$$\text{Pyramid} = \qquad ,, \qquad \text{Uranus.}$$

Or $\frac{1}{3}$ cube of 3 times perimeter $=$ Uranus.

Cube of Babylon $= 120^3$ stades,
$=$ distance of Belus.

Cube of Nineveh $= 150^3$ stades,
$=$ distance of Ninus.

Should the perimeter $= 11368$ units, then perimeter will $= \frac{1}{10000}$ part circumference $=$ the circumference of the fosse surrounding the teocalli of Xochicalco.

ROCK-CUT TEMPLES OF INDIA.

Temples of Elephanta.

The island of Elephanta, distant about 2 leagues from Bombay, has a circuit of about 3 miles, and consists of rocky mountains, covered with trees and brushwood. Near the landing-place is an elephant, as large as life, shaped out of the rock, and supposed to have given its name to the island.

Having ascended the mountain by a narrow path, we reach the excavation which has so long excited the attention of the curious, and afforded such ample scope for the discussion of antiquarians. With the strongest emotions of surprise and admiration, we behold four rows of massive columns cut out of the solid rock, uniform in their order, and placed at regular distances, so as to form three magnificent avenues from the principal entrance to the grand idol which terminates the middle vista; the general effect being heightened by the gloom, peculiar to the situation. The central image is composed of three colossal heads, reaching nearly from the floor to the roof, a height of 15 feet. It represents the triad deity in the Hindoo mythology, Brahma, Vishnoo, and Seeva, in the characters of the creator, preserver, and destroyer. The countenance of Vishnoo has the same mild aspect as that of Brahma; but the visage of Seeva is very different — severity and revenge, characteristic of his destroying attribute, are strongly depicted; one of the hands embraces a large Cobra de Capello; while the others contain fruit, flowers, and blessings for mankind, among which the lotus and pomegranate are readily distinguishable. The former of these, the lotus, so often introduced into the Hindoo mythology, forms a principal object in the sculpture and paintings of their temples, is the ornament of their sacred lakes, and the most conspicuous beauty in their flowery sacrifices. From the northern entrance to the extremity of the cave is about $130\frac{1}{2}$ feet, and from the east to the west side 133. Twenty-six pillars, of which eight are broken, and sixteen pilasters, support the roof. Neither the floor nor the roof is in the same plane, and consequently the height varies from $17\frac{1}{2}$ to 15 feet.

The caves of the Isle of Elephanta cannot be sufficiently admired; and when the immensity of such an undertaking, the number of artificers employed, and the extraordinary genius of its projector, are considered, in a country until lately accounted rude and barbarous by the now enlightened nations of Europe. Had this work been raised from a foundation, like other structures, it would have excited the admiration of the curious; but when the reflection is made, that it is hewn out, inch by inch, in the hard and solid rock, how great must the astonishment be at the conception and completion of the enterprise!

From the right and left avenues of the principal temple are passages to smaller excavations on each side, containing two baths, one of them elegantly finished; the front is open, and the roof supported by pillars of a different order from those in the large temple; the sides are adorned with sculpture, and the roof and cornice painted in mosaic patterns; some of the colours are bright. The opposite bath, of the same proportions, is less ornamented; and between them a room detached from the rock, containing a representation of the Lingam, or symbol of Seeva. Several small caves branch out from the grand excavations.

The great temple is $130\frac{1}{2}$ by 133 feet,

$$\text{or } 114 \quad \text{,, } 116 \text{ units,}$$

$$114^3, \&c. = \tfrac{1}{720} \text{ distance of the moon,}$$
$$(10 \times 114, \&c.)^3 = \tfrac{1000}{720} = \tfrac{100}{72} = \tfrac{50}{36},$$
$$(6 \times 10 \times 114, \&c.)^3 = \tfrac{50}{36} \times 6^3 = 300.$$

Cube of 60 times less side
$= 300$ distance of the moon $=$ diameter of orbit of Mercury.

$$116^3, \&c. = \tfrac{1}{72} \text{ circumference,}$$
$$(10 \times 116, \&c.)^3 = \tfrac{1000}{72} = \tfrac{500}{36},$$
$$(6 \times 10 \times 116, \&c.)^3 = \tfrac{500}{36} \times 6^3 = 3000.$$

Cube of 60 times greater side $= 3000$ circumference.
The height varies from $17\frac{1}{2}$ to 15 feet,

$$\text{mean height} = 16\tfrac{1}{4} \text{ feet} = 13 \cdot 9 \text{ units,}$$
$$\text{say } = 13 \cdot 8 \quad ,,$$

Then content of the interior of the temple will

$$= 113 \times 116 \times 13 \cdot 8 = \tfrac{1}{6000} \text{ distance of the moon,}$$
$$= \tfrac{1}{100} \text{ radius of the earth.}$$

The dimensions of the Indian and Egyptian temples are taken from the " Library of Entertaining Knowledge."

The Isle of Elephanta, celebrated for the remains of Hindoo mythological excavations and sculptures, contains at the end of the cavern, opposite the entrance, a remarkable Trimurti, or three-formed god. Brahma, the creator, is in the middle, with Vishnu, the preserver, on one side, and Siva or Mahadeva, the destroyer, on the other. The latter holds in his hands a Cobra-capella snake, and on his cap, among other symbols, are a human skull and a young infant. The under lip of all these figures is remarkably thick. The length from the chin to the crown of the head is 6 feet, and their caps are about 3 feet more. On each side of the Trimurti is a pilaster, the front of which is filled by a figure, 14 feet high, leaning on a dwarf; but both much defaced.

To the right is a large compartment, hollowed a little, and carved with a great variety of figures; the largest of which is 16 feet high, representing the double figure of Siva and Parvati, named Viraj, half male and half female. On the right of Viraj is Brahma, four-faced, sitting on a lotus; and on the left is Vishnu, sitting on the shoulders of his eagle Garuda. Near Brahma are Indra and Indrani on their elephant; and below, a female figure holding a chowry. The upper part of the compartment is filled with small figures in the attitude of adoration.- On the other side of the Tri-murti is another compartment, with the various figures of Siva, and Parvati, his wife ; the most remarkable of which is Siva, in his vindictive character, eight-handed, with a chaplet of skulls round his neck. On the right of the entrance of the cave is a square apartment, supported by eight colossal figures, containing a gigantic symbol of Mahadeva, or Siva, cut out of the rock. There is a similar chamber in a smaller cavern, which is almost filled with rubbish, but having the walls covered with sculpture.

The pillars and figures in the cave have been defaced by visitors, and by the zeal of the Portuguese, who made war on the gods and temples as well as on the armies of India. Fragments of statues strew the floor, columns deprived of their bases are suspended from the roof, and there are others split and without capitals. Opposite the landing-place is a colossal stone elephant, cracked and mutilated, from which the Portuguese named the island,—by the natives called Gharipoor. The entrance into the cave is 55 feet wide, its height 18 feet, and its length equal to its width.—*East India Gazetteer.*

Length of cave = breadth = 55 feet = 47·56 units.

$$(10 \times 47 \cdot 7)^3 = \tfrac{1}{10} \text{ distance of the moon.}$$
$$(10 \times 10 \times 47 \cdot 7)^3 = \tfrac{1000}{10} = 100.$$

Cube of   10 times side = $\tfrac{1}{10}$ distance of the moon.
Cube of   100   ,,   ,, = 100   ,,   ,,   ,,
Cube of 2 × 100   ,,   ,, = 800   ,,   ,,   ,,
                = diameter of the orbit of the earth.

Height = 18 feet = 15·55 units.

$$(10 \times 15 \cdot 9)^3 = \tfrac{1}{810} \text{ distance of the moon.}$$
$$(3 \times 10 \times 15 \cdot 9)^3 = \tfrac{1}{810} \times 3^3 = \tfrac{1}{10} \text{ ,,}$$
$$(10 \times 3 \times 10 \times 15 \cdot 9)^3 = \tfrac{1000}{10} = 100 \text{ ,,}$$
$$(2 \times 10 \times 3 \times 10 \times 15 \cdot 9)^3 = 800 \text{ ,,}$$

Cube of   30 times height = $\tfrac{1}{10}$ distance of the moon.
Cube of 300   ,,   = 100   ,,
Cube of 600   ,,   = 800   ,,
                = diameter of orbit of the earth.

Content $= 47\cdot7$ &c. $\times 47\cdot7$ &c. $\times 15\cdot9 = 36600$ units.

Cube of content $= 36600^3$

$\qquad\qquad = $ diameter of the orbit of Belus

$\qquad\qquad = $ twice cube of Babylon

$\qquad\qquad = $ cube of Nineveh

$\qquad\qquad = $ distance of Ninus.

$47\cdot7^2 \times 16\cdot1$ &c. $= 36600$ units.

$\qquad$ If length $= $ breadth $= 48\cdot6$ units,

$\qquad\qquad 600 \times 48\cdot6 = 29160$,

$\qquad$ distance of Belus $= 29160^3$,

$\qquad$ cube of 600 times side $= $ distance of Belus.

Content $= 48\cdot6 \times 48\cdot6 \times 15\cdot5 = 36600$.

Diameter of the orbit of Belus $= 36600^3$.

Cube of content $= $ diameter of the orbit of Belus

$\qquad\qquad\qquad = $ distance of Ninus.

$\qquad$ Cube of 600 times side

$\qquad = $ cube of 150 times perimeter

$\qquad = $ cube of 120 stades

$\qquad = $ cube of Babylon.

Cube of content $= $ cube of Nineveh.

About 14 miles to the north of Gayah, in the province of Babar, is a hill, or rather rock, in which is dug a remarkable cavern, now distinguished by the name of Nagurjenee. It is situated on the southern declivity, about two-thirds from the summit. Its entrance is 6 feet high and $2\frac{1}{2}$ broad, and leads to a room of an oval form, with a vaulted roof, 44 feet in length, 18 in breadth, and 10 in height at the centre. This immense cave is dug entirely out of the solid rock; and the same stone extends much further than the excavated part on each side of it, and is altogether full 100 feet in length.

This town is one of the holy places of the Hindoos to which pilgrimages are performed; having been either the birthplace or residence of Buddha, the great prophet and legislator of the nations east of the Ganges. From this circumstance it is usually termed Buddha Gayah.—*East India Gazetteer.*

Jones is of opinion that the existence of Buddha, or the ninth great incarnation of Vishnu, may be fixed at 1014 years B. C.

Length = 44 feet = 38 units,
Breadth = 18 feet = 15·5 units,

$$(10 \times 37·9)^3 = 379^3 = \tfrac{1}{20} \text{ distance of moon,}$$
$$(20 \times 10 \times 37·9)^3 = \tfrac{1}{20} \times 20^3 = 400.$$

Cube of 200 times length

= 400 times distance of the moon
= distance of the earth.

$$(10 \times 15·3 \text{ &c.})^3 = 153^3 \text{ &c.} = \tfrac{1}{300} \text{ distance of moon,}$$
$$(30 \times 10 \times 15·3)^3 = \tfrac{1}{300} \times 30^3 = \tfrac{900}{10} = 90.$$

Cube of 300 times breadth = 90 distance of the moon,
16 cubes = 1440 circumference = distance of Mercury.

Length + breadth = 37·9 + 15·3 &c. = 53·2 &c.

$$(10 \times 53·3)^3 = 533^3 = \tfrac{7}{50} \text{ distance of the moon,}$$
$$(10 \times 10 \times 53·3)^3 = \tfrac{1000}{8} = 140,$$

2 cubes of 100 times 53·3

= 280 distance of the moon
= distance of Venus.

Height = 10 feet = 8·64 units,

$$(100 \times 8·65)^3 = 865^3 = \tfrac{1}{3} \text{ distance of the moon,}$$
$$(10 \times 865)^3 = \tfrac{1000}{3} = 600,$$

Cube of 1000 times height
= 600 times distance of the moon.
Distance of Mars = 604.

Temples of Salsette.

The excavations of the Island of Salsette, also contiguous to Bombay, are hewn in the central mountains. The great temple is excavated at some distance from the summit of a steep mountain, in a commanding situation. This stupendous work is upwards of 90 feet long, 38 wide, and of a proportionate height; hewn out of the solid rock, and forming an oblong square, with a fluted concave roof. The area is divided into three aisles by regular colonnades. Towards the termination of the temple, fronting the entrance, is a circular

pile"of solid rock, 19 feet high and 48 in circumference; most probably a representation of the lingam.

In this temple there are not many images, nor any kind of sculpture, except on the capitals of the pillars, which are, in general, finished in a very masterly style, and are little impaired by time. Several have been left in an unfinished state; and on the summit of others is something like a bell, between elephants, horses, lions, and animals of different kinds.

The lofty pillars and concave roof of the principal temple of Salsette present a much grander appearance than the largest excavation in the Elephanta; although that is much richer in statues and bas-reliefs. The portico of Salsette, of the same height and breadth of the temple, is richly decorated. On each side, a large niche contains a colossal statue, well executed; and facing the entrance are small single figures, with groups in various attitudes, all of them in good preservation. The outer front of the portico, and the area before it, corresponding in grandeur with the interior, are now injured by time, and the mouldering sculpture is intermingled with a variety of rock-plants. On the square pillars at the entrance are long inscriptions, the characters of which are obsolete, and which modern ingenuity has not yet succeeded in decyphering.

The whole appearance of this excavated mountain indicates it to have been a city hewn in its rocky sides, capable of containing many thousand inhabitants. The largest temple was doubtless their principal place of worship; and the smaller, on the same plan, inferior ones. The rest were appropriated as dwellings for the inhabitants, differing in size and accommodation, according to their respective ranks in society; or, as is still more probable, these habitations were the abode of the religious Brahmins, and of their pupils, when India was the nursery of art and science, and the nations of Europe involved in ignorance and barbarism.

The great temple,

90 by 38 feet
= 77 by 33 units

$331^3 = \frac{1}{30}$ distance of the moon

= diameter of the earth.

Cube of 10 times less side = diameter of the earth.

$775^3 = \frac{3}{7}$ distance of the moon.

$(7 \times 775)^3 = \frac{3}{7} \times 7^3 = 147.$

Distance of Mercury = 150 distance of the moon.

Cube of 70 times greater side = distance of Mercury.

Sum of 2 sides = $33 \cdot 1 + 77 \cdot 5 = 110 \cdot 6.$

$111^3 = \frac{1}{800}$ distance of the moon.

$(10 \times 111)^3 = \frac{1000}{800} = \frac{5}{4}.$

$(4 \times 10 \times 111)^3 = \frac{5}{4} \times 4^3 = 80.$

10 cubes of 40 times sum of 2 sides

or of 20 times perimeter

= 800 distance of the moon

= diameter of the orbit of the earth.

Or, greater side = 77 units,

$769^3 = 4$ circumference.

Sum of 2 sides = 111 units

$111^3 = \frac{1}{800}$ distance of the moon.

$(20 \times 111)^3 = \frac{1}{800} \times 20^3 = \frac{8000}{800} = 10.$

Cube of 20 times sum of 2 sides

or of 10 times perimeter

= 10 times distance of the moon.

Sides 77 by 33 units.

Less side to the power of 3 times 3 = $33 \cdot 2^9$

= distance of Ninus.

Greater side to the power of 3 times 3 = $77 \cdot 364^9$

= distance of a near fixed star.

See "Fixed Stars," Part X., Vol. II.

The pile of rock may not be cylindrical, but a circular obelisk.

Ellora.

The temples of Elephanta and Salsette are far surpassed by those of Ellora, which is in the province of Hyderabad, about 20 miles north-west from Aurungabad, the capital, and 239 east of Bombay. It may be considered as near the centre of India. Here we have a granite mountain, which is of an amphitheatre form, completely chiselled out from top to bottom, and filled with innumerable temples; the god Siva alone having, it is said, about twenty appropriated to himself. To describe the numerous galleries and rows of pillars which support various chambers lying one above another, the steps, porticoes, and bridges of rock over canals, also hewn out of the solid rock, would be impossible. The chief temple of this mountain is called Kailasa, which is entered under a balcony, after which we come to an ante-chamber, 138 feet wide, and 88 long; with many rows of pillars, and adjoining chambers, which may have been apartments for pilgrims, or the dwellings of the priests.

From this chamber we pass through a great portico, and over a bridge, into a huge chamber, 247 feet long and 150 broad, in the middle of which the chief temple stands on one mass of rock.

This temple itself measures 103 feet long and 56 wide; but its height is most surprising, for it rises above 100 feet in a pyramidal form. It is hollowed out to the height of 17 feet, and supported by four rows of pillars, with colossal elephants, which seem to bear the monstrous mass, and to give life and animation to the whole. From the roof of this monolith temple, which has a gallery or rock round it, bridges lead to other side arches, which have not yet been explored.

Chamber, 247 by 150 feet

$$= 212 \text{ by } 129 \text{ \&c. units.}$$
$$212^3 = \tfrac{1}{12} \text{ circumference.}$$
$$(12 \times 212)^3 = \tfrac{1}{12} \times 12^3 = 144.$$

Cube of 12 times side $= \frac{1}{10}$ distance of Mercury.

$$(10 \times 12 \times 212)^3 = \tfrac{1000}{10} = 100.$$

Cube of 120 times side $= 100$ distance of Mercury
$= $ diameter of the orbit of Uranus.

129^3 &c. $= \frac{1}{800}$ distance of the moon.

$$(10 \times 129^3) = \tfrac{1000}{800} = 2.$$

Cube of 10 times side $=$ diameter of the orbit of the moon.

Sum of 2 sides $= 212 + 129 = 441$ units.

$$440^3 = \tfrac{1}{4} \text{ circumference.}$$
$$(2 \times 440)^3 = \tfrac{2}{4} = 6.$$
$$(10 \times 2 \times 440)^3 = 6000.$$

Cube of 20 times sum of 2 sides $= 6000$ circumference.

6 cubes $=$ distance of Saturn.

36 cubes $=$ distance of Belus.

Chamber, 138 by 88 feet
$= 119\cdot3$ by $76\cdot18$ units.

119^3 &c. $= \frac{3}{800}$ circumference,

$$(10 \times 119)^3 = \tfrac{3000}{200} = 15.$$
$$(4 \times 10 \times 119)^3 = 15 \times 4^3 = 960.$$

3 cubes of 40 times side $= 2880$ circumference
$= $ diameter of the orbit of Mercury;

or, 12 cubes of 20 times side $=$ distance of Mercury,
less side $= 76\cdot18$ units.

$$(10 \times 75\cdot8)^3 = \tfrac{4}{10} \text{ distance of the moon.}$$
$$(10 \times 10 \times 75\cdot8)^3 = \tfrac{4000}{10} = 400.$$

Cube of 100 times less side $= 400$ distance of the moon
$= $ distance of the earth.

Sum of two sides $= 119\cdot8 + 75\cdot8 = 195\cdot6.$

$$100 \times 195\cdot6 = 19560.$$

Distance of Uranus $= 19560^3.$

Cube of 100 times sum of 2 sides $=$ distance of Uranus.

Chief temple, 103 by 56 feet
$= 89\cdot05$ by $48\cdot4$ units.

$$(10 \times 89\cdot2)^3 = \tfrac{50}{8} \text{ circumference.}$$
$$(2 \times 10 \times 89\cdot2)^3 = \tfrac{50}{8} \times 2^3 = 50.$$
$$(3 \times 2 \times 10 \times 89\cdot2)^3 = 50 \times 3^3 = 1350.$$

2 cubes of 60 times side = 2700 circumference
= distance of Venus;

$(6 \times 2 \times 10 \times 89 \cdot 2)^3 = 50 \times 6^3 = 10800$ circumference,
20 cubes of 120 times side = 216000 circumference,
= distance of Belus.

Less side = 48·4 units.

$(10 \times 47 \cdot 7)^3 = \frac{1}{10}$ distance of the moon.
$(10 \times 10 \times 47 \cdot 7)^3 = \frac{1000}{10} = 100$,,
$(2 \times 10 \times 10 \times 47 \cdot 7)^3 = 800$,,

Cube of 200 times side = 800 distance of the moon
= diameter of orbit of the earth.

Sum of 2 sides = 89·2 + 47·7 = 136·9 units.
$10 \times 136 \cdot 9 = 1369.$

Side of base of pyramid of Cholula = 1373 units.
Cube of perimeter of base = $(4 \times 1373)^3$
= distance of Mercury.

So cube of 40 times sum of 2 sides of temple, or of 20 times perimeter = distance of Mercury.

Distance of Mercury may be said to lie between 5460^3 and 5490^3.

Or, less side = 48·4 units
$10 \times 48 \cdot 4 = 484.$
$484^3 =$ circumference.
$(60 \times 484 \ \&c.)^3 = 60^3 \times$ circumference
= 216000 circumference
= distance of Belus.

Cube of 600 times less side = distance of Belus
= cube of Babylon.

Greater side = 89·05 units
if = 91
$60 \times 91 = 5460$

Distance of Mercury = 5460^3.

Cube of 60 times greater side = distance of Mercury.
Cube of 600 times less side = distance of Belus.

Sum of 2 sides = 48·4 + 91 = 139·4.
139^3 &c. $= \frac{1}{400}$ distance of the moon.

Cube of sum of two sides $= \frac{1}{400}$ distance of the moon

$$= \frac{1}{400^2} \text{ distance of the earth.}$$

Cube of perimeter $= \frac{1}{80}$ distance of the moon.

Cube of 10 times perimeter $= \frac{1000}{80} = 20.$

20 cubes of 10 times perimeter
   $= 400$ distance of the moon $=$ distance of the earth.

5 cubes of 20 times perimeter $= 800$ distance of the moon
   $=$ diameter of orbit of the earth.

Cube of 20 times sum of 2 sides
   $= 20$ times distance of the moon.

The excavated Brahminical temples in India are indicated by their square shape and flat roof ; those of the Buddhists, by their oblong form and vaulted roof.   The temple at Elephanta is formed like a cross with four short and equal arms, the three entrances being at the extremities of three of these ; the southern end being occupied by the triple-headed bust of Shiva.   This is a Brahminical temple, with a flat roof.

In the temples once sacred to Buddha at Canara, in Salsette, are seen lofty arched roofs.

One of the Brahminical temples at Ellora is 185 feet in length, 150 in breadth, and 19 in height.   It contains 28 pillars and 20 pilasters.   The area is more than one-third greater than that of Westminster Hall.   At Ellora are also seen small cubic temples.   The temple of Keylas, at Ellora, contains a pyramidal temple, 100 feet high, standing in the centre of the excavation.   In another part are two perfect obelisks, about 38 feet high, very light in appearance, and tastefully sculptured.   The roofs of the numerous temples all rise pyramidally to points.   Round the shafts of the columns are seen the Etruscan border.   This border is also found in Egypt and Central America, as well as in Etruria. The name of the race that achieved these wonderful excavations, as well as the dates, are unknown.

Here are found the pyramids and obelisks, as well as the cubic altars, in the temples of India, all cut from the living rock. Monolithic altars, both cubical and oblong, are found in Nubia and Egypt. In the adytum of a Nubian excavated temple near Wady is a large cubic stone. In the sanctuary of the temple at Debot, in Nubia, are two fine monolithic temples of granite, with the winged globe sculptured over each. Two small ones are seen in the central niche, or sanctuary, of one of the temples in the island of Philæ. Other monoliths have already been noticed.

Ellora Temple.

185 by 150 feet,

$= 159 \cdot 95$,, $129 \cdot 69$ units,

$159^3 = \frac{1}{270}$ distance of the moon,

$(3 \times 159)^3 = \frac{1}{270} \times 3^3 = \frac{1}{10}$,

$(10 \times 3 \times 159)^3 = \frac{1000}{10} = 100$.

3 cubes of 30 times greater side

$= 300$ times distance of the moon,
$=$ diameter of orbit of Mercury.

4 cubes $= 400$ distance of the moon $=$ distance of the earth.

129^3, &c. $= \frac{1}{800}$ distance of the moon,

$(10 \times 129$, &c.$)^3 = \frac{1000}{800} = 2$.

Cube of 10 times less side

$=$ diameter of orbit of moon.

150 cubes $=$,, Mercury.

150^3 cubes $=$,, Belus.

Height 19 feet $= 16 \cdot 4$ units

$(10 \times 16 \cdot 5$, &c.$)^3 = \frac{4}{100}$ circumference,

$(10 \times 10 \times 16 \cdot 5$, &c.$)^3 = \frac{4000}{100} = 40$.

Cube of 100 times height $= 40$ times circumference.

Content $= 159 \times 129 \times 16 \cdot 5 = 33686$ units

$3365^3 = \frac{1}{8}$ distance of Venus.

Cube of $\frac{1}{10}$ content $= \frac{1}{8}$ distance of Venus

$$(2 \times 3365)^3 = \text{distance of Venus.}$$

Height of pyramidal temple

$$= 100 \text{ feet} = 86\cdot4 \text{ units,}$$
$$(10 \times 86\cdot7)^3 = \frac{6}{10} \text{ distance of the moon,}$$
$$(10 \times 10 \times 86\cdot7)^3 = \frac{600}{10} = 600.$$

Cube of 100 times height $= 600$ distance of the moon
$$= 4 \text{ times distance of Mercury.}$$

Distance of Mars $= 604$ distance of the moon.

Height of obelisk $= 38$ feet $= 54$ cubits.

Sum of 2 sides $= 159\cdot95 + 129\cdot69$

$$= 289\cdot64 \text{ units,}$$
$$289^3 = \frac{2}{90} \text{ distance of the moon,}$$
$$(3 \times 289)^3 = \frac{2}{90} \times 3^3 = \frac{6}{10},$$
$$(5 \times 3 \times 289)^3 = \frac{6}{10} \times 5^3 = 75.$$

2 cubes of 15 times sum of 2 sides

$$= 150 \text{ distance of the moon} = \text{distance of Mercury,}$$
$$300 \text{ cubes} = \text{distance of Belus,}$$
$$(10 \times 3 \times 289)^3 = \frac{6000}{10} = 600 \text{ distance of the moon.}$$

Cube of 30 times sum of 2 sides
or of 15 times perimeter,
$$= 600 \text{ distance of the moon.}$$

Distance of Mars $= 604$,,

Sides are 159·95 by 129·69 units,

   if 159·2   ,,   126·4   ,,
$$60 \times 159\cdot2 = 9550.$$

Diameter of orbit of the earth $= 9550^3$
$$60 \times 126\cdot2 = 7584.$$

Distance of the earth $= 7584^3$.

Thus cube of 60 times greater side
$$= \text{diameter of orbit of the earth.}$$

Cube of 60 times less side
$$= \text{distance of the earth.}$$

The cubes of the sides are as 1 : 2.

Or sum of 2 sides $= 160 + 130 = 290$,
$$\text{if} = 291\cdot6.$$

Then $100 \times 291\cdot6 = 29160$.
Distance of Belus $= 29160^3$.
Cube of 100 times sum of 2 sides,
    or of 50 times perimeter,
    $=$ distance of Belus,
    $=$ cube of Babylon.

Ellora Temple.

185 by 150 feet,
$= 159\cdot95$,, $129\cdot69$ units,
$100 \times 159\cdot6 = 15960$,
distance of Saturn $= 15960^3$.

Cube of 100 times greater side
    $=$ distance of Saturn,
    $10 \times 129\cdot6 = 1296$.

Diameter of orbit of the moon $= 1296^3$.
Cube of 10 times less side
    $=$ diameter of orbit of the moon.

The rock-cut temples of India are generally supposed to be of higher antiquity than pagodas, or temples, built on the surface of the earth; but these perhaps exceed, in their dimensions and finish of the several parts, even the most wonderful specimens of Egyptian art.

The most common form of the Hindoo pagodas is the pyramidal, of which one of the most remarkable is that of Chalembaram, on the Coromandel coast, about 34 geographical miles south of Pondicherry, and 7 from the sea.

The whole temple, with its detached buildings, covers an area of 1332 by 936 feet, according to others 1230 by 960 feet, and is surrounded with a brick wall 30 feet high and 7 thick, round which there is another wall furnished with bastions. The four entrances are under as many pyramids, which, up to the top of the portal, 30 feet in height, are formed of freestone, ornamented with sculptured figures.

Above the portal, the pyramid is built of tiles or bricks, to the height of 150 feet, with a coat of cement upon it, which is covered with plates of copper, and ornaments of baked clay. On passing through the chief portico of the western propylæa, we see on the left an enormous hall with more than 1000 pillars, which are above 36 feet high, and covered with slabs of stone; this hall might have served as a gallery for the priests to walk about in, just as the hypostyle halls of the Egyptian temples. In the midst of these columns, and surrounded by them, is a temple called that of Eternity. On the right or south side, we see the chief temple, with halls of several hundred pillars at the east and west end, also supporting a flat roof of stone.

The pagoda itself rests on a basis 360 feet long and 260 broad, and rises to a surprising height. It is formed of blocks of stone 40 feet long, 4 wide, and 5 thick, which must have been brought about 200 miles, as there are no stone quarries in the neighbourhood.

The temple has a peristyle round it; and 36 of the pillars, which are placed in six rows, and form the portico, support a roof of smooth blocks. The columns are 30 feet high, and resemble the old Ionic order. The roof of the pyramid has a copper casing covered with reliefs referring to mythical subjects; the gilding which was once on it is still visible. In the middle of the courtyard there is a great tank, surrounded with a gallery of pillars, and also an inclosure round it of marble, well polished and ornamented with sculptures and arabesques. In the eastern part there is still another court surrounded with a wall, on the inside of which is a colonnade covered with large slabs of stone. Here also there is a pagoda, which is but little inferior in size to the larger one; but it contains only large dark chambers covered with sculptures, which have reference to the worship of certain deities, particularly Vishnoo.

The interior ornaments are in harmony with the whole; from the nave of one of the pyramids there hang, on the tops of four buttresses, festoons of chains, in length altogether 548 feet, made of stone. Each garland, consisting of twenty links, is made of one piece of stone 60 feet long; the links themselves are monstrous rings, 32 inches in circumference, and polished as smooth as glass. One chain is broken, and hangs down from the pillar.

In the neighbourhood of the pagodas there are usually tanks and basins lined with cement, or buildings attached for the purpose of lodging pilgrims who come from a distance. It is, however, often the case that the adjoining buildings, as well as the external ornaments in general, are in bad taste, and the work of a later age than the pagoda itself.

These two dimensions of the inclosure greatly differ. According to the last the two sides are 1230 by 960 feet,

$$\text{or} \quad 1061 \quad ,, \quad 830 \text{ units,}$$

$$829^3 = 5 \text{ circumference,}$$
$$1044^3 = 10 \quad ,,$$

Thus the cubes of the sides will be as $1 : 2$.
Sides are 830 by 1061 units,

$$\text{if } 842, \&c. \quad 1061,$$
$$9 \times 842, \&c. = 7584,$$

Distance of the earth $\qquad = 7584^3,$
$$9 \times 1061 = 9550,$$

Diameter of orbit of the earth $= 9550^3$.
Cube of 9 times less side $=$ distance of the earth.
Cube of 9 times greater side $=$ diameter of orbit of the earth.

Or sum of 2 sides $= 830 + 1061 = 1891,$
$$4 \times 1896 = 7584,$$

Distance of the earth $= 7584^3$.
The sides of the inclosure are also stated at

$$1332 \text{ by } 936 \text{ feet,}$$
$$= 1151 \quad ,, \quad 809 \text{ units,}$$
$$1148^3 = \tfrac{80}{6} \text{ circumference,}$$
$$(6 \times 1148)^3 = \tfrac{80}{6} \times 6^3 = 2880.$$

Or cube of 6 times side $= 2880$ circumference,
$$= \text{diameter of orbit of Mercury,}$$

$$816^3 = \tfrac{1}{2} \text{ distance of the moon,}$$
$$(2 \times 816)^3 = 4 \qquad \text{,,}$$
$$= 2 \text{ diameter of orbit of the moon.}$$

Or cube of 2 sides $= 2$ diameter of orbit of the moon.
Sum of 2 sides $= 1148 + 816 = 1964$ units

$$1964 = 7 \text{ distance of the moon,}$$
$$(3 \times 1964)^3 = 7 \times 3^3 = 199,$$
$$\tfrac{1}{2} \text{ distance of the earth} = 200,$$
$$(2 \times 3 \times 1964) = \tfrac{8}{2} = 4 \text{ distance of the earth.}$$

Or cube of 6 times sum of 2 sides $= 2$ diameter of orbit of the earth.

The pagoda is 360 by 260 feet,
$$= 311 \text{ ,, } 225 \text{ units,}$$
$$311^3 = \tfrac{1}{36} \text{ distance of the moon,}$$
$$(3 \times 311)^3 = \tfrac{1}{36} \times 3^3 = \tfrac{27}{36} = \tfrac{3}{4},$$
$$(10 \times 3 \times 311)^3 = \tfrac{3000}{4} = 750.$$

Cube of 30 times side $=$ 750.
10 cubes   - $= 7500 =$ distance of Uranus,
30 cubes   - $= 21600 =$,,   Belus,

$$225^3 = \tfrac{1}{10} \text{ circumference,}$$
$$(10 \times 225)^3 = \tfrac{1000}{10} = 100,$$
$$(6 \times 10 \times 225)^3 = 100 \times 6^3 = 21600.$$

Or cube of 60 times side $=$ 21600,
10 cubes   - $= 216000 =$ distance of Belus,
10 spheres   - $=$ $=$,,   Neptune,
10 pyramids   - $=$ $=$,,   Uranus.

Sum of 2 sides $= 311 + 225 = 536$ units

$$537^3 = \tfrac{1}{7} \text{ distance of the moon,}$$
$$(7 \times 537)^3 = \tfrac{1}{7} \times 7^3 = 49.$$

3 cubes of 7 times 2 sides $=$ 49×3
$$= 147.$$

Distance of Mercury $= 150$ distance of the moon.
Length of granite chain
$$= 548 \text{ feet} = 473 \text{ units,}$$

$$477^3 = \tfrac{1}{15} \text{ distance of the moon,}$$
$$(10 \times 477)^3 = \tfrac{1000}{10} = 100,$$
$$(2 \times 10 \times 477)^3 = 800,$$
$$= \text{diameter of the orbit of the earth.}$$

Thus cube of length of chain
$= \tfrac{1}{15}$ distance of the moon $= 6$ radii of the earth.

Cube of 10 times length $= 100$ distance of the moon,
Cube of 20   ,, $= 800$,,
  · $=$ diameter of the orbit of the earth.

Cube of perimeter of pagoda
$$(2 \times 537)^3 = \tfrac{8}{7} \text{ distance of the moon.}$$

Cube of perimeter of inclosure
$$= (2 \times 1964)^3 = 56 \text{ distance of the moon.}$$

Cubes of perimeters are
$$\text{as } \tfrac{8}{7} : 56 :: 8 : 392 :: 1 : 49 :: 1 : 7^2.$$

Cube of 3 times perimeter of inclosure
$$= (3 \times 2 \times 1964)^3 = 56 \times 3^3 = 1512 \text{ distance of the moon,}$$
$$= 10 \text{ times distance of Mercury,}$$
$$= \tfrac{1}{15} \quad\quad\quad \text{,,} \quad\quad\quad \text{Belus.}$$

Calling distance of Mercury $= 151$ distance of the moon.
Cube of 5 times perimeter
$$= (5 \times 2 \times 1964)^3 = 56 \times 5^3 = 7000 \text{ distance of the moon,}$$
$$= 10 \times (400 + 300),$$
$$= 5 \times 800 + 10 \times 300,$$

$= 5$ times diameter of orbit of the earth,
$+ 10$ times diameter of orbit of Mercury.

Some of the most striking proofs of the resemblance between a Hindoo and an Egyptian temple have been deduced from a comparison of this description with what has been said about the sacred buildings of Egypt. The pyramidal entrances of the Indian pagodas are analogous to the Egyptian propyla, while the large pillared rooms which support a flat roof of stone, are found frequently in the temples of both countries. Among the numerous divisions of the excavations of Ellora there is an upper story of the " Dasavatara," or the temple of Vishnoo's incarnations, the roof of which is supported by sixty-four square-based pillars, eight in each row. This chamber is about 100 feet wide, and somewhat deeper, and as to general design may be compared with the excavated chambers of Egypt, which are supported by square columns. The massy materials, the dark chambers, and walls covered with high-wrought sculptures; and the tanks near the temples, with their inclosure of stone, and the steps for the pilgrims, are also equally characteristic of a pagoda and an Egyptian temple. To this may be added the high thick wall, of a rectangular form, carried all round the sacred spot; it is, however, principally the massy structure of these surrounding walls which forms the point of comparison, as Greek temples had also a wall inclosing the sacred ground, and the temples and churches of all countries are, as a general rule, separated from the unhallowed ground, if not by strong walls, at least by some mark which determines the extent of the sacred precincts. Yet there is a further resemblance worth noticing between some of the Hindoo pagodas, and the great temple of Phtha at Memphis. The Egyptian temple had four entrances, or propyla, turned to the four cardinal points of the compass; which is also the case with the pagoda at Chalembaram, with another at Seringham, and probably others also. The pagoda at Chalembaram, according to Indian tradition, is one of the oldest in their country, and this opinion is confirmed by the appearance of the principal temple contained within the walls; but other parts, such as the pyramidal entrances, the highly finished sculptures, and the chain festoons, may be the work of a later date. It seems probable that this enormous religious edifice was the growth of many ages, each adding something to enlarge and perfect the work of former days.

Among the oldest pagodas are those of Devogiri (God's mountain), otherwise called Dowlutabad, in the neighbourhood of Ellora. There are three of a pyramidal form, without sculptures, and each surmounted by Siva's trident. But one of the finest specimens in India is the Great Pagoda of Tanjore, which is dedicated to the god Siva. It is considered one of the most magnificent in the Tanjore dominions, and,

indeed, is the finest specimen of the pyramidal temple in all
India. It is resorted to by vast multitudes on days of public
festival. Although this building is of a form that occurs
frequently in the Deccan (the southern part of the peninsula),
it differs materially both with regard to its external decoration and the form of its termination at the top. It is about
200 feet in height, and stands within an area inclosed by
high walls, the top of which, along their whole extent, is
decorated in the usual manner, with bulls sacred to the
divinity, to whose service the temple is devoted. The interior contains a chamber or hall that has no light except
from lamps.

Buildings of this shape are found also in the small island
of Ramiseram, between Ceylon and the continent of India.
The chief pagoda here has the form of a truncated pyramid.
The outer side of this pagoda has been painted red, a
practice, it should be remarked, common to the Egyptians
and Hindoos, both of whom are also in the habit of plaster-
ing the walls on which reliefs were to be executed.

But later discoveries have made known to us buildings
in the interior of Java, possessing the same characteristics
as some of the Hindoo temples.

The interior of this island, according to Heeren, particularly the south-east part, is rich in monuments of Indian
architecture and sculpture, which not only prove that these
arts were once diffused here, but were raised to a height
of perfection scarcely known on the continent. All these
monuments belong to the class of constructed buildings;
excavated temples are not found, so far as we yet know.
The largest edifices are at Brandanan, very near the
centre of the island. Five parallelograms, each larger
one including the next smaller, contain no less than 296
little temples or chapels. The whole was, without doubt,
dedicated to the Brahminical worship, and reminds us, in
its plan, of the pagodas at Seringham, with their seven-fold
inclosures. Whether there are any traces of Buddha worship
in Java, particularly at Boro-Bodo, is still doubtful.

At Djockdjocarta, Davidson informs us, are to be seen

many ancient residences of Javanese chiefs; among others the celebrated cratan or palace. It is surrounded by a huge wall, which incloses an area of exactly one square mile; outside the wall runs a deep broad ditch. Another curious building is that in which the sultans, in days of yore, used to keep their ladies; it is composed entirely of long narrow passages, with numerous small rooms on each side; each of which, in the days of their master's glory, was the residence, according to tradition, of a beautiful favourite. To prevent the escape of the ladies, or the intrusion of any gallants, the whole pile was surrounded by a canal, which used to be filled with alligators; the only entrance was by a sub-terraneous passage beneath this canal, and which ran under it for its whole length. When I visited the place, in 1824, the canal, passage, &c. were all in good order, though the latter was getting damp from neglect, — a proof that the masons and plasterers of Java, in old times, must have been very superior workmen.

Side $= 1$ mile $= 18\cdot79$ stades

$$8 \times 18\cdot79 = 150 \text{ stades.}$$

Cube of 8 times side,

$$\text{or of twice perimeter} = 150^3 \text{ stades,}$$
$$= \text{cube of Nineveh,}$$
$$= \text{distance of Ninus.}$$

The Capitoline hill is the smallest of the seven hills at Rome: its circuit at the base is not a mile. "In its form," says Burton, "it resembles, roughly speaking, a flat ellipse, whose greater diameter is equal to two of its shorter diameters; or, in other words, it resembles an oval half as broad as it is long. The general direction of its length is nearly north and south; the distance from the northern to the southern extremity, along the top, is about 1300 feet; and the breadth of the hill, at the middle of its length, about half as many. The top of the hill exhibits a peculiar conformation: instead of presenting one level surface, it rises at the two extremities into two summits, between which lies the rest of the hill, sunk a little lower, like a small plain or valley. This plain between the mountains was called by the ancient Romans the Intermontium, and is called Intermonzio at the present day. If we consider the Intermontium as itself a square hill, and the two summits as two higher semicircular hills joined on to its northern and southern sides respectively, we shall have a rough notion of the Capitoline mount, such as it would appear in its natural state."

Transverse diameter of ellipse = 1300 feet = 1124 units, say = 1130 units.

Conjugate diameter = $\frac{1}{2}$ 1130 units.

Cylinder having height = $\frac{1}{3}$ 1130 units, and diameter of base = 1130, will = $\frac{1}{3}$ 1130 × 1130² × ·7854 = 5 circumfer.

$\frac{2}{3}$ = inscribed spheroid = $\frac{10}{3}$,,
$\frac{1}{3}$ = ,, cone = $\frac{4}{3}$,,

Cylinder having height = 1130 units, and diameter of base = $\frac{1}{2}$ 1130, will = 1130 × 565² × ·7854 = $\frac{4}{?}$ circumfer.

$\frac{2}{3}$ = inscribed spheroid = $\frac{10}{?}$,,
$\frac{1}{3}$ = ,, cone = $\frac{4}{6}$,,

Cylinder having the height = diameter of base = 1130 units will = 1130³ × ·7854 = 10 circumference.

Distance of moon from the earth = 9·55 circumference.

1130³ &c. = $\frac{4}{3}$ distance of the moon.
565³ &c. = $\frac{1}{6}$,,
= 10 radii of the earth.

3 × 1130³ &c. = 4 distance of the moon.
(3 × 1130 &c.)³ = 27 × $\frac{4}{3}$ = 36 ,,
(10 × 1130)³ = $\frac{4}{3}$ 1000 = $\frac{10}{3}$ 400 ,,
or, cube of 10 times 1130 = $\frac{10}{3}$ distance of the earth.

Spheroid having height = $\frac{1}{2}$ 1130 and diameter of base = 1130 = $\frac{10}{3}$ circumference.

Spheroid : cube :: $\frac{10}{3}$ circumfer. : $\frac{10}{3}$ distance of the earth :: circumference : distance of the earth :: 1 : 3840.

This is all that we can attempt from the vague estimate of the transverse diameter being about 1300 feet.

At the foundation of Rome, we find a sacred enclosure of the Etruscan Druids, converted by the first Romans into a citadel; as the later Romans converted the Druidical enclosures of Britain into fortresses.

The elliptical outline of the Capitol at Rome is similar to that on Carrock Fell in Britain.

Malefactors were tumbled down headlong from the Tarpeian mount, as the victims were thrown down the Mexican teocalli.

When Romulus had founded his city on the Palatine hill, and was desirous of attracting inhabitants to it, one of the measures to which he resorted was that of declaring a part of the Intermontium of the opposite hill, lying between two little groves of oak trees, to be a sacred asylum, or place of refuge, for criminals and others who had been forced to flee from neighbouring communities, and even for runaway slaves. In the after ages of Rome, the place which this sanctuary occupied was long pointed out as one of the curious localities of the Capitoline Hill.   In Virgil's poem, Evander shows Æneas —

> —— " the forest which in after times,
> Fierce Romulus for perpetrated crimes
> A sacred refuge made."

Juvenal, in one of his Satires, thus chastises the pride of birth : —

> " And how high soe'er thy pride may trace
> The long-forgotten founders of thy race,
> Still must the search with that asylum end,
> From whose polluted source we all descend."

How like the grove of oaks, the sanctuary of the Druids, does this description of the Intermontium seem to be !

At that period no Roman temple had been erected on the mount.

Romulus, in the war with the Sabines, having slain with his own hands a king of one of the towns on the Anio, and stripped off his armour, the conqueror returned to his infant city, and ascended the Capitoline Hill, bearing the spoils of his slain enemy, and there, hanging them on an oak tree held sacred among the shepherds, he offered them, under the name of " spolia opima," or " rich spoils," to Jupiter, whom he had honoured with the epithet of " Feretrius," or "bearer of spoils." At the same time, he marked out the bounds of a temple, which he dedicated to the god, to be the seat of the " spolia opima" which thereafter should be offered by any leader of the Romans who might slay the king or commander of an enemy. " This," says Livy, " is the origin of the temple which, of all, was the first consecrated at Rome."

Shortly after, the Capitoline Hill seems to have first assumed the appearance of a fortress, encompassed with a ditch and palisade. When peace ensued between the Romans and Sabines, and the two nations became united into one people, the Sabines settled on the Capitoline, Saturnian, or Tarpeian Hill. The arx, or citadel of Rome, seems to have been afterwards formed on this hill : it originally occupied the southern summit, or that approaching towards the Tiber ; but as the entire mount was afterwards enclosed by walls and fortified, the appellation of arx became applicable indiscriminately to the whole.

Tarquinius Priscus selected one of the summits of the Tarpeian Hill for founding temples to Jupiter, Juno, and Minerva. But the ground chosen, it appears, was already occupied by several altars and chapels, which had been consecrated by the Sabines ; and the augurs were directed to ascertain if the deities to whom they were sacred would yield their place to Jupiter, Juno, and Minerva. The augurs were consulted, and allowed the removal of all, except the shrines of Terminus and Juventus, the gods of boundaries and youth. These deities stoutly refused to stir ; and their obstinate tenacity was received as a happy omen that the boundaries of the Roman land should never recede, and that the state should be for ever young. A second prodigy, still more remarkable, as indicating the future magnitude of the Roman dominion, followed upon digging for the foundations. A human head, with the face entire, " as of one newly slain," presented itself to the workmen. Tarquinius Superbus, who had succeeded Tarquinius Priscus, and employed Etrurian workmen, suspended the work, and called in the soothsayers. The meaning of the prodigy lay too deeply hidden for the native professors of the art, and reference was had to their Etruscan brethren. By these it was interpreted as an omen that the spot should be the "citadel of empire, and the head of things." The temple, — or the building, or both, — received accordingly the name of "Capitolium." At a subsequent period the name of the temple, and the summit on which it stood, was extended to the whole hill, and Capitolium was applied indifferently to all three, just as arx was applied to the other summit and the whole hill also.

Encouraged by these omens, Tarquinius proceeded on a scale of great magnificence; so that Livy says, "the booty of Pometia, which had been destined to carry the work to its summit, scarcely sufficed for the foundations." The people were forced to contribute their labour, receiving from the king a scanty measure of food in exchange; and we are told that they felt little aggrieved in having to build the temples of their gods with their own hands, though they worked unwillingly when compelled by the same monarch to complete the Circus Maximus and the great sewers of the city.

The Etrurian augurs resembled the Druids. An ancient sarcophagus lately found in Etruria had a human sacrifice unequivocally represented on both sides.

Pliny speaks of the Druids as practising magic, and being so great proficients of the art as to equal the Persian and Chaldean magi; "so that one would even think," he says, "that the Druids had taught it them."

Cæsar states that the institution of the Druids was supposed to have been brought from Britain into Gaul; and that those who wished to be better instructed generally made a voyage to Britain.

"Again," says Cæsar, speaking of the Gauls, "their great god is Mercury, of whom they have a number of statues, and believe him to be the conductor of travellers on their roads and journeys, the patron of merchants and commerce. After him, the gods most revered are Apollo, Mars, Jupiter, and Minerva, of whom they think for the most part like other people. They believe that Apollo banishes disease; that

Mercury presides over industry and the arts; that Jupiter holds the empire of heaven ; and that Mars is the arbiter of war. Generally they make a vow to sacrifice to Mars the spoils of the enemy ; and after victory they sacrifice animals, and other trophies they deposit in a place set apart ·for that purpose. In many cities are seen quantities of these spoils stored in consecrated places. It rarely happens that any one is so regardless of religion as to conceal the spoils he has taken, or to abstract what has been deposited. Penalties the most severe are attached to such crimes."

The statue of Jupiter which stood within the temple, according to Pliny, was originally of baked clay. About 300 years B. C. a statue of Jupiter was placed on the summit, with a chariot drawn by four horses: it was probably of bronze.

Reference has been made to the monolithic temples, both large and small. Two small stone chests are seen in one of the temples of Philæ. In the temple of Dabot, in Nubia, are two fine monolithic temples of granite, in the sanctuary : the winged globe is sculptured over each.

The stone chest of the Capitol contained sacred records.

Etrurian workmen, who may be classed with the wandering masons, were employed at the Capitol ; and Etrurian augurs were consulted.

The Romans felt little aggrieved when employed in building the temple; though they felt oppressed when compelled to work at other public buildings.

This religious feeling,— that the people were erecting temples to their gods, — was the secret of the concentrated physical power that enabled the kings and priesthoods to construct those stupendous monuments of labour, the pyramidal temples.

The Coliseum, commenced by Vespasian and finished by Titus, is the finest remain of Roman magnificence in the world. It is of an oval form, and was situated near the colossal statue of Nero, not far from the imperial palace. It was sufficient to contain eighty thousand people seated, and twenty thousand standing. The Coliseum occupies an elliptical area of nearly six acres : the greater diameter being about 615 feet English, and the less 510 feet.

The greater diameter of the elliptical area within is about 242 feet, and the less, 176 feet : leaving a circuit for seats and galleries of about 175 feet in breadth. The outward circumference when complete was about 1770 feet, enclosing an area of about 246000 feet. The interior ellipse was the arena, or place where the combatants engaged. The outer wall is 157 feet high in its whole extent.

Transverse diameter of greater ellipse = 615 feet = 531·5 units.

Conjugate diameter = 510 feet = 440·8 units.

$30 \times 531^2 = 15960 =$ distance of Saturn.

Cube of 30 times greater diameter = distance of Saturn.

2 cubes	"	"	"	=	" Uranus.
6 cubes	"	"	"	=	" Belus.

440^3 &c. $= \frac{1}{4}$ circumference.

2×440 &c.$^3 = \frac{1}{4} \times 2^3 = 6.$

$30 \times 2 \times 440$ &c.$^3 = 6000$

Cube of 30 times less diameter = 6000 circumference,

$= \frac{1}{4}$ distance of Saturn.

$= \frac{2}{14}$ " Uranus

$= \frac{2}{14}$ " Belus.

Sum of 2 diameters $= 531·5 + 440·8 = 972·3$.

$30 \times 972^2 = 29160^2 =$ distance of Belus.

Sphere $=$ " Neptune.

Pyramid $=$ " Uranus.

Sum of 2 diameters $= 972$ units $= 4$ stades

$=$ perimeter of tower of Belus.

$30 \times 4^3 = 120^2$ stades $=$ cube of Babylon.

Circumferences of circles having diameters 531 and 440

$= 1668$ and 1392.

Mean $= \frac{1}{2} (1668 + 1392) = 1530$ units.

Circuit of great ellipse by measurement $= 1770$ feet

$= 1530$ units.

$(4 \times 2 \times 440 \text{ &c.})^3 = 6 \times 4^3 = 384$ circumference.

10 cubes of 8 times less diameter = 3840 circumference
= distance of the earth.

Cube of sum of 2 diameters = 4^3 stades = 972^3 units
= 8 circumference.

Transverse diameter of internal ellipse
= 281 feet = 1 stade = 243 units.

Conjugate diameter = 176 feet = ½ stade
= 152 &c. units.

243^3 = ⅓ circumference, and $(2 \times 243)^3$ = circumfer.
152^3 &c. = $\frac{1}{32}$,, $(4 \times 152$ &c.$)^3$ = 2 ,,

Cubes of diameters are as 1 : 4.

1 stade = height of tower of Belus.
⅝ ,, = ,, temple of Chinla
1½ ,, = ,, pyramid of Cephrenes.

Circumference of circle diameter 152 units = 477.

477^3 = $\frac{1}{11}$ distance of the moon.
$(10 \times 477)^3$ = $\frac{4141}{41}$ = 110

Cube of 10 times circumference = 100 distance of moon.
Cube of 20 times ,, = 800 ,,
= diameter of the orbit of the earth.

Circuit of great ellipse = 153 units.
Less diameter of less ellipse = 153 ,,

Cubes of 153 and 153 will be as 1 : 1 +.
153^3 &c. = $\frac{1}{11}$ distance of the moon.
= ½ radius of the earth.

$(10 \times 153$ &c.$)^3$ = = ½ distance of the moon
= ½ &c. = = 20 radii of the earth.

Cube of less diameter of less ellipse = radius of the earth.
Cube of circuit of great ellipse = 2 ,, ,, earth.

$(3 \times 10 \times 153$ &c.$)^3$ = ,, ,, = distance of the moon.
$(5 \times 3 \times 10 \times 153$ &c.$)^3$ = 50 ,, ,, =

2 cubes of 153 times less diameter ,, ,, ,,
= 2250 distance of the moon = ,, ,,

tical area of nearly six acres; the greater diameter being about 615 feet English, and the less 510 feet.

The greater diameter of the elliptical area within is about 281 feet, and the less, 176 feet; leaving a circuit for seats and galleries of about 175 feet in breadth. The outward circumference when complete was about 1770 feet, enclosing an area of about 246661 feet. The interior ellipse was the arena, or place where the combatants engaged. The outer wall is 157 feet high in its whole extent.

Transverse diameter of greater ellipse = 615 feet = 531·5 units.

$$\text{Conjugate diameter} = 510 \text{ feet} = 440\cdot8 \text{ units.}$$
$$(30 \times 532)^3 = 15960 = \text{distance of Saturn.}$$

Cube of 30 times greater diameter = distance of Saturn.

2 cubes	,,	,,	,,	=	,, Uranus.
6 cubes	,,	,,	,,	=	,, Belus.

$$440^3 \&c. = \tfrac{1}{4} \text{ circumference.}$$
$$(2 \times 440 \&c.)^3 = \tfrac{1}{4} \times 2^3 = 6.$$
$$(10 \times 2 \times 440 \&c.)^3 = 6000.$$

Cube of 20 times less diameter = 6000 circumference,

$$= \tfrac{1}{6} \text{ distance of Saturn.}$$
$$= \tfrac{1}{12} \quad ,, \quad \text{Uranus}$$
$$= \tfrac{1}{36} \quad ,, \quad \text{Belus.}$$

Sum of 2 diameters = 531·5 + 440·8 = 972·3.

$$(30 \times 972)^3 = 29160^3 = \text{distance of Belus.}$$
$$\text{Sphere} = \quad ,, \quad \text{Neptune.}$$
$$\text{Pyramid} = \quad ,, \quad \text{Uranus.}$$

Sum of 2 diameters = 972 units = 4 stades
= perimeter of tower of Belus.

$$(30 \times 4)^3 = 120^3 \text{ stades} = \text{cube of Babylon.}$$

Circumferences of circles having diameters 531 and 440
= 1668 and 1392.

Mean = $\tfrac{1}{2}$(1668 + 1392) = 1530 units.

Circuit of great ellipse by measurement = 1770 feet
= 1530 units.

$(4 \times 2 \times 440 \text{ &c.})^3 = 6 \times 4^3 = 384$ circumference.

10 cubes of 8 times less diameter = 3840 circumference
    = distance of the earth.

Cube of sum of 2 diameters = 4^3 stades = 972^3 units
    = 8 circumference.

Transverse diameter of internal ellipse
    = 281 feet = 1 stade = 243 units.

Conjugate diameter = 176 feet = $\frac{5}{8}$ stade
    = 152 &c. units.

$243^3 \quad = \frac{1}{8}$ circumference, and $(2 \times 243)^3 = \quad$ circumfer.
152^3 &c. $= \frac{1}{32} \qquad$,, $\qquad (4 \times 152 \text{ &c.})^3 = \quad 2 \qquad$,,

Cubes of diameters are as 1 : 4.

1 stade = height of tower of Belus.
$\frac{5}{8}$,, = ,, teocalli of Cholula.
$1\frac{5}{8}$,, = ,, pyramid of Cephrenes.

Circumference of circle diameter 152 units = 477.

$477^3 \qquad = \frac{1}{10}$ distance of the moon.
$(10 \times 477)^3 = \frac{1000}{10} = 100 \qquad$,,

Cube of 10 times circumference = 100 distance of moon.
Cube of 20 times ,, = 800 ,,
    = diameter of the orbit of the earth.

Circuit of great ellipse = 1530 units.
Less diameter of less ellipse = 153 ,,

Cubes of 153 and 1530 will be as 1 : 1000.

153^3 &c. $= \frac{1}{300}$ distance of the moon
    = $\frac{1}{4}$ radius of the earth.

$(10 \times 153 \text{ &c.})^3 = \frac{1000}{300} = \frac{10}{3}$ distance of the moon
    $= \frac{10}{3} \times 60 = \frac{600}{3} = 200$ radii of the earth.

Cube of less diameter of less ellipse = $\frac{1}{4}$ radius of the earth.
Cube of circuit of great ellipse = 200 radii of the earth.

$(3 \times 10 \times 153 \text{ &c.})^3 = \frac{10}{3} \times 3^3 = 90$ distance of the moon.
$(5 \times 3 \times 10 \times 153 \text{ &c.})^3 = 90 \times 5^3 = 11250 \qquad$,,

2 cubes of 150 times less diameter, or of 15 times circuit,
    = 22500 distance of the moon = distance of Belus.

Diameters of less ellipse $= 243$ and 153 units.

Cylinder having height $= 153$　,,
and diameter of base $= 243$　,,

will $= 153 \times 243^2 \times \cdot 7854 = \frac{1}{16}$ circumference.

Cylinder having twice dimensions will $= \frac{1}{2}$ circumference.

Spheroid $= \frac{1}{3}$　　　,,

Cone　　$= \frac{1}{6}$　　　,,

and $243 \times 152^2 = \frac{1}{20}$　　,,

Cylinder having height $=$ diameter of base
$= 153$ &c. units　　　　　　　　$= \frac{1}{40}$ circumference.

Cylinder having height $=$ diameter of base
$= 10 \times 153$ &c. $= \frac{1000}{40}$　　　　$= 25$ circumference.

Cylinder having height $=$ diameter of base
$=$ twice circuit $= 2 \times 10 \times 153$ &c. $= 200$ circumference,
and cube of circuit $= 200$ radii of the earth.

Circuit^3 : cylinder
Circuit^3 : $(2 \text{ circuit})^3 \times \cdot 7854$
　　　1^3 : $2^3 \times \cdot 7854$
　　　1 : $6 \cdot 2832$
Radius : circumference.

Radius^3 : cylinder :: 1^3 : $2^3 \times \cdot 7854$
　　　　　　　1 : $6 \cdot 2832$

Radius : circumference
Diameter : 2 circumference.
Radius^2 : area of circle :: 1^2 : $2^2 \times \cdot 7854$
　　　　　　　　1 : $3 \cdot 1416$
Radius　　: $\frac{1}{2}$ circumference
Diameter : circumference.

Were the external elliptical walls of the Coliseum originally constructed by the augurs or Druids of Etruria, and afterwards, on their foundation, was the present structure erected by the Jews whom Titus led in captivity from Jerusalem?

In the papal reigns this structure was used as a quarry for building many of the present palaces. To prevent further destruction of the building, Pope Benedict consecrated the ruins. In the pontificate of Pius VII. we saw the cross erected, and heard a priest of the Church of Rome proclaiming the humane doctrine of Christianity in that arena where formerly the combats of gladiators and wild beasts were exhibited for the sport of imperial Rome.

In the same arena, at a still more early period, a concourse assembled from the seven hills of Rome, and the plains of Latium might probably have witnessed the awful spectacle of human beings sacrificed to propitiate the gods : and there they might have listened in terror to the prophecies and denunciations of the Druidical augurs, the expounders of religion and the laws by which they governed the people.

The Pantheon, once the pride of Rome, still remains one of the most magnificent and complete of all the ancient temples. Its portico is a model of perfection ; it is of the Corinthian order, as is the whole building. It is supported by sixteen columns of oriental granite ; the shaft of each is a single stone, 42 feet English in height ; eight are placed in front, the other eight behind. It is a question whether Agrippa built the whole of it, or only the portico. This circular temple was dedicated to all the gods. The diameter of the inside is nearly 150 feet English ; the walls are besides this 18 feet thick : so that the diameter of the whole is 186 feet.

The interior of the Pantheon has a diameter of nearly 150 feet

$$= 129 \cdot 64 \text{ units,}$$
$$1296^3 = \text{diameter of orbit of the moon.}$$

Or cube of 10 times diameter
$$= \text{diameter of orbit of the moon.}$$

Cylinder having height = diameter of base = 130, &c. units
$$= \tfrac{8}{5000} \text{ distance of the moon.}$$

Cylinder having 10 times dimensions
$$= \tfrac{8000}{5000} = \tfrac{8}{5} \text{ distance of the moon.}$$

Cylinder having 50 times dimensions
$$= \tfrac{8}{5} \times 5^3 = 200 \text{ distance of the moon,}$$
$$= \tfrac{1}{2} \text{ distance of the earth.}$$

Cylinder having 100 times dimensions
        = twice diameter of orbit of the earth.

Cube of 100 times diameter = 13000^3.

Distance of Jupiter = about 13040^3.

Thus distance of Jupiter : twice diameter of orbit of the earth

                 :: cube   : cylinder
                 :: pyramid : cone
                 :: square   : circle.

            Diameter = 129·6 units,
        Circumference = 407, &c.

            407^3, &c. $= \frac{1}{16}$ distance of the moon,
        $(4 \times 407, \&c.)^3 = \frac{1}{16} \times 4^3 = 4$,,

Cube of 4 times circumference = 4 times distance of the moon.

Cube of 4 times circumference = twice cube of 10 times diameter,

        $6^{12} = 1296^3$ = diameter of orbit of the moon.

The height of the Pantheon was originally equal diameter of base.

Thickness of walls = 18 feet.

External diameter = 186 feet = 161 units,

            $(3 \times 161)^3 = 483^3$ = circumference.

Cube of 3 times greater diameter = circumference, and cube of 10 times less diameter = distance of the moon.

Cylinder having height = diameter of base = 160, &c.
                = $\frac{3}{1000}$ distance of moon,
        Sphere $= \frac{2}{1000}$,,
        Cone $= \frac{1}{1000}$,,

Cylinder having height = diameter of base
        = 10 × 160, &c. = 3 distance of the moon,
            Sphere = 2   ,,
            Cone   = 1   ,,

Internal circumference = 407, &c. units,
                = height of pyramid of Cheops.

    10 × internal diameter = 1296 units,
                = twice side of base of pyramid.

Another account makes the thickness of the walls 20 feet: then external diameter will $= 188$ feet $= 163$ units,

$$163^3, \&c. = \tfrac{2}{30} \text{ distance of moon,}$$
$$(10 \times 163, \&c.)^3 = \tfrac{2000}{50} = 40.$$

10 cubes of 10 times diameter $= 400$ distance of moon,
$$= \text{distance of the earth.}$$

Circumference will $= 514$ units,

$$514^3 = \tfrac{1}{8} \text{ distance of the moon,}$$
$$(2 \times 514)^3 = 1 \qquad \text{,,}$$

Cube of twice circumference $=$ distance of the moon.

Thus the Pantheon appears to have been originally a temple dedicated to the one god of the Sabæans; and at a later period, during the Roman empire, to have been consecrated to all the gods of the Grecian mythology, which were derived from the Egyptians, just as the early temples in Egypt were dedicated to the only god of the Sabæans, and later temples to the gods of the Egyptians.

Hence it seems that Rome was an ancient city before its legendary founder, Romulus, was suckled by the wolf.

For these great works, as well as the Cloaca Maxima, were originally constructed by the Sabæans, or wandering masons, in an age anterior to the date of Roman history.

The Romans made use of the ancient buildings, or their foundations, in constructing these still existing monuments of the empire.

Pope Boniface IV. dedicated the Pantheon to the Virgin. In 830 Gregory IV. dedicated it to all the saints.

Middleton, in his celebrated letter from Rome, observes, on the subject of this change of name from "all the gods" of antiquity to "all the saints" of the church of Rome, " that the noblest heathen temple now remaining in the world is the Pantheon, or Rotunda, which, as the inscription on the portico informs us, having been impiously dedicated of old by Agrippa to Jove and all the gods, was piously consecrated by Pope Boniface the Fourth to the Blessed Virgin and all the saints. With this single exception, it serves as exactly all the purposes of popish as it did for the pagan worship, for which it was built. For as in the old temple, every one might find the god of his country, and address himself to that deity whose religion he was most devoted to; so it is the same thing now; every one chooses the patron whom he likes best; and one may see here different services going on at the same time at different altars, with distinct congregations around them, just as the inclinations of the people lead them to the worship of this or that particular saint."

In these instances we find that man, when he adores the invisible Creator, searches for some visible object on which he may fix the eye in prayer.

The Sabæans knelt before the pyramid and obelisk, as symbols of the laws of the Creator, when they worshipped the invisible God.

The sun, moon, and stars, the host of heaven, were adored in the Chaldæan and Assyrian plains. These bright luminaries, which were daily seen in the heavens, were obedient to the laws typified by the pyramid and obelisk, and regarded as the greatest and most sublime of the visible works of the Creator when they offered up their adoration to the throne of heaven.

The heroes of antiquity were raised to demigods, and received divine honours, for some signal benefits which they had conferred on mankind, as the invention of arts, the discovery of science, or something highly useful to social life.

Adoration and prayer are offered to saints, who have distinguished themselves by a life agreeable to heaven, uncommon piety, and zeal for religion.

" The Keabé is the point of direction and the centre o. union for the prayers of the whole human race, as the Beithmâmour is for those of the celestial beings; the Kursy for those of the four arch-angels; and the Arsch for those of the cherubims and seraphims who guard the throne of the Almighty. The inhabitants of Mecca, who enjoy the happiness of contemplating the Keabé, are obliged, when they pray, to fix their eyes upon the sanctuary; but they who are at a distance from this valuable privilege are required only, during prayer, to direct their attention towards the hallowed edifice.

The believer who is ignorant of the position of the Keabé must use every endeavour to gain a knowledge of it; and after he has shown great solicitude, whatever be his success, his prayer is valid." (*D'Ohsson.*)

The Arab's prayer in the desert is from Southey's " 'Thalaba ": —

> "'Tis the cool evening hour;
> The tamarind from the dew
> . Sheathes its young fruit, yet green.
> Before their tent the mat is spread,
> The old man's awful voice
> Intones the holy Book.
> What if beneath no lamp-illumin'd dome,
> Its marble walls bedeck'd with flourish'd truth,
> Azure and gold adornment? sinks the word
> With deeper influence from the Iman's voice,
> Where in the day of congregation, crowds
> Perform the duty-task?
> Their Father is their Priest,
> The Stars of Heaven their point of prayer,
> And the blue Firmament
> The glorious Temple, where they feel
> The present Deity!"

The amphitheatre at Verona is inferior in size, but equal in materials and solidity to the Coliseum. The external circumference, forming the ornamental part, has been destroyed long ago, with the exception of one piece of wall, containing three stories of four arches, rising to the height of more than 80 feet. The pilasters and decorations of the outside are Tuscan. Forty-five ranges of seats, rising from the arena to the top of the second story of outward arches, remain entire, with the different vomitoria, and their respective staircases and galleries of communication. The whole structure is of blocks of marble, and presents such a mass of compact solidity as might have defied the influence of time, had not its power been aided by the more active operations of barbarian destruction.

The dimensions of the outward circumference is 1290 feet, the length of the arena 218, and its breadth 129. The seats are capable of containing 22,000 spectators.

Circuit of amphitheatre $= 1290$ feet,
Circuit of temple of Diana $= 1290$,,
                                    $= 1114$ units.

Cylinder having height $=$ diameter of base $=$ circuit $= 1114$ units, will

$\qquad = $ distance of the moon.

Breadth of theatre $= 129$ feet $= 111\cdot4$ units.

Cylinder having height $=$ diameter of base $=$ breadth $= 111\cdot4$ units, will

$\qquad = \frac{1}{1000}$ distance of the moon.

Cylinder having height $=$ diameter of base $= 10$ times breadth $= 1114$ units, will

$\qquad = $ distance of the moon.

Length of theatre $= 218$ feet,
Less side of temple $= 220$,,

$\qquad$ and 219, &c. feet $= 189\cdot5$ units,
$\qquad (40 \times 189\cdot5)^3 = 7580^3 = $ distance of the earth.

Cube of 40 times length of theatre $=$ cube of 40 times less side of temple

$\qquad = 7580^3 = $ distance of the earth.

Length $+$ breadth of theatre

$\qquad = 189\cdot5 + 111\cdot4 = 300\cdot9$ units,
$\qquad 300^3, \&c. = \frac{1}{40}$ distance of the moon,
$\qquad (10 \times 300, \&c.)^3 = \frac{1000}{40} = 25,$
$\qquad (2 \times 10 \times 300, \&c.)^3 = 25 \times 2^3 = 200$ distance of the moon.

Cube of 20 times sum of 2 diameters

$\qquad = 200$ times distance of the moon,
$\qquad = \frac{1}{2}$ distance of the earth.

Diameters of ellipse are $198\cdot5$ and $111\cdot4$ units.

Circumferences of circles having diameters $198\cdot5$ and $111\cdot4$ will $= 595$, &c. and 351.

$\qquad (3 \times 595)^3 = 50$ circumference.

Cube of 3 times circumference $= 50$ circumference of the earth.

$\qquad 351^3, \&c. = \frac{4}{100}$ distance of the moon,
$\qquad (10 \times 351, \&c.)^3 = \frac{4000}{100} = 40.$

Cube of 10 times circumference$=40$ distance of moon,
$$=\tfrac{1}{10} \qquad\text{,,}\qquad \text{earth.}$$

Sum of 2 circumferences$=595$, &c. $+351=946$, &c.

$$947^3, \text{&c.} = \tfrac{10}{4} \text{ circumference,}$$
$$(8\times 947, \text{&c.})^3 = \tfrac{10}{4}\times 8^3 = 3840.$$

Cube of 8 times sum of 2 circumferences
$$=3840 \text{ circumference}=\text{distance of the earth.}$$

The less diameter of the central arena at both Verona and Rome$=\tfrac{1}{10}$ the circuit of the amphitheatre.

Ephesus, a city of Ionia, built, as Justin mentions, by the Amazons; or by Androclus, son of Cordus, according to Strabo; or by Ephesus, a son of the river Cayster. It is famous for a temple of Diana, which was reckoned one of the seven wonders of the world. This temple was 425 feet long, and 220 broad. The roof was supported by 127 columns 60 feet high, which had been placed there by so many kings. Of these columns, 36 were carved in the most beautiful manner, one of which was the work of the famous Scopas. This celebrated building was not totally completed till 220 years after its foundation. There was above the entrance a huge stone, which, according to Pliny, had been placed there by Diana herself. The riches which were in the temple were immense, and the goddess who presided over it was worshipped with the most awful solemnity. This celebrated temple was burnt on the night that Alexander was born, and soon after it rose from ruins with more splendour and magnificence. Alexander offered to rebuild it at his own expense, if the Ephesians would place upon it an inscription which denoted the name of the benefactor. This generous offer was refused by the Ephesians, who observed, that it was improper that one deity should raise temples to the other.

Sides of temple
$$425 \text{ by } 220 \text{ feet,}$$
$$=367 \text{ ,, } 190 \text{ units,}$$

$$(100\times 366\cdot4)^3 = 36640^3 = \text{distance of Ninus,}$$
$$(40\times 189\cdot5)^3 = 7580^3 = \qquad\text{,,}\qquad \text{the earth.}$$

Cube of 400 times greater side

> = distance of the gods from the sun.

Cube of 40 times less side

> = distance of man from the sun.

Or cube of 40 times less side

> = 400 times distance of the moon,
> =   ,,   earth.

Sum of 2 sides = $425 + 220 = 645$.

Perimeter = $2 \times 645 = 1290$ feet,

> = 1114 units.

Cylinder having height = diameter of base = perimeter of temple

> = 1114 units will = distance of the moon.

Ægesta or Segesta, in Sicily, is said to have been founded by Æneas, and the work conducted by Ægestus, who gave the name to the city. Of the ruins of Segesta, the chief is a Doric temple of thirty-six columns, all perfectly entire, except one, which has been damaged by a stroke of lightning. This edifice is a parallelogram of 162 feet by 66.

> 162 by 66 feet,
>
> = 140 ,, 57, &c. units,
>
> 139^3, &c. $= \frac{1}{400}$ distance of the moon,
>
> $(20 \times 139, \&c.)^3 = \frac{1}{400} \times 20^3 = 20$.

20 cubes of 20 times greater side

> = 400 times distance of the moon,
> = distance of the earth,
>
> $(10 \times 57\cdot4)^3 = 574^3$, &c. $= \frac{4}{3}$ circumference,
>
> $(3 \times 10 \times 57\cdot4, \&c.)^3 = \frac{5}{3} \times 3^3 = 45$,
>
> $(2 \times 3 \times 10 \times 57\cdot4)^3 = 45 \times 2^3 = 360$.

Cube of 60 times less side = 360 circumference.

100 cubes = 36000 circumference = distance of Saturn.

200 cubes = distance of Uranus.

600 cubes =   ,,   Belus.

Sum of 2 sides $= 57$, &c. $+ 139$, &c. $= 196$, &c.

196^2, &c. $= \frac{7}{100}$ distance of the moon,

$(10 \times 196,$ &c.$)^2 = \frac{7000}{100} = 70$.

4 cubes of 10 times sum of 2 sides,

or of 5 times perimeter,

$= 280$ distance of the moon,

$=$ distance of Venus.

We have no means at present of knowing the measurement of the other great temples in Sicily; nor of the three great Doric temples at Pæstum, in Calabria. We recollect the magnificent temples at Pæstum all rise from well-defined platforms of masonry formed by three terraces or steps. It would be desirable to take the measurements of the steps and platforms, as well as of the temples themselves.

In architecture, as in everything else, says Gliddon, the Greeks and the Romans obtained their knowledge from their original sources in Egypt, where still existing ruins attest the priority of invention 1000 years before Greece, and 1500 years before Rome. These topics are now beyond dispute, and may be found in the pages of the Champollion school. Until the last few years they were utterly unknown in history.

PART VIII.

MONUMENTS IN CEYLON. — BRAZEN PALACE. — ENCLOSURE OF THE
SACRED BO TREE. — DAGOBAHS. — ADAM'S PEAK. — BURMESE
MONUMENTS. — SHOEMADOO PAGODA AT PEGU. — THE ORIGINAL
PAGODAS WERE OF THE HYPERBOLIC FORM. — THE GREAT DA-
GON PAGODA AT RANGOON USED AS A TEMPLE AND A FORTRESS.
— THE SACRED BOAT OR SHIP. — ASTROLOGERS. — THE RECUM-
BENT COLOSSAL MONOLITH MARBLE STATUE OF GAUDAMA, AT
AVA, AND THE TWO RECUMBENT STATUES PLACED, BY AMASIS,
ONE BEFORE THE TEMPLE OF VULCAN, AND THE OTHER AT
SAIS, WERE ALL OF EQUAL LENGTH. — OTHER COLOSSAL STA-
TUES. — GREAT BELLS. — WHITE ELEPHANTS. — BOODHISM. —
AMERICAN ANTIQUITIES. — FORTS. — TUMULI. — TEOCALLIS. —
PALACE OF MITLA. — ANCIENT CITIES IN YUCATAN. — RUINS OF PA-
LENQUE. — RUINS OF COPAN. — COLUMNAR IDOLS. — HILL FORTS
IN INDIA. — AFFGHAN FORTS. — EGYPTIAN FORTS. — LYDIAN AND
ETRURIAN TOMBS. — TOMB OF PORSENNA. — SEPULCHRE OF THE
HORATII AND CURIATII. — SARDINIAN TOMB. — CUCUMELLE IN THE
ROMAN MAREMMA. — GREAT CUCUMELLA AT VOLCI. — ETRUSCAN
DRAINAGE. — ETRURIAN AUGURS. — CEMETERIES. — SOCIAL SYS-
TEM. — SACERDOTAL AUTHORITY. — FINE ARTS. — DRUIDISM. —
CINGALESE DRUIDS. — DRUIDS OF BRITAIN AND GAUL. — MOUNDS
IN AFFGHANISTAN. — CATACOMBS AT ROME. — MOUNDS AT WARKA,
THE ERECH OF SCRIPTURE. — EARTHENWARE COFFINS. — TUMULI
NEAR KASSIA AND KESSARIA. — VARIOUS MODES OF SEPULTURE.
— EGYPTIAN TOMBS. — NUBIAN PYRAMIDS. — ANCIENT ARCHES.
— EGYPTIAN RITUAL. — SOULS OF THE DEPARTED WEIGHED IN
THE BALANCE OF TRUTH AND JUSTICE. — EMBALMING. — SCENES
OF ORDINARY LIFE PAINTED ON THE WALLS OF TOMBS. — GLASS.

Ceylon.

AT a period anterior to the Christian era, and to the discovery of Great Britain, Ceylon had attained a high degree
of civilisation and refinement. They scarcely appear in
their narrations to have entered on their career of civilisation,

ere we find them founding cities, building temples, and, above all, forming immense lakes for facilitating the operations of agriculture, which Uphan calls the true riches of a state. These extraordinary excavations rivalled the most remarkable labours of antiquity. The remains of those national monuments demonstrate an amount of population, and a state of prosperity, infinitely superior to what exists at present, or has for a long period existed in Ceylon. Not less striking than these lakes are the vast mounds, temples, and mausoleums, which are generally adjacent to their borders, and the remains of which at the present day attest the former splendour of the state.

In the first century of our era, about the year 63, the monarch Waahapp completed the walls of the city of Anooradhapoora, which the native historical records say were four gaws from north to south, and as many from east to west. A gaw is said to equal four English miles. Although the style of this account is essentially oriental, still the ruins of the walls, stupendous tanks, public buildings, and religious edifices, bear evidence of the enormous population which must have been required, to undertake and complete these gigantic structures.

The Brazen Palace, at Anooradhapoora, so called from the material with which the roof of the building was covered, was erected by Dootoogaimoonoo, who reigned 142 years before the present era, as an abode for priests. It was of a square form, each of its sides being 234 feet : its height was 270 feet. This building contained nine stories, in each of which were 100 apartments. The ruins now consist of 1600 granite pillars, in a greater or less state of preservation, which, being placed in forty parallel lines, form a square. These pillars vary in height, some being 11 feet above the ground, while others are 11½; those standing in the centre are delicately, but not elaborately chiselled, whilst the exterior ones are plain, and only half the thickness of those in the centre, which are nearly 2 feet wide, and 1½ thick ; on these pillars the stupendous fabric rested.

Within 1½ mile of these ruins are the gigantic remains of

several dagobahs, which rear their towering crests above the lofty trees in the surrounding jungle; these monuments are solid structures of brick, and were originally covered with chunam, but this incrustation has now fallen off the greater number of those edifices. The Ruwanwelli-saye is a dagobah of peculiar sanctity, and was commenced by Dootoogai-moonoo; tradition states that this mausoleum owes its erection to the following circumstance. During the time the Brazen Palace was being built, a stone pillar was found near the spot where the dagobah now stands. On this pillar a prediction was inscribed, which stated that where this stone was found a superb dagobah of 120 cubits in height would be built by a good monarch, who would be rewarded by Buddha for his piety both in this life and in the next, The dagobah stands in the middle of a square platform. whose sides are each 500 feet in length, the whole being surrounded by a moat 70 feet wide. The platform is paved with large slabs of granite, and the slopes towards the fosse are ornamented with massive pieces of sculpture, representing the heads of elephants, which project, as though the sculptor intended the beholder to imagine that the bodies of those huge creatures supported the superstructure. The Ruwanwelli-saye is now a conical mound of brickwork, overgrown with brushwood; still the stupendous ruin, which is 180 feet high, is regarded with peculiar interest both by the antiquarian and man of science, as it was to the spire of this dagobah that Sanghatissa the First, who reigned A. D. 243, placed a pinnacle of glass to serve as a protection against lightning.

This account will be found in the " Maha-Wansa," which was written in the middle of the fifth century, between 460 and 480, thus clearly proving the advanced state of science among the ancient Cingalese, and the knowledge they possessed of the non-conducting property of glass.

It is worthy of remark, that on the spire of Christchurch, at Doncaster (struck by lightning in 1836), a ball of glass had been placed, under the notion that glass, because a non-conductor, is also a repellent of lightning.

The ruin of the largest mausoleum which was ever built in Ceylon is to be seen at Anooradhapoora; it is called Abhaayagiri-dagobah, and was built by Wallagam Bahu, in the century preceding our era. The original height of this gigantic structure was 400 feet, the platform and moat being in proportion; the ruin is now 220 feet high, and the outer wall exceeds $1\frac{1}{4}$ mile in length. Trees of lofty stature cover the ruin, the only portion of brickwork perceptible being towards the summit.

The finest specimen of a mausoleum in Ceylon, although of smaller dimensions than the preceding, is the dagobah built over the collar-bone of Goutama Buddha, 300 years before the Christian era. The dagobah is low, broader at the summit than at the base, and is surrounded by four lines of slender stone pillars, twenty-six being placed in each line. The pillars are 23 feet high, have circular capitals, octagonal shafts, and square bases, the latter being narrower than the capitals. These graceful columns are ornamented with the most delicate and elaborate chiselling conceivable, and are so arranged on the platform of granite as to form the radii of a circle of which the dagobah is the centre. Antiquarians agree in admitting that this dagobah is the most elegant specimen of architecture in the island.

At Anooadhapoora there are eight large tanks, and many smaller ones, which are entirely cased with hewn stone.

There are numerous rock temples scattered over the island, but none either so large, or in the same state of preservation, as those at Dambool.

Side of the square platform on which the dagobah stands = 500 feet = 432 units,

$$(3 \times 432)^3 = 1296^3 = 6^{12} = 2 \text{ distance of the moon.}$$

Cube of 3 times side = 2 distance of the moon,

$$= \text{diameter of orbit of the moon,}$$

$$3^5 = 243, \text{ the Babylonian numbers.}$$

243 transposed, by placing the first numeral the last, = 432.

So cube of 3 times 3^5 transposed
$$= \text{diameter of orbit of the moon.}$$

The moat surrounding the platform is 70 feet wide $= 60 \cdot 5$ units.

External side of moat $= 432 + 2 \times 60 \cdot 5$,
$$= 553 \text{ units,}$$
$$554^3, \&c. = \tfrac{3}{4} \text{ circumference.}$$

2 cubes of side $=3$ times circumference.

Cube of twice side $= \tfrac{3}{4} \times 2^3 = 12$ circumference.

Cube of perimeter $= 12 \times 2^3 = 96$,,
$$= 10 \text{ distance of the moon.}$$

Cube of twice perimeter $= 80$,
$$= \tfrac{1}{8} \text{ distance of the earth.}$$

Cube of 6 times perimeter $= 80 \times 3^3$,
$$= 2160 \text{ circumference} = \tfrac{1}{100} \text{ distance of Belus.}$$

Side of Brazen Palace $= 234$ feet,
$$= 202 \text{ units,}$$
$$(3 \times 203, \&c.)^3 = 610^3 = 2 \text{ circumference.}$$

Cube of 3 times side $=$ twice circumference.

Should the side $= 204$ units,
  perimeter will $= 816$,,
$$816^3 = \tfrac{1}{2} \text{ distance of the moon,}$$
$$(2 \times 816)^3 = 4 \qquad \text{,,}$$

Cube of perimeter $= \tfrac{1}{2}$ distance of the moon,

Cube of 2 perimeter $= 4$,,
$$= \tfrac{1}{100} \text{ distance of the earth.}$$

Height of Brazen Palace $= 270$ feet,
$$= 233 \text{ units,}$$
$$231^3 = \tfrac{1}{80} \text{ distance of the moon,}$$
$$(2 \times 231)^3 = \tfrac{1}{10} \qquad \text{,,}$$
$$(20 \times 231)^3 = \tfrac{8000}{80} = 100.$$

Cube of height $= \tfrac{1}{80}$ distance of the moon.

Cube of 2 height $= \tfrac{1}{10}$,,

Cube of 20 height $= 100$,,

Cube of 40 height $= 800$,,
$$= \text{diameter of orbit of the earth.}$$

Cube of height $\quad=\frac{1}{80}$ distance of the moon,

$\quad\quad\quad\quad\quad\quad\quad=\frac{80}{80}=\frac{1}{4}$ radius of the earth.

Cube of 2 height $\quad=\frac{1}{4}\times8=6\quad\quad$,,

$\quad\quad\quad\quad\quad\quad\quad=3$ diameter of the earth.

The great king's temple is

$\quad\quad\quad\quad\quad\quad$ 178 by 80 feet,

$\quad\quad\quad\quad=153$, &c. ,, 68·5 units,

$\quad\quad\quad$ 153^3, &c. $=\frac{1}{300}$ distance of the moon,

$\quad$ $(10\times153, \&c.)^3=\frac{1000}{300}=\frac{10}{3}$ $\quad\quad$,,

Cube of 10 times greater side $=\frac{10}{3}$ distance of the moon.

Less side $=68\cdot5$ units

$\quad\quad\quad$ $(10\times68\cdot8)^3=688^3=\frac{3}{10}$ distance of the moon.

Cube of 10 times less side $=\frac{3}{10}$ distance of the moon,

$\quad$ $(10\times10\times68\cdot8)^3=\frac{3000}{10}=300$ $\quad\quad$,,

Cube of 100 times less side $=300$ distance of the moon,

$\quad\quad\quad\quad=$ diameter of orbit of Mercury.

Sum of 2 sides $=153$, &c. $+68$, &c. $=221$, &c.

$\quad\quad\quad$ 221^3, &c. $=\frac{1}{100}$ distance of the moon,

$\quad$ $(10\times221, \&c.)^3=\frac{1000}{100}=10$ $\quad\quad$,,

Cube of 10 times sum of 2 sides

$\quad\quad=10$ times distance of the moon.

Length of the wall at Dambool $=400$ feet $=346$ units,

$\quad\quad\quad$ 349^3, &c. $=\frac{1}{8}$ circumference,

$\quad\quad$ $(2\times349, \&c)^3=3$ $\quad\quad$,,

Cube of twice length $=3$ times circumference.

The sacred fanes of Dambool may be regarded as specimens of man's patience, ingenuity, and skill in the past ages, and are to be classed with the caves of Elephanta of India, and the pyramids in the sandy plains of Egypt. Those rock temples are vast in magnitude, their decorations, in a high state of preservation, are characteristic, and are maintained in thorough order by the attendant priests. The interior of the fanes of Dambool is concealed by a wall 400 feet in length, which is pierced for the reception of windows and doors.

Wallagan Bahu was the king who founded the rock temples, and the largest of these excavated religious edifices was commenced by him 86 years before the Christian era, and is called the Maha Rajah Wihare, or the Great King's Temple, in honour of the monarch. This magnificent cave is entered by an arched portal, on either side of which stand stone statues, which appear to scowl on the inquisitive intruder. The length of this excavation is 178 feet, the width 80, and the roof is 25 feet high at the loftiest part, which is at the front wall; the height of the cave gradually decreasing to the opposite wall, thus forming a complete arc of a circle. The whole surface, walls and roof, are painted in the richest and most brilliant colours imaginable, which appear perfectly fresh, though they have not been renovated for more than half a century. The paintings represent incidents in the life of Buddha, and historical subjects. Some of these are particularly interesting, as they illustrate the early history of Lanka-diva. The first represents the voyage of Wijeya and his 700 followers, the conquerors of Ceylon; the monarch and his train are represented in vessels totally devoid of sails, and having only lower masts. In another painting is pourtrayed the dedication of the island to Buddha; the peace and good feeling inculcated by his doctrines are exemplified under the allegorical symbol of a king patronising agriculture; the monarch is seen guiding a plough, which is drawn by elephants, priests following, who throw the grain into the furrow. This series of historical painting is continued down to the period of the arrival of the Bo-tree, the Delada, and other relics of Buddha; the building of Anooradhapoora and its religious edifices being duly set forth.

The temple is well lighted by numerous windows: every detail in the paintings and decorations can be brought under immediate inspection, and the whole are well finished, evincing both taste and skill. This sacred temple is dedicated to Buddha, and contains forty-eight statues of the god in different attitudes, which are of various dimensions, the greater number being larger, but none less than the natural stature of man. There is also an exquisitely proportioned dagobah, reaching to the roof, whose circular pedestal is embellished with four figures of Buddha, seated upon coiled cobra capellas. There are statues likewise of the gods Vishnu and Samen, the goddess Patine, and the kings Wallagan Bahu and Kirti Nissaanga.

These temples are under the charge of a certain number of priests, whose abodes, of a superior description, are below the caves on the south side of the rock, and are attached to the Asgiree Wiháre, at Kandy.

Anooradhapoora remained the seat of government until the termination of the eighth century, when it was abandoned, and Pollanarooa was then declared the seat of government and capital of the island. Until the twelfth century the city gradually increased in size; and its days of brilliant splendour were during the reigns of Prackrama Bahu the First, surnamed the Grand, who ascended the throne A. D. 1153, and Kirti Nissaangha; as it was by these monarchs that the public edifices were either completed or constructed. Prackrama constructed a succession of tanks, artificial lakes, and canals, which extended a distance of one hundred miles. The monarch gave his name to this stupendous and useful work, and the remains of the "rivers of Prackrama" can be seen and traced for a considerable distance. Pollanarooa was regarded as the capital till A. D. 1318, when it was finally abandoned, and all the magnificent structures, which then remained entire, were suffered to fall into decay, and are now surrounded by forests.

Historical records state that when Pollanarooa rose to its meridian of glory, the principal thoroughfares then extended to six gows, or twenty-four miles; and the lesser streets to four gows from the city into the suburbs.

The loftiest building at Pollanarooa is the Rankoot dagobah, which was built by the second queen of Prackrama Bahu. This mausoleum is covered with brushwood; and the slender form of the spire can be distinctly seen from a considerable distance, as the height of the ruin, from the platform to the extremity of the spire, is about 150 feet. The records state

the height of this dagobah originally to have been 120 car-
penters' cubits from the platform to the top of the spire, on
which was placed the golden umbrella.

120 × 2 feet 3 inches = 270 feet English.

Dondera, " the city of God," is the most southerly port of
the island.   The temples and remains which are here to be
seen are particularly interesting both to the antiquarian and
oriental scholar, as the ruins of an ancient edifice, situated on
a rocky point, commemorate the conquest of Ceylon by Rama,
by some supposed to be a fabulous being.   A solitary stone
pillar is all that remains perfect of this magnificent edifice.
The shape of this sole memento of the past is remarkably
singular, as the stone is formed alternately into squares and
octagons.   The eminent Oriental scholar, Jones, fixes the date
of Rama's existence about 1810 years before the Christian
era, and writes, " Rama, who conquered Silan (or Ceylon)
a few centuries after the flood."   The Cingalese annals assign
the date of 2387 B. C. as the period of Rama's reign in Lanka-
diva.

In the Ramayana, the oldest epic poem extant, is contained
the earliest notice to be met with in Oriental literature of the
Cinnamon Isle.   The Ramayana details the same events as
the Iliad of Homer ; — the abduction of another's wife, the
attempt of the enraged husband to regain his spouse, the long
and bloody wars that ensued, and the ultimate recovery of
the fair dame.

A short distance from the ruins of the Jaitawanarama, in
the midst of mouldering ruins and great trees, is the singular
temple of Gal-wihare, which is by far the finest specimen of
ancient Eastern sculpture in Ceylon.   Out of the face of a
huge granite rock, three figures of Buddha, two temples, and
a long inscription have been carved.   One of these statues is
of colossal dimensions, measuring 45 feet in length, in a reclining position, — the work having been separated from the
rock.   The second figure, which is standing, measures 24 feet.
The third is in a sitting position, and is 16 feet high, richly
ornamented, — having a number of fabulous animals at each

side, half alligator, half elephant,—and a profusion of elegant devices.

At the ruins of the Jaitawanarama is a colossal statue of Buddha, 50 feet in height.

The renowned city of Pollanarooa, with its extensive streets, varying from 16 to 24 miles in length, its busy bazaars, its luxurious palaces,—all have passed away. Cities, towns, and villages have disappeared; while the gigantic ruined tanks, many of them constructed at a period so remote as to be beyond the reach of tradition, and the magnificent stone temples, colossal statues, and lofty dagobahs, remain buried in the solitudes of the forest, tenanted by wild animals, whose haunts are seldom intruded on by man. Many of the tanks in Ceylon are upwards of 20 miles in length, situated in the most solitary and desolate parts of the island, buried in the depths of vast forests, neglected and unknown.

At the Aukane Wihare is a colossal statue of Buddha, measuring upwards of 50 feet in height, carved out of the face of an immense perpendicular block of granite. This gigantic figure is most admirably executed: the drapery hangs in graceful folds, and is as perfect as if fresh from the hands of the sculptor. It is joined at the back of the rock, for the purpose of support, and stands on a handsome pedestal elevated about 7 feet above the ground. On the right is placed a sculptured stone, representing a cobra capella with the hood extended; demon and serpent-worship being the most ancient of all the heathen superstitions of the East.

Annarahadapoora, founded in 437 B. C., was the capital of Ceylon for upwards of 1300 years, and where ninety kings are said to have reigned. It covered a space of 16 square miles, was surrounded by a wall 64 miles in circumference, and contained palaces, temples, water-courses, tanks, rice-fields, gardens, and forests. Its streets were wide, and of great extent; one of which extended as far as the sacred mountain of Mehintilai, a distance of seven miles, through which the procession of priests took place, amid all the pomp of ecclesiastical prosperity and princely munificence, the king and his nobles appearing in the train.

The Maha Wihare was erected by Tisso, 300 years B. C.   It stands in an enclosed space, 345 feet in length by 216 feet in breadth.   Here lie, scattered among huge trees, elegant bas-reliefs, mutilated statues, and broken pillars.   Out of the centre of a building of four terraces, each having a space of about 8 feet to stand on, the upper being the smallest, grows the Sacred Bo Tree (*Ficus religiosa*), or, Jaya Sri Maha Bodin-Wahansey, (the great, famous, and triumphant fig-tree,) which is an object of the greatest veneration among the Buddhists, and is visited by thousands of pilgrims from all parts of the island.   Before permitting you to ascend the ladder leading up to the sacred spot, the priests oblige you to take off your shoes, lest the holy ground should be polluted.

This is a branch of the tree under which Goutama sat the day he became a Buddhu.

Enclosure of the Sacred Bo Tree
$$= 345 \text{ by } 216 \text{ feet}$$
$$= 298 \text{ by } 186 \text{ &c. units.}$$
$$186^3 \text{ &c.} = \tfrac{3}{500} \text{ distance of the moon.}$$
$$(10 \times 186 \text{ &c.})^3 = \tfrac{3000}{500} = 6 \qquad ,,$$
$$\text{and } (10 \times 298)^3 = 4 \times 6 = 24 \qquad ,,$$

Cube of 10 times less side   =   6 distance of the moon.
Cube of 10 times greater side = 24   ,,
Sum of 2 cubes = 6 + 24   = 30   ,,

10 cubes of 10 times each of the 2 sides = 10×30
= 300 distance of the moon = diameter of orbit of Mercury.
Sum of 2 sides = 298 + 186 &c. = 484 &c.
484^3 &c. = circumference.

Sum of 2 sides = 2 stades.

Perimeter of the sacred enclosure = 4 stades = perimeter of the tower of Belus = $\frac{1}{4}$ perimeter of the square enclosure of the tower.

The cubes of the sides of the enclosure of the Maha Wihare are as 1 : 4.

The building in the centre has four terraces.   On the top of the platform stands the sacred Bo tree.   The tower of Belus had eight terraces.

Difference of sides $= 298 - 186 = 112$ units.
Cube of difference $= 112^3$ &c. $= \frac{1}{80}$ circumference.
$(20 \times 112$ &c.$)^3 = \frac{1}{80} \times 20^3$ $= 100$,,
Cube of 20 times difference $= 100$ circumference.
Cube of 60 times difference $= 2700$ circumference,
$= $ distance of Venus.
$= \frac{1}{80}$ distance of Belus.

The Jaitawanaroma dagobah, a brick structure, erected by Mahasen, A. D. 275, measures in height 265 feet, and, with the exception of the steeple, is covered with forest trees and impenetrable jungle.

265 feet $= 229$ &c. units.
229^3 &c. $= \frac{1}{90}$ distance of the moon.
$(30 \times 229$ &c.$)^3 = \frac{1}{90} \times 30^3 = 300$,,
Cube of 30 times height $= 300$ distance of the moon
$= $ diameter of the orbit of Mercury.

The most ancient of these structures is the Abayagirie dagobah, which was erected by King Wallagam Bahoo, B. C. 76, and measured in height 405 feet, but has gone greatly to decay. The entire structure is covered with dense wood.

Height $= 405$ feet $= 350$ units.
351^3 &c. $= \frac{2}{80}$ distance of the moon.
$(10 \times 351$ &c.$)^3 = \frac{2880}{8} = 40$,,
Cube of 10 times height $= 40$ distance of the moon.
10 cubes of 10 times height $= 400$,,
$= $ distance of the earth.

$(5 \times 351$ &c.$)^3 = \frac{2}{80} \times 5^3 = 5$ distance of the moon.
Cube of 5 times height $= 5$ times distance of the moon;
or, 349^3 &c. $= \frac{1}{8}$ circumference.
$(2 \times 349$ &c.$)^3 = 3$,,
Cube of twice height $= 3$ times circumference.

All the dagobahs seem to be solid structures, having no entrance in their sides, nor have any passages been found underground, which, from their gigantic dimensions, might have been supposed to exist. Their form is alike, from the huge Abagagirie dagobah to the miniature edifices which abound at Mehintilai. The great rock temples, colossal statues, beautiful pillars, exquisite sculptures, and wonderful tanks, some of them measuring 20 miles in circumference, demonstrate a state of prosperity at a very remote period of time, and fully prove the former greatness and splendour of the island. These interesting remains lie scattered in the deep solitudes of the forest; wild beasts prowl among the sacred edifices of the hallowed city, where the bear, cheetah, elephant, and elk abound. The trees are tenanted by the owl, peafowl, jungle cock, and parrot.

The highest mountain in Ceylon is Adam's Peak, which is estimated at 6450 feet above the level of the sea. It is 60 miles south of Colombo, and so lately as 1804 no European subject had ascended it. It is of a conical shape, like the Peak of Teneriffe, and is visible at sea, on the south-west coast, at a distance of 50 leagues. Two smaller peaks arise from the mountain, which, when viewed from some parts of the interior, appear to be of equal height with the principal one. This mountain equally claims the veneration of the Boodhist and Hindoo, the Mohammedan and the native Christian; each of whom consider it a place of peculiar sanctity, and has attached to its sacred locality some superstitious legend. The apex of the cone is frequently enveloped in clouds, and during the entire period of the southwest monsoon, is perfectly hid from them. The first European who scaled the summit of this celebrated mountain was Lieutenant Malcom, accompanied by a party of Malay soldiers.

The top of the peak is contracted to a small compass, being only 72 feet long by 54 broad, and is encircled by a parapet wall 5 feet high, generally very much out of repair. In the centre of this area is a large rock of ironstone, upon which the impression of Adam's foot is supposed to be traceable. By the Boodhists, however, the mark visible on this stone is declared to be the footprint of their divinity, the other statement being a Mahommedan tradition. The sacred spot is inclosed by a frame of copper, fitted exactly to its shape, ornamented with four rows of precious stones, and the whole is protected from the weather by a small wooden building, 12 feet long, 9 broad, and $4\frac{1}{4}$ high.

$$72 \text{ by } 54 \text{ feet,}$$
$$= 62 \cdot 2 \text{ by } 46 \cdot 7 \text{ units,}$$

$$610^3 = 2 \text{ circumference,}$$
$$477^3 = \tfrac{1}{10} \text{ distance of the moon.}$$

So that if the sides were about 71 by 55 feet,
Cube 10 times greater side would $= 2$ circumference.
Cube 10 times less side $\quad = \tfrac{1}{10}$ distance of the moon.
Cube of 100 times less side $= 100 \qquad$,,
Cube of 200 times less side $= 800 \qquad$,,
$\qquad\qquad\qquad = $ diameter of orbit of the earth.
10 times sum of 2 sides $= 610 + 477$,
$\qquad\qquad\qquad = 1087$ units.

50 times sum of 2 sides $= 5435$,
$\quad$ distance of Mercury $= 5460^3$.
10 times difference of 2 sides $= 610 - 477$,
$\qquad\qquad\qquad = 133$ units,

$$132^3, \&c. = \tfrac{1}{80} \text{ circumference,}$$
$$(10 \times 132, \&c.)^3 = \tfrac{1000}{80} = 20.$$

Cube of 10 times difference $= \tfrac{1}{80}$ circumference,
Cube of 100 $\qquad$,, $\qquad = 20 \qquad$,,

Boodhism is the most widely diffused religion in the world; embracing among its votaries the Cingalese, the Siamese, the Burmese, and other inhabitants of the Eastern peninsula, a large part of the vast population of China, and all the Mongolian nations of central and northern Asia. Tibet, however, is its great seat, and the special country of the Lamas, or professional priests of Boodh, who form a large portion of its entire population. Hither all who mean to be priests of Boodh flock to study in the colleges or monasteries with which the country abounds, and here are the most eminent chiefs of the Boodhist hierarchy; and above all the Delai-Lama, a pope of Boodhism, in whom, for the time, the spirit of Boodh is supposed to be incarnate, and at whose death a successor has to be chosen by lot, out of three candidates previously selected, by certain marks, from among the infants of all the families of the country, rich as well as poor.

Prinsep maintains that Boodhism, in very nearly its present state, has existed from a period long anterior to Christianity; that it is, in short, the actual system of theology and worship originated by the Indian sage Boodha Sakhya Muni, the date of whose death a variety of proofs fixes at B. C. 543.

Burmese Pagodas.

The object in Pegu that most attracts and most merits notice, says Symes, in his " Embassy to Ava," is the noble edifice of Shoemadoo, or the Golden Supreme. This extraordinary pile of building is erected on a double terrace, one raised upon another. The lower and greater terrace is about 10 feet above the natural level of the ground, forming an exact parallelogram; the upper and lesser terrace is similar in shape, and rises about 20 feet above the lower terrace, or 30 above the level of the country. I judged a side of the lower terrace to be 1391 feet, of the upper 684. The walls that surrounded the sides of the terrace, both upper and lower, are in a ruinous state; they were formerly covered with plaster, wrought into various figures; the area of the lower is strewed with fragments of small decayed buildings, but the upper is kept free from filth, and is in tolerable good order. There is reason to conclude that this building and the fortress are coeval, as the earth of which the terraces are composed appears to have been taken from the ditch; there being no other excavation in the city or in its neighbourhood that could have afforded a tenth part of the quantity.

The terraces are ascended by flights of stone steps, which

are broken and neglected. On each side are the dwellings of the Rhahaans, raised on timbers 4 or 5 feet from the ground; these houses consist only of a large hall; the wooden pillars that support them are turned with neatness; the roofs are covered with tiles, and the sides are made of boards; and there are a number of bare benches in every house, on which the Rhahaans sleep; but we saw no other furniture.

Shoemadoo is a pyramidal building, composed of brick and mortar, without excavation or aperture of any sort; octagonal at the base and spiral at the top; each side of the base measures 162 feet; this immense breadth diminishes abruptly, and a similar building has not unaptly been compared in shape to a large speaking trumpet.

Six feet from the ground there is a wide projection that surrounds the base, on the plane of which are fifty-seven small spires of equal size, and equi-distant; one of them measured 27 feet in height, and 40 in circumference at the bottom. On a higher ledge there is another row, consisting of fifty-three spires of similar shape and measurement.

A great variety of mouldings encircle the building; and ornaments somewhat resembling the fleur-de-lys surround the lower part of the spire; circular mouldings likewise gird it to a considerable height, above which there are ornaments in stucco not unlike the leaves of a Corinthian capital; and the whole is crowned by a tee, or umbrella, of open iron-work, from which rises a rod with a gilded pennant.

The tee or umbrella is to be seen in every sacred building that is of a spiral form; the raising and consecration of this last and indispensable appendage is an act of high religious solemnity, and a season of festivity and relaxation. The present king bestowed the tee that covers the Shoemadoo. It was made at the capital; and many of the principal nobility came down from Ummerapoora to be present at the ceremony of its elevation. The circumference of the tee is 56 feet; it rests on an iron axis fixed in the building, and is farther secured by large chains strongly rivetted to the spire. Round the lower rim of the tee is appended a

number of bells, which, agitated by the wind, make a con-
tinual jingling.

The tee is gilt, and it is said to be the intention of the
king to gild the whole of the spire.

All the lesser pagodas are ornamented with proportionable
umbrellas of similar workmanship, which are likewise encircled by small bells.

The extreme height of the edifice, from the level of the
country, is 361 feet, and above the interior terrace 331 feet.

On the south-east angle of the upper terrace there are two
handsome saloons, or kioums, lately erected, the roofs composed of different stages, supported by pillars; we judged
the length of each to be about 60 feet, and the breadth 30;
the ceiling of one is already embellished with gold leaf, and
the pillars are lackered; the decoration of the other is not
yet completed. They are made entirely of wood; the carving on the outside is laborious and minute; we saw several
unfinished figures of animals and men in grotesque attitudes,
which were designed as ornaments for different parts of the
building. Some images of Gaudma, the supreme object of
Birman adoration, lay scattered around.

At each angle of the interior and higher terrace there is a
temple 67 feet high, resembling in miniature the great
temple; in the front of that, in the south-west corner, are
four gigantic representations, in masonry, of Palloo, or the
evil genius, half beast, half human, seated on their hams,
each with a large club on the right shoulder. The pundit
who accompanied me said they resembled the Rakuss of the
Hindoos. These are guardians to the temple.

Nearly in the centre of the east face of the area are two
human figures in stucco, beneath an umbrella; one, standing, represents a man with a book before him and a pen in
his hand; he is called Thasiamee, the recorder of mortal
merits and mortal misdeeds; the other, a female figure kneeling, is Mahasumdera, the protectress of the universe, so long
as the universe is doomed to last; but when the time of
general dissolution arrives, by her hand the world is to be
overwhelmed and everlastingly destroyed.

Along the whole extent of the north face of the upper terrace there is a wooden shelf for the convenience of devotees who come from a distant part of the country. On the north side of the temple there are three large bells of good workmanship, suspended near the ground, between pillars; several deer's horns lie strewed around; those who come to pay their devotions first take up one of the horns, and strike the bell three times, giving an alternate stroke to the ground; this act, I was told, is to announce to the spirit of Gaudma the approach of a suppliant. There are several low benches near the foot of the temple, on which the person, who comes to pray, places his offering, commonly consisting of boiled rice, a plate of sweetmeats, or cocoa-nut fried in oil; when it is given, the devotee cares not what becomes of it; the crows and wild dogs often devour it in the presence of the donor, who never attempts to disturb the animals. I saw several plates of victuals disposed of in this manner, and understood it to be the case with all that was brought.

There are many small temples on the areas of both terraces, which are neglected and suffered to fall into decay. Numberless images of Gaudma lie indiscriminately scattered. A pious Birman who purchases an idol, first procures the ceremony of consecration to be performed by the Rhahaans; he then takes his purchase to whatever sacred building is most convenient, and there places it within the shelter of a kioum, or on the open ground before the temple; nor does he ever again seem to have any anxiety about its preservation, but leaves the divinity to shift for itself. Some of those idols are made of marble that is found in the neighbourhood of the capital of the Birman dominions, and admits of a very fine polish; many are formed of wood, and gilded, and a few are of silver; the latter, however, are not usually exposed and neglected like the others. Silver and gold are rarely used, except in the composition of household gods.

Should the shape of the umbrella over the head of Mahasumbera be of the hyperbolic form, it would denote that Mahasumdera, like Isis, represents gravitation.

On both the terraces are a number of white cylindrical

flags, raised on bamboo poles; the flags are peculiar to the Rhahaans, and are considered as emblematic of purity, and of their sacred function.   On the top of the staff is a henza, or goose, the symbol of both the Birman and Pegu nations.

The walls that formerly surrounded the terraces at Pegu were covered with reliefs in plaster.   The sides of the terraces of the teocallis in Mexico were ornamented with sculpture. Diodorus states that the palace at Babylon, which was also a citadel, was surrounded with three vast circular walls, which were ornamented with sculptured animals, richly painted in their natural colours on the bricks of which they were composed, and afterwards burnt in.   Here we find the process of enamelling described.

" A similar building has been compared to a large speaking trumpet."   How nearly this comparison agrees with the hyperbolic solid, when the axis passes through the centre of each ordinate, may be seen by reference to *Figs.* 49, or to 37, 38, where the axis does not pass through the centre.

The base of the speaking trumpet would appear to be the octagonal base, or base of the third terrace.   The base of the hyperbolic solid is the first, or lowest platform, the side of which $= 1202$ units, call 1.   The side of the base of the next, or second platform, $= \frac{1}{2}$.   The third platform may be the base of the trumpet, and greatest diameter $= \frac{1}{3}$.

So the series will be hyperbolic as 1, $\frac{1}{2}$, $\frac{1}{3}$, $\frac{1}{4}$, &c., like the hyperbolic solid in *Fig.* 49., which represents the velocity

$$\propto \frac{1}{D^2}.$$

It was traditionally believed that the temple of Shoemadoo was founded 2300 years ago.

Side of the lowest terrace $= 1391$ feet $= 1202$ units.

$$1202^3 = \tfrac{8}{9} \text{ distance of the moon.}$$
$$(5 \times 1202)^3 = \tfrac{8}{9} \times 5^3 = 200.$$

Cube of side $= \tfrac{8}{9}$ distance of the moon.

Cube of 5 times side $= 200,$
$$= \tfrac{1}{2} \text{ distance of the earth.}$$

Cylinder having height = diameter of base = 1202 units
= 12 circumference.

$$\text{Sphere} = 8 \quad \text{,,}$$
$$\text{Cone} = 4 \quad \text{,,}$$

If side of upper terrace = $\frac{1}{2}$ side of lowest terrace = 601 units, then cube of upper terrace

= $\frac{1}{8}$ cube of lowest terrace = $\frac{1}{5}$ distance of the moon,
= cube of Cephrenes.

5 cubes = distance of the moon.

Again, cube of twice perimeter of lowest terrace = $\frac{8}{5} \times 8^3$
= $\frac{4096}{5}$ distance of the moon,

about 4090^3 = diameter orbit of Jupiter.
5 cubes of 2 perimeter = diameter orbit of Jupiter.

Side of octagonal base = 162 feet = 140 units.

$$140^3 = \frac{1}{400} \text{ distance of the moon.}$$
$$(20 \times 140)^3 = \frac{1}{400} \times 20^3 = 20 \quad \text{,,}$$

Cube of 20 times side = 20 distance of the moon.
20 cubes of 20 times side = 20^3 = 400 ,,
= distance of the earth.

Cube of perimeter = $\dfrac{8^3}{400} = \dfrac{512}{400}$ distance of the moon.

Cube of 20 times perimeter = $\frac{512}{400} \times 20^3 = 10240$,,

$$\tfrac{1}{5} \text{ cube} = \frac{10240}{5} = 2048,$$
and distance of Jupiter = 2045.

Extreme height of edifice = 361 feet = 312 units, say = 314, &c.

Height × area base = 314, &c. × 1202^2 = 8 circumference, and sphere having diameter 1202 units = 8 circumference.

Height + side of base of lowest terrace = 314 + 1202 = 1516 units.

$$1516^3 = \tfrac{16}{5} \text{ distance of the moon.}$$
$$(5 \times 1516)^3 = \tfrac{16}{5} \times 5^3 = 400 \quad \text{,,}$$
$$= \text{distance of the earth.}$$

Cylinder having height = diameter base = 1202 = 12 circumference.

Cylinder having height = diameter = 4×1202, or 2 perimeter = $12 \times 4^3 = 768$ circumference = $\frac{1}{4}$ distance of earth.

Cube of $\frac{1}{2}$ $1202 = 601^3 = \frac{1}{4}$ distance of moon.

At Rangoon, Prome, Pagahm Mew, such temples appear numerous in the drawings made when the Burman empire was first invaded by the British.   Malcolm says there are in Rangoon more than 500 inferior pagodas (though some surpass in size any I have seen elsewhere), occupying as much space as the city itself, probably more.   Most of them stand a little out of the city, interspersed with groves embowering costly kyoungs and commodious zayats.   The latter are particularly numerous, to accommodate the hosts of worshippers who resort hither at certain seasons of the year.   Snodgrass describes two roads from Rangoon to the Shoedagon, which on either side are crowded with numerous pagodas, varying in size and richness according to the wealth or zeal of the pious architects.   These pagodas are all private property, every Burman, who can afford it, building one as an offering to Ghaudma; but, when once erected, little care or attention is afterwards paid to them, it being considered much more meritorious to build a new one, even of inferior size, than to repair the old; and numerous ruined towers and pagodas are, in consequence, found in every corner of the kingdom.   This explanation of the author may be applicable to the groups of pyramids found near Memphis, and in other parts of the world.

The Shoedagon, he adds, stands at the summit of an abruptly rising eminence, at the bottom of which, and at the distance of $2\frac{1}{2}$ miles, Rangoon is situated.   The conical hill upon which the pagoda stands is 75 feet above the road; the area on its top contains upwards of two acres, and in the centre of this space the pagoda is erected, in shape resembling an inverted speaking-trumpet, 338 feet in height, and surmounted with a cap made of brass, 45 feet high: the whole is richly gilded.   In the drawings opposite the great spiral temple at Pagahm Mew are seen other edifices without spires; the originals of these have apparently been constructed on the same principle as the hyperbolic spiral temples, and resemble some of the low edifices or temples of the Chinese, having only three or four terraces rising one above the other, the sides of the terraces apparently decreasing from the lowest in about the ratio of $1, \frac{1}{2}, \frac{1}{3}, \frac{1}{4}$. Their curved roofs may also have owed their origin to the hyperbolic curve. Snodgrass states that numerous pagodas and religious buildings alone distinguish Henzedah and Keoumzeik from the meanest villages; and, generally speaking, the remark holds good throughout the whole of Ava: the houses are much alike, and mostly built of the same materials; those of the chiefs and priests are alone distinguished by the number of roofs, one above another, and the other architectural insignia of their respective dignities and rank.

Perhaps these pagodas with spires might be called hyperbolic pagodas, to distinguish them from the pagoda like that at Nankin, which is an obelisk, and might be called an obeliscal pagoda. The Portuguese, it seems, were the first to give the name of pagodas to these edifices.

The Kioumdogee, or royal convent, is an edifice, says Symes, not less extraordinary from the style of its architecture, than magnificent for its ornaments, and from the gold that was bestowed on every part. It was composed entirely of wood, and the roofs, rising one above another, in five distinct stories, diminished in size as they advanced in height, each roof being surrounded by a cornice, curiously carved and richly gilded.

Judging from the varied and ornamented forms of these spires, as represented in the drawings, it would seem that these edifices form a series of copies continued through a long period after the principles of the original model had been lost sight of; as the spires might, perhaps, have originally been simple and unadorned, like the Egyptian obelisks before they were transferred to Rome, where they have since been disfigured by pontifical ornaments.

Yet the tee itself might originally have been intended as a repetition of the pagoda, and so placed on the top of the spire to denote its indefinite extension; as the truncated obelisk has a pyramid on the top, which denotes that the height wanting to complete the obelisk equals the square of the side of the base or area of the base of the pyramid.

The priests of Pegu resided within the court of the temple, as did the priests of Mexico.   These temples appear to have been used as places of defence.   On the death of Montezuma, the Spaniards attacked the great temple or teocalli of Mexitli, that stood on the site now occupied by the cathedral at Mexico. Cortes, with a buckler tied to his wounded arm, rushed among the combatants.   The Spaniards, encouraged by their general, forced their way up the steps, driving the Mexicans before them to the platform on the summit, where a dreadful carnage ensued.

The great Dagon Pagoda at Rangoon, in itself a fortress, was occupied by a battalion of Europeans, and "may be considered as the key of the British position," so says Major Snodgrass in his narrative of the Burmese War.

But we must again quote from the same authority :—

"Upon quitting the fort, the enemy retired upon the pagoda of Syriain, pursued by a part of the detachment along the narrow winding footpaths of the forest.   On reaching the pagoda, it was also found strongly occupied, with cannon pointing down every approach towards it from the jungle; and, — like most other buildings of the same description, — standing on a hill, surrounded by a wall, and accessible only by the regular flights of stairs which led to the interior; these also were strongly barricaded, and otherwise defended. The columns marched directly forward to the stairs, and had even partly ascended them, before a shot was fired, — the Burmese standing at their guns, coolly waiting the approach; but when at length the firing did commence, the soldiers, pushing briskly forward, soon closed upon the enemy."

The temple of Belus, at Babylon, was a place of strength, a kind of citadel, — so says Ammianus Marcellinus.

Heeren, in giving a general outline of the architecture and plans of Egyptian temples, remarks : "that on both sides of the saloons, as well as behind, were corridors which led into the chambers and apartments assigned for the abode of the priests.   The whole was again surrounded by an enclosure;

so that the number of walls effectually prevented the entrance to the sanctuary from being violated by the profane."

Greaves, describing the pyramid of Cephrenes, as he saw it more than 200 years ago, says: — "This pyramid is bounded on the north and west sides with two stately and elaborate pieces; which I do not so much admire, as that by all writers they have been pretermitted. About 30 feet in depth, and more than 1400 in length, out of a hard rock these buildings have been cut in a perpendicular, and squared by the chisel, as I suppose, for lodgings for the priests. The space within all of them is sometimes like a square and well-proportioned chamber, covered and arched above by the natural rock."

The temples or joss-houses of Ting-hai are said by recent travellers to be amongst the finest in China. On entering the large and deep gateway of the great temple, a colossal figure is seen seated on each side. After examining these seated giants, you pass to a large open quadrangle, one side of which is appropriated to the dormitories of the priests. Many colossal statues are described; but the principal one is that of Boodh seated on the lotus flower.

Another temple possessed some beautiful specimens of sculpture. Kwan-wyn, the goddess of mercy, riding on a dolphin in a troubled sea, distributing her acts of grace and exhibiting her power to save, would have been looked upon as a splendid work of art, had it been discovered in Greece instead of in a small Chinese island. The white elephant in this temple created much speculation among our orientalists, as it had hitherto been considered as peculiar to the Burmese and Siamese worship.

Much has been said of the white elephant of Burmah. Malcom states that there is now but one known to exist in the empire, — an old and remarkably fine animal, which has long been the pride of royalty at Ava. He seems to be an albino.

The great square in which stood the temple or teocalli of Mexitli is described by Acosta, or rather by De Solis on the authority of Acosta, as having four sides, and as many gates opening to the four winds. Close to the inside of the walls were the habitations of the priests, and of those who, under them, attended the service of the temple, with some offices, which altogether took up the whole circumference, without retrenching so much from that vast square but that eight or ten thousand persons had sufficient room to dance in it upon their solemn festivals.

Herodotus says, " In a chapel which stands below, within the temple of Babylon, a large image of gold, representing Jupiter sitting, is placed on a throne of gold, and a table of the same metal, all together weighing 800 talents, as the Chaldeans affirm. Without this chapel is an altar of gold. Besides these things, a statue of solid gold, twelve cubits high, stood formerly in the temple; but, not having seen this, I shall only relate what I heard from the Chaldeans; who say that Darius, the son of Hystaspes, having formed a design to take away the statue, had not courage to effect his purpose; but that Xerxes, the son of Darius, not only took the statue, but killed the priest who had forbidden him to remove it."

Already we have quoted Humboldt's account of the two teocallis of Teotihuacan. On the tops were placed two colossal statues of the sun and moon, which were of stone, and covered with plates of gold. These plates were carried away by the soldiers of Cortez.

" Vast sums," says Snodgrass, " are annually expended by the Burmese monarch and his court in building and gilding pagodas, in the middle of which images of Ghaudma, made of solid gold, are frequently buried, particularly in the splendid and very sacred buildings of this description in the neighbourhood of the capital."

The Burmese monarch is styled " Lord of earth and air." Sesostris was called " King of kings." It appears the Burmese not only have a golden god, but a golden king. In an answer from the chiefs, on the receipt of an order from the king of Ava, they say they " will surround the rebel strangers, and, by dint of your golden Majesty's excellent omnipotence, not one shall escape;—all shall be killed, destroyed, and annihilated."

The ship built of cedar-wood, and made an offering of by

Sesostris, was lined inside with silver, and outside with gold.

Malcom says, " Many of the Burmese boats contain forty or fifty men, and are perfectly gilded within and without, and even the oars. Some of them are intended to convey the king and royal family, and have handsome canopies." Snodgrass says, " The steam-vessel and some light boats which pushed up the river after the enemy's war-boats succeeded in capturing nine ; four of them were gilt."

Symes gives a drawing of the Shoepaundogee, or royal barge used by the king when he goes in state on the water; the length being 100 cubits (more than 150 feet). The king possesses a great variety of boats, but the Shoepaundogee is by far the most magnificent. More than 100 years before the embassy of Symes from England, France sent Chaumont on an embassy to Siam. This embassy was embarked in twelve gilded boats, and sailed across the river, which was entirely covered with floating spectators.

In one of the drawings by Moore of the great Dagon pagoda at Rangoon, taken during the first war, the description says, " The war-boat to the right is about 60 feet long, which had been deified or consecrated, in consequence of its having made an extraordinarily quick passage from Ummerapoora to Rangoon on some important occasion."

In a subterranean chamber near the pyramids of Ghiza are two boats sculptured in bas-relief, as seen in a drawing given in Breton's work.

Two immense boats are sculptured on the outside of the temple of Carnac. " One of them," says Richardson, " is 51 feet long, and has the head of a ram at each end. Another boat, 45 feet in length, is full of people, who are pushing it along with poles. Two such boats are represented by Denon, where the people of the first boat are pulling along the second boat.

" Once a year," says Diodorus, " the sanctuary or shrine of Zeus (Jupiter) at Thebes is taken across the river to the Libyan (the western) side ; and after a few days it is brought back, as if the deity were returning from Ethiopia." He

K 3

also mentions the ship of cedar-wood that Sesostris dedicated
to Ammon, the god of Thebes.   Heeren, after quoting this
passage about the holy ship, adds, "that this procession
appears to be represented in one of the great sculptured
reliefs on the temple of Carnac.   The sacred ship of Ammon
is on the river, with its whole equipment, and is towed along
by another boat.   It is, therefore, on its voyage.   This must
have been one of the most celebrated festivals, since, even
according to the interpretation of antiquity, Homer alludes
to it, when he speaks of Jupiter's visit to the Ethiopians, and
his twelve days' absence.   That such visits of the gods of the
colony to those of the parent state were common, and sure
proofs of national relationship, is well known from numerous
instances in the ancient world.   The forms only might be
different.   In one case this relationship might be commenced
by such a procession as we have described : in another, by the
actual mission of a sacred embassy.   When Alexander took
Tyre, says Arrian, he found there a religious mission from
Carthage, a Tyrian colony.   The same inference will apply
to all ages : a common religion is one of the strongest ties
among men, and tends, perhaps, more than any thing else to
perpetuate between two countries those friendly relations
which had their origin in a kindred blood.   A common religion
implies also, in some degree at least, a common language ;
and that this was the case with the Egyptians and Ethiopians
is a fact which cannot be doubted."

It appears the astrologers of the Burmese exercise the same
influence over passing events as did the astrologers of the
East in olden times.

He mentions the king's two brothers, with astrologers and
a corps of invulnerables, joining the army.   " Blindly superstitious in some points, Burmese of all ranks implicitly believe
in the predictions of these impostors.   The influence of the
moon upon the affairs of man is never doubted, and the calculations of the astrologers upon certain signs and indications
of that planet obtain universal credit.   From the fixing a pro-
pitious time for attacking a position, to the most ordinary
affair of life, nothing can prosper without consulting an

astrologer; these men are consequently found in every corner of the kingdom, and are held in the highest esteem and veneration by the people. By persons of rank, especially, these oracles are much favoured and respected; consulting them on all military operations, and abiding rigidly by their decisions. These predictions on some occasions, however, were productive of more evil than good to the cause they wished to serve; for although they seldom failed to inspire the troops with a degree of confidence, the publicity that attended their decisions not unfrequently found its way into our camp, and prepared us for the attack."

" Besides the Ponghees," says Malcom, "there are at Ava a considerable number of Brahmins, who are highly respected. They hold the rank of astrologers and astronomers to his majesty, in which they are supposed to be eminently skilled, and have committed to them the regulation of the calendar. They are consulted on important occasions, and give forth auguries, which are received with great confidence. The ancestors of the Brahmins appear to have come from Bengal at no distant period. Occasionally new ones come still."

Arrian informs us that Alexander, returning from India and having passed the Tigris on his way to Babylon, was met by the Chaldean magi, who, calling him apart from his friends, entreated him not to proceed on his journey to Babylon, telling him they were assured from the oracle of Belus that his entrance into the city at that time would be attended with ill consequences to himself. Yet Alexander availed himself of the oracle of Jupiter Ammon, which announced him as the son of Jupiter. It has been suspected that Alexander used the same means to obtain this response from Jupiter, that his father Philip employed when he consulted the oracle of Apollo at Delphos; which made Demosthenes exclaim that Apollo Philippised, or spoke what Philip ordered.

The night previous to the murder of Julius Cæsar, Calphurnia dreamed that the roof of her house had fallen in, and that he had been stabbed in her arms. Cæsar in early

K 4

life had been high-priest to Jupiter, and he, like Alexander, disregarded the evil omen.

We find that even Cortez appears to have been influenced by an astrologer to make the retreat on the night still distinguished in New Spain by the name of *noche triste,* the melancholy night.   De Solis tells us, that Cortez was against the night-march, but gave way to the majority in the council held on that occasion.   He admits, however, a singular fact, mentioned by the historians, that the mind of this extraordinary man was biassed by the vain predictions of an astrologer, a private in the army, who had advised him to march away that very night, "for that he should lose the greater part of his army if he suffered a certain favourable constellation to pass into another aspect." This man, known in the army by the name of the Necromancer, was among the slain.

The Mexicans on this occasion removed the wooden bridges over the canals, with a view to intercept the communication with the main land.

Semiramis intercepted the communication, in the night, between the two sides of the Euphrates, by removing some planks from the bridge.

The advantages of wooden bridges are that they can be easily erected and easily removed.

"Another novel and formidable reinforcement about this time joined the army from Ava, styled the king's invulnerables.   This corps consisted of several thousand men, divided, however, into many classes of warriors, of whom only a select band are entitled to the above appellation. They are distinguished by the short cut of their hair, and the peculiar manner in which they are tatooed, having the figures of elephants, tigers, and a great variety of ferocious animals indelibly, and even beautifully, marked upon their arms and legs; but to the soldiers they were best known by having bits of gold, silver, and sometimes precious stones, in their arms, probably introduced under the skin at an early age."

Let us next quote from Malcom, who, being a missionary,

is in some respects more minute in describing these pagodas than the soldier. Other extracts, that may appear to illustrate any subject previously noticed in these pages, will also be made.

Two miles from Rangoon is the celebrated pagoda, called Shoodagon. It stands on a small hill, surrounded by many similar pagodas, some fine zayats and kyoungs, and many noble trees. The hill has been graduated into successive terraces, sustained by brick walls; and the summit, which is completely levelled, contains about two acres.

Snodgrass says the conical hill on which this pagoda stands is 75 feet above the road, and the height of the pagoda 338 feet above the platform. It is not stated how these dimensions were obtained. In the view the terraces are not seen, being concealed by trees. Neither are their number nor dimensions given by either of the writers.

Malcom continues. "Before you stands the huge Shoodagon, its top among the clouds, and its golden sides blazing in the glories of an Eastern sun. Around are pompous zayats, noble pavements, Gothic mausoleums, uncooth colossal lions, curious stone umbrellas, gracefully cylindrical banners of gold embroidered muslin hanging from lofty pillars, enormous stone jars in rows to receive offerings, tapers burning before the images, exquisite flowers displayed on every side, filling the air with fragrance, and a multitude of carved figures of idols, worshippers, griffins, guardians, &c.

"Always in the morning men and women are seen in every direction kneeling behind their gift, and with uplifted hands reciting their devotions, often with a string of beads counting over each repetition. A gift once deposited is no more regarded. I have seen crows and dogs snatch the gift ere the offerer had well done his prayers, without the shadow of resistance being offered.

"Again. Desolate and diminished as is the city of Pegu, its Shoomadoo pagoda, and some of its appendages, are in good preservation and worthy of all admiration. It stands on a fine hill, of gradual ascent, the summit of which has been flattened into a plain of about three acres. The sides are sloped into two terraces, ascended by steps of hewn stone. The top is occupied not only by the great pagoda, but by zayats, kyoungs, trees, &c. The pyramid is of the usual form. The base consists of two octagonal stories, much larger than the pagoda itself, and wide enough to sustain each a ring of sixty pagodas, about 30 feet high, similar to each other, though not alike, and many of them much injured by time. The diameter of the octagonal base is 400 feet, and the entire height of the building 360 feet."

As Burmah is a country so little known to Europeans, we shall make further extracts from Malcom. " We went a little way beyond the city (Proome) to a fine hill, on which stands a pagoda not much smaller than that at Rangoon, and gilded from top to bottom. The ascent is by brick stairs, covered with a succession of zayats. In some respects it is a more interesting spot than the hill of Shoodagon. The city is more plainly seen, and the vicinity is far more beautiful, and the distant mountains form a fine back-ground. Around the pagoda are many smaller ones, containing beautiful marble images, some as large as life. A profusion of trees, gilded streamers, and other objects usually seen around pagodas, occupy the enclosure; and the whole air of the place is that of solemn antiquity. The bells struck by coming worshippers yielded deep, soft tones, and the chime from the lofty tee was particularly clear and sweet. The sun, descending with uncommon splendour, threw his mitigated rays under the roofs of the ancient temples, casting twilight pomp upon the stately idols in the deep niches; silence reigned among the retired terraces and time-worn shrines; the free fresh breeze diffused luxurious coolness, and, as the shade of evening gathered on, the place seemed just such as a devoted Boodhist would choose for his abstractions.

" The remains of the once magnificent Paghan stand in a region destitute apparently of the means of supporting human life. Such a locality, however, have some of the greatest cities in the world, and still more frequently the ruins of great cities. Man's presence and power can make a garden

in a desert, and his departure brings desolation over the
fairest scenes. The city is said to have been founded A. D.
107 ; but none of the ruins have ascribed to them a higher
date than A. D. 860. An American could scarcely assign
half this age to any building of brick. But these bricks are
uncommonly fine, the masonry exceedingly massive, and the
chunnam, or stucco with which they are coated, almost in-
destructible, in so mild a climate. The edifices, being regarded with religious veneration, have been preserved from
all intentional dilapidation. The plants and trees too, which
ever grace deserted edifices elsewhere, and, by insinuating
their roots into crevices, hasten their ruin, are here not seen.
This last peculiarity has been thought to arise from the influence of the adjacent earth-oil wells and springs on the
atmosphere.

" As would be expected by all who have seen a Burman
city, these ruins are of sacred edifices only. The frail
bamboo houses of the people perish almost as soon as deserted. I entered the place from the north, where a common
cartway crossed the crumbling ridge of a great wall. Gullies
and torrents cut up the environs on this side, and it is probable the city never extended over this region. Every spot,
however, which would accommodate a pagoda had one upon
it. Within the wall the ground is level, though very high,
and commanding a wide prospect. Here, for the first time,
I saw buildings which could be called temples ; many of the
pagodas being built hollow, with noble rooms devoted to
images and image worship. Some of these, as well as those
which are solid, are of the noblest description ; little injured
by time, with here and there some remains of the exterior
gilding in sheltered places. We entered some, and found
superb carved and gilded ceilings, sheltering at once great,
ghastly, half-crumbled gaudamas and herds of cattle. Marks
of fire in some showed them to be used by the people for
occasional homes, or perhaps by herdmen.

" I could not attempt to count these venerable piles. They
are thickly scattered, not only over all the site of the city,
but for miles round. Many of them are more than 100 feet

high.   One, which seems to have been occasionally repaired,
is 210 feet high.   The difference between their shape and
that of those in the lower provinces is very striking.   Instead
of the solid mass of masonry, rising with a tapering spire,
these are ponderous, wide-spread buildings, whose noble
interior entitle them to the name of temples.   The arches
are lofty, in both Grecian and Gothic forms, and the ceilings
in many cases gilded and ornamented with painting and
tracery.   The exterior is equally unlike the pagodas of
Pegu, from the profusion of laboured cornices, turrets, and
spires, which are scattered over the whole surface."

It will be noticed that both Grecian and Gothic lofty
arches are found in the temples at Paghan.

" Again.   It is evident that great reverence yet exists for
this spot; for many of the pagodas, of a size scarcely inferior to their venerable neighbours, are certainly modern,
and a few are new.   Such a feature in a landscape of ruins
is truly rare.   That the people should come to these abandoned shrines, and add others also, to be left unhonoured
by the passing throng, is perhaps accounted for by the fact,
that on this spot this religion was first proclaimed at Burmah.
Ah-ra-ham, the successful missionary of Boodhism, here
proclaimed its doctrines nearly 1000 years ago.   At this
place (then the metropolis), under the patronage of king
Ah-nan-ya-tha-mon-zan, he taught his ' new religion;' and
its spreading influence utterly supplanted polytheism, and all
the ancient superstitions.

" It has been said that in Burmah they have lost the art
of turning an arch, but this is wholly a mistake.   I have
seen many fine arches, of a large span, evidently erected
within a few years, and some not yet finished, constructed
wholly by Burman masons.   The stucco, which covers all
buildings, is put on with extraordinary durability, and generally with tasteful ornaments.   Floors and brick images
covered in this way have often a polish equal to the most
exquisitely wrought marble.   The mortar is made of the
best lime and sand, with a liberal mixture of jaggery, but
without hair.

" Though Burmans spend all their zeal on useless pagodas, there are near the capital some other structures of public utility. Some tanks have been constructed, which secure irrigation and consequent fertility to a fine region of adjacent country. One of these, near Makesobo, is truly a noble work. Across the little river at Ava and the marsh adjacent is a very long bridge, which I have not seen surpassed in India, and scarcely in Europe.

" Various other edifices, both civil and military, ornament the metropolis, and would do honour to any people."

Symes says well formed arches of bricks are still to be seen in the ancient temples, yet Birman workmen can no longer turn them. In latter ages wooden buildings have superseded structures of bricks and mortar.

The pagodas are said to vary in shape at different places. By reference to *figs.* 37. and 38. it will be seen how the outline of the hyperbolic curve may be varied.

" Ava, the ' golden city,' is surrounded by a wall 20 feet high, embracing a space of about 7 miles in circumference. Within this is a considerable area, enclosed by a better wall, with a broad, deep ditch, called ' the little city.' This space is chiefly occupied by the palace, hall of justice, council-house, and the dwellings of some of the nobility, but contains also some well built streets, and many inhabitants. The palace itself, and public buildings, are enclosed in a third wall, which is itself enclosed in a stockade. A very large part of the city is outside of these walls, on the margin of the rivers. On the east is the river Myet-nga, or little river, a fine stream, 150 yards broad, extending far into the interior. The Irrawaddy, opposite the city, is without islands, and compressed to a breadth of about 1100 or 1200 yards.

" The sacred edifices, as usual, are the prominent objects which on every side seize the attention. They are almost as numerous as at Paghan, and some of them of equal size.

" The pagodas are even more various in their shapes than at Paghan, and far surpass in taste and beauty any I have seen :

most of them are over 100 feet high, and some more than 200. Colossal images of bell-metal, marble, and brick covered with stucco, are innumerable. One, which had just been finished out of a solid block of white marble, is truly stupendous. I had no mode of taking his vast proportions, but measured his hand, and found the breadth 20 inches. As his proportions were just, this would make his height, had he been in a standing posture, about 35 feet."

Colossal recumbent statues are frequently met with in the Burmese empire. Compare this statue, cut out of a block of white marble, with the supine colossal statue mentioned by Herodotus as having been placed before the temple of Vulcan at Memphis by Amasis, and having a length of 75 feet. Also on the same basis he erected two statues of 20 feet each, wrought out of the same stone, and placed on each side of the same colossus. Another, like this, is seen at Sais, lying in the same posture, cut out of stone, and of equal dimensions.

Malcom estimates the length of the Ava statue at 35 feet English, which will $= \frac{1}{8}$ of 281 feet, or $\frac{1}{8}$ of a stade.

The statue at the temple of Vulcan was 75 feet in length, which will $= \frac{1}{8}$ of 600 feet of Herodotus, or $\frac{1}{8}$ of a stade.

Thus the two recumbent statues would be equal in length.

The clenched hand of red granite in the British Museum was brought from Egypt, and, according to Flaxman, it belonged to a statue 65 feet high when standing.

"The palace is entirely of wood. It consists of nearly 100 buildings, of different sizes, and occupies a space of about $\frac{1}{4}$ of a mile long, and almost as broad. The roofs have all the royal order of architecture. The hall of audience is in a sumptuous and convenient building, standing on a terrace of stone and mortar, which constitutes the floor, and is coated with stucco hard and polished. Lofty pillars, richly carved, support the roof, and, like the rest of the building, are covered with gold. The roof rises like a steeple, with many stages, and is 195 feet high.

"In looking at such buildings, or at the numerous boats of

his majesty or the nobility, of which every part, and even the oars, are covered with gold, one wonders whence all this wealth is derived, and is distressed that it should be so absurdly bestowed. The money expended in pagodas, kyoungs, temples, and gold and silver baubles, would fill the country with canals, bridges, and durable houses.

" Five miles south-west of Sagaing, and about a mile from the great manufactory of idols, is the Kyoung-moo-dau-gyee pagoda, famous for its size. Its shape is precisely like a thimble, 170 feet high, and 1000 feet in circumference at the base. It looks, in ascending the river, like a little mountain. An inscription within the enclosure gives the date of its erection, which corresponds to our A. D. 1626.

" The Mengoon pagoda, above Umerapoora, would be vastly larger if finished, surpassing some of the pyramids of Egypt. When not more than half advanced, the king grew so cool towards Boodhism, and had so exhausted his means and the liberality of the nobles, that he abandoned the undertaking. His Brahminical astrologers furnished him an excellent pretext by giving out that so soon as it was finished he would die, and the dynasty be changed. The lions were finished, and though intended, of course, to bear the usual proportion to the size of the edifice, they were 90 feet high. A huge bell was also cast for it, stated, in the 35th volume of the authorised Burman History or Chronicles, to weigh 55,500 viss (about 200,000 pounds); but the chief Woon-gyee declared to me that its weight was 88,000 viss.

" On the way to Umerapoora we saw the royal barges, and visited the pagodas and zayats of Shway-kyet-yet, or ' the scratch of the golden fowl.' Here Gaudama wears a form not given to him elsewhere, I believe, except in paintings, namely, that of a cock. The legend is, that when he was in that form of existence he was king of all fowls, and, passing that place, he scratched there! Hence the sanctity of the spot, and hence the noble structures that distinguish it! The face of the stone cocks which ornament the niches is somewhat human, the bill being brought up to his eyes, like a huge hooked nose."

Symes describes ornaments at the Shoemadoo somewhat resembling the fleur-de-lys. On the terraces white cylindrical flags, considered as emblematic of purity, waved from bamboo poles. Thus at Shoemadoo we find the fleur-de-lys and the white flag of France: at the Shway-kyet-yet, the Gallic cock.

We shall explain the origin of the fleur-de-lys in another work.

"The most meritorious deed is to make an idol, and this in proportion to its size and value; next, he who builds a pagoda; then, he who builds a kyoung, &c. Hence pagodas are innumerable. In the inhabited parts there is scarcely a mountain peak, bluff, bank, or swelling hill, without one of these structures upon it. Those of Pegu and Siam are all formed upon one model, though the cornices and decorations are according to the builder's taste. In general they are entirely solid, having neither door nor window, and contain a deposit of money, or some supposed relic of Gaudama. From the base they narrow rapidly to about midway, and then rise with a long spire, surmounted with the sacred tee. Some of these around Ava, and especially those at Paghan, are less tapering, and more resembling temples.

"Near all considerable cities are a number of zayats, which may be called temples, erected to contain collections of idols, amounting in some cases to hundreds. In general they are all colossal, and some very huge. In each collection will be found a recumbent image, 60, 80, or even 100 feet long, made of brick covered with stucco, and often gilded. Almost all the idols larger than life are thus formed; but so skilful are the artists in the working in lime, that the images have the appearance of polished marble. Groups of images, representing Gaudama walking with his rice-pot, followed by attendants with theirs, or illustrating some conspicuous action of his life, are not uncommon. The doors or gateways of religious edifices are generally guarded by huge Balus and lions, as they call them. Sometimes other images are added, as crocodiles, turtles, dogs, &c."

We find the pagodas, large and small, grouped together in

the Burmese empire, like the pyramids in other countries. As it is accounted a meritorious deed to build a pagoda, so it might have been esteemed an equally meritorious action to erect a pyramid. One is the reciprocal of the other, and both are symbols of the laws of gravity.

" Minderagyee, emperor of Burmah, conquered Arracan. Among the spoil on this occasion, the most valued articles, and those which perhaps had a large share in inducing the war, were a colossal bronze image of Boodh, and a cannon measuring 30 feet long, and 10 inches in calibre. These were transported in triumph to Amerapoorah, the then capital, and are still shown there with much pride.

" In casting bells, Burmah transcends all the rest of India. They are disproportionately thick, but of delightful tone. The raised inscriptions and figures are as beautiful as on any bells I have seen. They do not flare open at the mouth like a trumpet, but are precisely the shape of old-fashioned globular wine-glasses, or semi-spheroidal. Several in the empire are of enormous size. That at Mengoon, near Ava, weighs, as the prime minister informed me, 88,000 viss — more than 330,000 pounds! It seems almost incredible; but if any of my readers interested in such matters will make a computation for themselves, they will find it true. The bell, by actual measurement, is 20 inches thick, 20 feet high, including the ear, and 13 feet 6 inches in diameter. The weight was ascertained by the Burmese before casting, and its bulk in cubic inches proves them correct. It is suspended a few inches from the ground, and, like their other great bells, is without a tongue. That at Rangoon is not much smaller. It will be recollected that the largest bell in the United States does not exceed 5000 pounds. The Great Tom, at Oxford, in England, is 17,000 pounds; and the famous, but useless, bell at Moscow is 444,000 pounds."

This note is added:—" A friend, distinguished as a civil engineer, computed the weight, from this measurement, to exceed 500,000 pounds, supposing the bell-metal to consist of three parts copper and one part tin."

We find the great bell of Moscow weighs, according to

Cox, 432,000 pounds, and "exceeds in bigness every known bell in the world." "Its size is so enormous," says the writer, "that I could scarcely have given credit to the account of its magnitude if I had not examined it myself, and ascertained its dimensions with great exactness. Its height is 19 feet, its circumference at the bottom 21 yards 11 inches, its greatest thickness 23 inches. It was cast in the reign of the Empress Ann; but the beam on which it hung being burnt, it fell, and a large piece is broken out of it, so that it lately lay in a manner useless."

The great bell of Peking (measured by one of the Jesuits) was 14½ feet in height, and nearly 13 feet in diameter.

The French Jesuits went to view the principal pagoda in the city of Siam. It was low and narrow externally, covered all over with a metal called "calin." On entering, they saw nothing but gold. There was an idol 45 feet in height, and reaching to the roof, entirely composed of that precious metal. The missionaries, amid their admiration, were deeply grieved to think that one idol contained more gold than all the images of Catholic Europe put together. They also saw the white elephant, so celebrated in the annals of Eastern India. It made a very sorry appearance, being small, quite worn down, and wrinkled with age. It was kept, however, in the greatest pomp, and had a hundred men to attend on it. A curious mineral production consisted in a mine of loadstone, which the Jesuits visited. It attracted the pieces of iron with extraordinary force; but the needle in its vicinity became quite irregular. So far as could be judged from the direction of the iron instruments, the poles of the mines were from north to south.

Cæsar Frederick visited Pegu in 1568. The king's palace resembled a walled castle, gilded all over, and rising into lofty pinnacles. "Truly it may be a king's house." This monarch calls himself "the King of the White Elephants," and prizes these animals so highly, that if he knew one to be in possession of a neighbouring sovereign, he will make war in order to obtain it. He had only four, which were kept in the greatest state, having their meat served in gold and silver basins. There was also a black elephant, illustrious for its magnitude, being nine cubits high. He saw " a man of gold, very great, with a crowne, and four children of gold." There was also " a man of silver," who surpassed in height the roof of any house, and whose feet were as long as our traveller's whole body. There were besides other heathenish idols of a very great value. Buchanan saw at Ava an image composed of a single block of pure white alabaster, the magnitude of which may be conjectured from each finger being equal to the leg and thigh of a large man.

" Boodhism," remarks Malcom, " is probably at this time, and has been for many centuries, the most prevalent form of religion upon earth. Half the population of China, Lao, Cochin-China, and Ceylon ; all the Cambaja, Siam, Burmah, Thibet, Tartary, and Loo-choo ; and a great part of Japan, and most of the other islands of the southern seas, are of this faith. A system which thus enchains the minds of half the human race deserves the attention of both Christians and philosophers, however fabulous and absurd."

" Boodh is a general name for divinity, and not the name of any particular god. There have been innumerable Boodhs in different ages, among different worlds ; but in no world more than five, and in some not any. In this world there have been four Boodhs, of which Gaudama is the last. One is yet to come, namely, Aree-ma–day-eh.

" I have seen representations of Boodh of all sizes, from half an inch long to 75 feet, of wood, stone, brass, brick, clay, and ivory.

" The next Boodh is to appear in about seven or eight thousand years from the present time.

" No laws or sayings of the three first Boodhs are extant. Those of Gaudama were transmitted by tradition till 450 years after his decease, when they were reduced to writing in Ceylon, that is A. D. 94. These are the only sacred books of the Burmans, and are all in the Pali language, and called the Bedagat. The universe is there said to be composed of an infinite number of systems, called Sak-yas. These systems touch each other at the circumference, and the angular spaces

between them are filled with cold water.   Each side of these
spaces is 300 uzenas long.   Of these innumerable systems
some are constantly becoming chaotic, and reproducing themselves in the course of time.   Of these formations and dissolu-
tions there was never a beginning and will never be an end."

The missionary remarks, "that no false religion, ancient
or modern, is comparable to this.   Its philosophy is, indeed,
not exceeded in folly by any other; but its doctrines and
practical piety bear a strong resemblance to those of the
Holy Scripture.   There is scarcely a precept or principle in
the Bedagat which is not found in the Bible.   Did but the
people act up to its principles of peace and love, oppression
and injury would be known no more within their borders.   Its
deeds of merit are in all cases either really beneficial to mankind, or harmless.   It has no mythology of obscene and
ferocious deities; no sanguinary or impure observances; no
self-inflicting tortures; no tyrannising priesthood; no confounding of right or wrong, by making certain iniquities
laudable in worship.   In its moral code, its description of the
purity and peace of the first ages, of the shortening of man's
life because of his sins, &c., it seems to have followed genuine
traditions.   In almost every respect it seems to be the best
religion which man has ever invented."

American Antiquities.

It is stated in the *Penny Cyclopædia* that the square
forts, like the pyramids of Mexico, face the cardinal points.
When they have only one entrance it looks towards the east.
The walls are usually made of earth, but there are also one
or two instances where they are of stone.   In the interior of
the forts are mounds, which vary greatly in their dimensions.
Some are only 4 or 5 feet high, and 10 or 12 in diameter,
whilst others rise to the height of 80, 90, and some more
than 100 feet, and cover many acres.   Their base is round or
oval, and their shape that of a cone, but sometimes flat at the
top.   They are made either of stone or earth.   Many of
them are in the vicinity of, and sometimes within the walls

of, the fortifications, and it is thought that some of them thus situated have been used as stations to discover the approach of an enemy. But it is evident that the greater number of them are sepulchral monuments. In some of the lower ones great number of bones have been found. In the more elevated tumuli only a skeleton or two have been discovered. In the monuments of the last description some utensils and trinkets are usually found.

One of the larger of these tumuli is on the banks of the Ohio, 12 miles from the town of Wheeling in Virginia. Its figure is a truncated cone, measuring 295 feet at the base, 60 at the top, and 70 in perpendicular height. The height appears to have been originally greater, and the form more regular. There was found in this mound, besides three skeletons and trinkets that evinced no artistical talent, a small elliptical stone table, and twenty-four distinct characters arranged in parallel lines. It appears that they are not letters, but hieroglyphics.

Some very high tumuli are found in the neighbourhood of St. Louis, and among them are two which have two or three terraces or stages, which are considered as important in an historical point of view, as they seem to connect the antiquities, and consequently also the civilisation, of the ancient tribes that inhabited the United States with those of Mexico; for these tumuli approach in shape to the teocallis of the Mexicans.

In the vale of Mexico at Teotihuacan are two large pyramids which were consecrated to the sun and to the moon, and are surrounded by several hundred small pyramids, forming regular streets, which run exactly north and south, or east and west. The larger of the two pyramids is more than 160 feet in perpendicular height, and the other is more than 130 feet high. The base of the first is 900 feet long. The small pyramids which surround the two grand ones are from 30 to 40 feet high, and, according to the tradition of the natives, they were used as burial-places for the chiefs of the tribes. The two large teocallis have four stages or landings. The interior of these edifices consists of

L 3

clay mixed with numerous small stones; but this nucleus is enclosed by a thick wall made of a kind of pumice-stone. It is stated that on the platform of these edifices two colossal statues of the sun and moon were originally placed.

The largest, most ancient, and most famous of the Mexican teocallis is that of Cholula. It has four stages of equal height, and its sides front exactly the four cardinal points. It is 178 feet high, and each of the sides at the base is 1448 feet long. The teocallis or Mexican pyramids were at the same time temples and burial-places. A small chapel stood on the top of these pyramids.

The ruins of Santa Cruz del Quiché, in Central America, bear a great resemblance to the teocallis of Mexico and Chiapas, though the town was a fortress, and not a temple. It would appear that the different nations who succeeded one another in the possession of Anahuac had adopted the same kind of construction in their fortresses which is found in their religious buildings. The fortress of Xochicalco, between Mexico and Acapulco, is an isolated hill, 386 feet high, which has been surrounded by a ditch, and divided by the work of man into five stages or terraces, which are coated with masonry. The whole forms a truncated pyramid, whose four sides exactly front the four cardinal points. On the top of the hill is a flat space containing more than 12 acres, on which there are the ruins of a small building, which is supposed to have been a kind of watch-house.

Besides these pyramidal structures, there are ruins of buildings not very different from those erected in several parts of the old world. At the time when Humboldt visited America only one group of ruins of this description appears to have been known in Mexico, at Mitla, south-east of Oaxaca, which go under the name of the Palace, but since that time numerous ruins of this kind have been discovered. It does not, however, appear that, with the exception of Mitla, any of this description have been found in Mexico, or in the country west of the Isthmus of Tehuantepec, nor in the isthmus itself; they lie to the east of it, in countries which may be considered as forming parts of the peninsula of Yucatan. Stephens visited forty-four ancient cities, though his stay in the country was short. He is of opinion that these structures were erected by the ancestors of the present population, and at a period little anterior to the arrival of the Spaniards. It is not known how many there may be in other parts of the country, but they are certainly very numerous between 19° 45′ and 20° 45′, and especially between 20° and 20° 20′, on both sides of a low ridge of high grounds which in these parts run from west-north-west to east-south-east. Along the southern base of this ridge groups of ruins occur at the distance of 5 or 6 miles from one another, and appear to form a continuous series. The ruins are most numerous at Uxmál, Kabáh, Gabna, Kewick, Labpahk, and Chichen. Though no ruins of considerable extent appear on the shores of the Bay of Campeachy, some are found on those of the Bay of Honduras at Taloon (20° 12′ N. lat.), and in its neighbourhood at Tancar. Some inconsiderable ruins exist in the Island of Kankun, not far from Cape Catoche, the most northern point of Yucatan.

Travellers call these antiquities ruins of cities, probably under the first impression which such extensive remains make on those who see them. But whenever they have taken the trouble to make a plan of the ruins, it is found that there is only a small number of buildings. There is always one building of great extent, rather resembling the palaces of Europe than common dwelling-houses; and this edifice has received different names. At some places it is called the Governor's House, and at others the Cacique's House. This edifice exhibits a great quantity of architectural embellishments. There are columns of different sizes, corridors, paintings, ornaments in stucco, &c.

The front of the building is 300 feet long, and its width frequently exceeds 200 feet. The whole is so disposed as to form three or four terraces, the top of the whole being a large level space constituting the roof, which is enclosed with a low wall. The front of these buildings is generally orna-

mented with numerous sculptures.   This edifice is evidently
the principal object in every group of ruins.   It is surrounded by several other buildings, the use of which has not
been ascertained.   Among these outbuildings, as it were,
sometimes an edifice is found which may have been a temple;
but nothing has been produced which proves them to have
been places of public worship.   Generally there is one, and
sometimes two, pyramids near the palace, but even their use
is uncertain.

The most famous of these ruins are those of the city of
Palenque, as it is called, which lie near the boundary
between Mexico and Central America.   These ruins were
discovered in the middle of the eighteenth century, and from
that time it has always been stated that they cover a space
of 6 leagues in circumference and contain public works of
great magnificence.   It is now known that the ruins consist
only of a large building called the Palace, and four or five
other buildings of inferior size, in a tolerable state of preservation, with the remains of a few others so utterly dilapidated that it is impossible to say what they may have
been.   The palace stands on an artificial elevation of an
oblong form 40 feet high, 310 feet in front and rear, and
260 feet on each side.   The palace itself stands with
its face to the east, and measures 260 feet in front by 180
feet deep.   The height is not more than 25 feet, and it has a
broad projecting cornice all round.   There are no windows.
The front contains fourteen openings resembling gates, each
about 9 feet wide, and the intervening piers are between
6 and 7 feet wide.   The building is constructed of stone,
with a mortar of lime and sand, and the whole front has once
been covered with stucco and painted.   The piers are ornamented with spirited figures in bas-relief, but only six of
them remain.   The outer walls of the palace, as it were, are
formed by two parallel corridors running lengthwise on all
the four sides; they are about 9 feet wide.   The floors are
of cement, as hard as the best in the remains of the Roman
baths and cisterns.   The space enclosed by these corridors
contains four court-yards, separated from one another by

corridors of less extent, several sets of apartments, but connected again by passages between the corridors and rooms. The number of apartments exceeds twenty. The bas-reliefs in stucco and in stone, in the court-yards of the palace, attract attention partly on account of the manner in which they are executed, and partly on account of the style of the figures. In one of the court-yards is a tower having a base of 30 feet square; it has three stories, and is conspicuous for its height and proportions. Nearly contiguous to this great palace is one of inferior dimensions. It stands on a pyramidal structure 110 feet high on the slope. This building is 76 feet in front and 25 feet deep. It has five doors and six piers, all standing. The whole front is richly ornamented with stucco, and the corner piers are covered with hieroglyphics, each of which contains 96 squares. Besides these two tablets, there are in the corridors of the interior three others, likewise covered with hieroglyphics. The other two or three buildings are less remarkable; but they also contain a few bas-reliefs of value. All these buildings stand on the top of artificial mounds resembling pyramids, and the slopes of these mounds have evidently been faced with stone, which, however, has been thrown down by the growth of the trees which now cover them.

The ruins found to the east of the Isthmus of Chiquimula are distinguished from all other American antiquities by very marked characteristics. The most extensive of these ruins, and certainly the most remarkable, are those of the city of Copan, which are on the banks of a river of the same name, that joins the river Matagua from the south. This city was in existence at the time of the arrival of the Spaniards, and was destroyed by them on account of an insurrection, which happened among the natives some years after they had submitted to the foreigners. At present no human habitation is found among the ruins, and the whole site of the town is overgrown with large trees and underwood. The ruins are dispersed over a space about 1000 feet in length and 500 in width, and consist of the remains of strong and high walls constructed of massive hewn stones, and of several pyramidal buildings, but there are some square altars, of which one is sculptured on the four sides and the top, and of a considerable number of stone idols, most of them still standing, though a few have fallen to the ground. These idols have the shape of columns, and are from 12 to 20 feet high. They are mostly covered with sculptures on all four sides, from the base to the top. The sculptures are very rich and made with great labour and art. They are all of a single block of stone. Most of them present a human figure fantastically dressed and adorned, but they differ greatly in design. In a few the backs and sides are covered with hieroglyphics. The altars are also of a single block of stone. They are in general not so richly ornamented as the idols. The sculpture on the best preserved of these altars is in bas-relief, and this is the only specimen of that kind of sculpture found at Copan, all the rest being in bold alto-relievo. It is 6 feet square and 4 feet high, and the top is divided into thirty-six tablets of hieroglyphics. The sides of this altar are covered with sculptures representing each four human figures in sitting attitudes. There are, perhaps, no ruins which show greater art and ingenuity and more labour than the ruins of Copan, and they may in these respects be compared with the temples of Elephanta and Ellora in Hindostan. It appears that other ruins of a similar description occur in this part of Central America.

The following is a description of the hill-forts in India by an engineer.

" The spot fixed upon is generally a hill, or rather mountain, standing by itself in a plain, or so unconnected with its contiguous chain as to be out of reach of annoyance from that quarter. It is also such as to be from its declivity, or the scarped nature of its sides, particularly difficult of ascent. Where nature has provided a sufficient rampart no addition in the shape of walls is made; but in other parts works of defence, adapted to the form of the ground, are multiplied one within another, according as the parts are more or less precipitous. Much ingenuity is often displayed in this, and every advantage taken of projecting rocks, or other circumstances, in forming flank-defences, which generally consist of round towers as nearly at regular distances as the ground will admit of. These hill-forts, when viewed from a short distance, have generally a most formidable appearance; but, unless where nature has so formed the face of the rock as to render the ascent impossible, they are seldom so in reality. The works are of necessity so exposed that, if you can get sufficiently near to raise a battery against them, they are easily breached, notwithstanding the elevation you are compelled to give to the guns, while the irregularity on the sides of the hills affords facilities for forming lodgments close up to the walls. Most of these hill-forts have a town or pettah attached to them, surrounded by a wall of no great strength. These pettahs are generally situated on the plain close under the hill; the whole together being somewhat of the form of a jockey-cap, of which the fort or citadel forms the crown, and the town the rim or peak." — (*Twelve Years' Military Adventures.*)

The Affghan forts are thus described by Lynch. "In the centre of the basin of Ressenna is a large natural mound, on which are the remains of a fort, or castle; from the top of it a very fine view is commanded of all the forts scattered over the green lands of the basin, and from this mound I counted thirty forts: they are merely an *enceinte* of mud wall, built in the form of a square with a tower at each angle, and in some of them a high tower rising from the centre of the fort. On these towers, and also in the Huzzareh forts, which are in every way constructed similarly to those of the Affghans, just described, are fires lit and regular watches kept during the night; for these two tribes, differing alike in manners, religion, and language, are constantly annoying each other in every possible way."

According to Wilkinson forts were multiplied in the towns of Egypt in the same proportion as fortified temples were used as a means of defence, after the accession of the eighteenth dynasty.

. The following remarks on the five conical pillars on a massive substruction, common to the tombs of the two most powerful monarchs of Lydia and Etruria, are from the " Quarterly Review."

" The most remarkable monument of Lydia, Herodotus informs us, was the tomb of Alyattes, the father of Crœsus. It was a mound or tumulus of earth, raised upon a solid mass of masonry, and surmounted by five pyramidal columns or cones. The text of the historian, as Thiersch remarks, leaves us somewhat doubtful whether the crepis, or solid masonry, was a mere substruction, or was carried up through the mound of earth as a basement for the columns.

" The most remarkable monument of Etruria was the tomb of Porsena at Clusium. Its remains, as still extant in Varro's time, are described by him as exhibiting a massive stone basement, on the summit of which were five pyramidal columns or cones. The Etruscan tradition assigned various other marvellous super-additions ; but the above, as Thiersch remarks, was all that Varro saw, and, consequently, all that we have any valid authority to suppose ever existed.

" A third monument, offering the same peculiarity of a basement supporting five pyramidal columns, is that still extant on the Via Appia, between Albano and La Riccia, vulgarly known as the Sepulchre of the Horatii and Curiatii. Nibby, from the evidence of the five cones, conjectures it to have been that of Aruns, son of Porsena, who was slain in his father's assault on the town of Aricia. Thiersch, and all other leading authorities, agree with him in so far as to class it either as an ancient Etrurian structure, or (which is more probable) a later imitation of that peculiar model of sepulchral architecture.

" Another building of a similar form, but larger in size, is described by Quatremère de Quincy as extant in Sardinia, — a solid substruction, with five cones on the summit. That Sardinia was a colony or dependency of Etruria during its flourishing ages we learn upon other authority, the accuracy of which, if open to doubt, this monument would go far to confirm.

" But the closest parallel to the old Lydian model is that offered by the sepulchral tumuli called Cucumelle, spread in large numbers, and under considerable variety of form and structure, over the deserted plains of the Roman Maremma, once the cemeteries of the Etruscan cities of Volsci and Tarquinii. The true nature of these monuments has only been ascertained by the excavations of the last fifteen years. Their chief feature of distinction from the ordinary barrow is the crepis, or solid stone masonry, which presents in different instances examples of the two modes of structure to which Thiersch supposes Herodotus may refer in his description of the tomb of Alyattes. The plan of the ' great Cucumella ' of Volsci, according to the reports of the French and German architects by whom it was examined, corresponds, as these architects remark, so closely with that of the Lydian tomb, as at once to suggest the notion that it must have been erected upon the same original model. It consists of a solid stone basement seventy or eighty yards in diameter, supporting a tumulus surmounted by pyramidal cones, fragments of which are still strewed over the sides of the mound. The original number of these cones, even in the present dilapidated state of the monument, has been recognised by the intelligent observers above quoted to be five, standing on the summit of an equal number of massive towers carried up from the foundation through the centre of the tumulus, in the lower recesses of which are the sepulchral chambers. Within and around this, and other neighbouring tumuli, were found various pieces of sculpture, representing human figures, lions, griffins, harpies, &c., in a grotesque archaïc style. Several of these imaginary animals may be recognised among the figures of the Lycian monuments lately discovered by Fellowes."

None of the Tuscan monuments are more stupendous than their great drains, sewers, and water-courses. The sewerage of London is not more complete than that of some of the old towns of Tuscany, which had become ruins before Rome was built. " Besides the purifying of all the towns, and the draining of all the marshes, there are few lakes in Etruria, or in the states bordering on it," says Mrs. Gray, " which have not had their waters lowered ; and few rivers which have not had their channels deepened, straightened, and regulated by this extraordinary people.   Though the only two grand works extensively known are the Cloaca Maxima at Rome, and the Emissarium through the Hill of Albano, Italians are continually finding them in places where they have never before been suspected; and engineers, who alone are capable of appreciating their merits and their difficulties, may trace them now towards Chiusi, at Fiesole, and in the Lakes of Nemi and Gatano.   The Lake of Nemi has two *emissaria*, which have only lately come to light, and a very magnificent one was discovered at Gatano, in 1838, by Prince Borghese, in an attempt to drain that sheet of water.   Niebuhr was the first who investigated the old under-ground channels at Fiesole, in 1820.   In the state of Perugia, and in other parts of Tuscany, many *emissaria* still remain, by which land was formerly gained, and which continue to do their office at this day, owing to the consummate skill with which they have been constructed, though for ages they have been utterly neglected."

"It is from the cemeteries," says Dennis, "that we gain any real information concerning the internal life and character of the Etruscan people.   We can follow them from the cradle to the tomb; we see them in the bosom of their families, and at the festive board, reclining luxuriously amidst the strains of music and the time-beating feet of the dancers; and at their favourite games and sports, encountering the wild boar, or looking on at the race, at the wrestling-match, or other palæstric exercises; we behold them stretched on the death-bed,—the last rites performed by mourning relatives, the funeral procession,—their bodies laid in the tomb,—and the solemn festivals held in their honour.   Nor even here do we lose sight of them, but follow their souls to the unseen world, perceive them, in the hands of good or evil spirits, conducted to the judgment-seat, and in the enjoyment of bliss, or suffering the punishment of the damned.

"The leading feature in Etruscan society, which points most strongly to an Oriental origin, is the omnipresence of their religious creed, and the power possessed by that priestly aristocracy who were the sole ministers and interpreters of its rites and tenets. Yet there is much to distinguish the hierarchical as well as the religious institutions of Etruria from those of Egypt or Asia. Already, at the earliest period at which we have any knowledge of their social condition, all trace of an exclusively sacerdotal caste had disappeared. The chiefs and nobles of the land combined in their own persons the priestly character with that of the civil magistrate; and if they guarded with extreme jealousy the exclusive possession of the secrets and mysteries of their religion,— if they confined to their own class the functions of the augur or haruspex,—political expediency was at least as deeply concerned in this monopoly as religious superstition. The chief-priesthoods of individual deities were indeed hereditary in particular families; but so they were in many instances among the Greeks of the earliest ages; and there is no proof that the Lucumons of Etruria claimed the exclusive exercise of priestly functions upon any different grounds from those on which it was assumed by the primitive kings of Greece. On the other hand, the disappearance of the kingly office,— the fact that the Etruscans had already lost that monarchical constitution which is so remarkably characteristic of all Oriental races,— is in itself an argument of their social system, even if originally derived from the East, having undergone great modifications during the process of transmission.

"It was her system of spiritual tyranny," says Dennis, "that rendered Etruria inferior to Greece. She had the same arts, an equal amount of scientific knowledge, a more extended commerce. In every field had the Etruscan mind liberty to expand, save in that wherein lies man's highest delight and glory. Before the gate of that Paradise where the intellect revels unfettered among speculations on its own nature, on its origin, existence, and final destiny,— on its relation to the First Cause, to other minds, and to society in general,— stood the sacerdotal Lucumo, brandishing in one hand the double-edged sword of secular and ecclesiastical authority, and holding forth in the other the books of Tages, exclaiming to his awe-struck subjects,—' Believe and obey!' Liberty of thought and action was as incompatible with the assumption of infallibility in the governing power in the days of Tarchon or Porsena, as in those of Gregory XVI."

Niebuhr terms the Etrurians "a priest-ridden people." The secret of the priesthood, whom he characterises as "a warlike sacerdotal caste, like the Chaldæans," was the interpretation of lightning. "This, and other branches of divination, as reading fate in the entrails of victims, and, perhaps, in the flight of birds, was taught in schools. Their knowledge of medicine, physic, and astronomy was neither borrowed from the Greeks nor Carthaginians, but is believed to have been indigenous, and brought with them from the North, when they conquered a more ancient people, and established themselves in their country. The Etrurian mode of determining time was extremely accurate, and based on the same principles as the computation observed by the ancient Mexicans."

Dionysus of Halicarnassus tells us, though his account of Etruria has unfortunately been lost, that neither in language nor in manners had the Etruscans any resemblance to any other people.

Music, architecture, sculpture, painting, as well as engraving of gems, casting of metals, and the art of pottery, were familiar to the Etrurians, who are said to have been far advanced in civilisation before the Trojan War.

Mrs. Gray describes a large Etruscan sarcophagus containing what remained of a skeleton and armour of the head of the family of the Velthuri, and around him, in the sarcophagus, a strange assemblage of articles, besides utensils of bronze of all sorts of shapes and sizes, and a pair of loaded dice: lastly, on both sides of the sarcophagus there was unequivocally represented a human sacrifice.

The Druids, like the Lucumons, were augurs, and sacrificed man.

In the procession of souls the heads of both the good and evil genii are encircled with green serpents. Typhon, the angel of death, is represented with wings and two serpents tapering from the trunk to the lower extremities. There are doorways of the obeliscal form and obeliscal arches.

In Etruria we find the Typhon of the Egyptians associated with the green serpents of the Mexicans, and the doorways and arches both of the obeliscal form, and common to the three countries.

Traces of Druidical augury and human sacrifice form other connecting links in the chain of evidence tending to show that the religious institutions of both worlds had a common origin.

Captain Beechey states why human sacrifice was so usual among the Druids, as it continues to be in the despotic governments of the East. Tamehameha would not patronise the introduction of Christianity into Woahoo, because he thought that "the maxims of our religion would tend to deprive him of that despotic power which he exercised over the lives and fortunes of his subjects. The terror inspired by human sacrifices, and the absolute command which the superstition of his idolatrous subjects gave him, suited the plan of his government better than any other religion."— (*Voyage to the Pacific.*)

The Druids and Etrurian augurs both maintained their influence over the people by magic, affecting prophecy, miracle, and favour with heaven. They inspected the entrails of victims, foretold events, and, like the Chaldeans, told fortunes by the planets.

" Druidism is not extinct; it still exists in Ceylon, where it is termed Baliism. These Cingalese worshippers of the stars are few in number, and generally conceal their opinions. Townley says the worship consists entirely of adoration to the heavenly bodies, invoking them in consequence of the supposed influence they have on the affairs of men. The priests are great astronomers, and believed to be thoroughly skilled in the power and influence of the planets." (*Fosbroke.*)

Strutt mentions, from Speed, a sort of Druids who forbade the worship of idols or any other form intended to represent the Godhead.

" At the latter end of their time," says Rowlands, " they (the Druids) deflected from the unity of the Godhead, or their professed monotheism."

Clitarchus affirms that the Druids and the Gymnosophists were the first contemners of death.

The modern Cingalese Druids believe in the existence of a Supreme God, who is indifferent to the affairs of men. It is their concern to secure the favour and avert the displeasure of certain malignant spirits, whom they imagine to be constantly attendant on their persons, and to be the authors of all their evils. They place great confidence in their gorgrees, or amulets, and have sacred groves, trees, and huts. They sometimes pray on the graves of their fathers (as in Ossian), or under their sacred trees.

The figure in Montfaucon, called an Arch-druid, has an oaken crown and carries a sceptre: he is completely draped in a long mantle and flowing robes. An inferior Druid has no crown, but wears a sleeved tunic under a kind of surplice, and carries a crescent in his hand of the size of the moon at six days old; and that is the time when they cut the misletoe.

Borlase, besides the oaken wreath, says that the younger Druids were without beards, and that the old ones wore them very long. He adds, that stripes in the garments of figures, a known Phœnician costume, and their standing with rings or circles round their feet, are marks of Druids. He adds, that they passed through six different classes before they arrived at the summit of their dignity. The sixth was the Arch-druid, to which Montfaucon's figure applies. An inscription shows that they rose from the office of sacrist to others by interest; and that the priesthood descended from father to son.

We shall explain the origin of the crescentic emblem in another work.

According to Southey, the Druids, or priests of the ancient Britons, are said to have retained the belief of one Supreme God, all-wise, all-mighty, and all-merciful, from whom all things which have life proceed: though they feigned that there were other gods beside " Him in whom we live and move and have our being,"— Tentates, whom they call "the Father;" and Taranis, the thunderer; and Hesus, the god of battles; and Andraste, the goddess of victory; Hu, the mighty, by whom it is believed that Noah, the second parent of the human race, was intended; Ceridwen, a goddess in whose rites the preservation of mankind in the ark was figured; and Beal, or Belinus,—for the Phœnicians had introduced the worship of their Baal.

By the favour of these false gods the Druids pretended to foretell future events, and as their servants and favourites they demanded gifts and offerings from the deluded multitude. They were notorious above the priests of every other idolatry for the practice of pretended magic. They made the people pass through fire in honour of Beal, and they offered up the life of man in sacrifice. Naked women, stained with the dark blue dye of woad, assisted in these bloody rites. When the misletoe was discovered growing upon an oak, two white bulls were fastened by the horns to the tree; the officiating priest ascended, and cut the misletoe with a golden knife. The best and most beautiful of the flocks were selected for sacrifice.

Herodotus says: "All the Egyptians sacrifice calves, oxen, and bulls; but they are not permitted to sacrifice cows, because these are consecrated to Isis, whom they represent under the form of a cow, as Io is represented by the Greeks."

Cæsar, who passed ten years in Gaul, says,—"It is believed that the Druidical institution was introduced into that country from Britain, and that generally those go there who wish to be well instructed. The Druids exercise both a spiritual and temporal authority. Any one who refuses to submit to their decisions is excluded from participating in their sacrifices, which is regarded as the most severe punishment, because he is abandoned by all, and cannot then obtain justice. The Druids have a chief, who exercises the highest authority. They assemble at a certain period of the year on the confines of Carnutum (*Carnac*), in a consecrated place, and there give judicial decisions as to ·murder, the rights of inheritance, boundaries of land, &c. Some students remain twenty years under the discipline of their masters, and learn verses by heart which they are not permitted to write, though generally in

M 2

other public and private affairs the Greek characters are used. One of their principal maxims is that the soul never dies, but that at death it passes from one body to another : this, they think, highly contributes to promote virtue and make them disregard death. They treat besides of many other subjects, as the stars and their motions ; the magnitude of the earth ; the nature of things ; the greatness and power of the immortal gods ; and these subjects they teach their scholars. The Gauls are all very superstitious ; so that in severe diseases, and in great dangers incidental to war, they either sacrifice men, or vow that they will do so ; and in these sacrifices the Druids are employed by them to officiate. They imagine that the immortal gods cannot be appeased but by their offering life for life : they have even established public sacrifices of this kind. Others have an image of an enormous size made of wicker-work ; this they fill with living men ; afterwards they set fire to it, and consume them in the flames. They take for this purpose thieves and brigands, or people convicted of some other crime ; they think the sacrifice of such people is more acceptable to the immortals : but when there is a deficiency of these, they substitute the innocent for them.

"The Gauls say they are descended from Pluto ; this is a tradition they received from the Druids. On that account they measure time by the number of nights, and not by those of the days. The Germans have very different customs. They have neither Druids for their religion, nor sacrifices. They class only in the number of gods those they see, and from whom they experience visible assistance ; such as the sun, moon, and Vulcan ; they have no idea of others."

Cæsar says : " The Druids did not permit their religious doctrines to be recorded in writing ; these were recorded only in verses committed to memory, and so transmitted from one generation of priests to another."

Herodotus says : " The priests of Egypt made use of two sorts of letters ; one for sacred, the other for popular purposes." The Rosetta stone contains three inscriptions of the same import ; namely, one in hieroglyphics, another in the ancient and common characters of the country, and the third in Greek. It appears that this valuable relic records a decree of the Egyptian priests in honour of Ptolemy Epiphanes. Here we find the priests of Egypt, like the Druids of Gaul, recording public events, not connected with religious doctrines, in Greek characters. Again: here is a religion like that of the Aztèques, stained with blood of human victims offered as sacrifices before the assembled people. Were such sacrifices made by the Druids of Britain on the high place, the platform of Silbury Hill, as are related by the Spaniards to have been made on the platform of the teocalli when Cortez arrived in Mexico? The Aztèque priest opened the breast of the human victim, and took out the heart for an offering. Diodorus says of the Druids of Gaul,—" Pouring out a libation upon a man as a victim; they smite him with a sword upon the breast, near the diaphragm."

Divitiacus, the Gaulish king of the Edui, the friend and ally of Cæsar, was chief Druid as well as sovereign. Montezuma was also chief priest and sovereign of the Mexicans, and so were the Pharaohs of the Egyptians.

The Gauls were all very superstitious, and the Druids exercised over them the greatest influence. Herodotus says " the Egyptians were extraordinarily superstitious, even beyond any other people in the world."

The doctrine of the metempsychosis was taught by the Druids in the temple of Carnac in Gaul: that of immortality might have been taught in the temple of Carnac in Egypt.

The discipline of the noviciates in both hierarchies was rigid and austere, and had long to be endured before they could become candidates for authority.

The great god of the Druids is Mercury. They have a great many statues of him.

The Mercurial tombs were numerous about Syene in Egypt, according to Strabo.

Herodotus mentions that the Scythians sacrifice a prisoner of war to Mars by cutting his throat over a bowl; a libation of wine having previously been poured on his head. Also that prophets divine by willow rods.

M 3

" Near Sung-e-Masha, in Affghanistan," says Lynch, " my attention was attracted by a large block of black granite, about six feet high.   It was erect like a milestone, and on the side facing the road is a very curious inscription.   I copied the inscription and examined the locality, where there appeared a number of mounds.   I will not venture to say in what language the inscription is, or what it means; but the Sultan declares that the road at one time led to a large city in Ugeristan, and that formerly there were round towers all along the road, called *melees*, and that at some of them were stones with inscriptions like the present engraved upon them. The position of these mounds, called Subz Choob, which may possibly, like those at Nineveh and Babylon, indicate the site of a once flourishing city, commands a beautiful view of the valley of the Argundab.   It is in the entrance of a gorge in the mountains, through which a road leads into Ugeristan."

Sculpture was banished from the structure of the ancient Catholic Church.   Even sepulchral monuments were never seen within the walls of the building, which, according to the emphatic words of the fathers and councils, was not to be defiled by death and corruption.

Yet, according to Knight, it would appear that from the custom which had originated in the catacombs, — from the habit which the primitive Christians had acquired of visiting the graves of the martyrs, — it became a matter of necessity to associate the church with the tomb, and to provide a place of worship below ground as well as above.   This in several instances was accomplished at Rome by placing the church immediately above the catacombs, as at San Lorenzo and Santa Agnese ; or, as at St. Peter's, by placing the altar immediately above the spot to which the mortal remains of the Apostle had been removed.

Loftus, the first European who has visited the ancient ruins of Warka, in Mesopotamia, writes that Warka is no doubt the Erech of Scripture, the second city of Nimrod, and it is the Orchac of the Chaldees.   The mounds within the walls afford subjects of high interest to the historian and antiquarian : they are filled, nay, I may say, they are literally composed of coffins, piled upon each other to the height of forty-five feet. It has evidently been the great burial-place of generations of Chaldeans, as Meshad Ali and Kerbella at the present day are of the Persians. The coffins are very strange affairs; they are in general form like a slipper-bath, but more depressed and symmetrical, with a large oval aperture to admit the body, which is closed with a lid of earthenware. The coffins themselves are also of baked clay, covered with green glaze and embossed with figures of warriors, with strange and enormous coiffures, dressed in a long tunic and long under garments, a sword by the side, the arms resting at the hips, the legs apart. Great quantities of pottery and also clay figures, some most delicately modelled, are found around them; and ornaments of gold, silver, iron, copper, glass, &c., within.

A fine pillar at Kuhaon, set up in the reign of Skanda Gupta, is considered by Kittoe as a Jain monument; and there are remains of temples and tanks around, hitherto unnoticed. Near Kassia he visited a tumulus and the remains of a vihara and several chaityas. He considers the image called Mata Konwar to be a statue of Buddha, and not of Durga, as conjectured from the name. At Lukhunpoor he found tumuli varying from six to fifty feet in height, some constructed of brick and mud, and some of a kind of clay not found in the whole country round. The grand tumulus has been a chaitya of immense height, but has crumbled down, and is not more than 150 feet high and 300 yards in circumference. One of the tumuli having been undermined in digging for clay, fell in half two years ago, and in the centre was found an iron cylinder in an erect position, containing some large human bones. The noble pillar at this place, which is known as the Muttiah pillar, surmounted by a fine lion, he conceives to be the work of a western artist; and the inscription upon it, in Pali, of a later date than the pillar. At Auxuraj he found another fine mutilated pillar, the inscription upon which is identical with that on the Lukhunpoor column. He next went to Kessaria, where there is a large tumulus, and the remains of a town, viharas, and temples; which he considers to be identical with the Kusha Nagira of Fa Hian, the Chinese traveller.

All nations do something towards the speedy destruction or removal of the dead. The mode of effecting this is varied by the peculiar manners or prejudices of almost every nation. In some parts the dead are thrown over precipices, or abandoned to the deserts, woods, or ditches, to the hunger of wild beasts and vultures; and, in others, they are consigned to the rivers or seas, and become the prey of fishes. In the East Indies they are dried by fire, and then enveloped in cloths and deposited in the earth. In other parts of the same country the fire is suffered to consume the body altogether. The Parsees have two cemeteries, one white and the other black; in the one they bury those who have lived in the constant practice of virtue, and consign to the other those whose life has not been without reproach.

A few of the various practices of the natives of America may be noticed. The Arraques, who inhabit the south of Orinoco, suspend the corpse in its cabin until time has consumed its flesh; they then reduce the bones to powder, which they mingle with their drink; or they burn the body, and make the same use of the ashes. The Abipones of South America generally inter the dead under the shade of a tree; and when a chief or warrior dies, they kill his horses on the grave. After a time the remains are exhumed, and conveyed to a place more secret than the first. Some tribes make skeletons of the dead, and place them in a sitting posture, clothed with robes and feathers, in the cemetery, which is opened every year, the skeletons cleansed and clothed anew. Most of the tribes of the American continent strongly manifest the desire that their own bones and those of their fathers should rest in the land of their nativity. When the nomade tribes of South America wander many hundred miles from their proper boundaries, and one of their number happens to die, they reduce the body to a skeleton, which they place on the favourite horse of the deceased, and carry it with them till they arrive at the place of his family, however distant. It seems, indeed, that the different tribes are attached to particular districts, chiefly by the circumstance that the bones of their fathers are buried there. A North American chief indicated his aversion to a proposal for a cession of territory to the white man by asking, " Shall we say unto the bones of our fathers, ' Arise, and go into another land ? ' " In many tribes, when the encroachments of the white man drive them from their ancient domains, they exhume and take with them the bones of their ancestors and friends.

In early times the Assyrians and Babylonians covered the dead with wax previous to interment. The Egyptians embalmed the body, which they preserved with great care in houses, or in catacombs, devoted to this purpose.

The Moslems carefully keep up, even after death, the external distinctions between themselves and others which they so carefully assert during life. None but Turks are allowed to have the cypress in their cemeteries. Christians may plant any other trees ; but the Jews are allowed none. Again, Christians are not allowed to have perpendicular grave-stones, but they may and do raise decent oblong masses of masonry to support the inscribed horizontal slab, which the Jews are obliged to lay on the ground.

The ground occupied by cemeteries (cities of silence) is very extensive, owing to the dislike of the Turks to open the ground where it is known that a body has been interred. These " Fields of the Dead " are in the neighbourhood of Moslem cities, and apart from the saddening associations to which such spots give occasion they are commonly the most pleasing promenades which Eastern cities afford. The trees with which they are thickly planted in the western parts of Turkey afford a grateful shade. The women frequent the cities of silence very generally on Fridays, on which day they believe that their friends awaken to the consciousness of their former ties and relations.

It may be remarked that the custom of depositing the dead at some distance from the abodes of the living prevails among all people except those of Christendom. They only have been unable, until of late, to perceive the evils of intramural interment.

" The Egyptians," says Diodorus, "make small account of
the time of this life,— being limited ; but that which after
death is joined with a glorious memory of virtue, they highly
value.   They call the houses of the living inns, because they
inhabit them but a short time ; but the sepulchres of the
dead they term eternal mansions, because they continue with
the gods for an infinite space : therefore in the structure of
their houses they are not very solicitous, but in exquisitely
adorning their sepulchres they think no cost too great.
However, though the Egyptians were of opinion that as long
as the body endured the soul continued with it, yet it did
not quicken or animate the corpse, but remained there only
as an attendant or guardian, unwilling to leave her former
habitation."

Lepsius reckons 69 pyramids in the vicinity of Memphis,
all within a line of 56 miles, and 139 pyramids at and near
Meroë in Upper Nubia.

Upwards of 100 tombs of private persons scattered round
the pyramids have been opened by Lepsius, in which were
found a vast number of paintings representing the manners
and customs of the ancient Egyptians 5000 years ago.

" The Prussian Commission," remarks Perring, " have
gleaned the sites of 30 pyramids entirely unknown to preceding travellers.   Of these not a few are of very considerable extent, bearing evident traces of the mode in which
they were raised, and surrounded by ruins of temples and
extensive fields of tombs or burial grounds.   All these pyramids, without exception, belong to the ancient kingdom of
Egypt before the irruption of the Hyksos, who invaded
Lower Egypt about 2000 years B. C., and the whole of them
were erected (those at least between Aboorooash and Dashour)
by kings who reigned at Memphis.   To the same period belong the majority of effaced tombs of any importance which
surround them : this is evident from the fact that at a later
period the richest and most honourable families of the country,
who could display greater magnificence on their tombs, no
longer resided at Memphis, but at Thebes, which was also
the regal residence.

At what period, or in what country, the first pyramid was constructed as a monument of the science of astronomy, dedicated as a temple to religion, or a mausoleum to a king, conjecture itself must be silent.

The Nubian pyramids are generally of small dimensions. Most of these pyramids are remarkable for having porticoes attached to them, which seem to be a part of the original construction ; and the roofs of some of these porticoes have the complete arch with the key-stone.

" We may for the present," says Wilkinson, " be satisfied with the fact that the arch was in common use 3370 years ago, and rejoice that the name of Amunoph has been preserved on the stucco coating the interior of a vault at Thebes, to announce it, and to silence the incredulity of a sceptic.

" Though the oldest stone arch whose age has been positively ascertained dates only in the time of Psammetichus, we cannot suppose that the use of stone was not adopted by the Egyptians for that style of building previous to his reign, even if the arches in the pyramids of Ethiopia should not prove to be anterior to the same era. Nor does the absence of arch in temples and other large buildings excite our surprise, when we consider the style of the Egyptian monuments ; and no one who understands the character of their architecture could wish for its introduction."

Construction of Arches on the African Coast. — Temple gives the following account of the mode of building at Tunis : — " On speaking to the architect and engineers, and asking them to show me their plans, they at first did not seem to know what a plan was ; when it was explained to them, they declared they had nothing of the sort, and that, in fact, the Moors never make any previous to commencing a building ; but that they built by the eye a certain length of wall, and when this had been sufficiently prolonged, another was built at right angles to it, and so on. What is still more remarkable, their arches are all constructed by the eye, and have no framework to support them during the process, which is as follows. A brick, presenting its broad surface to view, is placed with its edge on the buttress where is to commence the spring of the arch ; another is made to adhere to it by means of a very strong cement made of gypsum peculiar to the vicinity of Tunis, which instantly hardens : on this brick is placed another in the same manner, and thus they proceed until the arch is completed.   I saw a vault thus made in less than an hour and a half.   These arches and vaults, when finished, are very graceful and correct in their proportions, and nothing can equal their strength and solidity. In building walls, an oblong frame about seven feet long, and as broad as the wall is intended to be, is placed on the foundations, and then filled with mortar and pieces of stone ; in a few minutes the frame is removed and placed in continuation of the line.   This method appears to have been adopted in the construction of Carthage."

At Monishwar, a town in Bejapoor, is a very handsome dome erected over a small square building, which in this province is effected in the following manner.   A mound of earth is raised, the intended height and shape of the dome or arch, over which the stones are placed, and when completed on the outside the support is removed.   The inhabitants have but little knowledge of the powers of mechanism.   When a large stone is to be raised, it is dragged up a slope of earth, made for the purpose, which is afterwards removed. — (*East India Gazetteer.*)

Gliddon describes the ritual as a collection of poems, hymns, and liturgical prayers, offered by, as well as for, the departed Egyptians, among whose cerements these papyri are found.   No translation of the whole has yet appeared.

Several more or less complete copies of it exist in hieroglyphical and in hieratic writings.   It doubtless received various modifications in the course of so many centuries ; each adding or extending some idea, which, in the previous epoch, was less distinctly defined.

This " ritual " was a formula of prayers and devotional exercises, of which the painted inscriptions on the mummy cases are, generally, extracts.   In Egypt, extracts from it are met with upon every object connected with death or religion, precisely in the same manner as in Mohammedan mosques we encounter passages from the Kurán, in Hebrew synagogues extracts from the Old, and in Christian churches from the New Testament.

It is divided into three parts: the first of which directs the prayers, ceremonies, and offerings to be used, while the body was carried from the embalmers to the tomb; the second narrates the adventures of the soul in Hades, after its separation from the body; and the third announces the return of the reunited soul and body to the celestial regions.

The doctrine taught is, that the body, when embalmed, becomes a statue or type of Osiris, and as such an object of worship. The tomb thus becomes a temple for costly offerings, made by the relations of the deceased to the deities, through the priestly guardians of the tomb. The doctrine of the state after death, appears to have been as follows: — During the seventy days that elapsed between death and burial, it was supposed that the soul was extinct, but, as soon as mummification was completed, it was resuscitated. It then ascended as a hawk, with a human head, to the new moon, and took a seat in the sun's boat, and, after undergoing many tribulations, trials, and sufferings, it arrived in the hall of Osiris, where it was weighed in the balance of Truth and Justice, and received its due award. Among the incidents of this journey was its appearance before the forty-two assessors, each of whom presided over one sin. To each the soul exclaims, in self-righteousness, "Bring forward my excellence; search out my sins!" and states that it has never committed such and such sins, thus — "I have defrauded no man; I have not prevaricated at the seat of justice; I have not made slaves of the Egyptians; I have not committed adultery," &c. &c.

Every provincial temple was provided with an establishment for the purpose of embalming. Here the bodies were delivered to the priests to be embalmed, and after seventy days restored to the friends to be carried to the place of deposit. The paintings on the tombs represent funeral processions, in which is seen the mummy transported in cars, or borne on sledges drawn by oxen, and attended by mourning friends. Sometimes this procession is made in boats, on the Nile, canals, or lakes; whence, in later times, probably arose the Greek fable of the boatman Charon.

St. Augustine remarks that the Egyptians alone believed in the resurrection, because they carefully preserve the bodies of their dead; for, says he, they have a custom of drying up the bodies and rendering them as durable as brass (alluding to his own time, A. D. 354—430).

Embalming did not entirely cease in the East until the seventh century after Christ, or the Muslim invasion. At the remote age of the fourth dynasty, the bodies, as in the case of king Menkare (Mycerinus), were prepared by saturation of natron, baked in ovens, and wrapped in woollen cloths. Bitumen began to be used after the conquest of Assyria by the Pharaohs of the eighteenth dynasty. Bandages of existing mummies, which in the generality of the first-class bodies vary from ten to thirty folds, have been known to reach as many as forty-six folds round the corpse, containing above 1000 yards of cloth, the weight of which exceeded 46 pounds of linen, varying in texture from good calico to superfine cambric. The mummy of a scribe, brought by Cailleaud from Egypt, on being unrolled produced nearly 350 square yards of linen cloth.

" On entering a tomb," says Gliddon, " we see the deceased surrounded by his family, who offer him their remembrances. The name, the profession, rank, and blood-relationship of each member of the family are written against him or her. The scenes of ordinary life are painted on the walls. Study, gymnastics, feasts, banquets, wars, sacrifices, death and funeral, are all faithfully delineated in these sepulchral illustrations of manners, which are often epic in their character. You have the song with which the Egyptian enlivened his labour in the field; the anthem that, when living, he offered to his Creator, and the death-wail that accompanied his body to the grave. Every condition, every art, every trade, figures in this picturesque encyclopædia, from the monarch, priest, and warrior, to the artisan and herdsman. Then these tombs are real museums of antiquities — utensils, toilet-tables, inkstands, pens, books, the incense-bearer, and smelling-bottle, are found in them. The wheat which the Egyptian ate, the fruit that adorned his dessert-table, peas, beans, and barley, which still germinate when replanted, are also discovered. The eggs, the desiccated remains of the very milk he had once used for his breakfast, even the trussed and roasted goose, of which the guests at his wake had partaken — all these evidences of humanity, and a myriad more, exist, in kind, in the museums of Europe. But not only do the scenes sculptured or painted on the temples or in the sepulchres furnish every detail concerning the Egyptians; they give us the portraits, history, geographical names, and characteristics of an infinitude of Asiatic and African nations existing in the days long anterior to the Exode — many of whom have left no other record of their presence on earth, and others, again, whose names are preserved in the Hebrew Scriptures."

Etruscan Glass. — " The rarities of Campana's collection which astonished me most," says Mrs. Gray, " were three small and most elegantly-formed beakers, of smalts or semi-transparent glass, the colours being blue, white, and yellow, in vandykes. The form was the most finished Greek, while the manufacture was identical with Egypt, and each stood upon a small and graceful stand of filagree gold. These and Galassi's are surely specimens of the gold and silver tazze of Etruria, so much renowned amongst the Greeks. As to the glass, I once saw afterwards the same sort at Corneto, found in a tomb at Tarquinia; but the vase was of a rude form in comparison, and very much broken."

The art of making glass, like the construction of the arch, has been supposed to have been unknown to the ancients. Both these generally received ideas appear now to have been erroneous. It is recorded by Pliny that a glass obelisk stood in the temple of Jupiter Ammon.

The antiquities found at Herculaneum, Pompeii, and at other places, may be seen in the museum at Naples. There are bread, and fruit, and the honey-comb; vases and vessels of ancient glass; candelabra and lamps; sacrificial vessels, common utensils for the kitchen, scales and weights of bronze, most elegant in workmanship and forms; inkstands, styles, and tablets; tickets for the theatre; the systrum and cymbals; essence bottles, rouge, and metallic mirrors; armour, and the toys of children; bells for browsing cattle; horse furniture; little figures of their household gods; dice, and bells to strike the hour.

The art of fabricating glass is of high antiquity. It has been conjectured that the ornaments placed in the ears of crocodiles, which Herodotus calls "stone pendants made by fusion or melting" were of glass. It may be well to remark that St. Hilaire confirms Herodotus even in so minute a matter as the piercing of the crocodile's ears. He found the anterior part of the covering of the ear of a mummy cro-codile pierced as if for the purpose of putting a pendant to it.

Perfection of Glass-manufacture among the Egyptians.
(From the Westminster Review.)

"The fact proved by the illustrations of Rossellini, by extant relics of glass-manufactory of Egypt in the British Museum, and by the extant confirmatory relics in various other museums, express the error of the ordinary and narrow ideas indulged in by historians on this subject. It is common to assert that, with the exception of some glass vessels of a great price, glass was little known and used till the time of Augustus, and never in windows until the fall of the Roman Empire. The fact is, that glass and porcelain, of equally fine quality as the modern, were made 1800 years B. C., under the eighteenth dynasty. They were, moreover, made in perfection. This is another startling allegation supported by good proof, but a more startling one must still be added. The glass-blowers of Thebes were greater proficients in the art than we are. They possessed the art of staining glass, which, although not wholly lost, is comparatively little known, and practised only by a few. Among the illustrations of Rossellini, there is a copy of a piece of stained glass of considerable taste of design and beauty of colour, in which the colour is struck through the whole vitrified structure; and there are instances of the design being equally struck through pieces of glass half an inch thick, perfectly incorporated with the structure, and appearing the same on the obverse as on the reverse side. In consequence of this fact it was that Winkleman truly asserted that the Egyptians of this time (the eighteenth dynasty) brought it to a much higher point of perfection than ourselves. In fact, after the decline of the art, Egypt became to Rome what Venice became afterwards to Europe. They imitated amethysts and other precious stones with wonderful dexterity; and, besides the art of staining glass, they must have been aware of the use of the diamond in cutting and engraving it. In Salt's collection in the British Museum in the time of Thothmos III., 1500 years B. C., a piece is beautifully stained throughout, and skilfully engraved with his emblazonment. The profusion of glass in Egypt is easily proved. Fragments have been found of granite which are covered with a coating of stained glass, through which the hieroglyphics of the stone appear. The relation that the bodies of Alexander and Cyrus were deposited in glass coffins, which has been considered as a fable, is thus analogically proved. But the profusion of the dearest glass-manufactures may be equally proved. Vast numbers of imitative precious stones in glass, made by the Theban jewellers, are to be found in all the museums of Europe. Among these are the false emeralds, in which they seem to have succeeded best. Diodorus Siculus says that coffins were commonly made of it in Ethiopia. The extensive character of the manufacture may also be inferred from a circumstance recorded by Pliny, that in the temple of Jupiter Ammon there was an obelisk of emerald, that is, of glass in imitation of emerald, 60 feet in height. The emerald hue which the glass-manufacturers of Europe gave to glass appears, from chemical analysis, to be imparted by oxide of copper; and the reds, used in imitation of rubies, or in staining plate-glass, appear to have been derived from minium.   All these facts prove the extensive knowledge of chemistry among the natives of old Thebes.   Glass bottles, nearly similar to our wine bottles in colour and measure, though in shape resembling the wide-mouthed bottles used in preserving fruit, may be seen in the British Museum, and are found in abundance in other European cabinets."

An extract from " Fraser's Magazine " will show that the art of colouring was also well known to the Egyptians.

" The tools of trade of the ancient Egyptians, with few exceptions, resemble those used in modern times.   But they startle the inspector by the grotesque character of being painted red and yellow in the illustrations.   Those, however, were their proper colours.   There are many tools of the same description, made of copper and brass, preserved in the Egyptian room of the British Museum.   They are elastic, do not oxidise, and have cut the hardest granite.   Must the capacity of producing this result be regarded as one among the lost arts?   The chemical knowledge displayed in the fabrication of the tools was equalled by the chemical knowledge evinced by the artisan, the tradesman, and the manufacturer.   The weavers used dyes, mineral and vegetable, and acetates of iron and of alum.   The dyers employed metallic oxides and mordants, both adjective and substantive.   The tanners showed equal chemical skill.   The painters employed vegetable extracts and mineral oxides; and the relics of glass extant, or attested, prove an equal chemical knowledge among the glass-blowers."

PART IX.

Temples in Lower Egypt.

ABOUT eight miles north-east of Samennud (the ancient Sebennytus) are the ruins of a magnificent temple, probably dedicated to Isis. It was built entirely of granite blocks, which must have been brought from the neighbourhood of Assouan, and was undoubtedly one of the most wonderful works of Egyptian art, as its ruins amply prove; though they are now heaped together in the greatest confusion, as if an earthquake had at one shock levelled the whole with the ground.

The temple was 300 feet in length and 100 wide. The capitals of the columns have been in the same style as those of the great portico or pronaos at Denderah, representing on each of the four sides the front face of Isis.

So little is known of the history of this great temple, that it is even doubtful what ancient site it occupies.

Sides are 300　 by 100　feet,

259·4 by 86·4 units,

if 254·4 by 86·9　 ,,

then, $100 \times 254·4 = 25440.$

Diameter of the orbit of Uranus $= 25440^3.$

$100 \times 86·9 = 8690.$

Distance of Mars $= 8690^3.$

Cube of 100 times greater side
　　　　$=$ diameter of the orbit of Uranus.

Cube of 100 times less side
　　　　$=$ distance of Mars.

Sum of 2 sides $= 254·4 + 86·9 = 341·3.$

Perimeter $= 682·6.$

10 perimeter $= 6826.$

Diameter of the orbit of Mercury $= 6880^3$;

or,　　　　　　　3×342 &c. $= 1028.$

Distance of the moon $= 1028^3.$

Cube of 3 times sum of 2 sides $=$ distance of the moon.

Otherwise, if the sides be 262 by 86·8 units,

$262^3 = \frac{1}{60}$ distance of moon $=$ radius of the earth,

$(6 \times 262)^3 = \frac{1}{60} \times 6^3 = \frac{36}{10},$

$(10 \times 6 \times 262)^3 = \frac{36000}{10} = 3600.$

Distance of Saturn 　$= 3750$

　　,,　　Mercury $=$ 　150

Difference $= \overline{3600.}$

Thus the cube of 60 times the side $262 =$ distance between Mercury and Saturn.

$(10 \times 86·8)^3 = \frac{6}{10}$ distance of the moon.

$(10 \times 10 \times 86·8)^3 = \frac{6000}{10} = 600.$

Or, cube of 100 times the side $86·8 = 600$ distance of moon; and distance of Mars $= 604.$

6 cubes $= 3600$

$=$ distance between Mercury and Saturn.

Hence the cube of 60 times the greater side = 6 times the cube of 100 times the less side.

Sum of 2 sides = 350.

$$350^3 = \tfrac{1}{25} \text{ distance of the moon.}$$
$$(25 \times 350)^3 = \tfrac{1}{25} \times 25^3 = 625.$$

6 cubes of 25 times sum of 2 sides = $6 \times 625 = 3750$

= distance of Saturn.

6^2 cubes = 22500 =   ,,   Belus.

$$(2 \times 350)^3 = \tfrac{8}{25} \text{ distance of the moon.}$$
$$(5 \times 2 \times 350)^3 = \tfrac{8}{25} \times 5^3 = 40.$$

7 cubes of 5 times perimeter = 280 distance of the moon
= distance of Venus.

10 cubes = 400 distance of moon = distance of the earth.

San, the ancient Tanis, and the Zoan of the Scriptures, though little known in profane history, attests by its ruins its former magnificence. It lies a few miles from the outlet of the canal of Moezz into the Lake Menzaleh, and on the east side of this canal. The mounds, formed of crumbling bricks, which have served as the enclosure of the temple, are about 1000 feet long and 700 wide; while the enclosures which mark the limits of the ancient city are conjectured to be about 5 miles in circuit.

1000 by 700 feet
= 864 by 605 units.

$$867^3 = \tfrac{1}{3} \text{ distance of the moon.}$$
$$601^3 = \tfrac{1}{9} \quad ,, \quad ,, \quad ,,$$

Cubes are as 1 : 3.

Sum of two sides = $867 + 601 = 1468$,
and $1482^3 = 3$ times distance of the moon.

If the dimensions within the walls were 867 by 601 units, without, or on the top of the walls, the dimensions might have been 1482 units for the sum of the two sides.

Within the enclosure are ruins of a massy propylon of red and grey granite, fragments of porticoes, columns, walls, obelisks, and statues, lying in confused heaps.

These extensive ruins lie in the midst of marshes, with no human habitation around them but a few miserable huts built of mud and reeds. Such is the present condition of a city whose origin is assigned to a very remote age, and which was once probably a royal residence of the Pharaohs.

Sum of 2 sides - - - - $= 1468$ units.
20 times sum, or 10 times perimeter - $= 29360$,,
Distance of Belus - - - - $= 29160^2$,,

$$1000 \text{ by } 700 \text{ feet} = 864 \text{ by } 605 \text{ units,}$$
$$\text{if } 869 \text{ by } 606 \text{ \&c.}$$
$$\text{then } 10 \times 869 = 8690$$
$$\text{distance of Mars} = 8690^3$$
$$9 \times 606 \text{ \&c.} = 5460$$
$$\text{distance of Mercury} = 5460^3.$$

Cube of 10 times greater side $=$ distance of Mars.
Cube of 9 times less side $=$ distance of Mercury.

$$\text{Sum of 2 sides} = 869 + 606 \text{ \&c.} = 1476.$$
$$(3 \times 1476)^3 = 80 \text{ distance of the moon.}$$

Cube of 3 times sum of 2 sides $= 80$ distance of the moon.

$$867^3 = \tfrac{3}{5} \text{ distance of the moon,}$$
$$(5 \times 867)^3 = \tfrac{3}{5} \times 5^3 = 75,$$
$$100 \times (5 \times 867)^3 = 7500.$$

Or 100 cubes of 5 times greater side
   $= 7500$ distance of the moon $=$ distance of Uranus,

$$300 \text{ cubes} = 22500 = \text{distance of Belus,}$$
$$601^3 = \tfrac{1}{8} \text{ distance of the moon,}$$
$$(5 \times 601)^3 = \tfrac{1}{8} \times 5^3 = 25,$$
$$(2 \times 5 \times 601)^3 = 25 \times 8 = 200.$$

Or cube of 10 times the less side
   $= 200$ distance of the moon $= \tfrac{1}{2}$ distance of the earth.

Pyramid having height $=$ side of base $= 1482$ units.
Content will $=$ distance of the moon.

Bubastis is thus described by Herodotus. The temple well deserves mention; for though others may be more spacious and magnificent, yet none can afford more pleasure to the eye. Except the entrance, it is surrounded by two canals that branch off from the river. Each canal is 1 plethron broad, shaded with trees on both sides. The portico is 10 orgyes in height, adorned with statues 6 cubits high, of excellent workmanship. Now the temple being in the middle of the city is looked down on from all sides as you walk round; and this happens to be so because the city has been raised, but the temple has not been moved, remaining in its original position. A wall goes quite round the temple, and is adorned with sculptures; within the enclosure is a grove of very tall trees planted round a large building, in which is the statue. The figure of the temple is a square, each side being a stade in length. In a line with the entrance is a road built of stone about 3 stades in length and 4 plethrons in breadth; on each side of it are exceedingly tall trees. The road leads to the temple of Hermes.

Hamilton remarks that Herodotus's description of " looking down on the temple" exactly corresponds to its present appearance.

The side of the temple = the side of the tower of Belus = 1 stade.

The cube of 1 side, or of 1 stade $= \frac{1}{8}$ circumference.

The cube of twice the side $= 1$ „

Height of portico = 10 orgyes,
$$= \tfrac{1}{10} \text{ stade} = 24 \cdot 3 \text{ units},$$
and $25^3 = \frac{1}{60}$ degree = 3 minutes.

Avenue 3 stades by 4 plethrons
$$= 729 \quad \text{„} \quad 162 \text{ units},$$

$$40 \times 729 = 29160,$$
Distance of Belus $= 29160^3$,

$$80 \times 163 = 13040,$$
Distance of Jupiter $= 13040^3$.

Cube of 40 times greater side
= distance of Belus = cube of Babylon.

Cube of 80 times less side
= distance of Jupiter.

N 4

Cube of 50 times greater side

$$= \text{distance of Ninus},$$
$$= \text{cube of Nineveh}.$$

Sum of 2 sides $= 729 + 163 = 892$ units

$$892^3 = \tfrac{50}{8} \text{ circumference},$$
$$(2 \times 892)^3 = 50,$$
$$(3 \times 2 \times 892)^3 = 50 \times 3^3 = 1350.$$

Cube of 6 times sum of 2 sides

or of 3 times perimeter $= 1350$ circumference,
$$= \tfrac{1}{3} \text{ distance of Venus}.$$

Cube of 6 times perimeter $= \tfrac{8}{2} = 4$ distance of Venus
$$= \tfrac{4}{80} = \tfrac{1}{20} \text{ distance of Belus}.$$

Breadth of canal $= 1$ plethron $= 40\cdot5$ units
$$(10 \times 40\cdot8)^3 = 408^3 = \tfrac{6}{10} \text{ circumference},$$
$$(10 \times 10 \times 40\cdot8)^3 = \tfrac{6000}{10} = 600.$$

Cube of 100 times breadth $= 600$ circumference.

The village of Metrahenny, half concealed in a thicket of palm-trees, about 10 miles south of Jizeh, on the east side of the river, marks the site of the great city of Memphis, once the rival of Thebes in magnitude and splendour. Yet, owing to its position, it has been so much exposed to plunder from the successive conquerors of the country, who have used it as a stone-quarry, that even its site has been matter of dispute. Independent, however, of the ruins that are still there, the situation is determined to correspond to that of Metrahenny by other evidence that is incontestable. Its remains are spread over an extensive place, on which may be seen blocks of granite, with fragments of columns, statues, and obelisks, which are all that remain of the great temple of Hephæstus (Phtha), and other sacred buildings of Memphis.

" High mounds," says Hamilton, " enclose a square of 800 yards from north to south, and 400 from east to west. The entrance in the centre of each side is still visible. The two principal ones face the desert and the river. We entered by the last, and were immediately much gratified by the sight of

thirty or forty large blocks of very fine red granite lying on the ground, evidently forming parts of some colossal statues, the chief ornaments of the temple."

$$\text{Sides } 400 \quad \text{by} \quad 800 \text{ yards}$$
$$= 1033 \cdot 5 \quad \text{,,} \quad 2067 \text{ units,}$$
$$\text{if } = 1042 \quad \text{,,} \quad 2084$$
$$\tfrac{1}{2} \, 1042 = 521$$
$$521^3 = \tfrac{4}{4} \text{ circumference,}$$
$$(2 \times 521)^3 = \tfrac{4}{4} \times 8 = \quad 10.$$

Cube of less side $\quad = \quad 10.$
Cube of greater side $\quad = \quad 80.$
Cube of perimeter $\quad = 270$
$\qquad\qquad\qquad\qquad = \frac{1}{10}$ distance of Venus.

If sides $= 1028$ by 2056 units.
Cube of less side $\qquad =$ distance of the moon.
Cube of greater side $\quad = 8 \qquad$,,
Cube of perimeter $\quad = 27 \qquad$,,
$(16 \times 1028)^3 = 16^3 \times 1 = 4096 \qquad$,,
Diam. of orbit of Jupiter $= 4090 \qquad$,,

Traces of the temple of Anteopolis extend 230 feet in length, 150 in breadth,

$$230 \text{ by } 150 \text{ feet,}$$
$$= 199 \quad \text{,,} \quad 129 \cdot 6 \text{ units,}$$
$$(10 \times 129 \cdot 6)^3 = \text{diameter of orbit of the moon,}$$
$$(100 \times 201, \&c.)^3 = \qquad \text{,,} \qquad \text{Saturn.}$$

Sum of 2 sides $= 129 \cdot 6 + 201, \&c. = 331$ units

$$331^3 = \tfrac{1}{30} \text{ distance of the moon,}$$
$$= \text{diameter of the earth.}$$

Thus cube of 10 times less side
$\qquad =$ diameter of orbit of the moon.
Cube of 100 times greater side
$\qquad =$ diameter of orbit of Saturn.
Cube of sum of 2 sides
$\qquad =$ diameter of the earth.

The magnificent temple of Denderah (Tentyra) is the most perfect of all existing monuments in Egypt. The remains cover a great extent, and consist of various buildings and propyla, besides the temple itself. They are enclosed, with the exception of one propylon, within a square wall, whose side is 1000 feet, and built of sun-dried bricks. The wall is in some parts 35 feet high, and 15 thick.

Side of square = 1000 feet = 864·6 units

$$867^3 = \tfrac{3}{5} \text{ distance of the moon,}$$
$$(10 \times 867)^3 = \tfrac{3000}{5} = 600,$$
$$(10 \times 867, \&c.)^3 = 604 = \text{distance of Mars.}$$

Cube of 10 times side = distance of Mars nearly.

$$(15 \times 867)^3 = \tfrac{3}{5} \times 15^3 = 2025 \text{ distance of the moon,}$$
$$(15 \times 867, \&c.)^3 = 2045 \qquad \text{,,}$$

Cube of 15 times side = 2045 ,,
= distance of Jupiter.

Distance of Belus = 11 times distance of Jupiter
= 37 &c. ,, Mars,
$$(5 \times 867)^3 = \tfrac{3}{5} \times 5^3 = 75 \text{ distance of the moon,}$$
$$(10 \times 5 \times 867)^3 = 75000.$$

$\tfrac{1}{10}$ cube of 50 times side = 7500 distance of the moon,
= distance of Uranus,
$\tfrac{1}{20}$ cube ,, = ,, Saturn,
$\tfrac{3}{10}$ cube ,, = ,, Belus,
$$10 \times 869 = 8690^3,$$
distance of Mars = 8690³.

Cube of 10 times side of square
= distance of Mars.

Length of temple 265 feet, breadth 140,
265 by 140 feet,
= 229, &c. ,, 121·5 units, or $\tfrac{1}{2}$ stade,
229³, &c. = $\tfrac{1}{90}$ distance of the moon,
$$(3 \times 229, \&c.)^3 = \tfrac{1}{90} \times 3^3 = \tfrac{3}{10},$$
$$(10 \times 3 \times 229, \&c.)^3 = \tfrac{3000}{10} = 300.$$

Cube of 30 times greater side
    $= 300$ times distance of the moon,
    $=$ diameter of orbit of Mercury.

Cube of 4 times less side
    $=$ cube of 2 stades $=$ circumference.

Sum of 2 sides $= 229$, &c. $+ 121 \cdot 5 = 351$ units
    351^3, &c. $= \frac{1}{25}$ distance of the moon,
  $(5 \times 351, \text{&c.})^3 = \frac{1}{25} \times 5^3 = 5.$

Cube of 5 times sum of 2 sides
    $= 5$ times distance of the moon.

The ruins of the temple of Hermopolis, or the great city of Mercury, afford a precise idea of the immense range and the high perfection the arts had attained in Egypt. The stones have preserved their original destination, without having been altered or deformed by the works of modern times, and have remained untouched for 4000 years! They are of freestone, of the fineness of marble, and have neither cement, nor mode of union, besides the perfect fitting of the respective parts. The colossal proportions of this edifice evince the power the Egyptians possessed to raise enormous masses.

The diameter of the columns, which are placed at equal intermediate distances, is 8 feet 10 inches; and the space between the two middle columns, within which the gate was included, 12 feet, which gives 120 feet for the portico; its height is 60 feet. Not any spring of an arch remains to throw light on the dimensions of the whole extent of the temple, or of the nave. The architecture is still richer than the Doric order of the Greeks. The shafts of the pillars represent fasces, or bundles; and the pedestal the stem of the lotus. Under the roof between the two middle columns are winged globes; and all the roofs are ornamented with a wreath of painted stars, of an aurora colour on blue ground.

Side of portico $= 120$ feet $= 102 \cdot 75$ units
    Height $= \quad 60 \quad ,, \quad = \quad 51 \cdot 35 \quad ,,$
  $(10 \times 102 \cdot 8)^3 = 1028^3 =$ distance of the moon.

Cube of 10 times side = distance of the moon

$(10 \times 51\cdot4)^3 = 514^3 = \frac{1}{8}$ distance of the moon.

Cube of 10 times height = $\frac{1}{8}$ distance of the moon.

The sides are as 1 : 2.

Cube of 10 times sum of 2 sides = $\frac{27}{8}$ distance of the moon.

Cube of 10 times perimeter	= 27	,,
Cube of 20 times perimeter	= 216	,,
Or cube of 10 times perimeter	= 3^3	,,
Cube of 20 times perimeter	= 6^3	,,

The temple of Apollinopolis **Magna** is described by Denon as surpassing in extent, majesty, magnificence, and high preservation, whatever he had seen in Egypt or elsewhere. This building is a long suite of pyramidal gates, of courts decorated with galleries, of porticoes, and of covered naves, constructed, not with common stones, but with entire rocks. This superb edifice is situated on a rising ground, so as to overlook, not only its immediate vicinity, but the whole valley.

On the right is the principal gate, placed between two huge mounds of buildings, on the walls of which are three orders of hieroglyphic figures increasing in their gigantic dimensions, insomuch that the last have a proportion of 25 feet. The inner court is decorated with a gallery of columns, bearing two terraces, which come out at two gates, through which is a passage to the stairs leading to the platform of the mounds. Behind the inner portico are several apartments and the sanctuary of the temple. A wall of circumvallation is decorated both within and without with innumerable hieroglyphics, executed in a very finished and laborious style. This magnificent temple appears to have been dedicated to the evil genius, the figure of Typhon being represented in relief on the four sides of the plinth which surmounts each of the capitals. The entire frieze, and all the paintings within, are descriptive of Isis defending herself against the attacks of that monster.

The modern village of Karnac is built on a small part of the site of a single temple. The smallest of the 100 columns of the portico alone is $7\frac{1}{4}$ feet in diameter, and the largest 12. The avenue of sphinxes, leading from Karnac to Luxor, is nearly half a league in length.

The village of Luxor is built on the site of the ruins of a temple, not so large as that at Karnac, but in a better state of preservation, the masses not having yet fallen through time and the pressure of their own weight. The most colossal parts consist of 14 columns of nearly 11 feet in diameter, and of two statues in granite, at the outer gate, buried up to the middle of the arms, and have in front of them two large and well-preserved obelisks.

The peristyle court of the Luxor is about 232 feet long by 174, containing a double row of columns along the four sides.

$$232 \quad \text{by} \quad 174 \text{ feet.}$$
$$= 200, \&c. \text{ by } 150, \&c. \text{ units.}$$

$$200, \&c. = \tfrac{1}{3} \, 601,$$
$$601^3 = \tfrac{1}{5} \text{ distance of the moon,}$$
$$200^3 \&c. = \frac{1}{5} \times \frac{1}{3^3} = \frac{1}{135}$$
$$\therefore (3 \times 200, \&c.)^3 = 601^3 = \tfrac{1}{5}$$
$$(10 \times 3 \times 200, \&c.)^3 = \tfrac{1000}{5} = 200.$$

2 cubes of 30 times side
$$= 400 \text{ distance of moon} = \text{distance of earth.}$$
$$150, \&c. = \tfrac{1}{4} \, 601,$$
$$150^3, \&c. = \frac{1}{5} \times \frac{1}{4^3} = \frac{1}{320} \text{ distance of the moon,}$$
$$(4 \times 150, \&c.)^3 = \tfrac{1}{320} \times 4^3 = \tfrac{1}{5}$$
$$(10 \times 4 \times 150)^3 = \tfrac{1000}{5} = 200.$$

2 cubes of 40 times side
$$= 400 \text{ distance of moon} = \text{distance of earth.}$$

Sum of 2 sides $= 200, \&c. + 150, \&c. = 351$ units,
$$351^3, \&c. = \tfrac{4}{100} \text{ distance of the moon,}$$
$$(10 \times 351, \&c.)^3 = \tfrac{4000}{100} = 40.$$

10 cubes of 10 times sum of 2 sides,
$$= 400 \text{ distance of moon} = \text{distance of earth.}$$

Cube of 3 times greater side
$$=(3 \times 200, \&c.)^3 = \tfrac{1}{4} \text{ distance of the moon,}$$
$$= \text{cube of Cephrenes.}$$

Cube of 3 times less side
$$=(3 \times 150, \&c.)^3 = 3^3 \times \tfrac{1}{324} \text{ distance of the moon,}$$
$$= \tfrac{27}{324} = \tfrac{1}{12}, \qquad\qquad \text{,,}$$
$$= \tfrac{1}{4} \text{ pyramid of Cephrenes.}$$

Thus 2 cubes of 40 times less side,
> $= 2$ cubes of 30 times greater side,
> $= 10$ cubes of 10 times sum of 2 sides,
> $=$ distance of the earth.

There is a ruin at Karnac, supposed to have been the tomb of Osymandyas, 530 feet long and 200 wide.

$$530 \text{ by } 200 \text{ feet,}$$
$$= 458 \text{ by } 173 \text{ units,}$$
$$458^3, \&c. = \tfrac{8}{9} \text{ circumference} = 320 \text{ degrees,}$$
$$174^3, \&c. = \tfrac{8}{162} \qquad \text{,,}$$

Cubes of the 2 sides are as $\tfrac{8}{162} : \tfrac{8}{9} :: 1 : 18$,

Sum of the 2 sides $= 458 + 174 = 632$ units, and $632^3 =$
$$\tfrac{20}{9} \text{ circumference,}$$
$$458^3 : 632^3 :: \tfrac{8}{9} : \tfrac{20}{9} :: 2 : 5.$$

At the extremity of this court, near to the entrance into the second, and on the left hand side, are the fragments of that enormous sitting statue described as the largest in Egypt. Ascending some steps we pass a second pylon, and enter a second court of the same dimensions as the first; it is the peristyle, having a double row of columns all round.

Sides 458 by 173 units.

$$458^3 = \tfrac{8}{9} \text{ circumference,}$$
$$(6 \times 458)^3 = \tfrac{8}{9} \times 6^3 = 192.$$

20 cubes of 6 times side $= 3840$ circumference,
$$= \text{distance of the earth.}$$

$$(15 \times 458)^3 = \tfrac{8}{9} \times 15^3 = 3000 \text{ circumference.}$$

$$(2 \times 15 \times 458)^3 = 3000 \times 2^3 = 24000,$$

3 cubes of 30 times greater side = 72000 circumference,

$\qquad$ = distance of Uranus,

9 cubes $\qquad$,, $\qquad$ = ,, Belus.

$\qquad (6 \times 15 \times 458)^3 = 3000 \times 6^3 = 648000$ circumference.

Cube of 90 times greater side = 648000 circumference.

$\qquad$ Pyramid = $\frac{1}{3}$ cube = 216000 circumference,

$\qquad$ = distance of Belus.

Cube of less side = $\frac{1}{18}$ cube of greater.

So cube of 90 times less side,

$\qquad = \frac{1}{18}$ 648000 = 36000 circumference,

$\qquad$ = distance of Saturn,

2 cubes $\qquad$,, $\qquad$ = ,, Uranus,

6 cubes $\qquad$,, $\qquad$ = ,, Belus.

Sum of 2 sides = 458 + 173 = 631 units,

$\qquad 632^3 = \frac{20}{9}$ circumference.

$\qquad (3 \times 632)^3 = \frac{20}{9} \times 3^3 = 60.$

Cube of 3 times sum of 2 sides = 60 circumference.

$\qquad (2 \times 3 \times 632)^3 = 60 \times 2^3 = 480.$

3 cubes of 6 times sum of 2 sides,

$\qquad$ or of 3 times perimeter,

$\qquad$ = 1440 circumference = distance of Mercury,

$\qquad (2 \times 2 \times 3 \times 632)^3 = 480 \times 2^3 = 3840$ circumference.

Cube of 12 times sum of two sides,

$\qquad$ or of 6 times perimeter,

$\qquad$ = 3840 circumference = distance of the earth.

Sides 458 by 173 units,

$\qquad 80 \times 458 = 36640.$

$\qquad$ Diameter of orbit of Belus = 36640^3,

$\qquad 40 \times 172 = 6880^3.$

$\qquad$ Diameter of orbit of Mercury = $6880^2.$

Cube of 40 times less side

$\qquad$ = diameter of orbit of Mercury,

Cube of 80 times greater side

$\qquad$ = diameter of orbit of Belus.

As has been stated, 6880^3 is somewhat less than the estimated diameter of orbit of Mercury, which will be nearly the cube of 40 times 173.

Sum of 2 sides $= 458 + 173 = 631$,
$$12 \times 632 = 7584.$$
Distance of the earth $= 7584^3$,

Cube of 12 times sum of 2 sides,
         $=$ distance of the earth.

There are twelve principal approaches to the temple of Karnak, each of which is composed of several propyla and colossal gateways or moles, besides other buildings attached to them, in themselves larger than most temples. The adytum consists of three apartments entirely of granite. The principal room, which is in the centre, is twenty feet long, sixteen wide, and thirteen high.

Three blocks of granite form the roof, which is painted with clusters of stars on a blue ground. The walls are likewise covered with painted sculpture. Beyond this are other porticoes and galleries, which have been continued to another propylon at the distance of 2000 feet from that at the western extremity of the temple.

Adytum.

    20 by   16, height 13   feet ,
   $= 17 \cdot 29$,, $13 \cdot 83$,   ,, $11 \cdot 24$ units,

$(100 \times 17 \cdot 16)^3 = 1716^3 = \frac{48}{9}$ circumference,
$(3 \times 100 \times 17 \cdot 16)^3 = \frac{48}{9} \times 3^3 = 1200.$

.30 cubes of 300 times greater side,
     $= 36{,}000$ times circumference $=$ distance of Saturn.

60 cubes $=$ distance of Uranus.

Less side $= 13 \cdot 83$ units,

    $(100 \times 13 \cdot 76)^3 = 1376^3$ $= \frac{24}{10}$ distance of moon,
$(5 \times 100 \times 13 \cdot 76)^3 = \frac{24}{10} \times 5^3 = 300$,,

Cube of 500 times less side,

$$= \quad \text{300 times distance of moon,}$$
$$= \quad \text{diameter of orbit of mercury.}$$

150 cubes = diameter of orbit of Belus,

  50 ,, =   ,,   ,, Uranus,

  25 ,, =   ,,   ,, Saturn.

Height $= 11 \cdot 24$ units

$$(100 \times 11 \cdot 24)^3 = 1124^3 = \tfrac{40}{4} \text{ circumference,}$$
$$(2 \times 100 \times 11 \cdot 24)^3 = \tfrac{40}{4} \times 2^3 = 100.$$

Cube of 200 times height
$$= \quad \text{100 times circumference.}$$

$$(3 \times 2 \times 100 \times 11 \cdot 24)^3 = 100 \times 3^3 = 2700 \text{ circumference.}$$

Cube of 600 times height,
$$= \quad \text{2700 times circumference,}$$
$$= \text{distance of Venus,}$$

80 cubes = distance of Belus.

Content $= 17 \cdot 16 \times 13 \cdot 76 \times 11 \cdot 24 = 2661$ units,

$$266^3 \text{ \&c.} = \tfrac{1}{6} \text{ circumference,}$$
$$(6 \times 266 \text{ \&c.})^3 = \tfrac{1}{6} \times 6^3 = 36,$$
$$(10 \times 6 \times 266 \text{ \&c.}) = 36{,}000.$$

Cube of   6 times content,
$$= \quad \text{36000 times circumference,}$$
$$= \quad \text{distance of Saturn ;}$$

or,   Cube of 6 times content,
$$= \quad 6^2 \times 10^3 \text{ circumference,}$$
$$= \quad \text{distance of 6th planet.}$$

Cube of $\tfrac{1}{10}$ content $= \tfrac{1}{6}$ circumference.

6 cubes of 6 times content
$$= \quad 6^3 \times 10^3 \text{ circumference,}$$
$$= \quad \text{distance of Belus,}$$
$$= \quad \text{6 times distance of Saturn.}$$

Adytum.

17·29 by 13·83 units,
if 17·2   „   13·65   „
then $400 \times 17·2 = 6880$,

Diameter of orbit of Mercury $= 6880^3$.
$400 \times 13·65 = 5460$,
distance of Mercury $= 5460^3$.

Thus cube of 400 times less side
$=$ distance of Mercury.

And cube of 400 times greater side
$=$ diameter of orbit of Mercury.

The cubes of the sides are as 1 : 2.

Sum of 2 sides $= 17·2 + 13·65 = 30·85$;
distance of Belus $= 30·7^9$, &c.

Sum of 2 sides to the power of 3 times 3
$=$ distance of Belus,
$=$ cube of Babylon.

Distance 2000 feet $= 1729$ units,
if $= 1720$ „
$4 \times 1720 = 6880$,
$6880^3 =$ diameter of orbit of Mercury.

Cube of 4 times distance
$=$ diameter of orbit of Mercury.

The width of the magnificent hypostyle hall of Karnac is
about 338 feet, and the length or depth (measured in the
direction of the axis of the building) 170¼ feet. " The
imagination," says Champollion, " which in Europe rises far
above our porticoes, sinks abashed at the foot of 140
columns of the hypostyle hall of Karnac."

338   by 170·5 feet,
$= 292$, &c. „   147, &c. units,

293^3, &c. $= \frac{2}{9}$ circumference $= 80$ degrees,
146^3, &c. $= \frac{2}{7\cdot 9}$ „ $= 10$ „

The sides of the hall are as 1 : 2.

The cubes of the sides are as 1 : 8.

Sides of the hall are 292, &c. by 147, &c.

$$\text{if } 291 \cdot 6 \quad \text{,, } \quad 145 \cdot 8,$$

$$100 \times 145 \cdot 8 = 14580,$$

$$\tfrac{1}{8} \text{ distance of Belus} = 14580^2.$$

$$100 \times 291 \cdot 6 = 29160,$$

$$\text{distance of Belus} = 14580^3.$$

Thus cube of 100 times less side
$$= \tfrac{1}{8} \text{ distance of Belus.}$$

Cube of 100 times greater side
$$= \text{distance of Belus,}$$
$$= \text{cube of Babylon,}$$

Sphere = distance of Neptune,
Pyramid =   ,,   Uranus,
$$= \text{diameter of orbit of Saturn.}$$

The sides are as 1 : 2.

The cubes are as 1 : 8.

The large edifice at Medinet-Abou, commonly called a palace, consists of a peristyle court (the second, there being one in front of it), on the north and south sides of which there is the usual kind of column, five on each side. On the east and west sides there are respectively eight square pillars, with caryatid figures in front of them facing one another. On the west side of this court is a second row of regular columns, behind the caryatid pillars and parallel to them. The whole length of this court from east to west is $123\tfrac{1}{2}$ feet, the breadth from north to south $144\tfrac{1}{3}$.

$$\text{Court } 123 \cdot 5 \quad \text{by } 144 \cdot 3 \text{ feet,}$$
$$= 106 \cdot 78 \text{ by } 124 \cdot 77 \text{ units.}$$

$$106^3, \&c. = {}_{9 \, 0 \, 0}\tfrac{1}{} \text{ distance of the moon,}$$
$$(10 \times 106, \&c.)^3 = \tfrac{1 \, 0 \, 0 \, 0}{9 \, 0 \, 0} = \tfrac{1 \, 0}{9},$$
$$(3 \times 10 \times 106, \&c.) = \tfrac{1 \, 0}{9} \times 3^3 = 30,$$

Cube of 30 times less side,
$$= 30 \text{ times distance of the moon.}$$

5 cubes $= 150$ times distance of the moon.
$\qquad = $ distance of Mercury.

$$\text{Greater side} = 124\cdot77 \text{ units,}$$
$$125^3 = \tfrac{9}{8000} \text{ distance of the moon,}$$
$$(10 \times 125)^3 = \tfrac{9000}{8000} = \tfrac{9}{8}$$
$$(10 \times 10 \times 125)^3 = \tfrac{9000}{5} = 1800,$$
$$(5 \times 10 \times 125)^3 = \tfrac{9}{8} \times 5^3 = 225.$$

100 cubes of 50 times side,
$\qquad = 22500$ times distance of the moon,
$\qquad = $ distance of Belus.

$$(10 \times 5 \times 10 \times 125)^3 = 225 \times 10^3 = 225000.$$
$\tfrac{1}{10}$ cube of 500 times side,
$\qquad = 22500$ distance of the moon,
$\qquad = $ distance of Belus.

Sum of 2 sides $= 106$, &c. $+ 125 = 231$, &c. units,
$\qquad 231^3$, &c. $= \tfrac{8}{700}$ distance of the moon,
$$(10 \times 231, \text{ \&c.})^3 = \tfrac{8000}{700} = \tfrac{80}{7}$$
$$(7 \times 10 \times 231, \text{ \&c.})^3 = \tfrac{80}{7} \times 7^3 = 3920.$$

3 cubes of 70 times sum of 2 sides,
$\qquad$ or of 35 times perimeter,
$\qquad = 11760$ distance of the moon,
$\qquad 11770 = $ distance of Neptune.

$$\text{Or court } 107 \text{ by } 125 \text{ units,}$$
$$\text{if} \quad 109\cdot2 \quad ,, \quad 126\cdot4.$$
$$50 \times 109\cdot2 = 5460,$$
$$\text{Distance of Mercury} = 5460^3.$$
$$60 \times 126\cdot4 = 7584,$$
$$\text{Distance of the earth} = 7584^3.$$

Thus cube of 50 times less side,
$\qquad = $ distance of Mercury.

Cube of 60 times greater side,
$\qquad = $ distance of the earth.

Sum of 2 sides $= 109\cdot2 + 126\cdot4 = 235\cdot6,$
$\qquad 235^3$, &c. $= \tfrac{6}{800}$ distance of the moon,
$$(10 \times 235, \text{ \&c.})^3 = \tfrac{6000}{800} = 12.$$

Cube of 10 times sum of 2 sides,
  or of 5 times perimeter,

  $= 12$ times distance of the moon.

Cube of 5×5 times perimeter,
  $= 12 \times 5^3 = 1500$ distance of the moon.

  5 cubes of 25 times perimeter,
        $= 7500$ distance of the moon,
        $=$ distance of Uranus,
  15 cubes $=$,,   Belus.

  or distance of Jupiter $= 23 \cdot 5^9$, &c.

$\frac{1}{10}$ sum of 2 sides to the power of 3 times $3 =$ distance of Jupiter.

Pococke and Hamilton suppose that the buildings of Medinet-Abou may be the Memnonium of Strabo. Belzoni found traces of a tank to the north of the small temple, which must have had statues all round it, as various fragments were discovered in making excavations. He found in this temple, also, stones with inverted hieroglyphics turned upside down, showing that it was built of the materials of an older edifice.

Others suppose these buildings to be the tomb of Osymandyas, described by Diodorus, who mentions two seated statues, each of a single stone, $40\frac{1}{2}$ feet high, being placed there.

$40\frac{1}{2}$ Babylonian feet $= 19\frac{3}{4}$ feet English.

The colossal head, now in the British Museum, called the head of Memnon, was found in the temple now commonly called the Memnonium, or temple of Memnon. The figure was in a sitting posture, like most of the Egyptian colossal statues, for Belzoni found it " near the remains of its body and chair." Though a statue of colossal size, it is very inferior in magnitude to some works of Egyptian art of this kind; its height from the sole of the foot to the top of the head, in its sitting position, having been probably about 24 feet, or somewhat less. The fragment in the Museum, which may be about one-third of the whole, is somewhat more than 8 feet in height.

From the court where the colossus was found, a flight of steps leads into an hypostyle hall of 10 columns in the breadth and 6 in the depth, the two centre rows containing, as usual, the largest pillars; they are 35 feet high and about 19 in circumference.

It is exceedingly difficult to procure exact measurements and descriptions of such buildings as those at Thebes, which is owing not only to the enormity of the masses, but also to the state of ruin in which many parts of those edifices are now lying. In the French plan, the whole length of the palace of Karnak, from the western extremity to the eastern wall, is about 1215 feet. This is the length of the real building itself, not taking into the account any propyla that may have existed on the eastern side, or any part beyond the walls of the edifice. The breadth of the narrowest part is 321 feet; the longest line of width being that of the front propylon, which has been already stated to be about 360 feet.

$$1215 \text{ feet} = 1049 \cdot 28 \text{ units,}$$
$$321 \text{ feet} = 277 \cdot 55 \quad \text{,,}$$
$$1028^3 = \text{distance of the moon,}$$
$$279^3 = \tfrac{1}{50} \qquad \text{,,}$$
$$\text{Length} = 1050 \text{ units,}$$
$$\tfrac{1}{2} = 525$$
$$525^3 = \tfrac{4}{3} \text{ circumference,}$$
$$(3 \times 525)^3 = \tfrac{4}{3} \times 3^3 = 36,$$
$$(10 \times 3 \times 525)^3 = 36000.$$

Cube of 30 times 525,
    or of 15 times length $= 36000$ circumference,
                 $=$ distance of Saturn,

| 2 cubes | - | - | $=$ | ,, | Uranus, |
| 6 cubes | - | - | $=$ | ,, | Belus. |

    Breadth $= 279$ units,
$$279^3 = \tfrac{1}{50} \text{ distance of the moon,}$$
$$(10 \times 279)^3 = \tfrac{1000}{50} = 20.$$

20 cubes of 20 times breadth $= 400$ distance of moon,
                        $=$,,   earth.

But the dimensions, like those of many other monuments, are too vague for consideration. For want of accurate measurements, we have been left to conjecture, and made hypothetical calculations ; these, however, may be corrected when the true dimensions have been ascertained : then, no doubt, many of the results will be found to be very different from these calculations, which have been made with a view of directing attention to the subject, and obtaining correct results. Many of the buildings noticed may have been constructed without reference to the cubes of their sides : also celebrated temples continued to have additions made to them in succeeding ages.

In measuring the monuments of great antiquity, it will be requisite to take the internal and external dimensions of the buildings, as well as of the surrounding walls, mounds, or fosses ; and likewise those of the Druidical structures and circles, with their surrounding mounds and trenches ; as well as the length and breadth of the avenues.

The temple of Edfou, though not the most ancient of the existing monuments, is one of the most imposing in its appearance, and one of the completest both in its great outline and its smaller details. It stands on the west side of the river (N. lat. 25°) on a small eminence on the plain, which has here an unusually low level. The temple is exceedingly encumbered with rubbish, both outside and inside.

The entrance is composed of two pyramidal moles, sometimes called propylæa by modern writers, each front of which is about 104 feet long and 35 wide at the base ; the moles are about 114 feet high. These dimensions of the base (104 by 35 feet) diminish gradually from the base to the summit, where the horizontal section is 84 by 20 feet. They are, in fact, truncated pyramids, with a rectangular base (not a square), and sides inclining less to one another than in the regular pyramids.

Sides of base 104 by 35 feet,
$$= 89 \cdot 9 \text{ by } 30 \text{ units,}$$
$$(10 \times 89 \cdot 9)^3 = 899^3 = \tfrac{2}{3} \text{ distance of the moon.}$$

o 4

3 cubes of 10 times side = diameter of orbit of the moon.
less side = 30 units,

$(10 \times 30) = 300$, and 300^3, &c. $= \frac{1}{40}$ dist. of moon.
$(10 \times 10 \times 30)^3 = \frac{1000}{40} = 25$.

6 cubes of 100 times side = 150 distance of the moon,
= distance of Mercury.

Sum of 2 sides $= 89 \cdot 9 + 30 = 119 \cdot 9$ units,
119^3, &c. $= \frac{3}{200}$ circumference,
$(10 \times 119,$ &c.$)^3 = \frac{3000}{200} = 15$,
$(4 \times 10 \times 119,$ &c.$)^3 = 15 \times 4^3 = 960$.

4 cubes of 40 times sum of 2 sides,
or of 20 times perimeter,
= 3840 circumference = distance of the earth.

Top section 84 by 20 feet,
72·63 by 17·3 units,
$(10 \times 72 \cdot 5)^3 = 725^3 = \frac{7}{20}$ distance of the moon,
$(10 \times 10 \times 72 \cdot 5)^3 = \frac{7000}{20} = 350$,
$(2 \times 10 \times 10 \times 72 \cdot 5)^3 = 350 \times 2^3 = 2800$.
Cube of 200 times side = 10 times distance of Venus.
less side = 17·3,

$(10 \times 17 \cdot 5,$ &c.$)^3 = 175^3$, &c. $= \frac{1}{200}$ dist. moon.
$(10 \times 10 \times 17 \cdot 5,$ &c.$)^3 = \frac{1000}{200} = 5$,
$(2 \times 10 \times 10 \times 17 \cdot 5,$ &c.$)^3 = 5 \times 2^3 = 40$.
10 cubes of 200 times side = 400 distance of the moon,
= distance of the earth.

Sum of 2 sides $= 72 \cdot 5 + 17 \cdot 5 = 90$,
$(10 \times 89 \cdot 9)^3 = 899^3 = \frac{4}{3}$ distance of the moon.

3 cubes of 10 times sum of 2 sides,
or of   5 times perimeter,
diameter of orbit of the moon.

Height 114 feet = 98·57 units,
$(10 \times 99 \cdot 2)^3 = 992^3 = \frac{2}{10}$ distance of the moon,
$(10 \times 10 \times 99 \cdot 2)^3 = \frac{2000}{10} = 900$.

Cube of 100 times height $=900$ distance of the moon,
$\frac{1}{6}$ cube   - $=150$,,
                               $=$ distance of Mercury,
25 cubes   - $=$,,   Belus.
   Greater side of base $=$ sum of 2 sides at top,
   Less side of base $=\frac{1}{3}$ greater side.

It is not stated whether or not the measurement at the top include the pylonic curved projection.

The portico consists of eighteen pillars, six in a row, the intercolumniation of the central ones, forming the doorway, being, as is usual, the greatest.

The whole height of the portico above the lowest level of the court is about 56 feet.

The external sides of the portico are

$$133 \quad \text{by} \quad 61 \cdot 3 \text{ feet,}$$
$$= 114, \&c. \text{ ,, } 53 \text{ units,}$$
$$114^3, \&c. = \tfrac{1}{720} \text{ distance of the moon,}$$
$$53^3, \&c. = \tfrac{1}{7200} \text{ ,,}$$

The cubes of the sides are as $1 : 10$.

Sides of the portico are

$$114, \&c. \text{ by } 53, \&c. \text{ units,}$$
$$114^3, \&c. = \tfrac{1}{720} \text{ distance of the moon,}$$
$$(6 \times 114, \&c.)^3 = \tfrac{1}{720} \times 6^3 = \tfrac{216}{720} = \tfrac{1}{3},$$
$$(3 \times 6 \times 114, \&c.)^3 = \tfrac{1}{3} \times 3^3 = 9,$$
$$(5 \times 3 \times 6 \times 114, \&c.)^3 = 9 \times 5^3 = 1125.$$

20 cubes of 90 times greater side
$$= 22500 \text{ distance of the moon,}$$
$$= \text{distance of Belus.}$$

$$53^3, \&c. = \tfrac{1}{7200} \text{ distance of the moon,}$$
$$(10 \times 53, \&c.)^2 = \tfrac{1000}{7200} = \tfrac{10}{72},$$
$$(6 \times 10 \times 53, \&c.)^3 = \tfrac{10}{72} \times 6^3 = \tfrac{2160}{72} = 30,$$
$$(5 \times 6 \times 10 \times 53, \&c.)^3 = 30 \times 5^3 = 3750.$$

Cube of 300 times less side
$$= 3750 \text{ distance of the moon,}$$

$=$ distance of Saturn,

2 cubes $=$,,   Uranus,

6 cubes $=$,,   Belus.

Sum of 2 sides $= 167$, &c. units

$$167^3, \text{&c.} = \tfrac{1}{24} \text{ circumference},$$

$$(6 \times 167, \text{&c.})^3 = \tfrac{1}{24} \times 6^3 = \tfrac{216}{24} = 9,$$

$$(2 \times 6 \times 167, \text{&c.})^3 = 9 \times 2^3 = 72,$$

$$(10 \times 2 \times 6 \times 167, \text{&c.})^3 = 72000.$$

Cube of 120 times sum of 2 sides

or of   60 times perimeter,

     $= 72000$ circumference $=$ distance of Uranus,

                     3 cubes $=$,,   Belus.

Thus 20 cubes of   90 times greater side

     $= 6$,,   300 times less side,

     $= 3$,,   120 times sum of 2 sides.

Or sides of portico 114, &c. by 53, &c. units,

          if $114 \cdot 7$,, $54 \cdot 6$,,

      then $60 \times 114 \cdot 7 = 6880$,

     diameter of orbit of Mercury $= 6880^3$.

         $100 \times 54 \cdot 6 = 5460$,

     distance of Mercury $= 5460^3$.

Thus cube of 60 times greater side

     $=$ diameter of orbit of Mercury.

Cube of 100 times less side

     $=$ distance of Mercury.

Or should less side $= 52 \cdot 1$ units,

         $60 \times 52 \cdot 1 = 3126$,

     $\tfrac{1}{10}$ distance of Venus $= 3126^3$.

Cube of 60 times less side

      $\tfrac{1}{10}$ distance of Venus.

Cube of 60 times perimeter

      $=$ distance of Uranus.

Sum of 2 sides $= 114 \cdot 7 + 54 \cdot 6 = 169$,

       40×168, &c. $= 6740$,

     distance of Venus $= 6740^3$.

Cube of 40 times sum of 2 sides
or of 20 times perimeter,
$$= \text{distance of Venus.}$$

Cube of 40 times perimeter
$$= 8 \text{ times distance of Venus,}$$
$$= \tfrac{1}{10} \text{ distance of Belus.}$$

The sides of the wall that enclose the adytum and hypostyle hall are

$$172 \quad \text{by } 55 \text{ feet,}$$
$$= 148 \cdot 7 \quad ,, \quad 47 \cdot 56 \text{ units,}$$
$$10 \times 148 = 1480,$$
$$\tfrac{1}{2} = \quad 740,$$
$$(3 \times 740)^3 = 10 \text{ distance of moon,}$$
$$(3 \times 2 \times 740)^3 = 10 \times 2^3 = 80.$$

10 cubes of 30 times greater side
$$= 800 \text{ distance of the moon,}$$
$$= \text{diameter of orbit of the earth.}$$

Less side $= 47 \cdot 56$ units,
$$(10 \times 47 \cdot 7)^3 = 477^3 = \tfrac{1}{10} \text{ distance of the moon,}$$
$$(10 \times 10 \times 47 \cdot 7)^3 = \tfrac{1000}{10} = 100,$$
$$(2 \times 10 \times 10 \times 47 \cdot 7)^3 = 800.$$

Cube of 200 times less side
$$= 800 \text{ times distance of the moon,}$$
$$= \text{diameter of orbit of the earth.}$$

Sum of 2 sides $= 148 \cdot 7 + 47 \cdot 56 = 196 \cdot 26$ units,
$$10 \times 196 \cdot 2 = 1962,$$
$$\tfrac{1}{2} = \quad 981,$$
$$981^3, \&\text{c.} = \tfrac{50}{6} \text{ circumference,}$$
$$(6 \times 981, \&\text{c.})^3 = \tfrac{50}{6} \times 6^3 = 1800,$$
$$(6 \times 981, \&\text{c.}) = 3 \times 2 \times 981 = 3 \times 1962 = 30 \times 196 \cdot 2$$
so $(30 \times 196 \cdot 2)^3 = 1800.$

20 cubes of 30 times sum of 2 sides
or of 15 times perimeter $= 36000$ circumference,
$$= \text{distance of Saturn.}$$

If greater side $= 148 \cdot 2$ units,
$$10 \times 148 \cdot 2 = 1482,$$

$1482^3 = 3$ distance of the moon,
$(4 \times 1482)^3 = 3 \times 4^3 = 192.$

20 cubes of 40 times greater side $= 3840$ circumference,
$\qquad\qquad\qquad\qquad = $ distance of the earth.

The great court is 161 feet by 133,
$\qquad\qquad$ 161 by 133 feet,
$\qquad\quad = 135{\cdot}2 \;,,\;\; 115$ units,
$\qquad\qquad 115^3 = \frac{4}{300}$ circumference,
$(10 \times 115)^3 = \frac{4000}{300} = \frac{40}{3},$
$(3 \times 10 \times 115)^3 = \frac{40}{3} \times 3^3 = 360.$

Cube of 30 times side $= 360$ circumference.

100 cubes $= 36000$ circumference $=$ distance of Saturn.
$\qquad\qquad 135^3, \&c. = \frac{8}{900}$ distance of the moon,
$(10 \times 135, \&c.)^3 = \frac{8000}{900} = \frac{80}{9},$
$(3 \times 10 \times 135, \&c.)^3 = \frac{80}{9} \times 3^3 = 60.$

5 cubes of 30 times side $= 300$ distance of the moon,
$\qquad\qquad\qquad\qquad = $ diameter of orbit of Mercury.

Sum of 2 sides $= 115 + 135, \&c. = 250, \&c.$ units,
$\qquad\qquad 251^3, \&c. = \frac{7}{80}$ circumference,
$(10 \times 251, \&c.)^3 = \frac{1000}{80} = 140,$
$(2 \times 10 \times 251, \&c.)^3 = 140 \times 2^3 = 1120.$

100 cubes of 20 times sum of 2 sides
$\qquad$ or of 10 times perimeter $= 112000$ circumference,
$\qquad\qquad$ distance of Neptune $= 113000 \qquad\qquad ,,$

External wall of the temple
$\qquad\qquad$ 415 by 154 feet,
$\qquad\quad = 358{\cdot}82 \;,,\; 133{\cdot}15$ units,
$\qquad\quad 361^3, \&c. = \frac{5}{12}$ circumference,
$(12 \times 361)^3 = \frac{5}{12} \times 12^3 = 5 \times 144 = 720.$

2 cubes of 12 times greater side $= 1440$ circumference,
$\qquad\qquad\qquad\qquad = $ distance of Mercury,

50	,,	,,	=	,,	Saturn,
100	,,	,,	=	,,	Uranus,
300	,,	,,	=	,,	Belus.

or $357^3 = \frac{1}{10}$ circumference.

less side $= 133 \cdot 12$ units,

133^3, &c. $= \frac{1}{48}$ circumference,

$(2 \times 133)^3 = \frac{8}{48} = \frac{1}{6}$,

$(6 \times 2 \times 133)^3 = \frac{1}{6} \times 6^3 = 36$,

$(10 \times 6 \times 2 \times 133, \&c.)^3 = 36000$.

Cube of 120 times less side $= 36000$ circumference,

$\qquad\qquad\qquad\qquad = $ distance of Saturn,

| 2 cubes | ,, | = | ,, | Uranus, |
| 6 cubes | ,, | = | ,, | Belus. |

Sum of 2 sides $= 361 + 133 = 494$ units,

$494^3 = \frac{1}{9}$ distance of the moon,

$(3 \times 494)^3 = \frac{1}{9} \times 3^3 = 3$.

Cube of 3 times sum of 2 sides
$\qquad = 3$ times distance of the moon.

Sides $358 \cdot 82$ by $133 \cdot 15$ units,

if 364, &c. ,, 136, &c.

40×364, &c. $= 14580$,

$\frac{1}{8}$ distance of Belus $= 14580^3$,

80×364, &c. $= 29160$,

distance of Belus $= 29160^3$,

40×136, &c. $= 5460$,

distance of Mercury $= 5460^3$.

Thus cube of 40 times greater side
$\qquad\qquad = \frac{1}{8}$ distance of Belus.

Cube of 40 times less side
$\qquad\qquad = $ distance of Mercury.

Sum of 2 sides $364 + 136 = 510$ units,

$\qquad\qquad 40 \times 510 = 20400$,

$\qquad$ distance of Uranus $=$ about 20300^3.

Cube of 40 times sum of 2 sides
$\qquad\qquad = $ distance of Uranus.

Hypostyle hall of 18 pillars
$\qquad$ Sides 67 by 34 feet,
$\qquad\qquad = 57 \cdot 92$,, $29 \cdot 4$ units,

$(10 \times 58,\ \&c.)^3 = \frac{9}{80}$ distance of the moon,

$(5 \times 10 \times 58,\ \&c.)^3 = \frac{9}{80} \times 5^3 = \frac{225}{10}$,

$(10 \times 5 \times 10 \times 58,\ \&c.)^3 = \frac{225000}{10} = 22500$.

Cube of 500 times greater side
$= 22500$ times distance of the moon,
$=$ distance of Belus.

Sphere =   ,,   Neptune,
Pyramid =   ,,   Uranus.

Less side = 29·4 units
$(10 \times 28\cdot9)^3 = 289^3 = \frac{1}{45}$ distance of the moon,
$(45 \times 10 \times 28\cdot9)^3 = \frac{1}{45} \times 45^3 = 2025$.

Cube of 450 times less side = 2025,
distance of Jupiter = 2045.

Sum of 2 sides = 58 + 28·9 = 86·9 units,
$(10 \times 86\cdot7)^3 = 867^3 = \frac{6}{10}$ distance of the moon,
$(10 \times 10 \times 86\cdot7)^3 = \frac{6000}{10} = 600$.

Cube of 100 times sum of 2 sides
or of 50 times perimeter,

$= 600$ times distance of moon,
$=$ 4   ,,   Mercury,
distance of Mars = 604 distance of the moon.

Sides 57·92   by 29·4 units,
if 57·3, &c. ,, 29·16 ,,
then $120 \times 57\cdot3$, &c. = 6880 ,,

diameter of orbit of Mercury = 6880³.
$1000 \times 29\cdot16 = 29160$,
distance of Belus = 29160³.

Thus cube of 120 times greater side
= diameter of orbit of Mercury.

And cube of 1000 times less side
= distance of Belus.

The adytum is   33 by 17 feet,
$= 28\cdot53$ by 14·7 units,

$(10 \times 14 \cdot 82)^3 = \frac{3}{1000}$ distance of the moon,
$(10 \times 10 \times 14 \cdot 82)^3 = \frac{3000}{1000} = 3$.

Cube of 100 times less side $= 3$ distance of the moon.
$(10 \times 28 \cdot 4)^3 = 284^3 = \frac{1}{5}$ circumference,
$(10 \times 10 \times 28 \cdot 4)^3 = \frac{1000}{5} = 200$,
$(6 \times 10 \times 10 \times 28 \cdot 4)^3 = 200 \times 6^3 = 43200$.

5 cubes of 600 times greater side,
$= 5 \times 43200 = 216000$ circumference $=$ distance of Belus.

Sum of 2 sides $= 28 \cdot 4 + 14 \cdot 82 = 43 \cdot 22$,
$(10 \times 43 \cdot 2, \&c.)^3 = 432^3, \&c. = \frac{4}{7}$ circumference,
$(7 \times 10 \times 43 \cdot 2, \&c.)^3 = \frac{4}{7} \times 7^3 = 245$,
$(2 \times 7 \times 10 \times 43 \cdot 2, \&c.)^3 = 245 \times 2^3 = 1960$.

10 cubes of 140 times sum of 2 sides,
or of 70 times perimeter,
$= 19600$ circumference,
19636 ,, $=$ distance of Jupiter.

Greater side $= 28 \cdot 53$ units,
and $28 \cdot 6^9 =$ distance of Neptune.

Or sides are $28 \cdot 53$ by $14 \cdot 7$ units,
if $29 \cdot 16$ by $14 \cdot 58$,
then $1000 \times 29 \cdot 16 = 29160$.
Distance of Belus $= 29160^3$,
$1000 \times 14 \cdot 58 = 14580$,
$\frac{1}{8}$ distance of Belus $= 14580^3$.

Thus cube of 1000 times greater side,
$=$ distance of Belus,
$=$ cube of Babylon,

and cube of 1000 times less side,
$= \frac{1}{8}$ distance of Belus.

The sides are as 1 : 2,
The cubes ,, 1 : 8.

The doorway of an Egyptian propylon is one of the most imposing parts of the architecture. In this instance, the

whole height, from the base of the doorway to the top of
the cornice, is 74½ feet, and the height of the entrance itself
about 51¾, leaving 22¾ for the architrave, the noble mould-
ing, the frieze, and the cornice that surmount it.   The
width of the doorway is the same all the way from the
bottom to the top, the whole width being 40⅓ feet, and
that of the passage itself 17¾.   The winged globe, flanked
on each side by the erect serpent, ornaments, as usual, the
frieze of the doorway.

Entrance Passage.

Height $= 51\cdot75$ feet $= 44\cdot74$ units,
Breadth $= 40\cdot3$,, $= 34\cdot84$,
Length $= 17\cdot75$,, $= 15\cdot34$,
Content $= 44\cdot74 \times 34\cdot84 \times 15\cdot34 = 23911$,
  Distance of Neptune $=$ about 23400^3.

$23911^{\frac{1}{3}} = 28\cdot8$,
$23400^{\frac{1}{3}} = 28\cdot6$,
  $28\cdot6^9 =$ distance of Neptune.
  Height $= 44\cdot74$,
  $(10 \times 44\cdot9)^3 = 449^3$, &c. $= \frac{1}{4}$ circumference,
$(5 \times 10 \times 44\cdot9)^3 = \frac{1}{4} \times 5^3 = 100$,
$(3 \times 5 \times 10 \times 44\cdot9)^3 = 100 \times 3^3 = 2700$.

Cube of 150 times height $= 2700$ circumference,
  $=$ distance of **Venus**,
80 cubes   ,, $=$,,   **Belus.**
Cube of 15 times height $= 100$ circumference,
360 cubes   ,, $= 36000$,
  $=$ distance of **Saturn.**

Cube of 30 times height $= 800$ circumference,
  45 cubes $=$ distance of **Saturn,**
  90 ,, $=$,,   **Uranus,**
  270 ,, $=$,,   **Belus.**
Cube of 90 times height $= 800 \times 3^3 =$ 21600 circumference,
10 cubes of 90   ,, $= 216000$,,
  $=$ distance of **Belus,**
10 spheres   ,, $=$,,   **Neptune.**

Greater side $= 34 \cdot 84$ units,

$(10 \times 34 \cdot 9, \&c.)^3 = 349^3, \&c. = \frac{3}{8}$ circumference,

$(2 \times 10 \times 34 \cdot 9, \&c.)^3 = \frac{3}{8} \times 8 = 3,$

$(10 \times 2 \times 10 \times 34 \cdot 9, \&c.)^3 = 3000$

$(6 \times 10 \times 2 \times 10 \times 34 \cdot 9, \&c.)^3 = 3000 \times 6^3 = 3 \times 216000$ circumference.

Cube of 1200 times side $\qquad = 3$ times distance of Belus,

$\frac{1}{3}$ cube $=$ pyramid $=$ distance of Belus.

otherwise $(10 \times 34 \cdot 4)^3 = 344^3 = \frac{3}{8 \cdot 0}$ distance of the moon,

$(2 \times 10 \times 34 \cdot 4)^3 = \frac{3}{8 \cdot 0} \times 2^3 = \frac{3}{1 \cdot 0},$

$(10 \times 2 \times 10 \times 34 \cdot 4)^3 = \frac{3 \cdot 0 \cdot 0}{1 \cdot 0} = 300.$

Cube of 200 times greater side,

$= 300$ times distance of the moon,

$=$ diameter of orbit of Mercury.

Less side $= 15 \cdot 34$ units,

$(10 \times 15 \cdot 3, \&c.)^3 = 153^3, \&c. = \frac{1}{3 \cdot 0 \cdot 0}$ distance of moon,

or $(10 \times 15 \cdot 0, \&c.)^3 = 150^3, \&c. = \frac{3}{1 \cdot 0 \cdot 0}$ circumference.

Taking greater side $= 34 \cdot 4,$

less side $= 15 \cdot 0,$

Sum $= 49 \cdot 4,$

$(10 \times 49 \cdot 4)^3 = 494^3 = \frac{1}{6}$ distance of the moon,

$(3 \times 10 \times 49 \cdot 4)^3 = \frac{1}{6} \times 3^3 = 3.$

Cube of 30 times sum of two sides,

3 times distance of the moon.

Height $= 44 \cdot 9$ units,

Then content will $= 44 \cdot 9 \times 34 \cdot 4 \times 15 = 23168$ units,

or content will $= 44 \cdot 9 \times 34 \cdot 9 \times 15 = 23505,$

Distance of Neptune $=$ about $\qquad 23400^3.$

Hence it appears that this temple of a distant epoch was entered by a portal that conducted the Sabæan from earth to heaven, or to the most remote of the planets now known, and only very recently discovered.

The solidity and grandeur of the temple accorded with the sublimity of the religion of the Sabæans, whose God was the creator and preserver of the universe.

2 less side $= 2 \times 15 \cdot 34 = 30 \cdot 68$ units,

Distance of Belus, $= 30 \cdot 7^9$,

$\frac{1}{2}$ greater side $= \frac{1}{2} \, 34 \cdot 9 = 17 \cdot 45$,

Distance of Mercury $= 17 \cdot 6^9$.

Thus twice less side to the power of 3 times 3
$$= \text{distance of Belus.}$$

Half the greater side to the power of 3 times 3
$$= \text{distance of Mercury.}$$

Sum of 2 sides $= 15 \cdot 34 + 34 \cdot 9 = 50 \cdot 24$,

mean $= 25 \cdot 12$,

Distance of Saturn   ,, $= 25 \cdot 2^9$,

or mean of the two sides to the power of 3 times 3
$$= \text{distance of Saturn.}$$

$\frac{1}{2}$ height $= \frac{1}{2} \, 44 \cdot 9 = 22 \cdot 45$,

$22 \cdot 45^9$ lies between Mars and Jupiter.

Should height $= 44 \cdot 3$ units,

$(10 \times 44 \cdot 3)^3 = 443^3 = \frac{8}{100}$ distance of the moon,

$(10 \times 10 \times 44 \cdot 3)^3 = \frac{8000}{100} = 80$.

5 cubes of 100 times height $= 400$ distance of the moon,
$$= \text{distance of the earth.}$$

$(5 \times 10 \times 44 \cdot 3)^3 = \frac{8}{100} \times 5^3 = \frac{1000}{100} = 10$,

Cube of 50 times height $= 10$ times distance of the moon.

$(10 \times 5 \times 10 \times 44 \cdot 3)^3 = 10 \times 10^3 = 10000$,

Cube of 500 times height $= 10000$ distance of the moon.

Sum of 2 sides $= 50 \cdot 24$ units,

height $= 44 \cdot 3$

$\overline{ = 90 \cdot 54,}$

$\frac{1}{4} = 23 \cdot 63$,

Distance of Jupiter $= 23 \cdot 6^9$,

or one-fourth (sum of 2 sides + height) to the power of 3 times 3 $=$ distance of Jupiter.

Height of doorway to the top of the cornice $= 74 \cdot 5$ feet $= 64 \cdot 4$ units,

$(10 \times 64 \cdot 7)^3 = 647^3 = \frac{1}{4}$ distance of the moon,

$(2 \times 10 \times 64 \cdot 7)^3 = \frac{8}{4} \quad = 2$,,

Cube of 20 times height = diameter of orbit of moon,
  „   10   „   = ¼ distance of moon,
                    = 15 radii of the earth.

$$\tfrac{1}{2} \text{ height} = \tfrac{1}{2} \, 64 \cdot 4 = 32 \cdot 2,$$

Diameter of orbit of Belus = 33·2⁹.

Height of entrance + breadth,

$$= 44 \cdot 74 + 34 \cdot 84 = 79 \cdot 58 \text{ units,}$$
$$(10 \times 79 \cdot 6)^3 = 796^3 = \tfrac{4 \cdot 9}{9} \text{ circumference,}$$
$$(3 \times 10 \times 79 \cdot 6)^3 = \tfrac{4 \cdot 9}{9} \times 3^3 = 120.$$

12 cubes of 30 times sum = 1440 circumference,
                    = distance of Mercury.

$$(9 \times 10 \times 79 \cdot 6)^3 = \tfrac{4 \cdot 9}{9} \times 9^3 = 3240.$$

6 cubes of 90 times sum,

$$= 6 \times 3240 = 19640 \text{ circumference.}$$

Distance of Jupiter = 19636.

Should the height of the doorway to the top of the cornice = 65·2 units,

$$65 \cdot 2 \times 200 = 13040,$$

Cube of 200 times height = 13040³ = distance of Jupiter.

In the hills near the town of Siout, now the chief place in Upper Egypt, are some magnificent tombs. Siout is most probably the ancient Lycopolis. Gau-el-Kebir (the great) is a small village on the east bank of the river (N. lat. 27°), remarkable for the remains of an ancient temple which had once been of considerable extent. The ruins are 300 feet long; but the portico only is standing. It consists of 18 columns, 8 feet in diameter, which, with their entablatures, are each 62 feet high.

$$300 \text{ feet } = 259 \text{ units,}$$

and
$$262^3 \&c. = \tfrac{1}{60} \text{ distance of the moon,}$$
$$= \text{ radius of the earth.}$$
$$(3 \times 262)^3 = \tfrac{27}{60}$$
$$(10 \times 3 \times 262)^3 = \tfrac{27000}{60} = 450.$$

Cube of 30 times length = 450 distance of the moon
$$= 150 + 400$$
$$= \text{ distance of Mercury + distance of the earth.}$$

50 cubes $= 22500 =$ distance of Belus,
50 spheres $\quad\quad = \quad\quad$,,   Neptune.

Or, 4×260 &c. $= 1042$ &c.
and 1042^3 &c. $= 10$ circumference,
$(10 \times 1042)^3 = 10000$,,

Cube of 40 times length $= 10000$ circumference
$\quad\quad = \frac{10}{36}$ distance of Saturn
$\quad\quad = \frac{10}{72}$,,   Uranus
$\quad\quad = \frac{10}{113}$,,   Neptune
$\quad\quad = \frac{10}{216}$,,   Belus.

Or, $266^3 = \frac{1}{6}$ circumference,
$(6 \times 266)^3 = \frac{1}{6} \times 6^3 = 36,$
$(2 \times 6 \times 266)^3 = 36 \times 2^3 = 288.$

10 cubes of 12 times length $= 2880$ circumference
$\quad\quad\quad = $ diameter of orbit Mercury.

$266^3 = \frac{1}{6}$ circumference,
$(60 \times 266)^3 = \frac{1}{6} \times 216000,$
$\quad\quad = \frac{1}{6}$ distance of Belus,
$\quad\quad = $ distance of Saturn.

Cube of 60 times length $=$ distance of Saturn.
300 feet $= \quad 259$ units
if length $= \quad 257$,,
$4 \times 257 = 1028$,,
Distance of the moon $= 1028^3$,,
Cube of 4 times length $=$ distance of the moon.

The little island of Philæ is one of the richest spots in Egypt in architectural beauty. The two great propylæ form the entrance to the court, and are similar to those at Edfou. They are 118 feet wide and 54 high. Still in front of the large propyla there is a gallery, 250 feet long, with a row of columns on the right and left.

Width 118,   height 54   feet,
$= 102\cdot2$,, $46\cdot7$ units.
$(10 \times 102\cdot8)^3 = 1028^3 = $ distance of the moon.

Cube of 10 times width = distance of the moon,
$\qquad$ 150 cubes = $\qquad$ „ $\qquad$ Mercury,
$\qquad$ 150^2 „ = $\qquad$ „ $\qquad$ Belus.
$(10 \times 47 \cdot 7)^3 = 477^3 = \frac{1}{10}$ distance of the moon.
$(10 \times 10 \times 47 \cdot 7)^3 = \frac{1000}{10} = 100$ $\qquad$ „
$(2 \times 10 \times 10 \times 47 \cdot 7)^3 = 800$ $\qquad$ „
Cube of 200 times height = 800 $\qquad$ „
$\qquad$ = diameter of orbit of the earth.

Sum of width + height = $102 \cdot 8 + 47 \cdot 7 = 150 \cdot 5$ units,
$\qquad$ 150^3 &c. $= \frac{3}{100}$ $\qquad$ circumference,
$(10 \times 150$ &c.$)^3 = \frac{3000}{100} = 30$ $\qquad$ „
$(2 \times 10 \times 150$ &c.$)^3 = 30 \times 2^3 = 240$ $\qquad$ „
6 cubes of 20 times sum = 1440 $\qquad$ „
$\qquad$ = distance of Mercury;
or, 150^3 &c. $= \frac{1}{320}$ distance of the moon,
$(32 \times 150)^3 = \frac{1}{320} \times 32^3 = \frac{1024}{10} = \frac{2048}{20}$.
20 cubes of 32 times sum = 2048 distance of the moon,
distance of Jupiter = 2045 $\qquad$ „
Length of gallery = 250 feet = 216 units,
$\qquad$ 216^3 &c. = $\qquad$ $\frac{8}{90}$ circumference,
$(3 \times 216$ &c.$)^3 = \frac{8}{90} \times 3^3 = \frac{24}{10}$
$(5 \times 3 \times 216$ &c.$)^3 = \frac{24}{10} \times 5^3 = 300$
Cube of 15 times length = 300 circumference.
9 cubes = 2700 = distance of Venus.

Cube of 30 times length = 2400 circumference,
30 cubes of 30 times length = 72000 $\qquad$ „
$\qquad$ = distance of Uranus.

Should length = 221 units,
$\qquad$ 221^3 &c. $= \frac{1}{100}$ distance of the moon.
$(10 \times 221$ &c.$)^3 = \frac{1000}{100} = 10.$ $\qquad$ „

Cube of 10 times length = 10 times distance of the moon.
15 cubes = 150 = distance of Mercury,
40 cubes = 400 = $\qquad$ „ $\qquad$ earth.

$\qquad$ Width of temple $102 \cdot 2$ units, if $102 \cdot 8$,
$\qquad$ Height $\qquad$ „ $\qquad$ $46 \cdot 7$ „ $\qquad$ $47 \cdot 7$,

then,
$$10 \times 102 \cdot 8 = 1028,$$
distance of the moon = 1028^3.
$$200 \times 47 \cdot 7 = 9550,$$
distance of the earth = 9550^3.

Thus cube of 10 times width = distance of moon,
and   cube of 200 times height = distance of the earth.

Sum of $102 \cdot 8 + 47 \cdot 7 = 150 \cdot 5,$
$$4 \times 150 \cdot 5 = 602,$$

$601^3 = \frac{1}{4}$ distance of the moon,
$(10 \times 601)^3 = \frac{1000}{8} = 200.$

Cube of 40 times sum = 200 distance of the moon,
= $\frac{1}{2}$ distance of the earth.

Gallery = 216 units;
if = 217   ,,
$$40 \times 217 = 8680,$$
Distance of Mars = about 8690^3.

Cube of 40 times length = distance of Mars;
or, $(3 \times 216)^3 = 648^3 = \frac{1}{4}$ distance of the moon,
Cube of 3 times length = $\frac{1}{4}$,,
Cube of 6 times length = $\frac{8}{4} = 2$,,
= diameter of orbit of the moon.

The Nubian rock-cut temples between the First and Second Cataract are of great antiquity.

The most remarkable of these temples is the one at Ipsambul, which was opened by Belzoni, who says,—"We entered first into a large pronaos, 57 feet long and 52 wide."

57 by 52 feet
= 49 ,, 45 units,

$48 \cdot 4^3 = \frac{1}{1000}$ circumference; $484^3 =$ circumference
= 2 pyramid of Cheops,

$45 \cdot 6^3 = \frac{1}{1200}$ circumference; $456^3 = \frac{10}{12}$ circumference
= 2 pyram. of Cephrenes.

Cubes of sides are as 5 : 6.

" The outside of the temple is magnificent.   It is 117 feet wide and 86 high ; the height from the top of the cornice to the top of the door being 66 feet 6 inches, and the height of the door 20 feet. There are four enormous sitting colossi, the largest in Egypt or Nubia, except the Great Sphinx at the Pyramids, to which they approach in the proportion of nearly two-thirds. Their height is about 50 feet, not including the caps, which are about 14 feet."

Height of a statue, including the cap, $= 50 + 14 = 64$ feet $= 55$ units,
and $54^3 = \frac{1}{2}$ degree $= 30$ minutes.

Height without the cap $= 50$ feet $= 43$ units, and $42 \cdot 9^3$ $= \frac{1}{4}$ degree $= 15$ minutes.

$$\text{The cubes are as } 1 : 2.$$

Doorway 66·5 and 20   feet
$\qquad = 57 \cdot 49 \qquad 17 \cdot 29$ units,
$\frac{1}{2} = 28 \cdot 74,$
$\qquad\quad 28 \cdot 6^9 = $ distance of Neptune,
$\qquad\quad 17 \cdot 6^9 = \qquad\quad , \qquad$ Mercury.

$$\text{Height } 57 \cdot 49 \text{ units,}$$
$$(10 \times 57 \cdot 5)^3 \times 575^3 = \tfrac{1}{40} \text{ distance of the moon,}$$
$$(2 \times 10 \times 47 \cdot 5)^3 = \tfrac{1}{40} \times 2^3 = \tfrac{1}{5} \qquad \text{,,}$$
$$(10 \times 2 \times 10 \times 57 \cdot 5)^3 = \tfrac{10000}{5} = 1400 \qquad \text{,,}$$

$\frac{1}{5}$ cube of 200 times height $= \frac{1}{5}$ 1400 distance of moon,
$$= \qquad 280 \qquad \text{,,}$$
$$281 = \qquad \text{,,} \quad \text{Venus.}$$

$$\text{Height } = 17 \cdot 29 \text{ units,}$$
$$(10 \times 17 \cdot 5 \text{ \&c.})^3 = 175^3 \text{ \&c. } = \tfrac{1}{200} \text{ distance of moon,}$$
$$(10 \times 10 \times 17 \cdot 5 \text{ \&c.})^3 = \tfrac{1000}{200} \qquad = 5 \qquad \text{,,}$$
$$(2 \times 10 \times 10 \times 17 \cdot 5 \text{ \&c.})^3 = 5 \times 8 \quad = 40 \qquad \text{,,}$$

10 cubes of 200 times height $= 400$ times distance of moon,
$$= \text{distance of the earth.}$$

$$\text{Whole height } = 57 \cdot 5 + 17 \cdot 5 = 75 \text{ units,}$$
$$(10 \times 74 \cdot 9)^3 = 749^3 \qquad = \tfrac{100}{27} \text{ circumference,}$$
$$(3 \times 10 \times 74 \cdot 9)^3 = \tfrac{100}{27} \times 27 = 100 \qquad \text{,,}$$
$$(3 \times 3 \times 10 \times 74 \cdot 9)^3 = 100 \times 27 = 2700 \qquad \text{,,}$$

Cube of 90 times whole height,
$$= 2700 \text{ circumference,}$$
$$= \text{distance of Venus.}$$

Cube of 180 times height $= 2700 \times 8 = 21600$.
10 cubes $= 216000$ circumference $=$ distance of Belus.

Pronaos 57   by 52   feet
$$= 49 \cdot 28 \text{ ,, } 44 \cdot 96 \text{ units,}$$
$$(10 \times 49 \cdot 4)^3 = 494^3 = \tfrac{1}{6} \text{ distance of the moon,}$$
$$(3 \times 10 \times 49 \cdot 4)^3 = \tfrac{1}{6} \times 3^3 = 3 \quad\quad \text{,,}$$

Cube of 30 times length
$$= 3 \text{ times distance of the moon.}$$

50 cubes $= 150$ distance of the moon,
$$= \text{distance of Mercury.}$$

Width 44·96 units,
$$(10 \times 45 \cdot 6) = 456^3 \quad = \quad \tfrac{10}{12} \text{ circumference,}$$
$$(12 \times 10 \times 45 \cdot 6)^3 = \tfrac{10}{12} \times 12^3 = 1440 \quad\quad \text{,,}$$

Cube of 120 times width $=$ distance of Mercury,
150 cubes   ,, $=$,,   Belus.

Sum of 2 sides $= 49 \cdot 4 + 45 \cdot 6 = 95$ units,
$$(10 \times 94 \cdot 7)^3 = 947^3 \quad = \quad \tfrac{30}{4} \text{ circumference,}$$
$$(2 \times 10 \times 94 \cdot 7)^3 = \tfrac{30}{4} \times 2^3 = \quad 60 \quad\quad \text{,,}$$
$$(4 \times 2 \times 10 \times 94 \cdot 7)^3 = 60 \times 4^3 = 3840 \quad\quad \text{,,}$$

Cube of 80 times sum of 2 sides
$$= 3840 \text{ circumference} = \text{distance of the earth.}$$

Outside of Temple.

Side 117   by 86   feet high
$$= 101 \cdot 16 \text{ ,, } 74 \cdot 36 \text{ units.}$$

$$(10 \times 102 \cdot 8)^3 = 1028^3 = \text{distance of the moon.}$$
Cube of 10 times side $=$ distance of the moon,
150 cubes   ,, $=$,,   Mercury,
150^2 ,,   ,, $=$,,   Belus.

Height 74·36 units,
$$(10 \times 75 \cdot 7)^3 = 757^3 = \tfrac{4}{10} \text{ distance of the moon,}$$
5 cubes of 10 times height $= 2$ distance of the moon
$$= \text{diameter of the orbit of the moon.}$$

$(10 \times 10 \times 75 \cdot 7)^3 = \frac{4000}{10} = 400$ distance of the moon.

Cube of 100 times height = distance of the earth.

Side + height = $102 \cdot 8 + 75 \cdot 7 = 178 \cdot 5$ units,

178^3 &c. $= \frac{1}{20}$ circumference,

$(10 \times 178$ &c.$)^3 = \frac{1000}{20} = 50$,,

$(6 \times 10 \times 178$ &c.$)^3 = 50 \times 6^3 = 10800$,,

20 cubes of 60 times sum

= 216000 circumference = distance of Belus.

Or, Height = 74·36 units,

$(10 \times 73 \cdot 8)^3 = 738^3 = \frac{10}{27}$ distance of the moon,

$(3 \times 10 \times 73 \cdot 8)^3 = \frac{10}{27} \times 27 = 10$,,

Cube of 30 times height
= 10 times distance of the moon.

75^3 &c. $= \frac{4}{3}$ degree $= 80$ minutes,

101^3 &c. $= \frac{10}{3}$,, $= 200$,,

7584^3 = distance of the earth.

Doorway 57·49 and 17·29 units
  if 57·33 &c. 17·2 ,,

$120 \times 57 \cdot 33$ &c. $= 6880$
$400 \times 17 \cdot 2 = 6880$

Diameter orbit of Mercury = 6880^3.

Cube of 120 times height from the top of the cornice to the door = cube of 400 times the height of the door = diameter of orbit of Mercury.

Outside of Temple.

Side 101·16 by 74·36 units high.
  if 102·8 ,, 75 84 ,,

then $10 \times 102 \cdot 8 = 1028$
  distance of moon $= 1028^3$
  $100 \times 75 \cdot 84 = 7584$
  distance of earth $= 7584^3$.

Thus cube of 10 times side
                    = distance of moon

and cube of 100 times height

$$= \text{distance of earth.}$$

Cube of 60 times sum $\quad = \quad \frac{1}{20}$ distance of Belus

,,   30   ,, $= \frac{1}{160}$,,

$$= \frac{80}{160} = \quad \frac{1}{2} \text{ distance of Venus.}$$

Since distance of Venus $= \quad \frac{1}{80}$ distance of Belus.

Sum $= 102 \cdot 8 + 75 \cdot 84 = 178 \cdot 64$

$$178^3 \ \&\text{c.} = \frac{1}{20} \text{ circumference}$$
$$(60 \times 178 \ \&\text{c.})^3 = \frac{1}{20} \times 60^3 = \frac{1}{20} 216000.$$

Cube of 60 times sum $= \quad \frac{1}{20}$ distance of Belus.

$$(10 \times 178, \&\text{c.})^3 = \frac{1000}{20} = 50.$$

Cube of 10 times sum $= 50$ circumference.

The smaller rock-cut temple at Ipsambul has been more completely examined than the large one.   The front, which is close to the river, and 20 feet above the present usual level of the water, is 91 feet long : the depth of the excavation, measured from the centre of the front to the extremity of the adytum, is 76 feet.   On the outside are six colossal figures, about 30 feet high, hewn out of the rock, a female figure being placed on each side between two male figures. They are in the usual attitude of standing colossi, with one foot advanced before the other.

Sides 91   by 76 feet

$\quad = 78 \cdot 6$,, $65 \cdot 8$ units

if $= 79 \cdot 8$,, $65 \cdot 2$

$$200 \times 79 \cdot 8 = 15960$$

distance of Saturn $= 15960^3.$

$$200 \times 65 \cdot 2 \quad = 13040$$

distance of Jupiter $= 13040^3.$

Cube of 200 times greater side

$$= \text{distance of Saturn.}$$

Cube of 200 times less side

$$= \text{distance of Jupiter.}$$

Sum of 2 sides $= 79 \cdot 8 + 65 \cdot 2 = 145$

$$60 \times 145 = 8700$$

about $8690^3 = $ distance of Mars.

Cube of 60 times sum of 2 sides,
  or of 30 times perimeter
      = distance of Mars.

A passage leads to the pronaos, a room 35 by 36·5 feet, supported by six square pillars, three on each side.

Sides 35   by 36·5 feet
    = 30·2 ,, 31·12 units:
  if = 30·5 ,, 32·4

then 20 × 30·5 = 610
              610^3 = 2 circumference.
    40 × 32·4 = 1296
              1296^3 = 2 distance of the moon.

Cube of 20 times less side = 2 circumference.
Cube of 40 times greater = 2 distance of the moon.
Sum of 2 sides by measurement
                = 30·2 + 31·12 = 61·32
                mean   = 30·66
    Distance of Belus   = 30·7⁹.

The temple of Dandour, in Nubia, is of small dimensions. It is a parallelogram, the front of which is 21¼ feet, and the length of the side 43¼.

      21·75 by 43·75 feet
    = 18·8   ,, 37·82 units.
  $(100 × 18·7)^3$ = 6 distance of moon
  $(5 × 100 × 18·7)^3$ = $6 × 5^3$ = 750.
  10 cubes of 500 times less side
          = 7500 distance of moon
          = distance of Uranus
  30 cubes   =   ,,   Belus.
  100 cubes of 100 times less side
          = 600 times distance of moon
          = distance of Mars.
    $(10 × 37·9)^3$ = $\frac{1}{20}$ distance of moon
    $(100 × 37·9)^3$ = $\frac{1000}{20}$ = 50
  $(2 × 100 × 37·9)^3$ = 50 × 8 = 400.

Cube of 200 times greater side
$\quad\quad$ = 400 times distance of moon
$\quad\quad$ = distance of earth.

Sum of 2 sides $= 37 \cdot 9 + 18 \cdot 7 = 56 \cdot 6$ units,
$\quad (10 \times 56 \cdot 6)^3 = \frac{1}{6}$ distance of moon.

Cube of 10 times sum of 2 sides,
$\quad\quad$ or of 5 perimeters $= \quad \frac{1}{6}$ distance of moon,
$\quad\quad\quad\quad\quad\quad\quad\quad\quad = 10$ radii of earth
$\quad\quad\quad\quad\quad\quad\quad\quad\quad = \quad 5$ diameters of earth.

$\quad (6 \times 10 \times 56 \cdot 6)^3 = \frac{1}{6} \times 6^3 = 36$ distance of moon,
$(5 \times 6 \times 10 \times 56 \cdot 6)^3 = 36 \times 5^3 = 4500.$

5 cubes of 300 times sum of 2 sides,
$\quad\quad$ or of 150 times perimeter
$\quad\quad\quad\quad = 22500$ times distance of moon,
$\quad\quad\quad\quad = $ distance of Belus.

$\frac{1}{2} 37 \cdot 9 = 18 \cdot 95$ units,
$\quad\quad$ and $18 \cdot 9^9 = $ distance of Venus.

$\frac{1}{2}$ sum of 2 sides $= \frac{1}{2} 56 \cdot 6 = 28 \cdot 3$,
$\quad\quad$ and $28 \cdot 6^9 = $ distance of Neptune.

Sides of temple $18 \cdot 8$ by $37 \cdot 82$ units,
$\quad\quad\quad\quad$ if $18 \cdot 96 \;,, \; 37 \cdot 92$

then $\quad\quad\quad\quad\quad 200 \times 18 \cdot 96 = 3792$
$\quad\quad \frac{1}{8}$ distance of earth $= 3792^3$
$\quad\quad\quad\quad\quad 200 \times 37 \cdot 92 = 7584$
$\quad\quad\quad$ distance of earth $= 7584^3.$

Thus cube of 200 times less side
$\quad\quad\quad\quad = \frac{1}{8}$ distance of earth,

and cube of 200 times greater side
$\quad\quad\quad\quad = $ distance of earth.

$\quad$ The sides are as $1 : 2$
$\quad\quad\quad$ cubes $\;,, \quad 1 : 8.$

Temples in Upper Nubia.

The most interesting monument between the second and third cataracts is the temple of Soleb, which stands on the west bank of the river, and about 400 yards distant from it, in lat. 20° 25′.

According to Waddington, there is an entrance exactly opposite the gate of the temple, on each side of which two walls lead up to the remains of two sphinxes: one, which is grey granite, has the ram's head, and is six feet in length; the other is so much broken as to be nearly shapeless. Further on is a flight of stairs leading to the temple; two other sphinxes have been posted in front of it, of which there remains a part only.

The front of the portal, which is far from perfect, is about 175 feet long; the width of the staircase before it, 57 feet.

The first chamber is 102 feet 6 inches in breadth by 88 feet 8 inches in depth: round three sides of it runs a single row of pillars, and at the furthest end has been a double row, making in all thirty columns, of which seven are still standing and perfect: the diameter of their base is 5 feet 7 inches, and their height about 40 feet. They are inscribed with hieroglyphics only. The space between them and the wall of the temple has been covered with a roof, which is now fallen in. Jupiter Ammon appears twice among the fallen figures. The sculptures on the temple are described as being of the very best style, though in some parts they have been left unfinished.

The second chamber is described as having a single row of twenty-four columns round it; but no dimensions of the side are given.

The front of the portal is about 175 feet.

$$175 \text{ feet} = 151 \ \&\text{c. units}$$
$$150^3 \ \&\text{c.} = \tfrac{3}{100} \text{ circumference.}$$
$$153^3 = \tfrac{1}{300} \text{ distance of moon}$$
$$= \tfrac{1}{8} \text{ radius of earth.}$$

First chamber 102·5 by 88·7 feet

$$= \quad 88·6 \quad ,, \quad 76·7 \text{ units.}$$

$(10 \times 76·8)^3 = \quad 768^3 = 4 \text{ circumference}$

$(10 \times 87·9)^3 = \quad 879^3 = 6 \qquad ,,$

$(100 \times 76·8)^3 = 4000 \text{ circumference} = \frac{1}{5} \text{ distance of Saturn}$

$(100 \times 87·9)^3 = 6000 \qquad ,, \qquad = \frac{1}{5} \qquad ,,$

Sum of 2 sides $= 76·8 + 87·9 = 164·7$ units.

Should the 2 sides of the basement of the temple $= 165·6$ units,

$$(10 \times 165·6)^3 = 1656^3 = 40 \text{ circumference.}$$

Cube of 10 times sum of 2 sides $= 40$ circumference.

Cube of 10 times perimeter $= 320$ circumference.

12 cubes $= 12 \times 320 = 3840$ circumference

$$= \text{ distance of earth.}$$

Otherwise 88^3 &c. $= \frac{1}{100}$ circumference $= \frac{2}{4}$ degree

77^3 &c. $= \frac{1}{124} \qquad ,, \qquad = \frac{6}{9} ,,$

or $\qquad \frac{1}{3} 88 = 29·33$

and $29·2^9 = $ distance of Neptune.

$\frac{1}{3} 76 = 25·33$

and $25·2^9 = $ distance of Saturn.

$\frac{1}{3}$ the greater side to the power of 3 times 3 $=$ distance of Neptune.

$\frac{1}{3}$ the less side to the power of 3 times 3 $=$ distance of Saturn.

We have since called $28·6^9 = $ distance of Neptune.

Front $\qquad\qquad = 151$ units

$90 \times 151 = 14590$

$\frac{1}{8}$ distance of Belus $= 14580^3$.

Cube of 90 times front $= \frac{1}{8}$ distance of Belus

Cube of 180 times front $= 1 \qquad\qquad ,,$

First Chamber.

Sum of 2 sides $= 164·7$ units

$80 \times 163 \quad = 13040$

distance of Jupiter $= 13040^3$.

About half an hour south of the village of Soleb, in Upper Nubia, on the west side of the Nile, there are considerable remains, called by the natives Gorganto, according to Rüppel. In all probability these remains were once a royal residence, as the plan, which can easily be made out, is altogether different from that of other Egyptian temples: the entrance of this building is turned to the east, and some few hundred steps from the Nile. All the parts follow one another regularly along the axis. The front part is a massive wall, containing a court 192 feet long and 107 broad. Here there are two lion-sphinxes, of granite, with outstretched paws, near the entrance.

The first court is terminated by two prismatic towers (propyla), leading to a second court, which is about 76 feet deep, 92 wide, and ornamented all round with a row of colossal columns. On the west side a double row of pillars form a kind of peristyle. After this we come to a second court, of the same width as the preceding, and 86 feet deep. A colonnade runs round its inner wall. In the north-western angle there is a small door which leads to no particular chamber.

The palace ends in a chamber 40 feet deep and 54 wide, with a flat roof, once supported by twelve colossal pillars. The capitals have their decorations in imitation of palm-branches; and in the pillars of both courts the type is that of trunks of palm-trees tied together, as in the great temple of Luxor. There are hieroglyphics on the pillars and archi-traves, well cut, but not very numerous. The whole building is much damaged: of seventy pillars which once ornamented it only nine remain, standing in different places.

The material of all the parts is sandstone. Near the palace is a small mole in the Nile, built of large blocks of freestone. When we add to this description the fact that the name of Ramses the Great is found in this palace, we may obtain a probable date as to its high antiquity; and this con-clusion we may apply to enlarge our conceptions of the extent of the Sesostrid empire and the architectural taste of its monarchs. Perhaps in no country of the world so readily as in Egypt do we recognise the natural types which man has applied to the purposes of architectural use and ornament. Every traveller, whose eye has been accustomed to measure and compare, detects, without any difficulty, in the varied forms of Egyptian capitals and pillars the few simple and graceful models which nature offers for imitation on the banks of the Nile.

$$\text{Court, 192 by 107 feet}$$
$$= 166 \text{ by } 92 \cdot 5 \text{ units,}$$

$$167^3 = \tfrac{1}{24} \text{ circumference,}$$
$$(6 \times 167)^3 = \tfrac{1}{24} \times 6^3 = \tfrac{36}{4} = 9$$
$$(20 \times 6 \times 167)^3 = 9 \times 20^3 = 72000 \text{ ;}$$

Cube of 120 times greater side = 72000 circumference
$$= \text{distance of Uranus,}$$

3 cubes	,,	=	,, Belus,
3 spheres	,,	=	,, Neptune.

$$(10 \times 93 \cdot 3)^3 = 933^3 \qquad = \qquad \tfrac{1}{4} \text{ distance of the moon,}$$
$$(10 \times 10 \times 93 \cdot 3)^3 = \tfrac{1}{4} \times 1000 = 750 \qquad \text{,,}$$
10 cubes of 100 times less side = 7500   ,,
$$= \text{distance of Uranus,}$$

30 cubes	,,	=	,, Belus,
30 spheres	,,	=	,, Neptune.

$$\text{Court } 76 \text{ by } 92 \text{ feet}$$
$$= 65 \cdot 7 \text{ by } 79 \cdot 5 \text{ &c. units,}$$

$$(10 \times 64 \cdot 8)^3 = 648^3 = \tfrac{1}{4} \text{ distance of the moon,}$$
$$(10 \times 81 \cdot 5)^3 = 815^3 = \tfrac{1}{2} \qquad \text{,,}$$

$$\text{Court } 86 \text{ by } 92 \text{ feet}$$
$$= 74 \text{ &c. by } 79 \text{ &c. units,}$$

$$(10 \times 75 \cdot 2)^3 = 752^3 = \tfrac{30}{8} \text{ circumference,}$$
$$(10 \times 81 \cdot 5)^3 = 815^3 = \tfrac{1}{2} \text{ distance of the moon.}$$

Sum of 2 sides = $75 \cdot 2 + 81 \cdot 5 = 156 \cdot 7$ units,
$$156^3 = \tfrac{1}{80} \text{ circumference,}$$
$$(10 \times 156)^3 = \tfrac{1000}{30}$$
$$(6 \times 10 \times 156)^3 = \tfrac{1000}{30} \times 216 = \tfrac{214000}{30}.$$

30 cubes of 60 times sum of 2 sides
or of 30 times perimeter
$= 216000$ circumference $=$ distance of Belus.

10 cubes $=$ distance of Uranus,
5 cubes $=$ distance of Saturn.

Court 192 by 107 feet
$= 166$ by 92·5 units,

165^3 &c. $= \frac{4}{100}$ distance of the moon,
$(10 \times 165$ &c.$)^3 = \frac{4000}{100} = 40,$
$(3 \times 10 \times 165$ &c.$)^3 = 40 \times 3^3 = 1080,$
$(2 \times 3 \times 10 \times 165$ &c.$)^3 = 1080 \times 2^3 = 8640.$

25 cubes of 60 times side
$= 8640 \times 25 = 216000$ circumference $=$ distance of Belus.

Less side $= 92·5$ units,

$(10 \times 92·5$ &c.$)^3 = 925^3$ &c. $= 7$ circumference.

Sum of 2 sides $= 165$ &c. $+ 92·5 = 257·5$ units,

257^3 &c. $= \frac{1}{20}$ circumference,
$(20 \times 257$ &c.$)^3 = \frac{1}{20} \times 20^3 = 1200.$

30 cubes of 20 times sum of 2 sides
or of 10 times perimeter $= 36000$ circumference
$=$ distance of Saturn;

or, sum $= 257·5,$
$4 \times 257 = 1028,$
distance of the moon $= 1028^3,$

cube of 4 times sum of 2 sides
or of 2 perimeter $=$ distance of the moon.

If sides $= 168·5$ by 94 &c. units,

$40 \times 168·5 \qquad = 6740,$
distance of Venus $\qquad = 6740^3.$
80×94 &c. $\qquad = 7584,$
distance of the earth $= 7584^3.$

40 by 54 feet
$= 34·58$ by 46·67 units,

$$\tfrac{1}{2} \, 24{\cdot}58 \; = \; 17{\cdot}29,$$

and $\qquad\qquad 17{\cdot}6^9 \; = \;$ distance of Mercury.

$$\tfrac{1}{2} \, 46{\cdot}67 \; = \; 23{\cdot}33,$$

and $\qquad\qquad 23{\cdot}5^9 \; = \;$ distance of Jupiter.

Sum of 2 sides $= 34{\cdot}58 + 46{\cdot}67 = 81{\cdot}25$ units,

$$10 \times 81{\cdot}25 \; = \; 812{\cdot}5,$$

and 815^3 &c. $= \tfrac{1}{4}$ distance of the moon

$= 30$ radii of the earth.

Perimeter (2×815 &c.)$^3 = \tfrac{8}{2} = \qquad$ 4 distance of the moon,

$\qquad$ (4×815 &c.)$^3 \qquad\quad = \quad$ 32 $\qquad\qquad$ „

$\qquad$ (8×815 &c.)$^3 \qquad\quad = \quad$ 256 $\qquad\qquad$ „

$\qquad$ (16×815 &c.)$^3 \qquad\quad = $ 2048 $\qquad\qquad$ „

and 2045

$\qquad\qquad\qquad\qquad\qquad = $ distance of Jupiter.

Thus the cube of 16 times the sum of the 2 sides

or of 8 times perimeter

$= $ distance of Jupiter.

Chamber 40 $\qquad$ by $\quad$ 54 feet

$\qquad\qquad = 34{\cdot}58$ „ $\quad$ $46{\cdot}7$ units,

$(10 \times 34{\cdot}3)^3 = 343^3 = \tfrac{1}{27}$ distance of the moon,

$(3 \times 10 \times 34{\cdot}3)^3 = \tfrac{1}{27} \times 27 = \; 1 \qquad\qquad$ „

Cube of 30 times less side $= $ distance of the moon,

150 cubes $\qquad - \qquad - \qquad = \qquad$ „ $\qquad$ Mercury,

150^2 cubes $\qquad - \qquad - \qquad = \qquad$ „ $\qquad$ Belus.

Greater side $= 46{\cdot}7$ units,

$(10 \times 46{\cdot}7)^3 = 467^3 = \tfrac{9}{10}$ circumference,

$(10 \times 10 \times 46{\cdot}7)^3 = \tfrac{900}{10} = 900,$

$(2 \times 10 \times 10 \times 46{\cdot}7)^3 = 900 \times 2^3 = 7200.$

5 cubes of 200 times greater side

$\qquad\qquad = \quad$ 36000 circumference $=$ distance of Saturn,

10 cubes $= \; 72000 \qquad\qquad$ „ $\qquad = \qquad$ „ $\qquad$ Uranus,

30 cubes $= 216000 \qquad\qquad$ „ $\qquad = \qquad$ „ $\qquad$ Belus.

Sum of 2 sides $= 34{\cdot}58 + 46{\cdot}7 = 81{\cdot}28,$

$$(10 \times 81\cdot6)^3 = 816^3 = \tfrac{1}{2} \text{ distance of the moon,}$$
$$(2 \times 10 \times 81\cdot6)^3 = \tfrac{2}{8} = 4 \qquad \text{,,}$$

Cube of 10 times sum of 2 sides
$$= \quad \tfrac{1}{2} \text{ distance of the moon,}$$
Cube of 10 times perimeter
$$= \quad 4 \text{ distance of the moon,}$$
100 cubes of 10 times perimeter
$$= 400 \text{ distance of the moon} = \text{distance of earth;}$$
or, $\tfrac{1}{10}$ cube of 100 times perimeter = ,,

Chamber 34·58 by 46·7 units.

$$\text{Sum} = 81\cdot28$$
$$\tfrac{1}{4} = 20\cdot64$$
Distance of Mars = 20·5⁹, &c.

At Mount Barkal, in Upper Nubia, the temples lie between the mountain and the river. One of them has been full 450 feet in length and 159 in breadth.

$$450 \text{ by } 159 \text{ feet}$$
$$= 389 \text{ by } 137\cdot6 \text{ units,}$$
$$393^3 = \tfrac{5}{90} \text{ distance of the moon,}$$
$$(3 \times 393)^3 = \tfrac{5}{90} \times 3^3 = \tfrac{15}{10}.$$

100 cubes of 3 times length = 150 distance of the moon
$$= \text{distance of Mercury.}$$

Again; $(10 \times 3 \times 393)^3 = \tfrac{15000}{10} = 1500,$
5 cubes of 30 times length = 1500 × 5

$$= 7500 \text{ distance of the moon} = \text{distance of Uranus,}$$

15 cubes - - - - = Belus,
15 spheres - - - = Neptune.

$$(10 \times 137\cdot6)^3 = 1376^3 = \tfrac{24}{10} \text{ distance of the moon,}$$
$$(10 \times 10 \times 137\cdot6)^3 = \tfrac{24000}{10} = 2400 \qquad \text{,,}$$
Cube of 100 times breadth = 2400.

Pyramid = 800 distance of the moon,
$$= \text{diameter of orbit of the earth;}$$
or $(4 \times 10 \times 137\cdot6)^3 = \tfrac{24}{10} \times 4^3 = 153\cdot6$ distance of moon.

$$(4 \times 10 \times 137\cdot3)^3 = 150 \text{ distance of the moon}$$
$$= \text{distance of Mercury.}$$

Cube of 40 times $137 \cdot 3 =$ cube of perimeter of pyramid of Cholula $=$ distance of Mercury.

Sum of 2 sides $= 393 + 137 \cdot 6 = 530 \cdot 6$ units.

$$533^3 = \tfrac{4}{3} \text{ circumference,}$$
$$(3 \times 533)^3 = \tfrac{4}{3} \times 3^3 = 36,$$
$$(10 \times 3 \times 533)^3 = 36000.$$

Cube of 30 times sum of 2 sides
    or of 15 times perimeter

$\qquad = 36000$ circumference $=$ distance of Saturn,

2 cubes	-	-	-	$=$,,	Uranus,
6 cubes	-	-	-	$=$,,	Belus,
6 spheres	-	-	-	$=$,,	Neptune,

100 cubes of 3 times length $\quad =$ distance of Mercury.
$\tfrac{1}{2}$ cube of 100 times breadth $\quad =$ distance of the earth ;

$\qquad$ or length $= 389$ units,
$\qquad 384^3$ &c. $= \tfrac{1}{2}$ circumference.

$\qquad$ Cube of length $= \tfrac{1}{2}$ circumference
$\qquad$ Cube of 2 lengths $= \tfrac{8}{2} = 4,$
$\qquad$ Cube of 10 times length $= \tfrac{1000}{2} = 500.$

$\qquad$ Breadth $= 137 \cdot 6$ units,

$$(10 \times 137 \cdot 6)^3 = 1376^3 = \tfrac{24}{10} \text{ distance of the moon,}$$
$$(5 \times 10 \times 137 \cdot 6)^3 = \tfrac{24}{10} \times 5^3 = 300.$$

Cube of 50 times breadth $= 300$ distance of the moon,
$\qquad\qquad\qquad\qquad = $ diameter of orbit of Mercury.

Sum of 2 sides $= 384 + 137 \cdot 6 = 521 \cdot 6,$

$$522^3 = \tfrac{10}{8} \text{ circumference,}$$
$$(2 \times 522)^3 = 10 \qquad\qquad \text{,,}$$

$\qquad$ Cube of perimeter $= 10 \qquad$,,
$$(3 \times 2 \times 522)^3 = 10 \times 3^3 = 270 \qquad \text{,,}$$

10 cubes of 6 times sum of 2 sides
$\qquad$ or of 3 times perimeter
$\qquad = 2700$ circumference $=$ distance of Venus.

$$(6 \times 2 \times 522)^3 = 10 \times 6^3 = 2160 \text{ circumference.}$$

100 cubes of 12 times sum of 2 sides

or of 6 times perimeter

$= 216000$ circumference $=$ distance of Belus

Sides of temple are

389   by 137·6 units,

if 391·2 by 137·6   ,,

then $50 \times 391·2 = 19560$,,

diameter of the orbit of Saturn $= 19560^3$,,

$50 \times 137·6 = 6880,$,,

diameter of orbit of Mercury $= 6880^3.$

Thus cube of 50 times greater side

$=$ diameter of the orbit of Saturn.

and cube of 50 times less side

$=$ diameter of orbit of Mercury.

The great temple of Mount Barkal is one of the most striking monuments south of Wada Halfa. The length of its axis is 500 feet all but 4 or 5 feet.

500 feet $= 429$ units,

425^3, &c. $= \frac{2}{3}$ circumference,

$(3 \times 425)^3 = \frac{2}{3} \times 3^3 = 18,$

$(10 \times 3 \times 425)^3 = 18000.$

2 cubes of 30 times length $= 36000$ circumference,

$=$ distance of Saturn,

4   ,,   ,, $=$,,   Uranus,

12   ,,   ,, $=$,,   Belus,

12 spheres   ,, $=$,,   Neptune.

A spacious court, which appears to have had a colonnade round it, is 126 feet long.

126 feet $= 108$, &c. units,

108^3, &c. $= \frac{1}{90}$ circumference,

$(3 \times 108, \&c.)^3 = \frac{1}{90} \times 3^3 = \frac{3}{10},$

$(10 \times 3 \times 108, \&c.)^3 = \frac{3000}{10} = 300,$

Cube of 30 times length $= 300$ circumference,

$= \frac{1}{9}$ distance of Venus,

$= \frac{1}{120}$,,   Saturn,

$= \frac{1}{240}$,,   Uranus,

$= \frac{1}{720}$,,   Belus.

q 3

Another court is 146 feet long.

$$146 \text{ feet} = 126, \&c. \text{ units,}$$
$$126^3, \&c. = \tfrac{5}{2700} \text{ distance of the moon,}$$
$$(3 \times 126)^3 = \tfrac{5}{2700} \times 3^3 = \tfrac{5}{100},$$
$$(10 \times 3 \times 126)^3 = \tfrac{5000}{100} = 50.$$

3 cubes of 30 times length $= 150$ distance of the moon,
$$= \text{distance of Mercury,}$$
8 „ „ $=$ „ earth,
or $(2 \times 10 \times 3 \times 126)^3 = 50 \times 8 = 400$ distance of the moon.
Cube of 60 times length $=$ distance of the earth.

Cube of length of great temple $= 425^3, \&c. = \tfrac{2}{3}$ circumference
$$(6 \times 425, \&c.)^3 = \tfrac{2}{3} \times 6^3 = 144.$$
10 cubes of 6 times length $= 1440$ circumference,
$$= \text{distance of Mercury.}$$

Length is less than 429 units,
if $= 424$,
then $60 \times 424 = 25440$,
diameter of orbit of Uranus $= 25440^3$.

Cube of 60 times length
$$= \text{diameter of orbit of Uranus.}$$

At El Maçaourah, a valley in the desert, about 9 leagues south of Chendy, in Ethiopia, there is a vast collection of ruins consisting of eight small temples and terraces, with a great number of small chambers. The circuit of these ruins is 2715 feet, and the whole was surrounded by a double enclosure. The chief temple is in the centre.

A few hundred yards from this place are seen two other buildings, one to the west and the other to the east. Near the eastern temple there are traces of a large tank, protected from the sand by mounds of earth all round it, which are probably artificial. This tank, like those in Egypt, was intended for the use of the temple when the sacred edifice was not near enough to the river to render the water of the Nile available for religious and other purposes. Though these ruins are so extensive, all is on a small scale, the buildings as well as the materials. The greatest temple is only 34 feet long: on the pillars are figures in the Egyptian style; others in the same portico are fluted after the Greek fashion. On the basis of one Calliaud thought he detected the remains of a zodiac. Time and the elements, which have destroyed the ancient Saba, seem to have been willing to spare the observatory of Meroe. Without making excavations it is easy to see the whole plan of the building. It is surprising in all these ruins so few hieroglyphics are found. Only the six pillars which form the portico of the central temple have hieroglyphics; all the other walls are without sculptures.

Circuit $= 2715$ feet $= 2347$ units,

$\qquad 235^3$, &c. $= \frac{9}{800}$ distance of the moon,

$(10 \times 235$, &c.$)^3 = \frac{9000}{800} = 12$.

Cube of circuit $= 12$ distance of the moon,

$\qquad (5 \times 10 \times 235$, &c.$)^3 = 12 \times 5^3 = 1500$.

Cube of 5 times circuit $= 1500$ distance of the moon,

$\qquad = 10$ times distance of Mercury,

$\qquad = \frac{1}{4} \qquad$,, $\qquad$ Uranus,

$\qquad = \frac{1}{15} \qquad$,, $\qquad$ Belus.

$\frac{1}{2}$ circuit $= \frac{1}{2}$ $2347 = 1173$ units,

$\qquad$ and $1178^3 = \frac{3}{2}$ distance of the moon,

$\qquad (5 \times 1178^3) = \frac{3}{2} \times 5^3 = \frac{375}{2}$.

20 cubes of 5 times $1178 = 3750$ distance of the moon,

$\qquad\qquad = $ distance of Saturn,

$\qquad (4 \times 1178)^3 = \frac{3}{2} \times 4^3 = 96$ distance of the moon.

3 cubes of twice circuit $= 96 \times 3 = 288$,

$\qquad$ distance of Venus $= 281$ distance of the moon.

Length of temple $= 34$ feet $= 29 \cdot 39$ units,

$\qquad (10 \times 29 \cdot 3$, &c.$)^3 = 293^3$, &c. $= \frac{7}{300}$ distance of moon,

$(10 \times 10 \times 29 \cdot 3$, &c.$)^3 = \frac{7000}{300} = \frac{70}{3}$.

12 cubes of 100 times length $= 280$ distance of the moon,

$\qquad$ distance of Venus $= 281 \qquad\qquad$,,

Otherwise, 293^3, &c. $= \frac{2}{9}$ circumference,
    or $(10 \times 29{\cdot}3$, &c.$)^3 = \frac{2}{9}$,
    $(3 \times 10 \times 29{\cdot}3$, &c.$)^3 = \frac{2}{9} \times 3^3 = 6$,
$(10 \times 3 \times 10 \times 29{\cdot}3$, &c.$)^3 = 6000$.

Cube of 300 times length $= 6000$ circumference,

$$= \frac{1}{6} \text{ distance of Saturn,}$$

$$= \frac{1}{6^2} \quad\quad ,, \quad\quad \text{Belus.}$$

Should circuit of ruins $= 2385$ units,
    2 circuit will $= 4770$,,
        $477^3 = \frac{1}{10}$ distance of the moon,
    $(10 \times 477)^3 = \frac{1000}{10} = 100$.

Cube of twice circuit $= 100$ distance of the moon,
Cube of 4 times circuit $= 800$,,
        $=$ diameter of orbit of the earth.

Length of temple $= 29{\cdot}39$ units,
        if $= 29{\cdot}16$,,
    $1000 \times 29{\cdot}16 = 29160$
distance of Belus $= 29160^3$.

Cube of 1000 times length
        $=$ distance of Belus.

The Pacific Ocean, extending in latitude from pole to pole, and in longitude over a whole hemisphere, exceeds the area of all the continents and islands of the globe. Over the surface of this vast ocean there are dispersed, at various intervals, about 680 islands, exclusive of New Holland, New Zealand, New Caledonia, New Ireland, and the Solomons.

The wandering masons, who have left traces of their monuments in the four quarters of the world, will be found to have traversed the great Pacific Ocean, made the circuit of the globe, and measured its circumference.

The great morai at Otaheite is described by the missionaries, in 1797, as an enormous pile of stone-work, in form of a pyramid, on a parallelogram area; having a flight of 10 steps quite round it, the first of which, from the ground, is 6 feet high, the rest about 5 feet; it is in length, at the base, 270 feet, and width 94 feet; at the top it is 180 feet long, and about 6 wide: the steps are composed partly of regular rows of squared coral-stones, about 18 inches high, and partly with bluish coloured pebble-stones, nearly quite round, of a hard texture, all about 6 inches diameter, and in their natural unhewn state: this is the outside. The inside, that is to say what composes the solid mass (for it has no hollow space), is composed of stones, of various kinds and shapes. It is a wonderful structure; and it must have cost them immense time and pains to bring such a quantity of stones together, and particularly to square the coral of the steps with the tools they had when it was raised; for it was before iron came among them; and as they were ignorant of mortar or cement, it required all the care they have taken to fit the stones regularly to each other that it might stand. When Banks, who accompanied Cook in his first voyage, saw this place there was on the centre of the summit a representation of a bird, carved in wood; and, close by it, the figure of a fish, carved in stone; but both are now gone, and the stones of the upper steps are in many places fallen; the walls of the court have also gone much to ruin, and the flat pavement is only in some places discernible. Banks, speaking of this court, says, the pyramid constitutes one side of a court or square, the sides of which are nearly equal; and the whole was walled in and paved with flat stones; notwithstanding which pavement, several plantains and trees, which the natives call etoa, grow within the enclosure. At present there is within this square a house, called the House of Eatooa, in which a man constantly resides. Banks further states that at a small distance to the westward of this edifice was another paved square, that contained several small stages, called ewattas by the natives, which appeared to be altars whereon they placed the offerings to their gods; and that he afterwards saw whole hogs placed upon these stages or altars.

Another morai is thus described: — "We set off with the

chief to see a morai, where it was said the ark of the Eatooa was deposited, and which had been conjectured by some writers to bear a similitude in form to the ark of the covenant. The morai stands on the north side of the valley, about a mile or more from the beach; it is erected on level ground, enclosed by a square wooden fence, each side of which may measure 30 or 40 yards. About one half of the platform, next the interior side of the square, is paved, and on this pavement, nearly in the middle, there stands an altar upon 16 wooden pillars, each 8 feet high; it is 40 feet long and 7 feet wide: on the top of the pillars the platform for the offerings is laid, with thick matting upon it, which, overhanging each side, forms a deep fringe all round it. Upon this matting are offerings of whole hogs, turtle, large fish, plantains, young cocoa-nuts, &c.; the whole in a state of putrefaction. A large space on one side of the fence was broken down, and a heap of rough stones laid in the gap; upon these stones, and in a line with the fence, were placed what they call tees; these were boards from 6 to 7 feet high, cut into various shapes. At a corner near this stood a house and two sheds, where men constantly attended. They entered the house and found at one end the little house or ark of the Eatooa; it was made exactly like those they set on their canoes, but smaller, being about 4 feet long, and 3 in height and breadth. As it contained nothing but a few pieces of cloth, they inquired where they had hid the Eatooa; they answered that it had been taken in the morning to a small morai near the water-side, but that they would immediately bring it, which they did in about half an hour. It was in shape exactly like a sailor's hammock lashed up, and composed of two parts, the larger one just the size of the house, and the lesser, which was lashed upon it, was about half that size: at the ends were fastened little bunches of red and yellow feathers, the offerings of the wealthy.

"On their way back they called to see the body of Orepiah, as preserved in a tupapow: he had not been many months dead, and was now in a perfectly dry state. The man to whom the performance of this operation was entrusted lived close by, and came near when he saw them. He seemed quite willing to oblige, and asked if they would like to see the body unshrouded; for, as it lay, nothing could be seen but the feet. Answering in the affirmative, he drew it out upon the uncovered stage, and took several wrappers of cloth off it, and placed the corpse in a sitting position. The body had been opened, but the skin every where else was unbroken, and, adhering close to the bones, it appeared like a skeleton covered with oil-cloth. It had little or no smell, and would, notwithstanding the heat of the climate, remain so preserved for a considerable time. The method they take for this is, to clear the body of the entrails, brain, &c. : then washing it well, they rub it daily outside and in with cocoa-nut oil, till the flesh is quite dried up; after which they leave it to the all-destroying hand of time. This tupapow was constructed by driving long stakes in the ground, over which was a thatched roof. On the adjoining trees, plantains and bread-fruit hung for the use of the dead."

Sides of base   270 by   94 feet
$$= 233{\cdot}4 \ ,, \ 81{\cdot}3 \text{ units}$$
233^3 &c. $= \frac{1}{600}$ distance of moon
$(10 \times 233)^3 = \frac{1000}{6000} = \frac{10}{6}.$

24 cubes of 10 times greater side
$$= 280 \text{ distance of moon} = \text{distance of Venus,}$$
or 3 cubes of 20 times greater side
$$= \text{distance of Venus,}$$
$(10 \times 81{\cdot}6) = \frac{1}{2}$ distance of moon.

2 cubes of 10 times less side $=$ distance of moon.

Sum of 2 sides $= 233$ &c. $+ 81{\cdot}6 = 314$ &c. units.
314^3 &c. $= \frac{2}{70}$ distance of moon
$(10 \times 314)^3 = \frac{2000}{70} = \frac{200}{7}.$

14 cubes of 10 times sum of 2 sides
$$= 400 \text{ distance of moon} = \text{distance of earth.}$$
$(10 \times 81{\cdot}6)^3 = \frac{1}{2}$ distance of moon
$(2 \times 10 \times 81{\cdot}6)^3 = \frac{8}{2} = 4.$

Cube of 20 times less side

$= 4$ distance of moon $= \frac{1}{100}$ distance of earth,

or 100 cubes of 20 times less side

$= 400$ times distance of moon $=$ distance of earth,

or cube of 200 times less side

$= 4000$ distance of moon $= 10$ times distance of earth.

We have seen an engraving of the burial-ground in one of the Sandwich Islands, "Cimetiere d'Atooi," in which is the outline of an obelisk, of considerable height and well-proportioned, formed with the branches of trees, or canes.

Belcher, in a voyage round the world, gives the drawing of an Indian tomb, on the north-west coast of America, in which is seen a pole erect, surmounted with the orb or globe and the obeliscal star, — like the sceptre, or St. Edward's staff, which is carried before the sovereign of England in the procession that precedes the coronation. The orb and obe liscal star are also put into the hand of the sovereign immediately before the crown is placed on his head.

The adoption of the Babylonian standard, based on a knowledge of the earth's circumference, to the monumental records of science prove that the Druids of Britain, the Persian Magi, the Brahmins of India, the Chaldees of Babylonia, the Egyptian Hierarchy, the Priests of Mexico and Peru, were all acquainted, as Cæsar says of the Druids, with the form and magnitude of the earth; or as Pomponius Mela states, with the form and magnitude of the earth and motion of the stars.

Hence it is evident that the world had been circumnavigated at an unknown epoch, and colonies formed in the old and new world, all making use of the same standard in the construction of their religious monuments. So the Babylonian or Sabæan standard may be said to have been universal.

At a later age the two worlds became lost or unknown to each other. When that event happened history is silent. Was the use of the compass at that period lost? When the compass became again known was America re-discovered?

The discovery of the compass in Europe is stated to have been made at the beginning of the fourteenth century; but it would appear to have been in use in the European seas before that period. Tropical America was discovered by Columbus about the end of the fourteenth century.

Gliddon remarks that "the priests of Egypt told Solon many things that must have humbled his Athenian pride of superior knowledge; but one fact that they told him, on geography, is so curious, in regard to the 'far West,' that it is worthy of mention.

"We know the maritime abilities of the Phœnicians, and we can adduce tangible reasons to show, that, by the orders of Pharaoh Necho, Africa had been circumnavigated, and the Cape of Good Hope, about 600 B. C., actually doubled, before it was in the year 1497 of our era discovered by Diaz and Vasco de Gama.

"The Egyptians had intercourse with Hindostan, the Spice Islands, and China, long before that period; and in maritime skill equalled, as in geographical knowledge they surpassed, all early nations. Now when Solon was receiving that instruction in the Egyptian sacerdotal colleges which rendered him the 'wisest of mankind,' (among the Athenians,) besides gleaning an insight into primeval history and geology that subsequently induced him to compose a great poem, wherein he treated on Attica before the Ogygian flood, and on the *vast island* which had sunk into the Atlantic Ocean, he was informed by Sonchis, one of the priests, of the existence of the Atlantic Isles; which, Sonchis said, were larger than Africa and Asia united." (See Plato.)

North America discovered in the tenth century. — Snorro Sturlonides, in his Chronicle of Olaus, published at Stockholm in 1697, states that those enterprising navigators, the Norwegians, planted a colony in Iceland as early as the year 874, and established some settlers on the coast of Greenland in 982, when they are represented as having proceeded towards the west, and, finding a more inviting coast, on which were some grape-vines, and in the interior some pleasant

valleys shaded with wood, they gave it the namo of Vineland, and settled some colonists there.

This statement has been considered as founded on ru-
mours, and so much involved in the obscurity of the past,
as to render the authenticity of the facts extremely doubtful.
But the publication, in 1838, of the work entitled " An-
tiquitates Americanæ," by the Royal Society of Northern
Antiquaries at Copenhagen, has given the contents of many
of the old Gothic MSS. preserved in the archives of Den-
mark.

This great work, it is said, presents a host of striking facts,
which prove beyond a doubt that America was discovered by
the Northmen in the year 986, and was repeatedly visited by
them during the two succeeding centuries. The nautical
and astronomical notices, preserved in some of the ancient
writings, are of the greatest importance in fixing the positions and latitudes of the places named. The identity of
Vineland with Massachussetts and Rhode Island is fully
established.

" Some think it very probable that Columbus, who visited
Iceland in the year 1477, was first made aware of the existence of another quarter of the globe by the people of that
island, and that in this way the idea of making a voyage of
discovery westwards was first suggested to his active mind.

" If Columbus had desired to seek a continent of which he
had obtained information in Iceland, he would not have
directed his course south-west from the Canary Islands.

" The Faroe Islands and Iceland must be considered the
intermediate stations and starting points for attempts made
to search Scandinavian America.

" The littoral tract of Vineland was made 125 years after
the first settlement of the Northmen in Iceland, when Lief
discovered that part of America which comprised the coast
line between Boston and New York. This was the principal settlement of the Northmen.

" The first Bishop of Greenland, Eric Upsi, an Icelander,
undertook, in 1121, a Christian mission to Vineland; and the
name of that colonised country has even been discovered in

national songs of the inhabitants of the Faroe Islands."
(Humboldt.)

Christian anchorites in the north of Europe explored and
opened to civilisation regions that had previously been inaccessible. The eagerness to diffuse religious opinions has
sometimes prepared the way for warlike expeditions, and
sometimes for the introduction of peaceful ideas and the
establishment of the relations of commerce.

Religious zeal, so strongly characteristic of the doctrines
promulgated in the systems of India and Egypt, was the
means of furthering in those regions the extension of geographical knowledge at an epoch long anterior to the date
of Christianity. This is evident from the still existing
monumental records left by these early missionaries of religion and civilisation, — the founders of settlements in both
hemispheres.

The Babylonian standard of these missions has been traced
through Asia, Egypt, Phœnicia, and along the Mediterranean
coasts. Druidical remains exist along the coast of Africa,
in Malta, Portugal, Jersey, and Guernsey; those of France
and the British Isles have already been noticed.

In Iceland are found circles of upright stones and stones
laid on each other, in a similar manner, though on a less scale,
than Stonehenge. Such circles are called domh-ringr, that is
doom-rings, or circles of judgment, because in these solemn
places courts were held of all kinds and dignities.

Greenland will be the next country, of which Cape Fare-
well is about equidistant between Iceland and the coast of
America. Reaching Newfoundland, cromlechs are found
there, as well as in several parts of the United States, and some
at a considerable distance from the coast. A stone circle is
situated upon a high hill, one mile from the town of Hudson,
in the state of New York, and is remarkable for the size of
the stones, and their position. Another is artificially placed
on a high rock upon the banks of the river Winnipigon.
This circle the Indians are accustomed to crown with wreaths
of herbage and with branches. A very fine cromlech, ten
feet broad, resting upon the apices of seven small conical

pillars, still exist at North Salem, New York. There is no monument or elevation near it from which the rock could have been thrown. The Indians have also stones of memorial or sacrifice. Captain Smith relates " that the Indians had certain altar stones, which they call Pawcorances; " these stand apart from their temples, some by their houses, others in the woods and wildernesses. Sacrifices are offered on these stones, when they return from the wars, from hunting, and upon other occasions. They are also crowned with oak and pine branches.

Herbet says that there was little difference between the Druids of Britain, the Magi of Persia, and the Brahmins of India. Higgins gives the following identities : — " Many of the Irish deities are precisely the gods of Hindostan. The Neil corresponds to the Hindoo Naut and the Neith of the Egyptians; Saman to Samanant; Bud to Boodhy; Can to Chandra; Ourhe, *i. e.* he who is, to Om or Aum; Esar to Eswara."

This last god, the Iswara of India, delighted with human sacrifices, was the Hesus of the Gauls and Britons; the Romans having Latinised the termination.

Chreeshna, the name of the Indian Apollo, is actually the old Irish name for the sun. The Irish had a deity called Cali. The altars on which they sacrificed to her are at this day named Leba Caili, or the bed of Cali of the Hindoos.

The Druidical remains have thus been traced from the Mediterranean along the western coast of Europe as far as Iceland, forming a chain of evidence of a former intercourse between the two worlds, the connecting links of which extend over the new as they have been found to do over the old world.

Dicuil, the Irish monk, who wrote in the time of Charlemagne, says that Iceland was then inhabited by British families.

The Irish, it would appear, were a commercial and navigating people when Tacitus wrote that Ireland was better known to merchants than even Britain.

The round towers in Ireland are described by Kohl " as

being built with large stones, and when seen at a distance look rather like lofty columns than towers, being from the base to the top nearly of the same thickness. They are now indeed by no means all of the same height, many having fallen into ruins, but those which remain tolerably complete are from 100 to 120 feet high, from 40 to 50 in circumference, and from 13 to 16 in diameter. At the base the wall is always very thick and strong, but becomes slighter towards the top. Within, the towers are hollow, without any opening but a door, generally 8 or 10 feet from the ground, and some very narrow apertures or windows, mostly four in number, near the top. These windows are usually turned towards the four cardinal points of the compass.

" In all parts of Ireland these singular buildings are found scattered about, all resembling each other like the obelisks of Egypt. The whole number of them is, at present, 118 ; of these 15 are in a perfect state of preservation, and of 36 little more than the foundation remains.

" In no part of Europe do we find any similar building of antiquity. In Scotland, it is said, two or three such towers exist, and these, it may be inferred, were reared by Irish colonists.

" In the far East we come to erections of the same character and dimensions ; the first thing that a traveller is reminded of on seeing an Irish round tower is a Turkish minaret. No authentic records exist to guide us to a knowledge of the time when these towers were built, or of the use for which they were intended. Everything proves that they have existed from a very remote antiquity, and the most opposite conclusions have been adopted with respect to the period and object of their erection.

" There is nothing very improbable in the hypothesis that these towers were built by the Phœnicians, who are known to have visited the island and to have exercised power there. Travellers have recently discovered in the Persian province of Masanderan towers precisely similar to those of Ireland ; and in India erections of a similar kind, dedicated to religious purposes, have also been met with. This, taken in connection with the shape of the Turkish minaret, makes it extremely probable that the round towers had an Oriental origin."

It appears from Bonnycastle's "Canada" that the remains of ancient civilisation traced in Mexico may extend in a chain much further north. "Singular discoveries are occasionally made in opening the Canadian forests, though it would seem that ancient civilisation had been chiefly confined to the western shores of the Andean chain, exclusive of Mexico only. In a former volume was described a vase of Etruscan shape, which was discovered during the operations of the Canada Company near the shores of Lake Huron, and vast quantities of broken pottery, of beautiful forms, are often turned up by the plough. I have a specimen of large size of an emerald green glassy substance, which was unfortunately broken when sent to me, but described as representing a regular polygonal figure; two of the faces, measuring some inches, are yet perfect. It is a work of art, and was found in the virgin forest in digging."

Humboldt, after describing the hill of Xochicalco, adds, the magnitude of these dimensions ought not to surprise us; on the ridge of the cordilleras of Peru, and on heights almost equal to that of Teneriffe, M. Bonpland and myself have seen monuments still more considerable. Lines of defence and entrenchments of extraordinary length are found in the plains of Canada.

The great number of monuments in the extensive western valley of North America, the magnitude of many of them, the objects of art which they are found to contain, indicate a more powerful and advanced race than that which was found scattered over it by the first European hunters; and that the era to which some of them belong is separated by many centuries from that of the European discovery is proved by an examination into the comparative age of the forest which now covers them.

The mounds indicate the existence of a very numerous, as well as a very advanced, population. Rafinesque is said to have ascertained the existence of five hundred ancient monuments in Kentucky alone, and fourteen hundred out of it, — most of which he had visited and surveyed in person. And they are spread over the whole basin of the Mississippi, from the confines of Mexico to those of the British possessions; though they reach the Atlantic border nowhere but in Florida. Some of these extend over five hundred acres of land; and many have the appearance of relics of cities, or of great settled encampments of a race long in possession of the soil.

Beyond the Alleghanies exist well defined traces of ancient fortified cities or camps, and great sepulchral tumuli, the work of unknown nations.

Barrows and other similar tumuli are also found in America, and are thus mentioned in the "Encyclopædia Americana:"—"In the valley of the Mississippi tumuli, or mounds of earth, are discovered in great numbers, of the origin and uses of which we are yet ignorant. Similar constructions also occur in Mexico. The barrows of the Mississippi valley have been found to contain bones, and are said to be composed of earth different from that of the surrounding country. They exhibit no trace of tools, and are, in fact, merely regular piles of earth, without brick or stone. They are commonly situated in rich plains or prairies. There is one near Wheeling, 70 feet in height, 30 or 40 rods in circumference at the base, and 180 feet at the top. There is a numerous group at the Chaokia, stated at about 200 in all, the largest of which is a parallelogram about 90 feet high and 800 yards in circuit. It has been asserted that the skulls found in these mounds resemble those of Peru."

Stephens and Calderwood found at Copan, in Central America, a wall almost 2 miles in length, and from 60 to 100 feet in height, which appeared to have been the outer wall of a city. They discovered there some temples, with the interior portions in a state of good preservation; all of them stood upon artificial mounds of a pyramidal form, from 80 to 100 feet in height. There were there immense sculptured figures of colossal proportions in a state of good preservation. The pedestals of these were covered with hieroglyphics, which differed from all others ever discovered, in this respect, that they were all formed of the human body in different postures, or of different parts of the human body. Fifteen miles from Copan is the city of Coriquan, where were found monuments much larger in size than at Copan, and more time-worn. One hundred miles further to the north and a little to the west, were the ruins of the city of Palenque; there are no monuments here, but there were other buildings of very great interest. In the centre of the city were the remains of a palace upwards of 600 feet in length, and standing upon an artificial pyramidal mound. Some of the rooms in the interior were found quite perfect, and on the sides of the room, 7 or 8 feet from the floor, were painted figures, of which the colours were still quite brilliant. There were also here some small temples covered with hieroglyphics of the same description as at Copan. At a short distance from Palenque is the city of Mitla. Quiché is another city, with a great temple or palace. Another city has recently been discovered, much larger than any hitherto described. These remains are scattered through the valley of the Mississippi.

Having traced the littoral route of the forgotten communication between Europe and America, let us next follow the tract of monumental records in an opposite direction through Northern Asia to America.

Having terminated the voyage from the Mediterranean to Vineland, let us now depart from the Pillars of Hercules and travel in the contrary direction to America.

Tyre was the most celebrated city of Phœnicia, and the ancient emporium of the world. Its colonies were numerous and extensive. It was, says Volney, the theatre of an immense commerce and navigation, the nursery of arts and science, and the city of perhaps the most industrious and active people ever known. In the period of their greatest splendour and perfect independence, says Heeren, Tyre stood at the head of the Phœnician cities. The kingdom of Carthage, the rival of Rome, was one of the colonies of Tyre. The building of Tyre and of the original temple of Melkarth (the Tyrian Hercules), would, according to the account which

Herodotus received from the priests, reach back 2760 years before our era.

The foundation of Tartessus and Gades, where a temple was dedicated to the wandering divinity Melkart (a son of Baal), and the colonial city of Utica, which was older than Carthage, remind us, says Humboldt, that the Phœnicians had already navigated the open sea for many centuries before the Greeks passed beyond the straits termed by Pindar the " Gadeirian gate." Tartessus was a town in Spain at the mouth of the Bœtis, where the sun was supposed to set ; or according to the poets, went to bed, and put up his horses, which he again yoked next morning in the east.

Gades (Cadiz) is said to have been founded by the Phœnicians 287 years before Carthage, 347 before Rome, and 1100 years before the Christian era.

Ships from Tyre and Sidon extended commerce far beyond that of any of the ancient states in the Mediterranean. They planted numerous colonies on the shores of the Mediterranean and Atlantic, and are said to have discovered England, and perhaps Ireland. Vellancy says, de Fontenu has proved that the Phœnicians traded with Britain before the Trojan war, 1190 years B. C.

Hanno, the Carthaginian, is said to have written in Punic a voyage round Africa. He left Carthage with a fleet of 60 ships, each 50 oars, and containing in all 30,000 persons, men and women in equal numbers. After passing the Pillars of Hercules, he planted colonies on the west coast of Africa, and then continued his voyage south. But Gosselin thinks the Carthaginians only went about 20 degrees south of the Pillars, and assigns the period about 1000 years B. C. This would make the foundation of Carthage of a much earlier date than is commonly assigned.

It was not till about 400 years after, or the beginning of the 6th century B. C., that the Phœnicians are said by Herodotus to have sailed from the Red Sea by order of Necho, king of Egypt, and in the third year to have arrived at the mouth of the Nile.

Herodotus, on the authority of the Egyptian priests, mentions this voyage, though he doubts its truth; but the most convincing argument of the truth of the report appears, says Volney, that the mariners who sailed round Lybia had the sun on their right hand. This was what appeared to be incredible to Herodotus.

Though the Carthaginians undertook voyages solely for the sake of discovery, yet, from a disposition they manifested to keep their discoveries private, their knowledge of geography, for the most part, perished with their power. The Carthaginians were very superstitious, and offered human victims to their gods.

Alexander by his father claimed descent from Hercules, and by his mother Olympias, of the royal house of Epirus, he traced his line to Achilles, the hero of the Iliad. It became a passion with Alexander to emulate Achilles' deeds and renown; and his first care, when he first landed in Asia upon the coast of Troy, was to pay magnificent funeral honours to the shade of the hero; during which he himself, in imitation of the ancient rites, ran naked and on foot round the barrow which covered the hero's remains —

> " That mighty heap of gathered ground,
> Which Ammon's son ran proudly round." — BYRON.

The barrows which are erected on the shores of the Hellespont to Hector and Ajax are, according to Kohl, exactly like the barrows which commemorate Odin and Thor, and other Scandinavian heroes.

When the traveller stands on the Scythian or Tartarian steppes, he sees these artificial hills stretching to a vast distance around. They vary greatly both in height and circumference; but, generally, when one of particularly elevated appearance occurs, there are seen around it other barrows of smaller dimensions. It may reasonably be supposed, that while the larger tumuli covered the remains of princes and heroes, the smaller contained the bodies of inferior dignitaries.

Holmes, in his " Sketches of the Shores of the Caspian," describes a dark coloured mound, rising abruptly from the plain, at Karatuppeh, and not far distant another small hillock, but not surrounded by habitations. The natives can give no satisfactory information with regard to these mounds. It is very evident that they are not natural elevations; and it is probable they may be the burial-places of the ancient kings of Hyrcania. I was afterwards told that one of them, near Astrabad, had been opened, and various rings, plates, knives, and cups of gold and copper, as well as some men's bones of a large size, had been found. My informant had seen them.

There are many tuppehs in Azerbijan, similar in shape, which, when opened, have been found to contain nothing but ashes. They are by some supposed to be the remains of villages of the ancient Guebres, or fire-worshippers. A Guebre village was built of mud-houses, ranged in a circle round the sides of a high mound, and on the summit of which stood a temple. In process of time both houses and temple have crumbled to their original dust, nothing remained but a mound of earth. The village of Karatuppeh is built all round the sides of the hillock, precisely in the manner of an old Guebre village, and has a very curious appearance.

Busbequius, a traveller of the 13th century, after coming in sight of the river Hebeus, arrived at Philippolis. The plain before that city was full of round hills of earth, or tumuli, like those that exist and are so celebrated in the plains of Troy. The Turks told him their nation had raised these tumuli as monuments of great battles, and to cover the graves of such as had fallen nobly in them. The Turks no doubt raised some of them, but many existed in ancient times. Herodotus mentions the erection of some of them, in this particular country, by the army of Darius, whilst on its march against the Scythians. They are found not merely in the plain of Philippolis, but all through Thrace. On the other side of the Balkan mountains they are seen scattered here and there all the way to the Danube; from the other side of the Danube they extend all along the shores of the Black Sea to the Crimea, whence, as is mentioned in the

Travels of Busbequius, they are to be traced through the Tartar deserts. Another branch of them runs across the plains of Poland and Russia; but, at one time or another, the practice of raising them seems to have been common in most Asiatic and European countries. It is quite certain that they are not all tombs. Even in comparatively recent times Turkish armies have been known to throw up many (and one or two larger than the largest in the plains of Troy) for the purpose of displaying on their summit the sandjak, or standard of Mahomet; and it is very probable that their Scythian or Tartarian ancestors had a somewhat similar custom.

In some burying-places in Tartary, Busbequius saw large towers built of burnt bricks, and others of stone, though no stone was to be found on the spot. As he went further east, he observed other kinds of sepulchres, consisting of large open spaces paved with stone, having four large stones placed upright on the corners of the pavement, and facing the four cardinal points.

Humboldt remarks that Busbequius was the first who recognised that the Huns, the Baschkirs (inhabitants of Paskatir, the Bachgird of Ibn Fozlan), and the Hungarians, were of Finnish (Uralian) race; and he even found Gothic tribes who still retained their language, in the strongholds of the Crimea.

Bell, who accompanied the Russian embassy from Petersburg to China, passed through Tobolsk to Tara, crossed the river Obi, and five days after arrived at Tomsk, on the banks of the river Tomm. To the south is a range of hills, beyond which is an extensive plain, covered with numerous tombs, erected seemingly in honour of departed warriors, and marking, as he supposes, the site of numerous battles. It is become a regular trade at Tomsk to go and dig these tombs, where they find not only armour and the trappings of horses, but gold, silver, and even precious stones. These have evidently been deposited according to the ancient custom of burying with deceased chieftains all his most precious effects.

In 1733, Russia sent an exploring mission to Siberia, but its primary object was to explore Kamtschatka. There were employed on this occasion many learned and ingenious travellers, among whom was Behring, so celebrated for his discoveries on the eastern seas of Asia. At Krasnoiarsk, on the banks of the Irtish, that runs into the Obi, they found the soil so rich that it will yield five or six successive crops without manure. A considerable quantity of antiquities, some of gold and silver, are dug from the tombs in the neighbourhood. Among the curiosities of Krasnoiarsk are some very extensive grottos, and a painted rock, the figures on which, however, do not surpass what might be made by the hand of a peasant.

In 1769, Pallas, in penetrating through Siberia, proceeded along the southern steppe, parallel to the Altai, and diversified by a chain of salt and bitter lakes. On descending the Tobol, near its junction with the Ouk, he came to a fine country on the banks of the Korrassoun, where he saw many bones of elephants, some of great size. Here too were a great number of open tombs, in which gold and silver ornaments had once been found; but every one had now been ransacked. This object of cupidity was said to have been the source whence the territory was first peopled; and, however the emigrants might have failed in the search, its superb pastures, and lakes abounding with fish, must have amply indemnified them.

Pallas proceeded by the rivulets Schaulba and Ouba, along the foot of the Altai, that vast and rich chain which rises near the east of the Caspian, and under various names traverses first the whole breadth of Asia, then turning to the north runs parallel to the shore of the continent, till it terminates at Behring's Straits. He considers it as the most considerable chain on the globe; and in its whole extent along the frontiers of Siberia it is eminently distinguished by metalliferous qualities. He was struck with the astonishing number of ancient works, carried on by the unknown people who once inhabited these tracts. There is not a productive spot throughout the Altai where their traces may not be found. Hence were doubtless derived those numerous metallic ornaments and utensils buried in the tombs on the Irtish. Descending that river, Pallas had an opportunity of surveying the ruins of Ablaikit, built by Ablai, a Kalmuc prince. It bears marks of having possessed all the magnificence that could be given to it by an uncivilised people. He counted forty-five idols, representing all that is most sacred among the Bourkans and the Kalmucs. Half of the figures were female; some of them were hideous, with inflamed features and countenances; others were monstrous, with ten faces and seven arms. They were variously formed, of copper, stone, and potter's earth; fragments of which were still found, but not in the same vast abundance as in the time of Gmelin. The edifice had been variously injured by the Russians and the Kirghises; and a squadron of cavalry, encamped near it, was just completing its destruction. Leaving the Irtish, and passing along the Altai, covered with perpetual snow, he came to Kolvian, the earliest forge established in this part of Siberia. The great scene of mining operations is now on the Schlangenberg, or Serpent Mountain, so called from the multitude of that description of animals which are found there. This mountain is situated about 60 miles from the Irtish, and 100 from the Obi; and appears from the course of the rivers on both sides to tower above all the rest of the Altai. It may be considered as an enormous mineral mass; whenever its covering of slate-rock is taken off, all the substances beneath are found to yield gold, silver, copper, and plumbago. Zinc, arsenic, and sulphur are also abundant. Since 1746, when this great source of wealth was first discovered, the openings made into the mountain are almost innumerable, being guided in several instances by the example set by the Tchouds, or ancient inhabitants, some of whose workings reached 60 feet deep. To give an idea of the richness of the Schlangenberg, it is stated between 1749 and 1771 to have produced 318 poods, or (at 36 pounds to each pood) 12,348 pounds of gold, and more than 324,000 pounds of silver. It still yields annually 36,000,000 pounds of mineral;

and the veins already discovered would be sufficient to supply the same quantity for twenty years to come.

As this kind of barrow-burial is not in those countries open to notice as an existing usage, it is a particular advantage to be able to recur to Herodotus, who speaks with a special reference to the people whose cemeteries have just been noticed, and whose account is confirmed by the discoveries of such travellers as have been able to acquaint themselves with the contents of these burial-hills. He says that when a king or chief died, the people assembled in great numbers to celebrate his obsequies. The body was taken to the district particularly appropriated to interments, where a large quadrangular excavation was made in the earth (in its dimensions more like a hall of banquet than a grave), and within it the body of the deceased prince was placed in a sort of bier. Daggers were laid at various distances around him, and the whole covered with pieces of wood and branches of the willow-tree. In another part of the same immense grave were deposited the remains of one of the late sovereign's concubines, who had been previously strangled; also his favourite servant, his baker, cook, housekeeper, and even his horses, — all followed him to the grave and were laid in the same tomb, together with his most valuable property, and, above all, a sufficient number of gold goblets. Our Saxon ancestors were content to think they should drink beer in the halls of Odin from the skulls of their enemies. After this the hollow was soon filled and surmounted with earth, every person being anxious to do his part in raising the hill by which his departed lord was honoured.

The following, besides its trait of manners and burial of armour, is curious in exhibiting the mode in which the tumulus was formed; the centre being apparently left open, and filled up last.

The Burial of Harald the Dane.

" When king Ring saw the chariot empty, he understood that king Harald was slain; he therefore caused a cessation of arms to be blown on the trumpets, and offered the Danish enemy peace and quarter, which they accepted. The next morning king Ring caused the field of battle to be carefully searched for king Harald's corpse, which was not found till the middle of the day, under a heap of slain. Ring caused it to be taken up, washed, and honourably treated according to the custom of those times, and laid it in Harald's chariot. A great mound was then raised, and the horse which had drawn Harald during the battle was harnessed to the car, and so the royal corpse was drawn into the mound. There the horse was killed; and king Ring caused his own saddle to be brought in, and gave it to his friend king Harald, praying him to use it in riding to dwell with Odin in Walhalla. After this he caused a great funeral feast to be celebrated, and at its conclusion begged all the warriors and chief men that were present to honour Harald by gifts and ornaments. Many precious things were thrown in, large bracelets and excellent arms; after which the mound was carefully closed and preserved, and king Ring remained sole governor over the whole kingdoms of Sweden and Norway." — *Anders Pryxeli's Sweden.*

Washington Irving mentions the burial of a beautiful female child among the Osages, American Indians, with whom were buried all her playthings and a favourite little horse, that she might ride it in the land of spirits.

" The inhabitants of Assam, in India beyond the Ganges, are idolaters; and it is an article of their faith that sinners suffer in a future state the pains of hunger and thirst; they therefore place food by the side of the corpse, and throw into the grave bracelets and other jewels and ornaments to purchase necessaries. The king is said to be interred with those idols of gold and silver which he worshipped when living; and an elephant, twelve camels, six horses, and a great number of hounds, are also buried with him, from an opinion that they may be of use to him in another world. In the performance of the funeral rites they are also said to exceed the Gentoos in barbarity; for not only the woman he loved best, but the principal officers of his household, are induced to poison themselves, that they may enjoy the honour of being interred with him and of serving him in a future state."— *Martyn's Geography.*

We have several instances of this cruel superstition being still practised in Africa. We shall only quote one. When a king in Guinea is buried, Bosman assures us, several of the slaves are sacrificed in order to serve him in the other world; as are his bossums or wives dedicated to his god. What was still more to be lamented, than the putting these miserable creatures to death, was the pain they endured in the execution. They pierced and cut them as in sport for several hours; he says he saw eleven put to death in this manner.

The cemetery of an Etruscan city was as large as the city itself. Above two thousand tombs have been opened in that of Tarquinia, and is computed by Avolta to have extended over sixteen square miles, and to contain not less than two million tombs; and yet it is surrounded on all sides by cemeteries of other cities of scarcely inferior extent. A common unpainted tomb consists of two vaulted chambers, small and low. On one side stands the sarcophagus, or bier, with its wreath, or arms, and around upon the walls are bronzes and terra-cotta. There are usually a number of vases on the ground near the sarcophagus. The subjects of the painted tombs are chariot-races, festivals, battles, in a spirited and lively coloured style, expressed, says Mrs. Gray, with a grouping and a spirit which is Greek and a mannerism which is Egyptian. The lids of the coffins have in some cases figures of men and women in alto-relievo, and in the coffins have been found a wreath of ivy, or of bay, in pure gold, or a helmet and spear; and in others something of gold or bronze, scarabæi, gems, jewellery, but rarely coins.

Tarquinia, Veii, Vulci, Tuscania, and other cities from the necropoli of which the vases and other Etruscan remains have been collected, are in the neighbourhood of Civita Vecchia, and within a day's journey from Rome.

The priests of Eklinga, in Rajast'han, all wear the distinguishing mark of the faith of Siva, which is a crescent on the forehead. Their hair is braided, and forms a species of tiara round the head, which is frequently adorned with a chaplet of the lotus-seed. Like the other ascetics they disfigure their bodies with ashes, and wear garments of a deep orange colour. Their dead are interred in a sitting posture, and the tumuli which are erected over them are generally of a conical form. "I have seen," says Tod, "a cemetery of these, each of very small dimensions, which may be described as so many concentric rings of earth, diminishing to the apex, crowned with a cylindrical stone pillar. One of the disciples of Siva was performing rites to the manes, strewing leaves of an evergreen, and sprinkling water over the graves."

Druidical or Celtic monuments may also be traced eastward from Asia Minor to Armenia, through Southern India to Macao, in China, and the island of Loochoo.

But to those who think that science could never have retrograded, and that in modern Europe only has the art of navigation obtained the power of conducting vessels over the broad Atlantic or Pacific Oceans, it may be shown that the ocean separating some parts of the old from the new world could have been traversed by two or three short voyages.

Humboldt remarks, since it is more than probable that the inhabitants of Asia and America passed the ocean, it may be curious to examine the breadth of the arm of the sea that separates the two continents, under the latitude of 65° 50′ north. According to the most recent discoveries made by the Russian navigators, America is so near Siberia, by Behring Straits, that by sailing from Cape Prince of Wales to Cape Tschoukotskay the distance between these two capes is but an arc of 44′, or $18\frac{1}{10}$ leagues, taking 25 to a degree. The Isle of Imaglin is nearly in the middle of this canal,— this isle is one of five nearer to the Asiatic coast.

Simpson, who journeyed across Arctic America, describes the Bow River as having a breadth of about one hundred and fifty yards, with a strong and deep current. This they crossed, baggage and horses, on a raft covered with willows, which, with like contrivances in overcoming other river difficulties, may remind one of the mode in which the Greeks passed the Hydaspes with Alexander, or crossed the Euphrates in the time of Cyrus.

Ferry, in his " Scenes in Mexico," mentions a party of Indian hunters descending the stream of the St. Pedro on rafts formed on large bundles of reeds, kept afloat by empty calabashes.

The connection between the Celtic tribes of Western Europe and the Scandinavians and Scythians of the north, are supposed to be conclusively shown by their barrows. The description of Herodotus of the mode in which they buried one of the kings has been confirmed in a remarkable manner by the contents of some barrows in Siberia opened by the Russian government. Herodotus mentions among other articles placed in the sepulchre " one of the king's wives strangled." To these they add cups of gold, because silver and brass are not used among them. This done they throw up the earth, and endeavour to raise a mound as high as they possibly can. In one which was opened, both the male and female body were laid on a sheet of pure gold, and covered with the same material. The gold weighed as much as forty pounds. In the barrows opened in England such costly materials are not found ; but considerable insight into the habits and manners of our British and Saxon progenitors, and the state of their arts and manufactures, has been obtained from the examination of their contents. In America there are large numbers of these tumuli ; it is stated that there are nearly 3000 of them, from 20 to 100 feet in height, between the mouth of the Ohio, the Illinois, the Missouri, and the Rio San Francisco. Some of these monuments are two or three stories high, and resemble in their form the Mexican teocallis, and the pyramids with steps of Egypt and Western Asia. Some are constructed of stones heaped together.

In the region comprehending Louisiana, Texas, Mississippi, and Florida, the south-western states of the American union, large mounds have been opened by Dickenson. One of them proved to be a vast cemetery, containing many thousand human skeletons, besides numerous stone implements, ornaments,

and other objects of interest.   In the course of these researches, Dickenson has collected a museum of 15,000 articles.
Among these are 60 crania of races entombed in the mounds,
and 150 perfect vases.   Some of the latter are said to be
equal to Etruscan or Grecian.   In the western states Davies
and Squier have made accurate measurements of 90 tumuli
or mounds, and have excavated 115.   Within these monuments they are said to have found implements and ornaments
of silver, copper, lead, stone, ivory, and pottery ; the last
mentioned fashioned into a thousand forms, and evincing a
skill in art which the existing race of Indians at the time of
the discovery could not approach.   In these tumuli were
also found marine shells, mica from the region of the primitive rocks, native copper from the shores of Lake Superior,
and galena from the Upper Mississippi.   These articles appear to indicate an extensive intercourse among the inhabitants of ancient America.   The gentlemen engaged in these
researches appear to have arrived at the following conclusions : — that the constructions of the tumuli were nearly
related to the Arctic race ; that only a small proportion of
the enclosures commonly called forts were reared for the
purpose of defence ; that a considerable number were in
some way connected with religious rites, but that the use of
by far the greater part cannot be conjectured in our present
state of information.   The tumuli in the western states are
thus classified by Bartlett : — 1. Tumuli of sepulture, containing a single skeleton, each inclosed in a rude sarcophagus
of timber, or an envelope of bark or matting, and occurring
in isolated or detached groups.   2. Tumuli of sacrifice, containing symmetrical altars of stone or burned clay, occurring
within or in the vicinity of inclosures, and always stratified.
3. Places of observation, or the elevated sites of temples or
structures occurring upon elevated or commanding positions.
    We have not seen the measurements of these tumuli.
    The " Louisville Journal" states that in the south-western
part of Franklin County, Mississippi, there is a platform or
floor, composed of hewn stone, neatly polished, some three
feet under ground.   It is about 108 feet long and 80 feet

wide. It extends due north and south, and its surface is perfectly level. The masonry is said to be equal, if not superior, to any works of modern times. The land above it is cultivated; but thirty years ago it was covered with oak and pine trees, measuring from two to three feet in diameter. It is evidently of very remote antiquity, as the Indians who reside in the neighbourhood had no knowledge of its existence previous to its recent discovery; nor is there any tradition among them from which we may form an idea of the object of the work or of the people who were its builders.

Sides 108 by 80 feet
$\qquad$ = 93·4 ,, 69 units

$(10 \times 93·4)^3 = 934^3 = \frac{3}{4}$ distance of moon
$(10 \times 68·8)^3 = 683^3 = \frac{3}{10}$,, .

Cubes of the sides are as 2 : 5.

Sum of 2 sides $= 68·8 + 93·4 = 162·2$ units.
$\qquad (10 \times 163·2)^3 = 1632^3 =$ 4 distance of moon
$(10 \times 10 \times 163·2)^3 \qquad = 4000$,, .

Cube of 10 times sum of 2 sides = 4 distance of moon
$\qquad = \frac{1}{100}$ distance of earth.

Cube of 100 times sum of 2 sides
$\qquad = 4000$ distance of moon
$\qquad = $ 10 times distance of earth.

The ruins of Central America can be traced from the West, in California, extending eastwards to the Ohio, then again southwards through Mexico to Yucatan. In the whole of this line numerous remains of pyramids are found. Another remarkable feature in these ruins are the numerous square stone pillars covered with bas-reliefs erected on each of their four sides. The average height is 25 feet, and they still stand erect in the midst of the debris of ruined architecture and perished vegetation which imbed their lower portions; in some places ruins have been found covered with soil to the depth of nine feet. In the front of these pillars sculptured stone altars stand, which are grooved to receive the blood of the human victims. The group of square stone columns and altar at Copan standing in a grove of trees, which seem to have been planted by the hands of man, reminds one strongly of the ruder Druidical remains in the Old World. The description of the pillars at Copan given by the Spaniards 300 years ago is equally applicable to them at this day. One of the figures they called the bishop.

The stone walled and arched roofed chapel at Calento was not known to the early Spaniards, though they passed close by it. In the middle is a stone altar for sacrifice. Among the sculptured reliefs, on one side of the chapel, is the prominent figure of a cross, or tree cross, having a bird on the top, and the head of a serpent at the bottom, gnawing the root.

The feathers that cover the gigantic scrolled serpent on the walls at Uxmal are those of the same bird, which is entirely green, and the feathers of its tail very long. Such feathers were found by Catlin still to be worn by a tribe of Indians as a distinguishing emblem of royalty. This bird is now very scarce, and only found in Guatemala. This serpent has the tail of a rattle-snake.

The western ruins about California are less ornamented than those about Mexico, and have been supposed to be of an earlier date. Among some of these ruins trees have sprung up, which, by their concentric rings, have been reckoned as five or eight hundred years old. Tools made of an alloy of copper and tin were used in arts and sculpture. The structure of the numerous Indian languages in America is said to be almost uniform, and different from any in the Old World, except that of Tchuktchi, the most eastern frontier of Asia, to which it bears a strong resemblance.

Some idols of stone are found in a place called Quirigua, which is situated on the banks of the river Montagu, several miles east of Encuentros, which is the place where the river is reached by the great road leading from the port of Ysabal to the town of Guatemala. The idols are exactly in the same style as those of Copan; but they are two or three times as high.

At this place is also found an obelisk, or rather a carved

stone, 26 feet above the ground, and probably 6 or 8 feet under. The sides represent figures of men, and are finely sculptured.

Vast regions of ancient ruins are said to have been discovered near St. Diego, and within a day's march of the Pacific Ocean, and at the head of the Gulf of California. Portions of temples, dwellings, lofty stone pyramids (seven of these within a square mile), and massive granite rings or circular walls round venerable trees, columns, and blocks of hieroglyphics, all speak of some ancient race of men, now for ever gone, their history actually unknown to any of the existing families of mankind.

From what has been stated, it would appear that a communication between Europe and America in a north-west direction from the Mediterranean, and another, in a north-east direction, between Asia and America, had been established between the two hemispheres at a remote period.

In a later age Columbus, by directing his course south-west from the Canary Islands across the Atlantic, discovered tropical America. This expedition, which manifested the perfect character of being the fulfilment of a plan sketched in accordance with scientific combinations, was safely conducted westward, through the gate opened by the Tyrians and Colœus of Samos, across the unmeasurable dark sea, " Mare tenebrosum " of the Arabian geographers.

Both Columbus and Amerigo Vespucci died in firm conviction that they had merely touched on portions of Eastern Asia.

The early missions from the Old to the New World may be supposed to have come from the mouth of the Nile or the Mediterranean, and across the Atlantic, to the mouth of the Mississippi : the mouths of both rivers are nearly in the same latitude, and the valleys of the two rivers abound with the remains of antiquity.

Columbus, in his first voyage, by sailing south-west from the Canary Islands, reached the island of Cuba. Between Cuba and Mexico, — the land of pyramids, — lies the Gulf of Mexico, which the Cyclopean masons might have crossed,

and erected teocallis in Mexico.   But in their course they
could leave no monumental records in the sea of darkness
where the sun set.   On the discovery, in modern times, of
the Canary Islands, the original inhabitants, known by the
name of Guanches, were in the habit of embalming their
dead, and depositing them in caves.   The Spaniards represent
the mode of embalming in the Canaries as being similar to
the process used by the Egyptians, as described by Herodotus.
When the preparations were completed, the body was sewn up
in goatskins and bandaged with leather : the kings and nobles
were placed in a sarcophagus made of a hollowed tree ; but
in all cases the corpse was deposited in a grotto destined for
that purpose.   They much resemble, when discovered in the
present day, those of Egypt in appearance ; but soon crumble
into dust when taken out of the skins in which they are
wrapped.   At Fer the catacombs are walled up, and domestic
utensils are found in them.

The most celebrated are those at Teneriffe, between Arico
and Guimar.   The interior is spacious, but the entrance is in
a steep cliff, and difficult of access.   There are niches in the
walls, in which the bodies are placed; and, when first discovered, there were upwards of a thousand mummies in the
place.   Humboldt says—" The many indications which have
come down to us from antiquity, and a careful consideration
of the relations of geographical proximity to the ancient un-
doubted settlements on the African shore, lead me to believe
that the Canary Islands were known to the Phœnicians,
Carthaginians, Greeks, and Romans,—perhaps even to the
Etruscans."   The same author thinks it probable that fully
2000 years elapsed from the foundation of Tartessus and
Utica by the Phœnicians to the discovery of America by the
northern course, that is to say, to Eric Randau's voyage to
Greenland, which was followed by the voyage to North
Carolina ; and that about 2500 years intervened before
Christopher Columbus, starting from the old Phœnician
settlement of Gadeira, made the passage by the south-west
route.

That the Phœnicians, or their descendants the Carthaginians, were competent to have made such voyages, and ultimately to have arrived in Mexico, may be shown by their having accomplished the circumnavigation of Africa. The Phœnicians were the first people along the Mediterranean shores that applied astronomical observations to navigation. They had remarked the fixed position of the Polar star during the general movement of the spheres. By this star they regulated their voyages, and such was their progress, from the time of Nechos to a period when other nations scarcely dared to quit the coasts, that they had departed from the Red Sea, made a voyage round Africa, and, at the end of the third year, arrived at the mouth of the Nile.

But those who constructed the first teocallis in Mexico knew that the earth was round, since they had measured its circumference : and, supposing that they first reached America by the northern line of coasts, they would necessarily infer that a shorter line existed between the Mediterranean and the same parallel of longitude. Hence it would appear highly probable that they would attempt a shorter passage by sailing in a westerly direction from the Mediterranean ; and, favoured by the trade-wind, they might have proved by trial what they had inferred by reason, and, like Columbus, have traversed the Atlantic by sailing west, guided by the Polar star or compass. With the latter it may fairly be presumed they were acquainted, since they placed the sides of the great teocallis and pyramids exactly opposite to the four cardinal points.

According to the following extract from the "Saturday Magazine," South America appears to have been visited by Europeans two thousand years ago. "It may not be improper here to mention a recent discovery, which seems to afford strong evidence that the soil of America was trodden by one of Alexander's subjects. A few years since there was found, near Monte Video, in South America, a stone with the following words, in Greek, written on it :—"During the reign of Alexander, the son of Philip, King of Macedon, in the sixty-third Olympiad, Ptolemy * * * "—The remainder of the inscription could not be deciphered. This stone covered an excavation which contained two very ancient swords, a helmet, a shield, and several earthen amporæ of large capacity.   On the handle of one of the swords was the portrait of a man, and on the helmet there was sculptured work representing Achilles dragging the corpse of Hector around the walls of Troy.   This was a favourite picture among the Greeks.   Probably this Ptolemy was overtaken by a storm in the Great Ocean (as the ancients termed the Atlantic), and driven on the coast of South America.   The silence of the Greek writers in relation to this event may easily be accounted for by supposing that in attempting to return to Greece he was lost, together with his crew, and thus no account of his discovery ever reached them."

It is stated that Lund, the Danish naturalist and geologist, has recently discovered, in the province of Minas-Geraes, a quantity of human bones, including some complete skeletons in the fossil state.   Nearly all the skulls bear the character of the present tribes of Brazil ; but in some the incisive teeth are exactly like the molar teeth, which circumstance has been remarked in some of the Egyptian mummies.

He has observed, in the numerous calcareous caverns of Brazil a quantity of human bones near those of different species of animals, some of which are now extinct.   He concludes from this fact that it is erroneous to regard the South American as a variety of the Mongolian race, who are supposed to have peopled the New World by emigration.

"The geological constitution of this continent shows," he says, "that it is anterior to what is called the Old Continent ; and the Mongolian race is but a branch of the American races, instead of being the primitive root."

Successive voyages might have been made across the great Pacific Ocean by sailing in an easterly direction from tropical Asia to central America.

The island of Macao lies on the extreme of the south coast of China.   East of Macao lie the Philippine Islands in the Chinese Sea, said to be more than 11,000 in number ; then the Ladrone and Caroline Islands in the Pacific ; next, the Sandwich group ;—all these, including Macao and the city of Mexico lie between the tropic of Cancer and the equator.

The connecting links of the Philippine Islands with the south of the equator and the Peruvian coast would be the numerous Hebrides, Friendly, Society, and Marquesas Islands. From the Marquesas to Peru would be a long voyage; and so would that between the Sandwich Islands and Mexico.

In the Pacific Ocean we find the rock idols of Christmas Island and of Pitcairn's, where no human foot was supposed to have trodden, till the mutineers of the " Bounty " landed, and found in the sculptured remains unequivocal proof that a people had anteriorly lived on that rock, and had there died or departed. Easter Island is remarkable for statues and stones roughly hewn, some of which are 27 feet high. The wicker obelisk at Atooi has been mentioned ; and the *morai*, or teocalli, at Otaheite, where ordinarily, though not always, human victims were selected from the criminals for sacrifice. There the priesthood perform the operation of circumcision on the top of a hill. So that in this island we find the teocalli and druidical sacrifices, such as Cæsar has described ; the high places where the Mahomedan, Jewish, and Egyptian custom of circumcision was practised, and adopted also by other nations of great antiquity. Herodotus mentions that circumcision was practised by the Colchians, Egyptians, and Ethiopians from time immemorial. Then he adds, "But whether the Ethiopians had this usage from the Egyptians, or these, on the contrary, from the Ethiopians, is a subject too ancient and obscure for me to determine."

Barrows is the name given to artificial hills, which were in ancient times generally constructed to commemorate the mighty dead. Such hills are usually formed of earth, but sometimes of heaped stones. In the latter form they are almost exclusively confined to Scotland, and are there called cairns. Barrows are found in almost every country, from America to the steppes of Tartary. Articles which are actually found in some tumuli, and most of them in those of this country, generally consist of stone and earthen coffins, urns of metal and earthenware, spears, swords, shields, bracelets, beads, mirrors, combs, and even coins and cloth.   Barrows have been found in New Caledonia, and in the country of the Hottentots.   Two very curious tombs on the barrow principle were discovered by Oxley, in 1817—1818 in the interior of New South Wales.   The principal of the two showed considerable art.   The form of the whole was semicircular; three rows of seats formed one-half, and the grave with the outer row of seats the other.   These seats or benches constituted segments of circles of from 40 to 50 feet, and were raised by the soil being trenched up between them.   The grave itself was an oblong cone, five feet high by nine in length.   This barrow was supported by a sort of wooden arch: the body was wrapped up in a great number of opossum skins, covered with dry grass and leaves, and lay about four feet below the surface.

Hodgkinson, who travelled and explored a region of Australia, as government surveyor, describes a grand ceremony, when the boys are inaugurated into the privileges of manhood.   After the preliminaries are settled, the blacks repair to the Cawarra ground.   This is a circular plot, about 30 feet in diameter, carefully levelled, weeded, and smoothed down.   It is, in general, situated on the summit of some round-topped hill, and the surrounding trees are minutely tattooed, and carved to such a considerable altitude that one cannot help feeling astonished at the labour bestowed on this work.   Many grotesque mummeries having been performed, the doctors or priests of the tribe take each a boy, and hold him for some time with his head downwards near the fire.   Afterwards, with great solemnity, they are invested with the opossum belt; and at considerable intervals between each presentation, they receive the nulla-nulla, the boomerang, the spear, &c.

Stokes witnessed at Port Stephen, in Australia, a corroborory, or dance performed in the night, by the natives, around lighted heaps of fuel.   The peculiar feature in this corrobory was the throwing of the kiley or boomerang, lighted at one end; the remarkable flight and extraordinary convolutions of which had a singular and startling effect.

Another trait in the character of the Australians deserves to be pointed out, which is their sculptured rocks. The natives are doubtless attracted to the Island of Depuch, one of the Forester group, partly by the reservoirs of water they find among the rocks after rain, partly that they may enjoy the pleasure of delineating the various objects that attract their attention on the smooth surface of the rocks. This they do by removing the hard red coating, and baring to view the natural colour of the green stone, according to the outline they have traced; much ability is displayed in their representations, the subjects of which could be discovered at a glance. The number of specimens was immense, so that the natives must have been in the habit of amusing themselves in this innocent manner for a long period of time. I could not help reflecting as I examined with interest the various objects represented, — the human figures, the animals, the birds, the weapons, the domestic implements, the scenes of savage life,—on the curious frame of mind that could induce them to repair, perhaps at stated seasons of the year, to this lonely picture-gallery, surrounded by the ocean wave, to admire and add to the productions of their forefathers. No doubt they expended in their works of art as much patience, labour, and enthusiasm, as ever was exhibited by a Raffaelle, or a Michael Angelo, in adorning the walls of St. Peter or the Vatican; and, perhaps, the admiration and applause of their fellow-countrymen imparted as much pleasure to their minds as the patronage of popes and princes, and the laudation of the civilised world to the great masters of Italy.

Brooke found the inhabitants of Borneo uncivilised and ignorant. They had been accustomed, since time forgotten, to bloody and barbarous practices,— murder, robbery, treachery, and almost every other vice. Yet they possess a religion, dark and imperfect though it be, founded on the original bases of all faith; one great God dwelling above the clouds, a future state of bliss for the good,—the happy hunting-ground of the American Indians, — and a place of punishment for the wicked.

Among the Caroline Islands in the Pacific ruined cities are said to exist, which are built with large square blocks of stone, and extending over a surface that must have contained a vast population. Now they are sunk below the level of the sea and situated on inclining banks, the tops of which form small islands of volcanic origin, which are still subject to the phenomena attending upon submarine fire. The parts above water seem to indicate, in many places, that a great surface had sunk into the sea, leaving summits above water; or the summits, with ruins upon them, are gradually returning to the surface.

Where did the people who have left these monumental proofs of civilisation in the Pacific come from? It has been asserted that vessels sailing from the eastern coast of Asia could not have discovered America, because junks like the Chinese could not have survived an attempt if perseveringly continued to cross the Pacific Ocean, and moreover that an attempt could not have been made at an early period for the want of the knowledge of the compass.

But a proof that a Chinese junk was able to have crossed the Pacific, is that one lately sailed from Canton, in China; rounded the Cape of Good Hope; touched at New York, in America; and finally arrived safely in London, where we examined her minutely.

A Japanese junk, having been blown out of her course was allowed to float at random for eight months, and when within 48 hours' sail of California an English ship sent a boat to the junk, and took out seven persons, the surviving number of a crew of forty. It was an open boat that brought the first intelligence of De Gama's safe arrival in India, — having gone the whole distance across the Indian Ocean, — round the Cape of Good Hope to Lisbon. Of the vessels that Columbus had on his first visit to America, only one was completely decked.

One of the boats, we cannot call her a vessel, that accompanied Drake on his first passage round Cape Horn was only 16 tons. Columbus in his second voyage found the sternpost of a vessel on shore at Guadaloupe. In 1798 an American merchant and a black boy, passengers from the East Indies in a British ship, traversed the Atlantic from off the African coast to Surinam, in South America, in an open boat or ship's gig, aided by the trade winds. Numerous instances might be adduced of Oceanian natives being scattered by the monsoons to immense distances from their homes, with and without women. Behring's Straits, between Asia and America, being scarcely 40 miles broad, could be crossed by the natives in seal-skin coracles, or on the winter's ice from the more desolate coast of Asia.

The Chinese ships are so constructed, remarks Wallace, that they may strike on a rock without sustaining any serious injury; and if a leak springs in one part, the cargo in another will not be damaged. These junks trade to all parts of the Eastern seas, and the compass used as in Europe; but with a needle pointing to the South, which is here considered as the attracting point.

Father Gaubil says, the directive power of loadstone was known to the Chinese under the dynasty of Han, which ended as early as the year after Christ 225, or about 1000 years before Paul the Venetian was in China. He also states that the variation of the compass was known to the Chinese as early as A. D. 1101.

Biot in his researches in the Chinese history, with a view of ascertaining the period at which the Chinese had the first knowledge of the compass, found a tradition mentioned of an instrument which pointed to the South 2700 years B. C. He remarks that, as the compass still points to the South in China, no alteration in the declination can have taken place in that country.

Gutzlaff, when a passenger in a junk from Siam to the north of China, noticed that the Chinese sailors, besides making an offering to an image of the " Queen of Heaven," worshipped the compass itself.

A recent account states that in some parts of China attention is paid in selecting the situation for burial, and the body is placed by the direction of the compass.

The religious, political, and scientific embassy, which Louis XIV. sent into Siam in 1684, had instructions to penetrate, if possible, into China. Having been shipwrecked on this voyage, they sailed in a Chinese junk for Ningpo. Here they suffered much from the superstitious habits of the Chinese sailors. As no savoury food was allowed to be eaten till it had first been offered to a little black idol, they were thus virtually interdicted from any thing better than plain boiled rice. They saw the sailors worshipping the very compass by which they steered, and even offered it meat.

"In a Chinese work (the historical Szuki of Szumathsian, a writer who lived in the early half of the second century before our era,) we meet with an allusion to the "magnetic cars," which the Emperor Tschingwang, of the ancient dynasty of the Tscheu, had given more than 900 years earlier to the ambassadors from Tunkin and Cochin China, that they might not miss their way on their return home. In the third century of our era, under the dynasty of Han, there is a description given in Hiutschin's Dictionary Schuewen, of the manner in which the property of pointing with one end towards the South, may be imparted to an iron rod by a series of methodical blows. A century later, under the dynasty of Tsin, Chinese ships employed the magnet to guide their course safely over the open sea; and it was by means of these vessels that a knowledge of the compass was carried to India, and from thence to the eastern coasts of Africa." (Humboldt.)

The Eugubian Tables, which Bentham believes to contain the invention of the compass by the Tyrrhenes, and the discovery of the colonisation of Ireland, were written in the reign of Numa or Romulus.

Volney, describing Arabia Felix, says "The Queen of Sheba dwelt at Mareb, the capital of the country of Saba. That Eupolemus, who was well acquainted with the history of the Jews, says, that David sent ships to work the gold mines of an island called Ourphe (Ophir), situated in the

Erythrean Sea, which is the name of the Arabic Ocean as far as the Persian Gulf. Then adds, but did not Eupolemus mean a celebrated island in those regions, called by Strabo Tyrinia (Tyrian Isle), where was to be seen under wild palm-trees the tomb of the King Erythras (that is, of the red king), who was said to have given his name to the Arabic Ocean, because he was drowned in it? We have here a Phœnician tale, the true meaning of which is, that the burning and red sun, which every evening was drowned in the ocean, was worshipped by the navigators who passed there, and who, in gratitude for a prosperous voyage, raised up a monument of the same description as that of Osiris, King, Sun, as well as Erythras. By representing this tomb as a considerable pyramidal tumulus, Strabo leads us to conjecture another motive of utility, that of raising on a flat coast a point of direction to mariners.

"From historical fragments, preserved by the Arabians, it appears that under the name of Arabians, children of Himiar, there existed in Arabia Felix, or Jemen, much more than 600 years before the age of David and Solomon, a civilised and powerful people, known to the Greeks at a late period by the name of Homerites or Sabeans. That long before the time of the Hebrews, those of Jemen had made remote expeditions, at one time to the coast of the Red Sea, by the interior of Africa, towards Tombout and as far as Morocco; at another time to the North, as far as the Caspian Gates, and sometimes to India. The Homerites pretend that the Queen of Sheba, Balquis, daughter of Had-had, built a palace at Mareb, and constructed the celebrated dyke of the lake of that city; but other Jemenders assure us that the dyke had been long constructed, and that Balquis only repaired it."

From these data, perhaps, in a little time, the site of the city of Mareb with its dyke and lake, as well as the pyramidal tumulus, may be discovered, since Aden, on the coast of Arabia Felix, has become a British station, and forms the connecting link by steam navigation between the Red Sea and India; as formerly the port called Arabia Felix, now

Hargiah, at the mouth of the river Sanaa, according to the Greeks, formed the connecting link of commerce between the Red Sea and Persian Gulf,—thence to India.   This port is supposed to have been the nearest to the residence of the Queen of Sheba.   Volney infers, after comparing a great number of historical and geographical probabilities, that Ophir was on the Arabian coast, at the entrance of the Persian Gulf.   Also, on this coast there still remains a town of Daba, which signifies gold ; and it is known by a number of passages from the ancients, collected by Bochart, that this country was formerly as rich in gold as Peru and Mexico at the present day.   Here is a country, perhaps, worthy of being explored for the remains of antiquity by the spirit of research that has already penetrated into other Eastern countries.

On the Arabian coast of the Persian Gulf, a river called Falg conducts to an ancient city in ruins called Ophor.   It is true this situation is not insular, according to Eupolemus ; but it is to be remarked, that in all the Arabian dialects, including the Hebrew, the same word signifies island and peninsula, according to Volney.   But the point of Oman, where Ophor stands, is a real peninsula, especially on account of the rivers that cut its basis.

At the mouth of the river that flows by the ruins of Ophor commences the great bank of pearls, the very ancient centre of a rich trade ; at the extremity of this bank are found two other islands, formerly called Tyr and Arad, and which, as Strabo says, had Phœnician temples : their inhabitants pretended that those of Tyr and Arad, in the Mediterranean, were descended from them.

One of the Homerite princes was surnamed Zou-l-Minar, Lord of the Pharos ; because, in an expedition to the country of the Negros (Africa), he erected towers supplied with lanterns, in order to again find his road across the ocean of sand.

We find a race of Sabæans, the Homerites, in Arabia Felix, and also a pyramid, and we may infer that, like other pyramids, the sides corresponded to the four cardinal points of the compass, with which not improbably they were acquainted, and by means of which they made remote expeditions, and carried on an extensive commerce with India and Africa.

If the Phœnicians were the descendants of these Sabæans, they would, like the English emigrants, have carried with them the knowledge of their fatherland, and, like the Americans, have established an extensive maritime commerce,—conducting their remote voyages by the compass. This extensive commerce might account for the prosperity of Arabia Felix at a remote period. The Arabs who visit Aden report that in the interior of Arabia Felix are the ruins of many cities, built by a race unknown.

The circumnavigation of the world has now become an ordinary occurrence; it may soon be made a voyage of pleasure by steamers. Lately Simpson has published a narrative of his overland journey round the world. He travelled from the Atlantic across Arctic America to the Pacific, and from the Pacific through Siberia to the British Channel. Before starting from the Russian port of New Archangel by a five months' journey through the Russian empire, he says, " I have threaded my way round nearly half the globe, traversing about 220 degrees of longitude, and upwards of 100 of latitude, barely one-fourth of this by the ocean." The circuit of the globe was made in 19 months and 26 days, and terminated at London.

Herodotus says he will not relate what he calls the fable of Abaris, a Hyperborean, who without eating is said to have carried an arrow all over the world; and adds, " I cannot refrain from laughing at those who have described the circumference of the earth, and wish to persuade us that the ocean extends all round it, and that the earth itself is round."

Herodotus, in numerous instances, as in the last, gives the statement as related to him by others, and then expresses his disbelief of what he has written. Yet, from being simply a reporter of what he heard, he has been called the too credulous historian. But when he laughs on being told that the earth is round and its circumference known, he might be called the too incredulous historian.

A ship never eats, neither does the compass, though we have seen the Chinese offering it food. A ship might have carried Abaris, who directed its course by the compass all over the world.

From this it would seem as if Herodotus had heard at different places, as at Babylon and Egypt, of the description of the form and measurement of the circumference of the earth, and moreover that the ocean extended round the world.

Jamblichus tells us that Pythagoras took from Abaris, the Hyperborean, his golden dart, without which it was impossible for him to find his way. But Porphyry, in his life of Pythagoras, makes the story more wonderful, and says that Abaris used to fly in the air, being carried by the dart given him by the Hyperborean Apollo. He further adds, that some people were of opinion Pythagoras could do the like.

A ship carrying Abaris might be said to fly by the wind filling the sails, while its course was directed by his arrow. For a ship with a compass need not sail along the coast, but would take the shortest course by crossing the sea, and as she was sinking below the horizon and no land near her, she would appear to the spectators on shore as if she were flying through the air.

From what has been stated it appears that ages ago astronomy, the polar star, the compass, the round figure of the earth and its circumference, were all known. When this knowledge was reacquired in Europe Columbus rediscovered America — possibly the lost Atalantis of the ancients.

When making some experiments in 1839, previously alluded to, and having found that we were able to attract and repel various substances without contact or external agency, we then tried if we could by self-agency give polarity to a common sewing needle. After subjecting the needle to experiment it was found on trial to point north and south. The experiment was repeated on other needles with like results. Next we tried a common needle without submitting it to any operation, and found that this needle also pointed north and south when floated on water. Then various new needles, bought at different places, without being subjected to operation, were tried in London, and in the country 20 miles distant, next on the shore of the Solway Firth, a large arm of the sea, between an amphitheatre of Scotch and English mountains. In all these trials the same results were uniformly obtained. Lastly, the same experiments were repeated among the mountains in Silesia, which form a continuation of the Carpathian chain, that bound the north of Hungary; there the sea was far remote, and the locality free from any lake, still the results were uniformly the same.

By the sea-coast numerous pieces of old iron, which we promiscuously met with, were found, with one exception, to point north and south when suspended in water.

Other results of a different kind were also obtained, but some of these varied at different places. We noted down all the experiments, intending to have repeated them, and tried others, but we were diverted from pursuing the path of inquiry further, by our attention being directed to other subjects.

The needle was fixed horizontally in the top of a waxed taper float, used in night lamps; the thin piece of cork floated on the water, and the needle above pointed N. and S.

The pieces of old iron were suspended in the water by means of a thread attached to a piece of cork-wood, which floated on the water, and the piece of iron in the water pointed N. and S.

So that a simple needle, or an old rusty nail, if properly adjusted, will make a compass.

How, then, can it be supposed that the ancients, so skilled in science, and particularly in astronomy, who built the sides of their pyramids corresponding to the cardinal points, could have been ignorant of the compass?

The figure is an Egyptian symbol of divinity. The inclination of the top of the rod very probably denotes the dip of the magnetic needle.

PART X.

PAGODA OF SERINGHAM. — BRAMBANAN IN JAVA. — VALLEY OF
NEPAUL. — CASHMERE. — PAGODA OF JUGGERNAUT. — CUBE OF
BABYLON. — PLANETARY DISTANCES REPRESENTED BY THE CUBE,
CYLINDER, SPHERE, PYRAMID AND CONE, IN TERMS OF THE CIR-
CUMFERENCE OF THE EARTH, AND DISTANCE OF THE MOON FROM
THE EARTH; ALSO BY THE NINTH ROOT OF THEIR DISTANCES. —
DISTANCES OF PLANETS REPRESENTED BY SPHERES AND BALLS OF
THREAD. — THE PARCÆ OR FATES. — EXTENT OF RAILWAY IN
GREAT BRITAIN. — DISTANCES OF FIXED STARS. — MAGNITUDE OF
PLANETS COMPARED. — PERIODIC TIME OF BELUS 432 YEARS. —
THE YUGES. — BELUS OF BABYLONIA LIKE OSIRIS OF EGYPT. —
WORSHIP OF JUPITER ONCE UNIVERSAL. — ANCIENT MYTHOLOGY.
— PERIODIC TIME OF NINUS 1200 YEARS. — ANTEDILUVIAN KINGS
AND PATRIARCHS. — REIGNS OF GODS AND MEN IN EGYPT. —
TRACES OF THE WORSHIP OF BEL OR BAAL IN AUSTRALIA, SCOT-
LAND, AND THE ISLE OF MAN. — THE GODS OF CARTHAGE. —
RAWUN THE TITAN CELEBRATED IN THE HINDOO ILIAD. — HINDOO
REFLECTIONS ON EUROPEAN ACHIEVEMENTS. — THE AZURAS AND
RASKSASAS OF THE HINDOOS LIKE GIANTS AND TITANS OF THE
GRECIAN MYTHOLOGY. — THE HEIGHT OF THE TITAN KOOMBHA-
KARNA EQUALLED THE CIRCUMFERENCE OF THE EARTH. — TITANIC
REPUTATION OF THE SABÆANS. — THE GIANTS OF THE OLD AND
NEW WORLD COMPARED. — BELUS THE CHIEF OF THE TITANS. —
THE TITANS OF GRECIAN MYTHOLOGY COMPARED WITH THE TI-
TANS OF CHALDÆA. — CUBE OF NINEVEH EQUALS DISTANCE OF
NINUS. — THE MAGI, GHEBRES, AND PARSEES. — KOYUNJUK TEPE
OPPOSITE MOUSOUL. — ASSYRIAN MOUNDS. — GATES OF WALHALLA.
DISTANCES OF FIXED STARS AND PLANETS. — HERO-GODS. —
COLOSSAL STATUES. — SARCOPHAGI IN THE PYRAMIDS. — ZO-
ROASTER, PYTHAGORAS, PLATO. — ELEUSINIAN MYSTERIES. — FIRE-
TEMPLE AT BALKH. — BRAHMINS, BOODHISTS, JAINS, AND SEIKS.

Seringham.

" THE pagoda of Seringham stands in the dominions of the
king of Tangore, in the neighbourhood of Trichinopoly, and

is composed," according to Orme, "of seven square enclosures, one within the other, the walls of which are 25 feet high, and 4 thick. These enclosures are 350 feet distant from one another, and each has four large gates, with a high tower, which are placed one in the middle of each side of the enclosure, and opposite to the four cardinal points. The outward wall is nearly four miles in circumference, and its gateway to the south is ornamented with pillars, several of which are single stones 35 feet long, and nearly 5 in diameter; while those which form the roof are still larger. In the inmost enclosures are the chapels. Here, as in all the other great pagodas in India, the Brahmins live in subordination which knows no resistance, and slumber in a voluptuousness that knows no wants; here, sensible of the happiness of their condition, they quit not the silence of their retreats to mingle in the tumults of the state; nor point the brand, flaming from the altar, against the authority of the sovereign or the tranquillity of the government. All the gateways are crowded with emblematical figures of their various divinities. No Europeans are admitted into the last square, containing the sanctuary of the supreme Veeshnu, and few have gone further than the third. In the war between the French and English in the Carnatic, this voluptuous slumber of the Brahmins was frequently interrupted; for the pagoda, being a place of considerable strength, was alternately taken possession of by the contending armies. On the first attempt to penetrate within the sacred enclosure, a venerable Brahmin, struck with horror at the thought of having a temple, so profoundly hallowed for ages, polluted by the profane footsteps of Europeans, took his station on the top of the grand gateway of the outermost court, and conjured the invaders to desist from their impious enterprises. Finding all his expostulations ineffectual, rather than be the agonising spectator of its profanation, he, in a transport of rage, threw himself upon the pavement below, and dashed out his brains."

There are seven square enclosures, and the distance between each = 350 feet, which call ¾ stade, or 351¼ feet.

Then the side of the least, or central square, will $=2 \times \frac{4}{4} = \frac{5}{2}$ stade, and the perimeter will $= 4 \times \frac{4}{2} = 10$ stades. The side of the external, or greatest square, will $= 7 \times \frac{4}{2} = \frac{35}{2} = 17\frac{1}{2}$ stades. The perimeter will $= 4 \times 17\frac{1}{3} = 70$ stades, and 1 mile 18·79 stades.

So the perimeter of the external square will nearly $= 4$ miles.

The perimeter of the least square $= 10$ stades $= 60$ plethrons.

The perimeter of the greatest square $= 70$ stades $= 7$ times 60 plethrons.

The sum of the perimeters of the walls of the 7 squares
$$= (1 + 2 + 3, \&c.) \times 10 \text{ stades},$$
$$= \tfrac{1}{2} \overline{n + 1} \cdot n \times 10,$$
$$= \tfrac{1}{2} 8 \times 7 \times 10 = 280 \text{ stades},$$
or nearly 15 miles.

The perimeters of the 7 squares $= 280 = 4 \times 70$ stades $= 4$ times the perimeter of the greatest square.

Suppose the 7 squares to be the bases of 7 cubes.

The side of the first square $= \frac{4}{2}$ stade $= 15$ plethrons $= 607\cdot5$ units, and the cube of 610 &c. units $= 2$ circumference.

Sum of the series of 7 cubes will
$$= (1^3 + 2^3 + 3^3, \&c.) \times 610^3$$
$$= (\tfrac{1}{2} \overline{n+1} \cdot n)^2 \times 610^3 = (\tfrac{1}{2} 8 \times 7)^2 \times 610^3$$
$$= 28^2 \times 610^3 = 784 \times 2 \text{ circumference}$$
$$= 1568 \text{ times the circumference.}$$

In another description the walls are said to be 4 or 5 feet thick, and height 25 feet. The great hall for pilgrims is supported by 1000 pillars, each cut out of a single block of stone.

Supposing the outer side of the wall of the first, or central square, $= 610$ units; then inner side of the wall will $= 2 \times 5 = 10$ feet $= 9$ units less than the outer side $= 610 - 9 = 601$ units.

So the cube of the outer side $= 610^3 = 2$ circumference, and cube of the inner side $= 601^3 = \frac{1}{5}$ distance of the moon.

Sum of the 7 external cubes
$$= 28^2 \times 610^3 = 784 \times 2 = 1568 \text{ circumference.}$$

Sum of the 7 internal cubes
$$= 28^2 \times 601^3 = 784 \times \tfrac{1}{5} = 156\cdot8 \text{ distance of the moon.}$$

Mean distance of Mercury $= 150$ or 151 distance of the moon.

The orbit of Mercury is very elliptical, the excentricity being nearly one-fourth the mean distance.

Possibly there might have been terraced walks round both sides of the walls, of such a breadth that the sum of the cubes of the sides of the 7 external terraces equalled the greatest distance of Mercury, and the sum of the cubes of the sides of the 7 internal terraces equalled the least distance of Mercury from the sun.

Sum of the 5 first of the internal series of cubes

$$= (1^3 + 2^3 + 3^3 + 4^3 + 5^3) \times \tfrac{1}{5}$$
$$= (\tfrac{1}{2}\, \overline{n+1} \cdot n)^2 \times \tfrac{1}{5}$$
$$= 15^2 \times \tfrac{1}{5} = 45 \text{ distance of moon.}$$

5th cube of internal series

$$= 5^3 \times \tfrac{1}{5} = 125 \times \tfrac{1}{5} = 25.$$

Cube of twice side $\qquad = 25 \times 8 = 200.$

Twice cube of twice side $= 400$ distance of the moon $=$ distance of the earth.

Sphere diameter 601 units $=$ circumference.

Cubes of external sides,

$$4^3 = 64.$$

Cube of 4th side $\qquad = 64 \times 2 = 128$ circumference.
Cube of 5 times side $\quad = 128 \times 5^3 = 16000.$
Cube of 15 times side $= 16000 \times 3^3$
$\qquad\qquad\qquad\qquad = 432000$ circumference
$\qquad\qquad\qquad\qquad =$ diameter of orbit of Belus.
$$5^3 = 125.$$

Cube of 5th side $\qquad = 125 \times 2 = 250$ circumference.
Cube of twice side $\quad = 250 \times 8 = 2000.$
Cube of 12 times side
$\quad$ or of 3 times perimeter $\qquad = 2000 \times 6^3$
$\qquad\qquad\qquad\qquad\quad = 432000$ circumference.
$\qquad\qquad\qquad\qquad\quad =$ diameter of orbit of Belus.
$$6^3 = 216.$$

Cube of 6th side $\qquad = 216 \times 2 = 432$ circumference.
Cube of 10 times side $= 432 \times 10^3$
$\qquad\qquad\qquad\qquad = 432000$ circumference.
$\qquad\qquad\qquad\qquad =$ diameter of orbit of Belus.
$\qquad\qquad$ 1 mile $= 4566$ units.

External side of 7th square $=610 \times 7 = 4270$ units, which is less than 1 mile.

If the side of a square $= 1$ mile, twice perimeter would $= 8$ miles

$$= 8 \times 18 \cdot 79 = 150 \cdot 32 \text{ stades.}$$

Greater side of Nineveh $= 150$ stades.

So the cube of Nineveh, which equals the cube of 150 stades, will equal the cube of 8 miles.

Malcom describes Seringham as " the famous pagoda, the most distinguished of the renowned seven. This proud monument of Hindoo art and wealth stands on an island made by the Cavery river dividing itself into two branches. The *sanctum sanctorum* of the numerous structures around is scarcely larger than a native's hut, but is highly adorned, and in some places gilded. It is enclosed within seven successive walls, 120 yards apart. These walls are of great strength, 25 feet high, and, besides common gateways, have twenty stupendous towers or pagodas over as many entrances. The outer wall is four miles in circumference. A multitude of sacred edifices are scattered about, among which are some vast halls. The flat roof of one of them is supported by 1000 slender pillars of carved granite. The pavement, stairs, and lower parts of the buildings generally, are of red and grey granite and sienite. The rough slabs had evidently been split. I was surprised to find that what was thought among us to be a modern invention had been practised here for ages.

" Griffins and tigers, gods and men, tolerably sculptured, adorned various parts. The cars, on which the idols were drawn on display days, stood in the bye-places. We saw no one performing any kind of worship.

" The intervals between the walls are occupied by streets of well-built houses, and present the common aspect of a busy town. The population is about 8300. Persians of all grades and occupations reside here, and carry on their business: a very large portion are Brahmins. The other inhabitants seemed chiefly to subsist by little shops. They made no objection to selling me unconsecrated idols, and whatever else I chose.

" A singular aspect is given to the place by scores, if not hundreds, of huge monkeys, which are seen at every glance. They are held sacred to Hunimaun, the divine ape, that conquered Ceylon for Rama. Of course they are not only unmolested, but well fed, and multiply without restriction. They looked on us from every wall, and frolicked on the trees, the images, and carved sides of the towers, often coming within a yard of us, without the semblance of fear. They are by no means peculiar to this temple, but abound in most Hindoo sacred places, and for the same reason.

" Pilgrims from all parts of India resort to this place for absolution from their sins; and as none come without an offering, the Brahmins live in voluptuous ease. The establishment receives also from the East India Company an annual stipend; still their rapacity is insatiate. Half-a-dozen of them, pretending to act as guides, followed us everywhere, begging with insolent pertinacity. Clerical mendicity is regarded as a virtue rather than a fault."

" At Brambanan, a village nearly in the centre of Java, are many extraordinary remains of Hindoo images, temples, and inscriptions. The area occupied by the ruins of all descriptions is equal to 10 miles. Over this entire surface there are scattered, at various distances, the ruins of several temples; but the most remarkable ruins are known to the natives by the name of the Thousand Temples. This collection constitutes a square group of buildings, each measuring about 250 paces. In the centre of the square stood one large temple, which was surrounded at equal distances by three square rows of smaller ones, each row but a few feet distant from the other. At each of the four cardinal points, where there appeared to have been once gates, were two gigantic statues, named by the Javanese Gopala, one of the names of Krishna. Each of these had a mace in his hand, and a snake twisted round his body.

" In the large temple there are no images; but from the remaining pedestals it appears there once were some. The inside

T 4

walls are adorned with the figures of the conch shell, of water vases, and of the sacred lotus, all indicating a Hindoo origin. On the outside of the large temple are figures of Brahmins. In some of the small temples there are still some images; and among the other ruins there is a group of large temples, one of which still contains an entire figure of Bhavani, and another of Ganesa; on an adjacent building are sculptured many Hindoo figures in relief. About a mile and a half distant from the Thousand Temples there is another cluster of buildings, close to which is an oblong slab of granite, 7 feet long and 3 broad, one face of which is covered with an inscription. Other stones and inscriptions are also scattered about.

"The stones of these buildings are of hewn granite, admirably well cut and polished, and laid on each other with great skill and nicety. No mortar has been made use of, but instead of it, the lower surface of each stone has a prominence which fits accurately into a groove in the upper surface of the one underneath, by which contrivance the stones are firmly retained in their situations. The roofs of the temples are all, like the rest of the building, of hewn granite; and it is in their construction that the greatest skill has been displayed. Every thing regarding these ruins is wrapped in the greatest obscurity."—(*East India Gazetteer.*)

Side of the square $= 250$ paces
$$= 6 \times 250 = 1500 = 2 \times 750 \text{ feet.}$$

Side of the base of Cheops' Pyramid
$$= 749 \text{ feet} = 648 \text{ units,}$$
$$648^3 = \tfrac{1}{4} \text{ distance of the moon,}$$
$$(2 \times 648)^3 = 2 \text{ distance of the moon.}$$

Thus the cube of the side of the square at Brambanan $=$ twice the distance of the moon from the earth $=$ diameter of the orbit of the moon.

$$75 \text{ cubes} = \text{distance of Mercury,}$$
$$200 \text{ cubes} = \text{distance of the earth.}$$

Cube of $\frac{1}{2}$ perimeter $= (4 \times 648)^3 = 16$ dist. of the moon.

25 cubes $= 400$

$= $ distance of the earth.

Cube of side $= (2 \times 648)^3 = 2$ distance of the moon.

$(5 \times 2 \times 648)^3 = 2 \times 5^3 = 250$

15 cubes of 5 times side $= 3750$

$= $ distance of Saturn.

Cube of 10 times side $= 2000$ distance of the moon.

In a narrative of a British surveying voyage, an excursion into the interior of the eastern part of Java is described by Jukes. The travellers examined the ruins of Singha Sari, consisting of temples, tombs, and colossal statues well executed. " There was a beautiful Brahmin bull lying down, about 4 feet long; human figures with elephants' heads; a fragment of a chariot drawn by several horses abreast, admirably sculptured; and many figures of Hindoo deities, with three or four heads and several pairs of arms. They seemed all to be cut from nearly the same kind of stone, and all bore the impress of the same style of art, and that one of no mean order. There was none of that excessively *outré* and indecent representations which are, I believe, frequent in the temples of India, and both the buildings and the sculptures bore the impress of great refinement of taste in the design, and much skill and carefulness in the execution. I must plead guilty to the most profound ignorance in architecture and sculpture generally, and to that of the Hindoos especially; but to my eye these ruined temples and statues were singularly beautiful and interesting, and they are worthy, I think, of far more study and attention than has hitherto been bestowed upon them. In the woods I found, as at Kedal, piles of old bricks of a much larger size and better material than the Javanese can now produce. These were the ruins either of the houses of the people or of the palaces of their kings. The imagination became busy in restoring their fallen glories, in picturing large cities, adorned with temples and palaces, seated on the plain, and in recalling the departed power, wealth, and state of the native kingdom that once flourished in a land so noble, so beautiful, and so well adapted for its growth and security.   That such a kingdom once existed is evident, not only from the detached ruins of so many separate parts of the valley, and the piles of brick in the forests, but from the ancient brick causeways still used as the principal roads of the country, and the ruins of large brick walls that are said to stretch from the southern side of Mount Kawi to the sea, fortifying the valley of Kediri, and thus defending the principal access to the plains of Malang from the west.   Any of these structures is far beyond the powers of the present inhabitants, if left to themselves, and bespeaks a people among whom civilisation and the arts had made no mean progress, and had had no short or temporary existence.   Whatever may have been the history of the people, it is entirely unknown, and scarcely mentioned even by tradition.

"Java is strewed with similar remains, and some of much greater extent and magnificence, from one end of the island to the other, as may be seen in Raffles' and Crawfurd's books, to which I must refer the reader ; merely observing that the outline sketches in the illustrations of those works, while they convey an idea of their forms and subjects, sufficient for our information on these points, by no means do full justice to the artistic beauties of the ruins and sculpture, and hardly attempt to pourtray those of the surrounding scenery."

The Hindoos are referred to by Herodotus in much the same manner as he speaks of the Pyramids, as existing without explaining their origin.   Their annals, partaking more of the character of fable than of truth, afford us no means of tracing their first rise.   Yet laws, literature, and religion aid us under such circumstances, and on all of them are to be found well known works of Hindoo antiquity.   The Vedas, a book of ancient hymns and prayers, supposed to have been collected in their present form, about the fourteenth century before the Christian era, throw much light on their attainments in philosophy, and even in science.   The doctrine of these works is theism, and they were supplanted in popular influence by the Puránas, which inculcate polytheism and idolatry. These last, composed of eighteen works by different authors, and of dates varying from the eighth to the sixteenth century, are now regarded as the Scripture of the Hindoos. They have accounts of creation, philosophical speculations, religious ceremonies, fragments of history, and legends of gods, heroes, and sages. The most perfect picture of the Hindoos is, however, afforded by the laws of Menu, drawn up, as is supposed, about the ninth century before the Christian era. This, which appears to be the greatest key to their history, is not the work of one period. Codes, as Elphinstone remarks, are never the work of a single age ; some of the earliest and rudest laws being preserved and incorporated with those of more enlightened times. Of Menu, the compiler of this work, nothing is known ; but its remote antiquity is gathered, as well from its antiquated style, as from some differences which it exhibits between the state of manners at that period and that existing from the time of Alexander to the present day. Thus no mention is made by Menu of the self-immolation of widows, and Brahmins are, by that code, permitted to eat meat, and to intermarry with women of inferior castes. The religion of the code, also, is theism of the Vedas, not the polytheistic idolatry of a later period. The community is divided by Menu into four castes, the sacerdotal, the military, the industrious, and the servile. The first three, though not equal, partake of certain rites ; the fourth and the outcasts are only considered as contributing to the welfare of others. These castes are named the Brahmins, the Cshatriyas, the Vaisyas, and the Sudras.

Although the Hindoos have no records deserving the name of history, the narratives of Alexander's expedition are striking testimonials to the antiquity of this people, as well as to the general permanence of oriental habits. The great peculiarity of the Hindoo system, the division into castes, is described, and the castes named. Their number is greater than at the present day, but Elphinstone observes that the Greeks subdivided two of the castes, and that, with this exception, the castes are the same as those mentioned in the laws of Menu. They describe the Brahmins (Brachmanes) with their ascetic observances; and Nearchus even explains their division into religious and secular. The early marriages of the females; the circumstance that the people live only on vegetables; the worship of the Ganges; the burning of widows on the funeral piles of their husbands; the brilliancy of their dyes; their skill in manufactures; their mode of catching and training elephants; their kinds of grain and manner of farming, are all as we now find them; and even their arms, with the exception of fire-arms, are the same as at present. The peculiar Indian bow, which Elphinstone says is now only used in the mountainous districts, which is drawn with the assistance of the feet, and which shoots an arrow six feet long, is minutely described, as are the long swords and iron spears, their powerful bits, and their admirable management of horses.

The books held sacred by the Hindoos leave scarcely any room to doubt that the religion of Brahma has been established from the most remote antiquity in the Nepaul valley, where there are as many temples as houses, and as many idols as inhabitants, there not being a fountain, river, or hill within its limits that is not consecrated to some one or other of the Hindoo deities. The popular religion in general differs nothing from the Hindoo doctrines established in other parts of India, excepting so far as the secluded nature of the country may have assisted to preserve it in a state of superior purity. The valley of Nepaul, in particular, abounds with temples of great sanctity, where newars, or peasantry, sacrifice buffaloes to Bhavani, and afterwards feed on the flesh with great satisfaction. The ancient history of Nepaul is very much clouded with mythological fable. The inhabitants have lists of princes for many ages back.

The Hindoos regard the whole of Cashmere as holy land; forty-five places are dedicated to Mahadeva, sixty-four to Vishnu, three to Brahma, and twenty-two to Durga (the wife of Mahadeva). In 700 places are carved figures of snakes, which they also worship.

We must pass the descriptions of several large Indian pagodas, as no others have any assigned dimensions, by merely observing that the pagoda of Juggernaut, according to Hamilton, is a circular structure, about 50 yards high, with the image of an ox larger than life cut out of an entire stone, and projecting from the centre of the building. The fore-part of this animal is alone visible. He describes the idol as an irregular pyramidal black stone. The Brahmins, according to Sonneret, carry its antiquity as far back as 4800 years. Sumnaut himself stands in his temple as an idol, composed of one entire stone 50 cubits in height, 47 of which were buried in the ground. According to the Brahmins, he had been worshipped on that spot 4000 or 5000 years.

According to De Marles, the shrine of the idol of Juggernaut is constructed of enormous blocks of granite, transported with incredible labour from the neighbouring mountains, and consists of a grotesque pyramidal structure, about 350 feet in height, and a spacious area, enclosed by a lofty wall. Around the interior of this wall there runs a gallery, supported by a double range of pillars, and forming 276 arcades. The four faces of the pyramid are covered with sculptured figures, and its apex crowned with ornaments of gilt copper, which flash and glitter in the sun. The interior of this stupendous structure, from which the light of heaven would appear to be excluded, is lighted up by a hundred lamps, which burn perpetually before the idol.

The height of the pyramid is about 350 feet, and $\frac{1}{4}$ of a stade = $351\frac{1}{4}$ feet = $2 \times \frac{1}{8}$ stade = twice the height of the teocalli of Cholula.

A pyramid having the height = $\frac{1}{4}$ stade, and side of base = twice the height = $\frac{2}{3}$ stade, will = $\frac{1}{3}$ circumference.

The Cube of Babylon.

The content of the tower of Belus = $\frac{1}{3}$ the cube of the side of the base = $\frac{1}{3}$ of a cubic stade = $\frac{1}{24}$ circumference.

So 1 cubic stade will = $3 \times \frac{1}{24} = \frac{1}{8}$ circumference.

The side of the square that enclosed the tower = 2 stades, and the cube of 2 stades = 8 cubic stades = circumference.

The walls of Babylon formed a square having the side = 120 stades. (*Herod.*)

$$120^3 = 1728000 \text{ cubic stades,}$$
$$\tfrac{1}{8} = 216000,$$

so the cube of the side of the square = 216000 times the circumference.

Circumference of earth = 24,899 miles.

Therefore the cube of the side, or 120^3 stades, will = 216000 × 24899 = 5378184000 miles.

The difference between 610^3 &c. units, which = 2 circumference, and the cube of $2\frac{1}{2}$, or $\frac{4}{4}$ stade, or 607·5 units, is about $\frac{1}{72}$ of 610^3 &c. units. Or 2 circumference will exceed the cube of $2\frac{1}{2}$ stades by about $\frac{1}{72}$ part.

In cubing the side of the square of Babylon, we have taken the cube of 2 stades, or 8 cubic stades, to = the circumference.

But the cube of 2 stades, or the cube of 846 units

$$= 114791256 \text{ cubic units,}$$
$$\text{and circumference} = 113689008.$$

So here the correction will be made by the addition of $\frac{1}{100}$ part to the distance obtained by this calculation.

$(2\frac{1}{2})^3$ stades is less than 2 circumference.

And 2^3 stades is greater than 1 circumference.

$$(2\tfrac{1}{2})^3 : 2^3 :: 5^3 : 4^3 :: 125 : 64.$$
125 is less than 2 × 64 or 128.

So the circumference will lie between half the cube of $2\frac{1}{2}$ stades and the cube of 2 stades.

So the cube of Babylon will = 537818400 + $\frac{1}{100}$ part = 5432 millions of miles.

In order to remember this number, count the four sides of the square of Babylon 1234; to each numeral add 1, which makes 2345; transpose, or read backwards, 2345, and we have 5432, the number of millions of miles which the cube of Babylon represents.

Let us compare the mean planetary distances with the cube of Babylon.

Cube = 5432,   Lost Planet = 5432.

$\frac{1}{2}$ = 2716,   Neptune   = 2850.

$\frac{1}{3}$ = 1811,   Uranus   = 1822.

$\frac{1}{6}$ = 905,   Saturn   = 906.

$\frac{1}{11}$ = 494,   Jupiter   = 494.

$\frac{1}{37\cdot4}$ = 145,   Mars   = 145.

$\frac{1}{57\cdot2}$ =   95,   Earth   =   95.

$\frac{1}{80}$ =   68,   Venus   =   68.

$\frac{1}{150}$ =   36,   Mercury   =   36.

Taking $\frac{1}{24}$ for the mean distance of the small planets between Mars and Jupiter, the series will be

$$1, \ \frac{1}{2}, \ \frac{1}{3}, \ \frac{1}{6}, \ \frac{1}{11}, \ \frac{1}{24}, \ \frac{1}{37\cdot4}, \ \frac{1}{57\cdot2}, \ \frac{1}{80}, \ \frac{1}{150}$$

of the cube.

The distance of Uranus exceeds the sum of the distances of all the other planets that are nearer to the sun. The distance of the lost planet Belus = 3 times the distance of Uranus from the sun.

' We have reason to think," observes Maclaurin, " that the fondness of the Pythagoreans and Platonists for geometry sometimes misled them, by inducing them to derive the mysteries of nature from such analogies of figures and numbers as are not only unintelligible to us, but in some cases seem not capable of any just explication. The use they made of the five regular solids in philosophy is a remarkable instance of this, and must have been a very important part of their scheme, if we may depend on the ancient commentators on Euclid, who tell us he was a Platonic philosopher, and composed his excellent elements for the sake of this doctrine.   But as it is a matter of pure speculation, we cannot conceive that there can be any analogy between it and the constitution of nature ; and they have not been successful who have of late endeavoured to explain this analogy, as we shall have occasion to show, when we come to give some account of Kepler's discoveries.   Nor is this the only instance, where a pursuit of analogies and harmonies has led us into errors in philosophy."

Cube		=	5432	Belus	=	5432
Inscribed sphere		=	2844	Neptune	=	2850
,,	pyramid	=	1811	Uranus	=	1822
Pyramid ¼ height		=	906	Saturn	=	906

The different great distances expressed in terms of the cube of unity have been represented by the cube and square based pyramid, the cylinder, sphere or spheroid, and cone. These five figures we suppose to have been the five regular bodies of the ancients, which were thought by the school of Alexandria to have been of such importance in the philosophy of former ages, that Euclid is said to have compiled his Elements of Geometry with the hopes of discovering them.

The planetary distances in terms of the earth's circumference will be, proximately,

Belus	=	cube of Babylon		=	216000 circumference.
Neptune		,,		=	113000 ,,
Uranus	= $\frac{1}{3}$	,,		=	72000 ,,
Saturn	= $\frac{1}{6}$	,,		=	36000 ,,
Jupiter	= $\frac{1}{11}$	,,		=	19636 ,,
Earth		,,		=	3840 ,,
Venus	= $\frac{1}{80}$	,,		=	2700 ,,
Mercury	= $\frac{1}{150}$	,,		=	1440 ,,

Distance of earth $= 2\frac{2}{3}$ distance of Mercury.
$= 2\frac{2}{3}$ 1440 $= 3840$ circumference.

Distance of Neptune $=$ sphere of Babylon,
$= \cdot5236 \times$ cube of Babylon,

$$= \cdot 5236 \times 216000 = 112997,$$
$$\text{or} = 113000 \text{ circumference.}$$

$2^{11} = 2048.$

Distance of Jupiter $= 2045$ distance of moon,
$$= 2^{11} \text{ nearly.}$$

Distance of Jupiter $= \frac{1}{11}$ distance of Belus,

∴ distance of Belus $= 11 \times 2^{11}$ distance of Moon.

Thus the distance of Jupiter and Belus may be expressed in terms of the numerals 1, 2.

Distance of earth $= 400$ distance of moon,
$$= 20^2 = 2^2 \times 10^2.$$

Distance of Belus $= 22500$ distance of moon,
$$= 15^2 \times 10^2.$$

Distance of earth : distance of Belus $:: 2^2 : 15^2,$

Distance of moon : distance of Belus $:: 1 : 22500$
$$:: 1 : 15^2 \times 10^2.$$

Distance of moon : distance of Mercury $:: 1 : 150$
$$:: 1 : 15 \times 10.$$

Distance of moon : distance of earth $:: 1 : 400,$
$$:: 1 : 2^2 \times 10^2.$$

Planetary distances from the sun in terms of the distance of the moon from the earth, and of the circumference of the earth.

Distance of Mercury $= 150$ distance of moon,

Earth $= \frac{8}{3}$ distance of Mercury $= 400$,,

$\frac{3}{2}$ distance of Earth $= 600$,,

Mars $= 604$,,

Moon	=	9·55	circumference	=	1	distance of moon.	
Mercury	=	1440	,,	=	150	,,	
Venus	=	2700	,,	=	281	,,	
Earth	=	3840	,,	=	400	,,	
Mars	=	5800	,,	=	604	,,	
Jupiter	=	19636	,,	=	2045	,,	
Saturn	=	36000	,,	=	3750	,,	
Uranus	=	72000	,,	=	7500	,,	
Neptune	=	113000	,,	=	11770	,,	

Belus $= 216000$ circumference $= 22500$ distance of moon.

22500 distance of moon $= 216000$ circumference;

or 150^2 „ $=$ 60^3 „

Distance of moon $= \dfrac{60^3}{150^2} = 9\cdot6$ circumference.

So that here all the distances of the moon, excepting the first line, are supposed to equal 9·6 circumference to avoid fractions.

The column of units to the ninth power will be somewhere about the planetary distances from the sun.

Mercury	-	-	-	-	-	17·6, &c. units.
Venus	-	-	-	-	-	18·9 „
Earth	-	-	-	-	-	19·6, &c. „
Mars	-	-	-	-	-	20·5, &c. „
* * *	-	-	-	-	-	
Jupiter	-	-	-	-	-	23·5, &c. „
Saturn	-	-	-	-	-	25·2 „
Uranus	-	-	-	-	-	27·1, &c. „
Neptune	-	-	-	-	-	28·6, &c. „
Belus	-	-	-	-	-	30·7, &c. „
Ninus	-	-	-	-	-	33·2.

The mean of three planetary distances from the sun, that of the earth being unity, are —

Neptune	$=$	30·0368000, nearly as 1
Uranus	$=$	19·1823900 „ $\frac{2}{3}$
Saturn	$=$	9·5387861 „ $\frac{1}{3}$

So that if 1 cylinder $=$ distance of Neptune
nearly $\frac{2}{3}$ or 1 sphere $=$ „   Uranus
$\frac{1}{3}$ or 1 cone $=$ „   Saturn.

Distance of Saturn from sun $= 9\cdot538$ times distance of earth from sun.

Distance of moon from earth $= 9\cdot55$ circumference.

Thus, circumference of earth : distance of moon :: distance of earth : distance of Saturn. The sphere of Babylon $=$ distance of Neptune, so a cylinder $=$ distance of Neptune will $=$ the sphere of Babylon.

3·1416 × distance of Saturn = distance of Neptune, or semi-orbit of Saturn = distance of Neptune.

3 × 3·1416 = 9·4248 = 3 semi-orbits of earth, and
9·5387 = distance of Saturn.
So 3 semi-orbits of earth = distance of Saturn,
25 times distance of Mercury = distance of Saturn,
25 radii of orbit of Mercury = 4 × 3·1416,
= 4 orbits of Mercury ;
so 4 orbits of Mercury = distance of Saturn,
60 semi-diameters of earth =   9·55 circumference = distance of moon,
9·55 circumference × 3·1416 × 2 =   60 circumference = orbit of moon,
and 60 × 24 = 1440 circumference = distance of Mercury.

or, 24 orbits of moon = distance of Mercury, and
24 × $\frac{480}{180}$, or 64 orbits of moon = distance of earth.

2 semi-diameters of orbit of Saturn = distance of		Uranus.
3 ,, ,, Uranus =	,,	Belus.
Thus, 60 semi-diameters of Earth =	,,	Moon.
24 orbits of Moon	= ,,	Mercury.
64 ,, ,, ,,	= ,,	Earth.
4 ,, Mercury ,,	= ,,	Saturn.
3 semi-orbits of Earth ,,	= ,,	Saturn.
1 ,, Saturn ,,	= ,,	Neptune.
2 semi-diameters of orbit of Saturn	= ,,	Uranus.
3 ,, ,, Uranus	= ,,	Belus.
3 diameters of orbit of Saturn	= ,,	Belus.
24 orbits of moon	= ,,	Mercury.
64 ,, ,, ,,	= ,,	Earth.
25 × 24 = 600 orbits of moon	= ,,	Saturn.
50 × 24 = 1200 ,, ,,	= ,,	Uranus.
150 × 24 = 3600 ,, ,,	= ,,	Belus.
4 orbits of Mercury	= ,,	Saturn.
8 ,, ,,	= ,,	Uranus.
24 ,, ,,	= ,,	Belus.

60 times circumference of earth = orbit of Moon.

60^2 times orbit of the Moon = distance of Belus.
60^3 times circumference of the earth = ,,
24 orbits of the Moon = distance of Mercury.
4 orbits of Mercury = ,, Saturn.
24 orbits of Mercury = ,, Belus.

Orbit of Moon : distance of Mercury,
:: orbit of Mercury : distance of Belus ;
distance of Moon : distance of Mercury,
:: distance of Mercury : distance of Belus.

3 semi-orbits of the earth = distance of Saturn.
3 orbits ,, = ,, Uranus.
9 ,, ,, = ,, Belus.

Distance of moon from earth = 9·55 circumference of earth.
Unity = 243×684^2 = 113689008 units = 684^2 stades = 24899 English miles = 21600 geographical miles.

*	circumf. of earth	-	=	1 circum.	cube root	= 1.
a.	dist. of moon from earth =		9·55	,,		= 2·12 &c.
1	,, Mercury from sun =		1440	,,		= 11·29 &c.
2	,, Venus ,,	=	2700	,,		= 13·9 &c.
3	,, Earth ,,	=	3840	,,		= 15·6 &c.
4	,, Mars ,,	=	5800	,,		= 17·9 &c.
5	,, Jupiter ,,	=	19636	,,		= 26·9 &c.
6	,, Saturn ,,	=	36000	,,		= 33·
7	,, Uranus ,,	=	72000	,,		= 41·6 &c.
8	,, Neptune ,,	=	113000	,,		= 48·3 &c.
9	,, Belus ,,	=	216000	,,		= 60.

The distance of Belus = 10 times as many circumferences of the earth as 1 circumference contains geographical miles.

Fig. 82. The radii of the series of spheres equal the cube root of the several planetary distances. So that the series of spheres will be proportional to the planetary distances.

If the diameter of the black sphere = 1, and the content = circumference of the earth,

Then the diameter of the next small sphere, *a*, = 2·12 &c., and content = distance of moon from earth.

The successive spheres have diameters equal the cube root

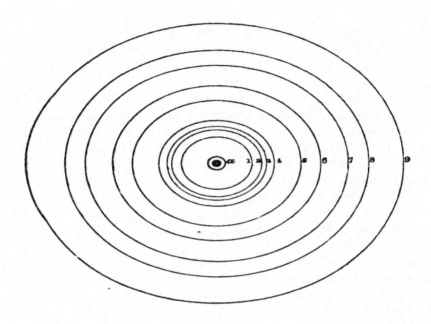

Fig. 82.

of the distances, and contents as the planetary distances from the sun.

Distance of moon from earth : distance of Mercury from sun :: distance of Mercury : distance of Belus.

u 3

Or sphere a : sphere 1 :: sphere 1 : sphere 9.

The concentric circles will represent spheres, cylinders, or cones ; and the circumscribing squares, cubes or pyramids.

This method of representing distances by spheres is simply representing distances by balls of thread.

If the black sphere equalled a ball of thread that would extend round the circumference of the earth, then the ball a would extend from the earth to the moon ; the ball 1 from the sun to Mercury ; and so of the remainder : the 9th ball or sphere would extend from the sun to Belus.

Owing to the recent great improvement in the art of manufacturing cotton by machinery, it is stated that one pound of Egyptian cotton can be spun, at Manchester, to the length of 238 miles, 1120 yards : so that 104 pounds of thread would reach round the globe.

Thus 104 × 216000, or 22464000 pounds of thread, would = 216000 circumference = distance of Belus.

In 1849 the quantity of cotton employed in the great manufacturing districts of England amounted to 775,000,000 pounds.

775,000,000 pounds of Egyptian cotton-thread would extend $5\frac{1}{2}$ times round the orbit of Belus.

The time of Belus' performing $5\frac{1}{2}$ revolutions round the sun will equal $5\frac{1}{2}$ × 432 = 2376 years ; the mean orbitular velocity of Belus being 9000 English miles an hour. So that if cotton, like the Egyptian, were spun at the rate of 9000 miles an hour, it would require 2376 years to spin 775,000,000 pounds. If the operation were continued only for 12 hours in each day, the time required for spinning the same quantity would = 2 × 2376 = 4752 years.

Cotton is now spun by machinery, and wound on spindles in the form of spheres, cylinders, and cones ; but it was formerly spun by the hand.

The Parcæ or Fates were powerful goddesses who presided over the birth and life of mankind. Some suppose that they were subjected to none of the gods but Jupiter ; whilst others suppose that even Jupiter himself was obedient to their commands. They are generally represented as three old women with chaplets made with wool and interwoven with the flowers of the Narcissus.

Some represent them as placed on radiant thrones, amidst the celestial spheres, clothed in robes bespangled with stars, and wearing crowns on their heads. They were three in number,— Clotho, Lachesis, and Atropos,— daughters of Nox and Erebus. Clotho appears in a variegated robe; on her head is a crown of seven stars; she holds a distaff in her hand reaching from heaven to earth. The robe which Lachesis wore was variegated by a great number of stars, and near her was placed a variety of spindles. Atropos was clothed in black; she held scissors in her hand, with clues of thread of different size, according to the length or shortness of the lives whose destinies they seemed to contain.

The poets of antiquity, in framing their preternatural stories, found it easy enough to describe men in a certain constitutional subjection to the deities, and those deities themselves in various degrees of subordination till they arrived at Jupiter, the Father of gods and men. But then came a difficulty. He was the son of Saturn; but how, and by what reaction of effects upon causes, the son came to be master of a still existing father, was a subject so difficult to be explained that the explanations were many and various. Then who was the father of Saturn? and so on. But when the genealogists had gone back as far as they could carry the patience of their readers, there arose a far more serious question than all,— which continually creeps out even in the popular mythology of Homer,—Who governed the gods? who imposed the laws, the objects, the bounds, and the goal of their dominions? who made them what they were? Hence the convenient fiction of the Fates, who governed gods and men, and whom Jupiter was supposed to consult and obey so assiduously that in some instances he assumes the character of the " wise man " of popular magic, who merely interprets a superior will. But then who made the Fates? Did they make events, or were events self-made, and the Fates an abstraction representing the order of events? In this way history, religion, poetry, and thought itself were lost in an interminable search for the First Great Cause, the true governor of the world, the ordainer of events, and the author of laws.

The extent of railway in Great Britain open in 1850 may be stated at 6381 miles of double and single line, which will be about 12,000 miles of single line. As each single line of railway consists of 2 rails, and as the length of the sidings have not been included in the estimate, the total length of iron rail laid down must exceed the circumference of our planet.

These lines are worked by nearly 2000 locomotives, which, in the course of a single year, collectively, travel over more than 32,000,000 of miles, — or in 3 years the whole distance from the earth to the sun, — or as much as $3\frac{1}{2}$ times round the world in a day; and carrying, in the course of a single year, not fewer than 60,000,000 passengers and 20,000,000 tons of goods. The number of passengers in a year exceed double the population of the kingdom. The length of rail, which exceeds 24,000 miles, would gird the world round with an iron band, weighing about 70 pounds a yard. This iron was raised from the mine, smelted, forged, and laid in the course of the last 15 years; whilst in the construction of the ways 250,000,000 cubic yards, or not less than 350,000,000 tons, of earth and rock have, in tunnel, embankment, and cutting, been moved to greater or less distances. The capital already raised by railway companies may be estimated at 236,000,000*l.* This sum exceeds one-quarter the National Debt of the United Kingdom.

Having compared the distances of the planets from Belus to Saturn with the cube, sphere, pyramid, and $\frac{1}{2}$ pyramid; let us compare, in like manner, the distances of the planets from Saturn to Mars. The cube of Belus = 120^3 stades = 1728000. Saturn = $\frac{1}{6}$ cube of Belus = 288000 = 36000 circumference = 66^3 stades = 906 millions of miles.

So, cube of Saturn	= 906,	Saturn	= 906
Inscribed sphere	= 474,	Jupiter	= 494
„ pyramid	= 302	* * *	
„ $\frac{1}{2}$ „	= 151,	Mars	= 145

Numerous small planets lie between Jupiter and Mars.

Distance of Mars : dist. of earth :: 145 : 95
Cylinder : sphere :: 145 : $\frac{2}{3}$ 145 :: 145 : 96·6
Distance of Venus : dist. of Mercury :: 68 : 36
Cube : sphere :: 68 : 68 × ·5236 :: 68 : 35·6

But the distance of Belus : distance of Neptune :: cube : sphere.

So, the distance of Venus : distance of Mercury :: distance of Belus : distance of Neptune.

Thus, the two planets nearest the sun are at the same relative distances from the sun and from each other, as are the two most remote planets.

Dist. moon : dist. Mercury :: dist. Mercury : dist. Belus
9·55 : 1440 :: 1440 : 216000
circum.

1 : 150 :: 150 : 150^2
Sphere a : sphere 1 :: sphere 1 : sphere 9

Thus, the relative distances of the moon from the earth, and the nearest planet from the sun, are the same as the relative distances of the nearest and most remote planets from the sun.

Of the four planets that have their distances represented by the first series of cube, sphere, pyramid, and $\frac{1}{2}$ pyramid, Neptune and Saturn have about 10 times the diameter of Mars and earth, each to each; Jupiter $\frac{1}{10}$ diameter of the sun; Uranus 11 times the diameter of Mercury.

Diameter of Neptune : diameter of Mars :: 41500 : 4100
,, Uranus : ,, Mercury :: 34500 : 3140
,, Saturn : ,, Earth :: 79160 : 7926
,, Sun : ,, Jupiter :: 882000 : 87000

Thus, magnitude of Sun : magnitude of Jupiter :: magnitude of Saturn : magnitude of earth :: magnitude of Neptune : magnitude of Mars :: 10^3 : 1^3 :: 1000 : 1 nearly.

Diameter of Uranus : diameter of Mercury :: 34500 : 3140
which is nearly as 11·29 : 1
the diameters of sphere 1 and black sphere.

So, magnitude of Uranus : magnitude of Mercury :: sphere 1 : black sphere.

Diameter of Mercury : diameter of Jupiter :: 3140 : 87000
:: 1 : 27·7
Diameter of black sphere : diam. of sphere 5 :: 1 : 26·9

Hence, magnitude of Mercury : magnitude of Jupiter :: black sphere : sphere 5 :: circumference of earth : distance of Jupiter nearly.

Also, magnitude of Uranus : magnitude of Mercury :: sphere 1 : black sphere :: distance of Mercury : circumference of earth.

∴ magnitude of Jupiter : magnitude of Uranus :: sphere 5 : sphere 1 :: distance of Jupiter : distance of Mercury.

Hence, if black sphere = magnitude of Mercury
sphere 1 will =   „   Uranus
„ 5 „ =   „   Jupiter

Or, if the black sphere diameter 1 = distance of Belus, then sphere 3, diameter 15·6, which nearly = 16, would equal the distance of a near fixed star from the sun.

But black sphere, diameter 1, = circumference of the earth, and sphere 3, diameter 15·6, = distance of the earth.

Hence, the circumference of the earth : distance of the earth from sun :: distance of Belus : distance of a near fixed star.

Diam. of earth	: diam. of the moon :: 7926	: 2160
Mag. of earth	: mag. of the moon :: 7926^3	: 2160^3
	nearly :: 50	: 1
Diam. Mercury	: diam. of the moon :: 3140	: 2160
Mag. Mercury	: mag. of the moon :: 3	: 1 nearly
Diam. of sun	: diam. of Mercury :: 882000	: 3140
Mag. of sun	: mag. of Mercury :: 22160000	: 1
Mag. of sun	: mag. of the moon :: 68000000	: 1
Diam. of sun	: diam. of the earth :: 110	: 1
Mag. of sun	: mag. of the earth :: 1331000	: 1
	nearly :: $1\frac{1}{3}$ million	: 1.

If the distance of Belus were represented by the black sphere, the distance of a near fixed star would be represented by sphere 3, and sphere S would represent a distance equal to 1000 times the distance of a near fixed star.

Or if the distance of Belus = 1^3
Distance of a near star = 16^3 = 4096
A remote distance = 160^3 = 4096000.

If 1 inch represented the circumference of the earth, 3·409 miles would represent the distance of Belus.

Magnitude of the sun : magnitude of Jupiter :: magnitude of Saturn : magnitude of the earth :: 10^3 : 1^3, nearly
:: sphere S : sphere 3.

The relative magnitude of the planets will be as the cube of their diameters, nearly as the spheres. (*Fig.* 83.)

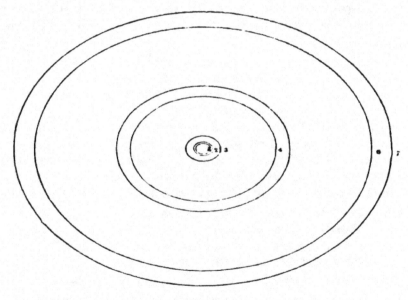

Fig. 83.

1.	Mercury	=	31 cubed =	29791
2.	Mars	=	41 =	68921
3. {	Venus	=	78 =	474522
	Earth	=	79 =	493039
4.	Uranus	=	345 =	41063625

5.	Neptune	=	415 cubed =	71473375
6.	Saturn	=	791	=	494913671
7.	Jupiter	=	870	=	658503000

Mars : Earth :: Neptune : Saturn :: 1 : 7.
Earth : Saturn :: Jupiter : Sun :: 1 : 1000.
Mars : Jupiter :: Neptune : Sun :: 1 : 9500.
Mars : Neptune :: Jupiter : Sun :: 1 : 1000.
Venus : Jupiter :: Saturn : Sun :: 1 : 1400.
Mercury : Uranus :: Venus : Jupiter :: Saturn : Sun :: 1 : 1400.
Earth : Sun :: 1 : 1400000.
Mars : Neptune :: Earth : Saturn :: Jupiter : Sun :: 1 : 1000.

These proportions may give some idea of the relative magnitude of planets, though they are far from being accurate.

Since P. T $\propto$ D$^{\frac{3}{2}}$,

P. T. of Belus : P. T. of Saturn :: 6$^{\frac{3}{2}}$: 1$^{\frac{3}{2}}$,

,,   : 10759 days :: 14·7 : 1,

,,   = 10759 × 14·7 = 158157 days,

,,   = 433 years.

So Belus would perform a revolution round the sun in about 433 years, say 432 years.

Then the Babylonian numbers 243, when transposed, will = 432 years for the periodic time of Belus.

432,000 years = the last Yug, or fourth age of the Hindoos.

So the last Yug will = 1000 times the P. T. of Belus.

3600 years = a sare,

and   1200 years = a divine year,

∴. 3600 × 1200 = 4320000 years

= a divine sare, or divine age, the great Hindoo period.

So a divine age will = 10000 times the P. T. of Belus.

Hence the times and distances may easily be recalled to mind, since 3^5 = 243, the Babylonian numbers; and 243 transposed by placing 2 the last, = 432, and 432 years = P. T. of Belus.

1000 times 432 = 432,000, the last Yug,

10,000 times 432 = 4,320,000, the divine age.

Distance of Belus = 120^3 stades
$$= 120^3 \times 243^3 = 1728000 \times 14348907$$
$$= 24794911296000$$

cubes of unity, which is almost 25 billions.

" Babylon had 100 gates, 25 on each side, all of solid brass." (*Herodotus.*)

The cube of one side = 25 billions of units.

Each side of the square enclosure of the tower of Belus = 2 stades = 486 units.

Cube of side = 486^3 =circumference.

If 486 units were equal to the internal side of the enclosure of the tower, and the thickness of the wall = 4 units, then the external side would $=486+8=494$ units.

Cube of external side $=494^3=\frac{1}{6}$ distance of moon.

Again, if the whole enclosure and tower stood upon an elevated platform which extended 10 units beyond the external side of the wall, then the side of the platform or terrace would $=486+8+20=514$ units.

Cube of side $=514^3=\frac{1}{8}$ distance of moon.
Cube of twice side $=1$ „
Cube of side of base of tower$=\frac{1}{8}$ circumference.
Cube of twice side $=1$ „

We have taken the distance of the moon from the earth to equal 60 semi-diameters of the earth $=30 \times 24899$ miles.

So 9·55 circumference $= 1085730026$ units,
but 9·57 „ $= 1088003806$ units
$=$ distance of moon by the cube of Cheops.

According to Herschel the mean distance of the centre of the moon from that of the earth is 59·9643 of the earth's equatorial radii, or about 237,000 miles.

The mean distance of Mercury from the sun is about 36,000,000 miles.

237000 miles$=$ distance of moon,
$152 \times 237000 = 36024000$ for distance of Mercury,
and $36000000 =$ distance „
$151 \times 36000000 = 5436000000$ for distance of Belus,
and $5432000000 =$ distance „

Thus 152 times the distance of the moon somewhat exceeds the distance of Mercury, and 151 times the distance of Mercury somewhat exceeds the distance of Belus.

So it may be said that the distance of Mercury = 151 times the distance of the moon, and the distance of Belus = 151 times the distance of Mercury.

The distance of the moon, according to the cube of Cheops, somewhat exceeds 237000 miles.

The distance of the moon = 4 cube of Cheops = 9·57 circumference = 238283 miles.

Mercury = 151 ×   238283 =   35980733,
Belus   = 151 × 35980733 = 5433090683,

which is very nearly 36,000,000 miles for the distance of Mercury, and very nearly 5,432,000,000 miles for the distance of Belus.

So,

distance of moon   = 4 cubes of Cheops = 9·57 circum.
  ,,   Mercury = 151 × 9·57 =   1445   ,,
  ,,   Belus   = 151^2 × 9·57 = 218205   ,,

It has been stated that 216,000 circumference for the distance of Belus would require to be corrected by the addition of about $\frac{1}{100}$ part.

For distance of Belus   = 5432 millions miles,
and circumference of earth = 24899 miles.

So 5432000000 ÷ 24899 = 218000 circumference.

These different estimates arise from taking

        242^3 &c. units = $\frac{1}{8}$ circumference,
or   (2 × 242, &c.)^3 = 1   ,,

and from taking 2 cubic stades, or (2 × 243)^3 to equal circumference, which answers for low numbers; but when the numbers become high, a correction becomes requisite, so that the cube of Babylon, or the cube of 120 stades, instead of equalling 216,000 circumference, when 2 cubic stades is made equal to circumference, will equal 218,000 circumference, when (2 × 242 &c.)^3 equal circumference; so that 120 cubic stades will equal 5432 millions of miles for the distance of

Belus. The periodic times corresponding to this distance equal 432 years, which is the elementary number of the great periods.

Regarding the epoch of the foundation of Babylon ancient authors differ in opinion, as we learn from Quintus Curtius that "Babylon was built by Semiramis, or, as is generally thought by Belus, whose palace is to be seen there." Berosus asserts that ancient Belus had long been the tutelar divinity of the country. The most remote of the Babylonian planets is so intimately associated with the Babylonian numbers, the walls of Babylon, and the pyramidal temple of Belus, that we think this lost planet may be designated by the name of Belus.

Both the Egyptian Osiris and the Babylonian Belus appear to have been regarded, at least, as hero-gods by the Sabæans, and not improbably they were originally one and the same divinity. The emblems of the divinity of Osiris are the symbols of the laws by which the planetary system is governed. The sun was worshipped by the Egyptians under the name of Osiris; by the Syrians under Bal; and by the Persians under Mithras. Polyhistor relates that, according to Berosus, Bel himself made the stars, the sun, the moon, and the other five planets.

Belus appears to have been adored at Babylon as Jupiter was by the Greeks. In fact Agathias, who wrote about 560, remarks, the Persians of former times adored Jupiter, Saturn, and the other gods of the Greeks, with this only difference, that they gave them other names, for with them Jupiter was Belus, Hercules was Sand-és, Venus was Anais, as is attested by Berosus and other writers who treat of the Mede and Assyrian antiquities. Herodotus informs us that the names of almost all the Grecian gods were originally derived from the Egyptians. The same author in his description of the pyramidal tower of Babylon calls it the temple of Jupiter Belus.

Pliny observes that Belus was regarded as the inventor of astronomy. Ctesias, speaking of the tower, calls it the temple of Jupiter, to whom the Babylonians gave the name of Belus. Akerman says that Bel or Baal was an epithet only, and not the name of a particular divinity. He refers to the Melita inscription, on which Melkart, the Phœnician Hercules, is styled the Baal of Tyr. Josephus tells us that Jezebel built a temple to the god of the Tyrians, whom they call Belus. A passage in Hosea shows that the Jews were in the habit of addressing the true God as their Baal. Milton, speaking of the divinities of the Assyrians and other nations, says they had general names of Baalim and Asteroth, those male, these female.

The entire organisation of Babylonia was attributed by tradition to Belus. Jupiter was regarded as the king of heaven and earth. His worship was universal, and surpassed in solemnity that of all the other deities. His temples were numerous, and he had many oracles, of which the most re-. nowned were those of Dodona in Epirus, and Ammon in the Libyan Desert. His names were numerous, as Osiris, Ammon, Baal, Belus, Zeus, Dios, Jeu, Jeud, Thor, Olympius, &c. The oak and the eagle were sacred to him; and, he was generally represented on a splendid throne of gold and ivory, with lightning and thunderbolts in one hand and a sceptre of cyprus in the other. His look was majestic, his beard long and flowing, and at his feet stood the eagle with expanded wings.

It may be remarked that the name of God is spelled with four letters in many different languages. In Latin it is Deus; French, Dieu; old Greek, Zeus; German, Gott; old German, Odin; Swedish, Gode; Hebrew, Aden; Dutch, Herr; Syrian, Adad; Persian, Syra; Tartarian, Edga; Slavonian, Bleg or Boog; Spanish, Dias; Hindoo, Esgi or Zeni; Turkish, Abdi; Egyptian, Aumn or Zent; Japanese, Zain; Peruvian, Liau; Wallachian, Zene; Etrurian, Chur; Tyrrhenian, Eber; Irish, Dieh; Croatian, Doha; Magarian, Oesc; Arabian, Alla; Duialtaan, Bagt. There are several other languages in which the word is marked with the same peculiarity.

Taylor, speaking of ancient mythology, says, " It is asserted that vices, diseases, and evil demons were esteemed deities by the ancients, and that the multitude of the gods, as an object of faith, was preposterous; the former of which assertions applies only to the corruption of the heathen religion during the decline and fall of the Roman empire; and the latter originates from a profound ignorance of ancient theology, and particularly of that of the Greeks.

" In the first place, the genuine key to this religion is the philosophy of Pythagoras and Plato, which, since the destruction of the schools of the philosophers by the emperor Justinian, has been only partially studied and imperfectly understood. For this theory was first mystically and symbolically promulgated by Orpheus, was afterwards disseminated enigmatically through images by Pythagoras, and was, in the last place, scientifically unfolded by Plato and his genuine disciples. The peculiarity of it also is this, that it is no less scientific than sublime; and that, by a geometrical series of reasoning, originating from the most self-evident truths, it developes all the deified progressions from the ineffable principle of things, and accurately exhibits to our view all the links of that golden chain, of which the deity is one extreme and body the other.

" The genuine pagan creed, as given by Maximus Tyrius, who lived under Marcus Antonius, is worthy of attention. ' There is one God, the king and father of all things, and many gods sons of God, ruling together with him. This the Greek says, and the barbarian says, the inhabitants of the continent, and he that dwells near the sea; and if you proceed to the utmost shores of the ocean, there too are gods rising very near to some and sitting very near to others.' By the rising and setting gods, he means the stars, which, according to the pagan theology, are divine animals, co-operating with the first cause in the government of the world."

Seven cubes, having their sides equal to the sides of the seven Seringham squares, will equal the distance of the nearest planet to the sun.

The cube, having the side equal to the side of the square

enclosure of the temple of Belus, will equal the earth's circumference.

The cube, having the side equal to the side of the square enclosed by the walls of Babylon, will equal the distance of the most remote planet known to the Sabæans when they built the pyramidal temple of Belus, and the celebrated walls of Babylon.

These famed walls were the monumental records of the astronomical triumph of the magi of Chaldæa, who were their only interpreters, and the sole depositories of science, which perished with a philosophical priesthood. Of the walls of the once mighty Babylon, one of the seven wonders of the world, no traces have been found.

$$1 \text{ year of Belus} = 1800 \text{ years of Mercury.}$$
$$= 432 \quad \text{,,} \quad \text{Earth.}$$
$$1 \text{ year of the gods} = 1200 \quad \text{,,} \quad \text{of man.}$$

If a planet were supposed to be about 113 times the distance of the earth from the sun,

the P. T. of earth would be to the P. T. of the planet
$:: 1\frac{1}{2} : 113\frac{1}{2} :: 1 : 1200$, so that one year of this planet would equal 1200 years of man.

The distance of the earth is about $\dfrac{1}{57 \cdot 2}$ part distance of Belus.

So the distance of this supposed planet would be about $\dfrac{113}{57 \cdot 2}$, or nearly twice the distance of Belus from the sun, or $5432 \times 1 \cdot 9755 = 10731$ millions of miles, which would equal about twice the cube of Babylon.

$$\text{P. T}^2 \text{ of earth : P. T}^2 \text{ of planet}$$
$$:: 1^2 : 1200^2 :: 1 : 1440000$$
$$\text{D}^3 \text{ of earth : D}^3 \text{ of planet}$$
$$:: 1^3 : 113^3 :: 1 : 1440000$$
$$\text{or P. T}^2 \propto \text{D}^3.$$

432 are Babylonian numbers.

Distance of planet = twice distance of Belus = 2×216000 = 432000 circumference.

432 years, the P. T of Belus, is the elementary number of 432000 years, the famous Chaldaic period of Berosus, a priest of the temple of Belus.

So in the period of 432000 years the earth would make 432000 revolutions round the sun.

$$\text{Belus } 432000 \div 432 = 1000 \text{ revolutions,}$$
$$\text{Planet } 432000 \div 1200 = 360 \qquad \text{,,}$$

1 revolution of the planet = 1200 years, and $3 \times 1200 = 3600$ years = a sare.

$$
\begin{aligned}
3600 \times 120 &= 432000 \text{ years} = \text{last yug.} \\
2 \times 3600 \times 120 &= 864000 \quad \text{,,} \quad = \text{3d.} \\
3 \times 3600 \times 120 &= 1296000 \quad \text{,,} \quad = \text{2d.} \\
4 \times 3600 \times 120 &= 1728000 \quad \text{,,} \quad = \text{1st.} \\
\hline
\text{Sum} &= 4320000, \text{ the Indian period for the}
\end{aligned}
$$

duration of the world.

In the " Asiatic Researches " we find that the Hindoos divided the maha-yug into four parts, which increase as 1, 2, 3, 4.

$$
\begin{aligned}
108,000 \text{ years} &= \text{1st age,} \\
216,000 \quad \text{,,} &= \text{2nd ,,} \\
324,000 \quad \text{,,} &= \text{3rd ,,} \\
432,000 \quad \text{,,} &= \text{4th ,,} \\
\hline
1080,000 \quad \text{,,} &= \text{maha-yug.}
\end{aligned}
$$

Each of these four ages being multiplied by 4 will = each of the four yugs, and four maha-yugs will = an Indian age, (the period assigned for the duration of the world).

$$
\begin{aligned}
432,000 \text{ years} &= \text{last yug,} \\
864,000 \quad \text{,,} &= \text{3rd ,,} \\
1296,000 \quad \text{,,} &= \text{2nd ,,} \\
1728,000 \quad \text{,,} &= \text{1st ,,} \\
\hline
4320,000 \quad \text{,,} &= \text{Indian age.}
\end{aligned}
$$

x 2

Or 1200 years $=$ 1 revolution of the supposed planet.

$$1200 \times 360 = \text{last yug,}$$
$$2 \times 1200 \times 360 = \text{3rd ,,}$$
$$3 \times 1200 \times 360 = \text{2nd ,,}$$
$$4 \times 1200 \times 360 = \text{1st ,,}$$
$$10 \times 1200 \times 360 = 4320000 \text{ years,}$$
or Indian period $=$ 3600 revolutions,
$=$ as many revolutions as there
are years in a sare.

The Chaldaic period $=$ $1200 \times 360 = 432000$ years $=$ 360 revolutions.

$$\text{Or } 360 \text{ revolutions} = \text{the 4th age,}$$
$$\tfrac{3}{4} \, 360 \text{ or } 270 \quad \text{,,} \quad = \text{ ,, 3rd ,,}$$
$$\tfrac{1}{2} \, 360 \text{ or } 180 \quad \text{,,} \quad = \text{ ,, 2nd ,,}$$
$$\tfrac{1}{4} \, 360 \text{ or } \; 90 \quad \text{,,} \quad = \text{ ,, 1st ,,}$$

Hence it would appear that the abode of the guardian gods of this solar system was supposed to be in a planet revolving round the sun, at a distance double that of Belus.

1 revolution $=$ 1200 years $=$ 1 year of the gods, and 1200 $\times$ 1200 $=$ 1440000 years $=$ a krite,
so 1200 revolutions $=$ a krite,
or P. T^2 $=$ a krite.

$$3 \times \text{P. } T^2 = 3 \times 1200^2 = 3 \times 1440000 = 4320000 \text{ years,}$$
$$\text{or} = 1200 \times 3600,$$
$=$ as many revolutions as there are years in a
sare.

Thus a krite $=$ P. T^2 $=$ as many revolutions as there are years in a revolution.

A Hindoo period $=$ $3 \times$ P. T^2 $=$ as many revolutions as there are years in a sare.

So 3 krites $=$ a Hindoo period.

In Hindostan it is believed, says Wallace, that the world has existed for 7,205,000 years, which period is divided into four ages that bear names conveying the same idea as the golden, silver, brass, and iron times of classical notoriety.

The present is the black age, and about 395,000 years of it remain.

The Sutee Yong, or age of purity, = 3,200,000 years. The Firtah Yong, or partial corruption, = 2,400,000 years. The Dwapour Yong, or partial depravity, = 1,600,000 years. The Kalli Yong, or depraved age, = 400,000 years. The four Yongs = 7,600,000 years.

It is believed that about 5000 years of the Kalli Yong have expired.

In the first age man lived 100,000 years; in the second 10,000; in the third 1000; and in this human life is limited to 100.

The Kalli Yong = 400,000 years.

The other Yongs are 4, 6, 8 times the Kalli Yong, and 4, 6, 8 are multiples of 2, 3, 4.

Five Krites = 5 × 1440000 = 7,200,000 = the time elapsed to the beginning of the Kalli Yong.

Three Krites = 3 × 1440000 = 4,320,000.

Ancient Christian writers, remarks Volney, complain of the difference of names and ages assigned by the Chaldean books to the antediluvian personages, by us called patriarchs, and by the Chaldeans kings. Syncellus has done us the service to preserve a list of them, copied from Alexander Polyhistor, or Abydenus, who themselves copied Berosus.

Chaldean antediluvian kings, according to Berosus.

Names.		Ages in sares.		In years.
Alor	-	10	-	36000
Alaspar	-	3	-	10800
Amelon	-	13	-	46800
Amenon	-	12	-	43200
Matalar	-	18	-	64800
Daon	-	10	-	36000
Evedorach	-	18	-	64800
Amphis	-	10	-	36000
Otiartes	-	8	-	28800
Xisuthrus	-	18	-	64800
Total		120		432000.

x 3

"These are the ten antediluvian kings whom the Chaldeans make to govern the world for 120 sares, equivalent to 432000 years.

"Thus the Chaldeans have left us a kind of enigma to explain. We must not be surprised if it has been misunderstood by many ancient and even modern authors, since its solution requires a knowledge of a very complicated astrological doctrine, which, long kept secret, has been too much neglected since its empire is at an end."

These ten kings appear to have been deified after death, and their reigns on earth to have been reckoned in divine years. So, by dividing these reigns by 1200, the number of years of man that = 1 year of the gods, we have the several reigns = 30, 9, 39, 36, 54, 30, 54, 30, 24, 54, total 360 years of man, which gives an average reign of 36 years instead of 43200 years.

Herodotus assigns 100 years for the reigns of three generations of Egyptian kings. So the average reign of a king will = $33\frac{1}{3}$ years. Cheops reigned 50, and Cephrenes 56 years.

The Indian period = 10 times the Chaldaic period.

The present Kalli Yong, or depraved age of Hindostan, limits the life of man to 100 years. In the preceding age, the Dwapour Yong, the life of man was limited to 1000 years.

Antediluvian patriarchs, according to Genesis.

Names.	Ages.
Adam	930
Seth	912
Enos	905
Cainan	910
Mahalaleel	682
Jared	895
Enoch	365
Methuselah	969
Lamech	777
Noah	950
Total	8484

The average age of these ten patriarchs = 848·4 years = 10 times 84·84 years.

The priests of Memphis read to Herodotus from a papyrus roll the names of 330 kings, the successors of men about whom nothing was known. Eighteen of these sovereigns were Ethiopians, and one an Egyptian woman. Mœris was the last of the 330.

When Hecatæus visited Thebes he mentioned to the Egyptian priests the imposing pedigree of the race to whom he belonged, with fifteen ancestors in an ascending line, and a god as the initial progenitor. But he was immeasurably surpassed by the priests, who showed him 341 wooden colossal statues representing the succession of chief priests in the temple in uninterrupted series from father to son, through a space of 11300 years. Prior to the commencement of this long period they said the gods dwelling along with men had exercised sway in Egypt; and they repudiated altogether the idea of men begotten by gods, or of heroes.

This will give 33 years and a fraction for an average reign in office.

The gods, according to Diodorus, reigned in Egypt for 18000 years; the last of this divine race being Horus, the son of Isis and Osiris. Then began the race of human kings, which comprised a period of near 5000 years from Men or Menes, the first mortal king, to the 180th Olympiad, or about 58 years B. C., when Diodorus visited Egypt.

The gods reigned 18000 years, or 5 sares.

According to the old Egyptian chronicle, Cronus and the other 11 divinities reigned together 3984 years. An average reign will equal 332 years.

Before these Helius — the Sun — the son of Hephæstus, reigned 30000 years.

Gods reigned 33984 years.

The Men, or Egyptians, commence their rule with Menes, the first Pharaoh, and continue through 31 successive dynasties to the invasion of Alexander, 332 B. C.

The average reign of these 12 divinities equals 332 years,

equal 10 times the average period of an Egyptian priest in office.

Abul Fazel, who visited the celebrated place of Hindoo worship, Juggernauth, on the sea-coast of Orissa, in 1582, says, "In the town of Pursottem, on the banks of the sea, stands the temple of Jugnaut, near which are the images of Kishen, his brother, and their sister, made of sandal-wood, which is said to be 4000 years old."

We do not know that any pyramid, teocalli, conical mound, or Druidical column, has been found in Australia, where we find the traces of ancient religion without monuments; but without monuments we have no chance of finding the standard of the tower of Belus in this island, though it has been traced round the world, and even found in the Pacific Isles. Such monuments may hereafter be found in Australia, the largest and least civilised island in the world, perhaps formerly the abode of science, where, after a long period of barbarism, civilisation, having followed the course of the sun from east to west, is again dawning.

The ancient missionaries of religion and civilisation planted the Babylonian standard with their pyramids and temples in all parts of the globe. It is only by these silent monuments that the ancient missions have been traced, after the lapse of ages, when all other records of their science and history had perished.

England has now planted her standard, extended her missions of religion, commerce, and civilisation on this vast island, which forms one of her numerous colonies on which the sun never sets.

Miles, in a paper read at the Ethnological Society, "On the Demigods and Dæmonia of Australia," says the worship of Baal ranks among the oldest and most generally diffused of ancient superstitions. It is the same as Bala of the Hindus. Ruler of the Air, Lord and Possessor of the Air, is its signification. In ancient times the summits of the hills were dedicated to the deities whose names had been forgotten, but which were still held sacred.

In the eastern part of Australia the summit of a mountain

is called Bool-ga; and Baal-Baal is the name of a place on the Murray; Baal is also the native word for fire. On the Loddon river the natives speak of a deity named Bin-Beal. Sun worship was practised among the inhabitants of Port Jackson when first discovered, and is called Baal. Governor Gray, in his vocabulary of the Swan river, gives "Boyal-ya, a sorcerer, the black witch of Scotland, a certain power of witchcraft. Boyal-ya-gaduk, possessing the power of Boyal. These people can transport themselves into the air at pleasure; they can render themselves invisible to all but other Boyal-ya-gaduks. If they have a dislike to a native, they can kill him by stealing upon him at night and consuming his flesh. All natural illness is attributed to these Boyal-ya-gaduks." The rites of Baal are marked by blood and human sacrifice. Balligan, in the Swan River dialect, is the infinitive mood of the verb to slay.

On the first of May a festival was held by the ancient Druids in honour of the Asiatic god Bel, or Baal, in which the power of the Eastern deity was symbolised by fire. Large fires were kindled on the mountain-tops, and the cattle of the surrounding country driven through them that they might be preserved from contagion and other evils till May-day next. On that day, likewise, all the hearth-fires were extinguished, that they might be rekindled from the sacred flame. The remains of this practice, but in an innocent and holyday form, still prevail in some parts of the Highlands of Scotland and the contiguous Lowlands. (Jameson.)

Train mentions, in his account of the Isle of Man, that the kindling of Baal fires, that is, celebrating the anniversary of the god Baal or Bel, was observed on the 1st of May, 1837, and that a trial, equivalent to a trial for witchcraft, went before a jury of Manksmen, in December, 1843.

There still survives in this island a fairy doctor, of the name of Teare, who is resorted to when all other aid fails. The messenger that is dispatched to him on such occasions is neither to eat nor drink by the way, nor even to tell any person his mission: the recovery is said to be perceptible from the time the case is stated to him. Farmers delay their sowing till Teare can come to bless the seed. Train has seen and conversed with this strange pretender.

The Carthaginians appear to have worshipped a multitude of deities, as Rollin observes from the preamble of a treaty they concluded with Philip of Macedon; wherein it is recited to be made in the presence of Jupiter, Juno, and Apollo; in the presence of the Demon or Genius of Carthage; in the presence of Hercules, Mars, Triton, and Neptune, and all the confederate gods of Carthage; in the presence of the sun, moon, and earth, rivers, meadows, waters, &c. But the gods chiefly invoked by them were the moon (called Cælestis and sometimes Urania) and Saturn, to which last they sacrificed their children, sometimes burning them, though they were usually content with making them pass through the fire.

When the Spaniards first arrived in America they found that their time, according to the Julian, was 11 days in advance of the Mexican time, and the Mexican year at that period, it is said, differed only 2 minutes and 9 seconds from the present estimated European year. A day consisted of 16 hours, a week of 5 days, a month of 20 days, a year of 18 months, making 360 days, to which 5 days or a week was added to complete the year. At the end of every 52 years an intercalation of $12\frac{1}{2}$ days was made.

Once in 52 years, their intercalary period, all the fires were extinguished, and a general mourning established. This was their most solemn religious ceremony, when all the priests assisted, robed in different dresses, according to the different deities to which they were dedicated or ordained. On the top of the teocalli, it is said, fire was elicited by friction from a victim's bones and a flint or stone knife: then a shout of acclamation followed, because the world was to be saved another 52 years from fire. The new fire was everywhere spread, from hand to hand, over the country.

The week of the Javanese is said to consist also of 5 days.

Rawun was a gigantic, many-armed, many-headed demon or Titan, a Hindoo Briareus, who, some thousand of years ago, was king of Lunka or Ceylon, and was slain by the god Rama at the end of the war, which is celebrated in the Ramayun, the Hindoo Iliad.

Rawun had, like Paris, carried off Sita, the wife of Rama. Rama and his brother Luxoomun, like the two Atrides, laid siege to the ravisher's capital, which they took and burned, as the Greeks did Troy; recovering the imprisoned beauty, and slaying the captor and all his family. Every exhibition of fireworks, transparencies, or other pyrotechny is, to this day, called Lunka by the Hindoos, as representing the superb conflagration of that city produced by one of Rama's most efficient allies, the monkey-god Hunoomun, commander of the army of monkeys, who assisted Rama's operations. Hunoomun allowed his tail, a tail of some miles long, to get in jeopardy among the besieged, and they imprudently wreaked their vengeance on this formidable member, by setting it on fire, and feeding the flame with all the available oil in the city. But as soon as it was well kindled, Hunoomun commenced wagging it to and fro through their capital, and thereby produced the most magnificent conflagration on record.

In this war Indragit, the son of Rawun, was slain by Luxoomun, Rama's brother. Indrajit had himself overcome the god Indra (the atmospheric Jove), and wrested the thunderbolt from him.

Indrajit's wresting the thunderbolt from Indra was perhaps like the discovery of Franklin, of whom it is said, metaphorically, *eripuit flumen cœlo.* " Indeed," says a writer in the *Dublin University Magazine,* " one is led to suspect that Rawun and his son were in reality men of great scientific resources. A remark on this subject was once made to us by a Hindoo, which is so curious that we here record it : — " The Hindoos, who watch and reflect on the proceedings and achievements of you Europeans, say that all your actions resemble those attributed in our Poorans, or religious poems, to giants and demons. Thus it is said in the Ramayun, that Rawun had taken several of the gods prisoners, and made them his household servants. The god

Agni (fire) was his cook, and dressed his food; the god Wayoo (wind) was his housemaid, and swept his chamber; the god Waroonu (water) was his gardener, and watered his trees; and so with the rest. You, too, have mastered and imprisoned these elements, and made them serve you. The wind works your ships; the ether (gas) lights your houses; you have harnessed the fire and water like horses to your carriages and your steamers; they work in your mills, and coin your money."

Besides the Hindoo deities who may be considered as the lawful tenants of heaven, there is a rebel race, called the Asuras and the Raksasas, who correspond nearly to the Giants and Titans of the Grecian mythology. But while the latter made only one grand attack on heaven, being baffled in which they remain for ever buried beneath the mountains which they had uprooted, the Indian rebels have obliged the gods to maintain a perpetual series of hard and doubtful conflicts. Nay, they have been often victorious, and have obtained temporary possession of the sky, till some lucky turn of fortune has driven them out, and restored the rightful possessors. The most huge and celebrated of these beings was Koombha-karna, whose house is said to have been 20,000 miles long, yet so inadequate to his dimensions, as to make it necessary to extend his bed through its whole length.

Bali having, by the sacrifice of 100 horses, conquered earth and a part of heaven, Vishnu, to deliver the world from his tyranny, appeared in the form of a Bramin, of dimensions so minute, that he could not step across the hole made by the foot of a cow. In this shape he presented himself before Bali, and proffered a request for so much ground only as he could cover by three strides. This apparently very modest petition being granted, Vishnu, suddenly resuming his natural dimensions, placed one foot upon earth, and another upon heaven. There remained then nothing but Bali himself, who was obliged to allow the third step to be made upon his own head, by which he was thrust down to the world of hydras.

Immediately subordinate to the great Hindoo Triad is Indra, invested with the lofty title of King of Heaven. He presides over the elements, and appears to occupy nearly the place of Jupiter in the Greek Mythology. His reign is not permanent, but is to continue only during 100 years of the gods. Indra is represented as a white man, with 100 eyes, sitting on an elephant, with a thunderbolt in his right hand, and a bow in his left. A splendid annual festival is celebrated in his honour throughout all Bengal.

The house of Koombha-Karna, one of the Titans, was 20000 miles long.

Circumference of earth = 21600 geographical miles.

The distance of the planets are measured by the earth's circumference.

So Koombha-Karna, with the aid of other Titans, may be supposed to have reached the skies. Ten such Titans would exceed the distance of the moon.

The mystery of the Titanic repute of the Sabæans was their religious and political power, derived from their astronomical knowledge, which enabled them to predict the eclipses of the sun and moon, and so to strike with astonishment and admiration the people, and even the kings at the time, totally ignorant of the causes, and greatly alarmed at the apparition of these phenomena. By these predictions the philosophical priesthood made themselves to be considered as initiated in the secrets, and associated in the science of the gods. These men of science were the priests of nature, and their religion was based on their researches, which were not less scientific than sublime. The earlier kings of Egypt possessed both priestly and royal dignity, and they assumed to themselves the titles of descendants of the gods.

We find the giants, in both the new and old world, defeated in their attempts to reach the heavens by building pyramids.

Figuratively, the pyramids were built to reach the heavens, since the type of the laws of nature, which extend to the heavens, formed their model.

The Sabæans were the Titans, — Cyclopian builders, or

wandering masons, whose monuments we have traced round the world.

These Sabæan missions planted the Babylonian standard and their religion everywhere; civilised mankind, and instructed them in the useful arts. The pyramids are their monumental records—historical they have none; but we may trace the footsteps of these missions by the traditions of nations handed down to us by Diodorus, who wrote about 58 years B. C., and remarks that, " Each nation, whether Greek or barbarian, has foolishly pretended to be the first to discover the comforts of human life, and to have preserved the tradition of its own history from the very origin of the world."

Humboldt says, in his *Monuments of America*, " After my return to Europe, in examining the Mexican manuscripts in the Vatican at Rome, I found this tradition preserved in the manuscript of Pedro de los Rios, a Dominican friar, who, in 1566, copied on the spot all the hieroglyphic paintings he could find.

" Before the great inundation which occurred 4080 years after the creation of the world, the country of Anahuac was inhabited by giants (Tzocuillixeque); all those who did not perish were turned into fish, with the exception of seven who concealed themselves in caverns. When the waters had subsided, one of the giants, Xelhua, surnamed the Builder, went to Cholula, where, in memory of the mountain Tlaloc, which had served as an asylum for himself and six of his brethren, he constructed an artificial hill in the form of a pyramid. He had the bricks made in the province of Tlamanalco, at the foot of the Sierra of Cocotl, and to transport them to Cholula, he placed a row of men, who passed them from hand to hand. The gods saw with anger this edifice, the summit of which was to reach the clouds. Irritated at the audacity of Xelhua, they launched fire against the pyramid; many of the workmen perished; the work was discontinued, and ultimately it was consecrated to the god of the air, Quetzalcoatl.

" This history recalls to mind the ancient traditions of the east, which the Hebrews have recorded in their sacred books.

"The father Rios, to prove the high antiquity of this fable of Xelhua, observed, ' that it was handed down in a song, which the Cholulains chanted at their festivals, and danced around the teocalli, and that the song began with the words *Tulanian hululaez*, which belong to no existing language in Mexico.' In all parts of the world, from the summit of the Cordilleras to the isle of Samothracia, in the Ægean Sea, fragments of primitive languages are preserved in religious ceremonies."

The belief in the dwarfing of mankind from early to later ages seems to belong to no country in particular. The present generation are pygmies compared to the generations of former ages, and the future will be pygmies compared with the present.

In the description of the ruins of Babylon, in Southey's "Thalaba," the same belief is alluded to:

> "A mighty mass remains ; enough to tell us
> How great our fathers were, how little we.
> Men are not what they were ; their crimes and follies
> Have dwarf'd them down from the old hero race
> To such poor things as we ! "

The Mussulmans are immutably prepossessed that as the earth approaches its dissolution, its sons and daughters gradually decrease in their dimensions. "As for Dagjial," they say, "he will find the race of mankind dwindled into such diminutive pygmies that their habitations in cities and all the best towns will be of no other fabric than the shoes and slippers of the present ages, placed in rank, and file in seemly and regular order, allowing one pair for two round families." (*Morgan's History of Algiers.*)

"The Cady then asked me, if I knew when Hagiuge was to come? ' I have no wish to know anything about him,' said I. ' I hope those days are far off, and will not happen in my time.' ' What do your books say concerning him?' says he, affecting a look of great wisdom. ' Do they agree with ours?' ' I don't know that,' said I, ' till I know what is written in your books.'   ' Hagiuge Magiuge,' says he, ' are little people, not so big as bees, or like the zimb, or fly of Sennaar, that come in great swarms out of the earth, ay in multitudes that cannot be counted ; two of their chiefs are to ride upon an ass, and every hair of that ass is to be a pipe, and every pipe is to play a different kind of music, and all that hear and follow them are to be carried to hell.' ' I know them not,' said I ; ' and, in the name of the Lord, I fear them not, were they twice as little as you say they are, and twice as numerous.   I trust in God I shall never be so fond of music as to go to hell after an ass for all the tunes that he or they can play.' "   (*Bruce*.)

These very little people, according to Thevenot, are to be great drinkers, and will drink the sea dry.

Belus is also made the chief of the Titans, according to the Syrian Mar Ibas, who found in the library of Arshak, eighty years after Alexander, a volume translated from Chaldean into Greek, entitled " The True History of the Ancient and Illustrious Personages."   It commences with Zerouan, Titan, and Yapetosth, and exposing in order the succession of illustrious men descended from these chiefs.

The text begins,—" They were terrible and brilliant those of the first of the gods, authors of the great good, and principals of the world and of the multiplication of men.   From them came the race of giants, with robust bodies, powerful limbs, and prodigious stature ; who, full of insolence, conceived the impious design of building a tower.   While working at it, a horrible and divine wind, excited by the anger of the gods, destroyed this immense mass, and threw among men unknown words, which excited tumult and confusion.   Amongst these men was the Japetic Haik, one of the most powerful giants.   He resisted those who pretended to the command over the other giants, and the gods, and excited a tumult against the impetuous effort of Belus. Mankind, scattered over the earth, lived in the midst of giants, who, stirred up by fury, drew their swords one against another, and struggled for the command : Belus, being successful, became master of almost all the earth."

The Titans of the Grecian mythologists heaped mountain upon mountain to attack the gods in heaven.

The Titans of Chaldea piled cube upon cube, or pyramid upon pyramid, to reach the planet of the celestial gods.

The cube of Babylon will = 3 pyramids, each = the distance of Uranus; and 2 cubes will = the distance of the supposed planet, = 6 such pyramids, each having the height = side of base = about 6 miles.

These Titans appear to have been giants in science and building, who, spread over the world, erected everywhere vast pyramidal temples and Cyclopean buildings, conformable to the Babylonian standard of measurement. They instructed mankind in religion, gave them laws, taught them agriculture and irrigation, so that the sterile soil became fertile, and the fertile soil more than doubled its produce. As the means of subsistence increased, civilisation expanded, and men became obedient to laws. Such were the benefits conferred on mankind by the early Sabæans, philosophical Titans, missionaries of religion and civilisation.

The Titans were not giants in stature, but gigantic in deeds.

The Tower of Belus and the walls of Babylon were less wonderful for their height and extent than for the wonders they could tell.

A distinction is made in the Grecian mythology between the Titans and giants; yet they were both the offspring of Cœlus and Terra.

Thessaly was the scene of battle of the giants against Jupiter. They tried to get up to heaven by piling mountains upon mountains, Ossa upon Pelion, and Pelion upon Olympus. The giants were at last defeated, and Jupiter drove them with his thunderbolts to Tartarus. The Titans made war against Saturn for taking their kingdom from their father Cœlus, to whom, as being their elder brother, it justly belonged; and the giants against Jupiter for confining their brothers the Titans to Tartarus.

P. T. Belus = 432 years, and 432 × 1000 = 432000 years.

P. T. of remote planet = 1200 years, and 1200 × 360 = 432000 years.

So 1000 revolutions of Belus = 360 revolutions of the remote planet = 432000 years, the Chaldaic period.

$$432000 \div 360 = 1200 = \tfrac{1}{3} \text{ Chaldean Sare,}$$
$$432000 \div 120 = 3600 = 1 \qquad\qquad ,,$$

Hence in 432000 years, a Chaldean period, or 120 sares, the remote planet would perform 360 revolutions, and Belus 1000.

In an Indian period of 4320000 years, or 1200 sares, the remote planet would perform 3600 revolutions round the sun, Belus 10000, and earth 4320000.

An Hindoo calpa of 432000000 years would = 360000 revolutions of the remote planet, and 1000000 of Belus.

Thus the P. T. of Belus, 432 years, is the elementary number of the great periods.

In 360 years of the gods, or 360 revolutions of the remote planet, or 120 sares, 10 of the guardian gods of the planets, or 10 deified antediluvian kings, might have been supposed to have governed the earth and other planets for a period of 432000 years.

This would make the average period of a god ruling the planets = 36 years of the gods.

P. T. Belus : P. T. supposed planet :: 432 : 1200
distance of Belus : distance of planet :: 432^3 : 1200^3
$$:: 57 \cdot 15 : 112 \cdot 36$$
$$2 \times 57 \cdot 15 = 114 \cdot 3$$

So the distances are nearly as 1 : 2, or as 4^3 : 5^3 :: 64 : 125
$$2 \times 64 = 128$$

$$4^3 : 5^3 : 120^3 \text{ stades} : 150^3 \text{ stades}$$
$$:: \text{distance of Belus} : \text{distance of planet,}$$

since cube of 120 stades = distance of Belus,
so cube of 150   ,,   =   ,,   planet.

The sides of Nineveh were 150 by 90 stades. Thus the cube of the greater side of Nineveh will equal the distance of supposed planet,—the abode of the gods,— which may be called Ninus.

$$\text{Mean of 2 sides} = \tfrac{1}{2}(150 + 90)$$
$$= 120 \text{ stades.}$$

Hence the cube of the mean of the 2 sides will
$$= \text{cube of Babylon.}$$
$$= \text{distance of Belus.}$$

The less side $= 90$ stades
$$120^3 \text{ stades} : 90^3 \text{ stades} :: 4^3 : 3^3$$
$$:: 64 : 27$$

$$90^3 \text{ stades} = \frac{27}{64} \times 120^3 \text{ stades} = \frac{27}{64} \times 216000 \text{ circumference}$$
$$= 91125 \qquad \text{,,}$$

Cube of 90 stades $= 91125$ circumference
$$\text{cylinder} = 71570 \qquad \text{,,}$$
distance of Uranus $= 72000 \qquad \text{,,}$

$\therefore 1$ cylinder $=$ distance of Uranus

3	,,	=	,,	Belus
6	,,	=	,,	Ninus
$\frac{1}{2}$	,,	=	,,	Saturn.

The Magi, Ghebres, and Parsees.

(FRASER'S PERSIA.)

The religion of the ancient Persians, says Fraser, originates in an age when history was lost in fable, and propagated by a succession of lawgivers of whom little except the names remain: we find it as the faith professed by a long series of brilliant dynasties, and maintaining itself through disaster and misfortune, till in our days it faintly appears in the persecuted sect of the Ghebres in Persia, or among the more fortunate and industrious Parsees of India.

The worship of the host of heaven was the earliest deviation from pure religion, the first step towards adopting a visible object of adoration instead of the unseen and inscrutable Being, of whose existence there is a witness in every heart; and such doubtless was the Sabæan ritual, the earliest religion of the Magi. The substitution of fire—the essence of light—in a form which might be constantly present, for the celestial bodies, is another and not an unnatural gradation in the progress of idolatry.

The worship of fire is, by the Persian writers, particularly Ferdusi, attributed to Hoshung, the third monarch of the Paishdadian or fabulous kings.   At all events its antiquity is not disputed ; but at whatever period it superseded the Sabæan or Chaldean faith, vestiges of the latter may be traced throughout every subsequent change, in that fondness for the delusive science of astrology, which, at the present moment, influences the people of the East as much as in the days of Nebuchadnezzar and Darius.

We shall not give a lengthened disquisition on the rites of the Magi.   It is enough to state that their principal doctrines were a belief in one god, all powerful, all good, beneficent, merciful and just, whose vicegerents were the planets, a fraternal affection for the whole human race, and a compassionate tenderness to the brute creation.

The ancient faith of Persia was restored or reformed by Zoroaster.   The Zendavesta, translated by M. De Perron, possesses the highest claim to authenticity, and comprehends in fact all that can be properly ascribed to the lawgiver himself.   This production, which, according to the Parsees, was dictated by inspiration, consisted, as their tradition asserts, of twenty-one books, of which only one, the twentieth, is preserved entire, while of the others only a few fragments exist.

The Avesta of Zoroaster sets out by declaring the existence of a great first principle, which is called Zirwan, an expression which is understood to denote time,—time without beginning and without end.   This incomprehensible being is author of the two great active powers of the universe : Ormuzd, the principle of all good, and Ahriman, the principle of all evil, were mingled together by a beneficent and omnipotent Creator, which has been as much controverted among the Magian priesthood as by modern metaphysicians.

According to the system of cosmogony in the Zendavesta, the duration of the present universe is fixed at 12,000 years, which is subdivided into four terms, each of which is appropriated to a peculiar series of events.

The six first angels of Ormuzd contended for more than

3000 years with the six deeves of Ahriman ; towards the termination of which Ormuzd called into being the heavens and their celestial systems,—the earth, with its complicated productions; and fire was given as the representative of that divine and original element which animates all nature. Serooch, the guardian of the earth, and Behram, armed with a mighty club and arrows, were formed to repel the attacks of Ahriman. Mythra, the mediator between Ormuzd and his creatures, and Rash or Rast, the genius of justice, with multitudes of spirits, were called forth to assist in repelling the powers of darkness, and angels were appointed to protect every being. The stars and planets, the months of the year, the days and even watches of the day had each their attendant spirit ; — all nature teems with them — all space is pervaded by them.

The system of cosmogony and theology of the Zendavesta promulgated by Zoroaster was, in all probability, compiled and reformed in some degree from the ancient religion of the Magi. The resurrection, however, is the true triumph of Ormuzd and his worshippers, and one of the most essential articles of their belief. The genii of the elements, which have received in deposit the various substances of the body, must render up their trust; the soul will recognise its earthly companion and re-enter it ; the juice of the herb Hom, and the milk of the bull Hezioak, will restore life to man, who then becomes immortal. Then takes place the final separation of the good and evil. The tortures of three awful days and nights, equal to an agony of 3000 years, suffice for the purification of the most wicked. The voice of the damned, ascending to heaven, will find mercy in the soul of Ormuzd, who will withdraw them from the place of torment. The world shall melt with fervent heat, and the liquid and glowing metals shall purify the universe, and fit all beings for everlasting felicity. To the just this ordeal proves as a pleasant bath of milk-warm water ; the wicked, on the other hand, shall suffer excruciating agonies, but it will be the last of their miseries. Hell itself and all its demons shall be cleansed ; Ahriman, no longer irreclaimable, will be converted to goodness, and become a ministering spirit of the Most High.

The doctrines and practice of the Ghebres and Parsees of the present day differ little from this code. They adore Ormuzd as the author of all good; they inculcate purity in thought, word, and action. They reverence all the angels, subordinate spirits, and agents of that good principle; and endless prayers are prescribed in their liturgies, with all the solemn words to be used, not only for important occasions, but also in the most trifling functions of life. The visible objects of their veneration are the elements, especially that of fire; and light is regarded as the noblest symbol of the Supreme Being, who is without form or limits. The sun, moon, planets, and stars, and even the heavens themselves, obtain peculiar respect; and in praying they turn to them, and especially to the rising sun. They have no temples nor images, nor paintings of Ormuzd or his angels. The Atish-Khudahs are merely edifices for guarding the sacred fire from defilement or extinction; in these the flame is kept burning; it is approached with the greatest reverence, and their most awful rites are practised before it. These houses are so constructed that the sun's rays never fall on the sacred fire.

The priests are of various classes, Dustoors, Mobuds, and Herboods. The first are of the highest order, for there are now neither Dustooran-Dustoor, nor Mobud-Mobudan (high-priests), and they are the doctors and expounders of the law. The others are of inferior rank, and are chiefly employed in performing certain menial offices in the fire-houses. The priesthood is hereditary in families of a particular tribe; they have no fixed salaries, being paid voluntarily for each service as it occurs, and many of them follow secular occupations.

The Parsees do not tolerate polygamy, unless the first wife prove barren, nor do their laws allow concubinage. They cannot eat or drink out of the same vessel with one of a different religion, nor are they fond even of using the cup of another, for fear of partaking of his sins. Their religion, however, admits of proselytism. They have no fasts, and reject everything of the nature of penance. God, they say, delights in the happiness of his creatures; and they hold it meritorious to enjoy the best of everything they can obtain. Their faith inculcates general benevolence; to be honest in bargains; to be kind to one's cattle and faithful to masters; to give the priests their due, physicians their fees; and these last are enjoined to try their sanitary experiments on infidels before practising on Parsees.

It is well known that they neither burn nor bury their dead. They have circular towers, called dockmehs, in which are constructed inclined planes; and on these they expose the bodies, courting the fowls of the air to feed upon them. They even draw auguries regarding the happiness or misery of the deceased, according as the left or right eye is first picked out by the vultures.

The Parsees attribute many wonderful influences to the Zendavesta, and pretend that it contains the principles of all arts and sciences, although they are concealed under symbols and mysteries.

The reign of Yezdijird III., which commenced A. D. 632, was distinguished by events infinitely more important than the fall of a tyrant or the change of a dynasty; for the same torrent that swept the race of Sassan from a throne which they had occupied more than 430 years, abolished the ancient religion of Zoroaster, and established a law which has effected one of the most striking moral changes on mankind that the world has ever witnessed.

In the year of the Christian era 569, and during the reign of the great Nooshirwan, was born Mohammed, the future lawgiver and prophet of Arabia; and forty years thereafter, in the reign of that monarch's grandson, he commenced the promulgation of those doctrines which were destined in so short a time to regulate the policy, the morals, and the religion of Asia. In twenty years after his death the whole of Arabia, Egypt, Syria, and Persia had been forced to receive the Koran, Africa had been invaded, and the Roman eagles had fled before the crescent of the Saracens.

While the arms of Persia were everywhere triumphant, and while their monarch was revelling in the excess of en-

joyment and the pride of insolent security, the first mutter-
ings of that storm were heard which was to overthrow the
fabric of the Sassanian power.   On the banks of the Karasu
the emperor received from Mohammed a letter requiring him
to abjure the error of that faith in which his fathers had
lived, and to embrace the religion of the one true God, whose
prophet he declared himself to be.   The interpreter read,
—"In the name of the most merciful God; Mohammed, son
of Abdallah, and apostle of God, to Khoosroo, king of Persia."
Thus it began.   "What!" cried the proud barbarian, "does
my slave dare to put his name before mine?"   Then he
seized the letter and tore it into fragments.   The answer was
sent to his lieutenant at Yemen, instead of Medina.   "I am
told there is in Medina a madman, of the tribe of Koreish,
who pretends to be a prophet.   Restore him to his senses : if
you cannot, send me his head."

When the messenger of Mohammed returned to Medina,
and told him that the great monarch had torn up his letter
without reading it, his master simply replied, "Even so shall
Allah rend his empire in pieces."   And these few words
spoke the oracle of destiny.   In less than ten years from the
scornful tearing of that letter by Khoosroo, the lieutenants of
the unknown "madman" ruled in Jerusalem, Alexandria and
Damascus, as well as in Mecca and Medina.

In their first attack the Arabs were repulsed, and in one
memorable action they lost their imprudent though zealous
leader, Abu Obeid.   But the disasters which attended the
passage of the Euphrates were repaired on the plains of
Cadesia (or Kudseah); and the glories of Persia sank for
ever when the celebrated standard of the Durufsh e Kawanee
fell into the hands of the Moslems, and their scimiters scattered the followers of Zoroaster as the sand of the desert is
driven by the whirlwind.   The plunder was increased almost
"beyond the estimate of fancy or of numbers" by the sack
of Madayn; "and the naked robbers of the desert," says
Gibbon, "were suddenly enriched beyond the measure of
their hope or knowledge."

Thus ended the dynasty of the Sassanides, and with it, as a national faith, the religion of the Magi.

Since the obelisk represents the distance and periodic time of a planet's revolution round the sun, and as unity in the obelisk $= \frac{2\,3\,\frac{1}{2}}{2\,4\,\frac{1}{3}}$ foot, or nearly 14 inches, which is about the distance between the steps of a ladder, or the radlines of a ship, the time of ascent to the planet Ninus, the abode of the gods, is very poetically described by Southey, in the "Curse of Kehama," where Ereenia ascends to Mount Calasay.

> " Yet he hath pass'd the measureless extent
> And pierced the Golden Firmament ;
> For Faith hath given him power, and Space and Time
> Vanish before that energy sublime.
> Nor doth eternal Night
> And outer Darkness check his resolute flight ;
> By strong desire through all he makes his way,
> Till Seeva's Seat appears, . . . behold Mount Calasay !

> " Behold the Silver Mountain ! round about
> Seven ladders stand, so high, the aching eye,
> Seeking their tops in vain amid the sky,
> Might deem they led from earth to highest Heaven.
> Ages would pass away,
> And worlds with age decay,
> Ere one whose patient feet from ring to ring
> Must win their upward way,
> Could reach the summit of Mount Calasay.
> But that strong power that nerved his wing,
> That all-surmounting will,
> Intensity of faith and holiest love,
> Sustain'd Ereenia still,
> And he hath gain'd the plain, the sanctuary above.

> " Lo, there the Silver Bell,
> That, self-sustain'd, hangs buoyant in the air !
> Lo ! the broad Table there, too bright
> For mortal sight,
> From whose four sides the bordering gems unite
> Their harmonising rays,
> In one mid fount of many-colour'd light.
> The stream of splendour, flashing as it flows,
> Plays round, and feeds the stem of yon celestial Rose !
> Where is the Sage whose wisdom can declare
> The hidden things of that mysterious flower,

That flower which serves all mysteries to bear ?
The sacred Triangle is there,
Holding the Emblem which no tongue may tell ;
Is this the Heaven of Heavens, where Seeva's self doth dwell ?"

Round about the mountain stand seven ladders, by which
you ascend a spacious plain, in the middle whereof is a bell
of silver, and a square table, surrounded with nine precious
stones of divers colours. Upon the table lies a silver rose,
called *Tamara Pua*, which contains two women as bright
and fair as a pearl; one is called *Brigasiri*, i. e. *the Lady of
the Mouth;* the other *Tarasiri*, i. e. *the Lady of the Tongue*,
—because they praise God with the mouth and tongue. In
the centre of the rose is the *triangle* of *Quivelinga*, which they
say is the permanent residence of God.—*Baldæus.*

Ravana, by his power and infernal arts, had subjected all
the gods and demigods, and forced them to perform menial
offices about his person and household. The whole *nava-
graha* (the *nine planetary* spheres) sometimes arranged themselves into a ladder, by which, they serving as steps, the
tyrant ascended his throne.—*Moore's Hindu Pantheon.*

The number of planets within the orbit of Ninus, the
abode of the gods, is 9.

The number of planetary distances from the earth to
Ninus is 7.

So, the ascent from the earth to Ninus, the Heaven of
Heavens, would be through 7 planetary distances by means
of 7 obeliscal ladders.

The 9 precious stones of divers colours denote the 9
planets that revolve within the orbit of Ninus, over which
preside the guardian gods of our system.

The distance of Ninus from the sun is about 50 billions of
units, or obeliscal steps.

The other emblems seen by Ereenia in the Sanctuary of
Seeva will be explained in a future work.

" We read in Eubulus that Zoroaster was the first who,
having chosen in the mountains near Persia a cavern agree-
ably situated, consecrated it to Mithra, creator and father of
all things; that is to say, he distributed this cave into

geometrical divisions, representing climates and elements, and imitated in part the order and arrangement of the universe by Mithra. From hence came the custom of consecrating caves to the celebration of mysteries, and hence the idea of Pythagoras and Plato, of calling the world a cave, a cavern. (*Porphyrus, de antro Nympharum.*)

"It was after this model that the Persians, according to Celsus, represented the ceremonies of Mithra, the double motion of the fixed stars and planets, with the passage of souls in the celestial circles or spheres. To denote the properties or attributes of the planets, they showed a ladder, along which were 7 gates, and afterwards an 8th at the upper extremity.

"This valuable fragment proves that the theology of this chief of a sect, like that of the Egyptians and Chaldeans, and of all the ancients in general, was, as we learn from Plutarch and Cheremon, nothing but the study of nature, and of its acting principles in the celestial and terrestrial bodies." (*Volney's Ancient History.*)

Mahomet's Night Journey through the Seven Heavens.

"From Mecca Mahomet was carried by the aerial flight of Al Borak, the white horse, having eagle's wings, with the swiftness of lightning to the holy temple at Jerusalem. After he had prayed in company with the prophets, a ladder of light was let down from heaven, until the lower end rested on the Shakra, or foundation-stone of the sacred house, being the stone of Jacob. Aided by the angel Gabriel, Mahomet ascended this ladder with the rapidity of lightning.

"Arrived at the first heaven, Gabriel knocked at the gate, announced the mission of Mahomet, who was welcomed, and the gate was opened. A description of this heaven is given, in which Mahomet met Adam.

"They ascended to the second heaven. Gabriel, as before, knocked at the gate; it was opened, and they entered. They continued their ascent through the successive heavens, till they came to the seventh. Gabriel could go no further. Mahomet now travelled, quicker than thought, an immense space; passing through two regions of dazzling light, and one of profound darkness, when he found himself in the presence of Allah, from whom he received many of the doctrines contained in the Koran.

" By the ladder of light he descended to the temple of Jerusalem, where he found Borak, and was borne back in an instant to the place whence he was first taken."

Rich, in describing the mounds on the supposed site of Nineveh, opposite the town of Mousoul, mentions one which he supposes may have been the monument of Ninus. " It is situated near the centre of the western face of the enclosure, and is joined, like the others, by a boundary wall: the natives call it Koyunjuk Tepè. Its form is that of a truncated pyramid, with regular steep sides and a flat top: it is composed, as I ascertained from some excavations, of stones and earth, the latter predominating sufficiently to admit of the summit being cultivated by the inhabitants of the village of Koyunjuk, which is built on it at the northeast extremity. The only means I had at the time I visited it of ascertaining its dimensions was by a cord which I procured from Mousoul. This gave 178 feet for the greatest height, 1850 feet the length of the summit east and west, and 1147 feet for the breadth north and south. In the measurement of the length I have less confidence than in the others, as I fear the line was not very correctly preserved, and the east side is in a less perfect condition than the others. It is almost superfluous to add, that the mount is wholly artificial."

Height to platform $=$ 178 feet $=$ 153·7 units.

$$\left. \begin{array}{l} 1 \text{ side } = 1850 \text{ feet} = 1585 \cdot 7 \\ 2 \text{ side } = 1147 \quad ,, \quad = \quad 991 \cdot 6 \end{array} \right\} 2577 \text{ units.}$$

Perimeter $= 2 \times 2577 = 5154.$

Perimeter of base of lowest terrace of Cholula

$$= 4 \times 1254 = 4980 \text{ units.}$$

Perimeter of pyramid of Cholula, or 4 times base of circumscribing triangle $=$ 5492 units

Cube of 5492 $=$ distance of Mercury.

Height to platform of Cholula
$$= 153 \text{ units, and } 152 = \tfrac{5}{8} \text{ stade.}$$

Hence it would appear that the heights of Cholula and Ninus are equal, and that the perimeters of the platform of Ninus and base of Cholula pyramid may also have been equal.

Or cube of perimeter = distance of Mercury.

The cubes of the perimeter of the lower terraces might have equalled greater planetary distances.

The sides of the terraces have not formed squares, but oblongs like the walls of the city of Nineveh.

The sides of the platform are as
$$991 : 1585 \text{ units,}$$
$$:: 10 : 16 \quad \text{,,} \quad .$$

The sides of the walls of Nineveh, said to have been built by Ninus, were as $90 : 150$ stades,
$$9 : 15 \quad \text{,,} \quad .$$

The cube of the greater = distance of Ninus.
The cube of the mean = ,, Belus.

Diodorus gives the dimensions of Nineveh 150 stades for each of the two larger sides of the quadrangle, and 90 stades for each of the two less sides; making a circuit of 480 stades. This enclosed space might contain not only a populous city, but moreover gardens and arable lands. Diodorus and Quintus Curtius mention that there was space enough within the precincts of Babylon to cultivate corn for the sustenance of the whole population, in case of a siege, besides gardens and orchards. Many cities in the East, such as Damascus and Isphahan, are .thus built; the amount of the population being greatly disproportionate to the site they occupy, if computed according to rules applied to European cities.

Layard remarks that had the Assyrians, so fertile in invention, so skilful in the arts, and so ambitious of great works, dwelt in a country as rich in stone and costly granites and marbles as Egypt or India, it can scarcely be doubted

that they would have equalled, if not excelled, the inhabitants of those countries in the magnitude of their pyramids,
and in the magnificence and symmetry of their rock temples
and palaces. But their principal settlements were in the
alluvial plains watered by the Tigris and Euphrates. On
the banks of these great rivers, which spread fertility through
the land, and afford the means of easy and expeditious intercourse between distant provinces, they founded their first
cities. On all sides they had vast plains, unbroken by a
single eminence until they approached the foot of the Arme-
nian hills.

As there were no natural eminences in the country, artificial mounds were made, on which were built the temples
of the gods, and the palaces of kings. Hence the origin of
those vast solid structures which have defied the hand of
time; and, with their grass-covered summits and furrowed
sides, rise like natural hills in the Assyrian plains.

The custom of erecting an artificial platform, and building
an edifice on the summit, existed among the Mexicans,
although they inhabited a hilly country.

Such a mode of building still exists among the inhabitants
of Assyria. On the summit of some old platform they erect
a rude castle, and the huts are built at the foot. There are
few ancient mounds containing Assyrian ruins which have
not served for the sites of castles, or villages built by the
Persians or Arabs.

These ancient mounds were not made by hastily heaping
up earth, but regularly and systematically built with sun-
dried bricks. Thus a platform, thirty or forty feet high,
was formed; and upon it they erected the royal or sacred
edifice. Were these magnificent mansions or temples? The
examination of the sculptures prove the sacred character of
the king. The priests or presiding deities (whichever the
winged figures so frequently found in the Assyrian monuments may be) are represented as waiting upon, or adminis-
tering to, him; above his head are the emblems of divinity
— the winged figure within the circle, the sun, the moon,
and the planets. As in Egypt he may have been regarded as

the representative, on earth, of the deity; receiving his power directly from the gods, and the organ of communication between them and his subjects, as mentioned by Diodorus. All the edifices hitherto discovered in Assyria have precisely the same character; so that we have most probably the palace and temple combined; for in them the deeds of the king and the nation are united with religious symbols, and with the statues of the gods. Layard could find no trace of the exterior architecture of these edifices.

Smirke, in his remarks on the bas-reliefs lately received from Nimroud, says, here we have a lofty castle with fortified turrets; a gateway, having a circular head; circular headed windows on an upper story; crenulated battlements; overhanging parapets with embrasures; a well defined chevron ornament forming the archivault of the entrance gateway; masonry of perfect workmanship equal to that of the best period of Greek art. The time is not far distant when the best informed antiquaries doubted the existence of any arch older than 100 years B.C.

In Anders Pryxell's Sweden, we find the Scandinavians associated with the same religion as that of the early Egyptians, the Brahminical and Buddhist system, which also formed that of the Druids.

According to the Edda, Walhalla has 540 gates, and 540 × 800, the number of Einherien that can march together out of each gate, gives 432,000.

Here, again, the number 432,000 accords with the Chaldaic cycle, which is the elementary number of the secular yugs so often mentioned in the Brahminical and Buddhist systems.

The ancient Mexicans divided the year into weeks of five days each.

$$1 \text{ day} = 24 \text{ hours} = 1440 \text{ minutes,}$$
$$= 86400 \text{ seconds,}$$
$$5 \text{ days} = 5 \times 86400 = 432000 \text{ seconds.}$$

The number of seconds in a Mexican week accords with the number of years in a Chaldaic cycle.

The ancient Mexican year consisted of 18 months, and

each month of 20 days, to which 5 days, or one week, was added to complete the year, conformably to the Egyptian method.

The intercalation was made every 52 years by the addition of a cycle of 13 days.

The odd week of the Mexicans was the odd 5 days during which Semiramis reigned.

The French in the Republic divided the year into 12 months of 30 days each, and added 5 more at the end to complete 365 days for the year.

Fixed Stars.

The number of stars seen by the naked eye may be about 4000; but when the telescope is turned upon them, the blue depths are sown with light, and, like the particles of dust rendered visible by a sun-beam, stars flash upon the glass. Each little space is a separate kingdom of glory. In whatever direction the telescope is directed, a spangled vault seems to fill it. Each star, though presenting a mere point of light to the eye, is believed to be a sun of magnitude, perhaps, equal to our own, and accompanied by a planetary system of which it is the centre.

According to Sturve's most recent investigations, the velocity of light is 166,072 geographical, or about 192,000 English miles a second; consequently about a million times greater than the velocity of sound. From a Centauri, 16 Cygni, and a Lyræ, a ray of light requires respectively 3, $9\frac{1}{4}$, and 12 years to reach us from these bodies.

If the distance of Belus be to a near fixed star as

Cube of side : cube of 4 times perimeter of Babylon

$$:: 1 : 16^3$$
$$:: 1 : 4096,$$

then light passing from Belus to the sun would equal about 470 minutes; from star 3·6, &c. years.

So the cube of 4 times perimeter of Babylon will represent the distance of a near star.

The time required for light to travel from the nearest fixed star is estimated by Herschel at $3\frac{1}{4}$ years.

Distance of Belus : distance of star :: 1 : 4096 :: distance of moon : 2 distance of Jupiter.

∴ 2 distance of Belus : distance of star,
:: 2 ,, moon : 2 ,, Jupiter.

Or distance of Ninus : distance of star,
:: ,, moon : ,, Jupiter,
:: sphere a : sphere 5 (*fig.* 82.).

So the distance of a star, the light from which takes 3·6, &c. years to reach our system, will be represented by the cube of 4 times perimeter of the walls of Babylon

$=$cube of 1920 stades,
$=$cube of 102, &c. miles English.

Distance of Belus $=$ 5432 millions of miles,
,, star $=$ 4096 times distance of Belus.

So distance of star will equal about 22 billions of miles English.

The distance of Belus equals about 25 billions of units.

Instead of comparing vast distances by roots cubed, they may be compared by roots to the 9th power :

For terrestrial or monumental distances when cubed, or raised to the third power, represent celestial distances.

So monumental distances when raised to the power of 3 times 3, or the ninth power, equal celestial distances.

Thus monumental distances are the roots of celestial distances.

Distance of Belus : distance of a near fixed star
:: 1 : 16^3
:: $30·7^9$: $30·7^9 \times 16^3$
:: $30·7^9$: $30·7^9 \times 2·52^9$
:: $30·7^9$: $77·364^9$,
or :: 1 : $2·52^9$.

Since $30·7^9 =$ distance of Belus in units,

So $77 \cdot 364^9 =$ distance of a near fixed star in units, and $33 \cdot 2^9 =$ distance of Ninus.

Or since distance of the moon : distance of Jupiter

:: distance of Ninus : distance of star ;

so   1 : 2048   ::   45000 : 92160000 times distance of the moon.

Thus distance of a near fixed star equals about 92 million times distance of the moon.

Magnitude of sum equals about 70 million times magnitude of the moon.

The great rock-cut temple at Salsette has the sides
$$90 \text{ by } 38 \text{ feet,}$$
$$= 77 \text{ ,, } 33 \text{ units.}$$

Less side to the power of 3 times 3
$$= 33 \cdot 2^9 = \text{distance of Ninus.}$$

Greater side to the power of 3 times 3
$$= 77 \cdot 364^9 = \text{distance of a near fixed star.}$$
See " Salsette," vol. ii. page 76.

> " High over-head, sublime,
> The mighty gateway's storied roof was spread,
> Dwarfing the puny piles of younger time.
> With deeds of days of yore
> The ample roof was sculptur'd o'er,
> And many a god-like form there met the eye,
> And many an emblem dark of mystery.
> Such was the city, whose superb abodes
> Seem'd scoop'd by giants for the immortal gods.
> Now all is silence dread,
> Silence profound and dead,
> The everlasting stillness of the deep."
>
> SOUTHEY.

The periodical revolution of the comet Encke is about $3\frac{1}{4}$ years, which is about the time of light passing from the nearest fixed star to our system.

The sarcophagus in the pyramid of Cheops, Vol. I. page 241., has the external nearly equal twice the internal content, by Vyse's measurement ; where dist. Uranus $= 26 \cdot 9^9$ &c. instead of $27 \cdot 1^9$ &c.

Internal content to the power of 3 times $3 = 27^9 =$ distance of Uranus.

External + internal content

$$= 3 \text{ times internal content.}$$

3 times (internal content) to the power of 3 times 3 $= 3 \times 27^9 =$ distance of Belus.

(3 times internal content) to the power of 3 times 3 $= (3 \times 27)^9 = 81^9$.

The distance 81^9 would require nearly $5\frac{1}{2}$ years for light to travel.

Thus distance of Uranus $= 27^9$

$$= (3 \times 3 \times 3)^{3 \times 3} = 3^{27},$$
$$\text{distance of Belus} = 3 \times (3 \times 3 \times 3)^{3 \times 3} = 3^{28},$$
$$\text{astral distance} = (3 \times 3 \times 3 \times 3)^{3 \times 3} = 3^{36}.$$

These distances expressed in terms of 3 will be too little, for the distance of Uranus will equal about $27 \cdot 1^9$, &c.

Among the infinite multitude of stars in the remote region of the Galaxy, Herschel estimates that the light of innumerable individuals must have occupied upwards of 2000 years in travelling over the distance which separates them from our system.

If the light from a Centauri take 3 years to travel to our system, the distance will equal about the cube of 98 miles, or $1 \cdot 42$ degrees.

If the light take 2000 years to travel from a star to our system, the distance will equal $2000 \div 3 = 666$ times the distance of a Centauri $= 666$ times the cube of 98 miles.

$$1 :: 666 : 1^3 :: 8 \cdot 73^3 : 98^3 : 855^3 \text{ miles.}$$

So the distance of the remote star will equal a cube having the side $= 855$ miles English $= 12 \cdot 4$ degrees.

The so-called fixed stars are said to have translatory motions. Our sun, according to Argelander, belongs, with reference to proper motion in space, to the class of rapidly moving fixed stars. But other astronomers do not admit that either the absolute or relative motion of the sun has been proved.

z 2

The apparently infinite distances of stars, or the extent of space in the heavens, is too vast for imagination. The Hindoo attempt to define heavenly space may be quoted from Southey's " Curse of Kehama " —

> " Veshnoo a thousand years explor'd
> The fathomless profound,
> And yet no base he found ;
> Upward, to reach its head,
> Ten myriad years the aspiring Brama soar'd,
> And still as up he fled,
> Above him still the Immeasurable spread.
> The rivals own'd their Lord,
> And trembled and ador'd."

" Contemplated as one grand system, astronomy is the most beautiful monument of the human mind, the noblest record of its intelligence. Seduced by the delusion of the senses, and of self-love, man considered himself for a long time as the centre of the motion of the celestial bodies, and his mind was justly punished by the vain terrors they inspired. The labour of many ages has at length withdrawn the veil which covered the system. Man appears on a small planet, almost imperceptible in the vast extent of the solar system, itself only an insensible point in the immensity of space. The sublime results to which the discovery has led may console him for the limited space assigned him in the universe. Let us carefully preserve, and even augment, the number of these sublime discoveries, which form the delight of thinking beings. They have rendered important services to navigation and astronomy, but the great benefit has been that they have dissipated the alarms occasioned by extraordinary celestial phenomena, and destroyed the errors springing from the ignorance of our true relation with nature ; errors so much the more fatal, as social order can only rest on the bases of these relations. *Truth, justice,* these are its immutable laws. Far from us be the dangerous maxim, that it is sometimes useful to mislead, to enslave, and to deceive mankind, to ensure their happiness. Cruel experience has at all times proved, that with impunity these sacred laws can never be infringed." (*La Place.*)

The walls of Babylon and the Tower of Belus record the deeds of these hero-gods, "the race of giants who sprung from the terrible and brilliant race of the first of the gods, principals of the world and the multiplication of men."

Since the height of the tower equalled one stade, or the height of fifty men, how great must have been the multiplication of men to equal the distance of a fixed star?

The circumference of the earth $= 684^2 = 467856$ stades,
$=$ height of $467856 \times 50 = 23,392,800$ men,
40 times circumference $= 935,712,000$,,

which is about the entire population of the world; so that if each individual equalled the height of 2 orgyes, or 5·62 feet English, the whole population of the globe would extend forty times round the earth, or about four times distance of the moon, or twice diameter of the orbit of the moon.

Distance of Mercury	$=$	36 millions of miles,	
,,	Venus	$=$ 68	,,
,,	Earth	$=$ 95	,,
,,	Neptune	$=$ 2853	,,
,,	Belus	$=$ 5432	,,
,,	Ninus	$=$ 10735	,,
Diameter of Sun		$=$ 882000 miles.	

Taking the distance of Mercury at 35, &c.
Venus   69, &c.
Earth   97, &c.

we get the following mean proportionals.

$\frac{1}{2}$ diameter of the sun : $\frac{1}{2}$ diameter orbit of Mercury,
:: $\frac{1}{2}$ diameter orbit of Mercury : $\frac{1}{2}$ diameter orbit Neptune,

diameter of sun : $\frac{1}{2}$ diameter orbit of Venus,
:: $\frac{1}{2}$ diameter orbit of Venus : $\frac{1}{2}$ diameter orbit of Belus,

diameter of sun : $\frac{1}{2}$ diameter orbit of the earth,
:: $\frac{1}{2}$ diameter orbit of the earth : $\frac{1}{2}$ diameter orbit of Ninus.

z 3

It has been shown, proximately,

diameter of the sun : $\frac{1}{2}$ diameter orbit of the earth,

:: diameter of the moon : $\frac{1}{2}$ diameter orbit of the moon,

:: diameter of the earth : diameter of the sun,

so diameter of the earth : diameter of the sun,

:: diameter of the sun : $\frac{1}{2}$ diameter orbit of the earth.

:: $\frac{1}{2}$ diameter orbit of the earth : $\frac{1}{2}$ diameter orbit of Ninus.

Also diameter of the earth : diameter of the sun,

:: diameter orbit of the earth : diameter orbit of Ninus,

and diameter of the moon : diameter orbit of the moon,

:: diameter of the sun : diameter orbit of the earth.

Taking 110 diameters of the earth to = diameter of sun, then $110^3 \times$ diameter of the earth

$$= 110^2 \times \text{diameter of the sun}$$
$$= 110 \ \times \tfrac{1}{2} \text{ diameter orbit of the earth}$$
$$= \qquad \tfrac{1}{2} \text{ diameter orbit of Ninus.}$$

$\frac{1}{2}$ diameter of sun : $\frac{1}{2}$ diameter orbit of Saturn :: 1 : 2042,

$\frac{1}{2}$ diameter orbit of moon : $\frac{1}{2}$ diameter orbit of Jupiter

:: 1 : 2045,

$\therefore \frac{1}{2}$ diameter of sun : $\frac{1}{2}$ diameter orbit of Saturn,

:: $\frac{1}{2}$ diameter orbit of moon : $\frac{1}{2}$ diameter orbit of Jupiter,

or $\frac{1}{2}$ diameter of sun : $\frac{1}{2}$ diameter orbit of moon,

:: $\frac{1}{2}$ diameter orbit of Saturn : $\frac{1}{2}$ diameter orbit of Jupiter.

We now see how the Titans, in order to reach the heavens, piled mountain upon mountain to form enormous cubes, which, when divided into cubes of unity, would represent celestial distances.

So it would appear that the Titans were a race of Sabæans, like the Magi, who predicted eclipses, and so were thought to hold communion with the gods. Their knowledge of chemistry enabled them to perform wonders before the astonished multitude, who held them in reverential awe, which was still further increased by the exercise of their religious and judicial functions, and by their practice of astrology and magic.

Their authority was acquired and maintained by rigidly restricting knowledge of the sciences to the sacred institutions, which became exclusively the depositories of all science.

In both Egypt and Chaldea we find, at very remote epochs, the traditions of gods and giants living among men, civilising and instructing them in agriculture.

The hero-gods of antiquity were men who had greatly distinguished themselves by deeds of arms, remarkable piety, and benevolence, or intellectual superiority. Many such had colossal or gigantic statues erected to them, and from traditional accounts they were held in veneration by posterity as giants and gods.

Colossal statues were also erected to the divinities of Eastern mythology.

Ancient genealogies were not, as among modern nations, valuable from the number of their mortal progenitors, but from the nearness of descent from the divine parent. The fewer the links between them and the gods, the more illustrious was the family. Plato was regarded by many of his admirers as the son of Apollo.

We shall notice some statues as huge as the race of giants in olden time.

The Daïri, or spiritual emperor of Japan, was supposed to be descended from the Kami, or demi-gods, who, in obedience to the will of heaven, peopled Japan.

The tendency of the human mind to combine spiritual and temporal power has been frequently alluded to. But in an early state of society, when the principles of government are scarcely, if at all, understood, it seems a very natural result that temporal power should be submitted to, because enforced by sanctions which claim a spiritual or divine origin.

The principles of Buddhism were introduced into Japan from China. The original or primitive religion of Japan still exists, though much disfigured. The adherents of this religion, says Golownin, believe that they have a preference before the others, because they adore the ancient peculiar divinities called Kami, that is, the immortal spirits or children

z 4

of the highest being, who are very numerous. They also adore and pray to saints who have distinguished themselves by a life agreeable to heaven, fervent piety, and zeal for religion. They build temples to them. The spiritual emperor is the head and high-priest of this religion.

Jedo, being the residence of the emperor and the court of Japan, is a very populous city, being supposed to contain from a million to a million and a half of inhabitants. On this subject the Japanese indulge in great exaggeration. They showed us, says Golownin, a plan of the capital, and told us that a man could not walk in one day from one end of it to the other.

The next city is Meaco, the residence of the Daïri, or spiritual emperor. It is an inland city, and is supposed to contain about half a million of inhabitants.

Saris, in the beginning of the 17th century, says, " Meaco is one of the greatest cities in Japan, and a place of mighty trade. The most magnificent temple in the whole country is at Meaco. It is as long as the body of St. Paul's (London) was before it was burned, and as lofty, with an arched roof, supported by mighty pillars, in which stands an idol of copper, which reaches as high as the roof." According to Herbert, his chair is 70 feet high and 80 broad, his head big enough to hold fifteen men, and his thumb was 40 inches round. This temple stands on a high hill, and on each side of the ascent are fifty pillars of free-stone, ten paces from each other, and on the top of every pillar is a lanthorn, which makes a fine show in the night. Xavier, in 1553, says he was informed that Meaco, previous to some devastation which it had suffered, actually contained 180,000 houses. Kæmpfer states that it contained 6000 temples, and that he took a whole day riding through, from one end to the other, though not exactly in a straight line.

In the road between Surungo and Jedo stands the idol Dabis, made of copper, in the form of a man sitting upon his legs and extending his arms, and is 22 feet high. The engraving represents Dabis placed upon a pedestal, and sitting cross-legged.

The Kaffirs of Bactria. — In the midst of the lofty mountains bordering on the northern limits of Affghanistan dwells a singular race of people, utterly unlike in religion, manners, and complexion all the nations by which they are surrounded. They are celebrated for their beauty, have ruddy complexions, blue eyes, and fair hair; they drink wine, sit on chairs, use tables and worship idols; while all their neighbours are dark men, with black eyes and hair, who abhor wine, sit and eat on the ground, and are zealous Mohammedans. Their language is as different from that of their neighbours as is their appearance. These interesting accounts excited Elphinstone and Burns to make further enquiries among the Mohammedans, as no European has endeavoured to see these people in their mountain fastnesses, from which it appears that they believe in one god, whom they call Imra, or Daghám; but they have also many idols of wood and stone, representing great men of former days, to whom they pay a sort of inferior adoration. This species of canonisation has frequently been granted in recent times to such men as have exercised largely the virtues of liberality and hospitality, to which the Kaffirs attach great reverence. The number of inferior gods is thus very great, but many are peculiar to separate tribes.

" Sravana Belgula, a village in the Mysore territories, is celebrated as being the seat of the Jain worship, once so prevalent over the South of India. Near the village are two rocky hills, on one of which, named Indra Betta, is a temple of the kind named Busty, and a high place with a statue of Gomuta Raya, the height being 70 feet 3 inches. The Jains agree with the Bhuddists, or Sangutas, who equally deny the divine authority of the Vedas, and who in a similar manner worship certain pre-eminent saints, admitting likewise as subordinate deities the whole pantheon of the orthodox Hindoos. These two sects (the Jains and the Bhuddists) differ in regard to the history of the personages whom they have deified ; and it may hence be concluded that they had distinct founders, but the original notion seems to have been

the same. All three agree in the belief of transmigration."
(*East India Gazetteer.*)

Jomard saw near Syene a block of granite, which had been intended for a colossus, about 68 feet high.

68 feet French will exceed, and

68 feet English will be less than 100 cubits.

Impey describes a colossal Jain image, cut in bas-relief in the side of a rock in the Satpoora range of mountains. The image measures 72 feet 8 inches to the knees, and from the other sculptured proportions, the total height must be 90 feet 10 inches, which makes it the largest image in India.

Impey visited Bang and Woon, in both of which he collected many inscriptions of historical interest; and in the former place he discovered several large Vihars and Dhagopas, which induces him to conjecture that Bang must have been the Dakkhinagiri Vihar, mentioned in the Mahawanso, as the place from which 30,000 disciples of Buddha went to Ceylon.

At Kermen-Shah, in Kourdistan, is an arcade, 30 feet deep, and about 70 high, cut out of a mountain of solid rock. Above is an equestrian statue, having an height from the head of the man to the foot of the horse at least 60 feet. The Persians say that this represents an hero who lived long before the time of Alexander, and was renowned for his valour and extraordinary size. His wife, on a horse, is also represented by his side, but she is less. It appears that these figures are the work of the same hero, and they pretend that he has engraven upon the rocks of many of the mountains, reliefs to immortalise his victories. Indeed such are seen in different places on the road to Ispahan. (*La Perse, par Henry.*)

Symes, at Logatherpoo Prau, formerly the residence of the Seredaw, or high priest of the Birman empire, saw the colossal statue of Gaudma.

" The area on which the temple stands is a square, surrounded by an arcade of masonry; on each side, nine cubical towers are erected, and several buildings are enclosed within the arcade. The temple in which the stupendous idol is placed differs from other pyramidal buildings, by having an arched excavation that contains the statue. On entering this dome, our surprise was greatly excited on beholding such a monstrous representation of the divinity. It was a Gaudma of marble seated on a pedestal, in its usual position. The height of the statue from the top of the head to the pedestal on which it sat was nearly 24 feet; the head was 8 feet in diameter, and across its breast it measured 10; the hands were 5 or 6 feet long; the pedestal, which was also of marble, was raised 8 feet from the ground. The neck and left side of the image were gilded, but the right arm and shoulder remained uncovered. The Birmans asserted, that this, like every other Gaudma which I had seen of the same material, was composed of one entire block of marble; nor could we on the closest inspection observe any junction of the parts. The building had evidently been erected over the statue, as the entrance could scarcely admit the introduction of the head."

The colossal statue of San Carlo Borromeo, which stands near the Lake Maggiore, in the north of Italy, is 66 feet high, and made of hammered copper, but the hands, feet, and head, are of bronze. The figure stands on a granite pedestal 46 feet high, which, added to that of the colossus, gives a total height of 112 feet. By means of a circular staircase in the interior of the statue, the curious may ascend into the saint's head, and look out of the windows of his eyes on the noble prospect before them.

The height of the brazen colossus of Apollo, or image of the sun, at Rhodes, was 70 cubits (Pliny). 70 cubits of Babylon = about 50 feet English.

The making of metal statues was a branch of art known in very high antiquity, although we know but little of the modes in which the process was conducted. It is supposed that the earliest brass statues were made of hammered metal, and not cast in a mould. Pausanias describes a statue of Jupiter, by Learchus, which was made of hammered pieces of brass, fastened together by means of pins or keys. Another process, though less probable, is supposed to have been, to hammer pieces of metal together until they formed a solid mass, and then hewing the statue out of the mass. Two statues of solid gold, one of Bacchus, and the other of Diana, are spoken of by the same writer, and it is supposed these were formed in a similar manner. A third mode adopted appears to have been, to carve a model or skeleton in wood, somewhat smaller than the required statue, and to hammer plates of metal on it, so as to give it the appearance of a metal statue, without using such a quantity of costly material.

In a chamber cut out of the solid rock, in the pyramid of Cephrenes, Belzoni found a sarcophagus of the finest granite. It was surrounded by large blocks of granite apparently intended to prevent its removal. Like the sarcophagus in the pyramid of Cheops it was destitute of hieroglyphics. The lid was half removed; and amidst a quantity of earth and stones were found some bones, which proved to be those of a bull. From an Arabic inscription on the wall of the chamber, it appears that some Arab rulers of Egypt had opened the pyramid, and closed it again.

The dimensions of the sarcophagus are

External.

Length ....8 ft. 7 in. $=$ 7·42 units.
Breadth.........3 ,, 6½ ,, $=$ 3·06 ,,
Height ....3 ,, 0 ,, $=$ 2·59 ,,
Content.................... $=$ 58·8 ,,
$\frac{1}{3} =$ 19·6 ,,
Distance of earth ...... $=$ 19·6^9 ,,
10 times breadth .... $=$ 30·6 ,,
Distance of Belus...... $=$ 30·7^9 ,,
10 times height............ $=$ 25·9 ,,
Distance of Saturn ... $=$ 25·2^9 ,,

Internal.

Length ....7 ft. 4 in. $=$ 6·05 units.
Breadth.........2 ,, 2½ ,, $=$ 1·9 ,,

Depth .... 2 ft. 5 in. = 2·08 units
    Content................... = 23·9   ,,
    Distance of Jupiter ... = 23·5⁹ &c.
5 times length .... = 30·25 ,,
    Distance of Belus...... = 30·7⁹ ,,
10 times breadth .... = 19   ,,
    Distance of Venus..... = 18·9⁹ ,,
10 times depth .... = 20·8 ,,
    Distance of Mars ...... = 20·5⁹ &c.

SARCOPHAGUS IN MYCERINUS' PYRAMID.

Exterior.

Length ....8 ft. 1 in. = 6·91 units.
Breadth.........3 ,, 1 ,, = 2·66   ,,
Height ....2 ,, 11 ,, = 2·52   ,,
3 times length .... = 20·73 ,,
    Distance of Mars.... ... = 20·5⁹&c.,,
10 times breadth .... = 26·6 ,,
    Distance of Uranus...... = 27·1⁹ ,,
10 times height .... = 25·2 ,,
    Distance of Saturn ...... = 25·2⁹ ,,

Interior.

Length .... 6 ft. 5 in. = 5·54 ,,
Breadth......... 2 ,, 0½ ,, = 1·76 ,,
Depth........... 2 ,, 0½ ,, = 1·76 ,,
6 times length .... = 33·24 ,,
    Distance of Ninus....... = 33·2⁹ &c.
10 times breadth .... = 17·6 ,,
    Distance of Mercury.... = 17·6⁹ ,,
10 times depth × breadth = 30·9 &c.
    Distance of Belus........ = 30·7⁹ &c.
    External content...... = 46·31 ,,
              ½ = 23·15 ,,
Distance of Jupiter...... = 23·5⁹ ,,
    Internal content ...... = 17·11 ,,

Distance of Mercury .... $= 17\cdot6^9$ units.
23·5 + 17·6 .... $= 41\cdot1$,,
Mean .... $= 20\cdot5$,,
Distance of Mars......... $= 20\cdot5^9$,,

In one of the excavated sepulchral apartments near Thebes, Bruce saw the prodigious sarcophagus, according to some, of Menes ; or, as others assert, of Osimandyas.   It is 16 feet high, 10 long, and 6 broad, and of one single piece of red granite.   Its cover, broken on one side, was still upon it, and had on the outside a figure in relief.

Content $= 16 \times 10 \times 6$ feet

$= 13\cdot8 \times 8\cdot46 \times 5\cdot4 = 645$ &c. units.

Cube of content $= 648^3 = \frac{1}{4}$ distance of the moon.
Cube of twice content $=$ twice distance of the moon.
If content $= 13\cdot04 \times 8\cdot67 \times 5\cdot46 = 624$ units,

$623^3 = \frac{2}{9}$ distance of the moon,
$(3 \times 623)^3 = \frac{2}{9} \times 3^3 = 6.$

Cube of   3 times content $= 6$ times distance of the moon,
Cube of 1000 times height $= 13040^3 =$ distance of Jupiter,
Cube of 1000 times length $= 8670^3 =$,,   Mars,
Cube of 1000 times breadth $= 5460^3 =$,,   Mercury.

If the thickness of the cover $= \cdot8$ unit, the less content would $=$ that of the sarcophagus without the cover, and the greater content that of the sarcophagus with the cover.

$13\cdot04 + 8\cdot67 + 5\cdot46 = 27\cdot17$ units,
Distance of Uranus $= 27\cdot1^9$ &c.

So sum of height + length + breadth to the power of 3 times
3 $=$ distance of Uranus.

3 times (sum to the power of 3 times 3)
$=$ distance of Belus.

(3 times sum) to the power of 3 times 3
$=$ an astral distance.

Or, distance of Uranus $= 27^9$ $= (3 \times 3 \times 3)^{3 \times 3}$ $= 3^{27}$
distance of Belus $= 3 \times 27^9$ $= 3 \times (3 \times 3 \times 3)^{3 \times 3} = 3^{28}$
astral distance $= (3 \times 27)^9 = (3 \times 3 \times 3 \times 3)^{3 \times 3} = 3^{36}$

In an adjoining gallery Bruce found the fresco painting of a man playing on an elegant harp.

In raising such small dimensions as those of the sarcophagi to the ninth power, so as to represent planetary distances, minutely accurate measurements will be required. Also the ninth roots of the distances in the table will require correction, for they are not accurate.

"Zoroaster or Zerdusht, the great reformer of the sect of the Persian Magi, between whose doctrines and those of Brahma," writes Maurice, "I shall hereafter, in many points, trace a striking resemblance, amidst the gloom of a cavern, composed his celebrated system of theological institutions, which filled twelve volumes, each consisting of one hundred skins of vellum, and was called the Zend-Avesta."

According to Ulug-Beg, quoted by Hyde, Zoroaster was the greatest mathematician and astronomer that the East in those remote periods ever saw. He had so far penetrated into the great arcana of nature, and had raised the Magian name to such a height, that, in the darker ages which succeeded, they were supposed to possess supernatural knowledge and powers; and hence the odious name of magic has ever since been bestowed upon arts that seemed to surpass human power to attain, and that of magicians upon those who practised them. In the union of astronomy and theology, which were sister sciences in those days, may perhaps be found an explanation of cavern-worship.

According to Prideaux, the renowned philosophers, Epictetus and Pythagoras, who was himself the scholar of Zoroaster, sought wisdom in the solitary cave.

If one of the distinguished Zoroasters should have lived at so late a period as the time of Pythagoras, and Pythagoras been instructed by him, this will readily account from what source Pythagoras derived his metempsychosis, astronomy, and magic. His belief in the transmigration of the soul into different bodies is generally admitted, as he was the first that taught that doctrine in Greece.

"It was Pythagoras," observes Arago, "that enriched almost all the great views upon which science rests at the present day. It was he who discovered the system of the world to which Copernicus has left his name. It was he that first conceived the bold idea that the planets are inhabited globes, like that on which we tread ; and that the stars which people the immensity of space are as many suns, destined to dispense heat and light to planetary systems that gravitate round them. He also regarded comets, not as fugitive meteors in the atmosphere, but as permanent stars that revolve round the sun according to laws proper to them."

" A sketch of the life of Pythagoras," says Maurice, " will show that he enjoyed opportunities, so much desired, of being instructed in the science and mysteries of the East; and that he, so much more qualified than any other Grecian whose name has reached us, appears to have been the first that introduced this Eastern knowledge into Europe.

"Let us commence our retrospect with the travels of Pythagoras, who flourished in the sixth century B. C.

"According to the account of his disciple Jamblichus, the first voyage of Pythagoras in pursuit of knowledge, after the completion of his academical exercises at Samos, was to Sidon, his native place, where he was early initiated in all the mysterious rites and sciences of Phœnicia,—a country whence the elder Taut emigrated to Egypt, and where the profound Samothracian orgia and the Cabiric rites were first instituted. From Phœnicia our philosopher travelled into Egypt, and there, with an unabated avidity for science, as well as with an unexampled perseverance, continued, under the severest possible discipline, purposely imposed upon him by the jealous priests of that country, during two-and-twenty years, successively to imbibe the stream of knowledge at Heliopolis, at Memphis, and at Diospolis or Thebes. Astonished at his exemplary patience and abstinence, the haughty Egyptian priesthood relaxed from their established rule of never divulging the arcana of their theology to a stranger ; for, according to another writer of his life, Diogenes Laertius, he was admitted into the inmost adyta of their temples, and there was taught those stupendous truths of their mystic philosophy which were never before revealed to any foreigner.

He is said to have submitted to circumcision that he might more rigidly conform to their dogmas and leave no point of their recondite sciences unexplored. It was during this long residence and seclusion among the priests of the Thebais that he rose to that high proficiency in geometrical and astronomical knowledge to which no Greek before him had ever reached, and few since have attained.

" But all the aggregate of Egyptian wisdom could not satisfy the mind of Pythagoras, whose ardour for science seems to have increased with the discouragements thrown in the way of his obtaining it. He had heard of the Chaldæan and Persian Magi, and the renowned Brachmanes in India, and he was impatient to explore the hallowed caves of the former and the consecrated forests of the latter. He was meditating this delightful excursion at the time that Cambyses commenced his celebrated expedition against Egypt, which terminated in the plunder of its treasuries, the slaughter of its gods, and the burning of its temples. During the remainder of the period of his abode in Egypt he had the mortification to be a spectator of all those nameless indignities which his patrons and instructors underwent from that subverter of kingdoms and enemy of science. Pythagoras himself was taken prisoner, and sent with other captives to Babylon. The Chaldæan Magi, however, at that metropolis received with transport the wandering son of science. All the sublime arcana inculcated in the ancient Chaldaic oracles, attributed to the elder Zoroaster, were now laid open to his view. He renewed, with intense ardour, those astronomical researches in which the Babylonians so eminently excelled, and learned from them new ideas relative to the motions, powers, properties, and influences of the heavenly bodies, as well as their situations in the heavens, and the vast periods they took to complete their revolutions.

" Babylon must have been at that particular period the proudest and most honoured capital upon earth, since it is evident from Hyde that both the prophet Ezekiel and the second Zoroaster, the friend of Hystaspes, whom Porphyry calls Zaratus (a name exceedingly similar to the oriental appellation of Zaratusht), resided there at the same time. The former, attached to the man who had submitted in Egypt to one fundamental rite prescribed by the Jewish law, instructed him in the awful principles of the Hebrew religion; the latter made him acquainted with the doctrines of the two predominant principles in nature, of good and evil, and unfolded to his astonishing view all the stupendous mysteries of Mithra. Twelve years, according to Porphyry, were spent by Pythagoras in this renowned capital, from which, when he had regained his liberty, determined to complete his treasure of Asiatic literature, he sought the distant, but celebrated, groves of the Brachmans of India. Among that secluded and speculative race he probably carried to the highest point of perfection attainable in that age those astronomical investigations to which he was so deeply devoted: by them he was probably instructed in the true system of the universe, which to this day is distinguished by his name; among them he greatly enlarged the limits of his metaphysical knowledge; and from them he carried away the glorious doctrine of the immortality of the soul, which he first divulged in Greece, and the fanciful doctrine of the metempsychosis.

" That Pythagoras, having been conducted to Babylon among the prisoners of Cambyses, was instructed by the Persian Magi, and particularly by Zoroaster, the first or principal depository of all secret and divine sciences, is a gross anachronism, says Volney; since Pythagoras, born in 608 B. C., was eighty-four when Cambyses conquered Egypt in 525. Jamblichus, who compiled the life of Pythagoras from a great many authors, about the year 320, repeats the same tradition.

" Plato, who followed Pythagoras, being born about 430 years B. C., must also have contributed to the information of the Greeks; since, besides the honour and advantage of having had Socrates for his guide and preceptor, he was instructed in all the intricate doctrines of the Egyptian philosophy. On the death of that martyr to the cause of truth, he travelled first into Italy and then into Egypt, as well to mitigate the anguish he felt for the loss of so excellent and wise a man, as to increase the treasures of knowledge with which his mind was already so amply stored. Cicero expressly informs us that in visiting Egypt his principal aim was to learn mathematics and ecclesiastical speculations among the barbarians; for by this disgraceful appellation the fastidious Greeks stigmatised all foreign nations. He travelled, says Valerius Maximus, over the whole of that country, informing himself, by means of the priests, during his progress, of geometry in all its various and multiform branches, as well as of their astronomical observations. From the sages of the Thebais, Pausanias affirms he learned the immortality of the soul; and from the style and tenour of his writings, it is pretty evident that he was deeply versed in the sacred books attributed to Hermes Trismegist."

"Maurice remarks that among the foreigners of the Greek nation that resided in Egypt, the two most celebrated were Pythagoras and Plato; and the philosophical dogmas promulgated by them on their return to Greece, as well as their mode of promulgating them, affords very ample evidence of the fact. These great men were in Egypt, the former in the sixth century before Christ, and the latter in the fifth, when the Egyptian system of religion and philosophy still flourished. Although they might not be able to penetrate into all the profound arcana of their mysterious erudition, these favoured disciples of the old Egyptian hierophants had seen enough of their enigmatical learning to transport back with them into Greece the same symbolical mode of instruction. Porphyry tells us that the former of these philosophers, during his various travels through Asia and Africa, learned arithmetic from the Phœnicians, geometry from the Egyptians, astronomy from the Chaldæans, and theology from the Persians. And what is here recorded relative to his attachment to the mysterious mode of dogmatising in Egypt, is founded on fact, may be proved from the circumstance, that on his return to Samos, after a residence of two-and-twenty years in that country, though he erected a school for the public study of philosophy within the city, yet he himself resided without the city in a cavern, where he delivered his more mystical and profound discourses; after the very same manner in which the more deep and recondite sciences of Egypt were alone taught, by her sequestered sacerdotal tribe, amid the gloomy adyta and subterraneous grottoes of the Thebais.

"In regard to Plato, we cannot but attribute to the same cause that spirit of mysticism which pervades the whole of his sublimely obscure theology, as well as that devotion to the favourite science of the Egyptians, which dictated the motto inscribed in large characters over the academy : " Let none ignorant of geometry enter this place."

Porphyry informs us that the cave of Zoroaster resembled the world fabricated by Mithra; in the lofty roof of which the signs of the zodiac were sculptured in golden characters; while through its spacious dome, represented by orbs of different metals, symbolical of their power and influences, the sun and planets performed their ceaseless and undeviating revolutions.

Porphyry himself, writes Maurice, was one of the profoundest critics and scholars that the schools of Greece ever bred, and deeply initiated in all the mystic rites of the ancient recondite philosophy and abstruse metaphysics.   He acquaints us that, according to Eubulus, Zoroaster, first of all among the neighbouring mountains of Persia, consecrated a natural cave, adorned with flowers and watered with fountains, in honour of Mithra, the father of the universe.   For he thought a cavern an emblem of the world, fabricated by Mithra; and in this cave were geometrical symbols, arranged in the most perfect symmetry, and placed at certain distances, which shadowed out the elements and climates of the world.   Again, they erected in these caverns a high ladder, which had seven gates, according to the number of planets through which the soul gradually ascended to the supreme mansion of felicity.

" These," remarks Maurice, " are not the only passages in which the gradual ascent of the soul through the planets or spheres of purification is indicated in the Geeta.   They are, however, sufficient for our purpose; and in proof that the

Indians actually had, in the remotest eras, in their system of theology, the sidereal ladder of seven gates, so universally made use of as a symbol throughout all the East, I have now to inform the reader of the following circumstance: there exists at present, in the King's library at Paris, a book of paintings entirely allusive to the Indian mythology and the incarnations of Veeshnu, in one of which is exhibited this very symbol, upon which the souls of men are represented as ascending and descending, according to the received opinion of the sidereal metempsychosis in Asia."

The same writer, quoting the mysteries of the Eleusinian worship, as described by Apuleius and Dion Chrysostome, who had both gone through the awful ceremony of initiation into the greater mysteries, mentions, that after the whole fabulous detail was solemnly recanted by the mystagogue, a divine hymn, in honour of *eternal and immutable truth,* was chanted, and the profounder mysteries commenced.

" The Eleusinian aspirant, after ablution, was clothed in a linen vestment, the emblem of purity; and we are informed in the Indian register (*Ayeen Akbery*), that the Brahmin candidate, in the first stage of probation, was arrayed in a linen garment without suture. But the mystic temple itself, as described by Apuleius, was ' *œdes amplissima ;*' according to Vitruvius, it was '*immani magnitudine ;*' and according to Strabo, it was capable of holding as large a number as a theatre. If these several authors had intended to describe the pagodas of Elephanta and of Salsette, could they have done it with more characteristic accuracy? — temples, of which the former, according to Niebuhr, is a square of 120 feet, and in the latter of which, if we are rightly informed in the Archæologia, the grand altar alone is elevated to the astonishing height of 27 feet. The gloomy avenues surrounding them have also been particularised, in which an overwhelming dread and horror seized the benighted wanderer; and with respect to the gaudy shows and splendid scenery occasionally displayed to the view of the initiated in their recesses,—who that beholds the superb decorations, the richly painted walls, and carved imagery in the modern pagodas,—who that considers the beauty of the colours and the ingenuity of the devices conspicuous in many of the manufactures of India, whether in gold or silver enamel, in boxes curiously inlaid with ivory, in carpets of silk richly flowered, and linens stained with variegated dies,—can possibly entertain a doubt of the ability of the ancient Indians strikingly to portray, on canvas or otherwise, the allegorical visions in which the genius of the nation takes so much delight,—the amaranthine bowers, in which beatified spirits are supposed to reside, and the Elysian plains of Eendra's voluptuous paradise?

" The initiated in the Grecian temples were crowned with myrtles; and Herodotus informs us that the Persian priests of Mithra, and consequently those of India, were decked with a rich tiara wound about with the same foliage, and that the arch-priest sang the theogony or ode, reciting the origin of the gods. The Hierophant, that is, the revealer of sacred things in the Eleusinian mysteries, was arrayed in the habit, and adorned with the symbols, of the great Creator of the world, of whom in those mysteries he was supposed to be the substitute, and revered as the emblem.

" The professed design," adds Maurice, " both of the Indian, the Egyptian, and the Eleusinian mysteries, was to restore the fallen soul to its pristine state of purity and perfection; and the initiated in those mysteries were instructed in the sublime doctrines of a supreme presiding Providence, of the immortality of the soul, and the rewards and punishments of a future state. But the Brahmans, in their profounder speculations on the being and attributes of God, initiated their pupils into mysteries still more refined: they inculcated upon their minds the necessity, resulting as a natural consequence from that doctrine, of not only restraining the violence of the more boisterous passions, but of entirely subduing the gross animal propensities by continued acts of abstinence and mortification, and of seeking that intimate communion of soul with the great Father of the universe, which, when in its most elevated point of holy transport, is in India denominated the absorbed state; this, and the subjugation of the passions and the mortification of the body, ever have been, and are at this day, carried to such an height of extravagance as is absolutely inconceivable by those who have not been spectators of it, and is such as far exceeds the most boasted austerities of Romish penitents.

" The prevailing doctrine of the metempsychosis was indisputably propagated in the schools of India long before it was promulgated in those of the Egyptian and Grecian philosophers. The following passage from the Sacontala, relative to the migrating soul, forms the concluding sentence to that beautiful drama. " May Seeva, with the azure neck and red locks, eternally potent and self-existing, avert from me the pain of another birth in this perishing world, the seat of crimes and of punishments ! "

" The principal fire-temple, and the usual residence of Zoroaster and of his royal protector, Darius Hystaspes, was at Balkh, the capital of Bactria, the most eastern province of Persia, situated on the north-west frontiers of India. We are told by A. Marcellinus that Hystaspes himself, and most probably not unattended by the illustrious Archimagus, did personally penetrate into the secluded regions of Upper India, and, in disguise, visited the deep solitudes of the forest, amidst whose peaceful shades the Brachmans exercise their lofty genius in profound speculations, and that he was there instructed by them in the principles of mathematics, astronomy, and the pure rites of sacrifice. These various doctrines, to the utmost extent of their inclination to impart and his own abilities to retain them, he afterwards taught the Magi, all which, together with the science of divination, those Magi traditionally delivered down to posterity through a long succession of ages. That part of India which Hystaspes visited was, doubtless, Cashmeer, where in all probability the genuine religion of Brahma flourished longest without adulteration.

" Abul-Fazil, who several times visited, together with the Emperor Akber, that delightful country, and therefore wrote not from the report of others but as an eye-witness, I can

A A 4

answer," says Maurice, " that such vestiges actually do exist there. In the account which the *Ayeen Akbery* gives of Cashmeer, there is a very interesting relation inserted of a most amiable race of religious devotees who are denominated Reyshees, and who are said to be the most respectable people of that country. These people, according to Abul Fazil, do not suffer themselves to be fettered by traditions; they revile no sect that may differ from them in religious opinions, nor do they meanly supplicate alms, like the wandering mendicants of the south. They abstain from all animal food; they devote their lives to unblemished chastity, and they make it their constant and benevolent employment to plant the road with fruit-trees for the refreshment of weary and fainting travellers. Now the word Reyshee signifies in Sanscrit a holy person, and in the principles and conduct of these devotees may surely be traced the mild, the beneficent, the uncorrupted religion of the great Brahma.

" It may fairly be concluded that Hystaspes was incited by the representation of his friend and counsellor Zoroaster to pay this private visit to the Brachmans, and that Zoroaster himself had frequently before visited that ' *nemorosam solitudinem* ' in which, Marcellinus informs us, they dwelt. It is a conclusion equally fair that the latter zealously copied the manners and habits of living of those whose austerity and wisdom he so ardently admired. When, therefore, we find Zoroaster, as he is represented by Porphyry, previously to his assuming the prophetic character, retiring to the gloom of a lonely cavern in Media, and ornamenting that cavern with various astronomical symbols and mathematical apparatus, displaying and teaching what he had there probably seen and been instructed in, ' *Bracmanorum monitu, rationes mundani motus et siderum ;* ' when we find him in Persia reviving with additional splendour the ancient but decayed worship of the sun and fire ; especially when, upon a more full investigation of the matter, we discover in the mountainous regions of India which he visited that the excavations were equally numerous and prodigious ; and, in the very midst of those mountains, according to the express words of Abul Fazil, who had in all probability personally examined them in his various excursions with Akber into that neighbourhood, that no less than 12,000 recesses were cut in the solid rock, all ornamented with carving and plaster-work, and remarkable for three astonishing idols, — the first representing a man 80 ells in height, the second a woman 50 ells in height, and the third a gigantic child 15 ells in height; when we read that in Cashmeer, after the defection of the inhabitants from their original simplicity and purity of worship, there were no less than ' 700 places where the figures of a serpent,' that ancient hieroglyphic emblem of the sun, were worshipped ;—on a due consideration of all these circumstances united together," adds Maurice, " it is impossible to avoid supposing that at the period alluded to the secret mysteries both of the Hindoo religion and the Hindoo sciences were performed and taught in the gloom of subterraneous retreats, hollowed. for that purpose out of the rock, and decorated with similar sculptures and ornaments; that the mystic rites performed in them were those in honour of elemental fire, and that the prevailing religion of the nation was the worship of the sun.

" The Mithratic worship in caverns continued longest in Persia. The Persians thought it impious to erect temples to the deity;. they continued, therefore, to perform this worship by night in the native and obscure cavern, and by day under the resplendent canopy of heaven."

That Maurice associates the pyramid with the fire-worship will be seen from the following quotation : — " How shall we explain so singular a phenomenon as that the pyramidal temple, symbolical of the solar ray, should rise with almost as bold an elevation in Mexico as in Egypt; and that the Peruvians should adore the sun with as much ardour as anciently did the Magi in Persia and the Brahmins of India ? "

Maurice gives from Montfaucon a drawing of an ancient sacrifice to the sun sculptured in a grotto or cavern near the modern town of Babain, in Upper Egypt. The rock has been excavated by the chisel to the height of 50 feet, and is 50 feet in width and 6 in depth.

Maurice thinks that these mysterious celebrations were the real origin of all those mystic rites which, in succeeding ages, throughout Asia as well as Europe, in Persia, in Greece, and in Rome, passed under the various denominations of Mithraic, Orphic, Eleusinian, and Bacchic. Also that the mysteries of both Osiris and Mithra are only copies of the ancient worship of Surya, the solar fire, which originally was adored in Chaldæa, or Syria, as the noblest object in nature, and as the purest symbol of the Deity in the whole extent of creation.

" If the Persian and the Hindoo legislator were not in reality the same person, which I strongly suspect they were," adds Maurice, " under two distinct appellations, it must be owned that the principles of their theology are wonderfully similar. Brahme, the great one, is the supreme, eternal, un-created God of the Hindoos. Brahma, the first created being, by whom he made and governs the world, is the prince of the beneficent spirits. He is assisted by Veeshnu, the great preser-ver of men, who has nine several times appeared upon earth, and under a human form, for the most amiable and benefi-cent purposes. Veeshnu is often called Creeshna, the Indian Apollo, and in character greatly resembles the Mithra of Persia ; the prince of the benevolent Dewtah has a second coadjutor in Mahadeo, or the destroying power of God ; and these three celestial beings, or, to speak more correctly, this threefold divinity, armed with the terrors of the Almighty power, pursue throughout the extent of creation the rebellious Dewtahs, headed by Mahasoor, the great malignant spirit who seduced them, and dart upon their flying bands the Agnyastra, or fiery shafts of divine vengeance." '

Volney remarks, " that the science of the magi consisted in astronomy and judiciary astrology, that is, in predictions, divinations, and prophecies attached to that art ; that it con-sisted also in certain chemical and physical knowledge, by means of which they performed phenomena that were pro-digious and miraculous for the mass of the people. This science gradually became an art of imposture and charlatanry, which received in its bad sense the name of magic, which we give it. In this respect, that is, as an art of evocations, of enchantments, of metamorphoses, effected by certain practices, it is much more ancient than Zoroaster, as it is very justly observed by the Persians, since it was the basis of the power and influence of the Egyptian, Chaldæan, Brahmin, and Druid priests; in a word, of all the priests of antiquity.

" The name of Kaldeans, mentioned already in Abram's time, as denoting an ancient nation, signifies conjuror, and proves the existence and practice of the art amongst a people which, as Ammianus Marcellinus says, was at first but a sect, and became afterwards, by its increase, a numerous and powerful nation. Now if, as is true, this sort of magic and magicians extends to thousands of years, it must, by confounding it with Zoroasterism, that Eudoxus and Hermippus have put back its founder to 5000 years before the war of Troy, or 6000 before Plato.

" After Cambyses, son of Cyrus, the mage Smerdis, as is known, usurped the throne by a substitution of person and name. Darius, with other conspirators, having killed him, there ensued a general proscription of the magi, who were massacred over the whole empire, and the recollection of this massacre was preserved in an anniversary called Magophony. It is evident that after this massacre, the terrified tribe of the magi was at the discretion of Darius, son of Hystaspes. If, afterwards, this king was proved to be called a mage doctor, he found it therefore prudent to re-establish them; but though he re-established them, he remained the master of their persons and property; he appointed their officers, the highpriests, the mobeds, &c."

This description of the Brahmins, and that of the Druids previously noticed, may be compared with Symes' account of the Boodhists.

" The groves before mentioned are objects of no unpleasing contemplation; they are the retreats of such Rhahaans or priests as devote themselves to religious seclusion, and prefer the tranquillity of rural retirement to the noise and tumult of a town.

" In the choice of a residence they usually select the most

retired spots they can find, where shady trees, particularly the tamarind and banyan, protect them from the noon-day sun.   In these groves they build their kioums, and here they pass their solitary lives.

" All kioums or monasteries, whether in town or country, are seminaries for the education of youth, in which boys of a certain age are taught their letters, and instructed in moral and religious duties.   To these schools the neighbouring villagers send their children, where they are educated gratis, no distinction being made between the son of the peasant and him who wears the tsaloe, or string of nobility.   A piece of ground contiguous to the grove is enclosed for a garden, where they sow vegetables and plant fruit trees : the Indian sweet potatoe and the plantain, being the most nutritious, are principally cultivated ; the charity of the country people supply them abundantly with rice, and the few necessaries which their narrow wants require.   Abstracted from all worldly considerations, they do not occupy themselves in the common concerns of life.   They never buy, sell, or accept of money."

The reception of Symes by the Seredaw, or chief priest, is thus described.   "He received us with much politeness, and in his looks and demeanour affected more liveliness and complaisance than any of the fraternity I had hitherto seen.   I presented him my offering, which consisted of a piece of yellow cloth, the sacerdotal colour ; some sandal-wood, and a few wax candles covered with gold leaf.   He asked several questions respecting England, such as how long the voyage usually was thence to India ; being told this he observed that we were an extraordinary people to wander so far from home.   I noticed the magnificence of the kioum : he replied, that such sublunary matters did not attract his attention ; he was on earth but as a hermit.   I desired his prayers ; he said they were daily offered up for the happiness of all mankind, but that he would recommend us to the particular protection of Gaudma.   He made some observations on our appearance, which I did not understand, and he even smiled — a relaxation unusual in a Rhahaan."

" There is every reason to believe," says Wallace, " that originally the worship of Brahma did not differ materially from that of Zoroaster's followers, or the disciples of Budha; and that the disgusting images of beasts and monsters were then unknown which at present shock the sight in every part of India. Surya, or the sun, was the great object of worship in Hindostan in early times. I have seen his image, that of a well-shaped man, in a most ancient temple in the fortress of Kantkote, in the province of Cutch. He holds a sun in each hand, and has behind him four diminutive attendants, with instruments something like tridents.

" Indeed, the gross deviations from the simplicity of the Brahmanical institution occasioned several successful attempts at reformation. In an age so early as to baffle the research of antiquarians, Budha apostatised; and, denying the divine origin of the Vedas, began to worship God under the form of a circle. It does not, however, appear that the followers of Budha ever became very numerous in Hindostan; but in all the neighbouring countries, that faith soon superseded ancient idolatry, and still holds its ground, having the great Lama of Tibet for its head. The Budhists are not divided into castes at present, except on the island of Ceylon, where, it is said, they still adhere to the Brahmanical classification, with merely placing the warriors before the priests.

" In the reformation of Budha, the discipline of Brahma was much relaxed, and a considerable latitude given in the use of food; but the founder of Jainism made the care of animal life one of his most particular injunctions, establishing it as the divine will that nothing should be deprived by man of its existence, and teaching that the world was never created. Their idea of time is therefore the most complex that can be conceived. They offer no sacrifice in their religious rites, which are simple ceremonies, conducted by priests in two sorts of temples. One is covered, and much like the Hindoo pagoda; the other is open above, having merely a high wall round colossean statues of much respected men: such are to be seen at Kurcul, in the province of Canara, and at Baligole, in Mysore. The Jains believe nothing but what they can perceive; and the only objects they worship are the deified spirits of holy men, who are represented in a state of divine abstraction in their temples, on altars of white marble.   I have seen several of these temples at Guzerat, and the following is a brief description of one.

" The images are of white marble coarsely sculptured, but with tolerable proportions.   There are ten of them seated on an altar, all exactly in the same posture.   The centre one, on an upper pedestal, was larger than life, to which the others bore an exact resemblance, though different in size.   These idols were situated in the temple, under a great pyramid, to which you enter by first going up a fine flight of steps, and passing through two circular, or rather octagonal apartments, over which there are large domes.   The first impression is, that you stand before representations of women with large ears; but on inquiry it will be found they are all intended for men, and that the form is merely feminine, to show the superior beauty a spirit acquires by transformation from flesh.

" It is impossible to describe the solemn grandeur of the *sanctum sanctorum*, in which the idols are placed, when lighted with large brass chandeliers, with attendant priests, while the great hall in the centre, as well as the two wings and the vestibule, are crowded with worshippers, who go through a number of salutations, prostrations, and ceremonies.   I was permitted to go close up to the images, upon leaving my boots at the great dome; and certainly, amidst all that surrounded me, I felt a considerable degree of awe and respect.   Indeed, a man of sensibility, in the presence of even marble statues that represent a state of mental abstraction, in which the Hindoos conceive there is real perfection, as the likeness of God, feels an elevation of sentiment towards the great Creator, who has so visibly revealed himself in every atom that meets human optics, and yet lies so completely veiled with his own magnificence as to be seen by different imaginations in a vast variety of particular forms. Such a man, so situated, is apt to be impressed with the Brahmanical idea, that all forms of natural adoration must be pleasing to God; and, while he pities the delusion of mortal inconsistencies, he will enlarge the sphere of his charity, and believe that a pure heart, under any mode of faith, will meet with favour in the sight of the Almighty.

" That Jain worship was a reformation in Brahmanism cannot be doubted. Any one will admit its pretensions to superior purity who compares the simple form of it to the complicated system of Hindooism and the monstrous idols which the Brahmanical Pantheon displays, many of which are too shocking for delicacy to describe. It would be uninteresting to exhibit such monsters, and it seems only necessary to observe that they are obviously creations of grossness and ignorance, which have crept into Brahmanism in its day of degeneracy; for originally there is nothing very repugnant to human reason in its construction. Even in some of its incarnations, particularly that of Chrishna, there is a remote resemblance to the history of our Saviour.

" At Guzerat the tribe called Banyans are very numerous. They have a great respect for animal life, and establish hospitals for the old and sickly of the brute creation. Here are also numerous establishments of Jains, who carry fans made of feathers to frighten away insects, lest they should inadvertently deprive anything that exists of life.

" The last attempt, made by a native of India, to substitute a new form of worship in Hindostan in room of the Brahmanical institution was made by Nanac, the founder of the Seiks, towards the middle of the fifteenth century. He was born at a village called Tulwandy, in the province of Lahore. His great success in converting the Hindoos to pure Deism proves that they may be roused by persuasion alone to change their religion, and imbibe principles of enthusiastic republicanism, with more ease than is generally supposed. The Seiks, or disciples of Nanac, are now very numerous; and besides nearly the whole province of Lahore, they have the Punjâb, part of Mooltan, and the greatest share of the country between the Jumna and the Sutleje. Their converts are permitted to retain the manners and customs of their castes in a great measure. The ceremony of initiation is a solemn oath to devote themselves to the use of the sword in defence of the state. The priests are called Immortals, and preside in a great assembly which meets, in prosperous times, at Amritsir, where the chiefs, having taken a sort of sacrament, by eating together of consecrated cake, transact the business of the government, which is a theocracy. But this invisibility has induced each chief to constitute himself the head of the state, and, therefore, the Seiks are weakened by internal divisions and constant struggles for power."

PART XI.

BABYLON. — MUJELIBÈ.— BIRS NIMROUD, THE SUPPOSED TOWER OF
BELUS.— EGYPTIAN BABYLON.— EFFLORESCENT SALTS.— BREADTH
OF THE EUPHRATES AT BABYLON. — BAGDAD. — LEANING TOWER
OF MOSUL. — ARCHED GATEWAYS AT NIMROUD. — TUNNEL UNDER
THE EUPHRATES COMPARED WITH THE SUBTERRANEAN PASSAGES
IN PERU, AND THE OLD NORMAN CASTLES IN ENGLAND. — THAMES
TUNNEL.— TUNNEL IN EGYPT.— MEXICAN TUNNEL AND CANAL. —
MEXICAN AND PERUVIAN AQUEDUCTS.— CANAL THROUGH THE
PROMONTORY OF MOUNT ATHOS.— HEIGHT OF GUADAMA, CON-
FUCIUS AND ARTACHÆUS.— BRIDGES.— MOUND OF NINUS.—
GREAT BABYLONIAN WORKS. — WALLS OF BABYLON.— ROMAN
MOVING TOWERS. — BRIDGE OVER THE EUPHRATES AT BABYLON.
— CONSTRUCTION OF THE TUNNEL.— CIRCUIT OF THE EXCAVATED
LAKE. — GREAT ANTIQUITY OF THE TOWER OF BELUS, OF THE
PAGODA AT NANKIN, AND OF THE SHOOMADOO PRAW AT PEGU.—
SEMIRAMIS DESCRIBES HER GREAT WORKS. — SEMIRAMIS AND
NAPOLEON I. CONTRASTED. — EXTENT OF BABYLON COMPARED
WITH OTHER ASIATIC CITIES.— THE WALLS OF PEKIN.— PARIS.—
CIRCUIT OF ROME. — EXTENT OF LONDON.— ISPAHAN. — MEMPHIS.
— NANKIN AND PAGODA.— QUANSAI.— HONG-CHEU-FU.— CHINESE
CANALS.— BRIDGES. — ARCHWAYS.— BEJAPOOR. — KERBELA.—
JEDDO. — THEBES.— GREAT WALL OF CHINA.— ROMAN WALLS IN
BRITAIN. — HIGHROADS IN PERU, EGYPT, AND INDIA.— EXTENT
OF THE QUAYS AT BABYLON, LIVERPOOL, AND PETERSBURG. —
CHINESE IMPERIAL CANAL.— MODERN EGYPTIAN CANAL.— KOO-
TUB MINAR AT DELHI.— FEROZE COTELAH.— BOLOGNA TOWERS.
— ST. MARK'S AT VENICE. — ANTWERP.— LEANING TOWER AT
PISA.— GERALDA AT SEVILLE. — KOOTSABEEA AT MOROCCO. —
CHIMNEYS IN THE MANUFACTURING DISTRICTS. — BRIDGES. —
RAILWAY ENGINEERING. — TRAJAN'S BRIDGE OVER THE DANUBE.
— ROADS. — SUSPENSION BRIDGES. — BRIDGE OF BOATS. — APPLI-
CATION OF IRON TO ARCHITECTURAL PURPOSES.

Babylon.

RICH remarks "that those who have investigated the antiquities of Babylon have laid much stress on the authority of

Diodorus, probably adverting more to the quantity than the quality of the information he supplies. He was never on the spot! he lived in an age when, as he tells us, its area was ploughed over! he has therefore recourse to Ctesias; and it must be owned that the want of discrimination in the ancients, and the credulity of Diodorus himself, were never more strongly exemplified than in his choice of a writer who confounds the Euphrates with the Tigris, and tells us that Semiramis erected a monument to her husband, which from the dimensions he specifies must have been of superior elevation to Mount Vesuvius, and nearly equal to Mount Hecla. If these are not " fairy tales," I certainly know not to what the term can be applied. When an author can in so many instances be clearly convicted of ignorance and exaggeration, we are certainly not justified in altering what is already before our eyes, to suit his description. We have only the very questionable authority of Ctesias for the second palace, and the wonderful tunnel under the river; but even he does not say whether the tower of Belus stood on the east or west side. Herodotus, who will ever appear to greater advantage the more he is examined and understood, is the only historian who visited Babylon in person; and he is in every respect the best authority for its state in his time. The circumference he assigns to it has been generally deemed exaggerated; but after all we cannot prove it to be so. He says nothing to determine the situation of the palace (for he speaks but of one) and temple; he has no mention of east or west, or of proximity to the river. It is true it has been attempted to establish from him, that the temple was exactly in the centre of one of the hollows into which the city was divided by the river. Strabo, as might be expected, contains much fewer particulars than Herodotus; and the other Grecian and Roman historians still less. They are consequently of little use in topographical inquiry. It appears, therefore, that none of the ancients say whether the tower of Belus was on the east or west of the Euphrates; that its position in the centre of the city, or even of one of its divisions, is by no means clearly made out; and while the description of the best ancient author involves no difficulties, the only particulars which embarrass us are supported by the sole testimony of the worst.

" The Mujelibè, 5 miles distant from Hilla, supposed by Pietro della Valle to have been the tower of Belus, is an oblong shape, irregular in its height, and the measurement of its sides, which face the cardinal points; the northern side being 200 yards in length, the southern 219, the eastern 182, and the western 136 ;—the elevation of the south-east or highest angle, 141 feet. The western face, which is the least elevated, is the most interesting on account of the appearance of building it presents. Near the summit it appears a low wall, with interruptions, built with unburnt bricks mixed up with chopped straw or reeds ; and on the north side are also some vestiges of a similar construction. The south-west angle is crowned by something like a turret or lantern : the other angles are in a less perfect state, but may originally have been ornamented in a similar manner. The western face is lowest and easiest of ascent ; the northern the most difficult. All are worn into furrows by the weather, and in some places, where several channels of rain have united together, these furrows are of great depth, and penetrate a considerable way into the mound. The summit is covered with heaps of rubbish, in digging into some of which, layers of broken burnt brick cemented with mortar are discovered, and whole bricks with inscriptions on them are here and there found ; the whole is covered with innumerable fragments of pottery, brick, bitumen, pebbles, vitrified brick or scoria, and even shells, bits of glass, and mother-of-pearl.

" The modern town of Arbil," adds Rich, " has an artificial mount at least as large as the Mujelibè, and much higher. This mount, which is of the highest antiquity, and probably existed in the days of Alexander, has been crowned by a succession of castles of different ages. The present is a Turkish building, and contains within its walls (as the others doubtless did) a portion of the town, consisting of two mahallas or parishes : the remainder of the town is situated at the foot of the mount, and would, if abandoned, in a few years leave not a single vestige behind.   Precisely the same observation holds good of the still more considerable city and castle of Kerkook.

" The governor of Hilla informed me of a mound as large as the Mujelibè, situated 35 hours to the southward of Hilla; and that a few years ago, a cap or diadem of pure gold, and some other articles of the same metal, were found there.

" In the western desert bearing north-west from the top of the Mujelibè, is a large mound called Towereij.   In the same desert, two leagues to the west of Hilla, is the village of Tahmasia, built by Nadir Shah, where, it is said, are some trifling mounds; this village must occupy part of the site of Babylon.   From the top of the Mujelibè in a southerly direction, at a great distance, two large mounds are visible, with whose names I am unacquainted.   Five or six miles to the east of Hillah is Al Hheimar, which is a curious ruin, as bearing, on a smaller scale, some resemblance to the Birs Nimroud.   The base is a heap of rubbish, on the top of which is a mass of red brickwork, between each layer of which is a curious white substance which pulverises on the least touch.   I have not yet visited Al Hheimar."

" To these ruins I add one which, though not in the same direction, bears such strong characteristics of a Babylonian origin, that it would be improper to omit a description of it in this place,—I mean Akerkouf, or, as it is more generally called, Nimrod's Tower; for the inhabitants of these parts are fond of attributing every vestige of antiquity to Nimrod, as those of Egypt are to Pharaoh.   It is situated ten miles to the north-west of Bagdad, and is a thick mass of unburnt brick-work of an irregular shape, rising out of a base of rubbish; there is a layer of reeds between every fifth or sixth (for the number is not regular) layer of bricks.   It is perforated with small square holes, as the brickwork at the Birs Nimroud; and about half way up on the east side is an aperture like a window : the layers of cement are very thin, which, considering it is mere mud, is an extraordinary circumstance. The height of the whole is 126 feet ; diameter of the largest part 100 feet; circumference at the foot of the brickwork, above the rubbish, 300 feet : the remains of the tower contain 100,000 cubic feet. To the east of it is a dependent mound, resembling those at the Birs and Al Hheimar."

These appear to be the dimensions of Ives, who saw and minutely described this building at Aggarkuff in 1758. It stands, sublime and solitary, on a plain about nine miles from Bagdad, amidst masses of ruined buildings that extend the whole length of the way from Bagdad, and which are supposed to be the remains of the ancient Seleucia. He intimates that if the foundation could be got at, it would be considerably larger than 300 feet in circumference.

The bricks of which it is composed are all $12\frac{1}{3}$ inches square and $4\frac{1}{2}$ thick, cemented together with a bituminous substance abounding plentifully in the neighbourhood, and intermixed with layers of reeds.

$$1\tfrac{1}{2} \text{ cubit} = 12\cdot645 \text{ inches,}$$
$$\tfrac{1}{2} \text{ cubit} = 4\cdot215 \quad \text{,,}$$

" It now remains," says Rich, " to notice the most interesting and remarkable of the Babylonian remains, viz., the Birs Nimroud. If any building may be supposed to have left considerable traces, it is certainly the pyramid or tower of Belus, which, by its form, dimensions, and the solidity of its construction, was well calculated to resist the ravages of time, and, if human force had not been employed, would, in all probability, have remained to the present day, in nearly as perfect a state as the pyramids of Egypt. Even under the dilapidation which we know it to have undergone at a very early period, we might reasonably look for traces of it after every other vestige of Babylon had vanished from the face of the earth. When, therefore, we see within a short distance from the spot fixed on, both by geographers and antiquarians and the tradition of the country, to be the site of ancient Babylon, a stupendous pile, which appears to have been built in receding stages, which bears the most indisputable traces both of the violence of man and the lapse of ages, and yet continues to tower over the desert, the wonder of successive

B B 3

generations,—it is impossible that their perfect correspondence with all the accounts of the Tower of Belus should not strike the most careless observer. I am of opinion that this ruin is of a nature to fix of itself the locality of Babylon, even to the exclusion of those on the eastern side of the river.

"The whole height of the Birs Nimroud above the plain to the summit of the brick wall is 235 feet. The brick wall itself, which stands on the edge of the summit, and was undoubtedly the face of another stage, is 37 feet high. In the side of the pile, a little below the summit, is very clearly to be seen part of another brick wall, precisely resembling the fragment which crowns the summit, but which still encases and supports its part of the mound. This is clearly indicative of another stage of greater extent. The masonry is infinitely superior to anything of the kind I have ever seen; and, leaving out of the question any conjecture relative to the original destination of the ruin, the impression made by the sight of it is, that it was a solid pile, composed in the interior of unburnt brick and, perhaps, earth or rubbish; that it was constructed in receding stages, and faced with fine burnt bricks, having inscriptions on them, laid in a very thin layer of lime cement; and that it was reduced by violence to its present ruinous condition. The upper stories have been forcibly broken down, and fire has been employed as an instrument of destruction, though it is not easy to say precisely how or why. The facing of fine bricks has been partly removed and partly covered by the falling down of the mass which it supported and kept together. So indisputably evident is the fact of the whole mass being, from top to bottom, artificial, that I should as soon have thought of writing a dissertation to prove that the Pyramids are the work of human hands as of dwelling on this point. Indeed, were there anything equivocal in the appearance of the mound itself, the principles of physical geography utterly forbid the supposition of there being an isolated hill of natural formation in ground formed by the depositions of a river.

"The Birs Nimroud is in all likelihood at present pretty

nearly in the state in which Alexander saw it, if we give any credit to the report that ten thousand men could only remove the rubbish, preparatory to repairing it, in two months. If, indeed, it required one half of that number to disencumber it, the state of dilapidation must have been complete. The immense masses of vitrified brick which are seen on the top of the mound appear to have marked its summit since the time of its destruction. The rubbish about its base was probably in much greater quantities, the weather having dissipated much of it in the course of so many revolving ages; and, possibly portions of the exterior facing of fine bricks may have disappeared at different periods.

" The only building which can dispute the palm with the Mujelibè is the Birs Nimroud, previous to my visiting which I had not the slightest idea of the possibility of its being the Tower of Belus; indeed, its situation was a strong argument against such a supposition : but the moment I had examined it, I could not help exclaiming, " Had this been on the other side of the river, and near the great mass of ruins, no one could doubt of its being the remains of the tower."

Taking for granted the site of Babylon to be in the vicinity of Hilla, the choice will be divided between two objects, the Mujelibè and the Birs Nimroud, as to which was the tower of Belus.

Total circumference
            of the four sides of the Birs = 2286 feet.
            of the Mujelibè   -   = 2111 „ .

" The variations in the form of the Mujelibè from a perfect square are not more than the accidents of time will account for ; and the reader will best judge from my description whether the summit and external appearance of this ruin correspond in any way with the accounts of the tower."

The height of the platform, or highest part of the tower of Belus, from the base was 1 stade, or 281 feet.

The height of the Birs Nimroud from the plain to the summit of the solid mass of brickwork equals 235 feet.

The perimeter of the four sides of the square area in which

the tower stood equalled $4 \times 2 = 8$ stades $= 8 \times 281 = 2248$ feet.

The total circumference of the four sides of the Birs $= 2286$ feet.

Side of square $= \frac{1}{4} 2286 = 571\cdot5$ feet
$$= 494 \quad \text{units}$$
494^3 &c. $= \frac{1}{9}$ distance of moon.

Cube of external side of the square enclosure
$$= \frac{1}{9} \text{ distance of moon.}$$
$(3 \times 494)^3 = \frac{1}{9} \times 3^3 = 3.$

Cube of 3 times side
$$= 3 \text{ times distance of moon.}$$
$(5 \times 3 \times 494)^3 = 3 \times 5^3 = 375$ distance of moon.

Cube of 15 times side $= \frac{1}{10}$ distance of Saturn.

10 cubes $=$ distance of Saturn
20 „ $=$ „   Uranus
60 „ $=$ „   Belus.

If the external side of the square enclosure $= 494$ units,

Cube of external side $= \frac{1}{9}$ distance of moon,

Cube of internal side $=$ circumference,

Cube of side of base of external pyramid $= \frac{1}{60}$ distance of moon.

Cube of side of base of internal pyramid $= \frac{1}{8}$ circumference.

The external cubes will be as 20 : 3
and the internal cubes   „   8 : 1.

" The Mujelibè appears to be, like the ruin at Nineveh, rather an artificial mound than a mass of decayed building. At the foot of the Mujelibè, about seventy yards from it, on the northern and western sides, are traces of a very low mound of earth, which may have formed an enclosure round the whole. A passage filled with skeletons has been found in the Mujelibè."

The tower was formed by a succession of terraces.

The Birs appears to be constructed in receding stages.

In another part, Rich says, "the Birs Nimroud is a mound of an oblong form, the total circumference of which is 762 yards. At the eastern side it is cloven by a deep furrow, and is not more than 50 or 60 feet high; but at the western side it rises in a conical figure to the elevation of 198 feet, and on the summit is a solid pile of brick 37 feet high by 28 in breadth, diminishing in thickness to the top, which is broken and irregular, and rent by a large fissure extending through a third of its height. It is perforated by small holes disposed in rhomboids.

"At the foot of the mound a step may be traced, scarcely elevated above the plain, exceeding in extent by several feet each way the true or measured base; and there is a quadrangular enclosure round the whole, as at the Mujelibè, but much more perfect and of greater dimensions. At a trifling distance from the Birs, and parallel with its eastern face, is a mound not inferior to that of the Kasr in elevation, but much longer than it is broad."

The side of the square enclosure of the tower = 2 stades = 486 units

$$485^3 = \text{circumference.}$$

The step that surrounds the base exceeds by several feet each way the measured base.

If the side of the square formed by the step = 494 units

$$494^3 = \tfrac{1}{4} \text{ distance of moon.}$$

But should the side of the terrace formed by the step = 514 units,

then $514^3 = \tfrac{1}{8}$ distance of moon

$$(2 \times 514)^3 = \tfrac{1}{8} \times 2^3 = \tfrac{8}{8} = 1.$$

Cube of twice side = distance of moon.

Cube of side of square enclosure

$$= 485^3 = \text{circumference,}$$

or cube of side of base of tower

$$242^3 \text{ \&c.} = \tfrac{1}{8} \text{ circumference}$$

$$(2 \times 242 \text{ \&c.})^3 = \tfrac{8}{8} = 1.$$

Cube of twice side of base = circumference.

Welstead says: — " Having ridden about 4½ miles across a plain covered with nitrous efflorescence and intersected by the traces of some ancient canals, we reached the base of the Birs Nimroud. It assumes a pyramidal form, the sides being steep and rugged and devastated by torrents. Fragments of walls occur at different heights, and on the summit an upright portion rears itself, and presents at a distance the appearance of a huge tower. I scrambled over the ruins of the crest of the hill, which is elevated 180 feet above the level of the plain. To the northward stand the mounds of Mujelibè and El Kara. That on which I had taken my stand contains, it is supposed, the ruins of the temple of Belus. I shall content myself with describing what I saw, leaving to others its application. The base of the mound on which I stood covers a space of 2,000 feet in circumference, and the whole roof would appear to be composed of one or many buildings: the whole was formerly encircled by a wall, the remains of which in the plains below may be traced. On the summit of the hill a mass remains entire, 40 feet in height and 13 in thickness. This is constructed of furnace dried bricks of a yellow colour, cemented together with a mortar so adhesive that although but three lines of an inch in thickness it is impossible, without breaking the brick, to separate them. Traces of fire are observable on the wall itself, which has been rent in twain by some violent convulsion, and also on such portions of it as lie strewn on the face of the hill, the surface of which exhibits a blue and cindery appearance. Indeed there is every reason to believe, from the action of the same element in many other places, that the final destruction of the building was caused by fire. To scarcely any other cause could we attribute the destruction of such immense masses as these buildings must have been, into the almost undistinguishable mass of ruins they now present. Mingled with others of a ruder kind we still find bricks inscribed with the cuneiform character, fragments of pottery, bitumen, and other portions of vitreous matter imbedded in clay. Contiguous to the Birs there is a Kubbet or tomb bearing the name of Ibraham Gholil, and the Arabs preserve a tradition that there Ibraham cast Nimrod into a flaming furnace, from which he escaped unharmed.

" The next day I visited the mounds containing the remains of Eastern Babylon; three by their magnitude are distinguished from the remainder. 1. El Hamra, the red. 2. Mujelibè. 3. El Kasir, or the Castle, is supposed to occupy the site of the great palace of Semiramis; its ruins cover a space half a mile in length and nearly the same in breadth, and rise to an average of about 90 feet above the level of the plain. The greater part of this structure appears of brick, containing large portions of chopped straw, but it has evidently been cased with those furnace dried, which are of better quality; in other respects the mass does not differ in appearance from the Birs.

" The Mujelibè forms an oblong mound, either side measuring 250 yards. Here, as with the pyramids of Egypt and the buildings at Persepolis, the sides face the cardinal points. From a distance the whole wears the same broken and rugged appearance as the other mounds. The upper ridge, though more tabular, is nevertheless very uneven. Here also there are walls and other indications of buildings : but time and the elements, aided by the spoiling hands of man, have exercised their usual desolating effects; a deep fissure on the SE. side would also indicate that it had been subjected to some violent convulsion of nature.

" Quitting the Mujelibè, an hour's ride eastward brought me to a pyramidal mound 70 feet in height, and about 300 yards in length. In the bricks with which it is constructed it does not differ from the Kasir; but from the situation of this fragment on the verge of the ruins, I conceive it not impossible it may have formed a portion of the long-looked-for wall. Various travellers and geographers with immense labour have sought on slenderer grounds or mere conjecture to identify the mound of Mujelibè with the remains of the tower of Babel; others, again, have sought that remarkable edifice at Birs Nimroud.

" After a careful survey I am compelled to admit that I could arrive at no satisfactory conclusion. Notwithstanding its magnitude, I saw little to warrant our looking for any very perfect remains of the tower."

The Mujelibè forms an oblong mound, either side measuring 250 yards.

250 yards = 750 feet.

Side of base of Cheops' pyramid

= 749 feet = 648 units.

The cube of the side   = 648^3 = $\frac{1}{4}$ distance of moon.

Rich says at the foot of the Mujelibè, about 70 yards from it, on the northern and western sides, are traces of a very low mound of earth, which may have formed an enclosure round the whole.

If the distance of this mound were 73 yards

= 219 feet = 190 units,

then one side would

= 749 + (2 × 219) = 1187 feet
= 648 + (2 × 190) = 1028 units,

and 1028^3 = distance of moon.

Thus the cube of the side of the base of the Mujelibè will = $\frac{1}{4}$ distance of moon, and the cube of the side of the inclosure will = distance of moon.

The cubes of the sides will be as 1 : 4.

Rich says the elevation of the south-eastern or highest angle is 141 feet. $\frac{1}{4}$ stade = $140\frac{1}{2}$ feet.

The sides of the Mujelibè, as well as the sides of Cheops' pyramid and the Mexican teocallis, face the cardinal points.

The pyramidal mound 300 yards in length, which Welsted thinks is not impossible to have been part of the long-looked-for wall = 70 feet in height.   100 cubits = $70\frac{1}{4}$ feet.

At Babylon we have the following distances represented in cubes and sections.

Tower of Belus   = $\frac{1}{24}$ circumference.
Cube of side of base   = $\frac{1}{8}$,,
Cube of side of square enclosure = 1   ,,

Cube of the side of the base of the Mujelibè

= $\frac{1}{4}$ distance of moon.

Cube of the side of the square enclosure

= distance of moon.

A section of the cube of Babylon having height = $\frac{8}{10}$ of the height of the tower = distance of Mercury.

A section, height = twice the height of external pyramid = distance of earth.

A section, 20 times height of tower = distance of Saturn.

A section, 40 times the height = distance of Uranus.

Cube of Babylon = distance of Belus.

Cube of side of base of external pyramid of the tower

$$= 262^3 \text{ \&c.} = \frac{1}{60} \text{ distance of moon}$$
$$= \text{radius of earth.}$$

Fostat, or Old Cairo, about three miles from Grand Cairo, stands on the site of a town called Babylon, built according to tradition by some Babylonians whom Sesostris had carried captive, and who revolted. In Strabo's time it was a Roman military station.

The Deïr-el-Nassara comprehends a vast enclosure, the walls of which are sixty French feet high; the construction appears very ancient, and the walls seem to have formed part of the fortifications of this ancient Babylon. The convent is inhabited by Coptic monks.

The height of these walls has also been said to equal 70 English feet, which = 100 cubits.

A correspondent of the " Literary Gazette" gives the following measurements, obtained by levelling:—

Mujelibè of Rich (S.E. angle), 108 feet Eng.

El Kasr (the palace and hanging gardens of Rich), 40 feet to Athlet's tree, and 25 feet to the highest point, S.E.

Amran Ibn Ali (rough calculation), 54 feet.

There is another point on the mound of the Mujelibè, a little retired from the angle at the crest taken, which by rough measurement was found to be 12 feet higher, giving a total of 120 feet. The surface of the top of the mound dips at an angle of 3 degrees towards the Euphrates.

The height of the Birs Nimroud appears to have been pretty accurately estimated by Rich at 235 feet from the plain below to the top of the masonry — the height of the mound 198 feet, and that of the masonry on the top 37 feet.

$$\text{Height of tower} = 1 \text{ stade} = 281 \text{ feet,}$$
$$\text{Height of a terrace} = \tfrac{1}{8} 281 = 35\tfrac{1}{8}$$
$$\overline{}$$
$$\text{Height of 7 terraces} = 245\tfrac{7}{8}$$

" The eastern face of Birs Nimroud," says Porter, " presents two stages of hill; the first showing an elevation of about 60 feet, cloven in the middle into a deep ravine, and intersected in all directions by furrows channelled there by the descending rains of succeeding ages. The summit of this first stage stretches in rather a flattened sweep to the base of the second ascent, which springs out of the first in a steep and abrupt conical form, terminated on the top by a solitary standing fragment of brickwork, like the ruin of a tower. From the foundation of the whole pile to the base of this piece of ruin measures about 200 feet, and from the bottom of the ruin to its shattered top are 35 feet. On the western side, the entire mass rises at once from the plain in one stupendous, though irregular, pyramidal hill, broken, in the slopes of its sweeping acclivities, by the devastation of time and rougher destruction. The southern and northern fronts are particularly abrupt."

Height from foundation to the base of the ruined tower = 200 feet.

Height of ruined tower = 35 feet.

Height of 6 terraces of Belus = $6 \times 35\tfrac{1}{8} = 210\tfrac{6}{8}$ feet.

2 more are wanting to make 8.

So $2 \times 35\tfrac{1}{8}$ - - = $70\tfrac{2}{8}$
$$\overline{}$$
Whole height - - = 281

The traces of the western bank of the Euphrates are now no longer discernible. The river overflows unrestrained; and the very ruins, with every appearance of the embankment, have been swept away. The ground there is low and marshy, and presents not the slightest vestige of former buildings of any description whatever. (*Buckingham.*)

Morasses and ponds tracked the ground in various parts. For a long time after the general subsiding of the Euphrates, great part of the plain is little better than a swamp. (*Porter.*)

Fredrick, of whose journey it was the principal object to search for the remains of the wall and ditch that had encompassed Babylon, states, that neither of these had been seen by any modern traveller. " All my inquiries among the Arabs," he adds, " on this subject completely failed in producing the smallest effect. Within the space of 21 miles in length, along the banks of the Euphrates, and 12 miles across its breadth, I was unable to perceive anything that could admit of my imagining that either a wall or a ditch had existed within this extensive area. If any remains do exist of the walls, they must have been of greater circumference than is allowed by modern geographers. I may probably have been deceived; but I spared no pains to prevent it. I never was employed in riding and walking less than eight hours for six successive days, and upwards of twelve on the seventh.

" The plain near Babylon is covered with nitrous efflorescence and intersected by the traces of some ancient canals."

Henniker says, in the vicinity of the temple at Bæris, in Nubia, the surface of the earth is covered with a lamina of salt and sand mixed, and has the appearance as if a ploughed field had been flooded over, then frozen, and the water drawn off from under the ice.

One of the lakes about the city of Mexico, built on the site of the Aztec Venice, was salt water, the others fresh; these have lately greatly subsided. Humboldt says waters formerly inundated the plains, and purified a soil strongly impregnated with carbonate and muriate of soda. At present, without settling into pools, and thereby increasing the humidity of the Mexican atmosphere, they are drawn off by an artificial canal into the river Panuco.

In the time of Montezuma, and long afterwards, the suburbs were celebrated for the beautiful verdure of their gardens; but these places now, and especially the plains of San Lazaro, exhibit nothing but a crust of efflorescent salts. The fertility of the plain, though yet considerable in the southern part, is by no means what it was when the city was surrounded by the lake. A wise distribution of water, particularly by small canals, for irrigation might restore the ancient fertility of the soil.

The earliest account of the supposed ruins of Babylon we know of, is given by Eldred, who left London on Shrove Monday, 1583, with six or seven other honest merchants. From Aleppo he went in three days to Birrah, on the Euphrates, where that river " is first gathered into one channel," instead of those numerous branches which, in its early course, procured the name of " the thousand heads." The stream is here about the breadth of the Thames at Lambeth, and running almost as swift as the Trent. They hired a bark to sail down. In their way the Arabs came to them with provisions, the women swimming out with milk on their heads. " Their haire, apparell, and colour, are altogether like those vagabond Egyptians, which heretofore have gone about in England." On the way he passed " the olde mighty citie of Babylon, many old ruins whereof are easily to be seen by day-light, which I, John Eldred, have often beheld." He notices in particular the tower of Babel, which he describes as a quarter of a mile in circuit, and about the height of St. Paul's, " but it sheweth much bigger." It was built of large sun-dried bricks, cemented by courses of " mattes made of canes," as entire " as though they had been laid within one yeere."

Eldred on his return spent forty-four days in ascending the Euphrates from Bassora to Bagdad. He then joined a caravan going to Aleppo. " Passing the Euphrates near Hit, he saw a valley wherein are many springs throwing out abundantly at great mouths a kind of black substance like unto tarre, which serveth all the country to make staunch their barkes and boates " (bitumen). He adds — " These springs make a noise like unto a smith's forge in the blowing and puffing out of this matter, which never ceaseth night nor day. The vale swalloweth up all heavy things that come upon it."

The comparison made by Eldred must have had reference to old St. Paul's. In 1309 the height of the tower is stated to have been 260 feet, and the height of the wooden spire 272 feet, making the height of the whole steeple 532 feet. But in 1561 the wooden spire was entirely consumed by lightning. So we conclude he compared the height of the Babylonian tower with that of the stone tower of St. Paul's, 260 feet in height.

The tower of Belus = 281 feet or 1 stade in height, and side of base = 1 stade.

The perimeter of the base = 4 stades = 1124 feet.

The circuit of the Babylonian tower = ¼ mile = 1320 feet.

The extract does not inform us at what part of the Euphrates this mighty tower was seen.

The breadth of the Euphrates at Birrah, estimated to equal the breadth of the Thames at Lambeth, will accord pretty well with the length of the bridge at Babylon, which, according to Ctesias, equalled 5 stades, and 5 stades of Herodotus = 1405 feet.

The Westminster bridge over the Thames, near Lambeth, has 15 stone arches, and a length of 1223 feet.

Strabo says the Euphrates was a stade in breadth at Babylon.

Rich makes the breadth at Hillah to equal 450 feet.

Xenophon, who forded the Euphrates himself, affirms, that the river is 4 stades broad at Thapsacus, above 500 miles higher than Babylon.

Rich remarks that the Euphrates rises at an earlier period than the Tigris; in the middle of winter it increases a little, but falls again soon after; in March it rises again, and in the latter end of April is at its full, continuing so till the end of June. When at its height it overflows the surrounding country, fills the canals dug for its reception, without the slightest exertion of labour, and facilitates agriculture in a surprising degree. The ruins of Babylon are then inundated

so as to render many parts of them inaccessible, by converting the valleys among them into morasses. But the most
remarkable inundation of the Euphrates is at Felugiah, 12
leagues to the westward of Bagdad, where, on breaking
down the dyke which confines the waters within their proper
channel, they flow over the country and extend nearly to
the banks of the Tigris, with a depth sufficient to render
them navigable for rafts and flat-bottomed boats. The
Tigris is a much more rapid river than the Euphrates.

Bagdad was founded by the Caliph Abu Jaafer al Mansur,
in the year 763 A. D., whether on the site of a former city or
not is unknown, observes Chesney, but it is agreed that
the materials were drawn from Ctesiphon and Seleucia.
The existing ancient remains in Bagdad are very few; but
these few far exceed any of the modern structures in solidity
and elegance. There are three or four mosques, the oldest
of which was built by Mansur's successor in the year 785,
and has now only remaining a minaret which is said to be
the highest in the city, near the centre of which it stands.

In Bagdad, as in all other Turkish cities, the only public
buildings of note are the mosques, the khans or caravan-
serais, and the bazaars. There are said to be about 100
mosques in the town; but not more than 30 are distinguished, in a general view of the city, by domes and minarets. The domes are remarkable not less for their unusual
height than for being covered with glazed tiles of various
colours, chiefly green, blue, black, and white, disposed with
considerable taste. The minarets, which are more massive
in their structure than those of Constantinople, and are
without the conical termination which the latter exhibit, are
also glazed, but in better taste than the domes, the colour
being of a light brown, with a different colour to mark the
lines formed by the junction of the bricks. These lofty
minarets and beautifully-shaped domes reflect the rays of
the sun with very brilliant effect. Some of the most ancient
towers are nearly surrounded by the nests of storks, the
diameter of which nearly corresponds with that of the
structure.

The climate of Bagdad is salubrious, but intensely hot in summer. A drop of rain scarcely falls at Bagdad later than the beginning of May, or earlier than towards the middle of September. After the end of September the rains are copious for a time, but the winter is, on the whole, dry. Nevertheless, the autumnal rains at Bagdad and other parts of the country are so heavy that the Tigris, which sinks generally during the summer months, again fills its channel and becomes a powerful and majestic stream. This occurs again in the spring, when the snows dissolve on the distant mountains. The low lands on both sides of this river and the Euphrates are then inundated; and when the fall of snow has been very great in the preceding winter, the country between and beyond the two rivers, in the lower part of their course, assume the appearance of a vast lake, in which the elevated grounds look like islands, and the towns and villages are also insulated.

The communication between the two parts of the city divided by the Tigris is by means of a bridge of 30 pontoons. Another mode of communication is by means of large round baskets, coated with bitumen, which are the wherries of the Tigris, Euphrates, and Dialah. The river is about 750 feet wide, in full stream, at Bagdad, and the rapidity of its course varies with the season. Its waters are very turbid, although perfectly clear at Mosul, and until the Great Zab enters the Tigris.

The ruins and foundations of old buildings, and even the lines of streets, may be traced to a great distance beyond the present walls of the town. On the western side these remains extend nearly to Agerkuf, or the " Mound of Nimrod," as it is called by the natives. This structure must originally have stood at no great distance from the gates of the ancient city. It is now reduced by time to a shapeless mass of brickwork about 126 feet in height, 100 feet in diameter, and 300 feet in circumference at the lower part, which, however, is much above the real base.

At Mosul, opposite to the site of Nineveh, a mosque stands in the centre of the city, with a leaning tower similar

c c 2

to the famous one at Pisa, but not in the same style of architecture and elegance. It is said that on Mahommed entering the city the tower bowed.

At Nimroud arched gateways are continually represented in bas-relief.

According to Diodorus, the tunnel under the Euphrates at Babylon, attributed to Semiramis, was vaulted. It was cased on both sides; that is, the bricks were covered with bitumen; the walls were 4 cubits thick. The width of the passage was 15 feet; and the walls were 12 feet high to the spring of the vault.

$$15 \text{ feet of Herodotus} = 7 \text{ feet English,}$$
$$\text{and } 12 \quad \text{,,} \quad = 5\cdot62 \quad \text{,,}$$

Compare these dimensions with the subterranean passages that communicated between a Peruvian palace and fortress as given by Tschudi.

The fortresses give a high idea of the progress made by the ancient Peruvians in architectural art. These structures were surrounded by ramparts and trenches. The largest ones were protected by the solidity of the walls, and the smaller ones by difficulty of access. The approaches to them were chiefly subterraneous; and thereby they were enabled to maintain secret communication with the palaces and temples in their neighbourhood. The subterraneous communications were carefully constructed; they were of the height of a man, and in general from 3 to 4 feet broad. In some parts they contract suddenly in width, and the walls on each side are built with sharp pointed stones, so that there is no getting between them, except by a lateral movement. In other places they become so low that it is impossible to advance except by creeping on all fours. Every circumstance had been made a subject of strict calculation; it had been well considered how treasures might be removed from the palaces and temples to the fortresses, and placed securely beyond the reach of an enemy, — for in the rear of every narrow pass there were ample spaces for soldiers, who might dispute the advance of a whole army.

The Euphrates tunnel seems to have been, like the subterranean passages communicating with the old Norman castles, a way to escape danger.

The Thames tunnel, two miles below London bridge, connects Wapping and Rotherhithe, on opposite sides of the river. Cylindrical shafts, of 100 steps each, give the means of descent and ascent. This great work is 1300 feet long, and was completed in 1843, after various delays, in about nine years.

The principal apparatus was the shield, a series of cells, in which, as the miners worked at one end, the bricklayers built at the other, the top, sides, and bottom of the tunnel. The two arched passages are 16 feet 4 inches in width, with a path of 3 feet for pedestrians, and the whole is brilliantly illuminated with gas.

Another description makes the excavation 38 feet in breadth, and 22 feet 6 inches in height: the basis of the excavation, in the deepest part of the river, is 76 feet below high-water mark. The entire length between the two shafts is 1300 feet.

This tunnel forms a double roadway. It was completed in the reign of Queen Victoria.

The approaches for carriages have not yet been made: so that at present the tunnel is only used by foot passengers.

Another tunnel is mentioned by Herodotus to have been made by Nitocris, queen of Egypt.

Her brother, the late king, having been killed by the Egyptians, she resolved to revenge his death, and so had recourse to this artifice. Having caused a long road to be hollowed under ground, she invited to a banquet, under pretext of making some new building, a great number of the nobility, whom she judged to have been a party to the death of the king. When the guests were assembled there, by means of concealed canals, the river was let in and drowned the whole party.

The length of the bridge over the Euphrates at Babylon, according to Ctesias, was 5 stades.

5 stades of Herodotus $= 5 \times 281 = 1405$ feet.

If the length of the tunnel under the Euphrates were the same, then the Thames tunnel will be to the Euphrates tunnel :: 1300 : 1405 feet in length.

Burnt bricks and bitumen only are stated to have been used in constructing the Euphrates tunnel.

Burnt bricks and Roman cement formed the entire arched tunnel under the Thames.

In Mexico an excavation was made to carry off the waters of the lakes of Zumpango and San Christoval, which formerly overflowed into that of Tezcuco, swelling the latter so as to endanger the safety of the city of Mexico. The first project was to construct a tunnel, or subterranean gallery, to turn off the course of the river Guantitlan, and drain the lake of Zumpango. It was begun in November, 1607, by the engineer Enrico Martinez; and 15,000 Indians were compelled to toil at the work for eleven months, during which they were treated with the most unfeeling severity, till at length a subterranean passage was effected upwards of 20,000 feet in length. The first tunnel, however, filled up, owing to the caving in of the earth; and it was at length determined to make an open cut through the hill of Nochistongo, which, after encountering great difficulties and more vexatious delays, was completed in the year 1789, at the cost of the lives of some thousands of Indians.

This canal, cut through clay, marl, gravel, and sand, is from 100 to 130 feet deep, and, at the summit, between 200 and 300 feet wide. Its length, from the sluice of Vestideros to the fall of the river of Tula, is upwards of 67,000 feet, or more than $4\frac{1}{2}$ leagues. The capital is still, however, exposed to inundations from the north and north-west, in the event of any sudden swelling of the lakes in that direction through continued rains, or any sudden or extraordinary melting of the snow on the mountains.

This canal, or drain, in its actual state, says Humboldt, is undoubtedly one of the most gigantic hydraulical operations ever executed by man. We look upon it with a species of admiration, particularly when we consider the nature of the ground, and the enormous breadth, depth, and length of the aperture. If this cut were filled with water to the depth of 30 feet, the largest vessels of war could pass through the range of mountains which bound the plains of Mexico to the north-east. The admiration which this work inspires is mingled, however, with the most afflicting ideas. We call to mind, at the sight of the cut of Nochistongo, the number of Indians who perished there, either from the ignorance of the engineers, or the excessive fatigue to which they were exposed in ages of barbarity and cruelty. We examine if such slow and costly means were necessary to carry off from a valley closed on all sides so inconsiderable a mass of water; and we regret that so much collective strength was not employed in some greater and more useful object,— in opening, for example, a passage through some isthmus which impedes navigation.

Humboldt says the formation of the subterranean canal, for draining the lakes near Mexico, was commenced in 1607, and that 15,000 Indians were constantly occupied for eleven months. At the end of that period the gallery was completed, its length being more than 6600 metres, or 1·48 league, taking 4443 metres to a league; the breadth 3·5 metres, and height 4·2 metres. He then compares this canal with other subterranean canals more recently constructed. The canal Du Midi, in France, is the next mentioned, but no dimensions given. The length of the canal joining the Thames and Severn is stated at 4000 metres: that of Bridgwater, near Worsley, including its different ramifications, extends 19,220 metres, a length equal to two-thirds the breadth of the straits between Dover and Calais. The length of the Picardy canal will be, when finished, 13,700 metres. The Hartz gallery extends a distance of 10,438 metres.

Near Forth the workings of the coal mines extend more than 3000 metres under the sea, without being exposed to any infiltrations.

The river Forth runs into the Firth of Forth at Stirling: both the river and Firth flow above the coal strata.

Two aqueducts supply Mexico with pure water. One has arches that extend 3300 metres: the other extends

10,200 metres, one-third of which the water is conducted over arches. The ancient city of Tenochtitlan had aqueducts not less considerable at the commencement of the siege by the Spaniards. The great aqueduct that brought the water from Santa-Fe may still be traced; it has a double set of tubes, made of baked earth, of which one set conveyed the water while the other underwent repairs. It may be observed, that the five lakes in the valley of Mexico were more or less impure. The water of the lake Tezcuco contained the greatest quantities of muriate and carbonate of soda, says Humboldt. These lakes supplied the canals with water for navigation.

Lorenzana, describing the aqueducts, says, the greatest and best constructed that the natives had made is the aqueduct of the city of Tezcuco. One still admires the traces of a great embankment that was raised to increase the surface of the water. One cannot but generally admire the industry and activity employed by the ancient Mexicans and Peruvians for irrigating the arid soils. On the coast of Peru I have seen the remains of walls upon which water was conducted to a distance of more than 5000 or 6000 metres, from the foot of the cordilleras to the coast. The conquerors of the 16th century have destroyed these aqueducts; and this part of Peru, like Persia, has again become a desert and void of vegetation. Such is the civilisation the Europeans have introduced among a people whom they please to call barbarians.

Herodotus mentions a canal excavated by Xerxes in order to avoid the danger to his fleet of rounding the promontory of Mount Athos. That such a work was ever undertaken has been doubted, and the veracity of Herodotus on this subject disputed. But the testimony of Gouffier, Hunt, and Leake, and the recent examination by Spratt, who thus describes the work, place the matter at rest. The central part of the isthmus, through which the canal was cut, is hilly, and, from the uncertainty which must have existed as to the nature of these hills and the obstacles they might oppose, we learn to estimate the boldness of the monarch's design. That part of the isthmus through which the canal is cut is a bed of tertiary sands and marls; so that the work of the Persian king, so extolled by ancient authors, is insignificant, compared to many works of the present day. Evidences of the work are still to be seen in different places, more particularly towards the centre of the isthmus, where there is a succession of swampy hollows which run in nearly a straight line across, and are from 2 to 8 feet deep, and from 60 to 90 broad; these may be traced nearly to the top of the rise, where all evidences of the canal are destroyed by a road leading to the promontory. Two or three other tracks or paths cross the site of the canal at different points, and have a similar effect. The highest part of the isthmus through which the canal was cut is 51 feet above the sea. The traces of the canal are less visible on the northern portion of the isthmus, but still a chain of hollows can be traced, having decidedly an artificial character. Through the plain the traces have disappeared, and the mouths of the canal have been obliterated by the action of the sea and its sands. The distance between the two shores is 2500 yards, but the canal, being slightly oblique, was somewhat longer than this.

Herodotus makes the isthmus about 12 stades over, forming a plain intermixed with some little hills.

12 stades of Babylon = 1124 yards.

So that the breadth of 2500 yards is more than twice 12 stades of Babylon.

Artachæus, the director of the canal, was the tallest of all the Persians, and wanted only the breadth of 4 fingers to complete the height of 5 royal cubits. (*Herodotus.*)

We have supposed a royal cubit of Babylon to equal ·9366 feet English.

So 5 royal cubits will only = 4·683 feet,
7 ,, will = 6·556 ,,
calling the breadth of 4 fingers = 3 inches.

Then 7 royal cubits — the breadth of 4 fingers
= 6 feet 6 inches — 3 inches
= 6 feet 3 inches for the height of Artachæus, if he

were 7 royal cubits of Babylon, less the breadth of 4 fingers, in height.

The deified Confucius, most holy teacher of ancient times, died B. C. 479. He is stated to have been more than 9 cubits in height; and, whatever may have been the cubit in those days, he was universally called " the tall man." (*Morrison.*)

9 Babylonian cubits = 6·33 feet English.

Gaudama was born about B. C. 626. His height when grown up was 9 cubits.

Bitumen, besides having been used in the buildings at Babylon, appears also to have been applied in coating the sides of vessels.

The Russian embassy to China in 1693, on reaching Tong-chou, observed the river to be covered with junks, having masts of bamboo with sails of rush, and cemented, instead of pitch, with a species of glutinous earth.

The proposed iron bridge over the Tyne at Newcastle is to have a carriage road of 1,380 feet in length. The bridge will consist of six river arches, and four land arches on each side. The iron arches will be supported on piers of solid stone masonry. The piers will be 48 feet by 16 feet 6 inches in thickness, and in extreme height about 131 feet, or nearly $\frac{1}{2}$ stade, from the foundation, having an opening in the centre through each, so that to the spectator at a distance the bridge will appear to rest on pillars.

The tubular bridge over the Nile at Benha is to have ten arches, and to be 870 feet in length. The Egyptian railway is to pass over it.

Diodorus, who quotes Ctesias, says that Semiramis raised at Nineveh, over the tomb of her husband Ninus, a mound of earth 9 stadia high and 10 broad.

9 stades would be 9 times height of tower of Belus.

If instead of stades read plethrons, then the height will = 9 plethrons.

The height of the pyramid of Cheops = 10 plethrons:

$$10 \text{ plethrons} = 405 \text{ units,}$$
$$408^3 \text{ &c.} = \tfrac{6}{10} \text{ circumference.}$$

A pyramid having height = side of base = 408 &c. units will = $\frac{1}{3}$ of $\frac{6}{10}$ = $\frac{6}{30}$ = $\frac{1}{5}$ circumference;

or, $\frac{9}{10}$ stade = $\frac{9}{10}$ 243 = 218·7 units.

If a pyramid have height = side of base = 221 &c. units nearly = $\frac{9}{10}$ stade,

then cube of side of base = 221^3 &c. = $\frac{1}{100}$ distance of moon.

Pyramid = $\frac{1}{300}$ distance of moon = $\frac{6}{300}$ = $\frac{1}{5}$ radius of earth.

A pyramid having height = side of base

= $\frac{10}{10}$ = 1 stade = 243 units.

Cube of side of base = 242^3 &c. = $\frac{1}{8}$ circumference.

Pyramid = $\frac{1}{24}$ circumference = 15 degrees.

The two pyramids will be similar.

The internal pyramid will = $\frac{1}{300}$ distance of the moon.

The external pyramid will = $\frac{1}{24}$ circumference = the internal pyramid of the tower of Belus.

Herodotus describes Babylon as standing in a spacious plain, and perfectly square, having a front on every side of 120 stades, which makes the whole circumference equal to 480 stades. "This city, so great in dimensions, is more magnificently built than any other we know. In the first place, a wide and deep fosse, always supplied with water, encompasses the walls, which are 200 royal cubits in height and 50 in breadth; every royal cubit containing three digits more than the common measure. Here I shall give some account how the Babylonians employed the earth that was taken out of so large a fosse, and in what manner the wall was built. As they opened the ground and threw out the earth, they made bricks and baked them in furnaces. The cement they used was a bituminous substance heated on the fire, and every thirty rows of bricks were compacted together with an intermixture of reeds. With these materials they first lined the canal, and afterwards built the wall in the same manner. Certain edifices, consisting only of one floor, were placed on the edges of the wall, fronting each other; and a space was left between these buildings sufficient for turning

a chariot with four horses abreast. In the circumference of
the walls one hundred gates of brass are seen, with entablatures and supporters of the same metal.

Babylon consists of two parts, separated from each other
by the river Euphrates, which, descending from the mountains
of Armenia, becomes broad, deep, and rapid, and falls into
the Red Sea.

The walls were brought down on both sides to the river,
with some inflexion at the extremities, from whence a rampart
of brickwork was extended along the edge of the river on
both sides. The houses of Babylon are three or four floors
in height, and the principal streets pass in a direct line
through the city. The rest, traversing these in several places,
lead to the river; and little gates of brass, equal in number
to the lesser streets, are placed in the ramparts which border
the stream. Within the first wall, which is fortified with
towers, another is built, not much inferior in strength, though
not altogether so thick.

Besides these, the centre of each division is walled round,
containing in one part the royal palace, which is very spacious
and strong; and in the other the temple of Jupiter Belus,
being a square building of the length of two stades on every
side, and having gates of brass, as may be seen in our time.
In the midst of this temple stands a solid tower.

The height of the walls = 200 royal cubits, say = 100
above the fosse.

The royal cubit exceeds the common cubit by 3 digits.

If the common cubit = 8·43 inches, a Grecian digit, by the
tables, = ·7554$\frac{11}{16}$ inch English ;

so 3 digits will = 2·2662 inches,

and 100 royal cubits = $100 \times \overline{8·43 + 2·2662}$
$$= 1069·62 \text{ inches}$$
$$= 89·135 \text{ feet English.}$$

If 100 royal cubits = 93·66 = 93$\frac{2}{3}$
$$= \tfrac{1}{3} \text{ stade,}$$

then 100 common cubits : 100 royal cubits :: $\frac{1}{4}$: $\frac{1}{3}$ stade
$$:: 3 : 4.$$

Thus a royal cubit will $= \frac{4}{3}$ 8·43 $=$ 11·24 inches English, and 300 royal cubits will $=$ 281 feet $=$ 1 stade

$$= 400 \text{ common cubits}$$
$$= 600 \text{ Babylonian feet}$$

∴ 1 royal cubit will $=$ 2 Babylonian feet.

Thus the height of the walls above the banks of the canal will $=$ 200 Babylonian feet, or 100 royal cubits.

The height of the tower of Belus $=$ 1 stade $=$ 300 royal cubits $=$ 100 orgyes.

So $\frac{1}{3}$ the height will $=$ 100 royal cubits $=$ the height of the walls of Babylon from the banks of the canal.

Ctesias reckons 50 orgyes for the height of the great wall of Babylon. But 50 orgyes, according to Herodotus, $=$ 200 cubits $= \frac{1}{2}$ stade $=$ 140$\frac{1}{2}$ feet English.

As the walls were formed by the earth excavated from the canal and baked on the spot, the canal would necessarily be deep; and it is probable that Herodotus and Ctesias meant the height taken from the bottom of the canal to the summit of the rampart, and that the depth of the canal equalled the height of the wall above the plain.

So that the height of the wall would be $\frac{1}{2}$ of 200, or 100 cubits, or 70$\frac{1}{4}$ feet English, for Ctesias' statement; and $\frac{1}{2}$ of 200, or 100 royal cubits, or 93$\frac{2}{3}$ feet English, for that of Herodotus.

Herodotus, in describing the two pyramids in the middle of the Lake Mœris, says "they are raised 50 orgyes above the water, and are as much concealed below as they are exposed above." This would make the whole height of each pyramid $=$ 100 orgyes, or 1 stade, the height of the tower of Belus.

If the height of the wall from the plane $=$ 200 royal cubits $= \frac{2}{3}$ stade, the height of the wall from the plane would $= \frac{2}{3}$ the height of the tower of Belus.

But if the height of the wall above the plane $=$ 200 Babylonian feet, or 100 royal cubits, the height of the wall would $= \frac{1}{3}$ the height of the tower.

Only a portion of the soil obtained by excavating the canal

might have been made into bricks for building the outer part of the walls, and the remainder might have been used for filling up the middle part between the brickwork ; so that all the soil obtained by digging the canal would be used in the construction of the walls. Thus the contents of the walls would equal the content of the surrounding canal.

Ctesias makes the walls of Babylon form a perfect square, each side being 90 stades in length, and the four sides, or circuit, = 360 stades. Thus the circuit of Herodotus will be to the circuit of Ctesias as 480 : 360 :: 4 : 3.

So that the dimensions of both the height and circuit of the walls given by Herodotus are ⅓ greater than those by Ctesias.

We have here compared the dimensions of Herodotus and Ctesias ; but we have always used the table of measures given by Herodotus, and compared it with the Babylonian standard- deduced from the tower of Belus and the various measurements of Herodotus.

Arrian, in describing Alexander's expedition, says the part of the wall of Tyre, against which Alexander directed the attack from wooden towers, was 150 feet high.

To overcome these walls, the Macedonian towers were made so high that the Tyrians had to build wooden towers on the walls, so that they might still have the advantage of height for defence.

By the Table, the Grecian foot = 12·0875 inches English.

So the height of that part of the wall of Tyre would exceed 140½ feet English, the whole height of the walls of Babylon, according to Ctesias.

It may also be noticed, that Alexander's ships were obliged to use chains instead of cables, because the Tyrians sent armed ships openly, and divers secretly, to cut the ships from their moorings. Thus it appears that the chain-cable was used by Alexander.

The height of a Roman moving tower is stated by the architect Vitruvius, when he directs the smallest of them not to be less than 90 feet high and 25 broad, the top to be ⅕ smaller, and to contain ten stories each, with windows.

The largest was 180 feet high and 34 broad, and contained 20 stories.

To this quotation from an account of Pompeii is appended the following note. "These numbers are so enormous, so much beyond the height of any wall, that we would suspect some error in the reading but for their coherence. One cannot allow much less than 9 feet for a story."

The Roman foot = 11·604 inches English. So that if the height of the walls of Babylon had equalled 200 royal cubits, or 187½ feet English, according to Herodotus, the height of the walls of Babylon would have exceeded 174 feet English, the height of the largest Roman moving towers.

FOUNDATION OF BABYLON.

Ctesias' Account. — *Assyrian System.* After the death of Ninus, Semiramis, passionately fond of every thing that had an air of grandeur, and ambitious of surpassing the glory of kings who preceded her, conceived the project of building an extraordinary city in Babylonia. For that purpose she collected from all quarters a multitude of architects and artists of all kinds, and prepared great sums of money and all the necessary materials; having afterwards made in the whole of her empire a levy of two millions of men, she employed them in forming the enclosure of the city by a wall 360 stades in length, flanked by a great many towers, taking care to leave the Euphrates in the middle of the ground. Such was the magnificence of her work that the breadth of the walls was sufficient for the passage of six chariots abreast. The height was fifty orgyes. Clitarchus, and the writers who followed Alexander, assign to the height only fifty cubits; adding that the breadth was little more than that of two chariots abreast. These authors say that the circuit was 365 stades, because Semiramis wished to imitate the number of days in the year. These walls were made of raw brick, cemented with bitumen. The towers, of a proportionate height and breadth, amounted to 250. Between the walls and houses the space left free was two plethrons broad.

Semiramis, to accelerate the work, imposed on each of her favourites (or most devoted servants) the task of one stade, with all the necessary means, and the additional condition of having it finished in one year.

The principal works attributed by Ctesias to Semiramis are : —

First. The great wall of enclosure and fortification, 360 stades in length.

Second. A quay constructed on each bank of the river. This wall was as broad as that of the city, and 160 stades in length.

Third. The bridge composed of stone piers and beams extended on these piers; the length was five stades, and breadth thirty feet.

Fourth. Two castles placed at the issues of the bridge. The western castle had a triple circuit of high strong walls, the first of which, constructed of burnt bricks, was sixty stades in circumference; the second, within the former, described a circle of forty stades; its wall was fifty orgyes high by 300 bricks broad, and the towers were seventy orgyes in height. On the unburnt bricks were moulded animals of all kinds, coloured so as to represent living nature. In fine, a third interior wall, forming the citadel, was twenty stades in circumference, and surpassed the second wall in breadth or thickness and length (?) [probably should be, surpassed in breadth and height.]

Fifth. Semiramis also executed another prodigious work : it was to dig in a low ground a great square basin or reservoir, thirty-five feet deep, having each of its sides three hundred stades in length and lined with a wall of burnt brick cemented with bitumen. When this work was finished, they turned the river into this basin, and immediately constructed, in haste, in its bed, left dry, a gut or covered gallery, extending from one castle to the other. The vault of this tunnel, formed of burnt brick and bitumen, was four cubits thick : the two supporting walls had a thickness of twenty bricks, and under the inner curve a height of twelve feet; the breadth of this tunnel was fifteen feet. All this work was performed in seven days; after which the river resuming its course, Semiramis could pass over dry-footed under the water, from one to the other of her castles. She placed at both entrances to this gallery brazen gates, both of which subsisted until the time of the kings of Persia, successors of Cyrus.

Lastly, she built, in the midst of the city, the temple of Jupiter, to whom the Babylonians gave the name of Belus. Historians not agreeing concerning this edifice, which besides is in ruins, we can say nothing positive about it: only it appears that it was excessively lofty, and that it was by means of it that the Chaldeans, addicted to the observation of the stars, acquired an exact knowledge of their risings and settings. (Diodorus describes this temple as having been built with brick and bitumen.)

Now time has destroyed all these works: only a part of this vast city has some houses inhabited; all the rest consists of land that is ploughed. There was also what was called the Hanging Garden; but this was not a work of Semiramis, —it was that of a certain Syrian king, who, in later times, built it for one of his concubines born in Persia. This woman, wishing to have verdant hills, persuaded the king to construct this fictitious landscape in imitation of the natural views in Persia. Each side of the garden was four plethrons long.

Such is the account of Ctesias, or of the ancient books he consulted. The exaggeration of certain details, such as two millions of men being constrained to labour, diminishes very much our confidence in them; but the limits between the possible and the true are not easily to be defined.

Account of Berosus and Megasthenes.   Chaldean System.
— To Nebuchadnezzar are attributed:—

First. The palace of the hanging gardens;

Second. The fortress of Teredon;

Third. The sluices and dykes against the reflux of the Persian Gulf;

Fourth. The basin and flood-gates in favour of the city of Siparis;

Fifth. The reparation of the wall of the great enclosure of Babylon;

Sixth. The application of brazen gates to these walls;

Seventh. The reparation of the castle with triple enclosure, and the reconstruction of the eastern castle on a similar plan.

Eusebius, in his "Evangelical Preparation," has preserved the following passage from Megasthenes, a Greek historian, contemporary with Seleucus-Nicator, king of Babylon, until the year 282 B. C., who sent Megasthenes as his ambassador to Sandracottus (Tchandra-Goupta), one of the kings of India residing at Palybothra: — "Babylon was built by Nebuchadnezzar: at the commencement the whole country was covered with water, and was called a sea; but the god Belus having drained the land and assigned limits to each element, surrounded Babylon with walls, and afterwards disappeared. At a later period the enclosure, distinguished by its brazen gates, was constructed by Nebuchadnezzar: it subsisted until the time of the Macedonians." Afterwards Megasthenes adds:—"Nebuchadnezzar become king, in the space of fifteen days surrounded the city of Babylon with a triple wall, and turned aside the canals called Armakale and Akrakan, coming from the Euphrates; afterwards, in favour of the city of Siparis, he dug a lake twenty orgyes in depth and forty parasangs in circumference. In it he constructed sluices and floodgates, called regulators of riches, for the irrigation of their fields, and also prevented the inundations of the Persian Gulf, by opposing them with dykes, and the irruption of the Arabs, by constructing the fortress of Teredon. He ornamented his palace by erecting a hanging garden, which he covered with trees."

Very soon after Megasthenes, a learned man of Babylon, Berosus, born of a sacerdotal family, professed the same opinion; and, because his astrological predictions and writings of various kinds rendered him so celebrated, the Athenians erected a statue for him with a golden tongue.

Berosus's interesting work, entitled "Chaldaic Antiquities," being lost, it is to the Jewish historian, Flavius Josephus, that we are indebted for the fragments relative to this question. (*Volney.*)

The circuit of the lake = 40 parasangs. A parasang of Herodotus = 30 stades.

Thus the circuit of the lake will = 40 × 30 = 1200 stades.

The circuit of Lake Mœris = 3600 stades.

Both lakes were formed as reservoirs for the purpose of irrigation.

Herodotus attributes five great works to Nitocris.

First, she dug above Babylon, for the Euphrates, a new bed which rendered its course so tortuous, that navigators passed successively three times in three days near the town of Arderica. The special object of this work was to prevent the progress of the Medes.

Second, she constructed in the city and on both sides of the river a quay in brick.

Third, she constructed in the bed of the river, when drained, piers of a bridge, on which were placed during the day planks, which were taken off at night, to prevent the inhabitants of one side from robbing those of the other.

Fourth, she dug an immense lake, 420 stades in circumference, to turn into it the waters of the river in inundations.

Fifth, with the earth taken out of the lake, she erected a large embankment to confine the Euphrates.

None of these works are attributed by Berosus to Nabukodonasar; but several appear to be confounded with those of Semiramis.

Volney says, "We are of opinion that Ctesias and the Perso-Assyrian books were authorised to say that Semiramis founded that great city, because, in fact, it appears she built, from their foundations, the walls and gigantic works which, even in their decline, astonished the army of Alexander, eight centuries and a half after the foundation, and 330 years before our era. The assent of the best authors, of the geographer Strabo among others, who had in his possession all the papers of the process, leaves no doubt upon the subject: but on the other hand, Berosus appears to us equally well founded, in asserting that, long before Semiramis, there existed a Babel or Babylon, that is, a palace or temple of the god Bel, from which the country derived its name of Babylonia, and whose temple, according to the custom of ancient Asia, was the rallying point, the pilgrimage, the metropolis of all the population subjected to its laws; at the same time that the temple was the asylum, the fortress of the priests of the nation, and the antique and no doubt original seminary of those astronomical studies, that judiciary astrology, which rendered those priests so celebrated under the name of Chaldeans, at an epoch whose antiquity can no longer be measured.   If the Babylonian nation is described to us as having been divided into four castes, after the manner of Egypt and India, which division is of itself a proof of great antiquity, we have a right to say that before Ninus there existed the caste of Chaldæan priests, similar in every respect to those of the Indian Brahmins."

The porcelain pagoda at Nankin has nine stories.   It appears that a pagoda had been, at various times, erected on the spot where the present tower stands.   Records of these pagodas are still retained as far back as the second century of the Christian era.

A *cast* iron pagoda, still standing, is said to be 1700 years old.

The Rhahaans assert that the temple of Shoemadoo Praw, at Pegu, was begun 2300 years ago, and built by successive monarchs.

The height = 361 feet.

Each side of the octagonal base = 162 feet.

The circumference of the tee = 56 feet.

Volney, speaking of Semiramis, says: " We should read in Diodorus the remaining actions of that prodigious woman, and see how, after founding her metropolis, she created in a few months, in Media, a palace and an immense garden, and undertook afterwards against the Indians an unsuccessful war, from whence she returned to Assyria to construct works, the curious details of which are given by Moses of Chorene in his history of Armenia.   So great was her activity and renown, that after her all great works in Asia were attributed by tradition to Semiramis. Alexander found her name inscribed on the frontiers of Scythia, then looked on as the limits of the habitable world. It is no doubt this inscription which Polyænus has handed down to us, in his interesting collection of anecdotes. Semiramis speaks herself : —

" Nature gave me the body of a woman ;
But my actions equalled me
To the most valiant of men (to Ninus).
I governed the empire of Ninus,
Which towards the East touches the river Hinaman (the Indus) ;
Towards the South the country of incense and myrrh (Arabia-felix) ;
Towards the north Sakkas (Scythians),
And the Sogdians (Samarkand).
Before me no Assyrian had seen the sea ;
I have seen four where no one goes,
So distant are they ;
What power opposes their overflowings ?
I compelled the rivers to flow where I desired ;
And I desired only where they could be useful.
I rendered fruitful the barren land,
By watering it with my rivers :
I created impregnable fortresses ;
I pierced with roads inaccessible rocks ;
I paved with my own money highways,
Where before were seen only the footsteps of wild beasts,
And in the midst of these occupations
I found time enough for me
And for my friends."

In this table, so simple and so grand, the dignity of expression and propriety of facts seem to vouch themselves for the truth of the monument. We therefore cannot admit the opinion of some writers, who consider Semiramis as a mythological personage of India or Syria."

The lives of Semiramis and Napoleon I. produce by comparison or contrast lights and shades too striking to be passed over without observation.

Both distinguished themselves by personal bravery in early life, and so rose to political power by military success.

Semiramis, when wife to Memnon, a general in the Bactrian war, led a forlorn hope, scaled a fortress, and planted the standard of victory on the walls of the capital.

Napoleon, when husband to Josephine, and general in the Italian campaign, seized a standard, rallied the troops at the contested bridge at Arcoli, and won the day. Both well knew how to concentrate and direct the physical force of empire in the execution of vast projects. So both became great conquerors, constructors of bridges, and makers of roads.

Both were twice married, first in military and again in royal rank.

Ninus wished to marry Semiramis during the life of her first husband, Memnon.

Napoleon married Marie Louise during the life of his first wife Josephine.

The glory of Semiramis became more brilliant after her matrimonial alliance with royalty ceased. Napoleon's glory became less so after his matrimonial alliance with royalty commenced. Semiramis owed a throne to the king: Napoleon to the people. Both rose from the people, yet both surpassed the glory of kings, though they came as strangers in the realms they ruled.

Semiramis reigned five days in the year before her accession.

Napoleon reigned 100 days after his abdication.

Both sustained their first reverses in eastern campaigns.

Afterwards the queen appears to have successfully directed her energies to the internal government of her country, which ought to be the true glory of kings.

Lastly, both abdicated their thrones: Semiramis voluntarily, Napoleon involuntarily. Semiramis never resumed hers. Napoleon reclaimed his, and without opposition seated himself again on a throne. The son of Semiramis succeeded to the throne of Babylon: the son of Napoleon, though born king of Rome, was never seated on the throne of France.

Semiramis demanded of her husband the five surplus days of the year to be queen. It also appears that Semiramis obtained her wish, as Athenæus says, " finally she persuaded Ninus, in a festival, to allow her to reign five days."

It appears the Persians and the magi preferred the complete year of 365 days, without adding five to the 360, the astrological number, taken from the degrees in the circle.

Quintus Curtius says, " when Darius marched against Alexander, the magi made a procession, in which they were followed by 365 young men, all clothed in purple, representing the days in the year."

Diodorus, quoting Ctesias, says, " when Semiramis became marriageable she made, by her extraordinary beauty and talents, the conquest of one of the king's principal officers. This officer's name was Memnon ; having come to inspect the stud, he carried Semiramis to Nineveh, and had two children by her. The war of Bactriana ensued. Semiramis accompanied her husband in it. Ninus defeated the Bactrians in the open country, but he in vain besieged their capital, where they had shut themselves up, when Semiramis, disguised as a warrior, found means to scale the rocks of the fortress, and by a signal raised on the wall, gave notice of her success to Ninus's troops, who then made themselves masters of the town. Ninus, charmed with the courage and beauty of Semiramis, requested Memnon to yield her to him : the latter refused ; Ninus persisted, Memnon killed himself from despair ; and Semiramis became queen of the Assyrians."

Other accounts may be found in Volney's Ancient History, from which we have already often quoted.

Murray states, that if we except the fabulous exploits of Bacchus, and the doubtful ones of Sesostris, the first recorded attempt to conquer India was made by Semiramis. This proud and ambitious queen, to whom India was represented as the most fruitful and populous region of Asia, is said to have prepared one of those immense armies which the East only can furnish. Some accounts raise its numbers to 300,000 foot and 500,000 horse. She began by conquering Bactria, and spent three years in preparing for the passage of the Indus. She accordingly defeated the fleet of boats which had been prepared to oppose her, and transported her army to the eastern bank.   Here, however, she had to contend with an immense force, which had been actively collected from all India.   The Assyrian troops were particularly dismayed by the report of the great bodies of elephants trained to war, which formed the strength of the Indian armies. To dissipate their alarm, a species of elephant was constructed; a mass of hide being formed into the shape of his huge animals, and moved internally by the force of camels and men.   These machines, when brought into real battle, had the success which might have been anticipated.   At the shock of the mighty war elephants, their pseudo-antagonists instantly resolved into their component parts, and the scattered fragments fled in dismay.   The whole army followed, and the queen, severely wounded, was saved only by the swiftness of her horse.   She is said scarcely to have brought back a third of her army to Bactria.

Herodotus says the walls of Babylon were fortified with towers, but he does not state the number.   Ctesias says there were 250.

Taking the circuit of the walls at 25 miles, there would be 10 towers to a mile.

The length of the Chinese wall = 1500 miles, and number of towers = 25,000 ; this will allow of 16¾ towers for a mile.

Let us compare the extent of the walls of Babylon with those of Asiatic cities still existing, and particularly with those of China, which was a highly civilised empire when Babylon was great, and has so continued amidst the downfall of great empires to the present time, when the traces of the walls of Babylon have been sought for in vain.

The laws and regulations of the dynasty of Tcheou, drawn up as far back as the twelfth century before our era, and translated by Biot, shows, first, the extreme antiquity of the Chinese ; next, their curious manners and customs ; thirdly, their jealous seclusion from, and exclusion of, all other nations; then, again, their political, social, and commercial importance in the family of peoples ; then their extensive literature, which, according to good authorities, exceeds in extent and value that of any other country, living or extinct, together with the advanced education of the mass of the people, which makes them, as Medhurst tells us, "read more than any other in the world;" and finally, their having maintained their national existence amid all the vicissitudes and earthquake-like convulsions of innumerable centuries, having kept up many of their ancient laws and customs with strictness and tenacity, and after having with utter unconcern witnessed the gradual decay and eventual annihilation of the mighty kingdoms of antiquity, seen with calm indifference the birth and rise from barbarism to gigantic power of those of modern times.

The Chinese, 1200 years before Christ,—nearly 500 years before the foundation of Rome, about 300 years after the foundation of Athens, 400 years before the birth of Homer, and at the time when Assyria and Egypt were still flourishing empires, — were fully civilised, were capable of being governed by laws which, for wisdom, gentleness, and justice, and affectionate care of the people, cast completely into the shade those of ancient Greece and Rome.

The walls of Pekin are of the height of 50 cubits (Malte Brun), so that they hide the whole city, and are so broad, that sentinels are placed upon them on horse-back; for there are slopes within the city of considerable length, by which horsemen may ascend the walls, and in several places there are houses built for the guards. There are nine gates, but they are neither embellished with statues nor other carving, all their beauty consisting in their prodigious height, which at a distance gives them a noble appearance. The arches of the gates are built of marble, and the rest with large bricks, cemented with excellent mortar. Most of the streets are built in a direct line; the largest are about 120 feet broad, and a league in length. Le père Artière, who visited the palace, says it is more than a league in circuit. The circuit of the city walls is called six leagues.

Davis makes the height of the walls of Pekin about thirty feet : they consist of a mound of earth encased with brick. The thickness of the walls at the base is 20 feet nearly.

The height of the walls is stated at 50 cubits, and at 30 feet English.

50 cubits of Babylon = 35 feet English.

Kircher describes the flying bridge in China, built from one mountain to another, as consisting of a single arch, 400 cubits long, and 500 cubits high.

400 Babylonian cubits = 1 stade = 281 feet English.

The span of the centre arch of the Southwark iron Bridge, London, is 240 feet.

Wallace says that the walls which surround Pekin, or a space of twenty-three square miles, are 40 feet high, and 20 feet thick at the bottom, rising like a pyramid to the breadth of 12 feet at the top. Along the walls stand high square towers, and outside of them there runs a deep fosse.

Taking the mean height of Davis and Wallace, we have $\frac{30+40}{2} = \cdot 35$ feet for the height of the walls, and 35 feet = $\frac{1}{8}$ stade = 50 cubits of Babylon.

So that at Pekin we find the walls formed by mounds of earth encased with bricks, and tapering from the base, as we supposed the walls of Babylon to have been built. Along the walls of Pekin are placed high towers, and outside the walls a deep fosse. Babylon had towers on the wall, which was surrounded by a deep fosse.

The area inclosed by the walls of Pekin is said to equal 23 square miles, which will be little more than half the area inclosed by the walls of Babylon, by taking the perimeter of the square at 480 stades, 25·54 miles, for then the enclosed area will = 41 square miles.

The circuit of the fortified walls of Paris equals 24·85 miles, and the height of the walls = 32·8 feet English.

" The most ancient portion of Pekin," observes Davis, " is that area to the north which is now called the Tartar city, or city of nine gates, the actual number of its entrances. To the south is another enclosure, less strictly guarded, as it does not contain, like the other, the emperor's residence. The whole circumference of the two combined is not less than twenty-five miles within the walls, and independently of suburbs. A very large portion of the centre of the northern city is occupied and monopolised by the emperor with his palaces, gardens, &c., which are surrounded by their own walls, and form what is called ' the prohibited city.' "

The dimensions of Nineveh, as given by Diodorus, were 150 stadia for each of the two larger sides of the quadrangle, and 90 for each of the two less sides, thus making the perimeter, or circuit, 480 stadia. Herodotus assigns 480 stadia for the circuit of the walls of Babylon, which equals 25 miles.

Salmon observes, that the Chinese have not arrived at any perfection in fortification yet; for they have no other works besides a wall strengthened with square towers, a deep ditch, sometimes dry, but commonly of running water, with some bulwarks or bastions, and a few pitiful iron guns upon their walls. There are nine gates in the Tartar city. .

The Chinese city is also walled round, and has seven gates, and a large suburb at every gate.

The emperor's palace stands in the middle of the Tartar city, and is an oblong square, about two miles in length, and one in breadth, defended by a good wall.

Marco Polo mentions the magnificent hunting-place of the Khan of Shandu (Shang-tu), in the Tartarian province of Kartschin. The park was 16 miles in circuit; the palace handsome, and built in a great measure of marble; to which was added a large tent-shaped pavilion of bamboo, which could be put up or taken down at pleasure. Polo proceeded with the Khan to Cambalu. Catha or modern China, and its capital Cambalu, now Pekin, had always been celebrated by early travellers as the most remarkable objects to be found on the continent of Asia. Accordingly, Cambalu was found to surpass in splendour all things that had yet been seen. The palace is surrounded by a wall and ditch 32 miles in circumference, each side being 8 miles long. Within this enclosure, however, are all the royal armouries, as well as fields and meadows well stocked with game. The proper palace is contained within a square of 4 miles in circumference; which space it entirely fills, with the exception of a large court in the middle. There is one story only, but the roof is very lofty, and entirely covered with painting and gilding, while dragons and various animals are carved on the sides of the halls. Contiguous to the palace is a mount entirely covered with the finest trees that can be collected from all parts of the empire. It is called the Green Mount; and the hollow left by the earth dug up for its construction is occupied by a lake. With regard to the city, it is divided into two, Cambalu Proper, or the old city, and Taidu, or the new city. This last had been built by Kublai, in consequence of his suspecting the fidelity of the inhabitants of Cambalu; and the two form what are now called the Chinese and Tartar cities. Taidu forms a complete square, each side of which is six miles in length; and the streets are laid out by the line in so straight a manner, that on entering one gate you see across to the other; and the whole city is arranged like the divisions on a chess-board.

The circuit of Ispahan, says Tavernier, taking the suburbs, is not less than that of Paris; but Paris contains ten times the number of inhabitants. It is not, however, astonishing that this city is so extensive and so thinly peopled, because every family has its own house, and every house its garden; so that there is much void ground. From whatever side you arrive, you first discover the towers of the mosques, and then the trees which surround the houses; at a distance, Ispahan resembles a forest more than a town.

At Ispahan, says Chardin, the walls, constructed of mud, have a circumference of 20,000 paces, which he calculated at 24 miles. It is built upon the Zeinderood, and artificially increased by another river, the Mahmood Ker; the stream is scanty in the summer months, but in the spring it attains a size equal to that of the Seine at Paris. Chardin affirms, that Ispahan was as populous as London in those days, during the reign of Shah Abbas the Great.

The fort of Agra, according to Orlich, is a mile in extent, and built entirely of red sandstone, with a double wall; the exterior one, towards the river, being 80 feet high, and the whole is surrounded with small bulwarks, and a moat 20 feet broad.

The nearly completed fortifications of an European city may also be noticed. In less than four years the continuous wall of the fortifications of Paris, with bastions at stated distances, over ground extremely varied in its surface, has been raised to the extent of 40,000 metres, being from 3 to 4 metres in thickness, and 10 metres in height. In front of this wall a wide and deep ditch has been dug, and scarps and counter-scarps formed, besides 80 kilometres, or 50 miles English, of strategic or military roads. This is not all; for outside this wall, 16 out of the intended 20 citadels have been constructed and militarily occupied. To complete this continuous wall, nothing remains but a comparatively small portion of the masonry work.

The extent of the walls of Paris = 40,000 metres = 24·85, &c. miles English.

The circuit of the walls of Babylon = 480 stades = 25·54 miles English.

Since there remains but a comparatively small portion of the walls of Paris to be completed, when finished, the circuits of the walls of Paris and Babylon will be very nearly equal in extent.

Height of the walls of Paris = 10 metres, = 32·8, &c. feet English.

Another description says : —" The fortifications of Paris form two new lines of defence round the capital. One is a continuous enclosure embracing the two banks of the Seine, intended to be bastioned and terraced with about 33 feet of encampment, faced with masonry ; 2 feet of the outer works with casements. The latter, the detached forts, are 17 in number, besides several detached trenches. The general plan of the continuous enclosure presents 91 angular faces, each about 1100 feet, with a continued fosse, or line of wet ditches, in front, lined with masonry : thence to the top of the embankments crowning the wall, on which is raised the artillery, is a height of about 46 feet (50 royal cubits).

" At different points are placed drawbridges, magazines, &c.,

and several military roads of communication have been formed. The distance of the regular zone or belt, from the irregular outline formed by the octroi wall of the city, varies from 700 yards to nearly 2 miles."

The area included between the old and new walls appears, by the plan, to equal or exceed the area of the present city : or the area enclosed by the new wall is double that enclosed by the old wall.

The circuit of the new wall of Paris equals the circuit of the wall of Babylon ; but only one half of the enclosed area is appropriated to the city of Paris, which contains a population of 1,000,000.

According to a third description, " The system of fortification adopted for the defence of Paris consists, first, of a continuous bastioned *enceinte*, revetted to the height of 35 feet, surrounded by a ditch, with *cuvette* 45 feet broad, and covered by a *contrescarpe* of masonry.   The gateways, to the number of fifty, are strong casemated barracks, containing batteries to flank the ditches and approaches, and form so many citadels. The ditch, by means of a barrage of the Seine, could be flooded to the depth of eight feet in forty-eight hours.

" The profile of the *enceinte* covers an extent of ground of about 400 yards, and its circumference a distance of 8 French leagues.

" The second line consists of seventeen detached forts, varying in their outlines and properties (but all constructed on the most approved principles of modern art), according to the nature of the localities, and connected with each other by strategic roads.   This exterior line, combined with the natural obstacles of the ground, and intersected by woods, rivers, and heights, embraces a circumference of upwards of 20 leagues.

" The distance between the two lines varies from 2000 to 7000 French metres.   The right bank of the Seine presents sixty-seven fronts, and the left twenty-seven.

" The exterior line is connected with the *enceinte* by strategic roads, which radiate the ground around the city.

" The armament of the *enceinte* requires 2000 guns of

heavy calibre; that of the detached forts 700. The powder magazines of the latter will contain 5,000,000 pounds of powder."

These fortified works enclose Paris, with a population of 1,200,000 souls, — the largest continental capital in Europe.

The simple wall that surrounded Paris before that city was recently converted into an immense fortress, has a circuit of about 15 miles. This wall has merely been loopholed and strengthened; and beyond it, at distances varying from a mile to a mile and a half, detached forts have been built, each capable of containing a thousand men. At present there stands a continuous rampart, more than 70 feet wide, faced with a wall upwards of 30 feet high, and a ditch in front of it 20 feet deep; the whole circuit of which measures nearly 24 miles. Outside this, at distances varying from one to three miles, are sixteen detached forts, of the most perfect construction, the smallest of which would hold 4000 men.

The circuit of Rome in the time of Vespasian was ascertained, by actual measurement, according to Pliny, to be 13½ Roman miles. The Roman mile was about 142 yards less than the English mile. So that this circuit of Rome will be less than the circuit of the wall enclosing Paris; and the circuit of the fortified rampart of Paris will be nearly equal to the circuit of the walls of Babylon.

Pliny also states, that Dinochares, the architect who laid out the plan of Alexandria, assigned to it a circuit of 15 miles; but there is no proof that the whole of this area was ever covered with houses. A fifth part of this space was, indeed, at the beginning assigned to the royal palace.

London is estimated to contain, in round numbers, 120 square miles, 2,500,000 inhabitants, and property assessed at more than 21,000,000l. a year.

London, not being a walled city, cannot be compared as other capitals have been by the circuit of their walls. But London and Paris have been compared by Darcy, the French Inspector of the Ponts and Chaussées, who has lately been in England. In his work we find the following particulars relative to the population, extent of the streets, &c., in Paris and London : —

" The total surface of London is 210,000,000 of square metres; its population, 1,924,000; number of houses, 260,000 ; extent of its streets, 1,126,000 metres ; surface of the streets, not including the foot pavement, 6,000,000 square metres ; extent of the sewers, 630,000 metres.   The total surface of Paris is 34,379,016 square metres; population, 1,053,879 ; number of houses, 20,526 ; extent of the streets, 425,000 metres ; surface of the streets, exclusive of the foot-pavement, 3,600,000 square metres; length of the sewers, 135,000 metres. Thus, in London every inhabitant corresponds to a surface of 100 square metres ; at Paris, to 34 square metres.   In London the average of inhabitants to each house is $7\frac{1}{2}$; at Paris, 34.   These details establish the difference that exists between the two cities; from which it appears that there is in London a great extent of surface not built over ; that the houses are not very high, and that almost every family has its own."

The Boulevards of Paris is the part where the greatest traffic takes place ; and the following are the results of Darcy on the subject : —

" On the Boulevard des Capucines there pass every twenty-four hours 9070 horses drawing carriages ; Boulevard des Italiens, 10,750 ; Boulevard Poisonnière, 7720 ; Boulevard St. Denis, 9609 ; Boulevard des Filles de Calvaire, 5856 ; — general average of about 8600.   Rue de Faubourg St. Antoine, 4300 ; Avenue des Champs Elysées, 8959."

" At London, in Pall Mall, opposite Her Majesty's Theatre, there pass at least 800 carriages every hour.   On London bridge, not less than 13,000 every hour.   On Westminster bridge the annual traffic amounts to not less than 8,000,000 horses."

The last census makes London to extend over an area of 78,029 acres, or 122 square miles : and the number of its inhabitants, rapidly increasing, was 2,362,236.

Thus the uninclosed area of London, including the suburbs, may be said to = 122 square miles.

The enclosed area of Babylon, exclusive of the suburbs, $=41$ square miles.

Thus the circuit of the walls of these four cities appear to be equal to each other: —

Ispahan $=$ 24 miles English.
Babylon $=$ 25·54 ,,
Paris $=$ 24·85 ,,
Peking $=$ 25 ,,

The length of the great wall of China $= 25 \times 60 = 1500$ miles.

The enclosed area of Peking is stated at 23 square miles.

The area of Babylon equals 41 square miles, nearly; reckoning the circuit to equal 480 stades.

If the circuit of the walls of Babylon equalled 486 stades, then 486 stades transposed and squared, or read backwards and squared, would $= 684^2$ stades $=$ circumference of the earth.

The circuit of the walls according to

Herodotus $=$ 480 stades
Ctesias $=$ 360 ,,
Clitarchus $=$ 365 ,,
Strabo $=$ 385 ,,
Curtius $=$ 368 ,,

The breadth of the walls, according to Ctesias, was sufficient for the passage of six chariots abreast. The towers, of a proportionate height and breadth, amounted to 250.

Clitarchus, and the writers who followed Alexander, assign only 50 cubits for the height of the wall, and that the breadth was little more than that of two chariots abreast.

The stade of the four last writers may have been different from the stade of Herodotus, the standard we have adopted in the important measurements of obelisks and pyramids. But in the Babylonian great works, when we have not the measurements of Herodotus given, we may use those of others in order to form some comparison between the vast works attributed to Semiramis and those of other nations.

In the days of Abdallatif, the ruins of Memphis occupied

the space of half a day's journey every way; and the learned physician of Bagdad was in ecstacies of admiration at the splendour of the sculptures. "At the end of seven centuries," says Miss Martineau, "the aspect of the place is this. From the village of Mitrahenny (which now occupies the site) can be seen only palm woods, a blue pond, rushes, and a stretch of verdant ground broken into hollows, where lie a single colossus, a single capital of a column, a half-buried statue of red granite, 12 feet high, and some fragments of granite strewn among the palms. This is all of the mighty Memphis!"

The Arabs, who visit Aden from a distance of 200 to 300 miles, describe the country to be beautiful, well-wooded and watered, in which are extensive towns with dense population, and numerous ruins of cities built with immense blocks of stone, which have not even a name among the Arabs, and of such antiquity that even the people or nation that built them is unknown.

Nankin is seated on the south bank of the river Yang-tse-kiang, which the tide ascends for more than 200 miles. When Nankin was the capital of the empire, it was said to have been the largest city in the world. To give an idea of its extent at that time, the Chinese historical records say, that if two horsemen were to go out in the morning at the same gate, and were to gallop round by opposite ways, they would not meet before night. This is certainly an exaggeration. The Jesuits, when surveying the town for the purpose of making a plan of it, found that the circuit of the exterior walls was 37 *lies*, or nearly 20 miles. This agrees pretty well with the description given by Ellis, who estimates the distance between the gate near the river and the Porcelain Tower at about 6 miles, and says that an area of not less than 30 miles was diversified with groves, houses, cultivation, and hills, and enclosed within the exterior walls, which forms an irregular polygon.

The present town consists of four principal streets, running parallel to one another, and intersected at right angles by smaller ones. Through one of the larger streets a narrow channel flows, which is crossed at intervals by bridges of a single arch. The streets are not spacious, but have the appearance of unusual cleanliness. The part within the walls, which is now only occupied by gardens and bamboo-groves, is still crossed by paved roads, a fact which tends to confirm the statement that the whole area was once built upon.

None of the buildings of Nankin are distinguished by their architecture, except some of the gates, and the famous Porcelain Tower, which is attached to one of the pagodas or temples. This building is octagonal, and of a considerable height in proportion to its base, the height being more than 200 feet, while each side of the base measures only 40 feet. It consists of nine stories, all of equal height, except the ground-floor, which is somewhat higher than the rest. Each story consists of one saloon, with painted ceilings; inside, along the walls, statues are placed; nearly the whole of the interior is gilded. Davis, however, says, it is porcelain in nothing but the tiles with which it is faced. At the termination of every story, a roof built in the Chinese fashion projects some feet on the outside, and under it is a passage round the tower. At the projecting corners of these roofs small bells are fastened, which sound with the slightest breeze. On the summit of the tower is an ornament in the form of the cone of a fir-tree; it is said to be gold, but probably is only gilt; it rests immediately upon a pinnacle, with several rings round it. This tower is said to have been nineteen years in building, and to have cost 400,000 taels.

Gough states the extent of the walls at about 20 miles in circumference, and their height as varying from about 70 to 28 feet. " It would not be easy to give a clear description of this vast city, or rather of the vast space encompassed within its walls. I shall, therefore, only observe, that the northern angle reaches to within about 700 paces of the river, and that the western face runs for some miles along the base of wooded heights rising immediately behind it, and is then continued for a great distance upon low ground, having before it a deep canal, which also extends along its southern face, serving as a wet ditch to both."

The extent of the walls of Nankin would therefore appear to be nearly equal that of the walls of ancient Babylon. The walls of both cities extend along the sides of canals. The height of part of the walls at Nankin is 70 feet.

$70\frac{1}{4}$ feet $= 100$ cubits of Babylon,
$93\frac{2}{3}$ feet $= 100$ royal cubits.

A large portion of the area enclosed by the walls appears to have been cultivated both at Nankin and Babylon.

Cunynghame believes the present population of Nankin to exceed 1,000,000. In going from the city to the Porcelain Pagoda he followed the course of a large canal, which in many places runs close under the walls, forming a ditch of immense magnitude and depth. At a rough calculation he makes the height of the tower, from the base to the golden pear-shaped ball at the summit, about 270 feet; and the lower story, including the balcony, about 40 paces in circumference. The structure is octagonal, and consists of nine stories, each of these the least degree smaller than the preceding, thus gradually becoming more slender towards the summit. Each apartment has its deity — one in the Bhuddist calendar, to which form of worship this temple is dedicated, the walls of every one being composed of gilt tiles, representing the same figure, Ma-tso-poo, or the Queen of Heaven. But in each department these tiles diminish in size conformably to the size of the room itself; from one to the other was a narrow staircase. When standing on the highest balcony, the golden pear was a few feet above his head, and placed on a light iron framework, from each side of which descended a chain to one of the eight angles of the roof.

The description sold at the pagoda makes the height 329 covils 4 inches. A pagoda had been, at various times, erected on the spot where the present Porcelain Tower stands, records of which are still retained as far back as the second century of the Christian era. The tower has never required repair, excepting when it was struck with lightning about forty-two years ago: still it retains all the freshness of a recently erected building.

The rough estimate of the height of the Nankin pagoda is

the same as that assigned to each of the two pagodas in Ceylon. The ditch under the walls of Babylon was broad and deep. At Nankin the ditch under the walls is of immense magnitude and depth.

This octagonal pagoda seems from the description to be of an obeliscal form. So that we may consider the obelisk, pagoda, and minaret all to have derived their proper symmetrical proportions from the same law that governs a body when falling freely by the force of gravity near the earth's surface. The Egyptian obelisk is quadrilateral; the Nankin pagoda octagonal; the Turkish minaret circular.

The Kootub Minar at Delhi is also of a circular form. It has twenty-seven sides, and an estimated height of 242 feet.

The Egyptian only can be admitted to have the true obeliscal form. All the others, like the modern obelisk, may be regarded as false representations.

The nine-storied pagodas of China, according to Davis, are connected with the religion of Fo, — the real meaning of the number never having been ascertained. Pagodas of seven stories are met with; and it is supposed that this number may convey a mystical allusion to the seven Budhas, who are said to have existed at different periods.

Davis and others suppose the height of the pagoda at Nankin to be about 200 feet.

The height is estimated at 270 and 200 feet.

Mean = 235 feet.

If height were 231, &c. feet,

height would = 329, &c. cubits of Babylon.

329 covils 4 inches is the Chinese height,

329, &c. cubits = 200 units.

Again. Nankin, which contains more than half a million of souls, was, under the Mings, the capital of all China. Its walls surround a city three times as large as Paris; but in the midst of its deserted streets are found ploughed fields, and grass grows on the quays which formerly boasted a triple line of ships. Nankin is situated in an immense plain, furrowed by innumerable canals. The fertile districts in its neighbourhood show a network of rivulets and navigable watercourses, and its own banks are planted with willows and bamboos.

In the province of Nankin grows the yellow cotton, from whence is made the material exported once in such large quantities to Europe. There, also, is raised the greater part of the rice consumed in the empire. Kiang-nan is unquestionably the brightest gem in the imperial diadem, and well it may be, since its fruitfulness is beyond belief. In Europe fertility is barrenness compared with it. Twice every year the fields of Kiang-nan are covered with crops, and fruits and vegetables grow uninterruptedly. Nankin itself is built in the water. It is a city like Rotterdam, surrounded by fertile marshes and waters abounding in fish. It has lost much of its former splendour: indeed, it looks like a village, notwithstanding its 500,000 inhabitants, when compared with the enormous enclosure in which it stands. But, narrow as it has become, it is still the city of learning and of pleasure.

Nankin was the capital of the Chinese empire to the end of the thirteenth century. Davis observes that the larger portion of the area within the wall, though no doubt thickly inhabited when this was the residence of the emperor, is now a mere waste, or laid out in gardens of vegetables, with occasional clumps of trees. The space enclosed is more irregular in shape than almost any other city of China, no doubt owing to the inequality of the surface; as the northern part of the city is composed in a great measure of lofty hills.

In the small proportion which the inhabited part bears to the whole area within the ancient walls, Nankin bears a striking resemblance to modern Rome; though the walls of Nankin are not only much higher, but more extensive, being about 20 miles in circuit. The unpeopled area of both these ancient cities are alike, in as far as they consist of hills, and remains of paved roads, and scattered cultivation; but the gigantic masses of ruin which distinguish modern Rome are wanting at Nankin, since nothing in Chinese architecture is lasting, except the walls of their cities.

The modern town of Nankin covers less than half of the

enclosed area. All the ancient palaces, observatories, temples, and sepulchres, were destroyed by the Tartars.

The main features of the Chinese cities are generally common to all of them, and also resemble those of Babylon. The cities of China are described as being formed on a regular plan, which is square whenever the situation and nature of the ground will admit. They are all enclosed by high walls; with large gates of more strength than beauty. Towers, which vary in elevation, but which are sometimes eight or nine stories high, and in form sometimes round, but more commonly hexagonal or octagonal, are built at regular distances; and, when practicable, a wide ditch filled with water surrounds the whole. The streets are in straight lines: the principal of them are about 35 feet wide, but the houses are meanly built, having rarely but one story above the ground-floor; so that the width of the streets, though not too much for the thronging population and bustle of a Chinese town, conduces but little to beauty and effect.

Among the descriptions of Marco Polo, we may refer to that of Kin-sai, or Hang-cheu-fu. Kin-sai, which signifies the celestial city, he extols as being pre-eminent to all cities in the world in point of grandeur and beauty, as well as from its abundant delights, which might lead an inhabitant to imagine himself in Paradise. It was then said to be 100 li in circuit, with streets broad and extensive, and squares or market-places of prodigious size, proportionate to the immense population. It was situated between a lake of sweet transparent water and a river of great magnitude, and traversed in every possible direction by canals, large and small, which carried with them all the filth of the city into the lake, and finally into the sea. These canals were traversed by almost innumerable bridges, without which there could have been no land communication from one place to another. Those thrown over the principal canals, and connecting the main streets of the city, had arches so lofty and so well built that vessels could pass under them without striking their masts, while carts and horses were passing over them.

Kin-sai, which was once the capital of southern China,

and, at the time of Marco Polo, the residence of the imperial court, has much declined since then, and has had its name changed.   As Hang-cheu-fu it is, however, described by modern travellers as a place of immense extent, intersected by numerous canals, and still containing an overflowing population.   The streets, though narrower, are paved as they were in the days of the Venetian traveller; now, as then, there are guards placed by night at the top of the lofty bridges, and on mounds or towers, to watch the breaking out of any fire, and to give and procure all the assistance necessary in a place where every house is built of wood; and on the outside of every house its occupant is obliged to hang a scroll or writing, containing the name of each individual of his family, whether male or female.   "When any person dies or leaves the house," says Marco Polo, "the name is struck out, and upon the occasion of a birth it is added to the list.   By these means, the great officers of the provinces and governors of the cities are at all times acquainted with the exact number of the inhabitants.   It is to be observed that the last ancient regulation, as well as that of the fire-police, is common to all the great Chinese cities.

On the side of the lake is a pagoda in ruins, which forms a remarkably fine object.   It is octagonal, built of fine hewn stone, red and yellow, of four entire stories, besides the top, which was mouldering away from age.   Very large trees were growing out of the cornices; it was about 200 feet high.   It is called the tower of the Thundering Winds, to which it would seem to have been dedicated, and is supposed to be 2500 years old.

One hundred li, according to Davis, equal 30 miles, which would be the circuit of Kin-sai.

The Jesuits, when they surveyed the city of Nankin, found the circuit of the exterior walls 37 lies, or nearly 20 miles.

Thus a li, according to Davis, $= \cdot 3$ mile,
        ,,   the Jesuits, $= \cdot 54$

"The capital called Quinsai, in China," says Murray, "completely dazzled the eyes of Marco Polo, and drew forth a description so splendid, that it has been one main ground upon which his veracity has been implicated. We cannot wonder if, on beholding a scene so far eclipsing all that he had seen in Europe, or even in the East, he should have been betrayed into a certain amplification; but allowing for this, all the leading features are justified by modern observation. Quinsai, he says, signifies the ' celestial city;' it is a hundred miles in circuit, has on one side a beautiful lake of clear water, and on the other side a large river, from which canals are distributed through all the streets of the town. To cross these, bridges are erected, amounting, it is said, to the number of 12,000; and while waggons are passing over, boats with masts are sailing beneath.

"It appears evident," adds Murray, "that Quinsai is the modern Hang-tcheu-fou, which, though now degraded into a provincial capital, still retains marks of having been such a city as Polo describes. The circuit of the walls is about sixty miles, and might once have been greater. The lake, the river, the numerous canals and bridges, though perhaps not quite so numerous, and the extensive manufactures of silk, which are noticed by Polo, all occur in the descriptions of the modern city."

In one of the descriptions of Hang-tcheu-feu, quoted from Marco Polo, the circuit is stated at 100 li.

In the other description, quoted from the same writer, the circuit is said to be 100 miles.

Thus it would appear that a li has been supposed equal to a mile.

Now 100 li, according to Davis, = 30 miles,
and 100 li, ,, to the Jesuits = 54.
for the circuit of Hang-tcheu-fu.

The circuit of Peking is stated by the translators of Marco Polo to equal 100 miles.

If for miles we say li, then the circuit of Peking will = 100 li,
= 30 miles, according to Davis's estimate of the li.

Davis himself says, the circuit within the walls of Peking is not less than 25 miles.

China is the oldest existing empire in the world, and there we have been enabled to trace cities like ancient Babylon.

These cities have walls and surrounding canals constructed like those of Babylon ; and the circuit of the walls of Peking, the capital of this empire, is not less than 25 miles, the same as that assigned to Babylon, and to the outer walls of Paris. Within the walls of both Peking and Babylon, a very large portion was occupied by the royal palaces and gardens, and in both, these royal domains were surrounded by their own walls.

The territory of the Chinese empire is described as extending 1400 miles from east to west, and as many from north to south, peopled by above 300,000,000 of persons, all living under one sovereign, prescribing their customs for a period far beyond the beginning of authentic history elsewhere, civilised when Europe was sunk in barbarism, possessed many centuries before ourselves of the arts which we deem the principal triumphs of civilisation, and even yet are not equalled by the industry and enterprise of the West in the prodigious extent of their public works, with a huge wall of 1500 miles in length, built 2000 years ago, and a canal of 700, four centuries before any canal had ever been known in Europe ; the institutions of the country, established for much above five-and-twenty centuries, and never changing or varying (in principle at least) during that vast period of time.

In sailing along the banks of the Peiho, the English embassy (Macartney's) were struck with the dead level of the country through which it flowed. The tide comes up 110 miles, and often causes the river to overflow. After passing through a crowd of shipping at Tiensing, they entered the great canal, here 100 feet wide. The canal, as they approached the Yellow River, presented a grand spectacle, being nearly 1000 feet broad, bordered with quays of marble and granite, with a continued range of houses; while both itself, and the various minor canals branching out of it, were covered with crowds of shipping. Some oblation was deemed needful to propitiate the genius of the Yellow River, before launching into its rapid stream. Fowls, pigs, wine, oil, tea flour, rice, and salt, were the chief component parts, and were carried to the forecastle, whence the liquids were poured into the river, while the meat was reserved for the captain and the crew.

Ellis, who accompanied the English embassy (Amherst's), sailed down the great river Yang-tse-Kiang, which he describes as truly majestic, and decidedly superior to the better known stream of the Hoangho, or Yellow River. This entirely agrees with the account long ago given by Marco Polo, who represents it as the greatest then known in the world.

Staunton, who accompanied the British embassy to China in 1792, says, in this most ancient empire, where upwards of two hundred millions of men have for ages been kept together under one government, knowledge and virtue alone qualify for public employment, and every person is eligible to rise to the highest honours ; for, although there are nine orders of mandarins, there is no such thing as hereditary rank ; there is no state religion, and no man is questioned on account of mere matter of opinion. The laws are, like the civil code of Rome, founded on the principle of universal justice, which the Creator has stamped on human understanding. There is every reason to believe that this empire has endured full 4000 years. It consists of fifteen provinces, exclusive of territories in Tartary and Thibet, spread over an area of about 3,350,000 square miles ; the whole of which is in a state of cultivation far beyond what is seen in the most civilised parts of Europe. The very mountains are, in places, tilled to their summits, and irrigated by artificial means ; the rivers are conducted in all directions across the country, forming fine canals, upon which thousands of families live in boats. There are many fine roads and curious bridges, but nearly all the magnificent edifices are for the public offices of the state, or for the honour of God, who is worshipped under various forms. Husbandmen are held in the highest estimation, and some of the Chinese emperors have risen from holding the plough. The fine arts have never advanced much in China. Their language is so difficult that few of them ever attain perfection in it : education is solely directed to wisdom, self-knowledge, and the science of life.   There are regular posts or modes of quick communication with all parts of the empire.   Justice is administered in every town, and criminals are punished with great severity : the form of oath is very solemn ; and is rendered striking by a piece of China ware being smashed with force on the ground, and similar destruction invoked on the soul and body for hesitation, evasion, or reservation in speaking the truth.   War is not cultivated as an art.   About 180 years ago the Tartars conquered the Chinese, and they have given four dynasties of emperors, without changing manners, customs, or forms.

The Chinese bridges are sometimes built upon barges strongly chained together, yet so as to be parted, and to let the vessels pass that sail up and down the river.   Some of them run from mountain to mountain and consist of one arch ; that over the Saffrany river is 400 cubits long and 500 high, though of a single arch, and joins two mountains. This may probably be the bridge mentioned by Kircher. In the interior parts of the empire there are said to be bridges still more stupendous.

The Spanish mission to China, in 1575, on entering Chinchew, passed one of the finest bridges in the world, 800 paces in length, and composed of stones 22 feet long by 5 feet broad.

Some of the Chinese arches are semi-circular, others the transverse section of an ellipse, and others again approaching to the shape of a horse-shoe.   In the ornamental bridges that adorn gardens and pleasure grounds, the arch is often of a height sufficient to admit a boat under sail, and the bridge is ascended by steps.

The commodiousness, length, and number of the Chinese ancient canals are stated to be incredible.

The chief of them are lined with hewn stone on the side, and so deep that they carry large vessels, and sometimes extend above 1000 miles in length.   They are furnished with stone quays, and sometimes with bridges of amazing construction.   These canals, and the variety that is seen upon their borders, render China delightful in a high degree, as well as fertile, in places that are not so by nature.

The archways erected to the memory of great men in China have square bases, like triumphal arches. Malte Brun states their number in China at 11,000, of which 200 are magnificent. The style of architecture resembles neither that of Greece nor Rome.

The propylons or towered gateways were common in Egypt, and are said still to abound in Thebes; they appear to have been sculptured with the representations of combats of chariots, horses and men, like triumphal arches, and dedicated to the deity in consequence of vows made previous to victory.

These may have given origin to Homer's poetic description of Hecatompylos, the city of 100 gates, whence by each gate 200 chariots and 2000 fighting men could be sent into the field. This would still seem more probable since Thebes appears to have had no walls.

The east wing of the northern front of the temple of Luxor has, represented on a great scale, a victory gained by one of the ancient kings of Egypt over their Asiatic enemies. The number of human figures introduced amounts to 1500; 500 on foot, and 1000 in chariots.

Diodorus said, the sun had never seen so magnificent a city as Thebes.

Wilkinson says those dwellings, which pretended to the character of mansions, had very large propylæ or gateways, such as belonged properly to temples, and false obelisks, (as we learn from the tombs), painted so as to imitate granite.

In the palace-temple of Rameses IV. colossal lion heads, like water-spouts, project from the walls, as in Gothic buildings, and there are many other points in this structure which remind one of the Gothic; for instance, the pinnacles of the outer walls, which are formed of shields ranged close to each other, present a magnificent appearance.

The fluted columns of Beni Hassan are of a character, says Wilkinson, calling to mind the purity of the Doric, which, indeed, seems to have derived its origin from Egypt.

The rocks of some of the grottos of Beni Hassan are cut into a slight segment of a circle, in imitation of the arch.

"After we had wandered from hall to hall, through the double and triple portico, where more than twenty different orders of columns alternated with each other, our attention was riveted on a painted hall, the peristyle of the principal temple at Philæ, which perhaps gave a more clear idea than any other of the former magnificence of the Egyptian temples, by the preservation of the liveliest colours, which seems almost miraculous in so exposed a situation. None of the fine columns in this hall resemble one another; every one shines in the splendour of different colours; every one displays diverse surprising elegancies of form, but all unite to combine one whole in the most perfect harmony.

"The rock temple at Yerf Husseim, near Philæ, bears on it the cartouches of Sesostris. The only hall is supported by two short fluted columns hewn out of the solid rock, such as are found solely in the most ancient temples of Egypt and Nubia, and which perhaps may have served as the first models of the later Doric style. The hieroglyphics on the columns, the pillars, and the ceiling, are merely painted.

"All the animals are admirably characterised by the artist, and no better representations can be found (of the giraffe, for instance), than there are here.

"Between Nubia and Dongola, on passing through the desert, we found again two of these fluted columns, which resemble the Doric, and they are the only ones which this temple seems to have had."—(*St. John.*)

"Bejapoor (Vijayapura, the impregnable), in the province of Bejapoor, when taken by Aurengzebe in person, A. D. 1689, stood on an extensive plain, the fort being one of the largest in the world. Between it and the city wall there was room for 15,000 cavalry to encamp. Within the citadel was the king's palace, the houses of the nobility, and large magazines, besides many extensive gardens, and round the whole a deep ditch, always well supplied with water. There were also without the walls very large suburbs and noble palaces. It is asserted by the natives, with their usual exaggeration, that during its flourishing state it contained 984,000 inhabited houses, and 1600 mosques.

" After its capture the waters of the reservoirs and wells in the fort decreased, and the country around became waste to a considerable distance. At present it exhibits almost nothing but ruins, which prove the vast magnitude of the city during its prosperous state.

" The outer wall on the western side runs nearly north and south, and is of great extent. It is a thick stone wall, about 20 feet high, with a ditch and rampart. There are capacious towers built of large hewn stones, at the distance of every hundred yards; but they are, as well as the walls, much neglected, having in many places fallen into the ditch, and being in others covered with rubbish.

" A mile and a half from the western wall is a town called Toorvee, built on the remains of the former city, and surrounded by magnificent piles of ruins, among which are the tombs of many Mahomedan saints, attended by their devotees. The court-way of the fort is from 150 to 200 yards broad; and the ditch; now filled with rubbish, appears to have been a very formidable one, excavated out of the solid rock on which the fort stands. The curtain is nearly 40 feet high from the berme of the ditch, entirely built of huge stones strongly cemented, and frequently adorned with sculptured representations of lions, tigers, &c. The towers flanking the curtain are very numerous, and of vast size, built of the same kind of materials. Measured by the counterscarp of the ditch, the fort is probably about eight miles in circumference. The curtain and towers in the southern face are most battered, as it was against these Aurengzebe raised his batteries.

" The fort in the interior is adorned with many handsome edifices, in rather better preservation than the fort, among which is the mausoleum of Sultan Mahmood Shah, with its dome of 117 feet diameter in its concavity, called by the natives the great cupola.

" The inner fort consists of a strong curtain, frequent towers of a large size, a fausse bray, ditch, and covered way; the

whole built of massy materials, and well constructed. The
ditch is extremely wide, and said to have been 100 yards,
but its original depth cannot now be discovered, being nearly
filled up with rubbish.

" The fort inside is a heap of ruins, none of the buildings
being in any repair, except a handsome little mosque built
by Ali Adil Shah. The inner fort was kept exclusively for
the palaces of the kings, and accommodation of their attend-.
ants. The first now contains several distinct towns, and
although so great a part is covered with ruins, there is still
room found for some corn-fields and extensive enclosures.
The inner fort, which is more than a mile in circumference,
appears but as a speck in the larger one, which, in its turn,
is almost lost in the extent occupied by the outer wall of the
city." (*East India Gazetteer.*)

The Sacred City of Kerbela.

M. Lottin de Laval, an archæologist of distinction, charged
by the French government with a scientific mission in the
East, has addressed a letter (which we find printed in the
Courrier d'Orient) to the venerable M. Champollion, giving
some particulars relating to an excursion made by him from
Musseïb to Kerbela. — " Kerbela, like Mecca," he says, " is
a holy city *par excellence* — possessed by the Schytes, who
have erected their superb tombs to their Imaums Hussein
and Abbas. Its entrance has been, from time immemorial,
interdicted not only to the Christians of the East, but even
to the Osmanlis, who are masters of the country. Scarcely
two years ago — before it was taken by Nedjid Pacha, — had
a Mussulman attempted to introduce himself, he would ine-
vitably have been murdered. Everything about the city was
a mystery — the nature of its government and its very site.
Each year 50,000 or 60,000 sectaries — sometimes 100,000
— flock thither from the most remote parts of Russia, from
Khorassan, the Great Bokhara, Cashmere, Lahore, and the
farther parts of India. *Sefer* is commonly the month of the
most celebrated pilgrimage. Numbers of caravans of Hadjis

arrive at Bagdad; and a curious sight it is to see those long
files of horsemen clad in picturesque costume, women hidden
beneath their thick veils, and dervises of every shade, mingled
with the Moukaris who conduct the famous *caravan of the
dead.*"

Furnished with the recommendations of the French ambassador at Constantinople, and of the Consul General of the
same country at Bagdad, M. Lottin de Laval determined
upon making an effort to penetrate into a city of which the
Orientals relate so many marvels. Crossing the Euphrates
at Musseïb by a bridge of boats, he turned west-by-south
across the Arabian desert; and arrived, after two hours'
march, on the banks of the Husseïnié — a great canal leading
from the Euphrates direct to Kerbela.

" On the left bank of the Husseïnié appeared plantations
of date trees; and shortly after these, the gardens commence.
During a march of several hours, the path traverses a forest
of huge palms; and the canal is bordered, on either side, by
apricot, plum, pomegranate, and lemon-trees in. flower —
with the vine twining everywhere among their branches;
presenting a rich scene of vegetation — still more enchanting
after a journey of ten days across the deserts of Babylon and
Arabia. We arrived, in the afternoon, at the gate, protected
by a formidable bastion; and over which towers, to the
south, the Mosque of Imaum Abbas, — whose cupola and
minarets, covered with painted and varnished porcelain, glit-
tered beneath the rays of a burning sun. There the order of
our march. was arranged, so as to have an imposing appearance in the eyes of the terrible and fanatic population of
Kerbela. Sadeg Bey, Mutsellim of the country, and one of
the most active and distinguished men of the empire, had
given us, at Hilla, a considerable escort of Arnauts and
Aguels — a very necessary precaution. A black Chawich
marched at our head, beating rapidly on two small tabors,
fastened to each side of his saddle — a mark, in this country,
of great honour. I followed next to this man; then
came my young companion and a Frenchman born at Bagdad,
succeeded by our Persian servants and our trusty horse-

men, lance or musket in hand. . . . The spectacle presented by this dreaded population was curious. At every step, we stumbled on pilgrims, mollahs, and green-turbaned Seïds (descendants of the Prophet). Women looked down upon us from the terraces. Every one rose at my approach, crossed his hands upon his breast, and then carried them to his mouth and to his head, giving me the salâm-aleïkoun. I suppose I must have played my part pretty well; for my aleïkoun-salâm was wonderfully well received, with no suspicion of the fraud. Clad like a Kurdish chief, with long beard, and arms at my girdle, and followed by my companion in the uniform of a superior officer of the Nizam, and M. Nourad, wearing his ordinary costume of an Arab of Bagdad, the Husseïnié, no doubt, fancied their new Mutsellim had arrived — Sadeg Bay having quitted Kerbela seven days before.

" I had been told that the two mosques of Kerbela were of unrivalled beauty — and I found it true: they exceed their fame. That of the Imaum Husseïn is the most sumptuous. A vast pile of masonry supports the cupola; and this cupola is entirely built in bricks of copper, about eighteen centimètres square, covered over with plates of gold of extreme purity. Three minarets spring up by the side of this sumptuous cupola, adorned with painted porcelain, enriched with flowers and inscriptions as far up as the Muezzin's gallery. Above this gallery are open colonnades on the two minarets which flank the southern gate; and these colonnades and the final shafts are gilt likewise. The interior is in harmony with this unheard-of splendour. The side walls are of enamelled porcelain, having a dazzling effect. Wreaths of flowers and friezes covered with inscriptions in Talik characters intermingle with remarkable elegance; and the cupola is adorned with mirrors, cut facet-wise, and with strings and pendents of pearls. The tomb of Husseïn is placed in the centre of this cupola. It is a square mass, of considerable height, — covered over with veils wrought in pearls mixed with diamonds, sapphires, and emeralds. Cashmere shawls are of no account. Around the tomb are hung marvellous sabres and kamas (poniards of Khorassan), profusely ornamented with precious stones — bucklers of gold, covered with diamonds — jewels, vases, and all that Asiatic luxury can conceive as most costly. Three balustrades protect this mausoleum. The first is of massive gold, wrought with great art. The two others are of massive silver, carved with the patience and skill of the Persian. The treasury of this mosque, before the taking of Kerbela, included riches incalculable; but Sadalla Pacha, after the massacre which took place near the tomb . . . . *paid his devotions* there for a space of five hours, with some Sunnite devotees like himself;—and it may be that Imaum Husseïn, irritated by such an outrage, removed to the seven heavens the treasure which had been collected during a period of three centuries — for certainly the *serdâbs* were afterwards found empty !

"The mosque of Imaum Abbas, situate to the east, has no wealth of gold, silver, or precious stones; yet, in my opinion, it is, in an architectonic point of view, far finer. Two minarets only flank its southern gate, and tower above its bold and magnificent cupola — built in porcelain, covered with wide arabesques of a very grand character, and with flowers of gold on a ground of tender green. When the hot sun of Araby darts its burning rays on this richly-coloured mass, the splendour and magnificence of the effect are such as thought can scarcely picture and no painting can convey. The body of the edifice is octagonal, — adorned in enamel of a lapis-lazuli tint, and enriched by interminable inscriptions in white. All around are pierced, moulded windows, retiring within indented frames; and the great door, of the same style — flanked by two galleries, sustained by light and graceful columns — projects boldly out, in a manner closely resembling the porch of our ancient basilicæ. The court of this mosque is vast, square, and pierced at each angle with gates of great richness. A fifth gate, less sumptuous, opening on a street which leads to the Date Bazaar, fronts this porch. The interior is simple: for Abbas detested luxury; and I have been told by Arab Schytes, that all the presents offered at his tomb are carried off in the night by genii, who deposit them in the *koubbé* of his brother Husseïn.

" From the terraces of the seraï, or fortress, of Kerbela — where I remained three days — the view of this city is extraordinary. It detaches itself vigorously and burningly from a forest of gigantic palm-trees, against which it is reared. On all sides float garments of dazzling colours over the terraces of the white Persian houses — the minarets and cupolas of enamel and gold glisten in the sun — pilgrims are praying, mollahs declaiming with tears the tragical end of their revered Imaums — caravans are coming and going — and, far in the distance, for background to this animated picture, is seen, on the reddened horizon, the long reach of the Arabian desert.

" I have already spoken of the ' caravan of the dead,' — and I have myself travelled in its silent company. The corpses, embalmed with camphor, which is the sacred scent of the Persians, and with certain spices, are wrapped in shrouds covered with inscriptions, very handsome and very dearly paid for to the mollahs of the Mosque of the Kasémé, near Bagdad. They are then laid in rude coffins, and placed on mules, — one of which often carries two of them. A Turcoman whom I questioned said he had been on his journey *a hundred and ten days !* He came from Kokhand, on the frontiers of Eastern China. Each sectary, well-to-do, in Persia or India, leaves a portion of his wealth to the mosques of Kerbela, that his body may be received there. There is a tariff, regulated by the place sought to be occupied by the body. It varies from five krans to five hundred (10,000 Bagdad piastres) — the maximum being applicable to those who desire to lie near the tomb of Husseïn. The fixed population of Kerbela numbers from nine to ten thousand ; but there is a considerable floating population, which pays enormous imposts to the Pacha of Bagdad. The air is very unwholesome, owing to the stagnant waters and the great quantity of corpses brought thither : — fever makes cruel ravages there, every year."

According to the Japanese, it takes 21 hours to make the

circuit of Jeddo, the capital of Japan. They affirm that it is 7 leagues in length and 5 in breadth. A river, according to Kempfer, traverses this immense capital, and supplies water not only to the fosses of the palace, but also to different canals. The city has neither walls nor fortifications; but the palace enclosure has a circuit of 5 leagues, according to Thunberg, formed of stone walls, with fosses and draw-bridges. He assigns to the city a circuit of 58 miles. The royal enclosure would alone form a considerable city : so that in oriental countries the population ought not always to be estimated according to the extent of the city.

Kempfer says the palace at Jeddo formed a species of fortified city in the heart of a general one, surrounded with a wall of freestone, and having the ornament of a lofty tower many stories high.

D'Anville and Denon state the circumference of ancient Thebes to have been 36 miles, and its diameter not less than 10½ miles. Others make the circuit of Thebes 27 miles, which will equal the circuit of Babylon, since 480 stades equals 26 miles nearly for the circuit of Babylon.

The extent of Thebes is reckoned by Diodorus at 150 stades, and 150 stades of Herodotus = 8 miles. Strabo says Thebes was at least 80 stades in length, which will equal 4½ miles. According to Wilkinson, traces of the former extent of the city are to be found at the present day for the length of 5¼ miles, and a breadth of 3 miles.

" The reign of Soter II., or Lathyrus, is remarkable," says Sharpe, " for the rebellion and the ruin of the once powerful city of Thebes. It had long been falling in trade and in wealth, and had lost its superiority in arms; but its temples, like so many citadels, its obelisks, its colossal statues, and the tombs of its kings, still remained. The hieroglyphics on the walls still recounted to its fallen priests and nobles, observes Tacitus, the provinces in Europe, Asia, and Africa which they once governed, and the weight of gold, silver, and corn which these provinces sent as a yearly tribute. The paintings and sculptures still showed the men of all nations and of all colours (*Rosellini*), from the

Tartar of the north to the negro of the south, who had graced the triumphs of their kings; and with these proud trophies before their eyes they had been bending under the yoke of Euergetes II. and Cleopatra Cocoe for about fifty years.

"One can therefore hardly wonder that, when Lathyrus landed in Egypt and tried to recall the troubled cities to quiet government and good order, Thebes should have refused to obey. For three years the brave Copts, intrenched within their temples, every one of which was a castle, withstood his armies; but the bows, the hatchets, and the chariots, could do little against Greek arms; while the overthrow of the massive temple walls, and the utter ruin of the city, prove how slowly they yielded to greater skill and numbers.

"Perhaps the only time before when Thebes had been stormed after a long siege, was when it first fell under the Persians; and the ruins which marked the footsteps of Cambyses had never been wholly repaired. But the fierce and wanton cruelty of the foreigners did little mischief, when compared with the unpitying and unforgiving distrust of the native conquerors. The temples of Tentyra, Apollinopolis, Latopolis, and Philæ show the massive Egyptian buildings can, observes Denon, when left alone, withstand the wear of time for thousands of years; but the harder hand of man works much faster, and the wide acres of Theban ruins prove alike the greatness of the city and the force with which it was overthrown; and this is the last time Egyptian Thebes is met with in the pages of history.

"The traveller now counts the Arab villages which stand within its bounds, and perhaps pitches his tent in the desert space in the middle of them. But the ruined temples still stand to call forth his wonder. They have seen the whole portion of time of which history keeps the reckoning roll before them: they have seen kingdoms and nations rise and fall; the Babylonians, the Jews, the Persians, the Greeks, and the Romans. They have seen the childhood of all that we call ancient; and they still seem likely to stand, to tell their tale to those who will hereafter call us the ancients."

" The system of ancient Egyptian fortification is illustrated by Wilkinson chiefly from the defences at Samneh. This consists of two remarkable forts, intended for the defence of the Egyptian frontier against the Ethiopians, which begin near the lower termination of the cataracts; each principal fort is accompanied by smaller ones. They bear a curious resemblance to the peculiarities of modern works, the glacis, scarps, counter-scarps, and even the ravelins in the ditches, being all similar. The material of their construction is the highly durable crude brick of the Egyptians. The height both of the walls and towers is about 50 feet; the former, 15 feet thick; the latter, square, and placed on each side (not, in the Roman manner, upon) the corner of the wall, or ranged like buttresses along the side. The fortress was commonly a square structure, with one or two main entrances and a sallyport; or, when near the river, a water-gate. The rampart was surmounted with round battlements usual in Egypt, and plainly copied from a row of shields. From the side most exposed to attack, a long wall projected, from 70 to 100 feet, of the same height as the rampart; upon which the besieged were enabled to run out, and sweep the faces or curtains by what would now be called " a flanking fire." This system of fortification, which is met with in many places in Egypt and Nubia, was in use as early as the thirteenth and fourteenth dynasties, but was superseded by the fortified temples. After the accession of the eighteenth dynasty every temple was likewise a fortress.

The length of the great wall of China is computed at more than 1500 miles; in height it varies from 20 to 25 feet; while the thickness is 15 feet. Towers, 48 feet high, are erected at distances of 100 yards from each other throughout its whole length; the number of towers being 25,000.

The country over which it passes is wild and hilly, and in some places it is built on the steep sides of mountains between 5000 and 6000 feet above the level of the sea; it surmounts their summits, and again descends into the valleys; in crossing a river it forms a ponderous arch: sometimes large tracts of boggy country opposed great obstacles to the progress of the architects, but all these difficulties were overcome by their perseverance, and the gigantic undertaking was completed in the space of five years. To accomplish this object the power of a despotic emperor was exerted, and every third man in the kingdom forced to labour at the work till it was finished. It is said to have been erected about 2000 years ago. In some spots where the natural aspect of the country is weak, the wall was doubled, and even trebled, to make up the deficiency.

The arch is used in the gateways of the great wall, as well as in bridges, and in the construction of monuments to the illustrious dead.

According to Davis, the Great Wall of China is built in the same way as we have supposed the walls of Babylon to have been built,—the exterior of brick, the interior of earth. The body of the wall of China consists of an earthen mound, retained on each side by walls of masonry and brick, and terraced by a platform of square bricks. The total height, including a parapet of 5 feet, is 25 feet, on a basis of stone projecting 2 feet under the brickwork, and varying in height from 2 feet to more, according to the level of the ground. The thickness of the wall at the base is 25 feet, diminishing to 15 at the platform. The towers are 40 feet square at the base, diminishing to 30 at the top, and about 37 feet in total height. At particular spots, however, the tower was of 2 stories and 48 feet high. The above description confirms, upon the whole, that of Grebillon about a century before. "It is generally," says he, "no more than 18, 20, or 25 geometrical feet high, but the towers are seldom less than 40."

The English embassy (Macartney's) on the fourth day after leaving Peking, saw, as it were, a line stretching over the whole extent of the mountain horizon; it was the Great Wall. On approaching, their astonishment was still increased at seeing this immense erection carried over a rugged barrier, ascending the highest mountains, and descending into the deepest valleys, with towers at the distance of every 100 steps. The transport of such massive materials to the height often of 5000 feet, the space of 1500 miles through which it continued, and the perfect preservation after a lapse of 2000 years, afforded all new subjects of wonder.

The British war-steamer Reynard lately anchored about 1000 yards distant from the Great Wall of China, when a party visited this stupendous work of human labour, which has its eastern termination on the shore of the Gulf of Leotong, about 120 miles north of the river Peiho, in lat. 40° 4' N., long. 120° 2' E. Viewed from the water, the terminus appears to consist of a fortress some 3000 yards in length, having a large gateway in the southern face. For about 800 yards from the fort the wall was in a very ruinous condition, the first part of it being little better than an embankment of sand, broken at intervals by projecting masses of ruined brickwork. At half a mile's distance from the fort, however, the wall commences to show a better state of preservation; here it was found to measure 39 feet across; the platform was covered with mould and variegated with flowers of every hue. The wall on the Tartar side, at this point, shows a fine well-built foundation of hewn granite, surmounted by a slanting brick facing, measuring together 35 feet in height; above this is a brick parapet, 7 feet high and 18 inches thick, divided by small embrasures at irregular intervals, from 8 to 13 feet apart.

At intervals, varying in distance from 200 to 500 yards, the wall is flanked on the Tartar side by towers of brick 45 feet square and 52 feet high. The one examined was entered from the wall by an arched granite doorway, 6¼ feet high and 3¼ broad. The construction of this arch was thought to be most remarkable, for the Chinese have long ceased to use keystones in their arches. A flat roof of the tower is surrounded by a parapet like that of the wall. The body of the tower is intersected at right angles by low arched vaults, each terminating in an embrasure, of which there are three on each outer face. From the construction of these vaults they seem to have been built for archers and spearmen, and not for any kind of artillery : there was no vestige of a parapet on the Chinese side of the wall, except on the low towers on this face, which intervene midway between those on the other, but are not vaulted. From this tower, which is the second inland, the wall continues apparently, more or less, in a ruined state for about three miles in a N.N.W. direction, over a fine undulating country. It then takes a sudden turn to the S. W., passing near a large town called Shan-hae-wei. Thence it ascends directly up a black rugged range of mountains, about 3000 feet in height, creeping up the side like a gigantic serpent, and disappearing over the summit of the ridge.

Before the party had proceeded more than a mile and a half inland three mandarins overtook them, and informed them that the Tartar general in command at Shan-hae-wei had come down to the fort, and that it was his wish they should proceed no further. They accordingly descended from the wall, and returned through the fields to the terminus. As all this part of China is still, by treaty, a sealed country, it may be years before another Englishman enjoys the same privilege.

The French accounts make the building of the wall to have extended over a much longer period ; and date the commencement 400 years before our era. But the great cooperation of physical power was made in the year 214 before Christ, when the emperor Thsin-Chi-Houang-Ti assembled along the line one third of the labouring population of the empire; so that operations were undertaken at all parts of the line at the same time, and finished in the course of one summer only. To accomplish this immense work, the generation of that period was sacrificed to the generations that succeeded.

The Romans built two walls in Britain, that of Severus, between England and Scotland, and that of Antoninus Pius in Scotland. The latter and less of the two is described by Stuart as a great military work, consisting, in the first place, of an immense fosse or ditch — averaging about 40 feet in width by some 20 in depth, which extended over hill and plain in one unbroken line, from sea to sea. Behind this ditch, on the southern side, and within a few feet of its edge, was raised a rampart of intermingled stone and earth, strengthened by sods of turf, which measured, it is supposed, about 20 feet in height and 24 feet in thickness at the base. The rampart was surmounted by a parapet, behind which ran a level platform for the accommodation of its defenders. To the southward of the whole was situated the military way — a regular causewayed road, about 20 feet wide, which kept by the course of the wall at irregular distances. Along the entire line were established, it is believed, nineteen principal stations or forts: the mean distance between each may be stated at rather more than two English miles. Along those intervals were placed many smaller castella or watch-towers, of which only some two or three could be observed in 1755.

Augustin Carete gives the following description of the royal highways in Peru. He says, " The Inca Guaynacava, marching with his army from Cusco to subdue the province of Quito, distant 500 leagues from the capital, met with great difficulties in his march over almost inaccessible rocks and mountains. Whereupon returning victorious, he caused a spacious way to be hewn out through the rocks, levelling the rough and uneven ground by raising it in some places 15 or 20 fathoms, and in others sinking it as much ; and in this manner carried on the work for 1500 miles (and future Incas continued it as far to the southward). He afterwards caused another way, of equal extent, to be carried through the plain country, 40 feet wide, which was defended by walls on each side. Along these ways were houses at certain distances, shady groves, and rivulets or reservoirs of water, for refreshment."

Tschudi states that " in the Puna there are many remains of the great high road of the Incas, which led from Cuzco to Quito, stretching through the whole extent of Peru. There is not in Peru, at the present time, any modern road in the most remote degree comparable to the Incas' highway.   The best preserved fragments which came under my observation were in the Altos, between Jauja and Tarma.   Judging from those portions, it would appear that the road must have been 25 or 35 feet broad, and that it was paved with large flat stones.   At intervals of about 12 paces distant one from another there is a row of smaller stones, laid horizontally and a little elevated, so that the road ascended, as it were, by a succession of terraces.   It was edged on each side by a low wall of small stones.

"Other remains of ancient Peru, frequently met with in these parts, are small buildings, formerly used as stations for the messengers who promulgated the commands of the Incas through all parts of the country.   Some of these buildings are still in a good state of preservation.   They were always erected on little hillocks, and at such distance apart, that from each station the nearest one on either side was discernible.   When a messenger was dispatched from a station, a signal was hoisted, and a messenger from the next successive station met him half way, and received from him the dispatch, which was in this manner forwarded from one station to another till it reached its destination.   A proof of the extraordinary rapidity with which these communications were carried on, is the fact, recorded on unquestionable authority, that the royal table in Cuzco was served with fresh fish, caught in the sea near the Temple of the Sun, in Lurin, a distance of more than 200 leagues from Cuzco.

"The messenger stations have, by some travellers, been confounded with the forts, of which remains are met with along the great Inca road.   The forts were buildings destined for totally different purposes.   They were magazines for grain, and were built by the Incas to secure to their armies in these barren regions the requisite supply of food.   They are broad round towers, with numerous long apertures for the admission of air."

"Besides the Mexican monuments, which are chiefly works of magnificence, others exist which attest the high degree of civilisation attained by the Toltecans, such as Cyclopean roads and bridges. The former of these were constructed of large blocks of stone, and frequently carried on a continued level, so as to be viaducts across valleys. There are also throughout Central America numerous excavations, or rock-hewn halls and caverns, called by the natives " granaries of the giants." They resemble the Cyclopean fabric near Argos, known by the name of the Treasury of Atreus, are generally dome-shaped, and the central apartment is lighted through an aperture in the vault. Other points of resemblance to Cyclopean masonry may be found in the doorways to these subterraneous galleries and apartments, which are similar to the Gate of Mycenæ; and also in the peculiar triangular arch formed by the courses of stone projecting over each other. Arches of this mode of construction are found in the cloisters of the building at Palenque. The remains of sculpture found in Mexico are numerous, and of great variety both of form and material." (*Penny Cyclopædia.*)

" On the road from Kosseir to Thebes are seen small square towers placed upon heights, inclining to the pyramidal but truncated form. They are found along the whole line of road, communicating with each other, according to the nature of it, at very unequal distances. They have evidently been signal stations. I do not think it improbable they are of great antiquity, as the road between Thebes and the Red Sea must have been known and frequented long before the time of the Ptolemies." (*Scenes and Impressions in Egypt.*)

The fine road made by the emperor Jehan-Guire from Agra to Lahore was planted with trees on both sides. This road was 250 leagues in length. " It has little pyramids or turrets," says Bernier, " erected every half league, to mark the ways, and frequent wells to afford drink to passengers, and to water the young trees."

The city of Xanthus contains some of the most ancient remains of architecture and sculpture in Asia Minor. Cyclopean walls of the finest kind, blended with later Greek work, still exist, and well-squared stones are scattered about in all directions. There are several gateways with their paved roads. The temples appear to have been very numerous, and, situated as they were along the brow of the cliff, must have combined with the natural advantages of the site to form one of the most beautiful cities. Columns, pediments, and friezes, in abundance, still remain, some standing, most of them fallen, many built into ancient walls, and heaps tumbled down the cliff, apparently overthrown by an earthquake. The Acropolis, or town on the top of the hill, evidently formed the city of the earliest inhabitants. The inscriptions and sculptures in this upper part of the city are all Lycian. The additions made to the city by the Greeks are lower down, and in this lower part the inscriptions and sculptures are mostly Greek. The tombs extend over miles of country to the south-east and west of the city, and are numerous on the opposite side of the river.

The whole of Lycia, once so populous, so full of cities, and so highly cultivated, is now in the most wild and desolate state. In Pliny's time there were thirty-six cities in Lycia, and there had been twice as many. The ruins of twenty-four cities have been discovered in recent times, thirteen by Fellowes, and eleven previously. Lions, leopards, bears, wolves, wild boars of enormous size, and large serpents, are abundant in the wooded districts.

Ctesias says Semiramis constructed, at a great expense, a wall on both sides of the river, as broad as that of the city, and 160 stades in length.

Taking the stade = 281 feet
160 stades = 8 miles and 906⅔ yards
= more than 8½ miles.

Liverpool, a town of recent commercial date, now possesses docks having an area of 111 acres. The whole length of the quays surrounding these docks equals 8 miles within a few yards. The length of the river wall is 2 miles and 823 yards. Both the walls of the quays and river are built with stone. So the river quays at Babylon would exceed the dock quays at Liverpool by about half a mile.

Since this estimate was made, the docks at Liverpool have increased, so that the extent of the quays at Liverpool will now exceed the length of the quays at Babylon.

Petersburg was begun by Peter the Great in 1703, and has now a population of 600,000. The Neva in its passage through the city separates into several arms, of which the four principal are named the Great and Little Neva, and the Great and Little Nefka. The traffic on these waters and on the canals is very great and animated. The scene along the noble quays by which they are bordered is one that the stranger tires not of gazing on. These quays are one of the most striking features of Petersburg; their total length is twenty miles, all built of granite. The canals, as they are called, but which are only smaller branches of the river, divide the city into numerous islands, and to connect one with another there are more than sixty bridges. Some are suspension bridges, but most are built of stone; and the latter have arched gateways at each end, as bridges used to have in old fortified cities. Over the main stream of the Neva there are none but bridges of boats, nine altogether, which are removed as soon as the winter frost begins to set in, and replaced as soon as the ice is firm, and renewed again in spring. The masses of ice brought down when the river breaks up are said to be such as would sweep away everything: hence it is that no permanent bridges have been built over the broad stream.

A bridge of boats would, from its evident simplicity, appear to have been the first means adopted for crossing a broad river passing through a flat country.

There is now constructing at Liverpool an iron bridge for the Neva at St. Petersburgh. The extreme length of the bridge from one abutment to the other will not be less than 1078 feet. This structure will consist of seven arches; the span of the centre one will be 156 feet. The Southwark iron bridge measures from one abutment to the other 708 feet, the span of the centre arch being 240 feet, exceeding the Sunderland iron bridge by 4 feet and the Rialto at Venice by 167 feet, or 11 feet more than the span of the Neva's bridge centre arch. The weight of the iron in the Southwark bridge is under 5400 tons. The weight of that of the Neva bridge will be little short of 10,000 tons. The

width of the carriage road or causeway of the Neva bridge
will be 50 feet; the width of the parapet or foot-walk 10
feet.

This iron bridge is intended to replace a bridge of boats
that has frequently been carried away by the ice floating
down the Neva.

Since writing the above this iron bridge has been erected
on granite piers.

$$
\begin{array}{lll}
\text{Length} & = & 1078 \text{ feet} \\
3\tfrac{1}{2} \text{ stades} & = & 1054\tfrac{3}{4} \text{ ,,} \\
\text{Centre arch} & = & 156 \text{ ,,} \\
\tfrac{1}{2} \text{ stade} & = & 140\tfrac{1}{2} \text{ ,,}
\end{array}
$$

According to Davis, the Imperial canal was principally
the work of Koblai Khan and his immediate successors. In
the MS. of a Mongol historian, Rashid-ud-Deen, written
A. D. 1307, there is the following curious notice of it : —

" The canal extends from Khanbalik (Peking) to Khinsai
and Zeytoon. Ships can navigate it, and it is forty days'
journey in length. When the ships arrive at the sluices,
they are raised up, whatever be their size, by means of
machines, and they are then let down on the other side of
the water." This is an exact description of the practice at
the present day, as may be seen by a reference to the
accounts of the two English embassies.

It must be observed, however, that although the canal has
been generally considered to extend from Tien-tsin, near
Peking, to Hangchou-foo in Che-keang, being about 600
geographical miles, the canal, properly so called, that is,
the Cha-ho, or river of flood-gates, commences only at Lint-
sing Chou in Shantung, and continues to the Yellow River.

One principle of this great work is its acting as a drain to
the swampy country through which it flows, from Tien-tsin
to the Yang-tse-keang. Being carried through the lowest
levels, and communicating with the neighbouring tracts by
flood-gates, it has rendered available much that would otherwise have been an irreclaimable swamp. The scientific skill of
the Jesuit missionaries accomplished a survey of the whole of

this fine country, on trigonometrical principles, so admirably correct as to admit of little improvement; and, with the exception of the British possessions in India, there is no part of Asia so well laid down as China.

A great Eastern work has lately been executed in the space of ten months. The Mahmoudie canal, which connects the port of Alexandria with the Nile near Fouah, was made by Mahomet Ali. It is 48 miles long, 90 feet broad, and 18 deep. It runs through a level country, and gives a facility for conveying the produce to the best port for exportation, and likewise serves for irrigating the adjacent land.

The extent of this canal equals twice that of the canal which surrounded the walls of Babylon.

The Hindoos represent Benares as the centre of all that is sacred, the focus of all that is wise, and the foundation of all that is good. Benares is called " the most holy city," from its being the supposed birth-place of Brahma.

Delhi is styled " the city of the kings of the world."

The Kootub Minar, still standing in the midst of the ruins of Old Delhi, has twenty-seven sides, and height 242 feet.

Heber supposes the height incomplete. " The Kootub Minar, the object of principal attraction, is really the finest tower I have ever seen, and must, when its spire was complete, have been still more beautiful."

This tower has five stories of unequal heights. The three lower .stories have their twenty-seven sides fluted. The upper stories are plain, and, from the drawing, seem circular.

By whom or for what purpose the tower of Delhi was erected is not known.

There is part of another tower, elsewhere described, which, if completed, would have exceeded in height the tower of Babel.

" There are near the Kootub Minar the remains of a much larger tower, which, if completed, would have been a most prodigious monument of human enterprise and labour. It is at its base nearly twice the circumference of the perfect tower, and has a winding passage, but without stairs, in the centre. It is not more than 40 feet high, but, had it been finished in due proportion, it would have been one of the greatest artificial wonders in the universe, next to the large pyramid in the vicinity of Grand Cairo."

The Kootub-Minar, according to Orlich, is 15 miles from Delhi, and was erected in 1193. This tower is 62 feet in diameter at the base, and rises to the height of 265 feet. It is divided into three stories, and the upper gallery is elevated 242 feet 6 inches above the ground. The lower story is about 90 feet high. A winding staircase of 383 steps conducts to the summit, from which may be seen the ruins of palaces, villas, mosques, sepulchres, and gardens of bygone ages: among these remains, 160 cupolas and towers may still be distinguished.

The present Delhi is built on the ruins of this decayed splendour. On the south are ruins which cover a space of 20 square miles. Delhi is now 7 miles in circumference, surrounded by walls of red sandstone, 30 feet high, and from 3 to 5 feet thick, with a moat of 20 feet broad, and has seven colossal arched gates.

The massive portico of the *Jamma* (mosque), which the Mahometans consider the wonder of the world, is flanked by two minarets, ornamented with Arabic inscriptions from the Koran: this portico leads to the marble halls, supported by angular columns, under the principal cupola. At the two extreme corners rise two minarets 150 feet high, between which and the principal gate two lofty domes project over the halls, adorned with ever-burning lamps.

The celebrated Feroze-Cotelah is one of these columns, of which Fabian speaks in his travels, 1400 years ago, and of which there is still one in the fort at Allahabad, and three others in the North Behar; one in the Terai, near the frontiers of Nepaul, the second not far from Bettiah, and the third on the river Gaudaki. They have all the same inscriptions in the ancient Pali or Deva-Magalhi language, and the Feroze-Cotelah has also inscriptions in Persian and Sanscrit. Prinsep succeeded in deciphering that in the Pali language. It is an edict of As-ò-ko, the Bhoodist king of all India, who lived from 325 to 288 years B. C., forbidding the destruction of living animals, and enforcing the observance of Bhoodism. The Feroze-Cotelah consists of one piece of brown granite; it is 10 feet in circumference, and, gradually tapering towards the summit, rises to the height of 42 feet.

An engraving of the Kootub-Minar represents it as having five stories; two less of marble above the three large ones of red stone.

The higher of the two leaning towers of Bologna, that of Asinelli, was built in 1109, and is 327 feet in height; $327\frac{4}{5}$ feet = 1 stade, and 1 plethron = $1\frac{1}{4}$ stade. The less tower, that of Garisenda, is 140 feet high; and $140\frac{1}{2}$ feet = $\frac{1}{2}$ stade.

Another description of the greater tower of Bologna makes its height = 376 feet; and 374·66 feet = 1 stade and 2 plethrons, or = $1\frac{1}{3}$ stade.

The height of St. Mark's tower or belfry, at Venice, is variously stated, from 300 to 350 feet. It is built of brick, and of a quadrangular form, with a pyramidal summit. The foundations of this stupendous tower, described by Evelyn as "exceeding deepe," were laid in the reign of Pietro Tribuno, who filled the office of Doge from the year 888 to 912; the body of it was not finished till the middle of the fourteenth century.

The height of the tower of the Antwerp cathedral is said to be 360 feet; $1\frac{1}{4}$ stade = $351\frac{1}{4}$ feet; but the tower of Antwerp differs from the other towers, since it is connected with the body of the cathedral. The campanile or tower of Venice is detached from the cathedral; and so are those at Florence, Pisa, and other Italian states; like as the single obelisk now standing before the temple of the Luxor.

The Leaning Tower at Pisa is inclined from the perpendicular rather more than 14 feet. It is built of marble and granite, and has eight stories, formed of arches, supported by 207 columns, and divided by cornices. The height is stated at 188 feet, and to have been built in 1174.

The leaning tower or belfry at Saragossa is built of brick, and its architecture is ornamental. The ascent to the top is by 280 steps. It was built in 1594.

All these towers appear to have been built pretty nearly about the same period, with the exception of those at Saragossa and Antwerp.

Davis, in describing the pagodas, observes, " that at Nanking is at the head of these monuments, which are of a religious nature, and, like the steeples of churches, were at first attached to temples.   Several still remain with the religious establishments to which they belong."

The great cathedral tower in Seville, called the Giralda, was built in 1196, by Abu Jussuff Yacub, when this city was the Moorish capital of Spain.   It was a " mueddin " tower, says Ford, to call the faithful to prayer, and was originally 250 feet high, the rich filigree belfry, which makes 100 feet additional, having been added to it in 1568. This was the tower-building age.   The Asinelli tower of Bolognia, 371 feet high, was erected in 1109, and the Campanile of St. Mark, at Venice, 350 feet high, in 1148.   The Giralda, like the Campanile, at Venice, is square: it is a most interesting as well as very elegant object, covered with a sunk Moorish pattern, and having light intersecting arches, resembling what has been called the Norman Saracenic.   The massive cathedral of Seville is the finest in Spain.

In the vast market-place of Morocco the stately tower of the great mosque, the Kootsabeea, stands towering above the countless minarets, whence the unity of God and Mohammed's mission are daily proclaimed.

The Kootsabeea is constructed like the Giralda of the cathedral of Seville, and built by the same famous Geber. (*Hay.*)

The heights of some of the circular chimneys in the manufacturing districts of Britain exceed 400 feet.

At Liverpool there is a chimney of this description, 309 feet high, 40 feet diameter at the base, and 9 feet at the top, of a perfect conical form.

There was a chimney near Warrington, in Lancashire, containing 3,500,000 bricks, weighing 3500 tons, and erected at a cost of 7000*L*   It was 406 feet high; 46 feet diameter at the base, and 17 at the top; and used in connexion with chemical works. The owners having no further use for it, resolved to bring it to the ground by the use of gunpowder; and, accordingly, charges were inserted under the base and fired; at the tenth explosion the structure fell into a heap of bricks.

We think another account stated that the chimney, having become inclined, so as to be considered dangerous, was destroyed.

There is a chimney at Glasgow 436 feet high, but of less diameter than the one near Warrington.

A chimney which had been erecting during the summers of four years at Wigan, in Lancashire, was completed when it had reached the height of upwards of 400 feet, or about 134 yards. Shortly after an inclination was observed from the sinking of the base, and a few months after its completion it fell across a canal in 1847.

The height of the hanging tower of Pisa, in Tuscany, is about 188 feet English. 200 royal cubits = $\frac{2}{3}$ stade = $187\frac{1}{3}$ feet.

The height of the outer wall of the Coliseum at Rome is about 160 feet English.

The height of the pedestal of the Monument, near London Bridge, is 40 feet, the height of the fluted Doric column 120 feet; together they equal 160 feet. The cone at the top with its urn equal 42 feet. The total height is 202 feet. 300 cubits = $\frac{1}{4}$ stade = $210\frac{3}{4}$ feet.

The tower at Konigsburg is 284 feet English, or about 1 stade in height.

The bronze column of Napoleon, in the Place Vendome, at Paris, formed on the model of that of Trajan at Rome, is 133 French feet, or 141, &c. English feet in height, without the statue, and $140\frac{1}{2}$ feet = $\frac{1}{2}$ stade.

So height   = $\frac{1}{2}$ stade,
            = 200 cubits,
            = 150 royal cubits,
            = 3 plethrons,
            = $\frac{1}{2}$ height of tower of Belus.

The height of the Pantheon, or St. Geneviève, at Paris, is 282 feet English, and 281 feet = 1 stade.

So height   = 1 stade,
            = 400 cubits,
            = 300 royal cubits,
            = 6 plethrons,
            = height of tower of Belus.

The extensive picture gallery, which connects the Louvre with the Tuileries, at Paris, is 227 toises, or 1452 feet English, in length.

The causeway to the pyramid of Cheops equals the length of the bridge of Semiramis over the Euphrates at Babylon = 5 stades = 1405 feet English.

The Pont de la Concorde, or Pont Louis XVI., is 600 feet English in length, which exceeds 2 stades, or 562 feet English.

The Pont Royal, opposite the Tuileries, consists of 5 stone arches, and measures 432 feet English in length, which exceeds $1\frac{1}{2}$ stade, or $421\frac{1}{2}$ feet.

The Pont d'Austerlitz, between the Boulevard of Bourbon and the Garden of Plants, has the arches of cast-iron supported by piles of stone. The length is 401 feet English, which is less than $1\frac{1}{2}$ stade.

The Pont de Grammont, between the quay of the Celestines and the island of Louvier, was constructed in 1824, and is the only wooden bridge in Paris; it consists of 5 arches, and is 140 feet English in length. $140\frac{1}{4}$ feet = $\frac{1}{2}$ stade.

The Pont d'Jena has 5 stone arches: the length is 467 feet English. 10 plethrons = $\frac{1 \cdot 0}{6}$ stade
        = $468\frac{1}{3}$ feet English
        = height to apex of Cheops' pyramid,
        = $\frac{5}{8}$ side of base.

The Chamber of Deputies, at Paris, formerly the Palais du Corps Législatif, adjoins, and originally formed part of the palace. Its principal entrance consists of a noble portico, with a colonnade of the Corinthian order on each side. The first court, 280 feet English long, and 162 broad, is surrounded by buildings of no distinct character; but the second, or court of honour, 140 feet by 96, presents several edifices of pleasing proportions.

The greater side of the first court equals nearly 281 feet = 1 stade = side of base of the tower of Belus.

The greater side of the less court equals nearly $140\frac{1}{3}$ feet = $\frac{1}{2}$ stade.

Should these stated measurements be nearly correct, a conception may be formed of the height of the tower of Belus, or the Babylonian stade.

The stone bridge at Tours, in France, has 15 elliptical arches, and is 1200 feet in length.

$$4\tfrac{1}{4} \text{ stades} = 1194\tfrac{1}{4} \text{ feet.}$$

Since 200 Babylonian feet

$$= 100 \text{ royal cubits,}$$

the number of feet may have been confounded with the number of royal cubits, and the height of the walls of Babylon stated at 200 royal cubits instead of 200 feet, or 100 royal cubits.

If so, the height, 100 royal cubits, or 200 feet, would = $93\frac{3}{4}$ feet English, which would seem more probable to have been the height of the walls of 25 miles circuit, than the enormous and apparently impracticable heights which have been assigned to them by some of the commentators of Herodotus.

Thus the height of the walls would = $\frac{1}{3}$ stade = $\frac{1}{3}$ the height of the tower of Belus.

Still Babylon, making allowance for exaggeration, was one of the strongest and most magnificent of the oriental capitals.

The length of the bridge of stone piers over the Euphrates, at Babylon, was 5 stades. (Ctesias.)

$$5 \text{ stades of Herodotus} = 5 \times 281 = 1405 \text{ feet.}$$

The Hungerford iron suspension bridge for foot passengers over the Thames, at London, has two piers of brick built in the river, each 80 feet high. The centre span between these two piers is $676\frac{1}{2}$ feet. The length between the abutments

1352¼ feet.   The height above high water at the centre of the span 32½ feet.

The navigation of the river was not in the least interrupted during the erection of this bridge, which was completed without a single accident, and without any scaffolding being erected for fixing the chains.   Wire ropes were hung from abutment to abutment, to which cradles were attached, which held the workmen and two windlasses, that raised the links from barges moored under the cradles.

$$\begin{aligned} \text{Height of each pier} &= \quad 80 \text{ feet,} \\ \tfrac{1}{4} \text{ stade} &= \quad 70\tfrac{1}{4} \\ \text{Length between the abutments} &= 1352\tfrac{1}{2} \\ 5 \text{ stades} &= 1405 \\ \text{centre span} &= 676\tfrac{1}{2} \\ 8\tfrac{1}{2} \text{ plethrons} &= 679. \end{aligned}$$

We felt interested in watching the progress of the erection of this iron chain suspension bridge ; as well as that of the new London Bridge, of five arches formed of massive blocks of granite.   This new bridge replaced the old one of nineteen stone arches.   We also frequently visited the tunnel during its construction under the Thames, while ships were sailing to and from all parts of the world over the heads of the workmen.   The formation of the tunnel excited much interest at the time ; and perhaps more on the Continent than even in England, though it was less wonderful to us than to others, who had not previously been in mines where tunnels formed by excavating coal extended under the sea.   Through these tunnels the coals were conveyed along iron railways by horse power to the shaft of the pit, 90 fathoms deep.

$$\begin{aligned} 94 \text{ fathoms} &= \ 564 \text{ feet} \\ 2 \text{ stades} &= \ 562 \quad ,, \ . \end{aligned}$$

These railways under ground had been in use many years before the first surface railway, for steam power, that between Liverpool and Manchester, was constructed.

The greatest work accomplished by the present race is the construction of railways.   The amount of engineering work that within the last ten years has been accomplished on more than 6000 miles of railway that in all directions thread the United Kingdom of Great Britain deserves a history of itself; not for the mere details of 400,000,000 tons of earth and rock moved in their construction, nor of the nearly 30,000 miles of iron rail laid down, nor the vast quantities of timber, stone, bricks, and iron made use of, but for the scientific knowledge that has been brought to bear upon them, the investigations to which they have given rise, the difficulties overcome, the apparent impossibilities accomplished, the ingenious contrivances brought into play in special localities, and the forethought, perseverance, and energy exercised in the laying down throughout the country of these time-saving iron highways.

No line in the kingdom comprises within the same distance so many of these triumphs of engineering skill as the eighty-four and a half miles between Chester and Holyhead. The railroad leaves Chester by a tunnel through the red sandstone rock, 405 yards in length. It reaches the Dee upon a viaduct of forty arches, crosses the Rhyddlan marshes, bores the great limestone promontory of Penmaen Rhos by a tunnel 530 yards in length, dives under the town and wall of Conway by a 90 yard tunnel, and through the basaltic and greenstone rocks of Penmaen Bach and Penmaen Mawr by tunnels 630 and 220 yards in length; a cast-iron girder viaduct carries it over a portion of the beach, and where it merges from the tunnels and runs over the Conway shore at the base of the high cliffs, it is protected by enormous sea-walls from the storm waves, and after the manner of the avalanche galleries of Switzerland, by a great timber gallery along the face of the cliffs from the crumbling rocks of the high and almost overhanging precipices. Then, on the way to Menai, three ridges of slate, greenstone, and primary sandstone hills, are cut through by tunnels 440, 920, and 726 yards in length; the valley of the river Cegyn is crossed by a viaduct 132 yards long and 57 feet in height; the Maldraeth Marsh is passed, and a ridge of rock, slate, and clay is bored by a tunnel 550 yards in length. Those eighty-four miles, in short, are full of what fifty years ago would have been called impossibilities. Neither marsh, nor mountain, nor rock, nor sea has stayed the course of the railway : it has forced its way and made its level through all impediments. But the works that render the Chester and Holyhead line above all others remarkable, are its bridges across the Conway estuary and the Menai Straits.

The viaduct on the Shrewsbury and Chester Railway across the Dee has 19 semi-circular arches of 60 feet span ; and the height from the bed of the river to the top of the parapet of the centre pier is 148 feet. Its length is 1532 feet. The piers are 13 feet thick, and 28 feet 6 inches long at the springing of the arch. The whole viaduct is founded on the solid rock, and is built of stone with the exception of the interior arching, which is built of hard fire-bricks.

The stone bridge over the Garonne at Bordeaux is one of the finest works of the kind on the Continent, and is 1593 feet in length. It has seventeen arches, the seven central arches having each a span of 87 feet ; the breadth between the parapets is 50 feet, and the roadway is nearly level. The difficulties attending the erection of this bridge were very great, owing to the depth of the river, which in one part is twenty-six feet at low water, with a rising tide of from twelve to eighteen feet, and a current which often flows with a velocity of seven miles an hour ; and to add to these obstacles there is a shifting and sandy bottom.

$$\text{Length} = 1593 \text{ feet}$$
$$5\tfrac{1}{2} \text{ stades} = 1545\tfrac{1}{2} \text{ ,, .}$$

The bridge at Foo-Choo-Foo, over the river Min-ho, about 30 miles from the river's mouth, has 36 arches. This Chinese bridge, which is built on diamond-shaped piles of granite, is said to be about 400 yards long, and 12 to 13 broad. There were formerly temporary shops constructed upon it, but they are now all removed.

There is a bridge across the river Cavery, communicating with the island Sivana Samudra, in the province of North Coimbetoor, which is formed of large columns of black granite, each about 2 feet in diameter, and twenty feet in length. This magnificent work is stated, in the " East India Gazetteer," to have formerly been 300 yards in length, but is now nearly destroyed. Directly opposite was the southern gate of a wall that surrounded the city, to which there was a flight of steps. The interior is now a jungle of long grass, with many banyan trees of great size; and the principal street may still be traced, extending from north to south about one mile in length. There are also the ruins of many Hindoo temples, great and small, and much sculpture of various sorts. In one apartment there is a statue of Vishnu, 7 feet long, in the best style of Indian carving. The figure is thick, with a pyramidical cap, the eyes closed, and seven cobra capella snakes forming a canopy over his head. The apartments are small and dark, and must be examined with torches, the principal statue being in the remotest chamber.

"It is by no means certain, however, that there was not a bridge across the Nile at Thebes; indeed, some of the sculptures which have been discovered of late years on the outside of one of the large edifices are, by some, supposed to prove very distinctly that there was one. An Egyptian monarch is represented approaching a river, which is shown to be the Nile, by the crocodiles, and peculiar kinds of fish depicted in it: he is returning with a train of captives from a foreign war; and accordingly, on the opposite side of the river, is seen a concourse of priests and distinguished men coming forth to greet his arrival. The river, upon which we look down with the usual bird's-eye view, is interrupted in the middle of its course by a broad band stretching across from bank to bank: this is apparently intended to represent a bridge; but as the view is of such a kind as to let us see no part whatever of the elevation of the structure, we are unable to say whether, supposing it to be really a fixed bridge, it was constructed with arches or simple beams. It is evidently to this bridge that the king is advancing; and we see at its foot, upon either side, something which may be taken for a gateway, — perhaps, the usual entrance into the town across the stream. The chief point of doubt is, whether the town into which the bridge leads is really meant for Thebes. Wilkinson considers it probable, but by no means certain, that it is so. Burton discovered it, and has given a lithograph of this curious piece of sculpture."

The natural difficulties must have very much opposed such an undertaking as the construction of a bridge over the Nile at Thebes, since the river itself, besides being deep and annually subject to a great overflowing, is said to be nearly a mile in breadth, or nearly 18·79 stades. The bridge over the Euphrates, at Babylon, was 5 stades in length.

We find that the arch was in use in Egypt nearly 3400 years ago, — or more than 1200 years before the period usually assigned as the date of its introduction among the Greeks. Yet though known, the arch, for the reasons afterwards assigned, might not have been used in constructing a bridge at Thebes.

"All the stones of a Chinese arch are commonly wedge-shaped," remarks Davis, "their sides forming radii which converge towards the centre of the curve. It is observable that, according to the opinion of Captain Parish, who surveyed and made plans of a portion of the Great Wall, no masonry could be superior to it. The arch and vaulted work were considered by him as extremely well-turned. The Chinese, therefore, must have understood the properties and construction of the arch long before the Greeks and Romans, whose original and most ancient edifices consisted of columns connected by straight architraves of bulk sufficient to support the incumbent pressure of solid masonry.

The breadth of the Nile at Cairo is stated at 2946 feet, which exceeds 10 stades, or 2810 feet.

The suspension chain bridge now being erected at Kief, across the river Dnieper, at the narrowest passage for several leagues, which, however, is still half an English mile in breadth, has five suspension piers in the river. This bridge, it is said, will be the largest in Europe, the length being fully half an English mile, and covering 140,000 square feet, which is considerably more than three acres.

$$\tfrac{1}{2} \text{ an English mile} = 2640 \text{ feet}$$
$$= 9·295 \text{ stades.}$$

So the length will be about 10 stades, or twice the

length of the bridge of Semiramis over the Euphrates at Babylon.

Hanging bridges appear to have been adopted in every country where the people had materials, and possessed sufficient ingenuity to manufacture flexible ropes from vegetable fibres, or from hides. They were found to have been in use from time immemorial in South America, when that country was first visited by Europeans.

In all the mountainous districts of India, Central Asia, and China, suspension bridges, formed of cables of vegetable substances, have, from the earliest times, been in use.

Tschudi describes two kinds of suspension bridges common in the mountainous districts of South America. The *soga* bridges are composed of four ropes, made of twisted cowhide, and about the thickness of a man's arm. The four ropes are connected together by thinner ones of the same material, fastened over them transversely. The whole is covered with branches, straw, and roots of the agave tree. On either side a rope, rather more than two feet above the bridge, serves as a balustrade. The puente de soga of Oroya is 50 yards long, and 1½ broad. It is one of the largest in Peru : but the bridge across the Apurimac, in the province of Ayacucho, is nearly twice as long, and it is carried over a much deeper gulph.

The *huaro* bridge consists of a thick rope, extending over a river, or across a rocky chasm. To this rope are affixed a roller and a strong piece of wood formed like a yoke ; and by means of two smaller ropes, this yoke is drawn along the thick rope which forms the bridge. The passenger who has to cross the huaro is tied to the yoke, and grasps it firmly with both hands; an Indian stationed on the opposite side of the river or chasm draws the passenger across the huaro.

Preparatory to the construction of the Niagara Falls Suspension Bridge, at a point nearly two miles below the Falls, and directly over the frightful rapids which commence here, was constructed a basket ferry, having a span of 800 feet, and the height of the rope 230 feet; height of each temporary tower 50 feet. The passengers were conveyed across the river, 250 feet deep.

Upon this spot has since been completed the permanent bridge ; and " its thousands of tons' weight of the strongest iron-cord the ingenuity of the ironmaster can devise find a support in iron-wrought anchors, built in the solid rock 100 feet below the surface."

Upon the very edge of the awful precipice which bounds each shore of the river are raised the stone towers, about 80 feet in height; and at a point about 100 feet in the rear of these huge towers are fastened the immense strands or ropes of wire which sustain the bridge in mid-air. These strands pass from their fastenings immediately over the tower upon each cliff; they pass thence across the chasm, and then over the top of the tower on the opposite shore, in the rear of which the ends are fastened into the rocks, as before described. The bridge is entirely supported by these strong strands of wire ; the platform is about 10 feet in width, and is composed of light planks, resting upon thin scantling, to which the wires are fastened.

Trajan's bridge across the Danube, in Hungary, was erected below the Rapids, or Iron Gate ; the piers were 20 in number, and formed of rolled stones and pebbles thrown into a caisson, then filled with mortar or Roman cement, and faced with brick. Adrian, his successor, broke down this bridge. Now thirteen truncated piers remain, and extend across the bed of the river, which violence, aided by floods and ice-shocks of 1700 winters, have not been able to destroy. The arches of Trajan's bridge were of wood : so were those of Napoleon's on the Simplon and Mount Cenis, and that of Semiramis across the Euphrates; the piers of all were of stone. The length of Trajan's bridge was nearly 3900 feet English, or nearly 14 stades. The same architect, Apollodorus of Damascus, who erected Trajan's column at Rome, also built this bridge over the Danube. The arch of Constantine, at Rome, was composed of the remains of that of Trajan. So it appears that both Napoleon and Trajan built bridges like Semiramis, and constructed their columns and triumphal arches like Sesostris. The obelisk and propylon were the column and triumphal arch of the Egyptian king.

Trajan also cut his way through the rock in constructing roads, like Semiramis and Napoleon. One of the greatest and most useful works of the Romans was the Roman road, or Via Trajana, which was formed along the sides of the Danube by cutting away the rock, and erecting a wooden-shelf-road against the wall of the rock. The platform rested partly on the ledge, and was partly supported by beams inserted into the sockets cut in the rock, and so doubled the breadth of the roadway by allowing the wood-work to over-hang the river; then, by roofing it over, a covered gallery or balcony was formed that extended for nearly 50 miles above the rushing river. Trajan, like Sesostris, has cut in the living rock, at Trajan's Tafel, records of his conquests. The tablet is supported by two winged figures, with a dolphin on each side, and surmounted by the Roman eagle.

Trajan's design was to unite the Trans-Danubian conquests of Rome with those on the south of the river. This may be regarded as the period of the greatest extent of the Roman empire; for after the bridge of Trajan was broken down, the Roman soldier never again crossed the Danube as a conqueror. So it would appear that each of these conquering sovereigns swayed the sceptre at the period when the dominion of empire was the highest.

Napoleon made two roads over the Alps, that of Mount Cenis and the Simplon. The latter took six years in completing, and more than 30,000 men were employed at one time. The number of bridges, great and small, between Brieg and Sesto amounts to 611. There are ten galleries, besides terraces, of massive masonry, miles in length. The breadth of the road is 25 feet, in some places 30, and the average rise nowhere exceeds 6 inches in 6½ feet. The construction of the road over the Simplon was decided upon by Napoleon immediately after the battle of Marengo, while the recollection of his own difficult passage of the Alps by the Great St. Bernard was said to be fresh in his memory.

The French Republican army was divided into six columns

in crossing the Alps : four moved upon Lombardy by the roads of the Great and Little St. Bernard, the St. Gothard, and the Simplon ; Napoleon himself, with the main body, crossing the Great St. Bernard ; two columns descended upon Piedmont by Mount Cenis and Mount Genèvre. At all periods of history the roads were practicable for travellers. Military bands have crossed these mountains ; and though the difficulties of the passage were considerable, they have been greatly exaggerated by the generality of historians.

In making a nine days' circuit of Mont Blanc, on foot, we crossed the Alps by the Great St. Bernard, where the greatest difficulty the French encountered was in transporting the artillery. The cannon were dismounted, placed on sledges, and dragged up by the men.

Hannibal, the Carthaginian general, with an army of infantry, cavalry, and armed elephants, passed the Alps on the side of Piedmont.

An obelisk (modern) stands at Arcoli, to commemorate the victory gained by Napoleon.

Layard discovered a small obelisk at Nimroud, supposed, by the reliefs, to commemorate the expedition of Semiramis to India.

At Ancona stands an antique triumphal arch of white marble, of good proportions, and well preserved, erected in honour of Trajan.

The Arch of Peace at Milan may be ranked among the most beautiful specimens of modern architectural sculpture. It adorns the Italian termination of that stupendous road made by Napoleon across the Alps, which is usually termed the Simplon, from the mountain of that name over which it is carried. The arch was also commenced by Napoleon, and was intended to have been a marble trophy of his victories. It was far from being complete at the time when he fell like a meteor from his throne.

The arch is built entirely of white marble, and finished in 1838. It is about 74 feet high, and almost as long, crowned with bronze figures on horseback at the corners, and a central piece of bronze-work representing Peace in a chariot drawn by six horses. There are three arcades; all of them are richly sculptured, and the largest is 44 feet in height. Four fluted Corinthian columns stand before each front, with half columns behind. These columns are 38 feet high, and each is cut out of a single block of Crevola marble.

$$\text{Height of a column} = 38 \text{ feet}$$
$$\tfrac{1}{8} \text{ stade} = 35\tfrac{1}{8}$$
$$\text{Height of the arch} = 74$$
$$\tfrac{1}{4} \text{ stade} = 70\tfrac{1}{4}$$
$$\text{Height of the cathedral at Milan} = 400$$
$$1\tfrac{1}{2} \text{ stade} = 421\tfrac{1}{2}$$
$$400 \text{ royal cubits} = 374\tfrac{2}{3}$$

At Medinet-Abou there is a hall of 10 columns in breadth and 6 in depth; the two centre rows contain the largest pillars; they are 35 feet in length and 19 in circumference. On the road from the quarry, whence the white marble was taken to build the cathedral at Milan, we saw one of these 38 feet columns, which ornament the triumphal arch, lying at the end of a wooden bridge over a torrent running in a very deep ravine, the sides of the rock being nearly perpendicular. The bridge was being strengthened before attempting to pass the column over it on rollers.

The spire of St. Stephen's, at Vienna, is said to be 465 feet high. Another account makes the height 453 feet.

$$456\tfrac{5}{8} \text{ feet} = 1\tfrac{5}{8} \text{ stade,}$$

=height of the pyramid of Cephrenes to the apex,
=height of the pyramid of Cheops to the platform.

$$468 \text{ feet} = \text{height to apex.}$$

The steeple of St. Michael's, at Hamburg, is said to be 456 feet high.

The following is a description of a Chinese road like that made by the Romans along the side of the Danube.

Salmon observes that the Chinese through the meadows and low grounds raise their ways to a great height, and in some places pave them; they cut passages through rocks and mountains, that carriages may pass the better; and on the sides of some steep mountains they make a kind of gallery with timber, which is very dreadful for strangers to look down from, but the country people ride over them without any apprehension.

The iron suspension bridge at Pesth, over the Danube, has a clear waterway of 1250 feet, the centre span or opening being 670 feet. The height of the suspension towers from the foundation is 200 feet, being founded in 50 feet of water. This is the first permanent bridge, since the time of the Romans, that has been erected over the Danube below Vienna.

$$4\tfrac{1}{2} \text{ stades} = 1264\cdot5 \text{ feet.}$$

The length of Trajan's bridge was nearly 14 stades.
The bridge of Semiramis was 5 stades in length.
The height of a tower = 200 feet.

$$187\tfrac{1}{3} \text{ feet} = 200 \text{ royal cubits,}$$

= height of the walls of Babylon according to Herodotus.

The bridge of Suen-tcheou, in the province of To-kien, is built over an arm of the sea, and supported by about 300 pillars. The length is stated at about 2500 feet, and the breadth 20. The stone-work from pier to pier, at the top, consists of large single massy stones.

Some of the Chinese bridges have been very much exaggerated in the accounts of Du Halde and the missionaries, remarks Davis, as appears from the later report concerning the bridge at Foo-chow-foo, visited during the unsuccessful commercial voyage of the ship Amherst, in 1832. " This same bridge, which proved a very poor structure after all, had been extolled by the Jesuits as something quite extraordinary."

The natural bridge of rock at Icononzo, in the Cordilleras, on the route from Santa-Fé de Bogota to Payayan in Quito, is formed of quartz rock. This surprising natural arch is, according to Humboldt, 48 feet in length, 40 in width, and 8 feet in thickness in the centre. By experiments carefully made on the fall of bodies, its height above the level of the water of the torrent has been ascertained to be about 320 feet. The depth of the torrent, at the mean height of the water, may be estimated at 20 feet.

At the distance of 60 feet below is another arch. " Three enormous masses of rock have fallen into such positions as enable them reciprocally to support each other. The one in the centre forms the key of the vault, — an accident which may have conveyed to the natives of this spot an idea of arched masonry, which was unknown to the people of the new world, as well as to the ancient inhabitants of Egypt."

The elevation of the bridges of Icononzo above the level of the sea is 2700 feet, somewhat more than half a mile. In concluding the description of these, Humboldt notices several other natural bridges, among which is that of the Cedar-creek, in Virginia. It is an arch of limestone, having an aperture of 90 feet, and an elevation of 220 above the level of the water of the creek. He considers this, as well as the bridge of earth, called Rumichaca, which is on the declivity of the porphyritic mountains of Chumban, in the South American province of Los Pastos; together with the bridge of Madre de Deos, named Dantcu, near Totonilco, in Mexico; and the perforated rock near Grandola, in the province of Alentejo, in Portugal, as geological phenomena, which have some resemblance to the natural bridges of Icononzo: but he doubts whether, in any other part of the world, there has yet been discovered an accidental arrangement so extraordinary as that of the three masses of rock, which, reciprocally sustaining each other, form a natural arch.

Syria abounds in caves, stalactical formations, deep recesses in the limestone, and dizzy ravines spanned by natural arches. Near the source of the Nahr el-kelb is a natural bridge, called by the natives Djessr-el-Khadjer, of the following dimensions: — Span, 180 feet; height from the water to the summit, 160 feet; breadth of the roadway, 140 feet; and the depth of the keystone, 20 feet.

Among the gigantic works produced by railway enterprise is the tubular bridge over the Menai Straits. The abut-

H H 2

ments, on each side of the Straits, are huge piles of masonry. That on the Anglesea side is 143 feet high and 173 long. The abutment on the Carnarvonshire side is nearly as large; but owing to the elevation of the ground the masonry is less in altitude. The wing walls of both terminate at the distance of 180 feet in splendid pedestals, and on each is a colossal lion couchant, of Egyptian design. These four lions are on a gigantic scale, each being 25 feet long, 12 feet high, though couched.

The distance between the Britannia tower, which stands on a rock in the centre of the Straits, and each of the side towers is 460 feet. The distance between the side towers and abutments is 230 feet. The base of each tower is 62 by 52 feet, height 198 feet above high-water, and each contains 210 tons of cast-iron girders. The several towers and abutments are externally composed of grey roughly-hewn Anglesea marble.

The length of one of the four greater tubes is 472 feet, being 12 feet longer than the greater span between the towers, and the greatest span yet attempted. Their greatest height is in the centre, 30 feet, and diminishing towards the end to 22 feet. Each tube consists of sides, top, and bottom, all formed of long, narrow wrought-iron plates, varying in length from 12 feet downwards. They are of the same manufacture as those for making boilers, varying in thickness from three-eighths to three-fourths of an inch. The rivets, of which 2,000,000 were used in the eight tubes, are more than an inch in diameter. They are placed in rows, and were put in the holes red hot, and beaten with heavy hammers. In cooling they contracted strongly, and drew the plates together so powerfully that it required a force from 4 to 6 tons to each rivet to cause the plates to slide over each other. The total weight of wrought-iron in a large tube is 1600 tons. This was floated on pontoons, and by means of the hydraulic press finally laid in its position.

The tube, if set on end, would reach 107 feet above the top of the cross of St. Paul's, and weigh as much as 26,000 men of 10 stones each.

The four lengths of each of the twin tubes riveted together equal 1513 feet, which far surpasses in size any piece of wrought-iron ever before put together, the weight being 5000 tons, or nearly equal to two 120-gun ships, having on board, ready for sea, guns, powder, shot, provisions, and crew. The two tubes together weigh 10,000 tons, through which trains speed as if it were a tunnel through solid rock on land, and not 100 feet in air above the roaring sea.

Previous to the bridge being opened a heavily laden train of coal waggons, weighing 240 tons, with three locomotive engines, was run through the tube at the ordinary rate at which such trains travel, from 10 to 12 miles an hour. The deflection caused by the load was found to be about three-fourths of an inch. Locomotives in steam were then passed through as fast as practicable, but only at 20 miles an hour, owing to the curves at each end. The deflection was the fraction of an inch, and the vibration scarcely perceptible; the tonnage weight of the tube itself acting in reality as a counterpoise or preventive to vibration.

This great work was completed in four years.

FEET.

The height of each tower above high water is stated at   198
200 royal cubits   -   -   -   -   =   187⅓
= height of the walls of Babylon. (*Herod.*)

The height of the abutment on the Anglesea side   =   143
½ stade   -   -   -   -   -   =   140½
= ½ height of the tower of Belus.

Length of a great tube   -   -   -   = 472
10 plethrons = ⅒ stade   -   -   -   = 468⅓
= height to apex of Cheops' pyramid,
= ⅝ side of base.

Length of the tubular part of the bridge   -   = 1513
5 stades   -   -   -   -   -   = 1405
= length of the bridge of Semiramis.

The whole length of the entire bridge, measuring from the extreme point of the wing walls of the Anglesea abutment to the extreme of the Carnarvon abutment, is 1833 feet; its greatest elevation, say at the Britannia pier, being 240 feet above low-water mark.

The first tubular bridge erected was the one over the Conway Estuary, which is 400 feet clear in length. The tube is 3 feet less in height than that of the Britannia. The tubes of both bridges were similarly constructed, floated, and raised to their permanent positions. At both Conway and the Menai, the depth of channel is 50 to 60 feet, the bottom rocky, the rise and fall of tide 20 feet.

About a mile from the great tubular bridge, for railway carriages, stands the Menai iron chain suspension bridge, erected in 1826. This bridge is partly of stone and partly of iron, and consists of seven stone arches, which connect the land with the two main piers that rise 53 feet above the level of the road, over the top of which the chains are suspended, each chain being 1714 feet from the fastenings in the rock. The roadway is elevated 102 feet above high-water level, and is 28 feet wide, divided into two carriage-ways of 12 feet each, with a foot-way between them of 4 feet. The distance between the piers, at the level of the road, is 551 feet. Another account makes the span 560 feet.

$$2 \text{ stades} = 562 \text{ feet,}$$
$$= \text{side of square enclosure of the tower of Belus.}$$

The suspension pier at Brighton, begun in 1822, runs into the sea 1014 feet from the front of the esplanade wall; the entire length being 1136 feet, which is divided into four spans or openings, of 255 feet each; the platform being 13 feet broad.

$$\text{Length} = 1136 \text{ feet.}$$
$$4 \text{ stades} = 1124 \quad ,,$$
$$= \text{perimeter of the square base of the tower of Belus.}$$

The high-level bridge, at Newcastle-upon-Tyne, has two roadways, one for carriages and foot passengers; and the other, at an elevation of 22 feet above it, with three lines of railway for locomotives. The carriage-road is 1380 feet in length on a straight line, and the locomotive is immediately

above, with the exception of a space at each end; the locomotive diverging at a point about 270 feet from each end.
Each diverging portion of the locomotive-way is supported
on a handsome colonnade, consisting of 20 metal pillars.

The bridge itself consists of 6 river arches, with 4 land
arches on each side — the former 124 feet 10 inches, and the
latter 36 feet 3 inches span; the land arches diminishing in
altitude from the foundation upwards, corresponding with the
steep bank on the river basin. These arches are constructed
of cast-iron, and supported on piers of solid masonry. The
piers are 48 feet by 16 feet in thickness, and in extreme
height 131 feet from the foundation, having an opening in
the centre through each. These piers are built on piles
piercing the bed of the river, about 50 feet on the north side,
and 20 feet on the south side.

Extreme height $= 131$ feet,
$\frac{1}{2}$ stade ,, $= 140\frac{1}{2}$,,
$= \frac{1}{2}$ height of the tower of Belus.

Length of carriage-road $= 1380$ feet,
5 stades ,, $= 1405$,,

$=$ the length of the bridge of Semiramis, over the Euphrates,
at Babylon.

The Patans and Moguls have left behind them vast monuments of their power in India. "I was at first surprised,"
remarks Wallace, "in travelling over the country, to observe
very few bridges; and those I saw in the Carnatic and Mysore were only composed of prodigious square stone pillars
placed on their ends in the river, and covered with smaller
stones. But I soon discovered that the great rivers are so
liable to overflow their banks during the monsoon, that
bridges over some of them could not be constructed, that
would withstand the impetuosity of the rush of waters. That
wonderful bridges were made in ancient times, we have evidence by the ruins of the magnificent bridge, 300 yards in
length, at Sivana Samudra. Ramma's bridge, which is said
to have united Ceylon to the continent, I do not mention,
because I believe it to be, like the Giant's Causeway, a natural

production.   At Jionpore, in the province of Allahabad,
there is a bridge of ten arches, over the Goomty river, which
has stood since the reign of Acber, although our troops have,
I am most credibly informed, frequently sailed over it during
the monsoon; and yet, though submerged for many days at a
time, it has suffered no damage from the current.   This bridge
is so complicated in its construction, that no native architect
could build or place one like it now.   There is another in
the province of Lucknow, over the Sye, of fifteen arches,
which is a fine specimen of Moorish architecture."

Burnes mentions that Runjeet Singh retained a fleet of
37 boats at Attock for the construction of a bridge across the
river, which is only 260 yards wide.   The boats are anchored
in the stream at a short distance from one another; and the
communication is completed by planks and covered with
mud.   Immediately below the fortress at Attock twenty-four
boats only are required; but at other places in the neighbourhood as many as thirty-seven are used.   Such a bridge
can only be thrown across the Indus from November to
April, on account of the velocity of the stream being comparatively diminished at that season; and even then the
manner of fixing the boats seems incredible.   Skeleton frame-
works of wood, filled with stone to the weight of 250 maunds,
and bound together strongly by ropes, are let down from
each boat, to the number of four or six, though the depth exceeds thirty fathoms, and these are constanly strengthened
by others to prevent accident.   Such a bridge has been completed in three days, but six is the more usual period; and
we are struck with the singular coincidence between this
manner of constructing a bridge and that described by Arrian, when Alexander crossed the Indus.   He there mentions
his belief regarding Alexander's bridge at Attock; and, except that the skeleton frame-works are described as huge
wicker-baskets, the modern and ancient manner of crossing
the river is the same.

In respect to the appropriation of iron to architectural
purposes, the evidences, with very few exceptions, are limited
to modern experience.   In China, however, it is recorded

that "suspension bridges," composed of iron chains and planks, have, at very remote periods, been constructed. The erection of one which is thrown over a very rapid torrent between two lofty mountains, on the road to Yun Nan, in the province of Koei Tcheou, and is stated to be still standing, is attributed to a Chinese general, so far back as the 65th of the Christian era; and although it has been customary hitherto to consider erections of this description as the works of engineering rather than of architecture, the circumstance of the construction so minute in its parts as that of a " chain bridge " enduring the wear, use, and the action of the elements during 1800 years, is a proof of the extraordinary durability of the material and the advantages offered by its use as a constituent of building.

There are also various traditions that the Chinese formerly erected temples of cast-iron, which material they possess the art of mending when cracked or broken in a manner infinitely superior to any now practised in Europe.

In the " voyage of the Nemesis," a British iron war steamer employed in the Chinese War, and the first that ever rounded the Cape of Good Hope, it is stated that at Chin-Keang there was recently discovered a pagoda made entirely of cast-iron, which has been called " Gutzlaff's pagoda," who is said to have been the first to find it out. It excited so much attention that an idea was at one time entertained of taking it to pieces and conveying it to England, as a remarkable specimen of Chinese antiquity; nor would this have been very difficult; for although it had seven stories, it was altogether little more than thirty feet high, each story being cast in separate pieces. It was of an octagonal shape, and had originally been ornamented in high relief on every side, though the lapse of ages had much defaced the ornaments. It was calculated by Gutzlaff that this remarkable structure must be at least 1200 years old, judging from the characters still found upon it. Whatever its age may be, there can be no question it proves the Chinese to have been acquainted with the art of casting large masses of iron, and of using them, both for construction and ornament, centuries before it was adopted in Europe.

Within the last seventy years this material has been much employed in the various departments of science and constructive art in England. The suspension and other bridges erected over the Menai Straits, and subsequently over the Thames at London, and elsewhere, the extensive iron-houses for the manufacture and repertory of gas, the great extent to which, of late years especially, it has been employed for the purpose of roof-plates, rafters, beams, staircases, doors, window frames, &c., on account of its affording security from fire, as well as infinitely greater strength and durability than timber, and also in substitution of stone for columns and other useful and ornamental parts of architecture, in consequence of its greater cheapness and durability, which latter and various other advantages attendant upon the employment of this material as a primary element of construction has of late years been further manifested by its general substitutoin for timber in the building of steam ships and the general purposes of naval architecture.

Several towers, composed entirely of iron, for lighthouses and similar purposes, have been recently constructed in London, of between 100 and 200 feet in height, and consisting of 10 or more stories, and subsequently exported to Jamaica and other countries. Also houses of various descriptions, having iron for the primary and almost sole constituent, have been exported, not only for manufactories and stores, but also for human dwellings.

The advantages of this material as a primary constituent of building is believed to have first suggested its employment by the inhabitants of the English East and West India colonies, where experience has fully proved its superiority over every other building material. In respect to the great safety of such constructions in the awful attacks of electricity with which those climates are so frequently visited, as, likewise, in case of earthquakes and similar convulsions of nature, wherein, in consequence of the necessary peculiarities of their construction, no less than the non-combustive properties of the material, houses composed of iron have been found to remain uninjured, when those of stone and brick have been levelled with the ground, and those of timber rapidly consumed by the fires which usually burst forth to increase the horror of such scenes.

A further inducement to the employment of iron for house-building in these and other tropical countries is, the counteraction of the effects of heat consequent upon the appropriation of double plates of iron, like the double courses of brick-work found at Pompeii, — by which a stratum of air being introduced between the surfaces, presents the most effectual resistance to heat. A stratum of air so interposed will also exclude the frost and cold. Such a correspondent advantage has occasioned the exportation of houses of this description to Russia and other northern countries.

The Ko-tow.

The Chinese, in performing the " Ko-tow " before the emperor, go down three times on their hands and knees, and each time strike the ground with their foreheads. This is the " three times three " practised by the emperor in worshipping heaven. His titles are the " Son of Heaven," the " Ten Thousand Years."—(*Davis.*)

Distance of Ninus $= 33 \cdot 2^9$

$$\text{say} = 33 \cdot 3^9 = 33 \cdot 3^{3 \times 3} = 33 \cdot 3^{3+3+3}$$

then 3 repeated 3 times (the last being a decimal) and raised to the power of 3 times 3,

$=$ distance of Ninus, the abode of the gods.

This distance is denoted by the three prostrations; and the three times three motions of the head made by the emperor in worshipping heaven, who is Pontifex Maximus, or high-priest of the empire.

The other title of the emperor is the " Ten Thousand Years."

10,000 years of Belus $=$ 4,320,000 years, a divine age, the great Indian period.

The Chinese say numbers begin at one, are made perfect at three, and terminate at ten.

THE END.

LONDON:
Printed by SPOTTISWOODE & Co.,
New-street-Square.

APPENDIX

TO THE

LOST SOLAR SYSTEM OF THE ANCIENTS.

BY JOHN WILSON.

LONDON:

LONGMAN, BROWN, GREEN, LONGMANS, AND ROBERTS.

1858.

LONDON :
PRINTED BY SPOTTISWOODE AND CO.
NEW-STREET SQUARE.

APPENDIX.

PRELIMINARY REMARKS.

A TRUNCATED Egyptian obelisk is a monolith, consisting of the shaft and pyramidal top. The shaft is the part intercepted by the top and base ordinates. The two adjoining sides are unequal in width, and the two opposite sides are of equal width. A vertical section made by a plane descending along the axis of the shaft, and parallel to the base ordinates of the greater sides, will form the greater section of the shaft, and a section made in like manner parallel to the base ordinates of the less sides will form the less section of the shaft. Each of these sections has a different apex above the top ordinates. The less axis of a section is the distance from the apex to the top ordinate; the greater axis is the distance from the apex to the base ordinate; so that each section has two axes. The height of the shaft equals the difference between the two axes of either section. The greater axis of a section = the less axis + height of shaft. The ordinate varies as the axis[1].

OBELISKS.

The axes of the ancient Egyptian obelisks, when perfect, were proportional to the mean distances of planets from the sun.

The dimensions of the pyramid on the top of a truncated obelisk are submultiples of the dimensions of other pyramids

A 2

which represent distances in terms of the diameter of the earth, and the distance of the moon from the earth.

CLEOPATRA'S NEEDLE.

(*At Alexandria.*)

Height of shaft, or axis intercepted by the top and base ordinates, equals 57·53 feet.

Greater Section.

Base ord. $= 8 \cdot 15$ feet
Top ord. $= 5 \cdot 15$,,
Base ord.$^2 = 8 \cdot 15^2 = 66 \cdot 42$
Top. ord.$^2 = 5.15^2 = 26 \cdot 42$
Difference of squares $= 40$.

The dimensions of the base ordinates are not taken quite at the bottom of the shaft, but on one side 3 feet, and $\frac{1}{4}$ inch above the bottom, and on the other side somewhat less, so the axis intercepted by the two measured ordinates will $=$ height of shaft $- 3$ feet $= 57 \cdot 53 - 3 = 54 \cdot 53$ feet.

L R, the latus-rectum, $\times$ intercepted axis $=$ difference of square of the 2 ordinates, or

$$\text{L R} \times 54 \cdot 53 = 40$$
$$\text{L R} = \frac{40}{54 \cdot 53} = \cdot 733.$$

Find height of apex above the top ord.

$$\text{Axis} \times \text{L R} = \text{ord.}^2 = \text{top ord.}^2$$
$$\text{Or, Axis} \times \cdot 733 = 26 \cdot 42$$
$$\text{Axis} = \frac{26 \cdot 42}{\cdot 733} = 36.$$

Thus, the less axis, or height of apex above the top ord. $=$ 36 feet.

Greater axis $=$ less axis $+$ height of whole shaft $= 36 + 57 \cdot 53$ $= 93 \cdot 53$ feet.

Less axis : greater axis :: 36 : 93·53.

Tabular distances of Mercury and Earth from the Sun are 37 and 95 millions of miles.

$$\text{And } 37 : 95 :: 36 : 92\cdot43$$
$$\text{Axes are as } \quad 36 : 93\cdot53.$$

Thus the axis from the apex to the top ord. : axis from the apex to the original base ord. :: distance of Mercury : distance of Earth.

Less Section.

Base ord. $= 7\cdot725$ feet
Top ord. $= 4\cdot708$
Base ord.$^2 = 7\cdot725^2 = 59\cdot7$
Top ord.$^2 = 4\cdot708^2 = \underline{22\cdot17}$
Difference of squares $= 37\cdot53$

L R $\times$ intercepted axis = difference of squares of the 2 ordinates, or

$$\text{L R} \times 54\cdot53 = 37\cdot53$$
$$\text{L R} = \frac{37\cdot53}{54\cdot53} = \cdot688.$$

Find height of apex above the top ordinate.

$$\text{Axis} \times \text{L R} = \text{ord.}^2 = \text{top ord.}^2$$
$$\text{Or, Axis} \times \cdot688 = 22\cdot17$$
$$\text{Axis} = \frac{22\cdot17}{\cdot688} = 32\cdot22.$$

Thus, less axis, or height of apex above the top ord. $= 32\cdot22$ feet.

Greater axis = less axis + height of whole shaft $= 32\cdot22 + 57\cdot53 = 89\cdot75.$

Less axis : greater axis :: $32\cdot22 : 89\cdot75$, which ratio is not proportional to the distances of two planets.

If from other measurements of this side of the obelisk the two axes should be found as 30 : 90, or as 1 : 3, then the axes would be as the distance of Uranus : the distance of Belus.

It appears that the stated measurements of Cleopatra's Needle by English travellers differ considerably, and again the French measures are different from those given on English authority.

Pyramidal Top of Cleopatra's Needle.

The two sides of the base of the pyramid, or the two top ordinates of the shaft

$$= 5\cdot15 \text{ and } 4\cdot708 \text{ feet}$$
$$= 4\cdot45 \text{ and } 4\cdot07 \text{ units.}$$

Height of pyramid $= 6$ ft. $6\frac{4}{5}$ in. $= 6\cdot566$ feet $= 5\cdot678$ units,
$$\text{Say} = 5\cdot53, \&c.,$$

Then height × base
$$= 5\cdot53, \&c. \times 4\cdot45 \times 4\cdot07.$$

Let a pyramid $= 100$ times these dimensions, then height × base,

Or, $553, \&c. \times 445 \times 407 = \frac{3}{32}$ dist. Moon.

Pyramid $= \frac{1}{3}$ of $\frac{3}{32} = \frac{1}{32}$,,
200 times (height × base)
$$= 2^3 \times \frac{3}{32} = \frac{24}{32} = \frac{3}{4} \text{ dist. Moon.}$$

Pyramid $= \frac{1}{3}$ of $\frac{3}{4} = \frac{1}{4}$,,
400 times (height × base)
$$= 2^3 \times \frac{3}{4} = \frac{24}{4} = 6 \text{ dist. Moon.}$$

Pyramid $= \frac{1}{3}$ of $6 = 2$,,
$$= \text{diameter orbit Moon} = 6^{12}.$$

St. Peter's Obelisk.

(In the Vatican Circus.)

Intercepted axis, or height of shaft from the base to the top ord. $= 77\cdot18$ feet. All the sides are said to be of equal width.

Base ord. $= 8\cdot83$ feet
Top ord. $= 5\cdot91$,,
Base ord.$^2 = 8\cdot83^2 = 78$
Top ord.$^2 = 5\cdot91^2 = 35$
Difference of squares $= \overline{43}.$

L R × intercepted axis = difference of squares of the 2 ordinates, or,

$$\text{L R} \times 77 \cdot 18 = 43$$
$$\text{L R} = \frac{43}{77 \cdot 18} = \cdot 557.$$

Find height of apex above the top ord.

$$\text{Axis} \times \text{L R} = \text{ord.}^2 = \text{top ord.}^2$$
$$\text{Axis} \times \cdot 557 = 35$$
$$\text{Axis} = \frac{35}{\cdot 557} = 62 \cdot 83.$$

Thus less axis, or height of apex above the top ord. $= 62 \cdot 83$ feet.

Greater axis = less axis + height of shaft $= 62 \cdot 83 + 77 \cdot 18 = 140$ feet.

Axes are as $62 \cdot 83 : 140$
And dist. Venus : dist. Mars :: 68 : 144.

Here the axes are not proportional to the distances of Venus and Mars, nor to any two planets.

It must be observed that the discrepancies about the dimensions of this obelisk are so great that Zoëga wished a more exact measurement could be made ; besides the shaft appears to have been broken in ancient times, and to have lost part of its length.

Pyramidal Top of St Peter's Obelisk.

All the sides of this obelisk are said to be of equal width, and the top ordinate to = about 5 ft. 11 in. $= 5 \cdot 916$ feet $= 5 \cdot 11$ units.

Height of pyramid $= 6$ feet $= 5 \cdot 2$ units,
then height × base,
$$= 5 \cdot 2 \times 5 \cdot 11^2.$$

Let a pyramid $= 100$ these dimensions,
then height × base,
or, $520 \times 511^2 = \frac{1}{8}$ dist. Moon.
Pyramid $= \frac{1}{3}$ of $\frac{1}{8} = \frac{1}{24}$,,
200 times (height × base) $= 2^3 \times \frac{1}{8} = \frac{8}{8} =$ dist. Moon.

▲ ◄

Pyramid $=\frac{1}{3}$ dist. moon.

$=\frac{6.0}{3}=20$ radii Earth $=10$ diameters.

2000 times (height $\times$ base) $=10^3 \times 1 = 1000$ dist. Moon.

CITORIO OBELISK.

(*On the Monte Citorio*.)

Axis, or height of shaft intercepted by the top and base ordinates $= 66\cdot37$ feet.

Base ord. $= 8$ feet
Top ord. $= 5\cdot09$
Base ord.$^2 = 8^2 \qquad = 64$
Top ord.$^2 = 5\cdot09^2 = 25\cdot9$
Difference of squares $= \overline{38\cdot1}$

L R $\times$ intercepted axis $=$ difference of squares of the 2 ordinates.

Or, L R $\times 66\cdot37 = 38\cdot1$
$$L R = \frac{38\cdot1}{66\cdot37} = \quad \cdot574.$$

Find height of apex above the top ordinate.

Axis $\times$ L R $=$ ord.$^2 =$ top ord.^{2}
Axis $\times \cdot574 = 25\cdot9$
$$\text{Axis} = \frac{25\cdot9}{\cdot574} = 45\cdot1.$$

Thus, less axis, or height of apex above the top ord. $= 45\cdot1$ feet.

Greater axis $=$ less axis $+$ height of shaft.

$= 45\cdot1 + 66\cdot37 = 111\cdot47$ feet.

Less axis : greater axis :: $45\cdot1 : 111\cdot47$
Dist. Mercury : dist. Earth :: $37 \quad : 95$
and $37 : 95 :: 45\cdot1 : 115\cdot8$
Axes are as $\quad 45\cdot1 : 111\cdot47$

On account of the corrosion of the shaft, the other base ordinate could not be measured.

This obelisk formerly stood in the Campus Martius; it was

there found buried in the ground and broken in four pieces, the lowest of which was so injured by fire that it was necessary to substitute in its place another block before it was erected on the Monte Citorio.

The measurements are Stuart's.

Pyramidal Top of the Citorio Obelisk.

The two top ordinates of the shaft, or the two sides of the base of the pyramid, are

$$5 \text{ ft. } 1\tfrac{74}{100} \text{ in.} = 5\cdot09 \text{ feet} = 4\cdot4 \text{ units}$$
$$\text{and } 4 \text{ ,, } 11\tfrac{3}{4} \text{ ,, } = 4\cdot98 \text{ ,, } = 4\cdot306$$
$$\text{Height } 5 \text{ ,, } \tfrac{578}{1000} \text{ ,, } = 5\cdot048 \text{ ,, } = 4\cdot363$$
$$\text{Say} = 4\cdot3$$
$$\text{then height} \times \text{base}$$
$$= 4\cdot3 \times 4\cdot4 \times 4\cdot306.$$

Let a pyramid $= 100$ times these dimensions,

$$\text{then height} \times \text{base,}$$
$$\text{or, } 430 \times 440 \times 430\cdot6 = \tfrac{3}{40} \text{ dist. Moon.}$$
$$\text{Pyramid} = \tfrac{1}{3} \text{ of } \tfrac{3}{40} = \tfrac{1}{40} \text{ ,,}$$
$$200 \text{ times (height} \times \text{base)} = 2^3 \times \tfrac{3}{40} = \tfrac{24}{40} = \tfrac{3}{5}$$
$$\text{Pyramid} = \tfrac{1}{3} \text{ of } \tfrac{3}{5} = \tfrac{1}{5} \text{ dist. Moon.}$$
$$= \tfrac{60}{5} = 12 \text{ radii Earth.}$$
$$= 6 \text{ diameters.}$$

The pyramid $= \tfrac{1}{40}$ dist. Moon
$$= 1,000,000 \text{ times the pyramidal top.}$$

The pyramid $= \tfrac{1}{5}$ dist. Moon
$$= 8,000,000 \text{ times the pyramidal top.}$$

FLAMINIAN OBELISK.

(In the Piazza del Popolo.)

Height of shaft, or axis intercepted by the top and base ordinates, equals about 73 feet at present.

Greater Section.

Base ord. $= 7 \cdot 83$ feet
Top ord. $= 4 \cdot 83$
Base ord.$^2 = 7 \cdot 83^2 = 61 \cdot 3$
Top ord.^{2} $= 4 \cdot 83^2 = 23 \cdot 3$
Difference of squares $= 38$

L R $\times$ intercepted axis $=$ difference of squares of the 2 ordinates.

Or, L R $\times 73 = 38$
L R $= \frac{38}{73} = \cdot 52$

Find height of apex above the top ordinate.

Axis $\times$ L R $=$ ord.$^2 =$ top ord.^{2}
Axis $\times$ $\cdot 52 = 23 \cdot 3$
Axis $= \dfrac{23 \cdot 3}{\cdot 52} = 44 \cdot 8$

Thus, the less axis, or height of apex above the top ord. $=$ 44·8 feet.

Greater axis, or height from apex to base ord. $=$ less axis $+$ height of shaft $= 44 \cdot 8 + 73 = 117 \cdot 8$ feet; but this obelisk has lost 3 palms $= 2 \cdot 2$ feet at the lower part; so add 2·2 feet to the greater axis for the part wanting, then the greater axis from apex to the original base ord. will $= 117 \cdot 8 + 2 \cdot 2 = 120$ feet.

Less axis : greater axis :: 44·8 : 120
and 36 : 95 :: 44·8 : 118·3
Dist. Mercury : dist. Earth :: 36   : 95.

Tabular distances of Mercury are 36 and 37 millions of miles.   Thus the axis from the apex to the top ord., and the axis from the apex to the original base ord., are nearly proportional to the distances of Mercury and the Earth.

Less Section.

Base ord. $= 6 \cdot 92$ feet
Top ord. $= 4 \cdot 08$
Base ord.$^2 = 6 \cdot 92^2 = 47 \cdot 88$
Top ord.^{2} $= 4 \cdot 08^2 = 16 \cdot 64$
Difference of squares $= 31 \cdot 24$

L R × intercepted axis = difference of squares of the 2 ordinates,

$$\text{L R} \times 73 = 31 \cdot 24$$
$$\text{L R} = \frac{31 \cdot 24}{73} = \cdot 428$$

Find height of apex above the top ord.

$$\text{Axis} \times \text{L R} = \text{ord.}^2 = \text{top ord.}^2$$
$$\text{Axis} \times \cdot 428 = 16 \cdot 64$$
$$\text{Axis} = \frac{16 \cdot 64}{\cdot 428} = 38 \cdot 87$$

Thus, less axis, or height of apex above the top ord. = 38·87 feet.

Greater axis = less axis + original height of shaft = 38·87 + (73 + 2·2) = 38·87 + 75·2 = 114·07

So less axis : greater axis :: 38·87 : 114·07, nearly as 1 : 3

and dist. of Uranus : distance of Belus :: 1 : 3.

Here the axis from the apex to the top ord., and the axis from the apex to the original base ord., are nearly as the dist. Uranus : dist. Belus.

Present dimensions of the Flaminian obelisk,

Height of shaft = 73 feet.

Greater Section.

Top ord. = 4·83, base ord. = 7·83.

Less Section.

Top ord. = 4·08, base ord. = 6·92.

Original Dimensions.

Height of shaft = 75·2 feet.

Greater Section.

Top ord. = 4·83, base ord. = 7·9.

Less Section.

Top ord. = 4·08, base ord. = 6·99.

Since the original greater axis of the greater section = 120, the corresponding

$$\text{ord.}^2 \text{ will} = \text{axis} \times L\ R$$
$$= 120 \times \cdot52 = 64\cdot2$$
$$\text{ord.} = 64\cdot2^{\frac{1}{2}} = 7\cdot9.$$

The original greater axis of the less section = 114·07,

$$\text{ord.}^2 = \text{axis} \times L\ R$$
$$= 114\cdot07 \times \cdot428 = 48\cdot82$$
$$\text{ord.} = 48\cdot82^{\frac{1}{2}} = 6\cdot99.$$

Mercati's measurement includes the pyramidal top in the height of the shaft, which together equal 78 feet 5 inches. We call the height of the shaft the distance between the top and base ordinates, which is equal to Mercati's shaft, less the pyramidal top. No mention being made of the height of the pyramid, we have supposed its height 5 feet 5 inches, making the height of the shaft = 78 ft. 5 in. — 5 ft. 5 in. = 73 feet.

Pyramidal Top of the Flaminian Obelisk.

The two sides of the base of the pyramid, or the two top ordinates

$$= 4\cdot83 \text{ and } 4\cdot08 \text{ feet}$$
$$= 4\cdot18 \text{ and } 3\cdot53 \text{ units.}$$

No mention is made of the height of the pyramid; but in an engraving the height exceeds the side of the base.

Suppose the height = 6·37 feet = 5·51 units,

$$\text{then height} \times \text{base}$$
$$= 5\cdot51 \times 4\cdot18 \times 3\cdot53.$$

Let a pyramid = 100 times these dimensions,

$$\text{then height} \times \text{base,}$$

or, 551, &c. $\times$ 418 $\times$ 353 = $\frac{3}{40}$ dist. Moon.

$$\text{Pyramid} = \tfrac{1}{3} \text{ of } \tfrac{3}{40} = \tfrac{1}{40} \qquad ,,$$

200 times (height $\times$ base)

$$= 2^3 \times \tfrac{3}{40} = \tfrac{24}{40} = \tfrac{3}{5} \text{ dist. Moon.}$$

$$\text{Pyramid} = \tfrac{1}{3} \text{ of } \tfrac{3}{5} = \tfrac{1}{5} \qquad ,,$$

$$= \tfrac{60}{5} = 12 \text{ radii Earth}$$
$$= 6 \text{ diameters.}$$

5 × 200 or 1000 times (height × base)

$$= 5^3 \times \tfrac{1}{4} = 75 \text{ dist. Moon}$$
$$= \tfrac{1}{2} \text{ dist. Mercury.}$$

2000 times (height × base)

$$= 2^3 \times 75 = 600 \text{ dist. Moon}$$
$$= \text{dist. Mars, nearly}$$
$$= \tfrac{3}{4} \text{ dist. Earth.}$$

5 × 2000 or 10,000 times (height × base)

$$= 5^3 \times 600 = 75,000 \text{ dist. Moon}$$
$$= 20 \text{ times dist. Saturn}$$
$$= 10 \quad ,, \qquad ,, \quad \text{Uranus.}$$

Thus 10,000 times (height × base)

$$= 10 \quad ,, \quad \text{dist. Uranus}$$
$$= \tfrac{10}{3} \quad ,, \qquad ,, \quad \text{Belus.}$$

To Construct a Truncated Obelisk.

Given the distance of Mercury : the distance of Earth :: 36 : 95, and the distance of Uranus : the distance of Belus :: 1 : 3, to construct an obelisk having the axes proportional to these distances, and the greatest axis equal to the greatest axis of the original Flaminian obelisk = 120 feet.

Greater Section.

Fig. 84. By similar triangles, 95 : 36 :: 120 : 45·47.

Height of shaft = difference of axes

$$= 120 - 45 \cdot 47 = 74 \cdot 53.$$

less axis = 45·47

greater axis = less axis + height of shaft

$$= 45 \cdot 47 + 74 \cdot 53 = 120.$$

Axes are as 45·47 : 120 :: 36 : 95

and dist. Mercury : dist. Earth :: 36 : 95.

Let L R = ·52, then determine the ordinates,

L R × less axis = top ord.^{2}

$$\cdot 52 \times 45 \cdot 47 \quad = 23 \cdot 64$$
$$\text{top ord.} = 23 \cdot 64^{\frac{1}{2}} \quad = 4 \cdot 86.$$

L R × greater axis = base ord.^{2}

$$\cdot 52 \times 120 \quad = 62 \cdot 4$$
$$\text{base ord.} = 62 \cdot 4^{\frac{1}{2}} \quad = 7 \cdot 9.$$

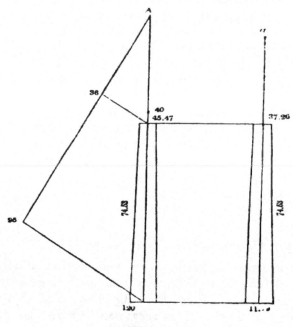

Fig. 84.

Less Section.

The greater axis being = 120, make the less axis = 40 ;
Then the axes will be as 40 : 120 :: 1 : 3.
Height of shaft = difference of axes
= 120 — 40 = 80.

The height of the shaft = 80, and the less axis, or height
of apex A above the top ord. = 40, if this side were taken independent of the other ; but both sections must have a common shaft equal the height of the other section = 74·53, so
that the shaft = 80, and axis = 40, must both be proportionally
reduced,

As 80 : 74·53 : 40 : 37·26.

Then 37·26 will equal the less axis, or height of apex *a*,
above the top of the common shaft.

Greater axis = less axis + height of shaft.
= 37·26 + 74·53 = 111·79.
Axes are as 37·26 : 111·79 :: 1 : 3
And dist. Uranus : dist. Belus :: 1 : 3.

Let L R = ·447, then find the ordinates.

L R × less axis = top ord.[2]
·447 × 37·26 = 16·65
top ord. = 16·65[1] = 4·08.

L R × greater axis = base ord.[3]
·447 × 111·79 = 49·95
base ord. = 49·95[1] = 7·07.

So the dimensions of this obelisk will be, height of shaft = 74·53 feet.

Greater Section.

Top ord. = 4·86, base ord. = 7·9.

Less Section.

Top ord. = 4·08, base ord. = 7·07.

The dimensions of the original Flaminian obelisk were, height of shaft = 75·2 feet.

Greater Section.

Top ord. = 4·83, base ord. = 7·9.

Less Section.

Top ord. = 4·08, base ord. = 6·99.

The axis of the greater section are as,
Dist. Mercury : dist. Earth.

The axis of the less section are as,
Dist. Uranus : dist. Belus.

Venus is placed between Mercury and the earth, and Neptune between Uranus and Belus.

Having determined the two sections, the proposed obelisk can be constructed, since the two sections of an obelisk are made by two planes at right angles to each other, descending vertically along the axis and parallel to the ordinates. Each section is supposed to be parabolic, having the ord. varying as axis^2, but the difference between the top and base ordinates being so small, compared with the height of the section or shaft, that the sides may be represented by straight lines. The shaft is not continued above the top ordinates where the axes of the two sections terminate, because each of these axes has a different apex, and, therefore, the obelisk is truncated.

LATERAN OBELISK.

(*Before the Church of St. John Lateran.*)

Present height of the shaft, or axis intercepted by the top and base ordinates = 97·5 feet.

Greater Section.

Base ord.   = 9·716 feet
Top ord.   = 6·77   ,,
Base ord.^{2} = 9·716^2 = 94·3
Top ord.^{2} = 6·77^2 = 45·8
Difference of squares = $\overline{48·5}$.

L R × intercepted axis = difference of squares of the 2 ordinates,

$$L\ R \times 97·5 = 48·5.$$

$$L\ R = \frac{48·5}{97·5} = ·5.$$

Find height of apex above the top ordinate,

Axis × L R = ord.^{2} = top ord.^{2}
Axis ×   ·5 = 45·8

$$Axis = \frac{45·8}{·5} = 91·6.$$

Thus, less axis, or height from apex to top ordinate = 91·6 feet.

Greater axis from the apex to the present base ord. = less axis + height of shaft = 91·6 + 97·5 = 189·1, to which add four palms = 2·9 feet, for the portion cut off from the lower part,

then the greater axis from apex to the original base ord. =
189·1 + 2·9 = 192 feet.

So, less axis : greater axis :: 91·6 : 192.

Tabular distances of Venus and Mars are 68 and 144
millions of miles.

And 68 : 144 :: 91·6 : 193·9
axes are as 91·6 : 192.

Thus, less axis : greater axis
:: distance of Venus : distance of Mars.

Less Section.

Base ord. = 9 feet
Top ord. = 5·66
Base ord.^{2} = 9^2 = 81
Top ord.^{2} = 5·66^2 = 32
Difference of squares = 49.

L R × intercepted axis = difference of squares of the two
ordinates,

$$L R \times 97·5 = 49$$
$$L R = \frac{49}{97·5} = \quad ·5$$

So the L R of the less section = the L R of the greater
section.

Find the height of apex above the top ordinate,

Axis × L R = ord.^{2} = top ord.^{2}
Axis × ·5 = 32
$$Axis = \frac{32}{·5} = 64.$$

Thus, less axis, or height of apex above the top ordinate =
64 feet.

Greater axis from the apex to the present base ord. = less
axis + height of shaft = 64 + 97·5 = 161·5, to which add four
palms = 2·9 feet, for the part wanting; then the greater axis
from the apex to the original base ord. = 161·5 + 2·9 = 164·4
feet. So, less axis : greater axis :: 64 : 164·4.

Distances of Mercury and Earth are 37 and 95 millions of
miles,

And 37 : 95 :: 64 : 164·3
axes are as 64 : 164·4.

Hence the axes of the less section are as dist. Mercury : dist. Earth ; and the axes of the greater section are as dist. Venus : dist. Mars.

Since both sections of this obelisk have the same latus-rectum, the axes of two different sections may be compared in the same way as the axes of one section,

As less axis of less section : less axis of greater section
:: 64 : 91·6
and 64 : 91·6 :: 68 : 97·32
dist. Venus : dist. Earth :: 68 : 95.

Less axis of greater section : greater axis of less section :: 91·6 : 164·4; dist. Mercury : dist. Venus :: 37 : 68, and 37 : 68 :: 91·6 : 168·34 ; axes are as 91·6 : 164·4.

Less axis of less section : greater axis of greater section

:: 64 : 192 :: 1 : 3
and dist. Uranus : dist. Belus :: 1 : 3

Since the original greater axes of the greater and less sections are 192 and 164·4, the original base ord. of the greater section will = 9·8, and of the less section = 9·07 ;

for L R × axis = ord.²
·5 × 192 = 96
ord. = 96ⁱ = 9·8

Original base ord. of greater section = 9·8.

Again, L R × axis = ord.²
·5 × 164·4 = 82·2
ord. = 82·2ⁱ = 9·07

Original base ord. of less section = 9·07.

So the original dimensions of the Lateran obelisk will be, height of shaft = 100·4 feet.

Greater Section.

Top ord. = 6·77, base ord. = 9·8.

Less Section.

Top ord. = 5·66, base ord. = 9·07.
The Lateran is the largest of all the obelisks.

Pyramidal Top of the Lateran Obelisk.

The two sides of the base of the pyramid, or the two top ordinates of the shaft

= 6·77 and 5·66 feet
= 5·854 ,, 4·89 units.

No measurement of the height is stated ; but the height is said to exceed the side of the base by about one-third.

If height = 8·35 feet = 7·58 units,
Then height × base
= 7·58 × 5·854 × 4·89.

Let a pyramid = 100 times these dimensions,
Then 758, &c. × 585·4 × 489 = $\frac{1}{5}$ dist. Moon.
Pyramid = $\frac{1}{3}$ of $\frac{1}{5}$ = $\frac{1}{15}$,,   ,,
= $\frac{60}{15}$ = 4 radii Earth
= 2 diameters.

Pyramid 15 times dimensions of this
= $15^3 \times \frac{1}{15}$ = 225 dist. Moon
= $\frac{1}{100}$,, Belus.

Pyramid 10 times dimensions of the last
= $10^3 \times 225$ = 225000 dist. Moon
= 10 times dist. Belus
= 30 ,, ,, Uranus
= 60 ,, ,, Saturn.

Thus, a pyramid 15,000 times dimensions of the top pyramid
= $15^3 \times 10^3$ dist. Moon
= 15 × 10^2 ,, Mercury
=   10 ,, Belus.

For dist. Moon : dist. Mercury :: dist. Mercury : dist. Belus.

Dist. Mercury = 150 dist. Moon.
Dist. Belus   = 150 ,, Mercury.

To construct a Truncated Obelisk.

Given the distance of Mercury 37, Venus 68, Earth 95, and Mars 144 millions of miles from the sun, to construct an obelisk, having the latus-rectum common to the two sections, so that not only the axes of the same section may be proportional to these distances, but also that the axes of different sections may be compared with planetary distances.

Fig. 85. Let the height from the base of the shaft to the apex A of the greater section = 192 feet, as in the Lateran

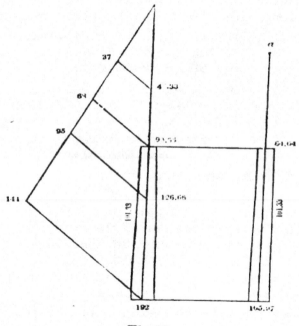

Fig. 85.

obelisk.   Join 144, the distance of Mars, and 192 ; to this line draw the other lines from 95, 68, 37, parallel ; then as 37, 68, 95, 144 are as the planetary distances, so, by similar triangles, will 49·33, 90·66, 126·66, 192, be also as the planetary distances.

Greater Section.

144 : 68 :: 192 : 90·66.

Less axis : greater axis :: 90·66 : 192.

Height of shaft = difference of axes

= 192 − 90·66 = 101·33

Axes are as 90·66 : 192 :: 68 : 144

And dist. Venus : dist. Mars :: 68 : 144.

Less Section.

144 : 95 :: 192 : 126·66

144 : 37 :: 192 :   49·33.

Less axis : greater axis :: 49·33 : 126·66.

Height of shaft = difference of axes

= 126·66 − 49·33 = 77·33.

Thus, 77·33 would be the height of the shaft to the axes 49·33 and 126·66 by taking this side, independent of the other; but the two sections have a common shaft, the height of which = 101·33 feet, the difference of the axis of the greater section, so that the less shaft must be made equal to the greater shaft, and the less axis proportionally increased,

as 77·33 : 101·33 :: 49·33 : 64·64.

Thus, 64·64 will be the less axis, or height of apex a above the top of the common shaft.

Greater axis = less axis + height of shaft

= 64·64 + 101·33 = 165·97.

So the axes of the less section will be as 64·64 : 165·97 :: 37 : 95, and dist. Mercury : dist. Earth :: 37 : 95.

Since the two sections of this obelisk have a common latus-rectum, an axis of one section may be compared with an axis of the other, as less axis of less section : less axis of greater section :: 64·64 : 90·66 :: 68 : 95·37, and dist. of Venus : dist. of Earth :: 68 : 95.

Less axis of greater section : greater axis of less section :: 90·66 : 165·97 :: 37 : 67·72, and dist. of Mercury : dist. of Venus :: 37 : 68.

Less axis of less section : greater axis of greater section ::

64·64 : 192 :: 1 : 3 nearly, and dist. of Uranus : dist. of Belus :: 1 : 3.

In the three last instances the two axes compared are those of different sections: but since both the greater and less sections have the same latus-rectum, the axes, ordinates, and areas of different sections, as well as the axes, ordinates, and areas of the same section, may be compared with each other; the two axes being as the distances of two planets from the sun, the corresponding ordinates will be inversely as the velocities, and the areas directly as the periodic times of the two planets.

The parabolic lines that bound the two sides of each section are represented by straight lines, for the difference of the two ordinates of the greater section only amounts to about 3 feet in 100, or $1\frac{1}{2}$ foot on each side of the axis.

Lastly, supposing the latus-rectum common to the greater and less sections = ·5 ; let us determine the four ordinates of the two sections.

$$\text{Height of shaft} = 192 - 90·66 = 101·33$$

$$A \quad \text{,,} \quad \text{of apex above shaft} = \quad 90·66$$

$$a \quad \text{,,} \quad \text{,,} \quad \text{,,} \quad = \quad 64·64$$

Greater Section.

$$L\,R \times \text{less axis} = \text{top ord.}^2$$
$$·5 \times 90·66 = 45·33$$
$$\text{top ord.} = 45.33^{\frac{1}{2}} = \quad 6·73.$$
$$L\,R \times \text{greater axis} = \text{base ord.}^2$$
$$·5 \times 192 = 96$$
$$\text{base ord.} = 96^{\frac{1}{2}} = 9·8.$$

Less Section.

$$L\,R \times \text{less axis} = \text{top ord.}^2$$
$$·5 \times 64·64 = 32·32$$
$$\text{top ord.} = 32·32^{\frac{1}{2}} = 5·69.$$
$$L\,R \times \text{greater axis} = \text{base ord.}^2$$
$$·5 \times 165·95 = 82·98$$
$$\text{base ord.} = 82·98^{\frac{1}{2}} = 9·11.$$

These are the four ordinates to the shaft having the height

of 101·33 feet ; the axes of the sections being proportional to planetary distances.

Thus, height of shaft of this obelisk = 101·33 feet.

Greater Section.

Top ord. = 6·73, base ord. = 9·8.

Less Section.

Top ord. = 5·69, base ord. = 9·11.

Compare these with the original dimensions of the Lateran obelisk, which are

Height of shaft = 100·4 feet.

Greater Section.

Top ord. = 6·77, base ord. = 9·8.

Less Section.

Top ord. = 5·66, base ord. = 9·07.

Both obelisks have a common latus-rectum = ·5, and in both the greater axis of the greater section = 192 feet.

In the Lateran obelisk we find the axes of the two sections were originally so proportioned, that not only the axes of one section were as the dist. of Venus : dist. of Mars, and of the other section as the dist. of Mercury : dist. of Earth ; but also that the axes of the two different sections were as the dist. of Venus : dist. of Earth, and also as the dist. of Mercury : dist. of Venus, and lastly as the dist. of Uranus : dist. of Belus.

It was Constantine, the father of Constantius, who first moved this obelisk from Heliopolis, the most learned college of the Egyptian priests, to Alexandria. The son was urged to vie with the glory of Augustus' achievements, who had brought two obelisks from Heliopolis, and to finish the work which his father had left incomplete. A ship was built to convey the obelisk to Rome ; the number of rowers employed were 300. The immense mass arrived in safety on the banks of the Tiber, and was erected in the Circus Maximus.

Pliny says, with respect to the two large obelisks at Rome in his time, one in the Campus Martius and the other in the Circus Maximus, " The inscriptions on them contain the interpretation of the laws of nature, the result of the philosophy of the Egyptians."

We now find that the dimensions of the obelisk, without any inscription, typify the laws of nature that govern the motions of planets round the sun, according to the theory of the philosophical priesthood of Heliopolis — the " City of the Sun."

The only obelisks we have met with having the dimensions of the shaft and ordinates stated, are Cleopatra's Needle at Alexandria, and the four obelisks at Rome.   Though the measurements of some of these obelisks may be incorrect, and the shafts mutilated, yet the results obtained from the stated dimensions show that the early Egyptian obelisks were so constructed as to indicate, not only the relative distances of planets from the sun, but also the laws they obey in their revolutions round that luminary, which was placed in the centre of the solar system of the ancients, as it now forms the centre of the modern system of Copernicus.

> " Dark has been thy night,
> Oh, Egypt ! but the flame
> Of new-born science gilds thine ancient name."

For a more particular account of these obelisks see Vol. I. Part III.

A Great Teocalli.

The journals announce the recent discovery of a great teocalli, or terraced pyramid.

" M. Ernest Pillon gives an account of the discovery by the French Consul, at Mossoul, who opened trenches through an enormous tumulus, which appeared to be formed by the falling down of a series of terraces.   He says: ' The wonders of wonders, the greatest sight that we can behold in these days, is Babel.   The present tower has lost six of its eight gradations or floors, and the two that remain are visible two leagues off. The quadrangular base is 194 metres on each side. The bricks of which it is built are composed of pure white clay, but slightly fired to pale yellow tint, which, before firing, was covered with characters. The pitch with which, we are taught, they were bound together is still found in a spring close by.' "

1 metre $= 39\cdot371$ inches English.

194 metres $= 636\cdot5$ feet ,,

$= 550$, &c. units.

If 195, &c. ,, $= 554$, &c. . ,,

Then cube of side of base $= 554^3$ &c. $= \frac{2}{3}$ circumference Earth. Pyramid having height $=$ side of base $= 554$, &c. units $= \frac{1}{3}$ of $\frac{2}{3} = \frac{2}{9}$ circumference.

If the side of base of the external pyramid $=$ height $= 601$ units,

Then 601^3 &c. $= \frac{1}{5}$ dist. Moon.

Pyramid $= \frac{1}{3}$ of $\frac{1}{5} = \frac{1}{15}$,, ,,

$= \frac{6.9}{18} = 4$ radii Earth.

$= 2$ diameters.

The internal pyramid $= \frac{1}{2}$ circumference Earth.

The external ,, $= 2$ diameters.

$= \frac{1}{15}$ dist. Moon.

The internal pyramid of Belus $= \frac{1}{24}$ circumference Earth.

The external ,, ,, $= \frac{1}{6}$ diameter.

$= \frac{1}{180}$ dist. Moon.

Thus, the two pyramids of the teocalli will be similar to the two pyramids of Belus; but the internal and external pyramids of the teocalli will be twelve times greater than the internal and external pyramids of Belus.

According to this supposition, the sides of the terraces of the teocalli will incline a little towards the apex, like the tower of Belus at Babylon (see Vol. I. p. 375), which also has eight terraces, and the height of the eight terraces $=$ side of base $=$ one stade $= 243$ units.

Cube of side of base of external pyramid of the teocalli,

$= 601^3$ &c. $= \frac{1}{5}$ dist. Moon

$= 6$ diameters Earth :

C

Cylinder having height = diameter of base = 601, &c. units,
= ½ circumference Earth.

sphere = ⅔   „   „

cone = ⅓   „   „

Thus, the cylinder of the external cube = the internal cube = ½ circumference. The sphere of the external cube = ⅔ the internal cube = circumference. The hemisphere of the external cube = the cone of the external cube = the pyramid of the internal cube = ⅓ circumference. The internal pyramid of the teocalli = the internal pyramid of Cheops = ½ circumference. The teocalli will have a greater height, but a less base than the pyramid of Cheops.

Proximate formula for the internal cube of the teocalli, which = 554^3, &c.

Say 555^3 = 3 times ⅓ circumference, or 5 repeated 3 times and raised to the third power = 3 times ⅓ circumference.

Pyramid = ⅓ of (5 repeated 3 times and raised to the 3rd power) = ⅓ circumference.

Proximate formula for the external cube of the teocalli, which = 601^3, &c.

Say $(2 \times 300)^3$ = 2 × 3 diameters Earth, or (twice 300) raised to the 3rd power = twice 3 times diameter Earth.

Pyramid = ⅓ of (twice 300) raised to the 3rd power = twice diameter Earth.

Here we find exemplified the method adopted by the ancients of representing distances by the cube, cylinder, sphere, cone, and pyramid. These five figures we suppose to have been the five regular bodies of the ancients, which were thought by the school of Alexandria to have been of such importance in the philosophy of former ages, that Euclid is said to have compiled his Elements of Geometry with the hopes of discovering them.

THE END.

LONDON : PRINTED BY SPOTTISWOODE AND CO., NEW-STREET SQUARE.

CPSIA information can be obtained
at www.ICGtesting.com
Printed in the USA
BVHW081603120819
555665BV00013B/1009/P